Learning

Strategies
for Success
in College
and Life

FIFTH EDITION

Robert S. Feldman
University of Massachusetts, Amherst

Mc
Graw
Hill

Connect
Learn
Succeed™

P.O.W.E.R. LEARNING: STRATEGIES FOR SUCCESS IN COLLEGE AND LIFE
Published by McGraw-Hill, a business unit of The McGraw-Hill Companies, Inc., 1221 Avenue of the
Americas, New York, NY, 10020. Copyright © 2011 by The McGraw-Hill Companies, Inc. All rights reserved.
Previous editions © 2000, 2003, 2007, and 2009. No part of this publication may be reproduced or distributed
in any form or by any means, or stored in a database or retrieval system, without the prior written consent of
The McGraw-Hill Companies, Inc., including, but not limited to, in any network or other electronic storage
or transmission, or broadcast for distance learning.

Some ancillaries, including electronic and print components, may not be available to customers outside the
United States.

This book is printed on acid-free paper.

1 2 3 4 5 6 7 8 9 0 RJE/RJE 1 0 9 8 7 6 5 4 3 2 1 0

ISBN 978-0-07-337516-8 (student edition)
MHID 0-07-337516-0 (student edition)
ISBN 978-0-07-730124-8 (annotated instructor's edition)
MHID 0-07-730124-2 (annotated instructor's edition)

Vice president/Editor in chief: *Elizabeth Haefele*
Vice president/Director of marketing: *John E. Biernat*
Sponsoring editor: *Alice Harra*
Developmental editor: *Kristin Bradley*
Editorial coordinator: *Vincent Bradshaw*
Marketing manager: *Keari Green*
Lead media producer: *Damian Moshak*
Digital developmental editor: *Kevin White*
Director, Editing/Design/Production: *Jess Ann Kosic*
Lead project manager: *Susan Trentacosti*
Senior production supervisor: *Janean A. Utley*
Senior designer: *Marianna Kinigakis*
Senior photo research coordinator: *Jeremy Cheshareck*
Photo researcher: *Allison Grimes*
Media project manager: *Cathy L. Tepper*
Interior design: *Maureen McCutcheon*
Typeface: *11/13 Minion*
Compositor: *Laserwords Private Limited*
Printer: *R.R. Donnelley*
Cover credit: *Jill Braaten*
Credits: *The credits section for this book begins on page 404 and is considered an extension of the copyright page.*

Library of Congress Cataloging-in-Publication Data

Feldman, Robert S. (Robert Stephen), 1947-
P.O.W.E.R. learning: strategies for success in college and life/Robert S. Feldman.—5th ed.
    p. cm.
    Includes index.
    ISBN-13: 978-0-07-337516-8 (student edition: alk. paper)
    ISBN-10: 0-07-337516-0 (student edition: alk. paper)
    ISBN-13: 978-0-07-730124-8 (annotated instructor's edition: alk. paper)
    ISBN-10: 0-07-730124-2 (annotated instructor's edition: alk. paper) 1. College student
orientation. 2. Study skills. 3. Life skills. 4. Success. I. Title. II. Title: POWER learning.
LB2343.3.F44 2011
378.1'98—dc22   2009046167

The Internet addresses listed in the text were accurate at the time of publication. The inclusion of a Web site
does not indicate an endorsement by the authors or McGraw-Hill, and McGraw-Hill does not guarantee the
accuracy of the information presented at these sites.

www.mhhe.com

Dedication

To my students, who make teaching a joy.

About the Author

ROBERT S. FELDMAN

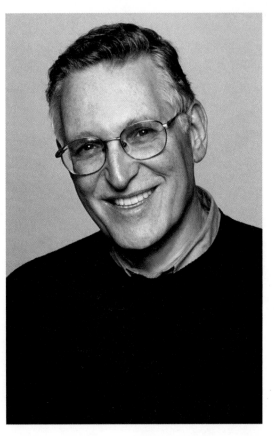

Robert S. Feldman still remembers those moments of being overwhelmed when he started college at Wesleyan University. "I wondered whether I was up to the challenges that faced me," he recalls, "and—although I never would have admitted it at the time—I really had no idea what it took to be successful at college."

That experience, along with his encounters with many students during his own teaching career, led to a life-long interest in helping students navigate the critical transition that they face at the start of their own college careers. Professor Feldman, who went on to receive a doctorate in psychology from the University of Wisconsin–Madison, teaches at the University of Massachusetts at Amherst, where he is the Dean of the College of Social and Behavioral Sciences. He directs *POWER Up for Student Success,* the UMass first-year experience course for incoming students.

Professor Feldman's proudest professional accomplishment is winning the College Outstanding Teaching Award at UMass. He also has been named a Hewlett Teaching Fellow and was Senior Online Instruction Fellow. He has taught courses at Mount Holyoke College, Wesleyan University, and Virginia Commonwealth University.

Professor Feldman is a Fellow of both the American Psychological Association and the Association for Psychological Science. He is a winner of a Fulbright Senior Research Scholar and Lecturer award and has written some 100 scientific articles, book chapters, and books. His books, some of which have been translated into Spanish, French, Portuguese, and Chinese, include *Improving the First Year of College: Research and Practice, Understanding Psychology,* 9/e, and *Development Across the Life Span,* 5/e. His research interests encompass the study of honesty and truthfulness in everyday life, development of nonverbal behavior in children, and the social psychology of education. His research has been supported by grants from the National Institute of Mental Health and the National Institute on Disabilities and Rehabilitation Research.

With the last of his three children completing college, Professor Feldman occupies his spare time with serious cooking and earnest, but admittedly unpolished, piano playing. He also loves to travel. He lives with his wife, who is an educational psychologist, in a home overlooking the Holyoke mountain range in western Massachusetts.

v

Table of Contents

PART 1 — Getting Started

3 Recognizing Your Learning Styles, Self-Concept, and Values 56

PART 2   Using P.O.W.E.R. for Academic Success

4 Taking Notes

5 Taking Tests

6 Building Your Reading Skills

7 Writing and Speaking

8 Memory

9 Choosing Your Courses and Major

10 Technology and Information Competency   255

PART 3   Life Beyond the Classroom

11 Making Good Decisions   *289*

12 Diversity and Your Relationships with Others   *313*

The valuable input we have received from the *P.O.W.E.R. Learning*'s reviewers, along with the feedback from the tens of thousands of students, the hundreds of instructors who used the prior editions, and classroom testing, have resulted in the addition of new and updated information, reflecting advances in our understanding of what makes students successful and changes in college instruction. The following sample of new and revised topics provides a good indication of the book's currency:

CHAPTER 1—P.O.W.E.R. LEARNING: BECOMING A SUCCESSFUL STUDENT

- Includes measurable Learning Outcomes (page 1)
- Revised Try It 2 on goals (page 7)
- New Speaking of Success feature (page 23)

CHAPTER 2—MAKING THE MOST OF YOUR TIME

- Includes measurable Learning Outcomes (page 28)
- Expanded coverage on controlling time (page 30)
- Updated discussion of personal styles of time management (page 31)

CHAPTER 3—DISCOVERING YOUR LEARNING STYLES, SELF-CONCEPT, AND VALUES

- Includes measurable Learning Outcomes (page 56)
- Greater emphasis on learning styles (page 57)
- Expanded discussion of self-concept (page 68)
- New Course Connections (page 70)

CHAPTER 4—TAKING NOTES

- Includes measurable Learning Outcomes (page 89)
- Completely revised discussion of notetaking tools (page 92)
- New information regarding notetaking and PowerPoints (page 99)
- New Speaking of Success feature (page 112)

CHAPTER 5—TAKING TESTS

- Includes measureable Learning Outcomes (page 116)
- Further discussion of test anxiety (page 122)
- New strategies for test taking (page 130)

CHAPTER 6—BUILDING YOUR READING SKILLS

- Includes measurable Learning Outcomes (page 145)
- New Try It 2 on Advanced Organizers (page 150)
- Additional information on writing while you read (page 155)
- New Course Connections feature (158)

New to the Fifth Edition

CHAPTER 7—WRITING AND SPEAKING

> Includes measurable Learning Outcomes (page 169)
> New table (7.1) that more effectively defines types of college writing (page 172)
> Updated information on public speaking (page 190)

CHAPTER 8—MEMORY

> Includes measurable Learning Outcomes (page 202)
> Updated coverage of memory (page 203)

CHAPTER 9—CHOOSING YOUR COURSES AND MAJOR

> Includes measurable Learning Outcomes (page 225)
> New support for Try It 2 on required courses (page 232)
> Revised Try It 3 on choosing courses (page 235)
> More on service learning (page 240)
> Identification of skills employers look for (page 250)
> New Speaking of Success feature (page 251)

CHAPTER 10—TECHNOLOGY AND INFORMATION COMPETENCY

> Includes measureable Learning Outcomes (page 255)
> New chapter opening example (page 256)
> Updated coverage of "You and Technology" (page 256)
> New Journal Reflections (page 257)
> "Technology and Your Academic Life" (page 257)
> More on e-mail (page 262)
> Nettiquette (page 263)
> Revised distance learning (page 267)

CHAPTER 11—MAKING GOOD DECISIONS

> Includes measurable Learning Outcomes (page 289)
> Expanded coverage of flexible alternatives (page 291)

CHAPTER 12—DIVERSITY AND YOUR RELATIONSHIPS WITH OTHERS

> Includes measurable Learning Outcomes (page 313)
> Updated Try It 1 on diversity in your college community (page 316)
> Dealing with friendship and diversity (page 325)
> New Speaking of Success profile on Lindsey Beck of Three Rivers Community College (page 335)

CHAPTER 13—MONEY MATTERS

> Includes measurable Learning Outcomes (page 339)
> More on identity theft (page 352)
> Expanded coverage on protecting your credit score (page 353)

CHAPTER 14—STRESS, HEALTH, AND WELLNESS

- ‣ Includes measurable Learning Outcomes (page 367)
- ‣ Signs of suicide in others (page 377)
- ‣ More on weight loss and diet (page 379)
- ‣ Expanded discussion of alcohol on college campuses (page 383)
- ‣ More on drug addiction (page 383)
- ‣ New Speaking of Success feature (page 393)
- ‣ Updated information for further reading (page 395)

Text Features: Achieving the Goals of **POWER** Learning

P.O.W.E.R. Learning provides a systematic framework for organizing the strategies that lead to success

P Prepare

O Organize

W Work

E Evaluate

R Rethink

P.O.W.E.R. Plan

Each chapter utilizes the principles of the **P.O.W.E.R. system (Prepare, Organize, Work, Evaluate, and Rethink),** so students can clearly see how easy it is to incorporate this effective process into their everyday routine. The P.O.W.E.R. plan illustration highlights the key steps for the corresponding chapter material.

Handy, updated **reference charts** appear throughout the text for quickly accessing and organizing important material.

table 7.1	Major Types of College Writing
Research paper	A paper requiring abstract, critical thinking supported through the collection of existing information. Often requires analysis and synthesis of the material to develop a conclusion.
Essay	A paper written from an author's personal point of view and arguing a particular point. It may take the form of a review, criticism, or personal recollection or it may argue a political viewpoint.
Critical review	Criticism of an argument, article, musical piece, or other work.
Journal	Personal reflections on class readings or assignments.

P.O.W.E.R. *Learning* offers a wide range of skill-building opportunities

Every chapter offers numerous **Try It** activities for gaining hands-on experience with the material covered in the chapter. These include questionnaires, self-assessments, and group exercises to do with classmates. The **Try It** activities, along with other assessment opportunities, are also available on the text's Web site at **www.mhhe.com/power**.

Every chapter includes an updated list of the three types of **resources** that are useful in finding and utilizing information relevant to the chapter: a list of on-campus resources, books, and Web sites. There are also exercises in using the Web, called **Taking It to the Net.** This material helps students study and retain important concepts presented in the chapter, as well as guide their future inquiry.

Every chapter includes a **Course Connections** box that shows students how to use the chapter's content to maximize their success in particular classes. The goals of *P.O.W.E.R. Learning: Strategies for Success in College and Life* are achieved through a consistent, carefully devised set of features common to every chapter. Students and faculty endorsed each of these elements.

P O W E R   Try It!

1 Get to Know Your College Advisor

It is helpful to get a feel for who your advisor is, so schedule a 15- to 30-minute appointment with him or her. Before you meet with your advisor, do some background research by looking at your college catalog. College catalogs usually provide information on the background of faculty and staff, listing their titles, where they went to college and graduate school, what departments they teach in, and what their areas of academic interest are. In addition, you can search the Web; some instructors have their own home pages that describe their background.

To learn more about your advisor, cover some of these topics when you meet:

Philosophy of college advising:

Words of advice:

Things to try at the college:

Things to avoid at the college:

After you have met with your advisor, consider the following questions: Do you have a better sense of your advisor as an individual? What things did you learn that can help you? How can you use your advisor's responses to take better advantage of what your college has to offer?

To Try It online, go to www.mhhe.com/power.

[RESOURCES]

ON CAMPUS

The college official that determines when classes meet is known as the Registrar. If you are having difficulty in scheduling your classes, the registrar's office may be helpful. In addition, your academic advisor can help you work out problems in enrolling in the classes you want.

For help with such issues as planning a study schedule for the upcoming term, dealing with multiple assignments due on the same date, or tips on dealing with competing academic and work demands, consult with your campus learning center. The staff can help you sort out the various options you may have.

IN PRINT

Stephen Covey's *The Seven Habits of Highly Successful People* (Fireside, 2004) and Alan Axelrod and Brian Tracy's *Eat That Frog! 21 Great Ways to Stop Procrastinating and Get More Done in Less Time* (Berrett-Kohler, 2007) offer practical, hands-on guides to time management.

TAKING IT TO THE NET

1 Complete a weekly organizer online. Find a site on the Web that offers shareware or freeware featuring a weekly planner (for example, **www.studygs.net/schedule/Weekly.html** or **www.printablecalendar.ca/**). Create a weekly schedule sheet for yourself based on this design. Be sure to write in all of your classes and any other regular obligations that you have. Be sure to set specific times in your daily schedule to study and do homework. (If you already use Outlook or another kind of communications software, use its calendar function to do the same thing.)

2 Make a master calendar for the term, using the same software you used for the exercise above. If your calendar does not provide this information automatically, you can go to Yahoo! (**dir.yahoo.com**), click on "Reference," then again on "Calendars." Here you'll find many links to different calendar-related information such as when holidays occur. Be sure to indicate dates when important assignments are due and when exams occur.

Study Time: How Much Is Enough?

What would you guess is the average number of hours instructors think you should be studying each week? In the view of instructors queried in a national survey, students should spend, on average, 6 hours per week preparing for *each* class in which they're enrolled. And if they're taking courses in the sciences and engineering, instructors expect their students to put in even more hours.[2]

Keep in mind that study time does not include actual class time. If you add that in, someone taking four classes would need 24 hours of outside class preparation and would be in class for 16 hours—for a total of 40 hours, or the equivalent of full-time employment.

If you've underestimated the amount of time instructors believe is necessary to devote to class preparation, you may need to rethink the amount of time you'll need to allocate to studying. You might also speak to your individual instructors to see what they believe is an appropriate amount of preparation. Although they may not be able to give exact figures, their estimates will help you to prioritize what you need to do to be a successful student.

Course Connections

P.O.W.E.R. *Learning* demonstrates the connection between academic success and success beyond the classroom

Acknowledging Others' Ideas: Academic Honesty and Plagiarism

As you move through the process of writing a paper, there are many temptations to cut corners. A friend may have written a paper the previous year on the same topic and offer to "lend" it to you . . . you may find a paper on the Web that addresses just what you intended to write . . . you and a friend may be enrolled in a very large class, and he may suggest that you each write part of the paper and "share" sections.

Don't yield to temptations such as these. Not only is honesty the best policy, but it's also the *only* policy in the world of academics. There's no greater academic sin than **plagiarism**, taking credit for someone else's words, thoughts, or ideas. In the academic world, plagiarism is about the same as stealing a stranger's car. Even if you just mean to "borrow" a passage, passing another person's work off as your own is totally wrong.

Furthermore, penalties for plagiarism are severe. In many colleges, plagiarism results in a comment on your transcript or can result in expulsion. You even could face legal charges, because almost all published material is copyrighted, which means that it is someone's *intellectual property*. If an author learns that you have used his or her writing as your own, the author has the right to take you to court and sue for damages.

If the moral and intellectual arguments against plagiarism don't convince you, here's the hard reality: It is likely you are going to get caught. Increasing numbers of instructors and colleges routinely use Web-based computer programs to check students' papers for plagiarism. The process is simple. Students turn in papers

Plagiarism
Taking credit for someone else's words, thoughts, or ideas

Due to increasing concern with **academic honesty and plagiarism,** *P.O.W.E.R. Learning* addresses the topic in several places and contexts, including acknowledging sources in writing papers and giving speeches and crediting material accessed online.

The **Career Connections** feature links the material in the chapter to the world of work, demonstrating how the strategies discussed in the chapter are related to career choices and success in the workplace.

P.O.W.E.R. Learning Meets the World of Work

Although the focus of the P.O.W.E.R. Learning system is on developing school success, its applications extend well beyond the classroom. In particular, the principles of P.O.W.E.R. Learning are useful in the world of work, and your ability to use them will provide you with keys to success in the workplace.

Skeptical? In *Career Connections* boxes in future chapters we'll explore how the principles we're discussing can help you choose an appropriate career and excel in the workplace. For now, though, take a look at these "help wanted" advertisements and online postings. They illustrate the importance of the components of P.O.W.E.R. Learning in the workplace.

Speaking of **Success**

NAME: **Shorena Kalandaris**
SCHOOL: **Smith College, Northampton, Massachusetts**

Shorena Kalandaris spent her high school years preparing to leave her native Republic of Georgia, located where Europe and Asia meet. She knew that she wanted to pursue college in the United States, and after graduation from high school, she enrolled in Smith College in Massachusetts.

Studying in the United States was not easy for Kalandaris. She was separated from her family in Georgia for long months at a time, and she had to quickly learn the skills necessary to take care of herself while away from her family.

"I have always had many interests and activities, but being alone here, I had to manage my time myself. I participate in competitive ballroom dance and had to balance that with my studies," noted Kalandaris.

Cultural differences proved challenging, and Kalandaris sought out other international students to cope with the unique challenges of her situation. She became involved in campus organizations that support international students, and she was active

in organizing activities for the international student community.

Kalandaris excelled at Smith, and she was nominated to be a candidate for the Goldman Sachs Global Leaders program. Young leaders from across the United States were chosen to attend leadership training from current global leaders, and they met with other students who had the same passion to make changes to their world.

Kalandaris plans to attend the London School of Economics for her junior year abroad, and she intends to return to Georgia after earning a graduate degree in economics. Ultimately, her goal is to work for the National Bank of Georgia to help improve the Georgian economy.

Says Kalandaris, "I would encourage students to have diverse interests, but to aim for quality experiences. Have a goal, because it is very easy to get distracted. Once you have a goal, the rest of your plan will fall into place."

www.mhhe.com/power   **CHAPTER FOURTEEN** Stress, Health, and Wellness   **393**

Many new **Speaking of Success** articles have been added that profile real-life success stories. Some of these people are well-known individuals, whereas others are current students or recent graduates who have overcome academic difficulties to achieve success.

P.O.W.E.R. Learning helps you develop critical thinking skills

Chapter 1 features a **P.O.W.E.R. Profile Assessment tool** that gives students a sense of where they stand—both numerically and graphically—in relation to the key topics addressed in the book. The "P.O.W.E.R. Profile" helps students identify their strengths and weaknesses and determine how they want to improve. Students can return to the P.O.W.E.R. Profile at the end of the course to assess and chart their progress.

Journal Reflections

My School Experiences

Throughout this book, you will be given opportunities to write out your thoughts. These opportunities—called Journal Reflections—offer a chance to think critically about the chapter topics and record your personal reactions to them. As you create your reflections, be honest, to yourself and to your instructor.

Completing these Journal Reflections provides a variety of benefits. Not only will you be able to mull over your past and present academic experiences, you'll begin to see patterns in the kind of difficulties—and successes!—you encounter. You'll be able to apply solutions that worked in one situation to others. And one added benefit: You'll get practice in writing.

If you save these entries and return to them later, you may be surprised at the changes they record over the course of the term. You can either write them out and keep an actual journal, or create your journal electronically at the P.O.W.E.R. Learning Web site at **www.mhhe.com/power**.

1. Think of one of the successful experiences you've had during your previous years in school. What was it?

2. What made the experience successful? What did you learn from your success?

3. Think of an experience you had in school that you could have handled more successfully, and briefly describe it. Why did it occur?

4. What could you have done differently to make it successful? What did you learn from it?

5. Based on these experiences of academic success and failure, what general lessons did you learn that could help you be a more successful student in the future?

The **Journal Reflections** feature provides students with the opportunity to keep an ongoing journal, making entries relevant to the chapter content. Students are asked to reflect and think critically about related prior experiences. These conclude with questions designed to elicit critical thinking and exploration.

The Case of . . .
The Time of His Life

Will Linz couldn't believe it. On the same day he had completed his term paper and handed it in, his instructor announced a test for the following week. When the class protested that the test hadn't been listed in the syllabus, the instructor murmured that she'd made a mistake and was sorry about the short notice.

Will panicked when he remembered that next week he also had to complete two lab reports he had put off because he had been working on his term paper. Even worse, next weekend was lost. He had promised—promised!—his girlfriend, who was working full-time, that he would go with her to her annual company picnic. Although he dreaded the thought of being with a bunch of people he barely knew, he'd finally agreed to go just last week.

As he was driving home thinking about all this, his car started to sputter and then stalled. That was it. He was unable to get it started. That was it. He sat there on the side of the road, feeling like his life had completely fallen apart and wondering how he'd ever get it back together again.

1. What might you tell Will that could help solve his predicament?

2. Is there anything Will could have done to prevent the situation he now faces from occurring in the first place?

3. What specific time management techniques might Will have employed in the past to avoid these problems?

4. What strategies might Will use now to take control over his limited time during the coming week?

5. What advice could you give Will to try to prevent problems in time management for his next term?

Each chapter ends with a **case study (The Case of . . .)** to which the principles described in the chapter can be applied. Case studies are based on situations that students might themselves encounter. Each case provides a series of questions that encourage students to consider what they've learned and to use critical thinking skills in responding to these questions.

P.O.W.E.R. Learning provides an engaging, accessible, and meaningful presentation

An appealing design and visual presentation highlight large, clear photos carefully selected to show the diversity of students as well as the latest in technological aids and devices.

Chapter-opening scenarios describe an individual grappling with a situation that is relevant to the subject matter of the chapter. Readers will be able to relate to these vignettes, which feature students running behind schedule, figuring out a way to keep up with reading assignments, or facing a long list of vocabulary words to memorize.

Key terms appear in boldface in the text and are defined in the margins. In addition, they are listed in a **Key Terms and Concepts** section at the end of the chapter, with accompanying page references.

[KEY TERMS AND CONCEPTS]

Retrieval (p. 203)

Rehearsal (p. 207)

Mnemonics (p. 208)

Acronym (p. 208)

Acrostic (p. 209)

Method of loci (p. 211)

Peg method (p. 211)

Visualization (p. 213)

Overlearning (p. 215)

Memory consolidation (p. 218)

All of these reviewed and tested features are designed not only to help understand, practice, and master the core concepts presented in this text, but also to collectively support the main goals and vision of this text, as demonstrated on the following pages.

The P.O.W.E.R. Resources

The same philosophy and goals that guided the writing of *P.O.W.E.R. Learning: Strategies for Success in College and Life* led to the development of a comprehensive teaching package. Through a series of focus groups, questionnaires, and surveys, we asked instructors what they needed to optimize their courses. We also analyzed what other publishers provided to make sure that the ancillary materials accompanying *P.O.W.E.R. Learning* would surpass the level of support to which instructors are accustomed. As a result of the extensive research that went into devising the teaching resources, we are confident that whether you are an instructor with years of experience or are teaching the course for the first time, this book's instructional package will enhance classroom instruction and provide guidance as you prepare for and teach the course.

Print Resources

INSTRUCTOR'S EDITION

(0-07-730124-2): The Instructor's Edition (IE), prepared by Joni Webb Petschauer and Cindy Wallace of Appalachian State University, contains the full text of the student edition of the book with the addition of notes that provide a rich variety of teaching strategies, discussion prompts, and helpful cross-references to the Instructor's Resource Manual. The IE has been completely redesigned in an effort to provide more frontline teaching assistance. Notes are easily laid out in the back of the text and include a myriad of additional class activities, teaching advice, and guidance toward a successful classroom. The fifth edition also includes three additional chapters on student athletes, career preparation, and transferring students that can be included in custom versions of *P.O.W.E.R. Learning*.

INSTRUCTOR'S RESOURCE MANUAL

(0-07-730123-4): Written by Joni Webb Petschauer and Cindy Wallace of Appalachian State University with additional contributions from experienced instructors across the country, this manual provides specific suggestions for teaching each topic, tips on implementing a first-year experience program, handouts to generate creative classroom activities, audiovisual resources, sample syllabi, and tips on incorporating the Internet into the course.

CUSTOMIZE YOUR TEXT

P.O.W.E.R. Learning can be customized to suit your needs. The text can be abbreviated for shorter courses and can be expanded to include semester schedules, campus maps, additional essays, activities, or exercises, along with other materials specific to your curriculum or situation. Chapters designed for student athletes, career preparation, and transferring students are also available.

STUDENT PLANNER

Updated annually, this convenient organizational tool is available as a stand-alone or with the student text. The planner provides daily tips for success, time-management techniques, a daily calendar, and contact information.

Human Resources

WORKSHOPS WITH AUTHOR AND AUTHOR TEAM

Are you faced with the challenge of launching a first-year experience course on your campus? Would you like to invigorate your college success program, incorporating the most recent pedagogical and technological innovations? Is faculty recruitment an obstacle to the success of your program? Are you interested in learning more about the P.O.W.E.R. system?

Workshops are available on these and many other subjects for anyone conducting or even just considering a first-year experience program. Led by author Robert Feldman, *P.O.W.E.R. Learning* Instructor's Resource Manual authors Joni Webb Petschauer and Cindy Wallace, or one of the McGraw-Hill *P.O.W.E.R. Learning* consultants, each workshop is tailored to the needs of individual campuses or programs. For more information, contact your local representative, or email us at **fye@mcgraw-hill.com.**

Digital Resources

LASSI: LEARNING AND STUDY STRATEGIES INVENTORY

The LASSI is a 10-scale, 80-item assessment of students' awareness about and use of learning and study strategies related to skill, will, and self-regulation components of strategic learning. The focus is on both covert and overt thoughts, behaviors, attitudes, and beliefs that relate to successful learning and that can be altered through educational interventions. Research has repeatedly demonstrated that these factors contribute significantly to success in college and that they can be learned or enhanced through educational interventions such as learning and study skills courses.

The LASSI provides standardized scores and national norms for 10 different scales. The LASSI is both diagnostic and prescriptive. It provides students with a diagnosis of their strengths and weaknesses compared to other college students in the areas covered by the 10 scales, and it is prescriptive in that it provides feedback about areas where students may be weak and need to improve their knowledge, attitudes, beliefs, and skills.

The LASSI is available in print or online at **www.hhpublishing.com.** Ask your McGraw-Hill sales representative for more details.

IMPLEMENTING A STUDENT SUCCESS COURSE

This innovative Web content (available on the OLC) assists you in developing and sustaining your Student Success course. Features include a "how to" guide for designing and proposing a new course, with easy-to-use templates for determining budget needs and resources. Examples of model programs are provided from two-year, four-year, and career schools. The site explores course goals, such as orientation and retention, and provides research data to support your proposal. Also included are materials to help sustain your course, such as faculty development programs and online resources.

COURSE CONTENT FOR YOUR LEARNING MANAGEMENT SYSTEM

The online content of *P.O.W.E.R. Learning* is supported by WebCT, eCollege. com, and Blackboard. Additionally, our PageOut service, free to qualified adopters, is available to get you and your course up and running online in a matter of hours! To find out more, contact your local McGraw-Hill representative or visit **www. pageout.net.**

P.O.W.E.R. LEARNING ONLINE LEARNING CENTER WEB SITE
(**www.mhhe.com/power**): Instructors and students will find materials such as downloadable resources, self-quizzes, online journal activities and assessments, case study assignments, Web exercises, and a rich bank of links for college success. Instructor's resources also include an EZ Test computerized test bank and chapter-by-chapter PowerPoint presentations. Also, new to this edition is the inclusion of an Asset Map that identifies ancillary material for instructors and aligned by Learning Outcome.

connect™ plus+

LESS MANAGING.
MORE TEACHING.
GREATER LEARNING.

What Is Connect *Plus+*?

McGraw-Hill Connect *Plus+* is a revolutionary online assignment and assessment solution providing instructors and students with tools and resources to maximize their success.

Through Connect *Plus+*, instructors enjoy simplified course setup and assignment creation. Robust, media-rich tools and activities, **all tied to the textbook's learning outcomes**, ensure you'll create classes geared toward achievement. You'll have more time with your students and less time agonizing over course planning.

Connect *Plus+* Features

McGraw-Hill Connect *Plus+* includes powerful tools and features that allow students to access their coursework anytime and anywhere, while you control the assignments. Connect *Plus+* provides students with their textbook and homework, **all in one accessible place.**

 Simple Assignment Management
Creating assignments takes just a few clicks, and with Connect *Plus+*, you can choose not only which chapter to assign but also specific learning outcomes. **Videos, animations, quizzes**, and many other activities bring **active learning** to the forefront.

▶ **Smart Grading**
Study time is precious and Connect *Plus+* assignments **automatically provide feedback** to you and your students. You'll be able to conveniently review class or individual student knowledge in an online environment.

▶ **Connect Plus+ eBooks**
McGraw-Hill has seamlessly **integrated eBooks** into their Connect *Plus+* solution with **direct links to the homework, activities, and tools**—students no longer have to search for content, allowing them more time for learning.

McGraw-Hill provides live instructor orientations for Connect *Plus+* to guarantee you will have a worry-free experience.

The POWER to Succeed!

The Power of Support!

Let the McGraw-Hill Student Success Team support your course with our workshop program.

> Planning to develop a First-Year Experience course from scratch?

> Reenergizing your First-Year Experience course?

> Trying to integrate technology in your class?

> Exploring the concept of learning communities?

We offer a range of author- and consultant-led workshops that can be tailored to meet the needs of your institution.

Our team of experts, led by *P.O.W.E.R. Learning* author Robert Feldman, can address issues of course management, assessment, organization, and implementation. How do you get students to commit to your program? How do you achieve support from your institution? How can you evaluate and demonstrate the effectiveness of your First-Year Experience course? These are questions that every program faces. Let us help you to find an answer that works for you.

Other workshop topics may include:

> Classroom Strategies for Enhancing Cultural Competence: The P.O.W.E.R. of Diversity

> Using Learning Styles in the Classroom

> Creating Student Success Courses Online

> Motivating Your Students

To schedule a workshop, please contact your local McGraw-Hill representative. Alternately, contact us directly at **fye@mcgraw-hill.com** to begin the process of bringing a P.O.W.E.R. Learning workshop to you.

The POWER to Create Your Own Text!

Do you want to:

> Only cover select chapters?

> Personalize your book with campus information (maps, schedules, registration materials, etc.)?

> Add your own materials including exercises or assignments?

> Address specific student populations, such as student athletes and transferring students?

P.O.W.E.R. Learning can be customized to suit your needs.[1]

WHY CUSTOMIZE?

Perhaps your course focuses on study skills and you prefer that your text not cover life issues such as money matters, health and wellness, or information on choosing a major. Whatever the reason, we can make it happen, easily. McGraw-Hill Custom Publishing can deliver a book that perfectly meets your needs.

[1]Orders must meet our minimum sales unit requirements.

WHAT WILL MY CUSTOM BOOK LOOK LIKE?

Any chapters from the *P.O.W.E.R. Learning* book that you include will be in full color. Additional materials can be added between chapters or at the beginning or end of the book in black and white. Binding (paperback, three-hole punch, you name it) is up to you. You can even add your own custom cover to reflect your school image.

WHAT CAN I ADD?

Anything! Here are some ideas to get you started:

> **Campus map** or anything specific to your school: academic regulations or requirements, syllabi, important phone numbers or dates, library hours.

> **Calendars** for the school year, for local theater groups, for a concert series.

> **Interviews** with local businesspeople or your school's graduates in which they describe their own challenges and successes.

> **Your course syllabus or homework assignments** so your students have everything they need for your course under one cover and you don't have to make copies to hand out.

SPECIAL CHAPTERS DESIGNED FOR THE UNIQUE NEEDS OF YOUR STUDENTS!

Three additional chapters are available for your customized text and have been designed to address the needs of specific student populations.

> *Strategies for Success for Student Athletes.* This chapter discusses the unique challenges of student athletes, such as managing school and team pressures, using resources and understanding eligibility, and knowing when and how to ask for help. It also addresses special concerns such as burnout, dealing with injury, and hazing.

> *Taking Charge of Your Career.* This chapter helps students determine the best career choices that fit personal goals. It provides important tips on how to develop a career portfolio, prepare a résumé and cover letters, and have a successful interview, including follow-up strategies.

> *Transfer Strategies: Making the Leap from Community College to a Four-Year School.* Designed for the potential transfer student, this chapter looks at the pros and cons of moving beyond a two-year degree and what personal decisions to make. It guides students through the transfer process, including applications, credit transfer, financial assistance, and transfer shock.

HOW DO I CREATE A CUSTOM BOOK?

The secret to custom publishing is this: *Custom Publishing Is Simple!*
Here are the basic steps:

> You select the chapters you would like to use from *P.O.W.E.R. Learning* with your McGraw-Hill sales representative.

> Together, we discuss your preferences for the binding, the cover, etc., and provide you with information on costs.

> We assign your customized text an ISBN and your project goes into production. A custom text will typically publish within 6–8 weeks of the order.

> Your book is manufactured and it is put into inventory in the McGraw-Hill distribution center.

> You are sent a free desk copy of your custom publication.

> Your bookstore calls McGraw-Hill's customer service department and orders the text.

You select what you want—we handle the details!
Contact us:

www.mhhe.com/power
Canada: 1-905-430-5034
United States: 1-800-446-8979
E-mail: fye@mcgraw-hill.com

With Gratitude

I am indebted to the many reviewers of *P.O.W.E.R. Learning* who provided input at every step of development of the book and the ancillary package. These dedicated instructors and administrators provided thoughtful, detailed advice, and I am very grateful for their help and insight. They include the following:

Miriam Frances Abety, Miami Dade College; Peg Adams, Northern Kentucky University; Angela Alexander, Nicholls State University; Mary Asher-Fitzpatrick, Cuyamaca College; Brenda Atchison, McLennan Community College; Rebecca Barr, Palomar College; Michelle Bates, Southeastern Louisiana University; Linda Blair, Pellissippi State Technical Community College; Judith Chaplain, Ozarks Technical Community College; Lisa Christman, University of Central Arkansas; Emily Cowdrick, Georgia Perimeter College–Lawrenceville; Margo Eden-Camann, Georgia Perimeter College; Louise Ericson, University of South Carolina–Upstate; Jo Ella Fields, Oklahoma State University–Oklahoma City; Connie Gulick, Central New Mexico Community College; Linda Hasty, Motlow State Community College; Bob Holdeman, University of South Carolina; Lois Darlene Hurd, Jefferson Community and Technical College, Southwest; Ann Iseda, Jackson Community College; Joel Jessen, Eastfield College; Cathi Kadow, Purdue University–Calumet; Linda Cooper Knight, College of the Albemarle; Judith Lynch, Kansas State University; Judith Miller, Blue Ridge Community College; David Neis, Southern Illinois University–Carbondale; Maria Parnell, Brevard Community College; Joanne Pinkston-McDuffie, Daytona Beach Community College; Angela Reeves, Mott Community College; Janice Reilly, Mesa Community College; Sherry Rhoden, Grand Rapids Community College; Dwight Rinehart, Reading Area Community College; Brieana Roumeliotis, California State University–Fullerton and Golden West College; Ryan Ruda, Garden City Community College; Dawn Shaffer, Central Piedmont Community College; Sharon Snyders, Ivy Tech Community College; Bruce Tucker, Santa Fe Community College; Douglas Watson, Weber State University; Kathie Wentworth, Tri-State University; Stephanie Foote, University of South Carolina, Aiken; Linda Burdsall, Jackson State Community College; Cheryl Burk, Wake Technical Community College; Terry Rafter Carles, Valencia Community College–East; Stephanie Crecca, Institute of Business and Medical Careers; Melanie Deffendall, Delgado Community College; Rebecca Ellison, Jefferson College; Charles Frederick, Jr., Indiana University; Jo Ann Jenkins, Moraine Valley Community College; Elvira Johnson, Central Piedmont Community College; Mahalia Johnson, Greenville Technical College; Elizabeth Kennedy, Florida Atlantic University; Kimberly Little, Southern Illinois University–Carbondale; Candace Maher, Central New Mexico Community College; Lucy Marrero, Santa Fe Community College; Al Matthews, North Lake College; Richard McMullen, Western Michigan University; Beryl Odom, Gadsden State Community College; Jody Owen, South Dakota State University; Mia Pierre, Valencia Community College-West; Karen Sumner, University of Sioux Falls; Francisca Uvah, University of West Florida.

The students in my own first-year experience courses (some of whom are shown here) provided thoughtful and wise advice. I thank them for their enthusiasm and eager willingness to provide constructive feedback.

Professors Cindy Wallace and Joni Webb Petschauer of Appalachian State University wrote the Instructor's Resource Manual and provided notes and tips for the Instructor's Edition. I thank both of them for their enthusiasm, good ideas, dedication, and friendship.

Edward Murphy, Ed.D., an educational testing expert, helped develop the exercises in the book, and I'm grateful for his excellent work.

John Graiff and Tolley Jones were a great help on every level in putting this book together, and I thank them for their willingness to go the extra mile. I could not have written this book without their support.

I am proud to be part of an extraordinary McGraw-Hill editorial, marketing, and sales team. My sponsoring editor, Alice Harra, has brought enthusiasm and intelligence to the project, and I welcome her good work.

I am especially grateful to Kristin Bradley, development editor, whose keen editorial eye, creativity, and wealth of good ideas has improved this book significantly. She is truly a delight to work with.

P.O.W.E.R. Learning author Bob Feldman and some of his first-year experience program participants.

There are several folks who, while no longer officially working on the project, still patiently answer my queries and offer their advice, for which I am extremely grateful. Andy Watts made superb contributions in extending the reach of *P.O.W.E.R. Learning,* and I'm very grateful for his work and even more for his friendship. Phil Butcher, Thalia Dorwick, David Patterson, Allison McNamara, and Alexis Walker were part of the team that developed the book, and I'm ever thankful for their efforts. Above all, I'm grateful to Rhona Robbin, the first development editor on the project, and sponsoring editor Sarah Touborg, who provided the impetus for the book. Certainly, the pages of *P.O.W.E.R. Learning* continue to reflect their many contributions.

Without a doubt, there is no better publishing group in the business than the one that worked on *P.O.W.E.R. Learning.* I count myself extremely lucky not only to have found myself a part of this world-class team, but to count each of them as friends.

In the end, I am eternally indebted to my family, both extended and immediate. Sarah, Josh, Julie, Jon, Leigh, Alex, and of course Kathy, thank you for everything.

Robert S. Feldman

Do you find that there's not enough time to accomplish all the things you want to do? Do you put off studying for tests until the last minute? Do you sometimes have trouble making decisions?

If so, you're not alone. *Every* first-year college student (as well as many returning students) encounters challenges such as these, and many others. That's where *P.O.W.E.R. Learning: Strategies for Success in College and Life* comes in. It is designed to help you to master the challenges you'll face in college as well as in life after college. The *P.O.W.E.R. Learning* system—which is based on five key steps embodied in the word *P.O.W.E.R.* (Prepare, Organize, Work, Evaluate, and Rethink)—teaches strategies that will help you become a more successful student and that will give you an edge in attaining what you want to accomplish in life.

But it's up to you to make use of the book. By familiarizing yourself with its features and using the built-in learning aids, you'll maximize its usefulness and be more likely to get the most out of it.

Familiarize Yourself with the Scope of *P.O.W.E.R. Learning*

Begin by skimming the Table of Contents, which provides an overview of the book. By reading the chapter titles, you'll get a sense of the topics that are covered and the logic of the sequence of chapters.

Then, Take Some Time to Flip through the Book

Choose a chapter that sounds interesting to you, skim a few pages, and see for yourself the kinds of practical information the book provides. Note that every chapter has the same diamond-shaped pattern:

Opening Prologue
Looking Ahead
The Main Body of the Chapter
Looking Back/Resources
Case Study

Get in Touch

I welcome your comments and suggestions about *P.O.W.E.R. Learning,* as well as the Web site that accompanies the book. You can write me at the College of Social and Behavioral Sciences at the University of Massachusetts, Amherst, Massachusetts 01003. Even easier, send me an e-mail message at **feldman@sbs.umass.edu.** I will write back!

A final word: *P.O.W.E.R. Learning* presents the tools that can maximize your chances for academic and life success. But remember that they're only tools, and their effectiveness depends on the way in which they are used. Ultimately, you are the one who is in charge of your future.

The start of college offers a wonderful point of departure. Make the journey a rewarding, exciting, and enlightening one!

Robert S. Feldman

CHAPTER 1

P.O.W.E.R. Learning: Becoming a Successful Student

Learning Outcomes

By the time you finish this chapter you will be able to

» LO **1.1**   Explain the benefits of a college education.

» LO **1.2**   Identify the basic principles of the P.O.W.E.R. Plan.

» LO **1.3**   Discuss how expert students use P.O.W.E.R. Learning to achieve college success.

The day has started off with a bang. Literally. As Jessie Trevant struggles sleepily to turn off her clock radio's continual buzzing at 8:35 a.m., she knocks it off the desk next to her bed. The loud bang as it hits the floor not only wakes her fully but also rouses her roommate, who grumbles resentfully.

Struggling out of bed, Jessie reflects on the day ahead. It's one of her most intense class days—four different classes, scattered across the campus. She also must put in several hours of work in the college bookstore, where she has a 15-hour-a-week job, and she knows she'd better get started on her history paper, due next week.

And then there's that biology test that she must take this morning.

After a quick shower, Jessie joins the flood of students making their way to classes. She glances at her biology textbook and feels a wave of anxiety flood over her: Will I do well enough? How will I manage to hold down a job and have enough time to study? Will I make friends here? Will it ever feel like home? Will I make my family proud? . . . *And underlying them all is a single challenge: Will I be successful in college?*

Looking Ahead

Whether academic pursuits are a struggle or come easily to you . . . whether you live on campus or commute . . . whether you are fresh out of high school or are returning to school many years after high school graduation—college is a challenge. Every one of us has concerns about our capabilities and motivation, and new situations—like starting college—make us wonder how well we'll succeed.

That's where this book comes in. It is designed to help you learn the most effective ways to approach the challenges you encounter, not just in college, but outside the classroom, too. It will teach you practical strategies, hints, and tips that can lead you to success, all centered around an approach to achieving college success: P.O.W.E.R. Learning.

This book is designed to be useful in a way that is different from other college texts. It presents information in a hands-on format. It's meant to be used—not just read. Write on it, underline words and sentences, use a highlighter, circle key points, and complete the questionnaires right in the book. The more exercises you do, the more you'll get from the book. Remember, this is a book to help you with your coursework throughout college, so it's a good idea to invest your time here and now. If the learning techniques you master here become second nature, the payoff will be enormous.

» LO 1.1 Why Go to College?

Congratulations. You're in college.

But *why*? Although it seems as if it should be easy to answer why you're continuing your education, for most students it's not so simple. The reasons that people go to college vary from the practical ("I want to get a good job"), to the lofty ("I want to learn about people and the world"), to the unreflective ("Why not?—I don't have anything better to do"). Consider your own reasons for attending college as you complete **Try It 1.**

Surveys of first-year college students show that almost three-quarters say they want to learn about things that interest them, get training for a specific career, land a better job, and make more money (see **Figure 1.1** on page 4). And, in fact, it's not wrong to expect that a college education will help people find better jobs. On average, college graduates earn about 75 percent more than high school graduates over their working lifetime. That difference adds up: Over the course of their working lifetimes, college graduates earn close to a million dollars more than those with only a high school degree. Furthermore, as jobs become increasingly complex and technologically sophisticated, college will become more and more of a necessity.

Why Am I Going to College?

Place a 1, 2, and 3 by the three most important reasons that you have for attending college:

_____ I want to get a good job when I graduate.

_____ My parents want me to go.

_____ I couldn't find a job.

_____ I want to get away from home.

_____ I want to get a better job.

_____ I want to gain a general education and appreciation of ideas.

_____ I want to improve my reading and study skills.

_____ I want to become a more cultured person.

_____ I want to make more money.

_____ I want to learn more about things that interest me.

_____ A mentor or role model encouraged me to go.

_____ I want to prove to others that I can succeed.

Now consider the following:

- What do your answers tell you about yourself?
- What reasons besides these did you think about when you were applying to college?
- How do you think your reasons compare with those of other first-year students who are starting college with you?

To Try It online, go to www.mhhe.com/power.

But the value of college extends far beyond dollars and cents. Consider these added reasons for pursuing a college education:

> **You'll learn to think critically and communicate better.** Here's what one student said about his college experience after he graduated: "It's not about what you major in or which classes you take. . . . It's really about learning to think and to communicate. Wherever you end up, you'll need to be able to analyze and solve problems—to figure out what needs to be done and do it."[1]

Education improves your ability to understand the world—to understand it as it now is, and to prepare to understand it as it will be.

> **You'll be able to better deal with advances in knowledge and technology that are changing the world.** Genetic engineering . . . drugs to reduce forgetfulness . . . computers that respond to our voices. . . . No one knows what the future will hold, but you can prepare for it through a college education. Education can provide you with intellectual tools that you can apply regardless of the specific situation in which you find yourself.

> **You'll learn to adapt to new situations.** College is a different world from high school. It presents new experiences and new challenges. Your adjustment to college culture will prepare you for future encounters with new situations.

> **You'll be better prepared to live in a world of diversity.** The racial and ethnic composition of the United States is changing rapidly. Whatever your ethnicity, chances are you'll be working and living with people whose backgrounds, lifestyles, and ways of thinking may be entirely different from your own.

figure 1.1

Choosing College

These are the most frequently cited reasons that first-year college students gave for why they enrolled in college when asked in a national survey.[2]

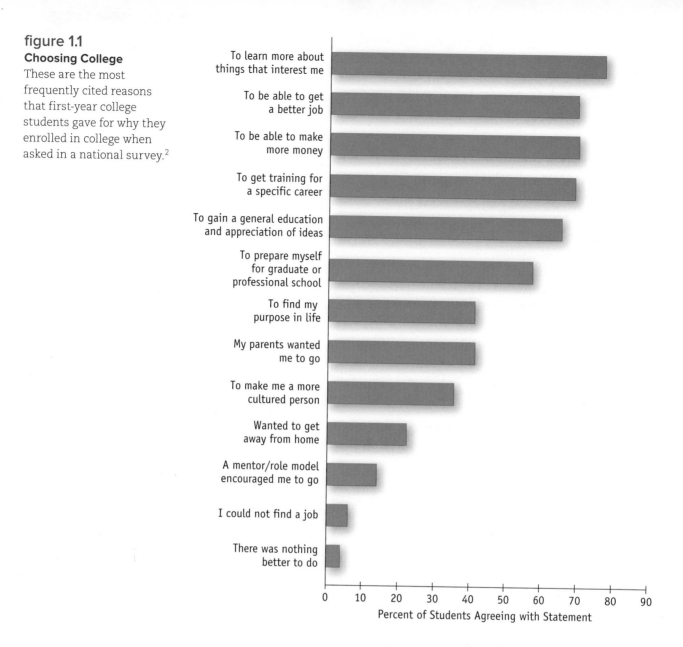

To learn more about things that interest me

To be able to get a better job

To be able to make more money

To get training for a specific career

To gain a general education and appreciation of ideas

To prepare myself for graduate or professional school

To find my purpose in life

My parents wanted me to go

To make me a more cultured person

Wanted to get away from home

A mentor/role model encouraged me to go

I could not find a job

There was nothing better to do

0 10 20 30 40 50 60 70 80 90

Percent of Students Agreeing with Statement

Community service

Making contributions to the society and community in which you live

> "Education is not the filling of a pail, but the lighting of a fire."
> —William Butler Yeats

Service learning

Courses that allow a student to engage in community service activities while getting course credit for the experience

You won't be prepared for the future unless you understand others and their cultural backgrounds—as well as how your own cultural background affects you.

> **You'll learn to lead a life of community service.** In its broadest sense, **community service** involves making contributions to the society and community in which you live. College provides you with the opportunity to become involved in community service activities, in some cases even getting course credit for it—a process called **service learning.** College also allows you to develop the skills involved in acting toward others with *civility* and respectful, courteous behavior.

> **You'll make learning a lifelong habit.** Higher education isn't the end of your education. Education will build upon your natural curiosity about the world, and it will make you aware that learning is a rewarding and never-ending journey.

> **You'll understand the meaning of your own contributions to the world.** No matter who you are, you are poised to make your own contributions to society and the world. Higher education provides you with a window to the

Journal Reflections

My School Experiences

Throughout this book, you will be given opportunities to write out your thoughts. These opportunities—called Journal Reflections—offer a chance to think critically about the chapter topics and record your personal reactions to them. As you create your reflections, be honest, to yourself and to your instructor.

Completing these Journal Reflections provides a variety of benefits. Not only will you be able to mull over your past and present academic experiences, you'll begin to see patterns in the kind of difficulties—and successes!—you encounter. You'll be able to apply solutions that worked in one situation to others. And one added benefit: You'll get practice in writing.

If you save these entries and return to them later, you may be surprised at the changes they record over the course of the term. You can either write them out and keep an actual journal, or create your journal electronically at the P.O.W.E.R. Learning Web site at **www.mhhe.com/power**.

1. Think of one of the successful experiences you've had during your previous years in school. What was it?

2. What made the experience successful? What did you learn from your success?

3. Think of an experience you had in school that you could have handled more successfully, and briefly describe it. Why did it occur?

4. What could you have done differently to make it successful? What did you learn from it?

5. Based on these experiences of academic success and failure, what general lessons did you learn that could help you be a more successful student in the future?

past, present, and future, and it allows you to understand the significance of your own contributions. Your college education provides you with a compass to discover who you are, where you've been, and where you're going.

In short, there are numerous benefits for attending college. To help you attain these benefits, it's time to introduce you to a process that will help you achieve success, both in college and in life beyond: P.O.W.E.R. Learning.

»LO 1.2 P.O.W.E.R. Learning: The Five Key Steps to Achieving Success

P.O.W.E.R. Learning itself is merely an acronym—a word formed from the first letters of a series of steps—that will help you take in, process, and make use of the information you'll acquire in college. It will help you to achieve your goals, both while you are in college and later after you graduate.

P.O.W.E.R. Learning
A system designed to help people achieve their goals, based on five steps: *Prepare, Organize, Work, Evaluate,* and *Rethink*

P.O.W.E.R. Plan

Prepare, Organize, Work, Evaluate, and Rethink. That's it. It's a simple framework but an effective one. Using the systematic framework that P.O.W.E.R. Learning provides (and which is illustrated in the P.O.W.E.R. Plan diagram) will increase your chances of success at any task, from writing a college paper to purchasing the weekly groceries.

Keep this in mind: P.O.W.E.R. Learning isn't a product that you can simply pull down off the bookshelf and use without thinking. P.O.W.E.R. Learning is a process, and you are the only one who can make it succeed. Without your personal investment in the process, P.O.W.E.R. Learning consists of just words on paper.

Relax, though. You already know each of the elements of P.O.W.E.R. Learning, and you may discover that you are already putting this process, or parts of it, to work for you. You've graduated from high school and been accepted into college. You may have also held down a job, had a first date, and registered to vote. Each of these accomplishments required that you use strategies of P.O.W.E.R. Learning. What you'll be doing throughout this book is becoming more aware of these strategies and how they can be used to help you in situations you will encounter in college and beyond.

P Prepare

Chinese philosopher Lao Tzu said that travelers taking a long journey must begin with a single step.

But before they even take that first step, travelers need to know several things: what their destination is, how they're going to get there, how they'll know when they reach the destination, and what they'll do if they have trouble along the way. In the same way, you need to know where you're headed as you embark on the intellectual journeys involved in college. Whether it be a major, long-term task, such as college attendance, or a more limited activity, such as getting ready to complete a paper due in the near future, you'll need to prepare for the journey.

Setting Goals

Before we seek to accomplish any task, all of us do some form of planning. The trouble is that most of the time such planning is done without conscious thinking, as if we are on autopilot. However, the key to success is to make sure that planning is systematic.

The best way to plan systematically is to use goal-setting strategies. In many cases, goals are clear and direct. It's obvious that our goal in washing dishes is to have the dishes end up clean. We know that our goal at the gas station is to fill the car's tank with gas. We go to the post office to buy stamps and mail letters.

Other goals are not so clear-cut. In fact, often the more important the task—such as going to college—the more complicated may be our goals.

What's the best way to set appropriate goals? Here are some guidelines:

➤ **Set both long-term and short-term goals. Long-term goals** are aims relating to major accomplishments that take some time to achieve. **Short-term goals** are relatively limited steps you would take on the road to accomplishing your long-term goals. For example, one of the primary reasons you're in college is to achieve the long-term goal of getting a degree. But in order to reach that goal, you have to accomplish a series of short-term goals, such as completing a set of required courses, taking a series of elective courses, and choosing a major. Even these short-term goals can be broken down into shorter-term goals. In order to complete a required course, for instance, you have to accomplish short-term goals, such as completing a paper, taking several tests, and so on. For practice in setting long- and short-term goals, complete **Try It 2.**

Long-term goals
Aims relating to major accomplishments that take some time to achieve

Short-term goals
Relatively limited steps toward the accomplishment of long-term goals

What Are Your Goals?

Before you begin any journey, you need to know where you are going. To plan your academic journey—and your later career—you first need to set goals. *Short-term goals* are relatively limited objectives that bring you closer to your ultimate goal. *Long-term goals* are aims relating to major accomplishments that take more time to achieve.

In this *Try It!*, think about your short- and long-term academic goals for a few minutes, and then list them. Because short-term goals are based on what you want to accomplish in the long term, first identify your long-term goals. Then list the short-term goals that will help you reach your long-term goals. An example is provided for each kind of goal:

Long-Term Goal #1 Get a college degree
    Related Short-Term Goals:
- Complete four courses with a grade of B or above each term
- _____
- _____
- _____
- _____

Long-Term Goal #2: _____
    Related Short-Term Goals:
- _____
- _____
- _____
- _____
- _____

Long-Term Goal #3: _____
    Related Short-Term Goals:
- _____
- _____
- _____
- _____
- _____

Long-Term Goal #4: _____
    Related Short-Term Goals:
- _____
- _____
- _____
- _____
- _____

Long-Term Goal #5: _____
    Related Short-Term Goals:
- _____
- _____
- _____
- _____
- _____

After you complete the chart, consider how easy or difficult it was to identify your long-term goals. How many of your long-term goals relate to college, and how many to your future career? Do any of your short-term goals relate to more than one long-term goal?

To Try It online, go to www.mhhe.com/power.

▸ **Recognize that who you are determines your goals.** Goal setting starts with knowing yourself. As you'll see when we focus on understanding yourself and your values—those qualities that you hold most desirable—in Chapter 3, it is self-knowledge that tells you what is and is not important to you. This understanding of yourself will help you keep your goals in focus and your motivation up when things get tough.

▸ **Make goals realistic and attainable.** Someone once said, "A goal without a plan is but a dream." We'd all like to win gold medals at the Olympics or star in rock videos or write best-selling novels. Few of us are likely to achieve such goals.

Be honest with yourself. There is nothing wrong with having big dreams. But it is important to be realistically aware of all that it takes to achieve them. If our long-term goals are unrealistic and we don't achieve them, the big danger is that we may wrongly reason that we are inept and lack ability and use this as an excuse for giving up. If goals are realistic, we can develop a plan to attain them, spurring us on to attain more.

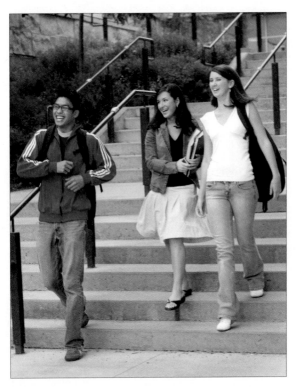

College is not an end-point, but part of a lifelong journey.

▸ **State goals in terms of behavior that can be measured against current accomplishments.** Goals should represent some measurable change from a current set of circumstances. We want our behavior to change in some way that can usually be expressed in terms of numbers—to show an increase ("raise my grade point average 10 percent") or a decrease ("reduce wasted time by two hours each week") or to be maintained ("keep in touch with my out-of-town friends by writing four e-mail messages each month"), developed ("participate in one workshop on critical thinking"), or restricted ("reduce my phone expenses 10 percent by speaking and texting less").

▸ **Goals should involve behavior over which you have control.** We all want world peace and an end to poverty. Few of us have the resources or capabilities to bring either about. On the other hand, it is realistic to want to work in small ways to help others, such as by becoming a Big Brother or Big Sister or by volunteering at a local food bank.

▸ **Take ownership of your goals.** Make sure that the goals you choose are your goals, and not the goals of your parents, teachers, brothers and sisters, or friends. If you're attending college only because others have told you to, and you have no commitment of your own, you'll find it hard to maintain the enthusiasm—not to mention the hard work—required to succeed.

▸ **Identify how your short-term goals fit with your long-term goals.** Your goals should not be independent of one another. Instead, they should fit together into a larger dream of who you want to be. Every once in a while step back and consider what you're doing today relates to the kind of person that you would ultimately like to be.

To get more practice in using these goal-setting principles, consider the goals that underlie taking a particular college class in which you are currently enrolled.

Course Goals

Think about one of the classes that you are taking this term. List your goals for the class in the first column below:

Goals for Class

**Goals in Order
of Importance**

The goals you've listed most likely range from the specific ("passing the class with a good grade") to the more general and vague ("becoming educated in the subject matter of the class").

Now, rank order them to determine which are the most important to you. Note that some of these goals may be short-term goals ("get a decent grade") and some represent longer-term goals ("complete all college requirements"). In addition, your goals may be specific ("get an A in the course") or relatively vague ("do well in the class").

Now consider the following:

- What is the difference between those goals that are most important to you and least important to you?

- Are your goals mostly short-term or long-term?

- How specific are your goals?

- What implications might your different goals have for your future success in the course?

WORKING IN A GROUP:

Compare your goals for the course with those of other students and consider the similarities and differences.

To Try It online, go to www.mhhe.com/power.

You probably have several goals for each course you are taking this term. Completing **Try It 3** will give you a chance to evaluate them.

⊙ Organize

By determining where you want to go and expressing your goals in terms that can be measured, you have already made a lot of progress. But there's another step you must take on the road to success.

The second step in P.O.W.E.R. Learning is to organize the tools you'll need to accomplish your goals. Building upon the goal-setting work you've undertaken in the preparation stage, it's time to determine the best way to accomplish the goals you've identified.

How do you do this? Suppose you've decided to build a set of bookshelves for one room in your house. Let's say that you've already determined the kind of bookshelves you like and figured out the basic characteristics of the ones you will build (the preparation step in P.O.W.E.R. Learning). The next stage involves gathering the necessary tools, buying the wood and other building materials, sorting the construction supplies, and preparing the room for the shelving project—all aspects of organizing for the task.

Similarly, your academic success will hinge to a large degree on the thoroughness of your organization for each academic task that you face. In fact, one of the biggest mistakes that students make in college is plunging into an academic project—studying for a test, writing a paper, completing an in-class assignment—without being organized.

The Two Kinds of Organization: Physical and Mental

On a basic level is *physical organization* involving the mechanical aspects of task completion. For instance, you need to ask yourself if you have the appropriate tools, such as pens, paper, and a calculator. If you're using a computer, do you have access to a printer? Do you have a way to back up your files? Do you have the books and other materials you'll need to complete the assignment? Will the campus bookstore be open if you need anything else? Will the library be open when you need it? Do you have a comfortable place to work?

Mental organization is even more critical. Mental organization is accomplished by considering and reviewing the academic skills that you'll need to successfully complete the task at hand. You are an academic general in command of considerable forces; you will need to make sure your forces—the basic skills you have at your command—are at their peak of readiness.

For example, if you're working on a math assignment, you'll want to consider the basic math skills that you'll need and brush up on them. Just actively thinking about this will help you organize mentally. Similarly, you'd want to mentally review your understanding of the causes of the American Civil War before beginning an assignment on the Reconstruction period that followed the war.

Why does producing mental organization matter? The answer is because it provides a context for when you actually begin to work. Organizing paves the way for better subsequent learning of new material.

Too often students are in a hurry to meet a deadline and figure they better just dive in and get it done. Organizing can actually *save* you time, because you're less likely to be anxious and end up losing your way as you work to complete your task.

Much of this book is devoted to strategies for determining—*before* you begin work on a task—how to develop the mental tools for completing an assignment. However, as you'll see, all of these strategies share a common theme: that success comes not from a trial-and-error approach but from following a systematic plan for achievement. Of course, this does not mean that there will be no surprises along the way, nor that simple luck is never a factor in great accomplishments. But it does mean that we often can make our own luck through careful preparation and organization.

W Work

You're ready. The preliminaries are out of the way. You've prepared and you've organized. Now it's time to get started actually doing the work.

Looking at the Big Picture

It's natural to view a college course as a series of small tasks—classes to attend, a certain number of pages to read each week, a few papers due during the term, three quizzes and a final exam to study for, and so on.

But such a perspective may lead you to miss what the course, as a whole, is all about. Using the P.O.W.E.R. Learning framework can help you take the long view of a course, considering how the class helps you achieve your long- and short-term goals (the *Prepare* step) and what you'll need to do to maximize your success in it (the *Organize* step). By preparing and organizing even before you step foot in the classroom for the first time, you'll be able to consider what it is that you want to get out of the course and how it fits into your education as a whole.

In some ways work is the easy part, because—if you conscientiously carried out the preparation and organization stages—you should know exactly where you're headed and what you need to do to get there.

It's not quite so easy, of course. How effectively you'll get down to the business at hand depends on many factors. Some may be out of your control. There may be a power outage that closes down the library or a massive traffic jam that delays your getting to campus. But most factors are—or should be—under your control. Instead of getting down to work, you may find yourself thinking up "useful" things to do—like finally hanging that poster that's been rolled up in a corner for three months—or simply sitting captive in front of the TV. This kind of obstacle to work relates to motivation.

Finding the Motivation to Work

"If only I could get more motivated, I'd do so much better with my " (insert *schoolwork, diet, exercising,* or the like—you fill in the blank).

All of us have said something like this at one time or another. We use the concept of **motivation**—or its lack—to explain why we just don't work hard at a task. But when we do that, we're fooling ourselves. We all have some motivation, that inner power and psychological energy that directs and fuels our behavior. Without any motivation, we'd never get out of bed in the morning.

We've also seen evidence of how strong our motivation can be. Perhaps you're an avid runner and you love to jog in the morning and compete in weekend races. Or maybe your love of music helped you learn to play the guitar, making practicing for hours a pleasure rather than a chore. Or perhaps you're a single mother, juggling work, school, and family, and you get up early every morning to make breakfast for your kids before they go off to school.

All of us are motivated. The key to success in and out of the classroom is to tap into, harness, and direct that motivation.

If we assume that we already have all the motivation we need, P.O.W.E.R. Learning becomes a matter of turning the skills we already possess into a habit. It becomes a matter of redirecting our psychological energies toward the work we wish to accomplish.

In a sense, everything you'll encounter in this book will help you improve your use of the motivation that you already have. But there's a key concept that underlies the control of motivation—viewing success as a consequence of effort:

Motivation

The inner power and psychological energy that directs and fuels behavior

Effort produces success.

Suppose, for example, you've gotten a good grade on your midterm. The instructor beams at you as she hands back your test. How do you feel?

You will undoubtedly be pleased, of course. But at the same time you might think to yourself, "Better not get a swollen head about it. It was just luck. If she'd asked other questions I would have been in trouble." Or perhaps you explain your success by thinking, "Pretty easy test."

If you often think this way—and you can find out if you do by completing **Try It 4**—you're cheating yourself. Using this kind of reasoning when you succeed, instead of patting yourself on the back and thinking with satisfaction, "All my hard work really paid off," is sure to undermine your future success.

A great deal of psychological research has shown that thinking you have no control over what happens to you sends a powerful and damaging message to your self-esteem—that you are powerless to change things. Just think of how different it feels to say to yourself, "Wow, I worked at it and did it," as compared with, "I lucked out" or "It was so easy that anybody could have done well."

In the same way, we can delude ourselves when we try to explain our failures. People who see themselves as the victims of circumstance may tell themselves, "I'm just not smart enough" when they don't do well on an academic task. Or they might say, "Those other students don't have to work five hours a day."

The way in which we view the causes of success and failure is, in fact, directly related to our success. Students who generally see effort and hard work as the reason behind their performance usually do better in college. It's not hard to see why: When they are working on an assignment, they feel that the greater the effort they put forth, the greater their chances of success. So they work harder. They believe that they have control over their success, and if they fail, they believe they can do better in the future.

Here are some tips for keeping your motivation alive, so you can work with your full energy behind you:

> **Take responsibility for your failures—and successes.** When you do poorly on a test, don't blame the teacher, the textbook, or a job that kept you from studying. Analyze the situation, and see how you could have changed what you did to be more successful in the future. At the same time, when you're successful, think of the things you did to bring about that success.

> **Think positively.** Assume that the strengths that you have will allow you to succeed and that, if you have difficulty, you can figure out what to do.

> **Accept that you can't control everything.** Seek to understand which things can be changed and which cannot. You might be able to get an extension on a paper due date, but you are probably not going to be excused from a college-wide requirement.

To further explore the causes of academic success, consider the questions in **Try It 5** on page 14, and then discuss them with your classmates.

> "The function of the university is not simply to teach bread-winning, or to furnish teachers for the public schools or to be a center of polite society; it is, above all, to be the organ of that fine adjustment between real life and the growing knowledge of life, an adjustment which forms the secret of civilization."
>
> W.E.B. DuBois, author,
> *The Souls of Black Folk*, 1903

E Evaluate

"Great, I'm done with the work. Now I can move on."

It's natural to feel relief when you've finished the work necessary to fulfill the basic requirements of an assignment. After all, if you've written the five

Try It! POWER

Who's in Charge?

4

To get a sense of your ideas of why things happen to you, check the statement from each of the pairs below that best describes your views:[4]

☐ 1a. In the long run, people get the respect they deserve in this world.

☐ 1b. Unfortunately, an individual's worth often passes unrecognized no matter how hard he or she tries.

☐ 2a. The idea that teachers are unfair to students is nonsense.

☐ 2b. Most students don't realize the extent to which their exam results are influenced by accidental happenings.

☐ 3a. I have often found that what is going to happen will happen.

☐ 3b. Trusting fate has never turned out as well for me as making a decision to take a definite course of action.

☐ 4a. In the case of the well-prepared student, there is rarely if ever such a thing as an unfair exam.

☐ 4b. Many times exam questions tend to be so unrelated to course work that studying is really useless.

☐ 5a. Becoming a success is a matter of hard work; luck has little or nothing to do with it.

☐ 5b. Getting a good job depends mainly on being in the right place at the right time.

☐ 6a. It is not always wise to plan too far ahead because many things turn out to be a matter of good or bad fortune anyhow.

☐ 6b. When I make plans, I am almost certain that I can make them work.

☐ 7a. In my case, getting what I want has little or nothing to do with luck.

☐ 7b. Many times I might just as well decide what to do by flipping a coin.

☐ 8a. Many times I feel that I have little influence over the things that happen to me.

☐ 8b. It is impossible for me to believe that chance or luck plays an important role in my life.

☐ 9a. What happens to me is my own doing.

☐ 9b. Sometimes I feel that I don't have enough control over the direction my life is taking.

☐ 10a. Sometimes I can't understand how teachers arrive at the marks they give.

☐ 10b. There is a direct connection between how hard a person studies and the grades he or she gets.

Scoring: Give yourself one point for each of the following answers and then add up your score:

1. a.   2. a.   3. b.   4. a.   5. a.   6. b.   7. a.   8. b.   9. a.   10. b.

Your total score can range from 0 to 10. The higher your score, the more you believe that you have a strong influence over what happens to you and are in control of your life and your own behavior. The lower your score, the more you believe that your life is outside of your control and what happens to you is caused by luck or fate.

If you score below 5 on this questionnaire, consider how rethinking your views of the causes of behavior might lead to greater success. In addition, consider how your values might influence your success.

To Try It online, go to www.mhhe.com/power.

double-spaced pages required for an assignment, why shouldn't you heave a sigh of relief and just hand your paper in to the instructor?

The answer is that if you stop at this point, you'll almost be guaranteed a mediocre grade. Did Shakespeare dash off the first draft of *Hamlet* and, without another glance, send it off to the Globe Theater for production? Do professional athletes just put in the bare minimum of practice to get ready for a big game? Think of one of your favorite songs. Do you think the composer wrote it in one sitting and then performed it in a concert?

5

Examining the Causes of Success and Failure

Complete this Try It while working in a group. First, consider the following situations:

1. Although he studied for a few hours the night before the test, Jack gets a D on a midterm. When he finds out his grade, he is disgusted and says to himself, "I'll probably never do any better in this course. I'd better just blow it off for the rest of the term and put my energies into my other classes."

2. Anne gets an A– on her history exam. She is happy, but when her instructor tells the class that they did well as a group and that the average grade was B+, she decides that she did well only because the test was so easy.

3. Chen gets a C on his first math quiz. Because he didn't do as well as he expected, he vows to perform better the next time. He doubles the amount of time he studies for the next quiz, but still his grade is only slightly higher. Distressed, he considers dropping the class because he thinks that he'll never be successful in math.

Now consider the following questions about each of the situations:

1. What did each student conclude was the main cause of his or her performance?
2. What effect does this conclusion seem to have on the student?
3. Taking an outsider's point of view, what would *you* think was the main cause of the student's performance?
4. What advice would you give each student?

Now consider these broader questions:

1. What are the most important reasons why some students are more academically successful in college than others?
2. How much does ability determine success? How much does luck determine success? How much do circumstances determine success?
3. If someone performs poorly on an exam, what are the possible reasons for his or her performance? If someone performs well on an exam, what are the possible reasons for his or her performance? Is it harder to find reasons for good compared with poor performance? Why?

To Try It online, go to www.mhhe.com/power.

Evaluation

An assessment of the match between a product or activity and the goals it was intended to meet

In every case, the answer is no. Even the greatest creation does not emerge in perfect form, immediately meeting all the goals of its producer. Consequently, the fourth step in the P.O.W.E.R. process is **evaluation,** which consists of determining how well the product or activity we have created matches our goals for it. Let's consider some steps to follow in evaluating what you've accomplished:

> **Take a moment to congratulate yourself and feel some satisfaction.** Whether it's been studying for a test, writing a paper, preparing a review sheet, or reading an assignment, you've done something important. You've moved from ground zero to a spot that's closer to your goal.

> **Compare what you've accomplished with the goals you're seeking to achieve.** Think back to the goals, both short-term and long-term, that you're seeking to achieve. How closely does what you've done match what you're aiming to do? For instance, if your short-term goal is to complete a statistics problem set with no errors, you'll need to check over the paper carefully to make sure you've made no mistakes.

> **Have an out-of-body experience: Evaluate your accomplishments as if you were a respected teacher from your past.** If you've written a paper, reread it from the perspective of that teacher. If you've completed a worksheet, think about what comments you'd write across the top if you were that teacher.

> **Evaluate what you've done as if you were your current instructor.** Now exchange bodies and minds again. This time, consider what you're doing from the perspective of the instructor who gave you the assignment. How would he or she react to what you've done? Have you followed the assignment to the letter? Is there anything you've missed?

> **Be fair to yourself.** The guidelines for evaluation will help you to determine just how much further work is necessary and, even more important, what work is necessary. Don't go too far, though: It's as counterproductive to be too hard on yourself as it is to be too easy. Stick to a middle ground, always keeping your final goal in mind.

> **Based on your evaluation, revise your work.** If you're honest with yourself, it's unlikely that your first work will satisfy you. So go back to *Work* and revise what you've done. But don't think of it as a step back: Revisions you make as a consequence of your evaluation bring you closer to your final goal. This is a case where going back moves you forward.

R Rethink

Even the Declaration of Independence underwent revisions before the final version was signed.

They thought they had it perfect. But they were wrong.

In fact, it was a $1.5 billion mistake—a blunder on a grand scale. The finely ground mirror of the Hubble space telescope, designed to provide an unprecedented glimpse into the vast reaches of the universe, was not so finely ground after all.

Despite an elaborate system of evaluation designed to catch any flaws, there was a tiny blemish in the mirror that was not detected until the telescope had been launched into space and started to send back blurry photographs. By then, it seemed too late to fix the mirror.

Or was it? NASA engineers rethought the problem for months, devising, and then discarding, one potential fix after another. Finally, after bringing a fresh eye to the situation, they formulated a daring solution that involved sending a team of astronauts into space. Once there, a space-walking Mr. Goodwrench would install several new mirrors in the telescope, which could refocus the light and compensate for the original flawed mirror.

Although the engineers could not be certain that the $629 million plan would work, it seemed like a good solution, at least on paper. It was not until the first photos were beamed back to Earth, though, that NASA knew their solution was A-OK. These photos were spectacular.

The daring mission to repair the Hubble space telescope was the culmination of months of rethinking how to fix the flaw in the telescope. It worked: A new time-lapse movie of images taken by the telescope showed the seasonal changes on Uranus, as well as other celestial wonders.

Critical thinking
A process involving reanalysis,
questioning, and challenge of
underlying assumptions

It took months of reconsideration before NASA scientists could figure out what went wrong and devise a solution to the problem they faced. Their approach exemplifies—on a grand scale—the final step in P.O.W.E.R. Learning: rethinking.

To *rethink* what you've accomplished earlier means bringing a fresh—and clear—eye to what you've done. It involves using **critical thinking,** thinking that involves reanalyzing, questioning, and challenging our underlying assumptions. While evaluation means considering how well what we have done matches our initial goals, rethinking means reconsidering not only the outcome of our efforts but also reconsidering our goals and the ideas and the process we've used to reach them. Critically rethinking what you've done involves analyzing and synthesizing ideas and seeing the connections between different concepts.

Rethinking involves considering whether our initial goals are practical and realistic or if they require modification. It also entails asking yourself what you would do differently if you could do it over again.

We'll be considering critical thinking throughout this book, examining specific strategies in every chapter. For the moment, the following steps provide a general framework for using critical thinking to rethink what you've accomplished:

> ➤ **Reanalyze, reviewing how you've accomplished the task.** Consider the approach and strategies you've used. What seemed to work best? Do they suggest any alternatives that might work better the next time?

> ➤ **Question the outcome.** Take a "big picture" look at what you have accomplished. Are you pleased and satisfied? Is there something you've somehow missed?

> ➤ **Identify your underlying assumptions, then challenge them.** Consider the assumptions you made in initially approaching the task. Are these underlying assumptions reasonable? If you had used different assumptions, would the result have been similar or different?

> ➤ **Consider alternatives rejected earlier.** You've likely discarded possible strategies and approaches prior to completing your task. Now's the time to think about those approaches once more and determine if they might have been more appropriate than the road you've followed.

> ➤ **What would you do differently if you had the opportunity to try things again?** It's not too late to change course.

> ➤ **Finally, reconsider your initial goals.** Are they achievable and realistic? Do your goals, and the strategies you used to attain them, need to be modified? Critically rethinking the objectives and goals that underlie your efforts is often the most effective route to success.

Completing the Process

The rethinking step of P.O.W.E.R. Learning is meant to help you understand your process of work and to improve the final product if necessary. But mostly it is meant to help you grow, to become better at whatever it is you've been doing. Like a painter looking at his or her finished work, you may see a spot here or there to touch up, but don't destroy the canvas. Perfectionism can be as paralyzing as laziness. Keep in mind these key points:

> ➤ **Know that there's always another day.** Your future success does not depend on any single assignment, paper, or test. Don't fall victim to self-defeating thoughts such as "If I don't do well, I'll never graduate" or "Everything is riding on this one assignment." Nonsense. There is almost always an opportunity to recover from a failure.

P.O.W.E.R. Learning Meets the World of Work

Although the focus of the P.O.W.E.R. Learning system is on developing school success, its applications extend well beyond the classroom. In particular, the principles of P.O.W.E.R. Learning are useful in the world of work, and your ability to use them will provide you with keys to success in the workplace.

Skeptical? In *Career Connections* boxes in future chapters we'll explore how the principles we're discussing can help you choose an appropriate career and excel in the workplace. For now, though, take a look at these "help wanted" advertisements and online postings. They illustrate the importance of the components of P.O.W.E.R. Learning in the workplace.

Prepare *Organize* *Work* *Rethink* *Evaluate*

CLINICAL DOCUMENTS SPECIALIST Job Code: GCD

CLINICAL RESEARCH ASSOCIATE II Job Code: GCD

> **Realize that deciding when to stop work is often as hard as getting started.** Knowing when you have put in enough time studying for a test, have revised a paper sufficiently, or have reviewed your answers adequately on a work-sheet is as much a key to success as properly preparing. If you've carefully evaluated what you've done and seen that there's a close fit between your goals and your work, it's time to stop work and move on.

> **Use the strategies that already work for you.** Although the P.O.W.E.R. Learning framework provides a proven approach to attaining success, employing it does not mean that you should abandon strategies that have brought you success in the past. Using multiple approaches, and personalizing them, is the surest road to success.

≫ LO 1.3 Are You Ready for College Success?

Maybe you're asking yourself why you should bother with P.O.W.E.R. Learning and the techniques that will be described in this book. You may believe that because you did OK in high school, you'll be just fine in college without changing the way you did things there.

But college isn't high school.[5]

In high school, you were probably told what you needed to learn from assignments; in college, it will be up to you to read and understand assignments on your own. You'll be tested on material in college that the professor may never once have mentioned in class.

High school teachers monitored your class attendance and graded all homework; in college, professors may not take attendance and may not look at every bit of homework—although they expect you to be in class and do all homework. And while you may be used to frequent tests in high school, in college you may have only a few exams, covering large chunks of material.

In high school, your time was mostly structured by others; in college, you have to manage it yourself. In a broader sense, in high school, you were told what your responsibilities were, while in college you're viewed as an adult who needs to figure out on your own what your responsibilities are.

In addition to differences in the style of instruction between high school and college, you're different, too. Whether you finished high school a few months ago or you deferred college and are returning after a lapse of many years, you are not the same person you were in high school. College offers a fresh start, with instructors who have no predetermined expectations about who you are.

But in order to get that fresh start, you need to have a clear sense of your own strengths and weaknesses. Accurately knowing who you are, and your own competencies, can help you focus on those strategies presented in future chapters that will be most beneficial to you. To get a more objective sense of your own strong and weak points, complete **Try It 6.**

Ultimately, to become an accomplished student, you must be open to change in yourself and to embrace success. The techniques for doing this are in this book, but only you can implement them. The road to success may not be simple or direct (see the *Speaking of Success* interview with C'Ardiss Gardner later in the chapter for a glimpse of one student's real-life journey), but there are few goals that are more important than attaining a college education.

Try It! **P O W E R**

Creating a P.O.W.E.R. Profile

6

Are you the student you aspire to be?

Before you can even think about answering that question, you need to know the kind of student you are—right now, at this very moment. Only by frankly facing your current strengths and weaknesses as fully as possible will you be able to know in what direction you should be heading.

To help you get a better understanding of who you are as a student, Try It 6 will take you through the steps of constructing your own **P.O.W.E.R. Profile.** The P.O.W.E.R. Profile is a way for you to take stock of where you stand in relation to the major topics that we'll be discussing in *P.O.W.E.R. Learning*—the characteristics that are most important for college success.

The P.O.W.E.R. Profile outlines key aspects of who you are. The Profile is just one of many possible profiles that could be drawn to describe you. For instance, you have a personality profile, a buying profile, a dating profile, a technology profile, and a variety of others. There is no "ideal" P.O.W.E.R. Profile; there are no right or wrong answers involved in creating one. Instead, as shown in the example in **Figure 1.2,** the P.O.W.E.R. Profile is a look at someone in relation to the 14 dimensions involved with student success (and, not so coincidentally, the key dimensions covered in each of the chapters in *P.O.W.E.R. Learning*).

The best way to maximize the usefulness of your P.O.W.E.R. Profile is to create one now, before you've gone beyond the first chapter of this book. Then, by completing a P.O.W.E.R. Profile at the end of the term, you can judge how much your profile has changed and in what directions. If you take to heart what you learn in your class and work carefully through the Try Its in the book and exercises, your profile will undoubtedly change in a positive direction. In the meantime, the P.O.W.E.R. Profile will give you an objective idea of where you stand right now on each of these dimensions.

To get started with your P.O.W.E.R. Profile, read each statement and judge how well it describes you, using these numbered descriptions:

1 = Doesn't describe me at all

2 = Describes me only slightly

3 = Describes me fairly well

4 = Describes me very well

figure 1.2
Sample P.O.W.E.R Profile

(continued)

Creating a P.O.W.E.R. Profile (continued)

6 Place your response on the line next to each of the questions. Take your time, answer the questions thoughtfully and, above all, truthfully. There are no right or wrong answers. Remember that the profile is not a test; it is for your own enlightenment only.

Dimension 1: College Rationale	
a. I understand why attending college is important to me. b. I have a clear short-term and long-term goals. c. My course selections are related to my goals. d. I know how to organize myself and get my work done. e. I accept that success or failure is in my own hands.	_____ _____ _____ _____ _____ **College Rationale Total** _____
Dimension 2: Time Use	
a. I know how to manage my time effectively. b. I understand how to set priorities for my time. c. I know how to say no to time wasters. d. I understand how to avoid procrastination. e. I consider myself to be a good time organizer.	_____ _____ _____ _____ _____ **Time Use Total** _____
Dimension 3: Self-Understanding	
a. I understand how I learn most effectively. b. I know how learning styles can affect academic success. c. I have a clear self-concept and understand who I am. d. I have a good sense of self-esteem. e. I know how to use a personal mission statement to guide important decisions.	_____ _____ _____ _____ _____ **Self-Understanding Total** _____
Dimension 4: Notetaking	
a. I take good notes during class lectures and discussions. b. My notes capture the speaker's main points. c. I know how to use active listening to focus in class. d. I can take good notes on what I read for my courses. e. I review my notes soon after I have written them.	_____ _____ _____ _____ _____ **Notetaking Total** _____
Dimension 5: Test-Taking	
a. I generally go to tests well prepared and reasonably calm. b. I understand how to tackle different kinds of test questions. c. I know how to control anxiety before and during testing. d. I usually leave time at the end of a test to check my work. e. I know how to use test results to improve my future test-taking.	_____ _____ _____ _____ _____ **Test-Taking Total** _____
Dimension 6: Reading	
a. I know my personal reading style and understand how it affects my reading. b. I understand how to use advance organizers in my reading. c. I know my attention span and understand how to stay focused. d. I know how to check for understanding while I read. e. I understand the importance of rereading and rethinking.	_____ _____ _____ _____ _____ **Reading Total** _____

Dimension 7: Writing & Speaking	
a. I know how to use the writing process to start and maintain the flow of my writing.	_____
b. I understand the importance of considering my audience in writing.	_____
c. I know how to outline, write a first draft, and revise my writing.	_____
d. I have strategies to overcome my fear of speaking in public.	_____
e. I have a good system for impromptu, unprepared oral presentations.	_____
	Writing & Speaking Total _____

Dimension 8: Memory	
a. I know my preferred memory style and use it to help me study.	_____
b. I know about rehearsal and overlearning and use them in my studies.	_____
c. I know how to link new information to information that I already possess.	_____
d. I am familiar with several memorization techniques.	_____
e. I know how to consolidate my memories to improve test performance.	_____
	Memory Total _____

Dimension 9: Choices	
a. I understand the options and choices available to me at my college.	_____
b. I know where I stand in terms of completing my course requirements.	_____
c. I know exactly what to do if there's a problem with my course selections or records.	_____
d. I am satisfied that my course choices are moving me in the right direction.	_____
e. I am confident that I will choose a major that makes sense in terms of my life goals.	_____
	Choices Total _____

Dimension 10: Technology	
a. I understand how to use computer applications effectively for my college work.	_____
b. I know how to use the Internet for communication, staying up to date, and research.	_____
c. I understand distance learning and know whether or not it's right for me.	_____
d. I know how to use library resources and the World Wide Web to gather information.	_____
e. I know how to evaluate the accuracy and reliability of information I have found.	_____
	Technology Total _____

Dimension 11: Decision Making	
a. I use a structured process for making important decisions.	_____
b. I know how to identify my goals and generate alternatives.	_____
c. I am good at assessing alternatives and making decisions I am happy with.	_____
d. I use an array of strategies for solving problems.	_____
e. I understand the most common obstacles to effective critical thinking.	_____
	Decision Making Total _____

Dimension 12: Relationships	
a. I understand the importance of diversity on campus and in the broader society.	_____
b. I have good relationships with people of many different backgrounds.	_____
c. I understand cultural competence and consider myself culturally competent.	_____
d. I know what it takes to build good relationships.	_____
e. I know how to handle conflict in my relationships.	_____
	Relationships Total _____

Dimension 13: Money	
a. I know my short- and long-term financial goals.	_____
b. I understand where my money comes from and where it goes.	_____
c. I know how to prepare a realistic budget and stick to it.	_____
d. I am realistic about the advantages and disadvantages of credit cards.	_____
e. I know where to go if I need financial aid for college.	_____
	Money Total _____

(continued)

Creating a P.O.W.E.R. Profile (concluded)

Dimension 14: Health	
a. I understand stress and know how to cope with it.	_____
b. I understand the importance of a good diet, exercise, and rest.	_____
c. I have strategies for avoiding the abuse of alcohol and other drugs.	_____
d. I am responsible about my sexuality and know how to stay sexually healthy.	_____
e. I know where to go to get help with all aspects of my health.	_____
	Health Total _____

Now you're ready to construct your P.O.W.E.R. Profile. Add up the numbers on each line to derive a total for each dimension. This total will range from 5 to 20. Finally, place a dot in each appropriate box on the chart in **Figure 1.3** corresponding to your score, and connect the dots to form your P.O.W.E.R Profile.

There—it's done. But it's really just a start. Your P.O.W.E.R. Profile is an objective way to mark the beginning of your journey through college. Its shape will continue to change and evolve the more years of school you have under your belt.

After taking some time to study your P.O.W.E.R. Profile and to maximize its usefulness, consider the following:

- Does your profile seem like an accurate reflection of your strengths and weaknesses as a student? Were there any surprises?
- To be a successful student, what do you think the "ideal" profile would look like?
- Most important, how can you use the results of the P.O.W.E.R. Profile to help you in the future? What are the most important areas for improvement? What strategies might you use to bring about those improvements?

figure 1.3
P.O.W.E.R. Profile

Your P.O.W.E.R. Profile chart with columns: College Rationale, Time Use, Self-Understanding, Notetaking, Test-Taking, Reading, Writing & Speaking, Memory, Choices, Technology, Decision Making, Relationships, Money, Health; rows scaled 20, 15, 10, 5.

Speaking of Success

NAME: C'Ardiss Gardner

SCHOOL: South Seattle Community College

HOME: Seattle, Washington

When C'Ardiss Gardner began college, she was already familiar with challenge. She became a mother at age 16 and chose to finish high school while working two jobs to support her infant.

Despite the challenges, Gardner not only finished her high school requirements early but also had enough credits to start at the local community college. When she started at South Seattle Community College, not only was she taking classes, but she was working two part-time jobs. But eventually, she was forced to delay her college plans to take a third job to support herself. For three years she juggled work and child rearing.

But Gardner also had plans. She got married and re-enrolled at South Seattle. After graduating with her associate's degree, she was accepted to four-year colleges around the country. She decided to move her family to the East Coast to attend Yale University. Gardner graduated from Yale with a B.A. in African-American Studies. She and her family returned to Seattle, where she now is raising three children, working as the registrar of a prep school, and

studying for a master's degree in education at Seattle University.

"Attending school as an African-American student with a small child was very challenging. I did not come from a community that supported or encouraged kids like me to go to college," said Gardner.

"Even something as simple as writing was enough to set me apart from the other students, who had spent years learning how to write at a college level. I had to learn those things, and it was very difficult," she noted. "One of the most important things I learned was to access as many resources as I could to help learn skills I was lacking. Professors offered help by reading my drafts before I turned essays or papers in. By accepting help, I was able to improve my writing skills and improve my grades."

The skills Gardner developed while at South Seattle Community College laid the groundwork for her future academic success and became the foundation upon which she has been able to build the rest of her life. Not only has she been able to continue her education, but she plans to use her skills to help pave the way for other students to access education.

www.mhhe.com/power   CHAPTER ONE   P.O.W.E.R. Learning: Becoming a Successful Student   23

Looking Back

What are the benefits of a college education?

> The reason first-year college students most often cite for attending college is to get a better job, and college graduates do earn more on average than nongraduates.

> College also provides many other benefits. These include becoming well-educated, learning to think critically and communicate effectively, understanding the interconnections between different areas of knowledge and our place in history and the world, practicing community service, and understanding diversity.

What are the basic principles of P.O.W.E.R. Learning?

> P.O.W.E.R. Learning is a systematic approach people can easily learn, using abilities they already possess, to acquire successful habits for learning and achieving personal goals.

> P.O.W.E.R. Learning involves **p**reparation, **o**rganization, **w**ork, **e**valuation, and **r**ethinking.

How do expert students use P.O.W.E.R. Learning?

> To *prepare,* learners set both long-term and short-term goals, making sure that their goals are realistic, measurable, and under their control—and will lead to their final destination.

> They *organize* the tools they will need to accomplish those goals.

> They get down to *work* on the task at hand. Using their goals as motivation, expert learners also understand that success depends on effort.

> They *evaluate* the work they've done, considering what they have accomplished in comparison with the goals they set for themselves during the preparation stage.

> Finally, they *rethink,* reflecting on the process they've used, taking a fresh look at what they have done, and critically rethinking their goals.

[KEY TERMS AND CONCEPTS]

Community service (p. 4)

Service learning (p. 4)

P.O.W.E.R. Learning (p. 5)

Long-term goals (p. 6)

Short-term goals (p. 6)

Motivation (p. 11)

Evaluation (p. 14)

Critical thinking (p. 16)

[RESOURCES]

ON CAMPUS

Every college provides a significant number of resources to help its students succeed and thrive, ranging from the activities coordination office to a multicultural center to writing labs. You can check them out on your college's Web site, catalog, or phone directory.

For example, here's a list of some typical campus resources, many of which we'll be discussing in future chapters:

- Activities/Clubs Office
- Adult and re-entry center
- Advising Center
- Alumni Office
- Art gallery
- Bookstore
- Career Center
- Chaplain/religious services
- Child Care Center
- Cinema/theater
- Computing center/ computer labs
- Continuing education
- Disability Center (learning or physical disabilities)
- Financial aid

- Fitness center/ gymnasium
- Health Center
- Honors program
- Housing Center
- Information Center
- Intramural sports
- Language lab
- Learning Center
- Lost and found
- Math lab
- Multicultural Center
- Museum
- Online education (distance learning) office
- Off-campus housing and services
- Ombudsman/conflict resolution

- Photography lab
- Police/campus security
- Post office
- Printing center
- Registration Office
- Residential Life Office
- School newspaper
- Student Government Office
- Student Affairs Office
- Study abroad/ exchange programs
- Testing Center
- Volunteer services
- Work-Study Center
- Writing lab

If you are commuting to school, your first "official" encounters on campus are likely to be with representatives of the college's Student Affairs Office or its equivalent. The Student Affairs Office has the goal of maintaining the quality of student life and ensuring that students receive the help they need. Student Affairs personnel often are in charge of student orientation programs that help new students familiarize themselves with their new institution.

If you are living on campus, your first encounter may be with representatives of the residence halls, often called the Residential Life Office. Their job is to help you settle in and orient you to campus. Your residence hall also probably has student residential advisors living on every floor; they can give you an insider's view of college life.

Whatever college representatives you deal with during your first days of college, remember that their job is to help you. Don't be shy about asking questions about what you may expect, how to find things, and what you should be doing.

Above all, if you are experiencing any difficulties, be certain to make use of your college's resources. Starting college is one of the biggest transitions that you'll ever experience in life, and it's a time when you should make use of whatever support your college offers.

IN PRINT

Navigating Your Freshman Year (Students Helping Students Series) (Prentice Hall, 2005), offers a wealth of information on college life from a student's vantage point.

For a variety of views of what it takes to be a successful college student, read *How to Survive Your Freshman Year: By Hundreds of College Sophomores, Juniors, and Seniors Who Did,* 3rd edition, published by Hundreds of Heads Books (2008).

Finally, to learn more about who your first-year classmates are across the United States, take a look at John Pryor and colleagues' *The American Freshman: National Norms for Fall 2008* (Higher Education Research Institute, 2009). The book provides a comprehensive look at the attitudes and opinions of first-year college students, based on the results of a national survey.

ON THE WEB

The following sites on the Web provide the opportunity to extend your learning about the material in this chapter. Although the Web addresses were accurate at the time the book was printed, check the *P.O.W.E.R. Learning* Web site [**www.mhhe.com/power**] for any changes that may have occurred.

> The University of Buffalo (**http://ub-counseling.buffalo.edu/adjusting.shtml**) Counseling Services offers a site on adjusting to campus life that includes links to relationships, health, and study skills.

> The U.S. Department of Education offers *Preparing Your Child for College: A Resource Guide for Parents* (**www.ed.gov/pubs/Prepare/index.html**). Though geared toward parents' concerns, the publication offers answers to a host of valuable questions such as "Why attend college?" and "What kinds of jobs are available to college graduates?"

> The Learn More Resource Center (**www.learnmoreindiana.org**) provides information on a variety of useful topics regarding adjustment to college life, including comments by students on their experiences. It covers such topics as where to live, how to select classes, how to study and learn, and much more.

TAKING IT TO THE NET

1 Find out what percent of the population of the United States has received an undergraduate degree, using search engines such as Google to find U.S. census information. (If you're unfamiliar with search engines on the Web, see Chapter 10 for suggestions that will get you started.) The Census Bureau site provides information about the level of education achieved by people over 25 years of age. How many men have received a bachelor's degree? How many women?

2 Consider the reasons for going to college. The U.S. Department of Education's "Think College" site (**www.ed.gov/students/prep/college/thinkcollege/edlite-index.html**) offers various rationales for continuing your education beyond high school. Were you aware of them prior to your enrollment in college?

The Case of . . .
Clueless in Seattle

It was during the second week of classes that the questioning started. Until then, Roger hadn't thought much about his decision to attend a large state college in a Seattle suburb. It had seemed like a good idea, and he was excited when he was accepted, but he couldn't really pinpoint why he was there.

And that was becoming a problem. As he was walking to class, he began to think about all that had happened to him in the last few weeks. First-year orientation . . . meeting his roommate, and trying to deal with his odd neatness . . . enrolling for classes . . . finding his way around campus . . . meeting an overwhelming number of new people, and trying to figure out where he fit in. Everyone else seemed to know what they were doing. Why didn't he?

It was overwhelming. He wanted to call his parents and tell them to come pick him up. He needed to sit on the porch where it was familiar and comfortable and not overwhelming and try to figure out what he should do. Nothing seemed to make sense. He began to question his decision to attend college. What was he going to do with his life? The question made him feel even more overwhelmed. Did he really need a college degree? With his computer skills, he could probably get a job right away. Hadn't his father's friend told him that he had a job waiting for him whenever he wanted it? At least then he'd be making money.

"Why bother," he thought to himself. "What an expense, and what a hassle. For what?" He realized, to his surprise, he had no real clue as to why he was in college.

1. What arguments could you provide Roger as to the value of a college education?

2. Do you think that Roger's doubts are common? Do people often attend college without thinking about it very much?

3. What might you suggest that Roger do to help deal with his doubts about the value of college?

4. Why might a student's doubts about the value of college be especially strong during the beginning weeks of college?

5. Do you share any of Roger's concerns about the value of a college education? Do you have additional ones? Did you think carefully about the reasons for attending college before you enrolled?

2

Making the Most of Your Time

Learning Outcomes

By the time you finish this chapter you will be able to

» **LO 2.1**   Discuss strategies to manage your time effectively.

» **LO 2.2**   Identify ways to deal with surprises and distractions.

» **LO 2.3**   Explain ways to balance competing priorities.

As Meadow Baresi stands in the long line at the cafeteria, she mentally goes over the things she needs to get done during the day: *Review notes for the 8:30 a.m. management quiz . . . work on philosophy paper . . . computer sci class at 11:15 a.m . . . pick up ticket receipts from last night's game . . . work at student affairs office from 1:00 to 4:00 . . . go to library to research philosophy paper.* She has the nagging feeling that there's something else she needs to do, but she can't put her finger on it.

She finally gets to the head of the line to pay for her bagel, which she's already half devoured. Glancing at a clock as she leaves the Commons, she gives up the thought of getting in some last-minute studying for her management quiz. It will be a minor miracle if she even makes it to class on time.

She's been up less than an hour, and already Meadow is running behind schedule.

Looking Ahead

Are your days like Meadow's? Are you constantly trying to cram more activities into less time? Do you feel as if you never have enough time?

You're not alone: Most of us wish we had more time to accomplish the things we need to do. However, some people are a lot better at juggling their time than others. What's their secret?

There is no secret. No one has more than 24 hours a day and 168 hours a week. The key to success lies in figuring out our priorities and better using the time we do have.

Time management is like juggling a bunch of tennis balls: For most of us, juggling doesn't come naturally, but it is a skill that can be learned. Not all of us will end up perfect jugglers (whether we are juggling tennis balls or time), but, with practice, we can become a lot better at it.

This chapter will give you strategies for improving your time management skills. After first helping you learn to account for the ways you currently use—and misuse—time, it gives you strategies for planning your time, including some ways to deal with the inevitable interruptions and counterproductive personal habits that can sabotage your best intentions. It will provide you with skills that are not only important for success in college but for your future life as well.

We also consider techniques for dealing with competing goals. There are special challenges involved in juggling the priorities of college work with other aspects of life, such as child rearing or holding a job.

≫ LO 2.1 Time for Success

Without looking up from the page, answer this question: What time is it?

Most people are pretty accurate in their answer. And if you don't know for sure, it's very likely that you can find out. Your cell phone may display the time; there may be a clock on the wall, desk, or computer screen; or maybe you're riding in a car that shows the time in the instrument panel.

Even if you don't have a timepiece of some sort nearby, your body keeps its own beat. Humans have an internal clock that regulates the beating of our heart, the pace of our breathing, the discharge of chemicals within our bloodstream, and myriad other bodily functions.

Time is something from which we can't escape. Even if we ignore it, it's still going by, ticking away, second by second, minute by minute, hour by hour. So the main issue in using your time well is, "Who's in charge?" We can allow time to slip by and let it be our enemy. Or we can take control of it and make it our ally.

By taking control of how you spend your time, you'll increase your chances of becoming a more successful student. Perhaps more importantly, the better you

Journal Reflections

Where Does My Time Go?

1. On the typical weekday, what time do you wake up? When would you prefer to wake up if you had the choice?

2. When do you typically go to bed on a typical weekday night? When would you prefer to go to bed if you had the choice?

3. Would you characterize yourself as a "morning person," who accomplishes the most in the early morning, or more as a "night person," who is most comfortable doing work in the evenings? What implications does this have for your scheduling of classes and when you do the most work?

4. If a day suddenly contained more than 24 hours, how would it change your life? What would you do with the extra time? Do you think you would accomplish more?

5. Generally speaking, how would you characterize your time management skills? What would be the benefit to you personally if you could manage time more effectively? What goals might you accomplish if you had more time at your disposal?

P **Prepare**
Learn where time is going

O **Organize**
Use a master calendar, weekly timetable, and daily to-do list

W **Work**
Follow the schedules you've put together

E **Evaluate**
Keep track of your short-term and long-term accomplishments

R **Rethink**
Reflect on your personal style of time management

P.O.W.E.R Plan

are at managing the time you devote to your studies, the more time you will have to spend on your outside interests. (You can get a sense of your own personal time style by completing **Try It 1** on page 31.)

The goal of time management is not to schedule every moment so we become pawns of a timetable that governs every waking moment of the day. Instead, the goal is to permit us to make informed choices as to how we use our time. Rather than letting the day slip by, largely without our awareness, the time management procedures we'll discuss can make us better able to harness time for our own ends. In short, time management doesn't confine us. On the contrary, it frees us to do the things we want and need to do.

P **Prepare**

Learning Where Time Is Going—and Where It Should Go

Before you get somewhere, you need to know where you're starting from and where you want to go. So the first step in improving your time management skills is figuring out how you're managing your time now.

Create a Time Log

"Where did the day go?" If you've ever said this to yourself, one way of figuring out where you've spent your time is to create a time log. A time log is the most essential tool for improving your use of time.

Try It! POWER

Find Your Time Style

1

Rate how well each of the statements below describes you. Use this rating scale:

1 = Doesn't describe me at all

2 = Describes me only slightly

3 = Describes me fairly well

4 = Describes me very well

	1	2	3	4
1. I often wake up later than I should.				
2. I am usually late for classes and appointments.				
3. I am always in a rush getting places.				
4. I put off big tasks and assignments until the last minute.				
5. My friends often comment on my lateness.				
6. I am easily interrupted, putting aside what I'm doing for something new.				
7. When I look at a clock, I'm often surprised at how late it is.				
8. I often forget appointments and have to reschedule them.				
9. When faced with a big task, I feel overwhelmed and turn my mind away from it until later.				
10. At the end of the day, I have no idea where the time went.				

Rate yourself by adding up the points you assigned. Use this scale to assess your time style:

10–15 = Very efficient time user

16–20 = Efficient time user

21–30 = Time use needs work

31–40 = Victim of time

To Try It online, go to www.mhhe.com/power.

A **time log** is simply a record of how you actually have spent your time—including interruptions. It doesn't have to be a second-by-second record of every waking moment. But it should account for blocks of time in increments as short as 15 minutes.

Look at the blank time log in **Try It 2** on page 32. As you fill out the log, be specific, indicating not only what you were doing at a given time (for example, "reading history assignment") but also the interruptions that occurred (such as "answered cell phone twice" or "switched to Internet for 10 minutes").

By looking at how much time you spend doing various activities, you now know where your time goes. How does it match with your perceptions of how you

Time log
A record of how one spends one's time

2

Create a Time Log

Keep track of the way you spend your time across seven days on time logs. Insert the amount of time you spend on each activity during each one-hour period for a single day. Do the same thing for every day of the week on separate time logs. **Be sure to make copies of this log before you fill it in for the first day.** You can print out copies at the *P.O.W.E.R. Learning* Web site at **www.mhhe.com/power.**

Analyze your log: After you complete your log for a week, analyze how you spend your time according to the major categories on the log. Add up the amount of time you spend on each category. You can also create other broad categories that eat up significant amounts of time.

Now consider the following:

1. What do you spend most of your time on?

2. Are you satisfied with the way that you are using your time? Are there any areas that seem to use up excessive amounts of time?

3. Do you see some simple fixes that will allow you to use time more effectively?

 WORKING IN A GROUP:

Compare your use of time during an average week with those of your classmates. What are the major differences and similarities in the use of time?

To Try It online, go to **www.mhhe.com/power.**

spend your time? Be prepared to be surprised, because most people find that they're spending time on a lot of activities that just don't matter very much.

≫LO2.2 Identify the "Black Holes" That Eat up Your Time

Do you feel like your time often is sucked into a black hole, disappearing without a trace?

Time Log

Day: _____   Date: _____

	personal care	food	classes	studies	work	recreation	sleep	other
6–7 a.m.								
7–8 a.m.								
8–9 a.m.								
9–10 a.m.								
10–11 a.m.								
11–12 (noon)								
12 (noon)– 1 p.m.								
1–2 p.m.								
2–3 p.m.								
3–4 p.m.								
4–5 p.m.								
5–6 p.m.								
6–7 p.m.								
7–8 p.m.								
8–9 p.m.								
9–10 p.m.								
10–11 p.m.								
11 p.m.–12 (midnight)								
12 (midnight)– 1 a.m.								
1–2 a.m.								
2–3 a.m.								
3–4 a.m.								
4–5 a.m.								
5–6 a.m.								

2

We all waste time, spending it on unimportant activities that keep us from doing the things that we should be doing or really want to do. For example, suppose when you're studying, your cell phone rings, and you end up speaking with a friend for a half hour. You could have (a) let the phone ring and not answered it; (b) answered, but told your friend you were studying and promised to call him or her back; or (c) spoken to him or her, but only for a short while. If you had done any of these things, you would have taken control of the interruption, and kept time from sinking into a black hole.

To get a sense of how your time is sucked into black holes, complete **Try It 3** on page 34.

Try It!

3

Identify the Black Holes of Time Management

The first 20 items on this list are common problems that prevent us from getting things done.[1] Check off the ones that are problems for you, and indicate whether you have control over them (controllable problems) or they are out of your control (uncontrollable problems).

	Big Problem for Me	Often a Problem	Seldom a Problem	Controllable (C) or Uncontrollable (U)?
1. Phone interruptions				
2. Drop-in visitors				
3. Texting				
4. Facebook and other social networking sites				
5. E-mail				
6. Inability to say no				
7. Socializing				
8. Snacking				
9. Errands and shopping				
10. Meals				
11. Children's interruptions				
12. Perfectionism				
13. Family appointments				

≫LO 2.3 Set Your Priorities

By this point you should have a good idea of what's taking up your time. But you may not know what you should be doing instead.

To figure out the best use of your time, you need to determine your priorities. **Priorities** are the tasks and activities you need and want to do, rank-ordered from most important to least important. There are no right or wrong priorities; you have to decide for yourself what you wish to accomplish. Maybe spending time on your studies is most important to you, or maybe your top priority is spending time with

Priorities
The tasks and activities that one needs and wants to do, rank-ordered from most important to least important

	Big Problem for Me	Often a Problem	Seldom a Problem	Controllable (C) or Uncontrollable (U)?
14. Looking for lost items				
15. Redoing mistakes				
16. Jumping from task to task				
17. Surfing the Web				
18. Reading newspapers, magazines, recreational books				
19. Car trouble				
20. Waiting for public transportation				
21. Other				
22. Other				
23. Other				
24. Other				
25. Other				

 WORKING IN A GROUP:

Examine the problems that affect each group member and then discuss these questions: Do time management problems fall into any patterns? Are there problems that at first seem uncontrollable that can actually be controlled? What strategies for dealing with such problems have you used in the past?

To Try It online, go to www.mhhe.com/power.

your family. Only you can decide. Furthermore, what's important to you at this moment may be less of a priority to you next month, next year, or five years from now.

For the purpose of effective time management in college, the best procedure is to start off by identifying priorities for an entire term. What do you need to accomplish? Don't just choose obvious, general goals, such as "passing all my classes." Instead, think about your priorities in terms of specific, measurable activities, such as "studying ten hours before each chemistry exam"—*not* "studying harder," which is too vague. (Look at the example of a priority list in **Figure 2.1** and also the *Course Connections* feature.)

Priority	Ranking
Study for each class at least 30 minutes/day	1
Start each major paper 1 week in advance of due date	2
Hand in each paper on time	1
Review for test starting a week before test date	2
Be on time for job	1
Check in with Mom once a week	3
Work out 3x/week	3

figure 2.1
Sample List of Priorities

Write your priorities on the chart in **Try It 4** on pages 38 and 39. After you've filled out the chart, organize it by giving each priority a ranking from 1 to 3. A "1" represents a priority that absolutely must be done; without it you'll suffer a major setback. For instance, a paper with a fixed due date should receive a "1" for a priority ranking; carving out time to take those guitar lessons you always wanted to take might be ranked a "3" in terms of priority. The important point is to rank-order your priorities to reveal what is and is not important to accomplish during the term.

Setting priorities will help you to determine how to make best use of your time. No one has enough time to complete everything; prioritizing will help you make informed decisions about what you can do to maximize your success.

Identify Your Prime Time

Take a look inward. Do you enthusiastically bound out of bed in the morning, ready to start the day and take on the world? Or is the alarm clock a hated and unwelcome sound that jars you out of pleasant slumber? Are you the kind of person who is zombielike by 10:00 at night, or a person who is just beginning to rev up at midnight?

Each of us has our own style based on some inborn body clock. Some of us are at our best in the morning, while others do considerably better at night. Being aware of the time or times of day when you can accomplish your best work will help you plan and schedule your time most effectively. If you're at your worst in the morning, try to schedule easier, less-involving activities for those earlier hours. On the other hand, if morning is the best time for you, schedule activities that require the greatest concentration at that time.

Each of us has an internal body clock that helps govern when we feel most alert. Becoming aware of your own body clock can help you schedule study sessions at times when you're able to work at peak efficiency.

Study Time: How Much Is Enough?

What would you guess is the average number of hours instructors think you should be studying each week? In the view of instructors queried in a national survey, students should spend, on average, 6 hours per week preparing for *each* class in which they're enrolled. And if they're taking courses in the sciences and engineering, instructors expect their students to put in even more hours.[2]

Keep in mind that study time does not include actual class time. If you add that in, someone taking four classes would need 24 hours of outside class preparation and would be in class for 16 hours—for a total of 40 hours, or the equivalent of full-time employment.

If you've underestimated the amount of time instructors believe is necessary to devote to class preparation, you may need to rethink the amount of time you'll need to allocate to studying. You might also speak to your individual instructors to see what they believe is an appropriate amount of preparation. Although they may not be able to give exact figures, their estimates will help you to prioritize what you need to do to be a successful student.

But don't be a slave to your internal time clock. Even night people can function effectively in the morning, just as morning people can accomplish quite a bit in the evening. On the other hand, listen hard to your internal time clock if you're tired much of the time. If you frequently feel sleepy, your body is giving you a simple, yet important, message: Get more sleep.

> "Time moves slowly, but passes quickly."
> Alice Walker, author, *The Color Purple*

⊙ Organize Mastering the Moment

You now know where you've lost time in the past, and your priority list is telling you where you need to head in the future.

Now for the present. You've reached the point where you can organize yourself to take control of your time. Here's what you'll need:

> - A **master calendar** that shows all the weeks of the term on one page. You don't need to buy one; you can make it easily enough yourself. It need not be great art; a rough version will do. The important point is that it must include every week of the term and seven days per week. (See the example of a master calendar in **Figure 2.2** on page 40.)

> - A weekly timetable. The **weekly timetable** is a master grid with the days of the week across the top and the hours, from 6:00 a.m. to midnight, along the side. This will permit you to write in all your regularly scheduled activities, as well as one-time appointments when they arise. (A blank weekly timetable is provided in **Figure 2.3** on page 41. You can also find it online at **www.mhhe.com/power.**)

> - A daily to-do list. Finally, you'll need a **daily to-do list.** The daily to-do list can be written on a small, portable calendar that includes a separate page for each day of the week. Or it can simply be a small notebook, with a separate sheet of paper for every day of the week. Whatever form your daily to-do list takes, make sure it's portable, because you'll need to keep it with you all the time.

The basic organizational task you face is filling in these three schedules. You'll need at least an hour to do this, so set the time aside. In addition, there will be some repetition across the three schedules, and the task may seem a bit tedious. *But every minute you invest now in organizing your time will pay off in hours that you will save in the future.*

Master calendar

A schedule showing the weeks of a longer time period, such as a college term, with all assignments and important activities noted on it

Weekly timetable

A schedule showing all regular, prescheduled activities due to occur in the week, together with one-time events and commitments

Daily to-do list

A schedule showing the tasks, activities, and appointments due to occur during the day

4

Set Priorities

Set your priorities for the term. They may include getting to class on time, finishing papers and assignments by their due dates, finding a part-time job that fits your schedule, and reading every assignment before the class for which it is due. To get started, list priorities in any order. Be sure to consider priorities relating to your school work, other work, family, social obligations, and health. After you list them, assign a number to each one indicating its level—giving a "1" to the highest priority items, a "2" to medium priority items, and a "3" to the items with the lowest priority.

List of Priorities	
Priority	**Priority Index**

Now redo your list, putting your number 1s first, followed by as many of your number 2s and 3s to which you feel you can reasonably commit.

Follow these steps in completing your schedule:

> **Start with the master calendar, which shows all the weeks of the term on one page.** In most classes, you'll receive a syllabus, a course outline that explains what the course is all about. Traditionally, a syllabus includes course assignments and their due dates and the schedule for tests that will be given during the term. Write on the master calendar every assignment you have, noting it on the date that it is due. If the instructor hasn't included due dates, ask; he or she probably already knows, or at least has a general idea, of the week that

Final List of Priorities	
Priority	
1.	
2.	
3.	
4.	
5.	
6.	
7.	
8.	
9.	
10.	
11.	
12.	

Now consider the following:

- What does this list tell you about your greatest priorities? Are they centered around school, friends and family, jobs, or some other aspect of your life?
- Do you have so many "1" priorities that they will be difficult or impossible to accomplish successfully? How could you go back to your list and trim it down even more?
- What does this listing of priorities suggest about how successful you'll be during the upcoming term?

To Try It online, go to www.mhhe.com/power.

various assignments will be due. Pencil in tentative assignments on the appropriate date.

Don't only put assignments on the master calendar. Also include important activities from your personal life, drawn from your list of priorities. For instance, if you're involved in a club that is bringing a guest speaker to campus, mark down the date of the event.

Finally, schedule some free time—time when you promise yourself you will do something that is just plain fun. Consider these days to be written

figure 2.2
Master Calendar Sample

	M	T	W	TH	F	SA	S
Sept.	7	8	9 Classes Start	10	11 Camping →	12	13
	14	Add/drop 15 ends	16	English 17 short paper due	18	19	20
	21	22	23	English 24 short paper due	Russian 25 quiz	26	27
	28	29	30 Psych exam	OCT 1 Music quiz English short paper due	1st Psych 2 paper due	3	4
	5	Music 6 paper due	7	English 8 short paper due	Russian 9 quiz	10	11
	12	13	14	Music quiz 15 English short paper due	16	17	18
	First-yr 19 seminar journal due	20	Psych 21 exam	English 22 short paper due Dad's bd—call	Theater 23 Midterm	Bartending 24 job	25
	Russian 26 midterm exam	English 27 midterm exam	28	Eng-short 29 paper due Music quiz	30	31	NOV 1
	2	3	4	English 5 short paper due	Russian 6 short paper due	7	Darcey's 8 Wedding!
	9	10	Holiday— 11 Veteran's Day	Eng-short 12 paper due Music quiz	Russian 13 quiz Psych exam	14	15
	First-yr 16 seminar group project due	17	Preregistration 18 for next semester	English 19 short paper due	20	21	22
	23	24	25	Thanksgiving 26	No Classes! 27	28	29
	30	DEC 1 Music paper due	2	English 3 short paper due	Russian 4 quiz	5	6
	First-yr 7 seminar final journal due	8	9	Music 10 quiz	Theater 11 project due Psych exam Last day of class!!	12	13
	English 14 final exam	Theater 15 final exam Russian final exam	16	Psych 17 final exam	Music exam 18 MY birthday!	19	20
	21	22	23	24	25 Xmas	26	27

in stone, and promise yourself that you won't use them for anything else except for something enjoyable. Just knowing that you have some down-time planned will help you to throw yourself into more demanding tasks. In addition, getting into the habit of allowing yourself time to relax and reflect on your life is as important as any other time management skill you may learn.

You now have a good idea of what the term has in store for you. In most cases, the first few weeks have few assignments or tests. But as the term rolls on—particularly around the middle and end of the term—things will get more demanding. The message you should take from this: *Use the off-peak periods to get a head start on future assignments.*

figure 2.3
Weekly Timetable
Make a single copy of this blank timetable or go to the *P.O.W.E.R. Learning* Web site (**www.mhhe.com/power**) and use the online version. Then fill in your regular, predictable time commitments.

Next, make as many copies as you need to cover each week of the term. Then, for each week, fill in the date on the left and the number of the week in the term on the right, and add in your irregular commitments.

Completing a master schedule also may help you head off disaster before it occurs. Suppose, for instance, you find that six weeks in the future you have two papers due and three tests—all in the same week!

After cursing your bad luck, it's time to take action. Begin to think of strategies for managing the situation, such as working on the papers or studying in advance. You might also try to change some due dates. Instructors are far more receptive to requests for extensions on papers if the requests are made well in advance. Similarly, it might be possible to take a test later—or earlier—if you make prior arrangements.

▶ **Now move to the weekly timetable provided in Figure 2.3.** Fill in the times of all your fixed, prescheduled activities—the times that your classes meet, when you have to be at work, the times you have to pick up your child at day care, and any other recurring appointments.

Once you've filled in the weekly timetable, as in the one on the next page, you get a bare-bones picture of the average week. You will still need to take into account the specific activities that are required to complete the assignments on the master calendar.

To move from your "average" week to specific weeks, make photocopies of the weekly timetable that now contains your fixed appointments. Make enough copies for every week of the term. On each copy, write the week number of the term and the specific dates it covers.

Using your master calendar, add assignment due dates, tests, and any other activities on the appropriate days of the week. Then pencil in blocks of time necessary to prepare for those events. (See a sample in **Figure 2.4**.)

How much time should you allocate for schoolwork? One very rough rule of thumb holds that every one hour that you spend in class requires, on average, two hours of study outside of class to earn a B and three hours of study outside of class to earn an A. Do the arithmetic: If you are taking 15 credits (with each credit equivalent to an hour of class per week), you'll need to plan for 30 hours of studying each week to earn a B average— an intimidating amount of time. Of course, the amount of time you must allocate to a specific class will vary from week to week, depending on what is happening in the class.

For example, if you estimate that you'll need five hours of study for a midterm exam in a certain class, pencil in those hours. Don't set up a single block of five hours. People remember best when their studying is spread out over shorter periods rather than attempted in one long block of time. Besides, it will probably be hard to find a block of five straight hours on your weekly calendar.

Similarly, if you need to write a paper that's due on a certain date, you can block out the different stages of the writing process that we'll describe in Chapter 7. You'll need to estimate how much time each stage will take, but you probably have a pretty good idea from previous papers you've written.

Some classes may need only a few hours of study in a given week. With good luck, heavy weeks in one class will be compensated for by lighter weeks in others.

Keep in mind that estimates are just that: estimates. Don't think of them as set in stone. Mark them on your weekly calendar in pencil, not pen, so you can adjust them if necessary.

But remember: It's also crucial not to overschedule yourself. You'll still need time to eat, to talk with your friends, to spend time with your family, and to enjoy yourself in general. If you find that your life is completely filled with things that you feel you must do in order to survive and that there is no room for fun, then take a step back and cut out something to make some time for yourself in your daily schedule. Finding time for yourself is as important as carving out time for what others want you to do. Besides, if you are overworked, you're likely to "find" the time by guiltily goofing off without really setting aside the time and enjoying it.

> **If you've taken each of the previous steps, you're now in a position to work on the final step of organization for successful time management: completing your daily to-do list.**

Weekly Timetable

Week of: 9/28   **Week #** 3

	Mon	Tues	Wed	Thurs	Fri	Sat	Sun
6–7 a.m.							
7–8 a.m.							
8–9 a.m.							
9–10 a.m.	9:05 Psych	9:05 Music	9:05 Psych	9:05 Music	9:05 Psych		
10–11 a.m.		↓		↓			
11–12 (noon)		11:15 English		11:15 English			
12 (noon)–1 p.m.	12:20 Theater	↓	12:20 Theater	↓	12:20 Theater		
1–2 p.m.	↓		↓				
2–3 p.m.							
3–4 p.m.	3:00 Russian		3:00 Russian		3:00 Russian		
4–5 p.m.	First-year seminar	Work		Work			
5–6 p.m.	↓						
6–7 p.m.							
7–8 p.m.		↓		↓			
8–9 p.m.							
9–10 p.m.							
10–11 p.m.							
11 p.m.–12 (midnight)							
12 (midnight)–1 a.m.							
1–2 a.m.							
2–3 a.m.							
3–4 a.m.							
4–5 a.m.							
5–6 a.m.							

figure 2.4
A Sample Weekly Timetable

Unlike the master calendar and weekly timetable—both of which you develop at the beginning of the term—complete your daily to-do list just one day ahead of time, preferably at the end of the day.

List all the things that you intend to do during the next day and their priority. Start with the things you know you *must* do and that have fixed times, such as classes, work schedules, and appointments. These are your first priority items. Then add in the other things that you *should* accomplish, such as an hour of study for an upcoming test, working on research for an upcoming paper, or finishing up a lab report. Finally, list things that are lower priority but enjoyable, setting aside time for a run or a walk, for example.

Don't schedule every single minute of the day. That would be counterproductive, and you'd end up feeling like you'd failed if you deviated from your schedule. Instead, think of your daily to-do list as a path through a forest.

figure 2.5
Sample Daily To-Do List

To-Do List for_____ (date)		
Item Item	Priority	✓ Completed
Call Chris to get English notes	1	✓
Meet with Prof. Hernandez	1	✓
Review Russian	1	✓
Work on outline for psych paper	2	✓
Return books to library	2	
Call Nettie	2	✓
Set up meeting with music group	2	
Meet Deena	2	
Do laundry	3	

If you were hiking, you would allow yourself to deviate from the path, occasionally venturing onto side tracks when they looked interesting. But you'd also be keeping tabs on your direction so you end up where you need to be at the end and not miles away from your car or home.

Like the sample daily to-do list in **Figure 2.5,** include a column to check or cross off after you've completed an activity. There's something very satisfying in acknowledging what you have accomplished.

W Work

Controlling Time

You're in luck: There is no work to time management—or at least not much more than you've already done. The work of time management is to follow the schedules that you've prepared and organized. But that doesn't mean it will be easy. Our lives are filled with surprises: Things take longer than we've planned. A friend we haven't spoken to in a while calls to chat, and it seems rude to say that we don't have time to talk. A crisis occurs; buses are late; computers break down; kids get sick.

The difference between effective time management and time management that doesn't work lies in how well you deal with the inevitable surprises.

There are several ways to take control of your days and permit yourself to follow your intended schedule:

> **Just say no.** You don't have to agree to every request and every favor that others ask of you. You're not a bad person if you refuse to do something that will eat up your time and prevent you from accomplishing your goals.
>
> Suppose, for example, a friend sees you in the library and asks to borrow the notes from a class that she missed yesterday and that you attended. It's not an unreasonable request. Here's the problem, though: You don't have your notebook with you, and you'd have to stop by your house to pick it up.
>
> Think through what the request entails. *It may be only 10 minutes to your house, but it's another 10 minutes back. That's 20 minutes. And then there's the time that you'll spend meeting her to give her the notes. And then the time*

it takes to meet her again, once she's copied the notes. Or suppose you decide to wait while she copies them. Overall, you may end up losing an hour.

The solution? You should probably say no to the immediate request. It's not unreasonable to tell your friend that you don't have the time today to get your notebook. You don't have to refuse her completely. She could stop by your house in the evening to pick up the notes, or you could bring them with you the next day. In short, there are ways to accomplish the goal of helping out your friend without wasting time and sabotaging your schedule.

▶ **Get away from it all.** Go to the library. Lock yourself into your bedroom. Find an out-of-the-way, unused classroom.

Any of these places can serve to isolate you from everyday distractions and thereby permit you to work on the tasks that you wish to complete. Try to adopt a particular spot as your own, such as a corner desk in a secluded nook in the library. If you use it enough, your body and mind will automatically get into study mode as soon as you seat yourself at it.

▶ **Enjoy the sounds of silence.** Although many students insist they accomplish most while a television, radio, or CD is playing, scientific studies suggest otherwise: We are able to concentrate most when our environment is silent. So even if you're sure you work best with a soundtrack playing, experiment and work in silence for a few days. You may find that you get more done in less time than you would in a more distracting environment.

▶ **Take an e-break.** Text messages, phone calls, Facebook status updates, instant messages, e-mail. Who doesn't love to hear from others?

We may not control when communications arrive, but we can make the message wait until we are ready to receive it. Take an e-break and shut down your communication sources for a period of time. Phone calls will be stored in voicemail, and text messages, IMs, Facebook updates, and e-mail will be saved on your phone or computer. They'll wait.

▶ **Use technology to save time.** Many things—from shopping for clothing to ordering groceries—can be accomplished quickly via the Web or telephone rather than in person.

▶ **Expect the unexpected.** Interruptions and crises, minor and major, can't be eliminated. However, they can be prepared for.

How is it possible to plan for surprises? Though it may still be too early in the term to get a clear picture of what sorts of unanticipated events you'll encounter, you should keep an eye out for patterns. Perhaps one instructor routinely makes surprise assignments that aren't listed on the syllabus. Maybe you're asked to work extra hours on the weekends because someone doesn't show up and you have to work overtime.

You'll never be able to escape from unexpected interruptions and surprises that require your attention. But by trying to anticipate them in advance, and thinking about how you'll react to them, you'll be positioning yourself to react more effectively when they do occur.

▶ **Combat procrastination. Procrastination,** the habit of putting off and delaying tasks that need to be accomplished, is like a microscopic parasite. It is invisible to the naked eye, but it eats up your time nonetheless.

It's 10:30 a.m. You've just come out of your German class. You know that there's going to be a test next week, and you've planned to go over the flash cards you made up last night. It's right there in your schedule: "10:30 a.m.—study German vocabulary." But you're thirsty after sitting in class, so you decide to go and buy yourself something to drink.

Procrastination
The habit of putting off and delaying tasks that need to be accomplished

"Hello and welcome to the game that'll be put off until tomorrow, but should've been played today."

As you head into the snack bar, you pass by the campus store, and you think about how you need to buy a couple of pens. After finding the kind of pen you like, you go to the checkout line. You pass by a rack of magazines, and, after leafing through a few, decide to purchase one. You can read it while you have your drink. You make your way to the snack bar, buy your soda, and sip it as you read the magazine.

Suddenly, a half hour has gone by. Because so much time has passed, you decide that it won't be worth it to start studying your German vocabulary. So you spend a little more time reading the magazine and then head off to your next class, which is at 11:00 a.m.

You can't control interruptions and crises that are imposed upon you by others. But even when no one else is throwing interruptions at us, we make up our own. Procrastination is a problem that many of us face. To identify whether you are a procrastinator, find your "Procrastination Quotient" (see **Try It 5,** page 47).

If you find yourself procrastinating, several steps can help you:

Break large tasks into small ones. People often procrastinate because a task they're seeking to accomplish appears overwhelming. If writing a 15-page paper seems nearly impossible, think about writing a series of five 3-page papers. If reading a 750-page book seems impossible, think of it as reading several 250-page books.

Start with the easiest and simplest part of a task, and then do the harder parts. Succeeding initially on the easy parts can make the harder parts of a task less daunting—and make you less apt to procrastinate in completing the task.

Substitute something easier for a more difficult task. If you have to write a letter, can you write a postcard instead? Sometimes it's possible to figure out an easier way to accomplish a task that works just as well.

Just begin! Sometimes the hardest part of an activity is simply getting started. So take the leap and begin the task, and the rest may follow more easily.

Work with others. Just being in the same physical location with others can motivate you sufficiently to accomplish tasks that you consider unpleasant and on which you might be tempted to procrastinate. For instance, studying vocabulary words can be made easier if you plan a study session with several of your classmates. Beware, though—if you spend too much time socializing, you lower the likelihood of success.

Keep the costs of procrastination in mind. Procrastination doesn't just result in delay; it may also make the task harder than it would have been if you hadn't procrastinated. Not only will you ultimately have less time to complete the task, but you may have to do it so quickly that its quality may be diminished. In the worst scenario, you won't even be able to finish it at all.

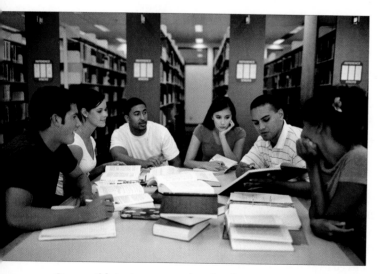

One antidote to procrastination is working in a study group. You'll be motivated by the presence of others who face the same challenges and assignments that you do.

Find Your Procrastination Quotient

Do you procrastinate?[3] To find out, circle the number that best applies for each question using the following scale:

Strongly agree	**4**	**3**	**2**	**1**	**Strongly disagree**

1. I invent reasons and look for excuses for not acting on a problem.

Strongly agree	**4**	**3**	**2**	**1**	**Strongly disagree**

2. It takes pressure to get me to work on difficult assignments.

Strongly agree	**4**	**3**	**2**	**1**	**Strongly disagree**

3. I take half measures which will avoid or delay unpleasant or difficult tasks.

Strongly agree	**4**	**3**	**2**	**1**	**Strongly disagree**

4. I face too many interruptions and crises that interfere with accomplishing my major goals.

Strongly agree	**4**	**3**	**2**	**1**	**Strongly disagree**

5. I sometimes neglect to carry out important tasks.

Strongly agree	**4**	**3**	**2**	**1**	**Strongly disagree**

6. I schedule big assignments too late to get them done as well as I know I could.

Strongly agree	**4**	**3**	**2**	**1**	**Strongly disagree**

7. I'm sometimes too tired to do the work I need to do.

Strongly agree	**4**	**3**	**2**	**1**	**Strongly disagree**

8. I start new tasks before I finish old ones.

Strongly agree	**4**	**3**	**2**	**1**	**Strongly disagree**

9. When I work in groups, I try to get other people to finish what I don't.

Strongly agree	**4**	**3**	**2**	**1**	**Strongly disagree**

10. I put off tasks that I really don't want to do but know that I must do.

Strongly agree	**4**	**3**	**2**	**1**	**Strongly disagree**

Scoring: Total the numbers you have circled. If the score is below 15, you are not a chronic procrastinator and you probably have only an occasional problem. If your score is 16–25, you have a minor problem with procrastination. If your score is above 25, you procrastinate quite often and should work on breaking the habit.

Now, consider the following:

- If you do procrastinate often, why do you think you do it?
- Are there particular subjects or classes or kinds of assignments that you are more likely to procrastinate on?
- Is there something that you are putting off doing right now? How might you get started on it?

 WORKING IN A GROUP:

Think about the last time you procrastinated. Describe it as completely as you can. What was the task? What did you do rather than doing what needed to be done? What could you have done to avoid procrastinating in this situation? Ask others what strategy they might suggest for avoiding procrastinating.

To Try It online, go to www.mhhe.com/power.

▸ **Balancing school and family demands.** If you are a full-time student and also have caregiver responsibilities for children or other family members such as aging parents, time management is especially challenging. Not only does your family demand—and deserve—substantial quantities of time, but juggling school and family obligations can prove to be more than a full-time job. However, there are some specific strategies that can help.

Dealing with childcare demands:

Provide activities for your children. Kids enjoy doing things on their own for part of the day. Plan activities that will keep them happily occupied while you're doing schoolwork.

Make spending time with your children a priority. Carve out "free play" time for your kids. Even 20 minutes of good time devoted to your children will give all of you—you and them—a lift. No matter how busy you are, you owe it to your children—and yourself—to spend time as a family.

Enlist your child's help. Children love to play adult and, if they're old enough, help you study. Maybe they can help you clear a space to study. Perhaps you can give them "assignments" that they can work on while you're working on your assignments.

Encourage your child to invite friends over to play. Some children can remain occupied for hours if they have a playmate.

Use television appropriately. Television viewing is not all bad, and some shows and DVDs can be not just engaging, but educational. The trick is to pick and choose what your children watch.

> "I had a friend who was concentrating in pre-med. He put off studying for his chem midterm until 10 p.m. the night before, spending his time instead at the movies and the campus hangout. After bombing the exam, he told us he did not have enough time to study. Basically, he gave himself an excuse to fail."
>
> **Thom McDade, student, Pomona College[4]**

Find the best child care or babysitters that you can. The better the care your children are getting, the better you'll be able to concentrate on your schoolwork. You may still feel guilty that you're not with your children as much as you'd like, but accept that guilt. Remember, your attendance in college builds a better future for your children.

Use your children's "downtime" effectively. If your children are young, use their nap time as a chance to catch up on schoolwork. Or consider getting up early, before your children wake up, for a period in which you will have fewer interruptions than later in the day.

Accept that studying will be harder with kids around. It may take you longer to study, and your concentration may suffer from the noise that kids make. But remind yourself what that noise represents: the growth and development of someone that you love. One day your children will be grown, and without a doubt there will be times that you'll miss their high level of energy and activity.

Dealing with the eldercare demands:

Encourage as much independence as possible on the part of older adults for whom you are responsible. Not only will it take some of the pressure off you, but it will be helpful to adults.

Ask for support from your siblings and other family members. Caring for an ill or aging parent should be a family affair, not a burden that falls on any one individual.

Determine what community resources are available. Local centers for aging may provide assistance not only to the elderly but also to their caregivers.

Respect your own needs. Remember that your own priorities are important. Elders for whom you are responsible will understand that you will sometimes need to put yourself first.

▸ **Balancing school and work demands.** Juggling school and a job can be exhausting. Not only must you manage your time to complete your schoolwork, but in many cases you'll also face time management demands while you are on the job. Here are some tips to help you keep everything in balance:

Make to-do lists for work, just as you would for your schoolwork. In fact, all the time management strategies that we've discussed can be applied to on-the-job tasks.

If you have slack time on the job, get some studying done. Try to keep at least some of your textbooks, class notes, or notecards always with you so you can refer to them. Of course, you should never do schoolwork without your employer's prior agreement. If you don't get permission, you may jeopardize your job.

Use your lunch hour effectively. Although it's important to eat a nutritious lunch and not to wolf your food down, you may be able to use some of the time alloted to you for lunch to fit in some studying.

Ask your employer about flextime. If your job allows it, you may be able to set your own hours, within reason, as long as the work gets done. If this is an option for you, use it. Although it may create more time management challenges for you than would a job with set hours, it also provides you with more flexibility.

Accept new responsibilities carefully. If you've barely been keeping up with the demands of work and school, don't automatically accept new job responsibilities without carefully evaluating how they fit with your long-term priorities. If your job is temporary and you're not planning to stay, you might want to respectfully decline substantial new duties or an increase in the number of hours you work. On the other hand, if you plan to continue in the job once you're done with school, then accepting new responsibilities may be more reasonable.

Always keep in mind why you're working. If you're working because it's your sole means of support, you're in a very different position from someone who is working to earn a bit of extra money for luxuries. Remember what your priorities are. In some cases, school should always come first; in others, your job may have to come first, at least some of the time. Whatever you decide, make sure it's a thoughtful decision, based on an evaluation of your long-term priorities.

⒠ Evaluate   Checking Your Time

Evaluating how you use your time is pretty straightforward: You either accomplished what you intended to do in a given period, or you didn't. Did you check off all the items on your daily to-do list? If you go over your list at the end of every day, not only will you know how successful your time management efforts have been, but you will be able to incorporate any activities you missed into the next day's to-do list.

The check-off is important because it provides an objective record of what you have accomplished on a given day. Just as important, it provides you with concrete reinforcement for completing the task. As we have noted, there are few things more satisfying than gazing at a to-do list with a significant number of check marks.

Career Connections

On-the-Job Time Management

Think you're busy now? Just wait: Once you are building your career and working at a full-time job, you may look back on your college years as a period of relative leisure.

For employees with a demanding boss who may, without warning, give them an urgent assignment due the next morning, time is always at a premium. This means that time management is an essential survival skill when developing your career. In fact, time management may be a talent that you'll need in the working world even more than you did while you were getting your college education.

When you are in school, most assignments are scheduled far in advance—usually at the start of the term. Most often, requirements are set forth plainly on a syllabus, and typically there are no new assignments added as the term moves forward. That means you can carefully map out your use of time over the term.

In the business world, things are often different. Crises occur, perhaps due to manufacturing problems or client demands, that require sudden flurries of work. In some jobs, you may be forced to drop everything you normally work on and pitch in on a sudden new task. As a result, your plans to complete your everyday work may be distrupted completely.

You'll also need to learn new time-management strategies on the job. For instance, if you supervise other employees, it may be possible to delegate some work to them, allowing them to help you complete assignments. Or sometimes it may be possible to deflect assignments brought to you by a boss to some other unit or department.

In short, time management is a skill that will help you build a successful career. Learning the basic principles of time management now will help you well beyond your years in college.

Of course, you won't always accomplish every item on your to-do list. That's not surprising, nor even particularly bad, especially if you've included some second- and third-level priorities that you don't absolutely have to accomplish and that you may not really have expected you'd have time for anyway.

Give yourself a virtual pat on the back for completing the things that you've accomplished. Successful time management is not easy, and if you've improved at all, you deserve to feel some personal satisfaction.

ⓡ Rethink | Reflecting on Your Personal Style of Time Management

At the end of the day, after you've evaluated how well you've followed your time management plan and how much you've accomplished, it's time to rethink where you are. Maybe you've accomplished everything you set out to do, and every task for the day is completed, and every item on your to-do list has a check mark next to it.

Or maybe you have the opposite result. Your day has been a shambles, and you feel as if nothing has been accomplished. Because of a constant series of interruptions and chance events, you've been unable to make headway on your list.

Or—most likely—you find yourself somewhere in between these two extremes. Some tasks got done, while others are still hanging over you. Now is the time to rethink in a broad sense how you manage your time by doing the following:

> **Reassess Your Priorities.** Are your long- and short-term goals appropriate? Are you expecting too much of yourself, given the constraints in your life? Reassess your priorities in order to be sure you're attempting to do what is

most important to you. As we'll discuss further in Chapter 3, you need to take into account your strengths, weaknesses, and values. You also need to seek to answer the question "Who am I?" in order to ensure that your priorities are optimal for *you*.

▶ **Reconsider Your Personal Style of Time Management.** We've outlined one method of time management. Although it works well for most people, it isn't for everyone. Some people just can't bring themselves to be so structured and scheduled. They feel hemmed in by to-do lists.

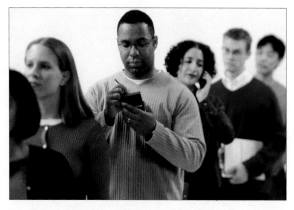

Managing your time effectively will allow you to make the most of every moment, helping you to accomplish the things that are most important to you.

If you're one of those people, fine. You don't need to follow the suggestions presented in this chapter exactly. In fact, if you go to your college bookstore or any office supply store, you'll find lots of other aids to manage your time. Publishing companies produce elaborate planners, such as DayTimers. In addition, software companies produce computerized time management software, such as Microsoft's Outlook or Novell's GroupWise, that reside on computers and wireless handheld devices such as a BlackBerry or iPhone. Many cell phones contain a calendar system and alarm, and they can be set to provide periodic reminders.

However you choose to manage your time, the important thing is to do so consistently. And remember that whatever approach to time management you take, it will work best if it is compatible with your own personal values and strengths. Keep experimenting until you find an approach that works for you.

▶ **Consider Doing Less.** If you keep falling behind, do less. There are only 24 hours in the day, and we need to sleep for about one-third of the time. In the remaining hours, it may be nearly impossible to carry a full load of classes and work full-time and care for a child and still have some time left to have a normal life.

Consequently, if you consistently fall behind in your work, it may be that you are just doing too much. Reassess your goals and your priorities, and make choices. Determine what is most important to you. It's better to accomplish less, if it is accomplished well, than to accomplish more, but poorly.

▶ **Do More.** Although it is a problem that many of us would envy, some people have too much time on their hands. Their classes may not be too demanding, or work demands may suddenly slacken off. If this happens to you, take advantage of your time. For example, you might use the extra time to simply relax and enjoy your more unhurried existence. There is a good bit to be said for having time to let your thoughts wander. We need to take time out to enjoy our friends, admire the flowers in the park, exercise, consider the spiritual side of our lives, and the like.

> "Our costliest expenditure is time."
>
> **Theophrastus, quoted in Diogenes Laertius's *Lives and Opinions of Eminent Philosophers*, tr. R.D. Hicks**

On the other hand, if you consistently have more time than you know what to do with, reflect on what you want to accomplish and add some activities that help you reach your goals. For example, consider becoming involved in a service-learning activity. Volunteer your time to the community. Consider taking an extra course during the next term.

But whatever you decide to do, make a real decision. Don't let the time slip away. Once it's gone, it's gone forever.

speaking of **success**

NAME: **Jasmin Rosario**

SCHOOL: **Vassar College, Poughkeepsie, New York**

Jasmin Rosario, who will be the first person in her family to graduate from college, has developed a philosophy that makes time management a number one priority.

"I think that some of the biggest rewards of college don't just involve academics, but come from the opportunities to be involved in a lot of other things," Rosario said.

A psychology major and art history minor, Rosario has taken that philosophy to heart. She is involved in numerous extracurricular activities, holds a campus job, and still maintains high grades.

However, her demanding schedule requires careful time management. "As a result of my involvement outside the classroom," she said, "I have to stay on top of my work, scheduling myself carefully."

"From the very beginning of the semester I'm already making a schedule and immediately know if I'm going to have two finals the same week or papers due on the same day," she added.

Rosario says that as soon as she gets class assignments, she writes them down. In addition, she also prepares weekly and monthly calendars and makes sure to prioritize her obligations.

"I always prioritize my commitments. Academics come first, followed by extracurricular activities and my campus job as a Wellness Peer Educator," she explained.

During periods of intense study, Rosario relieves stress by taking breaks, as well as socializing with other students and talking about anything other than academics.

"It's easy to get overwhelmed with all the work, so I think it's important to take breaks," she said. "For me the number one priority is to take care of myself. Work is work, but your health comes before everything else."

As a Wellness Peer Educator, Rosario has learned that it's important for students to know their limitations.

"Some students stress out and feel like they're in a box by giving too much to extracurricular activities. From the beginning, they have to know how much to give and to be very clear about it," she said.

Looking Back

How can I manage my time most effectively?

▸ Decide to take control of your time.

▸ Become aware of the way you use your time now.

▸ Set clear priorities.

▸ Use such time management tools as a master calendar, weekly timetable, and a daily to-do list.

How can I deal better with surprises and distractions?

▸ Deal with surprises by saying no, getting away from it all, working in silence, taking control of communications, using the phone to conduct transactions, and leaving slack in your schedule to accommodate the unexpected.

▸ Avoid procrastination by breaking large tasks into smaller ones, starting with the easiest parts of a task first; working with other people; and calculating the true costs of procrastination.

How can I balance competing priorities?

▸ Consider how your competing priorities relate to one another.

▸ Manage work time carefully, use slack time on the job to perform school assignments, use flextime, accept new responsibilities thoughtfully, and assign the proper priority to work.

[KEY TERMS AND CONCEPTS]

Time log (p. 31)

Priorities (p. 34)

Master calendar (p. 37)

Weekly timetable (p. 37)

Daily to-do list (p. 37)

Procrastination (p. 45)

[RESOURCES]

ON CAMPUS

The college official that determines when classes meet is known as the Registrar. If you are having difficulty in scheduling your classes, the registrar's office may be helpful. In addition, your academic advisor can help you work out problems in enrolling in the classes you want.

For help with such issues as planning a study schedule for the upcoming term, dealing with multiple assignments due on the same date, or tips on dealing with competing academic and work demands, consult with your campus learning center. The staff can help you sort out the various options you may have.

IN PRINT

Stephen Covey's *The Seven Habits of Highly Successful People* (Fireside, 2004) and Alan Axelrod and Brian Tracy's *Eat That Frog! 21 Great Ways to Stop Procrastinating and Get More Done in Less Time* (Berrett-Kohler, 2007) offer practical, hands-on guides to time management.

How to Do Everything with Microsoft Outlook (Osborne-McGraw-Hill, 2007), by Bill Mann, provides a quick, hands-on introduction to Microsoft's Outlook software, a popular time management program that is part of the Microsoft Office Suite.

Finally, Veronique Vienne and Erica Lennard's *The Art of the Moment: Simple Ways to Get the Most Out of Life* (Clarkson Potter, 2002) is an antidote to the impulse to schedule every minute of our days. The book celebrates taking time out and devoting it to oneself, providing a practical guide to rest and relaxation.

ON THE WEB

The *P.O.W.E.R. Learning* Web site at **www.mhhe.com/power** provides online versions of all the time management forms presented in this chapter. You can complete the forms online or download them and print out as many copies as you need. Although the Web addresses were accurate at the time the book was printed, check the *P.O.W.E.R. Learning* Web site [**www.mhhe.com/power**] for any changes that may have occurred.

➤ The University of Victoria's Office of Counseling Services provides two useful sites:
  • Effective hints on how to plan study time, ideas about when to study, as well as tips on how to study (**www.coun.uvic.ca/learning/time-management/**).
  • A handy self-management checklist that allows visitors to better achieve their goals with the time that they have (**www.coun.uvic.ca/learning/motivation/ self-management.html**). It also provides effective techniques for avoiding procrastination and distractions, two major obstacles to effective time management.

➤ From Penn State University, try this nifty online interactive time management exercise (**www.ulc.psu.edu/studyskills/time_management.html#time_management_ exercisetime_wasters**). This site also includes comprehensive links to a number of ways on how to manage your time while in college.

TAKING IT TO THE NET

1 Complete a weekly organizer online. Find a site on the Web that offers shareware or freeware featuring a weekly planner (for example, **www.studygs.net/ schedule/Weekly.html** or **www.printablecalendar.ca/**). Create a weekly schedule sheet for yourself based on this design. Be sure to write in all of your classes and any other regular obligations that you have. Be sure to set specific times in your daily schedule to study and do homework. (If you already use Outlook or another kind of communications software, use its calendar function to do the same thing.)

2 Make a master calendar for the term, using the same software you used for the exercise above. If your calendar does not provide this information automatically, you can go to Yahoo! (**dir.yahoo.com**), click on "Reference," then again on "Calendars." Here you'll find many links to different calendar-related information such as when holidays occur. Be sure to indicate dates when important assignments are due and when exams occur.

The Case of . . .
The Time of His Life

Will Linz couldn't believe it. On the same day he had completed his term paper and handed it in, his instructor announced a test for the following week. When the class protested that the test hadn't been listed in the syllabus, the instructor murmured that she'd made a mistake and was sorry about the short notice.

Will panicked when he remembered that next week he also had to complete two lab reports he had put off because he had been working on his term paper. Even worse, next weekend was lost. He had promised—promised!—his girlfriend, who was working full-time, that he would go with her to her annual company picnic. Although he dreaded the thought of being with a bunch of people he barely knew, he'd finally agreed to go just last week.

As he was driving home thinking about all this, his car started to sputter and then stalled. He was unable to get it started. That was it. He sat there on the side of the road, feeling like his life had completely fallen apart and wondering how he'd ever get it back together again.

1. What might you tell Will that could help solve his predicament?

2. Is there anything Will could have done to prevent the situation he now faces from occurring in the first place?

3. What specific time management techniques might Will have employed in the past to avoid these problems?

4. What strategies might Will use now to take control over his limited time during the coming week?

5. What advice could you give Will to try to prevent problems in time management for his next term?

3

Learning Outcomes

By the time you finish this chapter you will be able to

》 LO 3.1   Identify your learning style and how it affects your academic success.

》 LO 3.2   Explain self-concept and how it affects you.

》 LO 3.3   Create a personal mission statement.

》 LO 3.4   Recognize strategies for making wise personal decisions.

Discovering Your Learning Styles, Self-Concept, and Values

The transformation began when Shaniqua Turner got her first paper back from her English literature instructor. It wasn't the grade—which was good—that mattered so much, but what her instructor uttered, almost as an afterthought, as she handed the paper back to Shaniqua: "Nice job. Your insights were good, and you have great potential as a writer."

Shaniqua was thrilled. She had always thought of herself as having only modest talent in English and, although at one point she had harbored the fantasy of being a newspaper reporter, she had never felt she was good enough to make it.

But now something clicked: Maybe she did have the ability to succeed in a career involving writing.

Looking Ahead

Through the experiences we have in life, we build up a sense of our strengths and weaknesses, what we like and dislike about ourselves. In the process, the sense of who we are also affects the choices we make and the things that we do.

In this chapter you will be asked to consider various aspects of yourself. First you'll look at the ways in which you learn and how you can use your personal learning style to study more effectively.

You'll then explore who you are more broadly, considering the various aspects of your personality. You'll see how your self-esteem—the way you perceive your strengths and weaknesses—can lead to success or failure.

Finally, the chapter helps you investigate where you are headed. By creating your own personal mission statement, you'll begin to solidify the knowledge of who you are and where you would be happiest and most productive in the future.

» LO 3.1 Discovering Your Learning Styles

Consider what it would be like to be a member of the Trukese people, a small group of islanders in the South Pacific.

Trukese sailors often sail hundreds of miles on the open sea. They manage this feat with none of the navigational equipment used by Western sailors. No compass. No chronometer. No sextant. They don't even sail in a straight line. Instead, they zigzag back and forth, at the mercy of the winds and tides. Yet they make few mistakes. Almost always they are able to reach their destination with precision. How do they do it?

They can't really explain it. They say it has to do with following the rising and setting of the stars at night. During the day, they take in the appearance, sound, and feel of the waves against the side of the boat. But they don't really have any idea of where they are at any given moment, nor do they care. They just know that ultimately they'll reach their final destination.

It would be foolhardy to suggest that the Trukese don't have what it takes to be successful sailors. The fact that they don't use traditional Western navigational equipment when they're sailing does not mean that they are any less able than Western navigators.

Trukese sailors, who live on a small group of islands in the South Pacific, are able to navigate with considerable accuracy across great expanses of open seas, and they do so without the use of any of the standard navigation tools used by sailors in Western cultures. The navigational achievements of the Trukese sailors illustrate that there are multiple ways to attain our goals and that there is no single route to success.

Learning style

One's preferred manner of acquiring, using, and thinking about knowledge

Receptive learning style

The way in which we initially receive information

Read/write learning style

A style that involves a preference for written material, favoring reading over hearing and touching

Visual/graphic learning style

A style that favors material presented visually in a diagram or picture

What about academic success? Isn't it reasonable to assume that there are different ways to reach academic goals? Wouldn't it be surprising if everyone learned in exactly the same way?

Each of us has preferred ways of learning, approaches that work best for us. And our success is not just dependent on how well we learn, but on how we learn.

Learning styles reflect our preferred manner of acquiring, using, and thinking about knowledge. We don't have just one learning style, but a variety of styles. Even though our ability may be identical to someone else's, our learning styles might be quite different.

You probably already know quite a lot about your learning styles. Maybe you do particularly well in your biology classes while struggling with English literature. Or it may be the other way around. Because biology tends to be about natural processes, teachers present the subject as a series of related facts. English literature, however, requires you to think more abstractly, analyzing and synthesizing ideas.

Though we may have general preferences for fact-based learning or learning that requires more abstract thinking, we all use a variety of learning styles. Some involve our preferences regarding the way information is presented to us, some relate to how we think and learn most readily, and some relate to how our personality traits affect our performance. We'll start by considering the preferences we have for how we initially perceive information.

What Is Your Preferred Receptive Learning Style?

One of the most basic aspects of learning styles concerns the way in which we initially receive information from our sense organs—our **receptive learning style.** People have different strengths in terms of how they most effectively process information and which of their senses they prefer to use in learning. Specifically, there are four different types of receptive learning styles:

› **Read/write learning style.** If you have a **read/write learning style,** you prefer information that is presented visually in a written format. You feel most comfortable reading, and you may recall the spelling of a word by thinking of how the word looks. You probably learn best when you have the opportunity to read about a concept rather than listening to a teacher explain it.

› **Visual/graphic learning style.** Students with a **visual/graphic learning style** learn most effectively when material is presented visually in a diagram or picture. You might recall the structure of a chemical compound by reviewing a picture in your mind, and you benefit from instructors who make frequent use of visual aids such as videos, maps, and models. Students with visual learning styles find it easier to see things in their mind's eye—to visualize a task or concept—than to be lectured about them.

› **Auditory/verbal learning style.** Have you ever asked a friend to help you put something together by having her read the directions to you while you worked? If you did, you may have an auditory/verbal learning style. People with **auditory/verbal learning styles** prefer listening to explanations rather

Journal Reflections

How I Learn

How would you respond to the following learning situations?

1. Would you rather read a newspaper, listen to the news on the radio, watch it on TV, or click your way through it on a Web site? Why do you think you have this preference?

2. When you get a new piece of software or a new tool, do you like to read the instructions or just "play with it" until you get the hang of it?

3. Suppose a friend is teaching you a new and complex procedure (such as a new game or the way to use a piece of computer software). Do you prefer to get the "big picture" first or the details?

4. When you're in class, what do you do during lectures? Try to write down the instructor's exact words, draw diagrams and make tables, or jot down a few big ideas?

5. What do your answers to the previous questions reveal about the way you prefer to learn new information?

---

than reading them. They love class lectures and discussions, because they can easily take in the information that is being talked about.

▸ **Tactile/kinesthetic learning style.** Students with a **tactile/kinesthetic learning style** prefer to learn by doing—touching, manipulating objects, and doing things. For instance, some people enjoy the act of writing because of the feel of a pencil or a computer keyboard—the tactile equivalent of thinking out loud. Or they may find that it helps them to make a three-dimensional model to understand a new idea.

To get a sense of your own receptive learning style, complete **Try It 1** on page 60. But remember, having a particular receptive learning style simply means that it will be easier to learn material that is presented in that style. It does not mean you cannot learn any other way!

Receptive learning styles have implications for effective studying:

If you have a read/write style, consider writing out summaries of information, highlighting and underlining written material, and using flashcards. Transform diagrams and math formulas into words.

If you have a visual/graphic style, devise diagrams and charts. Translate words into symbols and figures.

If you have an auditory/verbal style, recite material out loud when studying. Work with others in a group, talking through the material, and consider tape recording lectures.

Auditory/verbal learning style
A style that favors listening as the best approach to learning

Tactile/kinesthetic learning style
A style that involves learning by touching, manipulating objects, and doing things

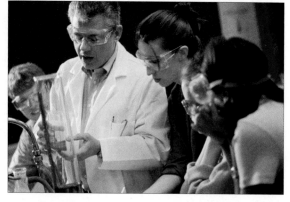

Learning styles reflect our preferred manner of acquiring, using, and thinking about knowledge. Tactile learners prefer hands-on learning that comes about through touching, manipulating, and doing things.

1

What's Your Receptive Learning Style?

Read each of the following statements and rank them in terms of their usefulness to you as learning approaches. Base your ratings on your personal experiences and preferences, using the following scale:

1 = Not at all useful
2 = Not very useful
3 = Neutral
4 = Somewhat useful
5 = Very useful

	1	2	3	4	5
1. Studying alone					
2. Studying pictures and diagrams to understand complex ideas					
3. Listening to class lectures					
4. Performing a process myself rather than reading or hearing about it					
5. Learning a complex procedure by reading written directions					
6. Watching and listening to film, computer, or video presentations					
7. Listening to a book or lecture on tape					
8. Doing lab work					
9. Studying teachers' handouts and lecture notes					
10. Studying in a quiet room					
11. Taking part in group discussions					
12. Taking part in hands-on classroom demonstrations					
13. Taking notes and studying them later					
14. Creating flash cards and using them as a study and review tool					
15. Memorizing and recalling how words are spelled by spelling them "out loud" in my head					
16. Writing down key facts and important points as a tool for remembering them					

	1	2	3	4	5
17. Recalling how to spell a word by seeing it in my head					
18. Underlining or highlighting important facts or passages in my reading					
19. Saying things out loud when I'm studying					
20. Recalling how to spell a word by "writing" it invisibly in the air or on a surface					
21. Learning new information by reading about it in a textbook					
22. Using a map to find an unknown place					
23. Working in a study group					
24. Finding a place I've been to once by just going there without directions					

SCORING:

The statements cycle through the four receptive learning styles in this order: (1) read/write; (2) visual/graphic; (3) auditory/verbal; and (4) tactile/kinesthetic.

To find your primary learning style, disregard your 1, 2, and 3 ratings. Add up your 4 and 5 ratings for each learning style (i.e., a "4" equals 4 points and a "5" equals 5 points). Use the following chart to link the statements to the learning styles and to write down your summed ratings:

Learning Style	Statements	Total (Sum) of Rating Points
Read/write	1, 5, 9, 13, 17, and 21	
Visual/graphic	2, 6, 10, 14, 18, and 22	
Auditory/verbal	3, 7, 11, 15, 19, and 23	
Tactile/kinesthetic	4, 8, 12, 16, 20, and 24	

The total of your rating points for any given style will range from a low of 0 to a high of 30. The highest total indicates your main receptive learning style. Don't be surprised if you have a mixed style, in which two or more styles receive similar ratings.

To Try It online, go to **www.mhhe.com/power**.

If you have a tactile/kinesthetic style, incorporate movement into your study. Trace diagrams, build models, arrange flash cards and move them around. Keep yourself active during class, taking notes, drawing charts, and jotting down key concepts.

Multiple Intelligences: Showing Strength in Different Domains

Do you feel much more comfortable walking through the woods than navigating city streets? Are you an especially talented musician? Is reading and using a complicated map second nature to you?

If so, in each case you may be demonstrating a special and specific kind of intelligence. According to psychologist Howard Gardner, rather than asking "How smart are you?" we should be asking a different question: "How are you smart?" To answer the latter question, Gardner has developed a *theory of multiple intelligences* that offers a unique approach to understanding learning styles and preferences.

The multiple intelligences view says that we have eight different forms of intelligence, each relatively independent of the others and linked to a specific kind of information processing in our brains:

> *Logical-mathematical intelligence* involves skills in problem solving and scientific thinking.

> *Linguistic intelligence* is linked to the production and use of language.

> *Spatial intelligence* relates to skills involving spatial configurations, such as those used by artists and architects.

> *Interpersonal intelligence* is found in learners with particularly strong skills involving interacting with others, such as sensitivity to the moods, temperaments, motivations, and intentions of others.

> *Intrapersonal intelligence* relates to a particularly strong understanding of the internal aspects of oneself and having access to one's own feelings and emotions.

> *Musical intelligence* involves skills relating to music.

> *Bodily kinesthetic intelligence* relates to skills in using the whole body or portions of it in the solution of problems or in the construction of products or displays, exemplified by dancers, athletes, actor, and surgeons.

> *Naturalist intelligence* involves exceptional abilities in identifying and classifying patterns in nature.

All of us have the same eight kinds of intelligence, although in different degrees, and they form the core of our learning styles and preferences. These separate intelligences do not operate in isolation. Instead, any activity involves several kinds of intelligence working together.

To get a sense of which intelligence you favor, complete **Try It 2** on page 64.

Personality Styles

Our learning styles are also influenced by our personality. Are you likely to try out for school productions? Or is the idea of getting on a stage totally lacking in appeal (if not completely terrifying)? Do you relate to the world around you primarily through careful planning or by spontaneously reacting?

According to the rationale of the *Myers-Briggs Type Indicator,* a questionnaire frequently used in business and organizational settings to place people in one of 16 categories, personality type plays a key role in determining how we react to different situations. Specifically, we work best in situations in which others—both students and instructors—share our preferences and in which our personality is most suited to the particular task on which we are working.

Four major personality dimensions are critical. Although we'll describe the extremes of each dimension, keep in mind that most of us fall somewhere between the end points of each dimension.

> **Introverts versus extraverts.** A key difference between introverts and extraverts is whether they enjoy working with others. Independence is a key characteristic of introverted learners. They enjoy working alone and they are less affected by how others think and behave. In contrast, extraverts are outgoing and more affected by the behavior and thinking of others. They enjoy working with others, and they are energized by having other people around.

> **Intuitors versus sensors.** Intuitors enjoy solving problems and being creative. They get impatient with details, preferring to make leaps of judgment, and they enjoy the challenge of solving problems and taking a big-picture approach. People categorized as sensors, on the other hand, prefer a concrete, logical approach in which they can carefully analyze the facts of the situation. Although they are good with details, they sometimes miss the big picture.

> **Thinkers versus feelers.** Thinkers prefer logic over emotion. They reach decisions and solve problems by systematically analyzing a situation. In contrast, feeling types rely more on their emotional responses. They are aware of others and their feelings, and they are influenced by their personal values and attachments to others.

> **Perceivers and judgers.** Before drawing a conclusion, perceivers attempt to gather as much information as they can. Because they are open to multiple perspectives and appreciate all sides of an issue, they sometimes have difficulty completing a task. Judgers, in comparison, are quick and decisive. They like to set goals, accomplish them, and then move on to the next task.

The Origins of Our Learning Styles

For many of us, our learning style preferences result from the kind of processing our brain "specializes" in. **Left-brain processing** concentrates more on tasks requiring verbal competence, such as speaking, reading, thinking, and reasoning. Information is processed sequentially, one bit at a time.

On the other hand, **right-brain processing** tends to concentrate more on the processing of information in nonverbal domains, such as the understanding of spatial relationships, recognition of patterns and drawings, music, and emotional expression. Furthermore, the right hemisphere tends to process information globally, considering it as a whole. Consequently, people who naturally tend toward right-brain processing might prefer visual/graphic learning styles.

Here are some key facts to remember about learning, personality, and processing styles:

> **You have a variety of styles.** As you can see in the summary of different categories of styles in Table 3.1 on page 66, there are several types of styles. For any given task or challenge, some types of styles may be more relevant than others. Furthermore, success is possible even when there is a mismatch between what you need to accomplish and your own pattern of preferred styles. It may take

Left-brain processing
Information processing primarily performed by the left hemisphere of the brain, focusing on tasks requiring verbal competence, such as speaking, reading, thinking, and reasoning; information is processed sequentially, one bit at a time

Right-brain processing
Information processing primarily performed by the right hemisphere of the brain, focusing on information in nonverbal domains, such as the understanding of spatial relationships and recognition of patterns, drawings, music, and emotional expression

Try It!

Your Sense of Intelligence

In this Try It, you will be able to get a sense of your own pattern of multiple intelligences. To start, place a check beside each statement that applies to you.

_____ 1. Sometimes people say that I am a born leader.

_____ 2. I am good at solving mazes and other visual puzzles.

_____ 3. My life would be much less meaningful without music.

_____ 4. I figure out how things work, and I can usually fix things when they break.

_____ 5. Conserving resources and sustainable growth are two of the biggest issues of our times.

_____ 6. I think about my life goals pretty often.

_____ 7. I love word games like Scrabble, anagrams, and crossword puzzles.

_____ 8. I keep track of advances in science.

_____ 9. I listen to music on a daily basis.

_____ 10. I am able to learn about things by touching them.

_____ 11. People often look to me to help resolve disputes.

_____ 12. I make lists of things that I want to accomplish.

_____ 13. I cherish my collection of books.

_____ 14. I enjoy thinking about big, philosophical questions.

_____ 15. I can recognize and name many different types of trees, flowers, and plants.

_____ 16. I am usually sensitive to color.

_____ 17. I keep a diary.

_____ 18. I have a good sense of rhythm. I can usually keep time to a piece of music.

_____ 19. Sometimes I can think without words, using just abstract ideas.

_____ 20. I seldom get lost, even in new places.

_____ 21. I am open to attending counseling sessions to learn more about myself.

_____ 22. Math and science are harder for me than English, social studies, and history.

_____ 23. People sometimes tell me that my mind works like a computer.

_____ 24. I am in good contact with my personal feelings.

_____ 25. When I am outside, I notice things like tracks, nests, and wildlife.

_____ 26. I am great at reading maps. I am usually the navigator.

_____ 27. When I talk with people, I often bring up things that I have read.

_____ 28. I like to garden and make things grow.

_____ 29. I can play one or more musical instruments.

_____ 30. I read whenever I have a free minute.

_____ 31. I am very systematic when I have to solve a problem.

_____ 32. I am pretty well coordinated.

_____ 33. I have pets, or at least I want to have them.

_____ 34. I have a good idea of my own strengths and weaknesses.

_____ 35. I have an appreciation for the arts.

_____ 36. I have three or more close friends.

_____ 37. I often tap out rhythms or sing melodies during the day.

_____ 38. I am a pretty good "do-it-yourselfer."

_____ 39. I am physically active at least three times a week.

_____ 40. I like to teach people what I know.

Using the scoring keys that follow, give yourself one point for each question that corresponds to the sentence you checked.

KEY: Types of Intelligences

Linguistic
Questions: 7, 13, 22, 27, 30
Number of these statements checked: _____

Musical
Questions: 3, 9, 18, 29, 37
Number of these statements checked: _____

Naturalist
Questions: 5, 15, 25, 28, 33
Number of these statements checked: _____

Logical-mathematical
Questions: 8, 14, 19, 23, 31
Number of these statements checked: _____

Bodily kinesthetic
Questions: 4, 10, 32, 38, 39
Number of these statements checked: _____

Interpersonal
Questions: 1, 11, 17, 36, 40
Number of these statements checked: _____

Intrapersonal
Questions: 6, 12, 21, 24, 34
Number of these statements checked: _____

Spatial
Questions: 2, 16, 20, 26, 35
Number of these statements checked: _____

Now fill in the summary chart below to compare your pattern of different kinds of intelligence.

Type of Intelligence	Score
Linguistic	
Musical	
Naturalist	
Logical-mathematical	
Bodily kinesthetic	
Interpersonal	
Intrapersonal	
Spatial	

Are you surprised by the pattern of strengths in the different kinds of intelligence described by Gardner? Why or why not? How do you think your profile affects the way you learn and your learning styles and preferences?

WORKING IN A GROUP:

Compare your patterns of strengths in the different types of intelligence. Ask others how their pattern affects their studying. How might working in a study group with students with a different pattern from yours affect the success of the study group?

To Try It online, go to **www.mhhe.com/power.**

table 3.1 Learning, Personality, and Processing Styles

All of us have particular learning, personality, and processing styles that we tend to rely on. At the same time, we also have capabilities in less-preferred styles. So, for example, although you may be primarily a read/write learner, you have the capacity to use auditory/verbal and tactile/kinesthetic approaches. Note in particular that the four categories of personality styles are considered independent of each other. For instance, you may be an extrovert and at the same time a sensor, a feeler, and a judger. Furthermore, although the "Using the Style" column suggests ways that students with a particular style can make the most of that style, you should also try strategies that work for styles different from your own.

Category	Type	Description	Using the Style[1]
Receptive Learning Styles	Read/write	A style that involves a preference for material in a written format, favoring reading over hearing and touching.	Read and rewrite material, take notes and rewrite them; organize material into tables; transform diagrams and math formulas into words.
	Visual/graphic	A style that favors material presented visually in a diagram or picture.	Use figures and drawings; replay classes and discussions in your mind's eye; visualize material; translate words into symbols and figures.
	Auditory/verbal	A style in which the learner favors listening as the best approach.	Recite material out loud when studying; consider how words sound; study different languages; tape record lectures; work with others, talking through the material.
	Tactile/kinesthetic	A style that involves learning by touching, manipulating objects, and doing things.	Incorporate movement into studying; trace figures and drawings with your finger; create models; make flash cards and move them around; keep active during class, taking notes, drawing charts, jotting down key concepts.
Multiple Intelligences	Logical-mathematical	Strengths in problem solving and scientific thinking.	Express information mathematically or in formulas.
	Linguistic	Strengths in the production and use of language.	Write out notes and summarize information in words; construct stories about material.
	Spatial	Strengths involving spatial configurations, such as those used by artists and architects.	Build charts, graphs, and flowcharts.
	Interpersonal	Found in learners with particularly strong skills involving interacting with others, such as sensitivity to the moods, temperaments, motivations, and intentions of others.	Work with others in groups.
	Intrapersonal	Strengths in understanding the internal aspects of oneself and having access to one's own feelings and emotions.	Build on your prior experiences and feelings about the world; use your originality.

| table 3.1 | Learning, Personality, and Processing Styles *(concluded)* |

Category	Type	Description	Using the Style
	Musical	Strengths relating to music.	Write a song or lyrics to help remember material.
	Bodily kinesthetic	Strengths in using the whole body or portions of it in the solution of problems or in the construction of products or displays, exemplified by dancers, athletes, actors, and surgeons.	Use movement in studying; build models.
	Naturalist	Exceptional strengths in identifying and classifying patterns in nature.	Use analogies based on nature.
Personality Styles	Introvert versus extravert	Independence is a key characteristic of introverted learners, who enjoy working alone and are less affected by how others think and behave. In contrast, extraverts are outgoing and more affected by the behavior and thinking of others. They enjoy working with others.	Experiment with studying in groups compared with working alone; consider your performance in class discussions compared with working on your own.
	Intuitor versus sensor	Intuitive people enjoy solving problems and being creative, often taking a big-picture approach. Sensors, on the other hand, prefer a concrete, logical approach in which they can carefully analyze the facts of the situation.	For intuitors, reflect on the personal meaning of material and seek out tasks that involve creativity. For sensors, seek out concrete tasks that involve the application of logical principles.
	Thinker versus feeler	Thinkers prefer logic over emotion, reaching decisions through rational analysis. In contrast, feelers rely more on their emotions and are influenced by their personal values and attachments to others.	Thinkers should seek to systematically analyze situations, attempting to identify patterns. For feelers, use emotional responses to reflect on material.
	Perceiver versus judger	Before drawing a conclusion, perceivers attempt to gather as much information as they can and are open to multiple perspectives. Judgers, in comparison, are quick and decisive, enjoying setting goals and accomplishing them.	Perceivers organize material sequentially and into component parts; for judgers, using goal-setting preferences facilitates learning.
Brain Processing Styles	Left-brain processing	Information processing that focuses on tasks requiring verbal competence, such as speaking, reading, thinking, and reasoning; information is processed sequentially, one bit at a time.	Organize material logically; identify patterns; make tables of key information; break material into component parts.
	Right-brain processing	Information processing that focuses on information in nonverbal domains, such as the understanding of spatial relationships, recognition of patterns and drawings, music, and emotional expression.	Identify patterns; use graphs and drawings; read aloud; create models.

more work, but learning to deal with situations that require you to use less-preferred styles is important practice for life after college.

> **Your style reflects your preferences regarding which abilities you like to use—not the abilities themselves.** Styles are related to our preferences and the mental approaches we like to use. You may prefer to learn tactilely, but that in itself doesn't guarantee that the products that you create tactilely will be good. You still have to put in work!

> **Your style will change over the course of your life.** You can learn new styles and expand the range of learning experiences in which you feel perfectly comfortable. In fact, you can conceive of this book as one long lesson in learning styles because it provides you with strategies for learning more effectively in a variety of ways.

> **You should work on improving your less-preferred styles.** Although it may be tempting, don't always make choices that increase your exposure to preferred styles and decrease your practice with less-preferred styles. The more you use approaches for which you have less of a preference, the better you'll be at developing the skills associated with those styles.

> **Work cooperatively with others who have different styles.** If your instructor asks you to work cooperatively in groups, seek out classmates who have styles that are different from yours. Not only will your classmates' differing styles help you to achieve collective success, but you can also learn from observing others' approaches to tackling the assignment.

Using Your Instructors' Teaching Styles

In the same way that each of us has preferred learning styles, instructors have their own styles of teaching, often based on their own personal learning styles. They may not even be aware of them, but their learning styles have an important impact on the way they teach—and that, in turn, will help determine how well you do in their classes.

Instructors who make frequent requests to "draw" or "diagram" may favor a more visual-graphic learning style. In contrast, if their tendency is to ask you to "list" or "discuss," or "analyze," they may be more in tune with a verbal/reading style.

Similarly, instructors who assign frequent projects that involve oral presentations and demonstrations might be indicating that their learning style is somewhat auditory. On the other hand, instructors whose assignments consist of frequent written work may have a more visual style. Work on "Instructor Styles" (**Try It 3**) to get a sense of your instructor's learning style, and look at the *Course Connections* feature on page 70 for strategies for dealing with what you find.

Learning styles are only one example of how the kind of person you are—your strengths and weaknesses, your likes and dislikes, your overall personality—affect your academic success. In fact, the totality of who you are is central in determining the path you follow in achieving success. Let's turn now to how an understanding of how the totality of who you are influences your college performance by considering self-concept.

» LO3.2 Self-Concept: "Who Am I?"

Of course you know who you are. You know your first and last name. You know where and when you were born, and you have no trouble identifying your ethnic background. You can probably recite your Social Security number with ease.

Try It! **POWER**

3

Instructor Styles

Working as a group with your classmates, try to determine your course instructor's learning style by answering the following questions:

1. What clues does the language your instructor uses give you about his or her learning style?

2. What assignments has the instructor scheduled, and what do they tell you about the instructor's learning style?

3. Are there constraints (such as class size, scheduling factors, school traditions) that also influence the instructor's teaching style, apart from his or her underlying learning style?

To Try It online, go to www.mhhe.com/power.

But if this is all that comes to mind when you think about who you are, you're missing a lot of the picture. There's a lot more to you than name, rank, and serial number. What makes you unique and special are your thoughts, your beliefs, your dreams. You have a unique history, and this set of experiences together with your genetic makeup—the combination of genes you inherited from your parents—is unlike anyone else's.

Our view of ourselves—our **self-concept**—has three parts:

1. Our physical self is both who we are physically—the color of our eyes or the curliness of our hair—and how we feel about our physical form. We all have our blemishes, protruding stomachs, long noses, or other physical quirks, but we don't all feel the same way about them.

2. Our social self is made up of the roles we play in our social interactions with others. As you're reading these words, you're not only a student but also a son or daughter, a friend, a citizen, and possibly an employee, a spouse, a lover, and/or a parent. Each of these roles plays an important part in defining your self-concept. Each also helps determine how you behave while acting in that particular role.

3. Finally, our self-concept also contains a personal self—our inner core, which is that private part of ourselves that no one knows about except us. It consists of the innermost thoughts and experiences that we may or may not choose to share with others.

Self-concept

People's view of themselves that forms over time, comprising three components: the physical self, the social self, and the personal self

[
"When I discover who I am, I'll be free."

Ralph Ellison, author
]

How Your Instructor's Teaching Style Can Guide Your Studying Strategies

Having a sense of your instructor's teaching style can help maximize your success in a course. It can give you insight into the kinds of test questions your instructor may favor and help you strategize about what to pay particular attention to when you're reading and studying course material.

If your instructor focuses on broad, conceptual views of material

- Be prepared for essay questions that ask you to pull different pieces of information together.
- Expect assignments in which you must synthesize different points of view into a coherent whole.
- As you read material, consider how different facts fit together into a broader picture.

If your instructor focuses on facts and details

- Prepare for tests by learning individual facts, which may be tested using multiple choice or fill-in test questions.
- Expect assignments that are very specific and detailed.
- Study by focusing on specific facts. For instance, consider creating note cards on which you write individual bits of information.

What if your preferred learning style doesn't match up with your instructor's teaching style? Then keep in mind that there are benefits to the discomfort that you may experience when your instructor emphasizes activities that don't match your own learning styles. Remember that real learning is often difficult and uncomfortable, and the practice you get with less-preferred learning styles in the end will make you a more accomplished student.

Self-Concept and Self-Fulfilling Prophecies

The way we view ourselves determines how we interact with others, what challenges we feel ready to take on, and our expectations for future success. If you see yourself as a successful student, you are likely to expect that you'll continue to be a successful student. On the other hand, if you see yourself as an incapable, inept student, your chances for future success are diminished.

In short, our self-concept can act as a self-fulfilling prophecy. A **self-fulfilling prophecy** occurs when we hold a belief or expectation that affects our behavior, thereby increasing the likelihood that our beliefs or expectations will come true. For instance, a person who views herself as a poor student may find herself thinking: "Why bother working hard? I'm no good as a student; that's just the way I am." It's easy to see how such a view could lead to a self-fulfilling prophecy: By not working hard, the student guarantees that the prophecy of poor performance comes true.

On the other hand, self-fulfilling prophecies can have positive effects. A person who sees herself as a good student will probably be motivated to study and complete assignments enthusiastically. Her view of herself can therefore bring about the expected behavior—in this case, success.

To get a clearer picture of your own self-concept:

> **Examine the roles you play.** To understand who we are, we need to understand the different roles that we play in life. Consider which of these roles are central to who you are—and who you want to be. Consider how an outsider

Self-fulfilling prophecy
A phenomenon that occurs when we hold a belief or expectation that affects our behavior, thereby increasing the likelihood that our beliefs or expectations *will* come true

might look at your actions, beliefs, and interests. How would that person characterize you?

> **Identify your strengths and weaknesses.** Look at yourself with a clear and objective eye, and consider what you do particularly well and what you don't do particularly well. If you're honest, you'll come up with several areas in which you need work—and many other areas in which you're already quite strong. Use **Table 3.2** on page 72 to help you organize your thoughts and build an initial inventory of your strengths and weaknesses.

IT'S ALWAYS 'GOOD DOG'—NEVER 'GREAT DOG.'

GREGORY

As you consider your strengths and weaknesses, don't place a value on them. The fact that you procrastinate and put off tasks doesn't make you a bad person, just as the fact that you're a good student doesn't necessarily make you a good person. The point in seeking to identify who you are is to determine your self-concept with accuracy, not to determine how good (or bad) a human being you are.

> **Construct your own definition of who you are.** Don't let what you believe others think about you determine what you think you're good at and bad at. See yourself through your own eyes, not someone else's.

> **Accept your entire self-concept.** If you're being honest with yourself, you'll find that there are parts of yourself that you like more than others. That's OK. Don't disown the parts you don't like; they're also part of who you are. Instead, accept that some parts of yourself need work, while others are the source of justifiable pride.

Make Sure Your Self-Concept Is Yours

Our own perceptions are not the only source of self-fulfilling prophecies. We sometimes permit others' views of who we are and their expectations about us to determine our behavior.

For example, if we think an instructor views us as a particularly hard worker, we may not want to disappoint him by slacking off. If we believe that our boss admires our persistence, we may be motivated to show her persistence when we're working on a difficult problem on the job.

> "Respect yourself if you would have others respect you."
>
> Baltasar Gracian, author

Responding to others' positive perceptions can be fine, for the results are good. But what happens if someone holds a negative view of who we are? What if we're constantly told that we're not working hard enough . . . or that we're not as smart as our older brother . . . or that we are the hard worker, but not the creative one?

The results can be devastating. If we consistently hear such messages about who we are, we can come to believe them. Even worse, our behavior can begin to reflect the negative messages. If we're constantly told that we don't work hard enough, we may in fact not work very hard. If we're told we're not as smart as someone else, we may begin to think of ourselves as not very bright. Or if someone tells us we're not creative, we may not try very hard to be creative.

In short, the negative messages that we hear from others can come to act as a prison, placing us in bondage to others' negative beliefs about who we are and what our capabilities are. It's crucial, then, not to buy into others' negative views of who we are. Our biggest help, and sometimes handicap, in this effort is self-esteem.

table 3.2 Inventory Your Strengths and Weaknesses

To get a clearer picture of your self-concept, complete an honest inventory of your strengths and weaknesses. To help you organize your thoughts, use the following table, adding brief examples.

Aspects of Self	Strengths	Weaknesses
Physical self		
Health and fitness		
Sports		
Nutrition and diet		
Appearance		
Other		
Social self		
Friend		
Son/daughter		
Lover/spouse		
Citizen/community member		
Employee		
Student		
Roommate		
Classmate		
Team or group member (e.g., sports, band, club)		
Other		
Personal self		
Personal experiences		
Unique traits		
Personality		
Spiritual self		
Habits		
Attitudes/opinions		
Ideas/thoughts		
Other		

≫ LO 3.3 Self-Esteem: Building a Positive View of Yourself

When you think about yourself as a student, you probably don't stop there. Instead, you may see yourself as a "good" student or maybe a "just OK" student. Similarly, when you consider yourself in the role of friend, you may view yourself as a "loyal-to-the-end" friend or maybe, in the opposite case, a "fair-weather" friend. In short, when we look inward at who we are, we don't just stop with a characterization of the different roles that we play in the world. Instead, we place a value on them. We see the various facets of our self-concept not in neutral terms, but as either positive or negative.

Self-esteem is the overall evaluation we give ourselves as individuals. It reflects the degree to which we see ourselves as individuals of worth and determines our general acceptance of ourselves. If we have high self-esteem, we generally feel respect for and acceptance of ourselves. On the other hand, if we have low self-esteem, we may lack respect for ourselves, reject parts of who we are, and judge ourselves negatively.

To get a sense of your own general level of self-esteem, complete the self-assessment in **Try It 4** on page 74.

Self-esteem
The overall evaluation we give ourselves as individuals

Why Self-Esteem Matters

People with high self-esteem are generally happier and better able to cope with adversity. High self-esteem provides a sense of security, because people with high self-esteem feel they are able to deal with problems that may arise. They also have a sense of **self-efficacy,** the expectation that they are capable of achieving their goals in many different kinds of situations. High self-esteem can also give people a sense of purpose and the belief that they are productive members of society.

In contrast, individuals lacking in self-esteem are more insecure, and their belief in their ability to reach their goals is weak. They feel less tied to others, and their sense of purpose is not firm. And when others are successful, people with low self-esteem may feel jealousy and envy.

Low self-esteem can produce a cycle of failure in which low self-esteem leads to low expectations, reduced effort, elevated anxiety, poor performance, and, finally, an affirmation of the low self-esteem that began the cycle in the first place. Such a cycle can be difficult to break (see **Figure 3.1** on page 75).

Self-efficacy
The expectation that one is capable of achieving one's goals in many different kinds of situations

Calvin and Hobbes   by Bill Watterson

Try It!

4 Measuring Your Self-Esteem

To get an informal estimate of your self-esteem, complete the following scale.[2]

Statement	Strongly Agree	Agree	Disagree	Strongly Disagree
1. On the whole, I am satisfied with myself.				
2. At times I think I am no good at all.				
3. I feel that I have a number of good qualities.				
4. I am able to do things as well as most other people.				
5. I feel I do not have much to be proud of.				
6. I certainly feel useless at times.				
7. I feel that I am a person of worth, at least the equal of others.				
8. I wish I could have more respect for myself.				
9. All in all, I am inclined to feel that I am a failure.				
10. I take a positive attitude toward myself.				

Scoring: For statements 1, 3, 4, 7, and 10, score as follows:

Strongly agree	= 4 points
Agree	= 3 points
Disagree	= 2 points
Strongly disagree	= 1 point

For statements 2, 5, 6, 8, and 9, score as follows:

Strongly agree	= 1 point
Agree	= 2 points
Disagree	= 3 points
Strongly disagree	= 4 point

Add your points together, and interpret the total as follows:

The highest possible score (i.e., an apparently very high level of self-esteem) is 40 points, and the minimum score (i.e., an apparently very low level of self-esteem) is 10. Most people score in the 30- to 40-point range. A much smaller number of people score in the 20s. A score of 10 to 20 is often found in people who suffer from chronic depression; those who score at this level should consider consulting a health care provider or call a 24-hour hotline such as 800-448-3000. Keep in mind that this is a very rough gauge of self-esteem and that scores will vary depending on a number of factors, including your mood when you complete the questionnaire.

Now consider the following:

- Do the results of the questionnaire match your own gut feelings about yourself?
- Do you think your self-esteem has changed? Do you have any ideas as to why?

To Try It online, go to www.mhhe.com/power.

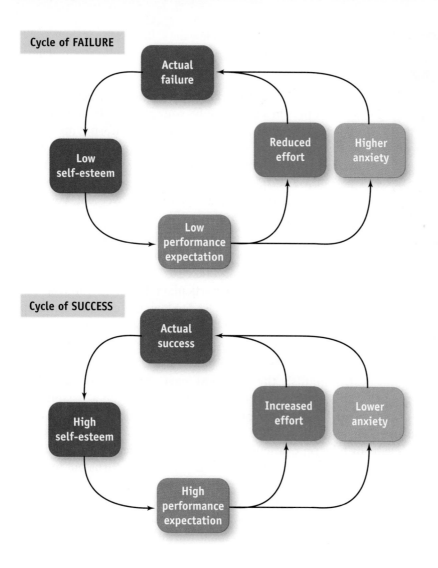

Cycle of FAILURE

Actual failure

Low self-esteem

Low performance expectation

Reduced effort

Higher anxiety

Cycle of SUCCESS

Actual success

High self-esteem

High performance expectation

Increased effort

Lower anxiety

figure 3.1

The Cycle of Failure and the Cycle of Success

Low self-esteem can lead to low performance expectations. In turn, low performance expectations can produce reduced effort and high anxiety, both of which can lead to failure—and ultimately reinforce the low self-esteem that started the cycle. In contrast, those with high self-esteem expect success, and that expectation leads to greater effort and lower anxiety, thereby increasing the likelihood of actual success. Ultimately, this success boosts self-esteem.

If a student with low self-esteem begins studying for a test believing that he is likely to do badly, he may put forth relatively little effort. Moreover, because he is virtually sure he is going to do poorly on the test, he may experience extremes of anxiety, feeling that (another) failure is lurking just ahead.

Ultimately, the combination of lack of effort and anxiety produced by his low self-esteem does him in, and he actually does do poorly on the test. But the cycle of failure is not yet complete: Rather than telling himself that low effort and elevated anxiety caused his poor test performance, he views it as an affirmation of his inferior ability. In turn, this misperception serves to reinforce his low self-esteem.

On the other hand, people with higher self-esteem find themselves in a cycle of success shown in **Figure 3.1.** Their higher expectations lead to increased effort and lower anxiety, making the probability of success greater. In turn, this helps affirm their higher sense of self-esteem that started the cycle.

Breaking the Self-Esteem Cycle of Failure

"OK," you may be saying to yourself, "I understand that self-esteem is important. But how am I supposed to ignore a lifetime of learning and improve my self-esteem?"

It's not a simple matter to shed a less-than-ideal view of ourselves and adopt a more positive one. And you certainly won't be able to change your basic conception

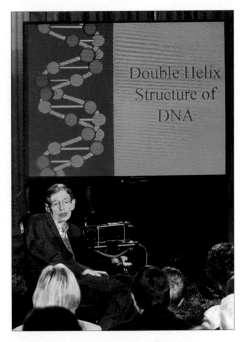

Physicist Stephen Hawking has overcome significant challenges in the physical realm to make ground-breaking intellectual contributions.

of yourself in the course of a few days. But there are steps you can take to bring yourself closer to an ideal level of self-esteem. They include the following:

> **Accept yourself, warts and all.** No one is perfect, and becoming a perfect person should not be your goal in life. If it were, you'd be doomed to failure, because you'd never measure up.

Accept the fact that there are certain aspects of yourself and your life that you're not pleased with. In fact, embrace your awareness of your displeasure: If you didn't realize that there were some things about yourself that needed improvement, you'd be out of touch with who you are.

> **Understand that everyone has value and self-worth.** Every individual has value and self-worth, some unique spark that sets him or her apart from everyone else. Examine yourself and your life, and get a picture of the particulars that make you you.

Low self-esteem can lead to low performance expectations. In turn, low performance can produce reduced effort and high anxiety, both of which can lead to failure—and ultimately reinforce the low self-esteem that started the cycle.

> **Distinguish the different parts of who you are.** No one is all bad, just as no one is all good. Maybe a person who never reached the level of success she wanted to in school turns out to be an excellent employee, the person who always seems to be asked to solve problems or take on challenges no one else can deal with. Another person may not be the kind of husband he wants to be, but turns out to be a terrific parent.

Understanding that you have failings in one arena of life doesn't mean that you can't be successful in others. It makes no sense to base your self-esteem on what you do worst in life, so don't make the mistake of focusing solely on your failings and minimizing your successes.

> **Don't just rely on—or wait for—others' praise.** Your self-esteem should not be solely dependent on the praise you get from others. Use your own judgment to evaluate the level of success you've achieved on a given task.

For instance, you know when you've done your best in writing a paper. If you feel proud of it, celebrate your accomplishment and take pride in it. Instead of waiting for your instructor's feedback, permit yourself to feel good about what you've done. Your self-esteem should be based on your own assessment of your accomplishments, not only on others' assessments.

> **Understand that building self-esteem is a lifelong undertaking.** It's taken a lifetime to develop whatever level of self-esteem you currently have. Your self-esteem is not going to change overnight.

Rebuilding self-esteem isn't easy. It's particularly hard to do at a time when you face a major life transition, such as the beginning of your college experience; your oldest friends and family may not be nearby, and the level of academic work you encounter presents new challenges. In fact, starting college presents a special opportunity to grow and develop. It's a new environment, giving you the opportunity to unlearn old patterns of behavior that have held you back and master new ones that will permit you to have a more positive view of yourself. Don't let low self-esteem keep you from becoming what you can be.

Preparing a Personal Mission Statement

The life that is unexamined is not worth living.

Twenty-five hundred years later, Plato's words are still true. If you never consider what you want out of life, what your dreams and aspirations are, and where you're heading, you're in danger of missing out on the most fundamental and meaningful parts of life. The day-to-day details of life will use up all your time, and you won't know exactly where it has gone.

One way to get a clearer picture of our life is to create a formal document—called a **Personal Mission Statement**—of what we actually hope to achieve during our lifetime. The P.O.W.E.R. framework provides a systematic series of steps (described below, and summarized in the P.O.W.E.R. Plan graphic) that can help us look inward and determine the way we wish to carry out our lives.

Personal Mission Statement
A formal statement regarding what a person hopes to achieve during his or her lifetime

P Prepare | Identifying Your Values

The first step toward understanding ourselves is to assess our underlying **values**—qualifies we see as most desirable and important—systematically. To do this, work through the following steps:

Values
The qualities we see as desirable and most important

1. Choose the five values that you hold most dear. Here are some examples, but don't necessarily restrict yourself to these: a comfortable life, an exciting life, a sense of accomplishment, world peace, beauty, equality, security, freedom, happiness, inner harmony, love, national security, pleasure, religion, self-respect, fame, friendship, wisdom, work, financial security, risk taking, being challenged.

2. For each value, answer each of these questions below: Why is it important to you, who taught it to you, how has it affected your behavior in the past, and in what ways can you affirm it through your future behavior?

Value #1 _____

Why it is important:

Who taught it to you:

How it has affected your past behavior:

In what ways you can affirm it through future behavior:

Value #2 _____

Why it is important:

Who taught it to you:

How it has affected your past behavior:

In what ways you can affirm it through future behavior:

Value #3 _____

Why it is important:

Who taught it to you:

How it has affected your past behavior:

In what ways you can affirm it through future behavior:

P Prepare
Identify your values

O Organize
Impose order on what motivates you

W Work
Create a personal mission statement

E Evaluate
Assess your personal mission statement

R Rethink
Reconsider your options

P.O.W.E.R. Plan

Value #4 _____

    Why it is important:

    Who taught it to you:

    How it has affected your past behavior:

    In what ways you can affirm it through future behavior:

Value #5 _____

    Why it is important:

    Who taught it to you:

    How it has affected your past behavior:

    In what ways you can affirm it through future behavior:

After you've identified your most important values, you'll be ready to move onto the organize step in developing a Mission Statement: determining what motivates you.

◉ Organize — Imposing Order on What Motivates You

Abraham Lincoln. Albert Einstein. Eleanor Roosevelt.

What is the common link among these three people? According to psychologist Abraham Maslow, each of them achieved **self-actualization,** a state of self-fulfillment in which people realize their highest potential in their own unique way.[3]

According to Maslow, self-actualization is the highest of the various needs that motivate our behavior. As you can see in the illustration in **Figure 3.2,** our underlying needs form a pyramid. At the bottom of the pyramid are our most basic needs, such as the biological needs that drive our behavior, including food, water, sleep, and sex. The basic needs are not much different from those that drive the behavior of nonhuman animals. The needs on the next higher level of the pyramid are safety needs; we need a safe, secure environment to function effectively.

But as humans are able to meet their more-basic survival needs, they have a chance to become acquainted with levels of need that relate to more-advanced qualities, such as the need for love. As the pyramid indicates, our love and belongingness needs come next: our need to form relationships with others and to look outside ourselves. We seek to give affection and to be contributing members of groups within society.

After these needs are fulfilled, we strive for the esteem of others. Esteem relates to the desire to develop a sense of self-worth. We want others to be aware of our competence and worth and to acknowledge our value in the world.

Only after we meet these physiological, safety, love and belongingness, and esteem needs can we strive for self-actualization. Although early views of self-actualization restricted this quality to a few well-known individuals, self-actualization is now generally regarded as a concept that can apply to any of us.

For instance, a parent with excellent nurturing skills who raises a family, a teacher who year after year creates an environment that maximizes students' opportunities for success, and an artist who realizes her creative potential might all be self-actualized individuals. The crucial characteristic of self-actualization is that we feel at ease with ourselves and satisfied that we are using our talents to the fullest.

Self-actualization

A state of self-fulfillment in which people realize their highest potential in their own unique way

"Authentic values are those by which a life can be lived."

Allan Bloom, author

Strive for self-fulfillment

Self-actualization

Be aware of and celebrate your successes

Esteem

Build social networks and relationships

Love and belongingness

Live in a secure environment

Safety needs

Eat well and get enough sleep

Biological needs

W Work   Creating a Personal Mission Statement

> *To make, distribute & sell the finest quality all natural ice cream & euphoric concoctions with a continued commitment to incorporating wholesome, natural ingredients and promoting business practices that respect the Earth and the Environment.*

> *To operate the Company on a sustainable financial basis of profitable growth, increasing value for our stakeholders & expanding opportunities for development and career growth for our employees.*

> *To operate the company in a way that actively recognizes the central role that business plays in society by initiating innovative ways to improve the quality of life locally, nationally & internationally.*[4]

You may have already guessed the name of the business that would make the statements reproduced above: Ben & Jerry's ice cream company. Like almost every other major organization, Ben & Jerry's has a mission statement, a series of statements about what the organization does and the principles that guide its corporate life.

What's good for Ben & Jerry's is good for you. Each of us should set out a personal mission statement, a description encompassing our own personal objectives, long-term goals, and guiding philosophy. It's a kind of personal constitution that sets out broad principles of how we wish to conduct our lives. It is a guideline that allows us to adapt our behavior to changes in our lives without straying from our overall direction and purpose.

A personal mission statement also helps us move from our abstract values and motivational needs to something concrete by providing the foundation for developing specific goals to guide our behavior. By making our values explicit, we are better able to formulate short- and long-term goals that reflect what is important to us.

For example, consider the following mission statement created by one student:

My mission is to use my personal abilities fully to become an engineer who will work on projects that will help others improve the quality of their lives. In addition, I hope to form meaningful relationships with others and to marry and raise children who will make their own contributions to society. Finally, I wish to participate in bettering the world by volunteering in organizations that will enhance the quality of my own community.

This mission statement reflects several underlying values and needs: the desire to use work to improve others' lives, the wish to form relationships with others, and the desire to make the world a better place. In some respects it is fairly specific (such as the desire to become an engineer and to marry and have children), while in others it is fairly vague (such as the wish to participate in organizations that can improve community life). The key point is that it provides a general framework, a way of evaluating whether any particular choice fits into this individual's overall personal mission.

To create your own personal mission statement, follow these three preliminary steps:

> **Summarize your most important values and motivational needs.** You've already assessed your values and motivational needs. Try to distill them into several key principles that will guide your life.

> **Consider what you want your major product to be.** Ben & Jerry's makes ice cream. What do you want to be known and remembered for? Your work? Your family? Your good deeds? Your relationships with others? Something you've created—art, photos, writings?

> **Reflect on the kind of person you want to be.** Do you wish to be kind, friendly, helpful, assertive, powerful, wealthy, altruistic?

Once you've completed these three steps, you're in a position to create your own mission statement. Write it in **Try It 5.**

E Evaluate Assessing Your Personal Mission Statement

After you've written a personal mission statement, consider whether it accurately captures what you are looking for out of life. Would a friend who knows you well see it as a valid reflection of who you are? Does the mission statement take a long-term view, reflecting not just where you are now, but where you wish to be in the future? Is it general enough to fit the many different circumstances in which you will find yourself?

Only you can determine the ability of your personal mission statement to capture what is important to you. If you feel it doesn't, rewrite it. Eventually you'll come up with a statement that illustrates what you feel makes you special.

R Rethink Reconsidering Your Options

Personal mission statements are not set in stone like the Ten Commandments. Instead, they should be considered living documents that you can change as you become clearer about what you want for yourself.

Write a Mission Statement

1. What are your most important values (e.g., comfort, environmental awareness, kindness to others, inner harmony, challenge, etc.)?

2. What are your motivational needs (e.g., love and belonging, esteem, self-actualization)?

3. In what general area or career do you wish to work?

4. What will be your most important "product," for which you want to be known and remembered (e.g., good deeds, wealth, power, prestige, artistic creations, business acumen, etc.)?

5. What kind of person do you want to be (helpful, kind, solitary, powerful, wealthy, etc.)?

6. In what sort of community do you want to live (large city, small city, small town, suburbs, country, woods, farm, etc.)?

7. With whom do you want to live (e.g., spouse, friends, children, etc.)?

8. What words describe your ideal lifestyle (e.g., sophisticated, woodsy, agricultural, down-home, laid back, ambitious, etc.)?

Now write your mission statement. You might, for example, state how you plan to achieve your motivational needs and realize your values through your chosen career. Next you might describe the sort of person you want to be and the "product" you plan to contribute to the world. Finally, you might describe your intended lifestyle, including the type of community you would like to live in and the nature of your ideal family.

To Try It online, go to **www.mhhe.com/power**.

PERSONAL MISSION STATEMENT

Prepared by: _____

Date: _____

That's why it's important to periodically revisit your personal mission statement, the final step in the P.O.W.E.R. Plan for creating a personal mission statement. When you do rethink your statement, ask yourself if it's still representative of your values and motivational needs. Consider whether it should be amended to reflect changes that have occurred in your life.

Even if you don't modify it, periodically reading your personal mission statement is important. It will remind you of who you are and what you are trying to get out of the one life you have.

» LO 3.4 To Thine Own Self Be True: No One Is Responsible for Your Life But You

"Don't take many English courses; they won't help you get a decent job." "How about pre-med? You'd make a great doctor." "Sign up for management classes so you'll be ready to join the family business when you graduate."

Sound familiar? Many of us have heard suggestions like these proposed by parents or others close to us. Such comments often sound quite reasonable.

Why, then, should suggestions like these be taken with great caution? The reason is they relate to decisions that you, and only you, should make. You are the one who must live with their consequences. You are the one who must live with yourself.

One of the worst reasons to follow a particular path in life is that other people want you to. Decisions that affect your life should be your decisions—decisions you make after you've considered various alternatives and chosen the path that suits you best.

Making your own decisions does not mean that you should ignore the suggestions of others. For instance, your parents do have their own unique experiences that may make their advice helpful, and having participated in a great deal of your personal history, they may have a clear view of your strengths and weaknesses. Still, their views are not necessarily accurate. They may still see you as a child, in need of care and protection. Or they may see only your strengths. Or, in some unfortunate cases, they may focus only on your flaws and shortcomings.

People will always be giving you advice. Ultimately, though, you have to make your own judgments about what's right for you, following your head—and your heart.

Identifying Your Interests

Creating a personal mission statement can help you think more productively about one of the most important decisions of your college career: identifying your profession. One way to jump-start this process is to systematically identify your current interests, a critical step in determining what kind of work will be most fulfilling and satisfying for you.

However, few of us are fully aware of the complete range of our interests, primarily because we don't take the time to systematically inventory them. Consequently, career advisor Richard Bolles[5] suggests answering the following questions in order to identify the scope of your interests:

- What are your favorite subjects and hobbies?
- What do you like to talk about most?
- When you go to a newsstand, what are the subjects of magazines that you are attracted to?
- When you read a newspaper, what section do you read first?
- If you're wandering around a bookstore, what kinds of books do you spend the most time looking at?
- When you surf the World Wide Web, what sites do you find yourself returning to regularly?
- When you watch TV game shows, what categories would you choose?
- If you were to write a book, what would you write about?
- When you get so engrossed in thought that you lose track of time, what is it you are thinking about?

Once you've got a better grip on your interests after answering each of these questions, the next step is to prioritize them, rank-ordering them from most interesting to least interesting. You can then use this rank-ordered list to investigate careers, seeking out work involving interests similar to your own. For example, if you have strong interests in the visual arts, you might explore careers involving graphic design, computer-assisted graphics, or architecture. If you avidly keep up with the news of the day, you might consider journalism or television news production. The critical point is to try to match what you like to do (as well as your learning and personality style strengths) with what you'll be doing when you're on the job. The closer the match, the happier and more successful you'll be.

 Career Connections

NAME: **Colin Powell**

SCHOOL: **B.A., The City College of New York;
M.S., George Washington University**

Few who knew Colin Powell when he was growing up would have guessed that he would become the highest-ranking military commander in the United States and later the country's Secretary of State.

The son of Jamaican immigrants, Powell characterizes himself as lacking drive while growing up in a poor South Bronx neighborhood in New York City. As he describes himself, "I was a happy-go-lucky kid, amenable, amiable, and aimless."

Although his parents, who had high educational expectations, urged him to transfer from his neighborhood high school to a more demanding school, his guidance counselor advised against it, citing his previous undistinguished academic performance. Powell ended up maintaining a C average in his neighborhood school, where simply showing up was largely what it took to pass.

But Powell's parents encouraged him to continue his education and apply to college. Bowing to their pressure, he entered The City College of New York, starting as an engineering major, and later switching to geology. Most important, though, Powell found a passion: participation in the college ROTC program, which provided training that allowed students to become officers in the military upon graduation. ROTC training provided him with a grounding, a sense that he had found what he was looking for in life.

When Powell graduated, he immediately entered the Army, distinguishing himself early on as a military leader. But he also came to feel he needed more education. Now more serious about education, he enrolled in a master's degree program in Government and Business Administration at George Washington University, earning nearly straight A's.

Returning to the Army after receiving his master's degree, Powell moved up rapidly through the ranks, ultimately moving into the highest military post in the country. After retiring from the military, Powell became the U.S. Secretary of State, serving four years in that position.

As a highly visible and successful black American, Powell understands that he is seen as a role model, particularly by young blacks. In his own words, "The message I give to young people as I talk in high schools essentially says, 'Do not let the fact that you're a minority or that you come from a different background or that you are trapped structurally somewhere serve as an anchor to keep you down. You've got to swim against it, you've got to climb against it.' The only thing I can do is tell them to reach down inside."[6] He certainly took his own advice.

Looking Back

What are my learning styles, and how have they affected my academic success?

> People have patterns of diverse learning styles—characteristic ways of acquiring and using knowledge.

> Learning styles include read/write, visual/graphic, auditory/verbal, and tactile/ kinesthetic styles (the receptive learning styles).

> The multiple intelligences view says that we have eight different forms of intelligence, each relatively independent of the others.

> Personality styles that influence learning are classified along dimensions of introversion/extraversion, intuition/sensing, thinking/feeling, and perceiving/judging.

What is self-concept, and how does it affect me?

> Self-concept is the understanding of the self that a person forms over time. Its major components are the physical, social, and personal selves.

> Self-concept is important because of the effects it has on people's attitudes and behavior. Self-concept can act as a self-fulfilling prophecy, in that people act in accordance with their self-concepts.

How does my level of self-esteem affect my behavior?

> Self-esteem is the overall evaluation we give ourselves as individuals.

> High self-esteem can lead to greater happiness, an enhanced ability to cope with adversity, a sense of security and confidence, and a sense of self-efficacy.

> Low self-esteem can lead to insecurity, low self-efficacy, and a cycle of failure.

How can I make wise personal decisions throughout life?

> A personal mission statement can be used to determine important values and to state the principles by which we intend to lead our lives.

> People's needs can be organized into a hierarchy in which the most basic and fundamental needs form the base of a pyramid and higher-order needs sit atop the basic needs.

> Although we should consider the ideas and opinions of others, we need to make our own decisions and choose our own path.

[KEY TERMS AND CONCEPTS]

Learning style (p. 58)

Receptive learning style (p. 58)

Read/write learning style (p. 58)

Visual/graphic learning style (p. 58)

Auditory/verbal learning style (p. 59)

Tactile/kinesthetic learning style (p. 59)

Left-brain processing (p. 63)

Right-brain processing (p. 63)

Self-concept (p. 69)

Self-fulfilling prophecy (p. 70)

Self-esteem (p. 73)

Self-efficacy (p. 73)

Personal Mission Statement (p. 77)

Values (p. 77)

Self-actualization (p. 78)

[RESOURCES]

ON CAMPUS

If you are interested in learning more about your pattern of learning styles, visit your campus counseling center or career center, where you may be able to take special assessment tests that can pinpoint your learning preferences and offer study strategies based on those preferences.

When dealing with the uncertainties of life and establishing your own sense of direction, it may help to speak to someone who has perspective and experience with college students. Here, too, a good place to start on campus is either a general counseling center or one that is designed to help students choose career paths. Mental health offices can also be helpful in putting you in touch with a therapist with whom you can explore issues revolving around your self-concept and self-esteem. Don't hesitate to get help. You are doing it for yourself.

IN PRINT

Gail Wood's book *How to Study: Use Your Personal Learning Style to Help You Succeed When It Counts* (Learning Express Press, 2000) provides an introduction to learning styles, offering tips and suggestions for making use of the way that you learn.

In addition, David Keirsey's *Please Understand Me II* (Prometheus Nemesis, 1998) and Linda Beren's *Understanding Yourself and Others* (Telos, 2006) offer insight into different personality types.

Don't Sweat the Small Stuff . . . and It's All Small Stuff (Hyperion, 2007), written by Richard Carlson, is a down-to-earth guide that is meant to help you sort out what is—and is not—important in your life.

ON THE WEB

Many sites on the World Wide Web provide the opportunity to extend your learning about the material in this chapter. (Although the Web addresses were accurate at the time the book was printed, check the *P.O.W.E.R. Learning* Web site [**www.mhhe.com/power**] for any changes that may have occurred.)

> Greg Kearsley, an instructional designer and online course developer at Walden Institute, has developed a useful site called "Explorations in Learning & Instruction: The Theory into Practice Database" (**tip.psychology.org/index.html**). This database contains short summaries of 50 major theories of learning and instruction.

> The University of Arizona's Learning Center site (**www.ulc.arizona.edu/selfassessment.php**) offers a number of self-assessments including a Learning Style Profile Generator and a Learning Style Assessment.

> An excellent set of guidelines on setting up a personal mission statement can be found at Kent State University's Ohio Literacy Resource Center site (**http://literacy.kent.edu/Oasis/Leadership/mission.htm**).

1   To help you write your own mission statement, Mental Help Net (an online guide to mental health, psychology, and psychiatry) offers a Web site entitled "Writing Your Own Philosophy of Life" (**www.psychologicalselfhelp.org/Chapter3/chap3_40.html**), in which a list of goals is grouped in three categories. Use your responses to help you create a mission statement.

2   Go to the University of South Florida's Counseling Center Web site entitled "Building Self-Esteem" (**http://usfweb2.usf.edu/counsel/b_psy/pdf/Building_Self.pdf**). Write down the six strategies listed there for enhancing your self-esteem. How do these suggestions compare to the suggestions offered in this book? Now use a search engine to locate other sources of information about raising self-esteem. (Possible search term: the phrase "raising self-esteem," in quotes.) Did you locate any other suggestions for raising self-esteem? How do they compare to the suggestions in this book?

The Case of . . .
The Instructor Who Spoke Too Much

Lana Carlson, a 26-year-old woman living in Carlsbad, Missouri, was at her wits' end. The instructor in her introductory psychology class spent each 50-minute lecture talking nonstop. He barely paused to acknowledge students' questions, and his only goal seemed to be to present as much material as possible. He even gave assignments in the same fast, nasal tone that he used throughout class.

If it weren't for her friend Darren Rubbell, who was in the same class, Lana would never have managed to figure out how to complete the assignments, which the professor never bothered to write down. The strange thing was that Darren didn't seem to have much trouble with the professor's endless talking. In fact, he claimed to enjoy the class a lot. He had no trouble following the lectures and understanding the assignments, seeming to absorb like a sponge the information the instructor was spouting.

1. Based on what you know about learning styles, what might be the source of Lana's difficulties?

2. What learning style does the instructor apparently assume all students have? Do you think this is one of Lana's learning styles? Why or why not?

3. How might the instructor change his presentation to accommodate diverse learning styles?

4. Why does Lana's friend Darren have so little trouble with the instructor's lectures?

5. Why do you think Lana has less trouble understanding Darren after class than she has understanding her instructor?

6. If you were Lana, what might you do to improve your situation?

Learning Outcomes

By the time you finish this chapter you will be able to

» LO **4.1**   Explain methods for effective note taking.

» LO **4.2**   Explain methods for taking notes in class.

» LO **4.3**   Apply techniques for taking notes from written materials.

Taking Notes

When he sat himself down in the front row of his biology class at the start of his second semester in college, Hill Taylor realized that something fundamental had changed.

In the past, Hill would have sat as far back in the classroom as he could. That's what he had done all through high school and the beginning of his first semester.

But then he received C's on three midterms.

In a notetaking workshop Hill enrolled in afterward, he learned the importance of active listening and taking good notes in class. He also learned that one way to become more engaged in class is to sit close to the instructor.

Trying out the strategies he was taught in the workshop, Hill found—a bit to his surprise—that they helped. By the end of the semester, he'd pulled his grades way up.

Looking Ahead

Hill Taylor's move from the back to the front of the classroom was both a source and a symbol of his academic success. Hill's ability to take good notes is also likely to pay future dividends, because notetaking skills not only help produce academic success in college but also contribute to career success.

In this chapter we discuss effective strategies for taking notes during class lectures, during other kinds of oral presentations, and from written sources such as textbooks. There's a lot more to good notetaking than you probably think—and a lot less if you view notetaking as essentially "getting everything down on paper." As we explore the ins and outs of notetaking, we'll pause along the way to discuss the tools of the notetaking trade, how to be an active learner, how to think your way to good notes, and how to deal with disorganized instructors.

P Prepare
Consider your goals

O Organize
Get the tools of notetaking together

W Work
Process—don't copy—information

E Evaluate
Think critically about your notes

R Rethink
Review your notes shortly after class to activate your memory

P.O.W.E.R. Plan

» LO 4.1, LO 4.2 Taking Notes in Class

You know the type: the student who desperately tries to write down everything the instructor says—no spoken word goes unwritten. And you know what you think to yourself: "If only I took such thorough notes—I'd do much better in my classes."

Contrary to what many students think, good notetaking does not mean writing down every word that an instructor utters. With notetaking, less is often more. We'll see why as we consider the basic steps in P.O.W.E.R. notetaking.

P Prepare Considering Your Goals

As with other academic activities, preparation is a critical component of notetaking. The following steps will prepare you for action:

> **Identify the instructor's—and your—goals for the course.** On the first day of class, most instructors talk about their objectives, what they hope you'll get out of the class, and what you'll know when it's over. Most restate the information on the class syllabus, the written document that explains the assignments for the semester. For example, they may say that they want you to "develop an appreciation for the ways that statistics are used in everyday life."

The information you get during that first session and through the syllabus is critical. If the instructor's goals aren't stated explicitly, you should attempt to figure them out. In addition to those "external" goals, you should have your own goals. What is it you want to learn from the course? How will the information from the course help you to enhance your knowledge, achieve your dreams, improve yourself as a person?

▶ **Complete assignments before coming to class.** Your instructor enthusiastically describes the structure of the neuron, recounting excitedly how neurons don't physically touch one another and how electrons flow across neurons, changing their electrical charge. One problem: You have only the vaguest idea what a neuron is. And the reason you don't know is that you haven't read the assignment.

Chances are you have found yourself in this situation at least a few times, so you know firsthand that sinking feeling as you become more and more confused. Because you can't follow the discussion, you can't get interested either, so the class seems boring, and you end up thinking about what you'll have for lunch or the movie you saw last night.

The moral: Always go to class prepared. Complete all of your reading and other assignments beforehand. Instructors assume that their students have done what they've assigned, and their lectures are based upon that assumption. It's virtually impossible to catch on to the gist of a lecture if you haven't completed the assignments.

▶ **Accept the instructor, despite his or her limitations.** Not every instructor is a brilliant lecturer. Accept the fact that, just as there are differences in skills among students, some instructors are more adept at lecturing than others. Ultimately, it's your responsibility to overcome a lecturer's flaws. A bad lecturer is not an excuse to do poorly or to give up. Don't let a miserable lecture style—or the fact that the instructor has a bad haircut or a mouth that droops to one side or wrinkled clothing—get in the way of your education. You're going to notice these things, but don't let them interfere with your goals. Good notetaking requires being prepared to listen to the material.

> "The highest result of education is tolerance."
> Helen Keller, author

▶ **Perform a preclass warm-up.** No, this doesn't mean doing stretches just before each class. As you head to class or settle into your seat, skim your notes from the previous lecture, looking over what the instructor said and where that lecture left off. You should also briefly review the main headings or summary section of any reading you've been assigned.

The warm-up doesn't have to be long. The goal is simply to refresh yourself, to get yourself into the right frame of mind for the class.

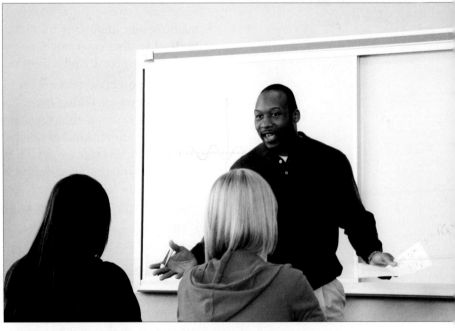

An engaging lecturer can make even the most complex material come alive in the classroom, whereas an instructor who is unorganized or dull can make coming to class sheer drudgery. No matter what the lecturer's style, however, you need to be prepared to take effective notes.

> **Choose a seat that will promote good note-taking.** You should certainly choose a seat that permits you to see and hear clearly, but there's more to your choice than that. Picking the right seat in a classroom can make a big difference.

Where is the best place to sit? Usually it's front and center. Instructors make more eye contact with the people near them, and they sometimes believe that the best, most-engaged students sit closest.

Furthermore, sitting in the back of the class may make you feel disengaged and out of touch with what is happening at the front of the room. In turn, this may make it easier for your mind to wander.

○ Organize Getting the Tools of Notetaking Together

Do you have a favorite pen? A preferred type of notebook?

By the time we reach college, most of us have developed distinct tastes when it comes to the materials we use in class. Although taking your favorite kind of notebook and pen to class will not make you a better notetaker, not having them certainly will interfere with your getting the most out of class.

There are several things to consider as you prepare for class:

> **Choose the appropriate writing utensil.** Generally, using a pen is better than using a pencil. Ink is less likely to smudge, and what you produce with ink is usually brighter and clearer—and therefore easier to use when studying. On the other hand, for math and science classes, where you may be copying down or even working through formulas in class, a pencil might be better, because it's easier to erase if you make a mistake when copying detailed, complex information.

Sometimes you may want to use a combination of pen and pencil. And in some cases you might use several different colors. One color—such as red—might signify important information that the instructor mentions will be on the test. Another color might be reserved for definitions or material that is copied from the board. And a third might be used for general notes on the lecture.

> **Choose a notebook that assists in notetaking.** Loose-leaf notebooks are particularly good for taking notes because they permit you to go back later and change the order of the pages or add additional material in the appropriate spot. But whatever kind of notebook you use, *use only one side of the page for writing; keep one side free of notes.* There may be times when you're studying that you'll want to spread out your notes in front of you, and it's much easier if no material is written on the back of the pages.

> **Consider using the Cornell Method of Notetaking.** According to educator Walter Pauk,[1] who devised the Cornell Method of Notetaking, the best way to take notes is to divide each notebook page into three sections. First, draw a line across the bottom of the page, an inch or two from the bottom. Second, draw a line down the left side of the page, about 2½ inches from the left-hand margin (illustrated in **Figure 4.1**).

To use the Cornell system, keep the notes you write in class within the largest area on the right-hand side of the page. Indent major supporting details beneath each main idea, trying to use no more than one line for each item, and leave space between topics to add information. Later, when you review your notes, you'll be able to jot down a keyword, catch phrase, or major idea

Notes taken in class

Memory   Intro Phych
                                                    10/16

	3 ways to store information
	sensory memory — everything sensed
aka working memory (like	short term memory — 15-25 sec.
Computer RAM)	Stored as meaning
	5-9 chunks
(like hard disk)	long-term memory — unlimited
Rehearsal : STM to LTM	rehearsal
	visualization
Chunking	Organize information into chunks:
	birds, instruments, body parts, etc.
	Mnemonics
Roy G. Biv	acronyms
Every good boy deserves fun	acrostics
30 days hath September	rhyming
Unfinished Symphony	jingles
pato, caballo	keyword technique
room and furniture	loci technique
sun, zoo, me, store...	peg method
	Using senses
	moving
	draw, diagram
	visualize

There are 3 types of memory (sensory, short-term, & long-term).
We can use chunking, mnemonics, & our senses to aid recall.

figure 4.1
A Notetaking Sample

In this example of a student's notes on a lecture about memory, she has used the Cornell Method of Notetaking; she has written the material in the right-hand column during class. Later, when reviewing her notes, she wrote down key pieces of information in the left-hand column and summarized the key points at the bottom.

Journal Reflections

How Do I Take Notes?

1. Describe your typical notetaking techniques in a few sentences. Do you try to write down as much of what the instructor says as possible? Do you tend to take only a few notes? Do you often find you need more time to get things down?

2. Overall, how effective would you say your notetaking techniques are?

3. In which classes do your techniques work best? Worst? Why?

4. Do your notes ever have "holes" in them—due to lapses of attention or times when you couldn't get down everything you wanted to? When do you usually discover them? What do you do about them?

5. How might the process of taking notes help develop a deeper understanding of the material being discussed?

on the left side of the page. Finally, you can use the area at the bottom of the page to summarize the key points covered on the page.

> **Consider the benefits of taking your textbook to class.** It's generally a good idea to take your textbook to class, unless your instructor advises you otherwise. Sometimes instructors will refer to information contained in it, and sometimes it's useful to have it handy to clarify information that is being discussed. You can also use it to look up key terms that may momentarily escape you. But don't, under any circumstances, use class time as an opportunity to read the textbook!

> **Consider the pros and cons of using a laptop computer to take notes in class.** There are several advantages: Legibility problems are avoided, and it's easy to go back and revise or add material after you've taken the notes.

There are also potential pitfalls. You may end up keyboarding more and thinking less. Or you may succumb to the temptation to check your e-mail or instant-message your friends, rather than listening to your instructor.

Because of their drawbacks, some instructors have strong feelings against the use of laptops in their class. Consequently, be sure to ask for permission before using your laptop to take notes.

Use these guidelines to make the most effective use of your laptop to take notes:

1. Make sure your computer battery is fully charged.

2. Use a computer that has a quiet keyboard so you don't annoy your fellow students, and make sure the built-in speaker is turned off. A tablet PC, which allows you to write on the screen in the same way you write with paper and pencil, may be the best choice.

3. Stay focused on your instructor. Avoid the temptation to play computer games, surf the Web, or respond to instant messages.

4. Finally, have an alternative, low-tech notetaking backup. Sometimes instructors present graphical material or formulas that are hard to input into a computer via a keyboard. And sometimes your computer may fail.

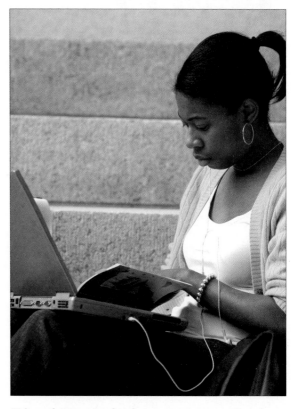

Using a laptop to take class notes ensures that they will be legible and that it will be easy to revise them after class. On the other hand, it's difficult to input graphical material, such as complex formulas, and there's also a danger that you'll be tempted to take too many notes.

W Work

Processing—Not Copying—Information

With pen poised, you're ready to begin the work of notetaking. The instructor begins to speak, and you start to write as quickly as you can, taking down as many of the instructor's words as possible.

Stop! You've made your first mistake. The central act in taking notes is not writing; listening and thinking are far more important. The key to effective notetaking is to write down the right amount of information—not too much and not too little.

Successful notetaking involves not just *hearing* what the instructor says, but *listening actively.* **Hearing** is the involuntary act of sensing sounds. The annoying drip of a faucet or the grating sound of a roommate's voice speaking on the phone in the next room are two examples of how hearing is both involuntary and often meaningless. In contrast, **active listening** is the voluntary act of focusing on what is being said, making sense of it, and thinking about it in a way that permits it to be recalled accurately. Listening involves concentration. And it requires shutting out competing thoughts, such as what we need to pick up at the grocery store or why our date last night was so terrific. (To get a sense of your own listening skills, complete **Try It 1** on page 96.)

Keeping the importance of active listening in mind, consider the following recommendations for taking notes:

▶ **Listen for the key ideas.** Not every sentence in a lecture is equally important, and one of the most useful skills you can develop is separating the key ideas from supporting information. Good lecturers strive to make just a few main points. The rest of what they say consists of explanation, examples, and other supportive material that expands upon the key ideas.

Your job, then, is to distinguish the key ideas from their support. To do this, you need to be alert and always searching for your instructor's **meta-message**—that is, the underlying main ideas that a speaker is seeking to convey, or the meaning behind the overt message you hear.

Hearing
The involuntary act of sensing sounds

Active listening
The voluntary act of focusing on what is being said, making sense of it, and thinking about it in a way that permits it to be recalled accurately

Meta-message
The underlying main ideas that a speaker is seeking to convey; the meaning behind the overt message

1

Determine Your Listening Style

Consider the following pairs of statements. Place a check next to the statement in each pair that more closely describes your style.

- [ ] 1a. When I'm listening in class, I lean back and get as comfortable as possible.
- [ ] 1b. When I'm listening in class, I sit upright and even lean forward a little.
- [ ] 2a. I let the instructor's words wash over me, generally going with the flow of the lecture.
- [ ] 2b. I try to guess in advance what the instructor is going to say and what direction the lecture is taking.
- [ ] 3a. I regard each lecture as a separate event, not necessarily related to what the instructor has said before or will say the next time.
- [ ] 3b. As I listen, I regularly ask myself how this relates to what was said in previous classes.
- [ ] 4a. When I take notes, I try to reproduce the instructor's words as closely as possible.
- [ ] 4b. When I take notes, I try to interpret and summarize the ideas behind the instructor's words.
- [ ] 5a. I don't usually question the importance of what the instructor is saying or why it's the topic of a lecture or discussion.
- [ ] 5b. I often ask why the content of the lecture is important enough for the instructor to be speaking about it.
- [ ] 6a. I rarely question the accuracy or logic of a presentation, assuming that the instructor knows the topic better than I do.
- [ ] 6b. I often ask myself how the instructor knows something and find myself wondering how it could be proved.
- [ ] 7a. I just about never make eye contact with the instructor.
- [ ] 7b. I often make eye contact with the instructor.

If you tended to prefer the "a" statements in most pairs, you have a more passive listening style. If you preferred the "b" statements, you have a more active listening style. Based on your responses, consider ways that you can become a more active listener.

To Try It online, go to www.mhhe.com/power.

> "I had tons of notes—I copied *every word* the professor said. Actually, I was so busy writing that I didn't understand a thing."
> **Student, Saint Joseph's University[2]**

How can you discern the meta-message? One way is to *listen for keywords*. Instructors know what's important in their lecture; your job is to figure it out, not just from what they say but from how they say it.

For instance, listen for clues about the importance of material. Phrases like "don't forget . . . ," "be sure to remember that . . . ," "you need to know . . . ," "the most important thing that must be considered . . . ," "there are four problems with this approach . . . ," and—a big one—"this will be on the test . . ." should cause you to sit up and take notice. Another good sign of importance is repetition. If an instructor says the same thing in several ways, it's a clear sign that the material being discussed is important.

Be on the lookout for nonverbal signals too. Does an instructor get excited about a particular topic? Does he or she seem unenthusiastic when talking about something? Use nonverbal cues to gauge the importance of a particular part of a message relative to other things being said.

Finally, listen for what is not being said. Sometimes silence is not just golden, but informative as well. By noting what topics are not being covered in class, or are presented only minimally, you can gauge the relative importance of ideas in comparison with one another.

This is where preliminary preparation and organization come in. The only way to know what's left out of a lecture is to have done the assigned readings in advance. Also, don't be fooled into thinking that if a topic is not covered in class, it's unimportant: Most instructors believe students are responsible for all material that is assigned, whether or not it's explicitly covered in class.

› **Use short, abbreviated phrases—not full sentences when taking notes.** Forget everything you've ever heard about always writing in full sentences. If you try to write notes in complete sentences, you'll soon become bogged down, paying more attention to your notes than to your instructor. In fact, if you use full sentences, you'll be tempted to try transcribing every word the instructor utters, which, as you now know, is not a good idea at all.

Instead, write in phrases, using only key words or terms. Save full sentences for definitions or quotes that your instructor clearly wants you to know word for word. For example, consider the following excerpt from a lecture:

> *There are two kinds of job analyses used by human resource experts: First, there are job- or task-oriented analyses, and second, there are worker- or employee-oriented analyses. Job analyses just describe the tasks that need to be accomplished by a worker. For example, heart surgeons need to be able to operate on patients in order to carry out their jobs. In contrast, employee-oriented job descriptions need to describe knowledge, skills, and abilities the employee must have to get the job done. For example, surgeons need to understand the different types of blood vessels in the heart in order to be successful. Most job analyses include elements of both job-oriented and employee-oriented types.*

If you were taking notes, you might produce the following:

2 kinds job analyses:
1. Job-oriented (=task-oriented): tasks needed to get job done. Ex: heart surgeon operates
2. Worker-oriented (=employee-oriented): knowledge, skills, abilities, etc. necessary to do job. Ex: surgeon knows blood vessels
Most j.a. a combination

Note how the lecturer used almost 120 words, while the notes used only around 35 words—less than one-third of the lecture.

› **Use abbreviations.** One way to speed up the notetaking process is through the use of abbreviations. Among the most common:

and *& or +*	with *w/*	without *w/o*
care of *c/o*	leads to; resulting in ⟶	as a result of ⟵
percent *%*	change Δ	number *#*
that is *i.e.*	for example *e.g.*	and so forth *etc.*
no good *n.g.*	question *?*	compared with *c/w*
page *p.*	important! *!!*	less than *<*
more than *>*	equals, same as *=*	versus *vs.*

figure 4.2
A Sample Outline

I. Difficulties faced by college students seeking affordable housing
  A. Students subjected to high rents close to campus
    1. Forced to share apartments
    2. Sometimes must live far from campus
  B. Made to sign harsh leases
II. Possible solutions
  A. College offers subsidized housing
    1. Advantage: Housing costs can be lowered
    2. Potential problems
      a. College becomes students' landlord
      b. College uses funds for housing instead of investing in education
  B. Rent control
    1. Advantage: Can provide fixed, reasonably priced rents
    2. Disadvantages
      a. Creates permanent expensive rent-control bureaucracy
      b. Landlords may neglect rent-control property
      c. Little incentive for owners to increase the number of rental units
      d. Strong competition for rent-fixed units
III. Summary
  A. Advantages and disadvantages to both solutions
  B. May need new, creative solutions

> **Take notes in outline form.** It's often useful to take notes in the form of an outline. An outline summarizes ideas in short phrases and indicates the relationship among concepts through the use of indentations.

When outlining, it's best to be formal about it, using roman numerals, regular numbers, and capital and small letters (see the example in **Figure 4.2**).

Or, if you prefer, you can also simply use outlining indentations without assigning numbers and letters.

Outlining serves a number of functions. It forces you to try to determine the structure of the lecture. Organizing the key points and noting the connections among them helps you remember the material better because you have processed it more. The effort involved in outlining also keeps your mind from drifting away from the lecture.

Use **Try It 2** on pages 100 and 101, "Outline a Lecture," to practice your outlining skills.

> **Copy key information written on the board or projected from overheads and PowerPoint slides.** If your instructor provides a definition, quotation, or formula, you probably should copy it. In fact, such prominently displayed material has "test item" written all over it. You might want to highlight such material in some way in your notes.

- **Take advantage of PowerPoint slides provided online by your instructor.** Some instructors will post their PowerPoint slides before class. If they do, print them out and bring them to class. You can use them as the basis for your notes, filling in the details provided during the lecture on the printout. Even if your instructor doesn't post the slides until after class, it's still a good idea to print them out and keep them with the notes you create in class. The combination of your notes and the PowerPoints will be invaluable when reviewing and studying the material.

- **Use different notetaking techniques for class discussions.** Not every course is structured as a lecture. Classes that are based less on lectures and more on class discussion pose greater challenges for notetaking.

  For example, a discussion of the use of tax support of private schools in a sociology class may raise a variety of issues. As students in the class offer their ideas, how much—and what—should you place in your notes?

  In such situations, the best approach is to take your cue from the course instructor. Often the instructor will pose some questions to get the discussion rolling. Note those questions—they're an important indicator of what the instructor is interested in. The instructor's reaction to particular comments is another clue. Listen to his or her responses. If the instructor responds enthusiastically to a particular point, you'll want to highlight it in your notes. (To practice taking notes during a discussion, go to **Try It 3** on pages 102 and 103.)

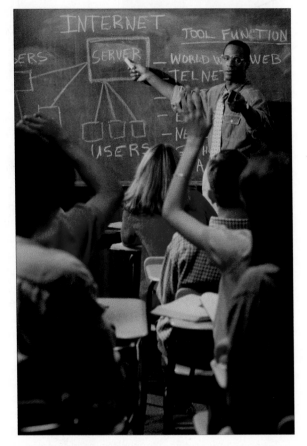

Asking questions in class does more than just provide you with the opportunity to clarify points you don't understand. It often will make you feel more a part of the class, and it will encourage other students to participate.

- **Pay particular attention to the points raised by instructors at the end of discussion and lecture classes.** Instructors often provide a summary of the discussion, which is worthy of inclusion in your notes.

- **Ask questions.** One of the most important things you can do during a class is to ask questions. Raising questions will help you evaluate, clarify, and ultimately better understand what your instructor is saying. Even beyond these critical goals, questions serve several other purposes.

  For one thing, raising questions will help you to personalize the material being covered, permitting you to draw it more closely into your own framework and perspective. Furthermore, when you ask a question and it is answered, you become personally engaged in what the instructor is saying. In very large classes, asking questions may be the only way that an instructor can get a sense of you as an individual.

  Questioning also increases your involvement in the class as a whole. If you sit back and never raise questions in class, you are much less likely to feel a real part of the class. Becoming an active questioner will rightly make you feel like you have contributed something to the class. Remember, if you are unclear about some point, it is likely that others share your lack of clarity.

Try It!

2 Outline a Lecture

Working with others in a group, take turns slowly reading sections of the following lecture to each other.[3] As the paragraph is being read, outline the main arguments in the space on page 101.

In 1985 Joseph Farman, a British earth scientist working in Antarctica, made an alarming discovery. Scanning the Antarctic sky, he found less ozone than should be there—not a slight depletion but a 30% drop from a reading recorded 5 years earlier in the Antarctic!

At first the scientist thought that this "ozone hole" was an as-yet-unexplained weather phenomenon. Evidence soon mounted, however, pointing to synthetic chemicals as the culprit. Detailed analysis of chemicals in the Antarctic atmosphere revealed a surprisingly high concentration of chlorine, a chemical known to destroy ozone. The source of the chlorine was a class of chemicals called chlorofluorocarbons (CFCs). CFCs have been manufactured in large amounts since they were invented in the 1920s, largely for use as coolants in air conditioners, propellants in aerosols, and foaming agents in making Styrofoam. CFCs were widely regarded as harmless because they were chemically unreactive under normal conditions. But in the thin atmosphere over Antarctica, CFCs condense on to tiny ice crystals; warmed by the sun in the spring, they attack and destroy ozone without being used up.

The thinning of the ozone layer in the upper atmosphere 25 to 40 kilometers above the surface of the earth is a serious matter. The ozone layer protects life from the harmful ultraviolet (UV) rays from the sun that bombard the earth continuously. Like invisible sunglasses, the ozone layer filters out these dangerous rays. When UV rays damage the DNA in skin cells, it can lead to skin cancer. Every 1% drop in the atmospheric ozone concentration is estimated to lead to a 6% increase in skin cancers. The drop of approximately 3% that has already occurred worldwide, therefore, is estimated to have led to as much as a 20% increase in skin cancers.

The world currently produces about 1 million tons of CFCs annually, three-fourths of it in the United States and Europe. As scientific observations have become widely known, governments have rushed to correct the situation. By 1990, worldwide agreements to phase out production of CFCs, by the end of the century had been signed. Nonetheless, most of the CFCs manufactured since they were invented are still in use in air conditioners and aerosols and have not yet reached the atmosphere. As these CFCs, as well as CFCs still being manufactured, move slowly upward through the atmosphere, the problem can be expected to grow worse. Ozone depletion has now been reported over the North Pole as well, and there is serious concern that the Arctic ozone hole will soon extend over densely populated Europe and the northeastern United States.

Finally, by asking questions in class, you serve as a role model for other students. Your questions may help break the ice in a class, making it easier for others to raise issues that they have about the material. And ultimately the answers that the instructor provides to others' questions may help you to better understand and/or evaluate your understanding of the material. (For tips on asking questions in class, see the **Course Connections** feature on page 104.)

Use Special Techniques for "Problem Instructors"

He talks too fast . . . she mumbles . . . he puts down people when they ask a question . . . she rambles and goes off on boring tangents . . . she explains things in a way that doesn't make much sense.

In the real world of the college classroom, not every instructor comes to class with a clear, compelling lecture and then presents it beautifully. All of us have suffered through lectures that are deficient in one or more ways. What should you do when you find yourself in such a situation?

Write your outline here.

 WORKING IN A GROUP

After you have outlined the passage, compare your outline with that of others who took notes on the same passage.

- Did you all agree on the main ideas of each passage?
- How do your notes differ from others', and what are the similarities?
- How might you improve your notes to better capture the main points?
- Would a different topic produce greater or fewer difficulties?

Collectively, produce what you believe is the ideal outline, and compare it to that produced by other groups.

To Try It online, go to www.mhhe.com/power.

1. *Remember that this too shall pass.* First, keep in mind that this is a temporary condition; your experience usually won't last more than one term. Most instructors are conscientious and well prepared, and unless you have enormously bad luck, the unpleasant experience you're having now will not be routine.

2. *Ask questions about the material.* Even if you have no idea what is going on in class—or especially if you have no idea—ask questions. You are not the only one struggling with the instructor's shortcomings. You will be doing everyone in the class a favor if you admit you're not following what an instructor is saying and ask for clarification.

3. *Ask—privately and politely—for the instructor to alter the way material is presented.* It is not bad classroom etiquette to ask an instructor to speak a little slower. Instructors sometimes get carried away with enthusiasm and begin speaking faster and faster without even being aware of it. Very often a reality check from a student will be welcome. But don't couch your comment in a way that makes the instructor feel inept ("Could you slow down;

Try It!

Take Notes during Discussions

Take notes on the following class discussion about the growth of English as a global language. Use cues from the instructor about the importance and accuracy of each point, and record in your notes only the key points that shed light on the topic.

Instructor: OK, so why is English so important globally, not just in English-speaking countries?

Alicia: Um, well, English is spoken by a lot of people. When I was in Denmark last summer, everyone spoke it. It just seems to be everywhere.

Instructor: OK. It's certainly a very widely used language. But we're trying to figure out why. We're looking for causes, not just symptoms, right? Anyone else? Bart?

Bart: Yeah, English is becoming, like, everyone's second language simply because it has established a good base. Not only did the *English* English people—you know, the British—spread the language all over through colonizing the world—you know, the sun never sets on the British Empire and all—but now America is everywhere, too. I mean, we're cool—our culture is cool and very influencing.

Instructor: Good, good. Yes, you've given two good reasons why English is widespread. The British Empire spread the language through parts of Asia, Africa, and the Caribbean in the 18th and 19th centuries, and modern U.S. culture is highly influential, which causes many people worldwide to welcome English. What else?

Catherine: Well, the way in which the American culture is spreading is very much language-centered. It's American movies and music that are everywhere, and these involve the language, not just the style. I mean, people know a lot more than how to say Coca-Cola and Nike, don't they? They listen to American CDs and movies, and they even produce songs and movies in English. So it's not just culture we're spreading, it's our language too.

Instructor: Exactly! The language is perhaps the most important aspect of the culture that we're distributing. Damon?

Damon: Yeah, I was just going to say, another thing that's caused the language to spread is global communications, which are just about always in English. Look at the language of aviation—pilots talk to each other in English, don't they? And the Internet. The universal language of the Internet is English. So if you want to communicate globally, and now everyone does because for the first time everyone *can*, you've got to pick up some English.

Rosario: Right. It's the universal second language. And it will only get more universal as American culture spreads further and other cultures develop to the point of being able to join the party—communicating, and buying stuff and listening to our music and so on. I mean, it's the biggest game in town, and it's spoken by the people with the biggest wallets. Money talks, you know. And now it talks American English.

Instructor: You've really hit it now. Language has always gone where the resources are. If someone has what you want, you'd better speak their language. Money speaks American English. Very well put, Rosario! Excellent discussion, folks.

you're going to fast and losing me"). Instead, keep the comment neutral, without placing blame. For instance, you might simply say, "I'm having trouble keeping up with you; would it be possible for you to speak a little more slowly?"

4. *Pool your resources.* Get together with other students in the class and work out a strategy for dealing with the situation. If an instructor speaks too fast and you just can't keep up with the flow of information, meet with your fellow students and compare what you've gleaned from the class. They may have understood or noted material that you missed, and vice versa. Together, you may be able to put the pieces of the puzzle together and get a fuller understanding of the material.

5. *Listen to the lecture again.* You might bring a digital or cassette voice recorder to class (but request the instructor's permission first!). Then, after class, you can play back the recording at your leisure. If you record it in a digital format, you could store it on your computer for a review before a test.

Were you able to identify the information that was most important? How would actually seeing the instructor's nonverbal reactions to the students' comments be helpful?

WORKING IN A GROUP:
Compare your notes on the discussion with these of your classmates. As a group, try to create an optimal set of notes, reflecting the most important points.

To Try It online, go to www.mhhe.com/power.

There's another option: Many instructors teach multiple sections of the same course. If this is the case, you might, schedule permitting, sit in on an additional section of the course. The second time around the information may become much clearer.

6. *Talk with the instructor after class.* If you feel totally lost after a lecture, or even if you've missed only a few points, speak with the instructor after class. Ask for clarification and get him or her to re-explain points that you missed. Such a dialogue will help you to understand the material better. But it will also do something more: help build your relationship with your instructor.

In the very rare case in which an instructor oversteps the bounds of decency, either by

If you've ever been totally lost following a lecture, you may have discovered that speaking with your instructor immediately after class was helpful. Most instructors are very happy to go over and clarify key points that they've covered during class. They also appreciate your initiative and interest.

Course
Connections

Asking Questions in Class

Even in a small class, raising your hand and asking a question can be intimidating. You may be afraid that you'll say something dumb, making it clear to the whole class just how out of it you are. Or maybe you're afraid that everyone will be staring at you. Or perhaps your concern is that your instructor and fellow classmates will resent your wasting valuable class time with your own trivial questions.

Although it may not be possible to fully banish such self-defeating thoughts, there are several strategies that you can follow to make it easier to raise the questions you have.

1. Sit in the front of the room. Sitting close to the instructor will make it easier to ask questions. Moreover, if you sit in the back of the room and ask a question, the students in front of you will likely swivel around and look at you. In that case, if you already feel intimidated, your feelings of anxiety may soar off the charts.

2. Write down your question before you ask it. If you anticipate that you'll stumble or forget what you want to say, write down your question before raising your hand. The idea is not to read it word for word, or even refer to it at all when you actually ask your question. But writing it will help you quickly organize your thoughts, and provide a safety net in case you freeze momentarily.

3. Ask a question early in the term. By starting to ask questions early on in the term, you'll establish yourself as a student who participates in class. In fact, try asking a question on the first day of class, which will make it considerably easier for you to ask questions later in the term.

4. Be one of the first students to ask a question after a class has started. One reason people give for avoiding asking a question is that others have already asked so many questions that there's no time, or that others have already addressed the issue.

Using these strategies will help you overcome the stage fright of asking your questions and permit you to participate fully in class discussions.

harshly putting students down, making discriminatory racial, ethnic, or religious remarks, or acting in a sexually harrassing manner, immediately report the matter to someone in the college administration. The appropriate person might be a department chair or dean of students. Such behavior is not only offensive, but in many cases illegal.

Keep a Balance between Too Many Notes and Too Few Notes

The key to effective notetaking is to keep a balance between too many and too few notes.

The best way to achieve this balance is by paying close attention in class. By being alert, engaged, and involved in class, you'll be able to make the most of the techniques we've discussed. The result: notes that capture the most important points raised in class and that will optimize your recall and mastery of the course subject matter (see a sample of two students' notes in **Figure 4.3**).

 E Evaluate

Thinking Critically about Your Notes

Toward the end of class, take a moment to look over your notes. Now's the time—before the class has ended—to evaluate what you've written.

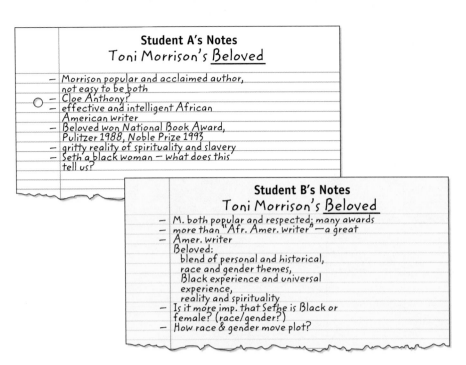

figure 4.3
Notes on a Lecture

Student A's Notes
Toni Morrison's Beloved

- Morrison popular and acclaimed author, not easy to be both
- Cloe Anthony?
- effective and intelligent African American writer
- Beloved won National Book Award, Pulitzer 1988, Noble Prize 1993
- gritty reality of spirituality and slavery
- Seth a black woman — what does this tell us?

Student B's Notes
Toni Morrison's Beloved

- M. both popular and respected; many awards
- more than "Afr. Amer. writer"—a great
- Amer. writer
  Beloved:
    blend of personal and historical,
    race and gender themes,
    Black experience and universal experience,
    reality and spirituality
- Is it more imp. that Sethe is Black or female? (race/gender?)
- How race & gender move plot?

After being sure you can answer "yes" to the most basic question—can I read what I've written?—ask yourself these questions:

- Do my notes do a good job of representing what was covered in class?

- Do they reflect the emphases of the instructor?

- Are there any key points that are not entirely clear?

- Do I need help clarifying any of the points my instructor made?

Evaluating your notes is a critical part of the notetaking process. You can get a sense of how effective your notetaking has been while you still have a chance to ask your instructor to clarify anything that is still not clear.

Perhaps, for example, you've left out a key word in a definition. Maybe you don't understand a concept fully, even though you've written about it in your notes. Possibly you've left out the third step in a list of six steps necessary to accomplish something.

If you look over your notes while you're still in class, you have time to ask your instructor for clarification. Or you can wait until the end of class and raise your question privately. Most instructors will be happy to answer questions from students who have obviously been actively listening. Just make sure that you add what they tell you to your notes so you'll be able to refer to them later. (To practice evaluating your notes, complete **Try It 4** on page 106.)

R Rethink   Activating Your Memory

The lecture has ended and class is over. You put the top on your pen, close your notebook, stash everything in your backpack, and head out for a cup of coffee before your next class.

Wait! Before you close up your notebook, finish the P.O.W.E.R. process. Rethink what you've heard. Spending 5 or 10 minutes reconsidering what you've written right now can save you *hours* of work later. The reason: Rethinking promotes the transfer of information into long-term memory (something discussed more in

Evaluate Your Class Notes

Take a set of notes you made recently during one of your classes and evaluate it on the following criteria.

Statement	Not Even Slightly	Slightly	Moderately	Pretty Well	Very Well
1. I can read my notes (i.e., they are legible).					
2. Someone else can read my notes.					
3. My notes are complete; I missed nothing important.					
4. My notes represent the key points that were covered in class.					
5. My notes reflect the instructor's emphases.					
6. The instructor's key points are clear and understandable.					
7. The notes contain only important points, with no extraneous material.					
8. I understand not only the notes but also the class content they reflect.					
9. Using only the notes, I will be able to reconstruct the essential content of the class in 3 months.					

 WORKING IN A GROUP:

What do your answers tell you about the effectiveness of your notetaking skills? What might you do differently the next time you take notes?

Evaluate and compare the notes you took during the previous 20 minutes of the class you are in now. How do your notes compare with those of the other members of your group?

To Try It online, go to **www.mhhe.com/power**.

Chapter 8). As you link the new information you've taken down to what you already know and then integrate it, you essentially plug this information into your memory in a much more meaningful way, which means you can remember it better and more easily.

If you looked over your notes to clarify and evaluate the information in them in class, you've already begun the process. But once class is over, you need to review the material more formally. Here's how to do it:

> **Rethink as soon as possible.** Time is of the essence! The rethinking phase of notetaking doesn't have to take long; 5 to 10 minutes are usually sufficient. The more critical issue is *when* you do it. The longer you wait before reviewing your notes, the less effective the process will be.
>
> There's no doubt that the best approach is to review the material just after the class has ended. As everyone else is leaving, just stay seated and go over your notes. This works fine for classes late in the day, when no other class is scheduled in the room. But what if you must vacate the room immediately after class? The next best thing is to find a quiet space somewhere nearby and do your rethinking there.
>
> In any case, don't let the day end without examining your notes. In fact, reconsidering material just before you go to sleep can be particularly effective.

> **Make rethinking an active process.** Some people feel the notes they take in class are akin to historical documents in a museum, with Do Not Touch! signs hanging on them. On the contrary, think of your notes as a construction project and yourself as the person in charge of the project.
>
> When you review your notes, do so with an eye to improving them. If any information is not entirely clear, change the wording in your notes, adding to or amending what's there. If certain words are hard to read, fix them; it won't be any easier to read them the night before a test—in fact, chances are you'll have even more trouble.
>
> If, on rethinking the material, you don't understand something, ask your instructor or a friend to clarify it. And when you receive an explanation, add it to your notes so you won't forget it. (You might want to use a different-colored pen for additions to your notes, so you'll know they came later.)

> **Think critically about the material in your notes.** As you review the information, think about the material from a critical point of view. Go beyond the facts and pieces of information, integrating and evaluating the material.
>
> In addition, as you rethink your notes, don't think of them only in terms of a single lecture or a single class. Instead, take a longer view. Ask yourself how they fit into the broader themes of the class and the goals that you and the instructor have for the semester. How will the information be useful to you? Why did the instructor emphasize a particular point?
>
> If you've configured your notes by leaving a 2½-inch column on the left-hand side of the page, now is the time to make use of that blank column. Write down keywords, significant points, major concepts, controversies, and questions. The process of adding this information will not only help you to rethink the material now, it will also provide guideposts when you study before a test.

Concept mapping

A method of structuring written
material by graphically grouping
and connecting key ideas and
themes

› **Create concept maps. Concept mapping** (Sometimes called "mind mapping") is a method of structuring written material by graphically grouping and connecting key ideas and themes. In contrast to an outline, a concept map visually illustrates how related ideas fit together. The pictorial summary gives you another handle to store the information in memory, and it focuses your thinking on the key ideas from the lecture.

In a concept map, each key idea is placed in a different part of the map, and related ideas are placed near it—above, below, or beside it. What emerges does not have the rigid structure of an outline. Instead, a "finished" concept map looks something like a map of the solar system, with the largest and most central idea in the center (the "sun" position), and related ideas surrounding it at various distances. It has also been compared to a large tree, with numerous branches and subbranches radiating out from a central trunk. (**Figure 4.4** presents a sample concept map.)

Building a concept map has several advantages. It forces you to rethink the material in your notes in a new style—particularly important if you used traditional outlining while taking the notes. In addition, it helps you to tie together the material for a given class session. Finally, it will help you to build a master concept map later, when you're studying the material for a final exam. (To practice in the techniques we've been discussing, see **Try It 5** on page 110, "Practice Your Notetaking Skills.")

»LO 4.3 Taking Notes as You Study

Weighing as much as five pounds, bulky and awkward, and filled with more information than you think anyone could ever need to know, it's the meat-and-potatoes of college life: your course textbook. You might feel intimidated by its size; you might be annoyed at its cost; you might think you'll never be able to read it, let alone understand, learn, and recall the material in it. How will you manage?

Study notes

Notes taken for the purpose
of reviewing material

The answer involves taking **study notes,** notes taken for the purpose of reviewing material. They are the kind of notes that you take now to study from later. (We'll consider research notes, notes that you take to write a paper or prepare a report, in Chapter 7 when we discuss writing papers.)

Several strategies are useful for taking study notes from written material such as magazines, books, journals, and Web sites. Which approach works best depends on whether you're able to write on the material you wish to take notes on.

Taking Notes on Material You Can Write On

Here are some suggestions for creating study notes for material you own, on which you're free to write on the material by underlining, highlighting, or writing in the margins:

› **Integrate your text notes into your study notes.** Start by annotating the pages, using the techniques that work best for you: highlighting, underlining, circling, making marginal notes. (These techniques are discussed in detail in Chapter 6; you may want to look ahead to that discussion.) Keep in mind that writing on the text, by itself, is not sufficient to promote learning—it's what you do next that counts.

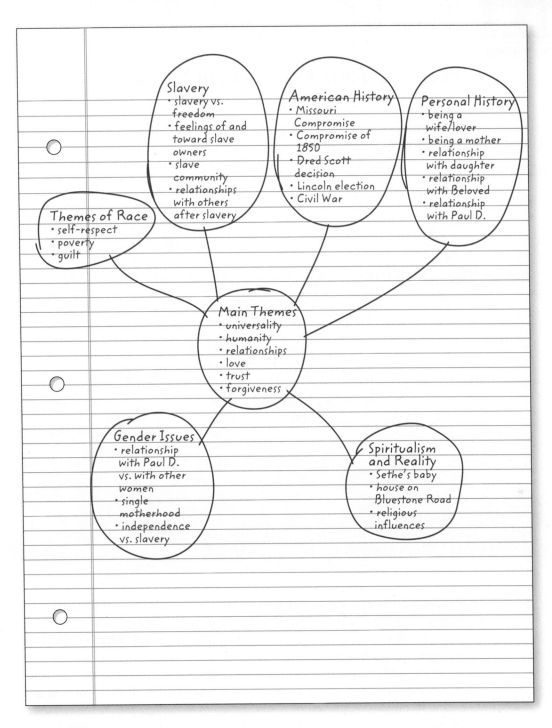

figure 4.4
A Concept Map of Toni Morrison's *Beloved*

Specifically, after you've finished reading and annotating the material, create study notes. The study notes should provide a summary of the key points, in outline form or in the form of concept maps. Either form of summary should supplement the annotations you've made on the printed page.

Furthermore, any notes you take should stand on their own. For instance, they should include enough information to be useful whether or not you have the book or article on hand.

POWER Try It!

5

Practice Your Notetaking Skills

Practice your notetaking skills, using any techniques you find helpful, in one of the classes in which you are enrolled this term. Use these notes to answer these questions:

1. Which specific techniques did I use in taking notes?

2. Which of the notetaking techniques detailed in this chapter was I unable to use, and why?

3. Could I take the notes I made in class and redo them, using one of the techniques in this chapter, such as creating a concept map?

After you have taken notes, use the techniques discussed in this chapter to evaluate and rethink them. Creating a concept map on a separate sheet of paper may be particularly helpful.

To Try It online, go to www.mhhe.com/power.

Flash cards
Index cards that contain key pieces of information to be remembered

> **Use flash cards.** If you feel confident that the annotations you've written in the book are sufficiently comprehensive, you might consider taking notes on flash cards. **Flash cards** are simply index cards that contain key pieces of information that you need to remember.
>
> Flash cards are particularly useful in subjects that present many small bits of information to remember, such as foreign language vocabulary words or scientific formulas. When you need to learn a list of foreign words, for instance, you can write a foreign word on one side of a card and its English meaning on the other side.
>
> One of the greatest virtues of flash cards is their portability. Because they are small, they can fit into your pocket or handbag, and you can look at them at odd times when you have a spare moment.

Taking Notes on Material You Are Unable to Write On

Taking notes on material that can't be written on is a different story. Library books, magazines, journal articles, and materials on library reserve that are shared with others require a different approach.

Taking Notes on the Job: Meetings of the Minds

For many people, meetings take up a good part of their professional workdays, and being able to take effective notes can provide a significant career advantage.

Meetings are similar to class discussions. During a meeting you will want to look for key topics and make note of the ideas that receive the most emphasis or enthusiastic response. Note these areas and keep them in mind as likely priorities.

During meetings, tasks are often assigned. Not only do you want to clearly note what you are to do and when you are supposed to do it, but keeping track of what others are doing will also be helpful, because you may need to get information from them or otherwise coordinate efforts. For instance, if you are assigned the task of managing the development of your company's Web site, you'll want to clarify in your notes who has agreed to do what portion of the task.

Taking notes when others are speaking also shows that you are paying attention to what the speaker is saying. It's a kind of compliment that suggests you find what the speaker is saying to be so important that you will want to refer to it later.

Finally, notetaking plays another role: It can make seemingly interminable meetings appear to proceed faster by providing something for you to do that's more active than simply listening. In short, not only can notetaking provide you with a clear record of what occurred in a meeting, but it can also keep you engaged in what is going on.

> **Approach the written material as you would a class lecture.** The techniques we discussed earlier for taking notes in class can all be adapted for taking notes from written material. In fact, the task is often easier, because, as is not the case with the spoken word, you'll be able to refer back to what was said earlier—it's in black and white in front of you.

> **Laptops can be especially helpful in creating study notes.** If you're a good keyboarder, it's often easier and quicker to take notes using a word-processing program. On the other hand, don't be lured into typing too much. You need to be just as selective in what you input into your computer as you would be in taking notes during a class lecture.

> **Use the tricks of the trade we discussed earlier for taking notes from a class lecture.** Look for key ideas, definitions, quotations, and formulas, and include them in your notes. Use the headings that are included in the text, such as chapter and section titles. Bold or italic type is also a clue that an important point is being made. Graphs and charts often provide critical information.

> **Use the same form of notetaking that you use in class lectures.** If you take notes in class using the two-column method (in which you reserve a 2½-inch column on the left-hand side of your paper for adding comments during later review of the notes), use that technique here as well. If you write your notes in outline form, create an outline based on the written material. If you often create graphics such as concept maps, create them now. The point is to produce notes that are consistent with those you take during class lectures.

speaking of **success**

NAME: **Valeska Chelminski**

SCHOOL: **Lesley College**

HOME: **Cambridge, MA**

When Valeska Chelminski was three years old, her parents were told that she would never graduate from college because she suffered from dyscalculia, a learning disorder characterized by difficulties with organization and math skills.

As a result of her condition, Chelminski struggled through school. Still, after high school, Chelminski tried attending a two-year technical college. However, after four years, she was still floundering, lacking the organizational and academic skills necessary to succeed in that environment. Although she considered giving up on higher education, instead she entered a program at Lesley College that teaches life skills to students with learning disabilities who have difficulty in mainstream college.

Entering this program was a turning point for Chelminski.

"As a college student, I have had to learn how to self-advocate in a way that says, 'Look, I have skills, but I need assistance in this other area,'" said Chelminski. "I have learned to organize myself with lists and daily, weekly, and monthly schedules. I have gotten permission to have longer time to take tests, and I acquired a mathematics tutor.

"As my confidence improved, something interesting happened in my English class. It seemed that in every class, someone came up to me for help," she added. "I realized I could actually help other students, and that was quite amazing. I discovered that language skills and writing come very easily to me. Now I work for the college disabilities services as a note-taker for students with other kinds of challenges."

"My view of disability," Chelminski continued, "is that all disabilities are gifts, and that I need to learn how to use my gift. For a long time I was defined by my disability; it was my identity. But now I know it is a part of me, but it is not me."

Looking
Back

What is effective notetaking?

> The central feature of good notetaking is listening and distilling important information—not writing down everything that is said.

How can I take good notes in class?

> Prepare for taking notes by identifying the instructor's and your own goals for the course, completing all assignments before arriving in class, and "warming up" for class by reviewing the notes and assignments from the previous class.

> Before writing notes, listen and think, processing the information that the instructor is attempting to deliver.

> Notes should be brief phrases rather than full sentences and, if possible, in outline form to reveal the structure of the lecture. Material written on the board should usually be copied word-for-word.

> Before leaving class, evaluate your notes, verifying that they are complete and understandable while there is still time to correct them. As soon as possible after class, actively rethink your notes.

What techniques apply to taking notes from written materials?

> Taking good study notes from written materials involves many of the principles that apply to taking good notes from oral presentations, although the source material can be consulted repeatedly, making it easier to get the information down accurately.

> Concept maps and flash cards can be helpful tools for notetaking from textbooks.

[KEY TERMS AND CONCEPTS]

Hearing (p. 95)

Active listening (p. 95)

Meta-message (p. 95)

Concept mapping (p. 108)

Study notes (p. 108)

Flash cards (p. 110)

[RESOURCES]

ON CAMPUS

If you are having difficulty taking class notes effectively, talk with your course instructor. Bring your notes with you soon after a class has ended, and let the instructor assess what you are doing correctly and what could stand improvement.

If your problems persist, and you have great difficulty translating the spoken word into notes, then there's a small possibility that you suffer from an auditory learning disability. Be tested by your college learning disabilities office or counseling office to rule this out.

IN PRINT

Judy Kesselman-Turkel and Franklynn Peterson's *Note-Taking Made Easy* (University of Wisconsin Press, 2003) provides a broad overview of how to take good notes in class, as does Bobbi DePorter and Mike Hernacki's *Quantum Notes* (Learning Forum, 2000).

In addition, Ron Fry's *Taking Notes* (Career Press, 1994) and *Noteworthy: Listening and Notetaking Skills* (2nd ed.), by Phyllis Lim and William Smalzer (William S. Hein & Co., 1996), provide a fine overviews of strategies for increasing your listening and notetaking expertise.

ON THE WEB

The following sites on the World Wide Web provide the opportunity to extend your learning about the material in this chapter. (Although the Web addresses were accurate at the time the book was printed, check the *P.O.W.E.R. Learning* Web site [**mhhe.com/power**] for any changes that may have occurred.)

▸ Brigham Young University's Career and Counseling Center offers this page (**http:// ccc.byu.edu/learning/note-tak.php**) on the Cornell Notetaking System. This notetaking system can help you improve the organization of your notes, while allowing you to make use of your existing strengths as a notetaker.

▸ A learning style model formulated by Richard M. Felder and Linda K. Silverman from North Carolina State University, The Index of Learning Styles is an online instrument used to assess preferences on four dimensions (active/reflective, sensing/intuitive, visual/verbal, and sequential/global) (**www.ncsu.edu/felder-public/ILSpage.html**).

TAKING IT TO THE NET

1 The best way to improve notetaking skills is to practice. Locate a current news story of interest on the Internet and take notes while reading it. Remember to leave the left margin large enough to add key points and summary information. One possible strategy is to go to the "News" section of the Yahoo! home page (**http://dir.yahoo.com**). Click on one of the news categories (e.g., Sports, Politics, Business, etc.) and look for a story that sounds interesting.

2 Taking notes during lectures is an important part of classroom learning, but keeping up with a speaker for an entire hour can be difficult. You can improve your notetaking skills for lectures by taking notes while listening to recorded speeches on the Internet. For example, go to an Internet site containing audio recordings of speeches (e.g., **www.electionspeeches.com**) and take notes while listening to a speech. Afterward, go back and indicate the key points and terms in the left margin of your notes. You can check your comprehension by comparing the speech to news articles reporting on it. (You can also check the articles for bias!)

The Case of . . .

The Human Dictation Machine

Everyone wanted to borrow Lila Bauman's notes.

If they missed a class, or even if they had been there but had just spaced out, other students in Lila's classes knew that they could find out what had happened in class by borrowing her notes. It was all there in black and white. The woman was virtually a human dictation machine. She spent her time in class in a whirlwind of notetaking, writing down seemingly every word her instructor uttered in a clear, meticulous script. By the end of a term, her notebooks were so lengthy that they approached the size of telephone books from a small city.

The strange thing, though, was that—despite her copious notes—Lila was only a mediocre student. Before tests she studied her notes thoroughly, but she never seemed to get grades higher than a C+. She didn't know why, especially in light of what she saw as her notetaking expertise.

1. How do you think Lila defines "good notetaking"?

2. Why does Lila's method of notetaking produce such poor results? What is she missing?

3. If you asked Lila to summarize the instructor's main ideas after a class lecture, how successful do you think she would be? Why?

4. Do you think it would be easy or hard to study for a final exam using Lila's notes? Why?

5. Do you think Lila evaluates her notes during or after class? Do you think she ever rethinks them? What questions would you ask to help her perform these steps?

6. In general, what advice would you give Lila on notetaking?

Taking Tests

Learning Outcomes

By the time you finish this chapter you will be able to

» LO **5.1**   Identify the kinds of tests you will encounter in college.

» LO **5.2**   Explain the best ways to prepare for and take various kinds of tests.

» LO **5.3**   Analyze the best strategies for answering specific kinds of test questions.

So it all comes down to a test.

That was the thought that ran through Imani Brown's mind as he got ready to start the most important test he had ever faced. Yes, he had taken tests all through his high school career, and yes, he had suffered through the S.A.T. to get into college.

But now, on the verge of starting his career as a high school teacher, he had one more hurdle to jump over. The state legislature had recently decided that all new graduates of teacher training programs had to pass a competency test before starting to teach.

Imani had wanted to be a teacher as long as he could remember; he simply had to pass.

Although he was fairly confident—he had studied hard—he couldn't relax altogether. He told himself that he had always done well on tests in the past; he wasn't going to fail now. But still . . .

Although many tests are not as critical as Imani Brown's teacher competency exam, tests do play a significant role in everyone's academic life. Students typically experience more anxiety over tests than over anything else in their college careers.

But tests don't have to be so anxiety producing. There are strategies and techniques you can learn to reduce your fear of test taking. In fact, learning how to take tests is in some ways as important as learning the content that they cover. Taking tests effectively does not just involve mastering information; it also requires mastering specific test-taking skills.

One of the most important goals of this chapter is to take the mystery out of the whole process of taking tests. To do that, you'll learn about the different types of tests and strategies you can start using even before you take a test. You'll gain insight into how different kinds of tests work and how best to approach them, and you'll also learn about the various types of test questions and strategies for responding most effectively to each type.

This chapter also explores two aspects of test taking that may affect your performance: test anxiety and cramming. You will learn ways to deal with your anxiety and keep cramming to a minimum—but you will also learn how to make the most of cramming, if you do have to resort to it.

The chapter ends with suggestions for evaluating your performance toward the end of a test and for using what you learn to improve your performance the next time around.

» LO 5.1 Getting Ready

Tests may be the most unpopular part of academic life. Students hate them because they produce fear, anxiety, apprehension about being evaluated, and a focus on grades instead of learning for learning's sake. Instructors often don't like them very much either, because they produce fear, anxiety, apprehension about being evaluated, and a focus on grades instead of learning for learning's sake. That's right: Students and instructors dislike tests for the very same reasons.

But tests are also valuable. A well-constructed test identifies what you know and what you still need to learn. Tests help you see how your performance compares to that of others. And knowing that you'll be tested on a body of material is certainly likely to motivate you to learn material more thoroughly.

Journal Reflections

How I Feel about Tests

1. How do you feel about tests in general?

2. What are your first memories of being in a testing situation? What were your feelings, and why?

3. What makes a test "good" and "bad" from your perspective?

4. What factors contribute to your success or failure on a particular exam? Which of these factors are under your control?

5. What strategies do you use when taking tests to maximize your performance? Which have been particularly effective, and why?

P Prepare
Ready
test-taking strategies

O Organize
Bring the right tools
to the test

W Work
Tackle the test

E Evaluate
Check your work

R Rethink
Reflect on what you've learned
when you get a test back

P.O.W.E.R. Plan

However, there's another reason you might dislike tests: You may assume that tests have the power to define your worth as a person. If you do badly on a test, you may be tempted to believe that you've received some fundamental information about yourself from the professor and the college, information that says you're a failure in some significant way.

This is a dangerous—and wrong-headed—assumption. If you do badly on a test, it doesn't mean you're a bad person. Or stupid. Or that you'll never do better again, and that your life is ruined. If you don't do well on a test, you're the same person you were before you took the test—no better, no worse. You just did badly on a test. Period.

In short, tests are not a measure of your value as an individual. They are only a measure of how well (and how much) you studied, and your test-taking skills. Tests are tools; they are indirect and imperfect measures of what we know. Someone with a great deal of knowledge can do poorly on a test; tension or going at too slow a pace can lead to unwelcome results in some cases. Another person may know considerably less and still do better on the test simply because he or she may have learned some test-taking skills along the way.

How we do on a test depends on a number of considerations: the kind of test it is, the subject matter involved, our understanding of test-taking strategies, and, above all, how well we prepare for it. Let's turn, then, to the first step in test-taking: preparation. (The five steps are summarized in the P.O.W.E.R. Plan on the left.)

Readying Your Test-Taking Strategies

Preparation for tests requires a number of strategies. Among the most important are the following:

Remember: Everything You Do in a Course Is Preparation for a Test

All the things you do during a course help to prepare you for a test. There is no surer way to get good grades on tests than to attend class faithfully and to complete all class assignments seriously and on time.

Preparing for tests is a long-term proposition. It's not a matter of "giving your all" the night before the test. Instead, it's a matter of giving your all to every aspect of the course.

Know What You Are Preparing For

Determine as much as you can about the test before you begin to study for it. The more you know about a test beforehand, the more efficient your studying will be.

To find out about an upcoming test, ask these questions:

› Is the test called a "test," "exam," "quiz," or something else? As you can see in **Table 5.1,** the names imply different things. For simplicity's sake, we'll use the term test throughout this chapter, but know that these distinctions exist, and they should affect the way you prepare.

› What material will the test cover?

› How many questions will be on it?

› How much time is it expected to take? A full class period? Only part of a period?

---

table 5.1   Quizzes, Tests, Exams . . . What's in a Name?

Although they may vary from one instructor to another, the following definitions are most commonly used:

Quizzes. A **quiz** is a brief assessment, usually covering a relatively small amount of material. Some quizzes cover as little as one class's worth of reading. Although a single quiz usually doesn't count very much, instructors often add quiz scores together, and collectively they can become a significant part of your final course grade.

Tests. A **test** is a more extensive, more heavily weighted assessment than a quiz, covering more material. A test may come every few weeks of the term, often after each third or quarter of the term has passed, but this varies with the instructor and the course.

Exams. An **exam** is the most substantial kind of assessment. In many classes, just one exam is given—a final exam at the end of the term. Sometimes there are two exams, one at the midpoint of the term (called, of course, a midterm) and the second at the end. Exams are usually weighted quite heavily because they are meant to assess your knowledge of all the course material covered up to that point.

---

table 5.2	Types of Test Questions
Essay	Requires a fairly extended, on-the-spot composition about some topic. Examples include questions that call on you to describe a person, process, or event, or those that ask you to compare or contrast two separate sets of material.
Multiple-choice	Usually contains a question or statement, followed by a number of possible answers (usually 4 or 5 of them). You are supposed to choose the best response from the choices offered.
True–false	Presents statements about a topic that are either accurate or inaccurate. You are to indicate whether each statement is accurate (true) or inaccurate (false).
Matching	Presents two lists of related information, arranged in column form. Typically, you are asked to pair up the items that go together (e.g., a scientific term and its definition, or a writer and the title of a book he wrote).
Short-answer	Requires brief responses (usually a few sentences at most) in a kind of mini-essay.
Fill-in	Requires you to add one or more missing words to a sentence or series of sentences.

> ▸ What kinds of questions will be on the test?
> ▸ How will it be graded?
> ▸ Will sample questions be provided?
> ▸ Are tests from previous terms available?
> ▸ How much does the test contribute to my final course grade?

Match Test Preparation to Question Types

Test questions come in different types (see **Table 5.2**), and each requires a somewhat different style of preparation.

> ▸ **Essay questions.** Essay tests focus on the big picture—ways in which the various pieces of information being tested fit together. You'll need to know not just a series of facts, but also the connections between them, and you will have to be able to discuss these ideas in an organized and logical way.

The best approach to studying for an essay test involves four steps:

1. Carefully reread your class notes and any notes you've made on assigned readings that will be covered on the upcoming exam. Also go through the readings themselves, reviewing underlined or highlighted material and marginal notes.

2. Play professor: Think of likely exam questions. To do this, you can use the key words, phrases, concepts, and questions that come up in your class notes or in your text. Some instructors give out lists of possible essay topics; if yours does, focus on this list, but don't ignore other possibilities.

"High school is memorization and regurgitation. Here you have to think."
Junior, Engineering Student, Notre Dame University[1]

3. Without looking at your notes or your readings, answer each potential essay question—aloud. Don't feel embarrassed about doing this. Talking aloud is often more useful than answering the question in your head.

You can also write down the main points that any answer should cover. (Don't write out *complete* answers to the questions unless your instructor tells you in advance exactly what is going to be on the test. Your time is probably better spent learning the material than rehearsing precisely formulated responses.)

4. After you've answered the questions, check yourself by looking at the notes and readings once again. If you feel confident that you've answered particular questions adequately, check them off. You can go back later for a quick review.

But if there are questions that you had trouble with, review that material immediately. Then repeat the third step above, answering the questions again.

⟩ **Short-answer and fill-in questions.** Short-answer and fill-in questions are similar to essays in that they require you to recall key pieces of information rather than finding it on the page in front of you. However, short-answer and fill-in questions—unlike essay questions—typically don't demand that you integrate or compare different types of information. Consequently, the focus of your study should be on the recall of specific, detailed information.

⟩ **Multiple-choice, true–false, and matching questions.** While the focus of review for essay questions should be on major issues and controversies, studying for multiple-choice, true–false, and matching questions requires more attention to the details.

Almost anything is fair game for multiple-choice, true–false, and matching questions, so you can't afford to overlook anything when studying. True, these kinds of questions put the material right there on the page for you to react to—Did Columbus land in 1492, or not?—rather than asking you to provide the names and dates yourself (as in the case of the essay question). Nevertheless, to do well on these tests you must put your memory into high gear and master a great many facts.

It's a particularly good idea to write down important facts on index cards like those in **Figure 5.1**. Remember the advantages of these cards: They're portable and available all the time, and the act of creating them helps drive the material into your memory. Furthermore, you can shuffle them and test yourself repeatedly until you've mastered the material.

Political reforms of progressive age: —direct primaries: people vote for whom they want to run; not appointed —initiative: people propose laws on their own —referendum: gov. proposes; people say yes or no —recall: people can remove politicians from office before they finish term	Endoplasmic reticulum (ER): Smooth ER—makes fats (lipids) Rough ER—has ribosomes which make proteins Together, they make membranes for whole cell (for plasma membrane, mitochondrion, etc.) Also make more of themselves.

figure 5.1
Using Index Cards

It also can be helpful to write the name of a particular concept or theory on one side of a note card, and then to generate and write an example of it on the other side. Studying the cards will ensure that you fully understand the concepts and theories and can generalize them to different situations.

Test Yourself

Once you feel you've mastered the material, test yourself on it. There are several ways to do this. Often textbooks are accompanied by Web sites that offer automatically scored practice tests and quizzes. (*P.O.W.E.R. Learning* does: Go to **www.mhhe.com/power** to try one!)

You can also create a test for yourself, in writing, making its form as close as possible to what you expect the actual test to be. For instance, if your instructor has told you the classroom test will be primarily made up of short-answer questions, your test should reflect that.

You might also construct a test and administer it to a classmate or a member of your study group. In turn, you could take a test that someone else has constructed. Constructing and taking practice tests are excellent ways of studying the material and cementing it into memory. (To be sure you're fully prepared for your next test, complete **Try It 1** on page 123.)

Deal with Test Anxiety

What does the anticipation of a test do to you? Do you feel shaky? Frantic, like there's not enough time to get it all done? Do you feel as if there's a knot in your stomach? Do you grit your teeth?

Test anxiety is a temporary condition characterized by fears and concerns about test taking. Almost everyone experiences it to some degree, although for some people it's more of a problem than for others. The real danger with test anxiety is that it can become so overwhelming that it can hurt test performance. (To assess your own test-taking style and the degree of anxiety around tests that you experience, see **Try It 2** on page 125.)

You'll never eliminate test anxiety completely, nor do you want to. A little bit of nervousness can energize us, making us more attentive and vigilant. Like any competitive event, testing can motivate us to do our best. You might think of moderate test anxiety as a desire to perform at your peak—a useful quality at test time.

On the other hand, for some, anxiety can spiral into the kind of paralyzing fear that makes their minds go blank. There are several ways to keep this from happening to you:

1. *Prepare thoroughly.* The more you prepare, the less test anxiety you'll feel. Good preparation can give you a sense of control and mastery, and it will prevent test anxiety from overwhelming you.

2. *Take a realistic view of the test.* Remember that your future success does not hinge on your performance on any single exam. Think of the big picture: Put the task ahead in context, and remind yourself of all the hurdles you've passed so far.

3. *Eat right and get enough sleep.* Good mental preparation can't occur without your body being well prepared.

4. *Learn relaxation techniques.* You can learn to reduce or even eliminate the jittery physical symptoms of test anxiety by using relaxation techniques. These techniques are covered in Chapter 14, but the basic process is straightforward: Breathe evenly, gently inhaling and exhaling. Focus your mind on a pleasant, relaxing scene such as a beautiful forest or a peaceful farm, or on a restful sound such as that of ocean waves breaking on the beach.

Complete a Test Preparation Checklist

It takes more than simply learning the material to prepare for a test. You also need a strategy that will help you understand what it is you are studying for. To do that, learn as much as you can about what the test will be like. The more you understand about the kind of test and what it will cover, the better you'll be able to target your studying.

To focus your studying, complete the following test preparation checklist before your next test.

TEST PREPARATION CHECKLIST

- ☐ I know whether it's a quiz, test, or exam.
- ☐ I know what kinds of questions will be on the test.
- ☐ I understand what material will be covered.
- ☐ I know how many questions will be on the test.
- ☐ I know how long I will have to complete the test.
- ☐ I know how it will be graded and how the grade contributes to my final course grade.
- ☐ I obtained sample questions and/or previous tests, if available.
- ☐ I formed or participated in a study group.
- ☐ I used different and appropriate preparation strategies for different types of questions.
- ☐ I read and studied my class notes.
- ☐ I composed some questions of the kind that will be on the exam.
- ☐ I answered essay questions aloud.
- ☐ I actively memorized facts and details.
- ☐ I made and used index cards.
- ☐ I created and used a test like the real test.

After completing the checklist, ask yourself these questions: How can I use this checklist to study more effectively for tests? How might completing the checklist change the way I previously have studied for tests? What new strategies might I follow in order to prepare for tests more effectively in the future?

To Try It online, go to www.mhhe.com/power.

5. *Visualize success.* Think of an image of your instructor handing back your test marked with a big fat "A." Or imagine your instructor congratulating you on your fine performance the day after the test. Positive visualizations that highlight your potential success can help replace images of failure that may fuel test anxiety.

What if these strategies don't work? If your test anxiety is so great that it's getting in the way of your success, make use of your college's resources. Most provide a learning resource center or a counseling center that can provide you with personalized help. (To focus on dealing with math test anxiety, see the **Course Connections** feature.)

Form a Study Group

Study groups are small, informal groups of students who work together to learn course material and study for a test. Forming such a group can be an excellent way to prepare for any kind of test. Some study groups are formed for particular tests, while others meet consistently throughout the term.

The typical study group meets a week or two before a test and plans a strategy for studying. Members share their understanding of what will be on the test, based

Study groups

Small, informal groups of students whose purpose is to help members work together and study for a test

Special Techniques for Dealing with Math Anxiety

For many students, the greatest test anxiety comes when they're taking a math test. Math seems to bring out the worst fears in some people, perhaps because it's seen as a discipline in which answers are either totally right or totally wrong, or because they've felt they've "hit the wall" and they'll never be able to understand a concept, no matter how hard they try.

Such feelings about math can be devastating, because they can prevent you from doing well even if you know the material. If you suffer from math anxiety, keep these things in mind:

- Math is like any other subject: The greatest component of success is the effort you put in, not whether you have a "math gene" that makes you naturally good at math. It's not true that you either are born "good at math" or not and that there's some "secret" about math that some people know and others don't.

- It's also not true that there's only one way to solve a math problem. Sometimes there are a variety of routes to coming up with a solution. And keep in mind that the solution to math problems often calls for creativity, not just sheer logic.

- It's a false stereotype that women are not as good at math as men, but it's a stereotype that many women buy into. Research has shown that when men do badly on a math test, they're most likely to think that they haven't put in enough effort. But when women don't do well on a math test, they're three times more likely than men to feel that they don't have enough ability to be successful.[2] That's an erroneous view of the world. Don't become a prisoner of stereotypes.

- Remember that math has practical uses. Some people are afraid of math because they view it as theoretical, with no practical value. But if you want to figure out the size of a room, how to calculate a tip in a restaurant, or how much interest you'll pay on a loan, you'll need to make use of geometry, arithmetic, and algebra.

- Finally, use these special strategies to deal with math problems on exams:

Before tests:

1. Math is cumulative, building on prior concepts and knowledge. Make sure you review math fundamentals before moving on to more advanced topics.

2. Ask questions in class. Don't be afraid that you'll ask the wrong question in the wrong way. Math instructors love their subject, and they want others to understand it.

3. Make use of review sessions and other study resources.

4. Practice, practice, practice. The more experience you have completing math problems under pressure, the better you'll do. Practice math problems using a timer in order to simulate an actual test.

5. Get rid of negative self-talk ("I'm a born math loser" or "This stuff is so hard I'm bound to fail") by identifying such negative thoughts and understanding the lack of logic behind them. Try to replace them with more positive thoughts ("I learned the basics of math, and this new material is just a logical extension of the fundamentals" and "If I'm confident and proceed methodically, I can succeed").

During tests:

1. Analyze math problems carefully. What are the known quantities or constants, and what pieces of information are missing? What formula(s) or theorem(s) apply?

2. For word problems, consider if they are similar to word problems that you've studied and mastered.

3. Consider drawing a diagram, graph, or probability tree.

4. Break down calculations into their component parts.

5. Check your math carefully.

6. Be neat and logical in your presentation, and show every step as you solve problems. Your instructor may give you partial credit if you lay out every step you're going through. In addition, some instructors require you to show your work.

Try It! **P O W E R**

2

Measure Your Test-Taking Style

Do you feel anxious at the very thought of a test, or are you cool and calm in the face of testing situations? Get a sense of your test-taking style by checking off every statement below that applies to you.

- ☐ 1. The closer a test date approaches, the more nervous I get.
- ☐ 2. I am sometimes unable to sleep on the night before a test.
- ☐ 3. I have "frozen up" during a test, finding myself unable to think or respond.
- ☐ 4. I can feel my hands shaking as I pick up my pencil to begin a test.
- ☐ 5. The minute I read a tough test question, all the facts I ever knew about the subject abandon me and I can't get them back no matter how hard I try.
- ☐ 6. I have become physically ill before or during a test.
- ☐ 7. Nervousness prevents me from studying immediately before a test.
- ☐ 8. I often dream about an upcoming test.
- ☐ 9. Even if I successfully answer a number of questions, my anxiety stays with me throughout the test.
- ☐ 10. I'm reluctant to turn in my test paper for fear that I can do better if I continue to work on it.

If you checked off more than four statements, you have experienced fairly serious test anxiety. If you checked off more than six statements, your anxiety is probably interfering with your test performance. In particular, statements 3, 5, 6, 7, and 10 may indicate serious test anxiety.

If, based on your responses to this questionnaire and your previous experience, your level of test anxiety is high, what are some of the steps described in this chapter that might be helpful to you?

To Try It online, go to www.mhhe.com/power.

---

on what an instructor has said in class and on their review of notes and text material. Together, they develop a list of review questions to guide their individual study. The group then breaks up, and the members study on their own.

A few days before the test, members of the study group meet again. They discuss answers to the review questions, go over the material, and share any new insights they may have about the upcoming test. They may also quiz one another about the material to identify any weaknesses or gaps in their knowledge.

Study groups can be extremely powerful tools because they help accomplish several things:

> They help members organize and structure the material to approach their studying in a systematic and logical way.

> They allow students to share different perspectives on the material.

> They make it more likely that students will not overlook any potentially important information.

> They force members to rethink the course material, explaining it in words that other group members will understand. As we will discuss in Chapter 9, this helps both understanding and recall of the information when it is needed on the test.

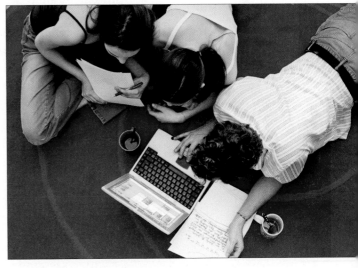

Study groups, made up of a few students who study together for a test, can help organize material, provide new perspectives, and motivate members to do their best.

> Finally, they help motivate members to do their best. When you're part of a study group, you're no longer working just for yourself; your studying also benefits the other study group members. Not wanting to let down your classmates in a study group may encourage you to put in your best effort.

There are some potential drawbacks to keep in mind. Study groups don't always work well for students with learning styles that favor working independently. In addition, "problem" members—those who don't pull their weight—may cause difficulties for the group. In general, though, the advantages of study groups far outweigh their disadvantages.

How do you form a study group? Follow these steps:

1. Identify motivated, enthusiastic classmates. Unenergetic classmates with negative attitudes do not make good study group members.

2. Include a variety of people. Involve classmates with different strengths in order to maximize what you can learn from them.

3. Choose a purpose for your study group. It might be to review class material and notes throughout the semester, meeting weekly. Or it might form to focus on test preparation and only meet prior to exams. Be clear on the focus when you form the group.

4. Don't make your study group too large. Groups larger than four or five people tend to get off task easily.

Regroup if necessary. If, after establishing your group, you find that the members don't function effectively, change membership or even disband your group. You want to make the most of a study group, and if it is not working well, think about starting over with a new group of classmates. (To set up your own study group, see **Try It 3.**)

Use Your Campus Learning or Tutorial Center Resources

Many colleges have a learning center, tutorial center, or other office that can help you study for a test. Often they are staffed by advanced students who have already taken courses that you're studying for. Take advantage of any opportunities you have to get the advice of such "expert" students. Not only can they provide you with general study strategies, but they can give you tips on a particular instructor's tests.

Don't wait until after you do badly on a test to visit your campus learning or tutorial centers. A visit prior to your first test is a good use of your time, even if you feel it's not essential. Just knowing what resources are available can boost your confidence.

Cramming: You Shouldn't, But . . .

Cramming
Hurried, last-minute studying

You know, of course, that **cramming**, hurried, last-minute studying, is not the way to go. You know that you're likely to forget the material the moment the test is over because long-term retention is nearly impossible without thoughtful study. But . . .

. . . it's been one of those weeks where everything went wrong.

. . . the instructor sprang the test on you at the last minute.

. . . you forgot about the test until the night before it was scheduled.

Whatever the reason, there may be times when you can't study properly. What do you do if you have to cram for an exam?

Don't spend a lot of time on what you're unable to do. Beating yourself up about your failings as a student will only hinder your efforts. Instead, admit you're

Try It! POWER

3

Form a Study Group

The next time you have to prepare for a test, form a study group with three to five classmates. They may have a variety of study habits and skills, but all must be willing to take the group seriously.

The first time you meet, compare notes about what is likely to be on the test and brainstorm to come up with possible test questions. If the instructor hasn't given you detailed information about the test (i.e., number and types of questions, weighting, etc.), one of you should be delegated to ask for it. Plan to meet once more closer to the test date to discuss answers to the questions you've come up with, share any new insights, and quiz each other on the material.

After you've taken the test and gotten your results, meet again. Find out if members felt the group was effective. Did the members feel more confident about the test? Do they think they did better than they would have without the group? What worked? What didn't? What could you do differently next time?

To Try It online, go to www.mhhe.com/power.

human and imperfect like everyone else. Then spend a few minutes developing a plan about what you can accomplish in the limited time you've got.

The first thing to do is choose what you really need to study. You won't be able to learn everything, so you have to make choices. Figure out the main focus of the course, and concentrate on it.

Once you have a strategy, prepare a one-page summary sheet with hard-to-remember information. Just writing the material down will help you remember it, and you can refer to the summary sheet frequently over the limited time you do have to study.

Next, read through your class notes, concentrating on the material you've underlined and the key concepts and ideas that you've already noted. Forget about reading all the material in the books and articles you're being tested on. Instead, only read the passages that you've underlined and the notes you've taken on the readings. Finally, maximize your study time. Using your notes, index cards, and concept maps, go over the information. Read it. Say it aloud. Think about it and the way it relates to other information. In short, use all the techniques we've talked about for learning and recalling information.

Just remember: When the exam is over, material that you have crammed into your head is destined to leave your mind as quickly as it entered. If you've crammed for a midterm, don't assume that the information will still be there when you study for the final. In the end, cramming often ends up taking more time for worse results than does studying with appropriate techniques.

Have you ever crammed for a test? If so, you know how exhausting it can be, and how easy it is to overlook crucial material. On the other hand, time pressures sometimes make cramming your only option. When that happens, there are strategies you can use to help you make the best use of limited time.

⊙ Organize — Facing the Day of the Test

You've studied a lot, and you're happy with your level of mastery. Or perhaps you have the nagging feeling that there's something you haven't quite completed. Or maybe you know you haven't had enough time to study as much as you'd like, and you're expecting a disaster.

Whatever your frame of mind, it will help to organize your plan of attack on the day of the test. What's included on the test is out of your hands, but you can control what you bring to it.

For starters, bring the right tools to the test. Have at least two pens and two pencils with you. It's usually best to write in pen because, in general, writing tends to be easier to read in pen than pencil. But you also might want to have pencils on hand. Sometimes instructors will use machine-scored tests, which require the use of pencil. Or there may be test questions that involve computations, and solving them may entail frequent reworking of calculations.

You should also bring a watch to the test, even if there will be a clock on the wall of the classroom. You will want to be able to pace yourself properly during the test. If you usually use a cell phone to determine the time, remember that some instructors may not allow you to look at them during the test.

Sometimes instructors permit you to use notes and books during the test. If you haven't brought them with you, they're not going to be of much help. So make sure you bring them if they're permitted. (Even for closed-book tests, having such material available before the test actually starts allows you a few minutes of review after you arrive in the classroom.) And don't be lulled into thinking an open-book test is going to be easy. Instructors who allow you to use your notes and books during a test may not give you much time to look things up, so you still need to study.

On the day of a test, avoid the temptation to compare notes with your friends about how much they've studied. Yes, you might end up feeling good because many of your fellow classmates studied less than you did. But chances are you'll find others who seem to have spent significantly more time studying than you, and this will do little to encourage you.

In addition, you might want to plan on panicking. Although it sounds like the worst possible approach, permitting yourself the option of spending a minute feeling panicky will help you to recover from your initial fears.

Finally, listen carefully to what an instructor says before the test is handed out. The instructor may tell you about a question that is optional or worth more points or inform you of a typographical error on the test. Whatever the instructor says just before the test, you can be sure it's information that you don't want to ignore.

Taking the Test

W Work   Tackling the Test

Take a deep breath—literally.

There's no better way to start work on a test than by taking a deep breath, followed by several others. The deep breaths will help you to overcome any initial panic and anxiety you may be experiencing. It's OK to give yourself over for a moment to panic and anxiety, but, to work at your best, use the relaxation techniques that we spoke about earlier to displace those initial feelings. Tell yourself, "It's OK. I am going to do my best."

Read the test instructions carefully. Even if instructors talk about what a test will be like beforehand, at the last minute, they may make changes. Consequently, it's critical to read the instructions for the test carefully. In fact, you should skim through the entire exam before you begin. Look at the kinds of questions and pay attention to the way they will be scored. If the point weighting of the various parts of the exam is not clear, ask your instructor to clarify it.

Knowing the point weighting is critical, because it will help you allocate your time. You don't want to spend 90 percent of your time on an essay that's worth only 10 percent of the points, and you want to be sure to leave time at the end of the test to check your answers.

An initial read-through will also help you verify that you have every page of the exam and that each one is readable. It may also provide you with "intra-test knowledge," in which terms defined or mentioned in one part of a test trigger memories that can help answer questions in another part of the test.

If there are any lists, formulas, or other key facts that you're concerned you may forget, jot them down now on the back of a test page or on a piece of scrap paper. You may want to refer to this material later during the test.

Once this background work is out of the way, you'll be ready to proceed to actually answering the questions. These principles will help you to do your best on the test:

> **Answer the easiest questions first.** By initially getting the questions out of the way that are easiest for you, you accomplish several important things. First, you'll be leaving yourself more time to think about the tougher questions. In addition, moving through a series of questions without a struggle will build your confidence. Finally, working through a number of questions will build up a base of points that may be enough to earn you at least a minimally acceptable grade.

> **Write legibly and only on one side of the paper.** If an instructor can't read what you've written, you're not going to get credit for it, no matter how brilliant your answer. So be sure to keep your handwriting legible.

  It's also a good idea to write your answers to essay questions on only one side of a page. This will allow you to go back later and add or revise information.

> **Master machine-scored tests.** Tests will sometimes be scored, in part, by computer. In such cases, you'll usually have to indicate your answers by filling in—with a pencil—circles or squares on a computer answer sheet.

  Be careful! A stray mark or smudge can cause the computer scanner to misread your answer sheet, producing errors in grading. Be sure to bring a good eraser in addition to a pencil; the biggest source of mistakes in machine grading is incomplete erasing.

  It's best to write your answers not only on the answer sheet, but also on the test itself (if the test is not intended for future reuse). That way you can go back and check your answers easily—a step you should take frequently. It's also a good idea to match up your answers on the test with the spaces on the answer sheet every five or so items. This will help you make sure you haven't skipped a space or gotten off track in some other way. If you catch such problems early, they're easy to fix.

  A variant of machine-scored testing is online testing. In such cases, you'll be taking an exam on a computer outside of class. Although we'll talk more about such tests in Chapter 10, for now keep in mind that you shouldn't wait until just before the final deadline to start your test. Technical difficulties may prevent you from logging in or having enough time to finish. In addition, be sure to have paper and pencil available. Even though you use the computer to record your answers, you'll want to be able to jot down ideas and notes and do calculations the traditional way: using paper and pencil.

> "Computerized test-scoring isn't perfect. Smudges can kill you. If your grade seems incorrect, ask to see the answer sheet."
>
> **Graduate, Physiology, Michigan State University[3]**

Every type of question requires a particular approach. Use these strategies below:

- **Essay questions.** Essay questions, with their emphasis on description and analysis, often present challenges because they are relatively unstructured. Unless you're careful, it's easy to wander off and begin to answer questions that were never asked. To prevent that problem, the first thing to do is read the question carefully, noting what specifically is being asked. If your essay will be lengthy, you might even want to write a short outline.

  Pay attention to keywords that indicate what, specifically, the instructor is looking for in an answer. Certain action words are commonly used in essays, and you should understand them fully. For instance, knowing the distinction between "compare" and "contrast" can spell the difference between success and failure. **Table 5.3** defines common action words.

  Use the right language in essays. Be brief and to the point in your essay. Avoid flowery introductory language. Compare the two sentences that follow:

  "In our study of world literature, it may be useful to ponder how The Canterbury Tales *came to represent such an important milestone in the field, and it will be seen that there are several critical reasons why it did have such an impact."*

  "The Canterbury Tales were groundbreaking for several reasons.*"

This second sentence says the same thing much more effectively and economically.

Essays are improved when they include examples and point out differences. Your response should follow a logical sequence, moving from major points to minor ones, or following a time sequence. Above all, your answer should address every aspect of the question posed on the test. Because essays often contain several different, embedded questions, you have to be certain that you have answered every part to receive full credit. (After reviewing Table 5.3, complete **Try It 4** on page 132.)

- **Short-answer and fill-in questions.** Short-answer and fill-in questions basically require you to generate and supply specific information in your own words. Unlike essays, which are more free-form and may have several possible answers, short-answer and fill-in questions are usually quite specific, requiring only one answer.

  Use both the instructions for the questions and the questions themselves to determine the level of specificity that is needed in an answer. Try not to provide too much or too little information. Usually, brevity is best.

- **Multiple-choice questions.** If you've ever looked at a multiple-choice question and said to yourself, "But every choice seems right," you understand what can be tricky about this type of question. However, there are some simple strategies that can help you deal with multiple-choice questions.

First, read the instructions carefully to determine whether only one response will be correct, or whether more than one of the choices may be correct. In most cases, only one choice will be right, but in some cases instructors may want you to check off more than one answer.

Turn to the first question and read it carefully. *Before you look at the possible answers, try to answer the question in your head.* This can help you avoid confusion over inappropriate choices.

table 5.3 Action Words for Essays

These words are commonly used in essay questions. Learning the distinctions among them will help you answer them effectively.

Analyze: Examine and break into component parts.

Clarify: Explain with significant detail.

Compare: Describe and explain similarities.

Compare and contrast: Describe and explain similarities and differences.

Contrast: Describe and explain differences.

Critique: Judge and analyze, explaining what is wrong—and right—about a concept.

Define: Provide the meaning.

Discuss: Explain, review, and consider.

Enumerate: Provide a listing of ideas, concepts, reasons, items, etc.

Evaluate: Provide pros and cons of something; provide an opinion and justify it.

Explain: Give reasons why or how; clarify, justify, and illustrate.

Illustrate: Provide examples; show instances.

Interpret: Explain the meaning of something.

Justify: Explain why a concept can be supported, typically by using examples and other types of support.

Outline: Provide an overarching framework or explanation—usually in narrative form—of a concept, idea, event, or phenomenon.

Prove: Using evidence and arguments, convince the reader of a particular point.

Relate: Show how things fit together; provide analogies.

Review: Describe or summarize, often with an evaluation.

State: Assert or explain.

Summarize: Provide a condensed, precise list or narrative.

Trace: Track or sketch out how events or circumstances have evolved; provide a history or timeline.

Try It!

4

Understand Action Verbs in Essay Questions

Answer the following questions about the Second Amendment to the United States Constitution by outlining your responses to them, paying attention to the different action verbs that introduce questions.

The Second Amendment states:

A well-regulated militia, being necessary to the security of a free State, the right of the people to keep and bear arms, shall not be infringed.

1. Summarize the Second Amendment to the Constitution.

2. Analyze the Second Amendment to the Constitution.

3. Discuss the Second Amendment to the Constitution.

How do your answers differ for the each of the questions? Which of the questions provoked the lengthiest response? Which of the questions could you answer best?

To Try It online, go to www.mhhe.com/power.

Next, *carefully read through every possible answer.* Even if you come to one that you think is right, read them all—there may be a subsequent answer that is better.

Look for absolutes like "every," "always," "only," "none," and "never." Choices that contain such absolute words are rarely correct. For example, an answer choice that says, "A U.S. president has never been elected without having received the majority of the popular vote" is incorrect due to the presence of the word "never." On the other hand, less-absolute words, such as "generally," "usually," "often," "rarely," "seldom," and "typically" may indicate a correct response.

Be especially on guard for the word "not," which negates the sentence ("The one key concept that is not embodied in the U.S. Constitution is . . ."). It's easy to gloss over "not," and if you have the misfortune of doing so, it will be nearly impossible to answer the item correctly.

If you're having trouble understanding a question, underline key words or phrases, or try to break the question into different short sections. Sometimes it is helpful to work backwards, *Jeopardy* style, and look at the possible answers first to see if you can find one that is clearly accurate or clearly inaccurate.

Use an **educated guessing** *strategy*—which is very different from wild or random guessing. Unless you are penalized for wrong answers (a scoring rule by which wrong answers are deducted from the points you have earned on other questions, rather than merely not counting at all toward your score), it always pays to guess.

The first step in educated guessing is to eliminate any obviously false answers. The next step is to examine the remaining choices closely. Does one response choice include an absolute or qualifying adjective that makes it unlikely ("the probability of war *always* increases when a U.S. president is facing political difficulties")? Does one choice include a subtle factual error? For example, the answer to a multiple choice question asking why Columbus took his journey to the new world that says "the French monarchy was interested in expanding its colonial holdings" is wrong because it was not the French, but the Spanish monarchy, that funded his journey.

> **True–false questions.** Although most of the principles we've already discussed apply equally well to true–false questions, a few additional tricks of the trade may help you with this type of question.
>
> Begin a set of true–false questions by answering the ones you're sure you know. But don't rush; it's important to read every part of a true–false question, because key words such as "never," "always," and "sometimes" often determine the appropriate response.
>
> If you don't have a clue about whether a statement is true or false, here's a last-resort principle: Choose "true." In general, more statements on a true–false test are likely to be true than false.

> **Matching questions.** Matching questions typically present you with two columns of related information, which you must link, item by item. For example, a list of terms or concepts may be presented in one column, along with a list of corresponding definitions or explanations in the second column. The best strategy is to reduce the size of both columns by matching the items you're most confident about first; this will leave a short list in each column, and the final matching may become apparent.

About Academic Honesty

It's tempting: A glance at a classmate's test may provide the one piece of information that you just can't remember. But you owe it to yourself not to do it. Copying from a classmate's paper is no different from reaching over and stealing that classmate's calculator or cell phone. It is a violation of **academic honesty,** one of the foundations of civility in the classroom, as well as in society. Unless the work you turn in under your own name is your work, you are guilty of academic dishonesty.

Educated guessing
The practice of eliminating obviously false multiple-choice answers and selecting the most likely answer from the remaining choices

Academic honesty
Completing and turning in only one's own work under one's own name

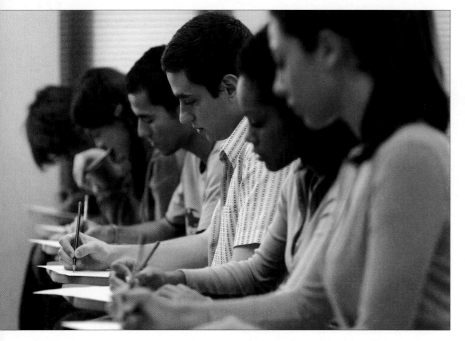

Academic honesty is the bedrock of college life. The risks of cheating—getting caught and causing damage to your academic future and sense of self-worth—far outweigh any momentary benefits.

Violations of academic honesty can take many forms. It may involve *plagiarism,* copying another's work and passing it off as your own. (We'll talk more about plagiarism in Chapter 7.) Academic dishonesty may also include using a calculator when it's not allowed, discussing the answer to a question, copying a computer file when it's unauthorized, taking an exam for another person, or stealing an exam. It can take the form of ripping a page out of a book in the library or lying to an instructor about the reason for a late paper. It includes using your textbook or conferring with a friend when taking a closed-book exam in an online, distance-learning course.

You may feel that "everyone does it," so cheating is not so bad. Wrong. Everyone doesn't do it, just as most people don't embezzle from their companies or steal from others. Although you may know of a few cases of exceptionally dishonest classmates, most of your classmates try to be honest—you just don't notice their honesty.

Whatever form it takes, academic dishonesty is just plain wrong. It lowers the level of civility in the classroom, it makes the grading system unfair, and it ultimately reduces the meaning of your grade. It certainly hinders academic and personal growth. It can't help but reduce one's self-esteem, and it robs the cheater of self-respect.

Finally, academic dishonesty violates the regulations of every college (rules that you should familiarize yourself with), and instructors feel it is their obligation to uphold standards of academic honesty. Violations of honesty policies will lead to any number of potentially devastating scenarios: failing the exam on which the cheating has taken place, failing the entire course, being brought before a disciplinary board, having a description of the incident permanently placed on your grade transcript, being placed on academic probation, or even being thrown out of school. A single instance of cheating can permanently prevent you from embarking on the career of your choice. Cheating is simply not worth it.

E Evaluate

Taking Your Own Final Examination

The last few minutes of a test may feel like the final moments of a marathon. You need to focus your energy and push yourself even harder. It can be make-or-break time.

Save some time at the end of a test so you can check your work. You should have been keeping track of your time all along, so plan on stopping a few minutes before the end of the test period to review what you've done. It's a critical step, and it can make the difference between a terrific grade and a mediocre one. It's a rare person who can work for an uninterrupted period of time on a test and commit absolutely

Tests for a Lifetime

If you think the last tests you'll ever have to take are the final exams just before you graduate from college, you're probably wrong.

For one thing, increasing numbers of professions require initial licensing exams, and some even require periodic exams to remain in good standing within the profession. For example, in some states, people who wish to become teachers must pass an exam, as in the case of Imani Brown described at the beginning of the chapter. Even experienced teachers are required to take periodic tests throughout their careers to remain in the teaching field.

In addition, you may have to take tests to continue your course of study for some professions. For example, if you are thinking about a career in medicine, law, or business, you'll need to take a national, standardized test (such as the MCAT or LSAT) to enroll in a postundergraduate program. How well you do on the test will determine whether you can go to graduate school and which graduate schools will accept you.

In short, good test-taking skills won't just bring you success in college. They're something that may benefit you for a lifetime as you pursue your career.

Career Connections

---

no errors—even if he or she knows the material backwards and forwards. Consequently, checking what you've done is crucial.

Start evaluating your test by looking for obvious mistakes. Make sure you've answered every question and haven't skipped any parts of questions. If there is a separate answer sheet, check to see that all your answers have been recorded on the answer sheet and in the right spot.

If the test has included essay and short-answer questions, proofread your responses. Check for obvious errors—misspellings, missing words, and repetitions. Make sure you've responded to every part of each question and that each essay, as a whole, makes sense.

Check over your responses to multiple-choice, true–false, and matching questions. If there are some items that you haven't yet answered because you couldn't remember the necessary information, now is the time to take a stab at them. As we discussed earlier, it usually pays to guess, even randomly if you must. On most tests, no answer and a wrong answer are worth the same amount—nothing!

What about items that you initially guessed at? Unless you have a good reason to change your original answer—such as a new insight or a sudden recollection of some key information—your first guess is likely your best guess.

Know When to Stop

After evaluating and checking your answers, you may reach a point when there is still some time left. What to do? If you're satisfied with your responses, it's simply time to tell yourself, "Let it go."

Permit yourself the luxury of knowing that you've done your best, and hand the test in to your instructor. You don't have to review your work over and over just because there is time remaining and some of your classmates are still working on their tests. In fact, such behavior is often counterproductive, because you might start overinterpreting and reading things into questions that really aren't there.

Disaster! I've run out of time! It's a nightmarish feeling: The clock is ticking relentlessly, and it's clear that you don't have enough time to finish the test. What should you do?

Stop working! Although this advice may sound foolish, in fact the most important thing you can do is to take a minute to calm yourself. Take some deep breaths to replace the feelings of panic that are likely welling up inside you. Collect your thoughts, and plan a strategy for the last moments of the test.

If there are essays that remain undone, consider how you'd answer them if you had more time. Then write an outline of each answer. If you don't have time even for that, write a few keywords. Writing anything is better than handing in a blank page, and you may get at least some credit for your response. The key principle here: Something is better than nothing, and even one point is worth more than zero points.

The same principle holds for other types of questions. Even wild guesses are almost always better than not responding at all to an item. So rather than telling yourself you've certainly failed and giving up, do as much as you can in the remaining moments of the exam.

R Rethink The Real Test of Learning

Your instructor is about to hand the graded exams back. All sorts of thoughts run through your head: How did I do? Did I do as well as my classmates? Will I be happy with my results? Will the results show how much I studied? Will I be embarrassed by my grade?

Most of us focus on the evaluative aspects of tests. We look at the grade we've received on a test as an end in itself. It's a natural reaction.

But there's another way to look at test results: They can help guide us toward future success. By looking at what we've learned (and haven't learned) about a given subject, we'll be in a better position to know what to focus on when we take future exams. Furthermore, by examining the kinds of mistakes we make, we can learn to do better in the future.

> "The test of any man lies in action."
>
> Pindar, author, *Odes*

When you get your test back, you have the opportunity to reflect on what you've learned and to consider your performance. Begin by actively listening to what your instructor says as he or she hands back the test. You may learn about things that were generally misunderstood by the class, and you'll get a sense of how your performance compares to that of your classmates. You also may pick up some important clues about what questions will be on future exams.

Then examine your own mistakes. Chances are they'll jump out at you since they will be marked incorrect. Did you misunderstand or misapply some principle? Was there a certain aspect of the material covered on the test that you missed? Were there particular kinds of information that you didn't realize you needed to know? Or did you lose some points because of your test-taking skills? Did you make careless errors, such as forgetting to fill in a question or misreading the directions? Was your handwriting so sloppy that your instructor had trouble reading it?

Once you have a good idea of what material you didn't fully understand or remember, get the correct answers to the items you missed—from your instructor, fellow classmates, or your book. If it's a math exam, rework problems you've missed. Finally, summarize—in writing—the material you had trouble with. This will help you study for future exams that cover the same material.

Finally, if you're dissatisfied with your performance, talk to your instructor—not to complain, but to seek help. Instructors don't like to give bad grades, and they may be able to point out problems in your test that you can address readily so you can do better in the future. Demonstrate to your instructor that you want to do better and are willing to put in the work to get there. The worst thing to do is crumple up the test and quickly leave the class in embarrassment. Remember, you're not the first person to get a bad grade, and the power to improve your test-taking performance lies within you. (Now, take a deep breath and complete **Try It 5.**)

Try It!

Take a Test-Taking Test

Take the following test on test-taking skills, which illustrates every question type discussed in this chapter. Answers to all questions except short-answer and essay questions are provided on page 143.

Before taking the test, think of the test-taking strategies we've discussed in the chapter and try to employ as many of them as possible.

MULTIPLE-CHOICE SECTION

Choose one of the possible responses following each question.

1. Tests are useful tools for which of the following purposes?
   a. Determining people's likely level of future career success.
   b. Indicating strengths and gaps in people's knowledge.
   c. Defining people's fundamental abilities and potentials.
   d. Evaluating people's individual worth and contributions.
2. One of the main advantages of study groups is that:
   a. Every individual must contribute equally to the group.
   b. Group members can help each other during the test.
   c. Each member has to memorize only a fraction of the material.
   d. Groups motivate their members to do good work.
3. Which of the following is a good way to deal with test anxiety?
   a. Visualizing success on the test.
   b. Drinking coffee or other stimulants.
   c. Telling yourself to stop worrying.
   d. Focusing on the importance of the test.

MATCHING SECTION

_____ 1. Essay question

_____ 2. Multiple-choice question

_____ 3. Matching question

_____ 4. Fill-in question

_____ 5. Guessing penalty

_____ 6. Cramming

_____ 7. Academic dishonesty

A. A question in which the student supplies brief missing information to complete a statement.

B. Hurried, last-minute studying.

C. A question in which the student must link information in two columns.

D. A question requiring a lengthy response in the student's own words.

E. Deduction of points for incorrect responses.

F. Representing another's work as one's own.

G. A question that requires selection from several response options.

FILL-IN SECTION

1. Fear of testing that can interfere with test performance is called _____.
2. The primary source of error on machine-scored tests is incomplete _____.

TRUE–FALSE SECTION

1. The best way to prepare for an essay test is to review detailed factual information about the topic. T _____ F _____
2. True–false questions require students to determine whether given statements are accurate or inaccurate. T _____ F _____
3. You should never permit yourself to feel panicky during a test. T _____ F _____
4. A good evaluation strategy toward the end of a test is to redo as many questions as time permits. T _____ F _____
5. In a multiple-choice question, the words "always" and "never" usually signal the correct response. T _____ F _____
6. If you run out of time at the end of a test, it is best to write brief notes and ideas down in response to essay questions rather than to leave them completely blank. T _____ F _____

SHORT-ANSWER SECTION

1. What are five things you should find out about a test before you take it?

2. What is academic honesty?

ESSAY SECTION

1. Discuss the advantages of using a study group to prepare for an examination.

2. Why is academic honesty important?

(Answers can be found on page 143 at the end of the chapter.)

After you have completed the test, consider these questions: Did you learn anything from taking the test that you might not have learned if you hadn't been tested? How effective were the test-taking strategies you employed? Were any types of strategies easier for you to employ than others? Were any types of questions easier for you to answer than others?

 WORKING IN A GROUP:

Exchange your essay responses with a classmate, and critique the essay. How do the responses of your partner compare with your own?

To Try It online, go to www.mhhe.com/power.

Columbia
COLLEGE CHICAGO

NAME: **Yajaira Gijon**

SCHOOL: **Columbia College Chicago, Chicago, Illinois**

As the first in her family to attend college, Yajaira Gijon faced unique challenges. The daughter of immigrants, it took her 10 years to achieve her goal of attaining a degree.

"I didn't pay much attention in high school, and my grades suffered," Gijon said. "But I pulled myself together after the death of a friend and decided to go to community college. My parents were surprised but very supportive."

Because Gijon worked full time at a graphics design company, she went to school at night. She could take only a few courses each semester.

After four years of part-time study at her community college, she decided to pursue a fine arts degree at Columbia College Chicago. It wasn't easy.

"The first semester was pretty tough," she said. "It was very competitive, and the instructors pushed you a lot. I wasn't used to that, and I had to rethink if I wanted to stay since I found it to be a frightening experience. But I told myself I just couldn't give up," Gijon added.

Realizing she needed to put extra effort into her studies, Gijon made a commitment to being more involved.

"What I had to do was educate myself more and learn more about the design field," she explained, "and so I joined a design group. I would go to the book store and pick up magazines and read through them looking for ideas. I also developed a sketch book and journal, jotting down my ideas and noting what the latest trends were."

College became an increasingly important part of Gijon's life. "Monday through Friday I would make an effort to be at school either at the library or lab, even if I didn't have classes," she said. "Being at school and seeing other students working hard motivated me."

Gijon eventually plans to attend graduate school. "I have an interest in teaching, and I feel really strongly that I'd like to come back and teach in my community and be a role model for others," she said.

"The sacrifices of my parents coming to this country inspired me to keep going," she added. "If they can do that, then I can achieve my goals."

Looking Back

What kinds of tests will I encounter in college?

> Although tests are an unpopular fact of college life, they can provide useful information about one's level of knowledge and understanding about a subject.

> There are several types of tests, including brief, informal quizzes; more substantial tests; and even more weighty exams, which tend to be administered at the midpoint and end of a course.

What are the best ways to prepare for and take various kinds of tests?

> Good test preparation begins with doing the course assignments, attending class regularly, and paying attention in class. It also helps to find out as much as possible about a test beforehand and to form a study group to review material.

> If cramming becomes necessary, focus on summarizing factual information broadly, identifying key concepts and ideas, and rehearsing information orally.

> When you first receive the test, skim it to see what kinds of questions are asked, figure out how the different questions and sections will be weighted, and jot down complex factual information that is likely to be needed for the test.

> Answer the easiest questions first, write legibly, use only one side of each sheet of paper, mark answer sheets carefully, and record answers in the test book as well as the answer sheet.

What are the best strategies for answering specific kinds of test questions?

> For essay questions, be sure to understand each question and each of its parts, interpret action words correctly, write concisely, organize the essay logically, and include examples.

> The best strategy for short-answer and fill-in questions is to be very sure what is being asked. Keep answers complete but brief.

> For multiple-choice questions, read the question very carefully and then read all response choices. Educated guessing based on eliminating incorrect response choices is usually a reasonable strategy.

> For true–false and matching questions, answer all the items that you are sure of quickly and then go back to the remaining items.

[KEY TERMS AND CONCEPTS]

Test anxiety (p. 122)

Study groups (p. 123)

Cramming (p. 126)

Educated guessing (p. 133)

Academic honesty (p. 133)

[RESOURCES]

ON CAMPUS

Colleges provide a variety of resources for students having difficulties with test-taking. Some offer general workshops for students, reviewing test-taking strategies. Furthermore, if you are planning to take a specific standardized test, such as the tests required for admission to business, law, or medical school, you may be able to sign up for a course offered through your college (or through such commercial organizations as Princeton Review or Kaplan).

If you are experiencing difficulties in a specific course, you may be able to find a tutor to help you out. Some colleges have tutoring centers or campus learning centers that can provide one-to-one assistance. You also can talk to your advisor, who may be able to point you in the right direction. It's also important to speak to your instructor, who more than likely has encountered many students with similar problems and may have some useful test-taking strategies.

If you find that you are experiencing significant test anxiety when taking a test or in the days leading up to it, talk to someone at your campus counseling center or health center. They can help you learn relaxation techniques and can provide counseling to help make your anxiety manageable.

IN PRINT

In *How to Ace Any Test* (Wiley, 2004), Beverley Chin provides a variety of techniques designed to improve your performance on any kind of test.

Eileen Tracy's *The Student's Guide to Exam Success* (Open University Press, 2006) gives an overview of strategies for test-taking success.

Finally, *Test Anxiety and What You Can Do About It* (National Professional Resources, 2005), by Joseph Casbarro is a professional guide to dealing with test anxiety, providing a variety of concrete suggestions.

ON THE WEB

The following sites on the World Wide Web provide opportunities to extend your learning about the material in this chapter. (Although the Web addresses were accurate at the time the book was printed, check the *P.O.W.E.R. Learning* Web site [**www.mhhe.com/power**] for any changes that may have occurred.)

➤ "The Multiple Choice Exam," an online handout from the University of Victoria's Learning Skills Program (**www.coun.uvic.ca/learning/exams/multiple-choice. html**), offers some valuable suggestions on how to approach multiple-choice exams. Several types of multiple-choice questions are described and strategies for answering them are explained. There are also helpful hints about what to look for in the wording of both the questions and the answer choices.

➤ "Simplified Plans of Action for Common Types of Question Words," another online handout from the University of Victoria's Learning Skills Program (**www.coun.uvic.ca/learning/essays/simple-answers.html**), gives examples of question words that are often found in essay assignments or in essay questions on exams. Possible "plans of action" for each of the question types are outlined. These outlines can be useful as a starting point for understanding how to approach essay questions.

➤ "Tactics for Managing Stress and Anxiety" (**www.coun.uvic.ca/personal/stress-anxiety.html**) offers several suggestions that you might find helpful in managing and reducing your level of stress and anxiety. The techniques may help you deal with test-related anxiety as well as academic anxiety in general. Not all of the techniques work for everyone. Try them and use the ones that work best for you.

TAKING IT TO THE NET

1 Seeing exams from other classes can help you get an idea of the kinds of questions that are often asked on exams. Use an Internet search engine to locate examples of exams from other colleges and universities. (One strategy would be to use the Google search engine—**www.google.com**—and type "examples of exams" [including the quotes] at the search prompt.) Look at several exams. How many of the questions on these exams were true–false? How many were multiple-choice? How many were essays?

2 Practice answering essay questions by comparing and contrasting the information different Web pages offer about the same topic. For example, go to AltaVista (**www.altavista.com/**) and enter the phrase "essay exams" (using quotes). Read the strategies for essay exams offered in the first two Web sites. Then write a paragraph describing the information both sites had in common, and another paragraph describing the information that was unique to each site.

[ANSWERS TO TEST ITEMS IN TRY IT 5
(ON PAGES 138–139)]

Multiple-choice: 1b, 2d, 3a

Matching: 1D, 2G, 3C, 4A, 5E, 6B, 7F

Fill-in: test anxiety, erasing

True–False: 1F, 2T, 3F, 4F, 5F, 6T

Short answer:

1. Possible answers include what the test is called, what will it cover, how many questions will be on it, how much time will it take, what kinds of questions will be on it, how will it be graded, will sample questions be provided, and are tests from prior terms available?

2. Academic honesty is completing and turning in only one's own work under one's own name.

Essay:

1. Strong essays would include a brief definition of a study group, followed by a discussion of the advantages of using study groups (including such things as helping to organize and structure material, providing different perspectives, and rethinking material). A mention of the disadvantages of study groups would also be reasonable.

2. After starting with a brief definition of academic honesty, the bulk of the answer should concentrate on the reasons why academic honesty is important and what are the drawbacks of academic dishonesty.

The Case of . . .
Too Many Questions, Too Little Time

There was no reason to panic, said Mia Varela to herself at the start of the test. The exam, a midterm in her Greek civilization class, contained 50 multiple-choice questions (each worth 1 point) and two short-answer essays (worth a total of 50 points). And she had 75 minutes to complete the test.

"Let's see," she said to herself. "At one and a half minutes per multiple-choice question, that would take 75 minutes. Hmm . . . that's no good. How about a minute for each one? Fifty minutes for the multiple-choice questions, leaving 25 minutes for the essays. That ought to work. I'll get the multiple-choice questions out of the way first."

But things didn't work out the way she planned. After an hour she had completed only 40 of the multiple-choice questions and hadn't even started on the essay questions. With only 15 minutes left, panic began to set in. She had trouble thinking. She began to be certain that she'd fail the test. She thought about how she hadn't studied enough. If only she'd worked harder. How could she explain this failure to her friends . . . to her parents . . . to herself? The thoughts kept coming, and time kept ticking away.

1. Is there evidence that Mia didn't study effectively for this type of test?

2. What was right about Mia's initial approach to the test?

3. What should Mia have done differently in calculating the amount of time to devote to each portion of the test? Why?

4. What should Mia have done to be aware of, and address, her timing problem sooner?

5. How should Mia have dealt with her panic? Were her thoughts productive or counterproductive? Why?

6. If you were in Mia's shoes, what would you do with only 15 minutes left in the test?

Learning Outcomes

By the time you finish this chapter you will be able to

» LO **6.1**   Explain how reading style and attention span affect reading.

» LO **6.2**   Identify how to improve concentration and read more effectively.

» LO **6.3**   Discuss how best to retain what you have read.

Building Your Reading Skills

"Read the first two chapters in your text by next Thursday."

"I've put three articles on reserve in the library. You'll need to have them read by our next class."

"Take a look at the first three Shakespeare sonnets in your book, and see if you can derive the major themes."

For Chris O'Hara, these reading assignments—handed down by different instructors on the same day in early October—felt like nails in his coffin. How was he supposed to finish all this reading in the next two days, in addition to studying for a Spanish test, writing a paper for history, and putting in eight hours at his part-time job?

Although the papers and tests were hard enough to deal with, it was the constant reading that was proving the most difficult challenge for Chris during his first term of college. He was a conscientious student who attempted to get everything done, but no matter how hard he tried, he just couldn't get everything read on time. When he pushed himself to read quicker and absorb more, he actually read and retained less. Thoughts about falling behind crowded out the meaning of whatever he was reading, and he had to go through the material all over again, slowing him down even more.

Looking Ahead

For students like Chris, reading assignments are the biggest challenge in college. The amount of required reading is often enormous. Even skilled readers may find themselves wishing they could read more quickly and effectively.

Fortunately, there are ways to improve your reading skills. In this chapter, we'll go over a number of strategies for reading more effectively. You'll assess your reading style and your attention span, consider what you should do before you even start reading an assignment, discover some ways of getting the most out of your reading, and learn how to retain what you've read.

» LO 6.1 Sharpen Your Reading Skills

What kind of reader are you? Ask yourself first of all about your reading *preferences:* What do you *like* to read, and why? What makes you pick up a book and start reading—and what makes you put one down?

Second, what's your reading *style?* Do you read at a comfortable pace and feel reasonably satisfied with how much you retain? Or do you plod through reading assignments, novels, and magazines and, like Chris, end up feeling that you're taking far too long? Perhaps you whip through chapters, devour books, and fly through the daily newspaper, but then find you can't recall the information as precisely as you'd like?

Before going any further, think about your own reading preferences by completing the **Journal Reflections,** and then consider your reading style—your characteristic way of approaching reading tasks—by completing **Try It 1** on the page 148.

Journal Reflections

My Reading Preferences

Think about what you like and don't like to read by answering these questions.

1. Do you read for pleasure? If so, what do you read (e.g., magazines, newspapers, novels, humor, short stories, nonfiction, illustrated books)?

2. What makes a book enjoyable? Have you ever read a book that you "couldn't put down"? If so, what made it so good?

3. What is the most difficult book you are reading this semester? Why is it difficult? Are you enjoying it?

4. Think about when you read for pleasure compared to when you read material for a class. How does the way you read differ between the two types of material?

5. Do you think there should be a difference between reading for pleasure and reading for a class? Why?

Read for Retention, Not Speed

You may have come across advertisements on the Web promoting reading "systems" that promise to teach you to read so quickly that you'll be reading entire books in an hour and whizzing through assigned readings in a few minutes.

Unfortunately it's not going to happen. For one thing, certain biological facts relating to the eye movements involved in reading simply prevent people from reading (and ultimately comprehending) so rapidly. Research has shown that claims of speed reading are simply groundless; it is unlikely that any system will overcome the built-in limitations of the human eye.

But even if it were physically possible to read a book in an hour, ultimately it probably doesn't matter very much. If we read too fast, comprehension and ultimately retention plunge. Reading is not a race, and the fastest readers are not necessarily the best readers.

The act of reading is designed to increase our knowledge and open up new ways of thinking. It can help us achieve new levels of understanding and get us to think more broadly about the world and its inhabitants. Speed matters far less than what we take away from what we've read. That's not to say we shouldn't try to become more efficient readers who comprehend and recall more effectively. Ultimately, though, the key to good reading is understanding—not speed.

1

Discover Your Reading Style

Use the following questions to learn *how* you read—that is, your characteristic reading style. Rate how well each statement below describes you. Use this rating scale:

1 = Doesn't describe me at all

2 = Describes me only slightly

3 = Describes me fairly well

4 = Describes me very well

	1	2	3	4
1. I often reread passages in books that I particularly like.				
2. I often read good passages aloud to whoever is around.				
3. I often stop while reading to check that I understood what I just read.				
4. If I come across a long, unfamiliar name, I try to sound it out and pronounce it correctly.				
5. If there's a word I don't understand, I look it up in a dictionary right away or mark it so I can look it up later.				
6. Before I start reading a textbook or other serious book or article, I look for clues about how it is organized.				
7. I often question what I'm reading and "argue" with the author.				
8. I often try to guess what the chapter I'm about to read will cover.				
9. I often write comments or make notes in books that I own.				
10. I'm always finding typographical errors in books and articles I read.				

Reading styles range from a very holistic (i.e., broad-brushstroke, noncritical) style to a very analytic (i.e., detailed, critical) style. Add up the points you assigned yourself. Use this informal scale to find your reading style:

10–12 = Very holistic reading style

13–20 = Mostly holistic reading style

21–28 = Mostly analytic reading style

29–40 = Very analytic reading style

How do you think your reading style affects the way you learn material in textbooks? Is your style related to the kinds of subjects you prefer? Do you think your reading style affects your leisure reading?

To Try It online, go to www.mhhe.com/power.

In describing how you can use the principles of P.O.W.E.R. Learning to become a better reader, we'll focus on the type of reading that is typically called for in academic pursuits—textbook chapters, articles, handouts, and the like. However, the same principles will help you get more benefit and enjoyment out of your recreational reading as well.

P Prepare | Approaching the Written Word

Preparation to begin reading isn't hard, and it won't take very long, but it's a crucial first step in applying P.O.W.E.R. Learning (summarized in the P.O.W.E.R. Plan on the right). Your aim in preparation is to become familiar with **advance organizers**—outlines, overviews, section objectives, or other clues to the meaning and organization of new material—provided in the material you are reading. Most textbooks have them built in; for an example, look at the start of every chapter in this book, which includes a chapter outline, plus a set of questions at the end of the "Looking Ahead" section. You can also create your own advance organizers by skimming material to be read and sketching out the general outline of the material you'll be reading.

Advance organizers pave the way for subsequent learning. They help you tie information that you already know to new material you're about to encounter. Ultimately, they can help us recall material better after we've read it.

In short, the more we're able to make use of advance organizers and our own prior knowledge and experiences, the better we can understand and retain new material. (To prove the value of advance organizers, complete **Try It 2** on page 150, "Discover How Advance Organizers Help.")

What's the Point of the Reading Assignment?

Before you begin an assignment, think about what your goal is. Will you be reading a textbook on which you'll be thoroughly tested? Is your reading supposed to provide background information that will serve as a context for future learning but that won't itself be tested? Is the material going to be useful to you personally? Realistically, how much time can you devote to the reading assignment?

Your goal for reading will help you determine which reading strategy to adopt. You aren't expected to read everything with the same degree of intensity. Some material you may feel comfortable skimming; for other material you'll want to put in the maximum effort.

Understand the Point of View of the Material Itself

What are you reading—a textbook, an essay, an article? If it is an essay or article, why was it written? To prove a point? To give information? To express the author's personal feelings? Knowing the author's purpose (even if his or her specific point and message aren't yet clear) can help you a great deal as you read.

Start with the Frontmatter

If you'll be using a text or other book extensively throughout the term, start by reading the preface and/or introduction and scanning the table of contents—what publishers call the **frontmatter.** Instructors often don't formally assign the frontmatter, but reading it can be a big help because it is there that the author has a chance to step forward and explain, often more personally than elsewhere in an academic book, what he or she considers important. Knowing this will give you a sense of what to expect as you read.

By reading the frontmatter, you can get inside the author's head, obtaining insight into the author's goals, values, and strategies in writing the book. You might

Advance organizers
Broad, general ideas related to material that is to be read or heard, which pave the way for subsequent learning

P.O.W.E.R. Plan

Frontmatter
The preface, introduction, and table of contents of a book

Try It!

2

Discover How Advance Organizers Help

Read this passage. What do you think it means?

The procedure is actually quite simple. First you arrange items into different groups. Of course, one pile may be sufficient, depending on how much there is to do. If you have to go somewhere else due to lack of facilities, that is the next step; otherwise, you are pretty well set. It is important not to overdo things. That is, it is better to do too few things at once than too many. In the short run this may not seem important but complications can easily arise. A mistake can be expensive as well. At first, the whole procedure will seem complicated. Soon, however, it will become just another facet of life. It is difficult to foresee any end to the necessity for this task in the immediate future, but then one can never tell. After the procedure is completed, one arranges the materials into different groups again. Then they can be put into their appropriate places. Eventually, they will be used once more and the whole cycle will then have to be repeated. However, this is a part of life.[1]

If you're like most people, you don't have a clue about what this all means. But suppose you had been given some context in advance, and you knew before reading it that the description had to do with washing laundry. Now does it all fall into place? Read the passage once more, and see how having an advance organizer (in this case, *washing laundry*) helps out.

To Try It online, go to www.mhhe.com/power.

also find information about the author's background, and perhaps even a photo. Use this material to "personalize" the author, to gain some insight into the kind of person he or she is. The information you obtain from the frontmatter will provide a mental "hook" on which you can hang the new ideas to which you'll be exposed. (For practice with frontmatter, do **Try It 3.**)

Create Advance Organizers

To provide a context for your reading, create your own advance organizers by skimming through the table of contents, which provides the main headings of what you will be reading. Textbooks often have chapter outlines, listing the key topics to be covered, which also provide a way of previewing the chapter content. As you read over the outline, you can begin to consider how the new material in the book may relate both to what you know and to what you expect to learn—from the reading assignment itself and from the course.

Textbooks also often have end-of-chapter summaries, and many articles include a final section in which the author states his or her conclusions. Take a look at these ending sections as well. Even though you haven't read the material yet and the summary probably won't make complete sense to you, by reading the summary, you'll get an idea of what the author covers and what is important.

Your instructor may also provide an advance organizer for readings. Sometimes instructors will mention things to pay particular attention to or to look for, such as "When you read Thomas Paine's *Common Sense,* notice how he lays out his argument and what his key points are." Sometimes they will say why they assigned a reading. Such information provides clues that can help you develop a mental list of the reading's key ideas.

However you construct advance organizers, be sure they provide a framework and context for what you'll be reading; this framework and context can spell the difference between fully comprehending what you read and misunderstanding it.

Now it's time to put all this practice to good use. Create an advance organizer for a textbook chapter in **Try It 4** on page 152.

Read the Frontmatter

Have you read the frontmatter of *this* book? Go there now. If you've already read it, review it. If you haven't, read it now. Then answer the following questions:

What are the goals of this book?

Who is the author, and what qualifies him to write this book?

Do you think the author has an understanding of students?

Do you think the author has an understanding of what students should do to become successful in their studies?

Is there anything in the frontmatter that made you curious? Does anything seem particularly interesting?

After reading the frontmatter, do you feel confident that you can learn what the author wants to teach? Do you feel that you *want* to learn it?

To Try It online, go to **www.mhhe.com/power**.

Organize ## Gathering the Tools of the Trade

It's obvious that the primary item you'll need to complete a reading assignment is the material that you're reading. But there are other essential tools you should gather, potentially including the following:

> Pencils or pens to write notes in the margin.

> Highlighters to indicate key passages in the text.

> A copy of the assignment, so you'll be sure to read the right material.

> A pad of paper and/or index cards for notetaking if the material is particularly complex. If you routinely use a word processor to take notes, get it ready.

> A dictionary. You never know what new words you'll encounter while you're reading. If a dictionary is not handy, you'll be tempted to skip over unfamiliar words—a decision that may come back to haunt you. Note that some word-processing software includes a dictionary; there are also many good dictionaries available online (e.g., Merriam-Webster's at **www.m-w.com,** where you will also find an online thesaurus). The point is to use what's available—but use something!

Try It!

Create an Advance Organizer

Use any information you have available to create an advance organizer for a chapter in a text that you are using this term. Skim the section headings in the chapter, read the chapter summary, consult the book's frontmatter, and recall anything your instructor may have said about the chapter.

Complete the following statements to prepare your organizer:

The general topics that are covered in the chapter are . . .

The most critical topics and concepts in the chapter are . . .

The most difficult material in the chapter includes . . .

Words, phrases, and ideas that are unfamiliar to me include . . .

Ways that the material in this chapter relate to other material that I've previously read in the text include . . .

Use this Try It as a starting point for advance organizers for future chapters in the book.

To Try It online, go to www.mhhe.com/power.

Give Yourself Time

There's one more thing you need to prepare successfully for a reading assignment: enough time to complete it. The length of reading assignments is almost never ambiguous. You will typically be given a specific page range, so you will know just how much material you will need to cover.

Now get a watch and time yourself as you read the first three pages of your assignment, being sure to pay attention to the material, not the time! Timing how long it takes to read a representative chunk of material provides you with a rough measure of your reading speed for the material—although it will vary even within a single reading assignment, depending on the complexity of the material.

You'll also need to consider an aspect of your personal learning style: your reading attention span. **Attention span** is the length of time that a person usually is able to sustain attention. People with long attention spans can read for relatively lengthy periods without getting jumpy, while those with shorter ones can only maintain attention for a short while. You can get a general sense of this by using **Try It 5,** "Discover Your Attention Span."

Use the three pieces of information you now have—the length of the assignment, your per-page reading speed at full attention, and your typical attention span—to estimate roughly how long it will take you to complete the reading

Attention span
The length of time that attention is typically sustained

Try It! POWER

5

Discover Your Attention Span

You should be aware of your attention span, the length of time you usually are able to sustain attention to a task, as you prepare for reading assignments. To get an idea of the length of your current attention span for reading, perform this exercise over the next few days.

1. Choose one of the textbooks that you've been assigned to read this semester.
2. Start reading a chapter, without any preparation, noting in the chart below the time that you start reading.
3. As soon as your mind begins to wander and think about other subjects, stop reading and note the time on the chart below.
4. Using the same textbook, repeat this process four more times over the course of a few days, entering the data on the chart below.
5. To find your reading attention span, calculate the average number of minutes across the five trials.

Trial #1   Starting time: _____   Ending time: _____

                  Number of minutes between start and end times: _____

Trial #2   Starting time: _____   Ending time: _____

                  Number of minutes between start and end times: _____

Trial #3   Starting time: _____   Ending time: _____

                  Number of minutes between start and end times: _____

Trial #4   Starting time: _____   Ending time: _____

                  Number of minutes between start and end times: _____

Trial #5   Starting time: _____   Ending time: _____

                  Number of minutes between start and end times: _____

Reading attention span (the average of the number of minutes in the last column, found by adding up the five numbers and dividing by 5) = _____ minutes

---

Ask yourself these questions about your reading attention span:

1. Are you surprised by the length of your reading attention span? In what way?
2. Does any number in the set of trials stand out from the other numbers? For instance, is any number much higher or lower than the average? If so, can you account for this? For example, what time of day was it?
3. Do the numbers in your trials show any trend? For instance, did your attention span tend to increase slightly over the course of the trials, did it decrease, or did it stay about the same? Can you explain any trend you may have noted?
4. Do you think your attention span times would be very different if you had chosen a different textbook? Why or why not?
5. What things might you do to improve your attention span?

To Try It online, go to www.mhhe.com/power.

assignment. For example, if you are asked to read 12 pages, you have found that you need approximately 4 minutes to read a page, and your reading attention span is, on average, 25 minutes long, you can expect your reading to take at least 60 minutes, assuming you'll take a short break when your attention begins to fade after 25 minutes.

In addition, you may need to interrupt your reading to look up words in the dictionary, get a drink, stretch, or answer the phone. You may also decide to break your reading into several short sessions, in which case your total reading time may be greater since you will have to get reacquainted with the reading assignment each time you sit down again.

» LO 6.2 ⬛ **W Work** ## Getting the Most Out of Your Reading

Finally, it's time to get down to work and start reading.

Obviously—because it's what you're doing at this very moment—you know how to read. But what's important is what you do while you're reading. Here are several things that will help you get the most out of the process of reading:

Stay Focused

The TV show you watched last night . . . your boyfriend forgetting to meet you at the bus stop . . . the replacement toothbrush you need to buy tomorrow . . . your grumbling stomach. There are a million and one possible distractions that can invade your thoughts as you read. Your job is to keep distracting thoughts at bay and focus on the material you are supposed to be reading. It's not easy, but there are things you can do to help yourself stay focused:

> **Read in small bites.** If you think it is going to take you 4 hours to read an entire chapter, break up the 4 hours into more manageable time periods. Promise yourself that you'll read for 1 hour in the afternoon, another hour in the evening, and the next 2 hours spaced out during the following day. One hour of reading is far more manageable than a 4-hour block.

> **Give yourself enough time.** If you plan to read a chapter of a book during a study session, make sure you check out how long the chapter is beforehand. Some book chapters are 24 pages in length; others are double that. Make sure you leave yourself enough time.

> **Take a break.** Actually, plan to take several short breaks to reward yourself while you're reading. During your break, do something enjoyable—eat a snack, watch a bit of a ball game on television, play a video game, or the like. Just try not to get drawn into your break activity to the point that it takes over your reading time.

> **Deal with mental distractions.** Sometimes problems have a way of popping into our minds and repeatedly distracting us. If a particular problem keeps

interrupting your concentration—such as a difficulty you're having on the job—try to think of an action-oriented strategy to deal with it. You might even write your proposed solution down on a piece of paper. Putting it down in words can get the problem off your mind, potentially making it less intrusive.

> **Manage interruptions.** You can't stop your roommate from receiving a cell phone call or—if you are a student who is also a parent—you can't prevent your children from getting a cut and needing immediate attention. But there are some things you can do to reduce interruptions and their consequences. For instance, you can schedule reading to coincide with periods when you know you'll be alone. You can also plan to read less critical parts of assignments (such as the summaries or book frontmatter) when distractions are more likely, saving the heavier reading for later. Or, if you are a parent with small children, you can get your child involved in an activity that they can perform independently.

If you are reading a long assignment, taking a break can be a reward and reinvigorate you.

Write While You Read

Writing is one of the most important aspects of reading. If you haven't underlined, jotted notes to yourself, placed check marks on the page, drawn arrows, constructed diagrams, and otherwise defaced and disfigured your book while you're reading, you're not doing your job as a P.O.W.E.R. reader.

The idea of writing on a book page may go against everything you've been taught in the past. (And of course you should never write on a library book or one that you've borrowed.)

However, once you've bought your book, *you own it and you should make it your own.* Don't keep your textbooks spotless so they will fetch a higher price if you sell them later. Instead, think of textbooks as documents recording your active learning and engagement in a field of study. In addition, you should look at your textbooks as the foundation of your personal library, which will grow throughout your lifetime. In short, writing extensively in your book while you're reading is an important tactic for achieving success.

The ability to add your own personal notes, underlining, and other annotations to a clean text while you're reading is one of the reasons it usually pays to buy new, rather than used, textbooks. Why would you want a stranger's comments on something you own? Can you really trust that person's judgment over your own regarding what's important to underline? New books allow you to mark them up in your own, personal style, without the distraction of competing voices.

However, before you start writing in your textbook, make sure you've bought the correct one. Look at each syllabus from your classes to ensure you've bought the appropriate text in the right edition. Sometimes there are multiple sections of a course, and each section uses a different text. Be sure the book you've bought matches the description in the syllabus.

Once you're sure you have the right book, make it your own. Write your name, e-mail address, and/or telephone number in the front of the book. If you misplace your book during the term, you want the person who finds it to be able to return it to you. It's also a good idea to orient yourself to each of your textbooks. Take a quick look at each of the books, examining the table of contents, introduction, and/ or preface (as we discussed earlier). Get a sense of the content and the general reading level of the book. Finally, get yourself online. Many textbooks contain a card or insert with a password that gives you access to online material. Follow the directions and enter the book's Web site, making sure the password allows you to register. If you have trouble making the site work, call the tech support number that should be included with the password.

After all this preliminary work, it's time to get started actually reading your text. What should you be writing while you are reading? There are several things you should write down:

> **Rephrase key points.** Make notes to yourself, in your own words, about what the author is trying to get across. Don't just copy what's been said. Think about the material, and rewrite it in words that are your own.

Writing notes to yourself in your own words has several consequences, all good. First, you make the material yours; it becomes something you now understand and part of your own knowledge base.

Second, trying to summarize a key point in your own words will make it very clear whether you truly understand it. It's easy to be fooled into thinking we understand something as we're reading along. But the true test is whether we can explain it to ourselves (or someone else) on our own, without referring to the book or article.

Third, the very act of writing engages an additional type of perception—involving the physical sense of moving a pen or pressing a keyboard. This will help you learn the material in a more active way.

Finally, writing notes and phrases will help you study the material later. Not only will the key points be highlighted, but your notes will also quickly bring you up to speed regarding your initial thoughts and impressions.

> **Highlight or underline key points.** Very often the first or last sentence in a paragraph, or the first or last paragraph in a section, will present a key point. (Remember those lessons about "topic sentences" you had in high school English classes? Writers really use them.)

Before you highlight anything, though, read the whole paragraph through. Then you'll be sure that what you highlight is, in fact, the key information. Topic sentences do not always fall at the beginning of a paragraph.

Be selective in your highlighting and underlining. A page covered in yellow highlighter may be artistically appealing, but it won't help you understand the material any better. Highlight only the key information. You might find yourself highlighting only one or two sentences or phrases per page. That's fine. *In highlighting and underlining, less is more.* One guideline: No more than 10 percent of the material should be highlighted or underlined.

If you want to use different-colored highlighters, that's fine, but be consistent in their use. For instance, some people use one color for important material that they already understand, and another for particularly difficult information.

> **Use arrows, diagrams, outlines, tables, timelines, charts, and other visuals to help you understand and later recall what you are reading.** If there are three examples given for a particular point, number them. If a paragraph discusses a situation in which an earlier point does not hold, link the original point to the exception by an arrow. If a sequence of steps is presented, number each step.

For example, after you have annotated *this* page of *P.O.W.E.R. Learning,* it might look something like what is shown in **Figure 6.1.**

Particularly if your learning style is a visual one, representing the material graphically will get you thinking about it—and the connections and points in it—in new and different ways. Rather than considering the material insert with a password that gives you access to online material. Follow the directions and enter the book's Web site, making sure the password allows you to register. If you have trouble making the site work, call the tech support number that should be included with the password.

After all this preliminary work, it's time to get started actually reading your text. What should you be writing while you are reading? There are several things you should write down:

> **Rephrase key points.** Make notes to yourself, in your own words, about what the author is trying to get across. Don't just copy what's been said. Think about the material, and rewrite it in words that are your own.

Writing notes to yourself in your own words has several consequences, all good. First, you make the material yours; it becomes something you now understand and part of your own knowledge base.

Second, trying to summarize a key point in your own words will make it very clear whether you truly understand it. It's easy to be fooled into thinking we understand something as we're reading along. But the true test is whether we can explain it to ourselves (or someone else) on our own, without referring to the book or article.

Third, the very act of writing engages an additional type of perception—involving the physical sense of moving a pen or pressing a keyboard. This will help you learn the material in a more active way.

Finally, writing notes and phrases will help you study the material later. Not only will the key points be highlighted, but your notes will also quickly bring you up to speed regarding your initial thoughts and impressions.

(1)
Use highlighter but less is more

Not more than 10% highlighted

Topic sentence

> **Highlight or underline key points.** Very often the first or last sentence in a paragraph, or the first or last paragraph in a section, will present a key point. (Remember those lessons about "topic sentences" you had in high school English classes? Writers really use them.)

Before you highlight anything, though, read the whole paragraph through. Then you'll be sure that what you highlight is, in fact, the key information. Topic sentences do not always fall at the beginning of a paragraph.

Be selective in your highlighting and underlining. A page covered in yellow highlighter may be artistically appealing, but it won't help you understand the material any better. Highlight only the key information. You might find yourself highlighting only one or two sentences or phrases per page. That's fine. *In highlighting and underlining, less is more.* One guideline: No more than 10 percent of the material should be highlighted or underlined.

If you want to use different-colored highlighters, that's fine, but be consistent in their use. For instance, some people use one color for important material that they already understand, and another for particularly difficult information.

(2)
> **Use arrows, diagrams, outlines, tables, timelines, charts, and other visuals to help you understand and later recall what you are reading.** If there are three examples given for a particular point, number them. If a paragraph discusses a situation in which an earlier point does not hold, link the original point to the exception by an arrow. If a sequence of steps is presented, number each step.

Use visuals →

For example, after you have annotated *this* page of *P.O.W.E.R. Learning,* it might look something like what is shown in **Figure 6.1.**

Particularly if your learning style is a visual one, representing the material graphically will get you thinking about it—and the connections and points in it—in new and different ways. Rather than considering the material

figure 6.1
Sample of Annotated Page

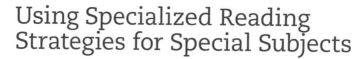

Course
Connections

Using Specialized Reading Strategies for Special Subjects

Although the approaches to reading we've been discussing cut across different subject areas, certain disciplines warrant specialized strategies. Consider the following:

- **Reading mathematics texts.** With their many formulas, math books can be especially intimidating. Although it may be tempting to skip over the formulas, that's a mistake. Look at them, think about them, annotate them, and make them concrete by substituting actual numbers for abstract letters.

- **Reading in a foreign language.** Use of a dictionary may be a big help when reading in a foreign language. But don't rely on it too much: If you can't remember the meaning of a word, first try to figure out what is being said from the context, and only then look it up. Also keep in mind this fundamental rule of language study: The more you immerse yourself in a language, the easier it will become.

- **Reading in the sciences.** Science textbooks can be daunting. Not only are they dense with words, but they include equations, tables, and graphs. As you are reading, make sure you understand the variables and equations that support the written word. Even the photos can be important and need to be studied.

  Be aware that the scientific method is the basis for much writing about scientific topics. In particular, scientists conduct experiments to support hypotheses, specific predictions that are derived from a theory. When reading about scientific research, try to identify the hypothesis that is being tested and what alternative hypotheses might be used.

- **Reading history texts.** History textbooks often include long, complex chapters. Before reading a chapter, pay particular attention to the chapter headings to get an overview of what is covered. Look at any maps, which will help you orient yourself to the chapter content. As you read a chapter, don't think of it in terms of a collection of dates and facts. Instead, think of larger trends and themes. Then you can use those trends and themes to organize dates and facts.

solely in verbal terms, you now add visual images. The act of creating visual annotations will not only help you understand the material better but also ease its later recall. Practice this technique on the sample textbook page in **Try It 6** on page 160.

> **Look up unfamiliar words in a dictionary.** Even though you may be able to figure out the meaning of an unfamiliar word from its context, use a dictionary anyway. This way you can be sure that what you think it means is correct. A dictionary will also tell you what the word sounds like, which may be important if your instructor uses the word in class. (Also see the accompanying **Course Connections** for more reading strategies.)

> **Use your own reading system.** If you've already learned a reading system in the past and it works for you, use it. Many students know the *SQ3R* method, which consists of five steps, designated by the initials *S-Q-R-R-R*. The first step is to *survey,* in which you give yourself an overview of the major points of the material. The next step is to *question.* Formulate questions about the material—either aloud or in writing—prior to actually reading a section of text. In the next step, *read* the material carefully and, even more important, actively and critically. While you are reading, answer the questions you have asked yourself. Critically evaluate material by considering the implications of what you are reading. The *recite* step involves describing

and explaining to yourself the material you have just read and answering the questions you have posed earlier. Finally, *review* the material, looking it over, reading end-of-chapter summaries, and answering the in-text review questions.

In addition to *SQ3R*, you can also make up your own system. The truth is that it doesn't really matter what system you use. What does matter is that you're systematic in the work of reading.

Dealing with Learning Disabilities

If you, like millions of people in the United States, have a learning disability of one sort or another, reading may prove to be particularly challenging. **Learning disabilities** are defined as difficulties in processing information when listening, speaking, reading, or writing; in most cases, learning disabilities are diagnosed when there is a discrepancy between learning potential and actual academic achievement.

One of the most common kinds of learning disabilities is *dyslexia,* a reading disability that produces the misperception of letters during reading and writing, unusual difficulty in sounding out letters, spelling difficulties, and confusion between right and left. Although its causes are not yet completely understood, one likely explanation is a problem in the part of the brain responsible for breaking words into the sound elements that make up language.

Another common disability is *attention deficit hyperactivity disorder* (or *ADHD*), which is marked by an inability to concentrate, inattention, and a low tolerance for frustration. For the 1 to 3 percent of college students and other adults who have ADHD, planning, staying on task, and maintaining interest present unusual challenges. These challenges are not only present in college but also affect job performance.

People with learning disabilities are sometimes viewed as unintelligent. Nothing could be further from the truth: There is no relationship between learning disabilities and I.Q. For instance, dozens of well-known and highly accomplished individuals suffered from dyslexia, including physicist Albert Einstein, U.S. General George Patton, poet William Butler Yeats, and—as we discuss in the **Speaking of Success** feature—writer John Irving.

By the time they reach college, most people with learning disabilities have already been diagnosed. If you do have a diagnosed learning disability and you need special services, it is important to disclose your situation to your instructors and other college officials.

In some cases, students with learning disabilities have not been appropriately evaluated prior to college. If you have difficulties such as mixing up and reversing letters frequently and suspect that you have a learning disability, there usually is an office on campus that can provide you with guidance. One place to start is your college counseling or health center.

Many sorts of treatments, ranging from learning specific study strategies to the use of medication, can be effective in dealing with learning disabilities. In addition, colleges that accept support from the federal government have a legal obligation to provide people with diagnosed learning disabilities with appropriate support. This obligation is spelled out in the Americans with Disabilities Act, and it provides important legal protections.

Learning disabilities
Difficulties in processing information when listening, speaking, reading, or writing, characterized by a discrepancy between learning potential and actual academic achievement

POWER Try It!

WORKING IN A GROUP

Mark Up a Book Page

6

First, working alone, read the excerpt in **Figure 6.2** on the opposite page. Then use the techniques we've discussed for marking up a page to highlight its key points.

Next, working in a group, compare and contrast your annotations with those of some classmates, and answer the following questions:

1. How do others' annotations differ from yours?

2. Why did they use the annotations they did?

3. Which annotation techniques worked best for you? Which did others prefer? Why?

4. How might these annotations help you to remember what is important?

5. If there were different sorts of material presented on the page, such as mathematical formulas, would you use different kinds of annotations?

To Try It online, go to www.mhhe.com/power.

The more parents speak to their children, the better their children's language skills.

Understanding Language Acquisition: Identifying the Roots of Language

Anyone who spends even a little time with children will notice the enormous strides that they make in language development throughout childhood. However, the reasons for this rapid growth are far from obvious. Two major explanations have been offered: one based on learning theory and the other on innate processes.

The **learning-theory approach** suggests that language acquisition follows the principles of reinforcement and conditioning discussed in Chapter 6. For example, a child who utters the word "mama" is hugged and praised by her mother, which reinforces the behavior and makes its repetition more likely. This view suggests that children first learn to speak by being rewarded for making sounds that approximate speech. Ultimately, through a process of shaping, language becomes more and more like adult speech (Skinner, 1957).

The learning theory approach is supported by research that shows that the more parents speak to their young children, the more proficient the children become in language usage (see Figure 8-11). In addition, higher levels of linguistic sophistication in parents' speech to their young children are related to a greater rate of vocabulary growth, vocabulary usage, and even general intellectual achievement by the time the children are 3 years of age (Hart & Risley, 1997).

On the other hand, the learning theory approach is less successful when it comes to explaining the acquisition of language rules. Children are reinforced not only when they use proper language, but also when they respond incorrectly. For example, parents answer the child's "Why the dog won't eat?" as readily as they do the correctly phrased question "Why won't the dog eat?" Both sentences are understood equally well. Learning theory, then, has difficulty in providing the full explanation for language acquisition.

Pointing to such problems with learning theory approaches to language acquisition, Noam Chomsky (1968, 1978, 1991), a linguist, provided a ground-breaking alternative. Chomsky argued that humans are born with an innate linguistic capability that emerges primarily as a function of maturation. According to his analysis, all the world's languages share a similar underlying structure called a **universal grammar.** Chomsky suggests that the human brain has a neural system, the **language-acquisition device,** that both permits the understanding of the structure of language and provides strategies and techniques for learning the unique characteristics of a given native language.

learning-theory approach: The theory suggesting that language acquisition follows the principles of reinforcement and conditioning

universal grammar: Noam Chomsky's theory that all the world's languages share a similar underlying structure

language-acquisition device: A neural system of the brain hypothesized to permit understanding of language

figure 6.2
Sample Page to Annotate

However, just because you are having trouble with reading assignments doesn't automatically mean that you have a learning disability. Not only is the kind of reading you do in college more difficult than what you did in high school, but there's also more of it. It's only when reading represents a persistent, long-term problem—one that won't go away no matter how much work you do—that a learning disability becomes a possible explanation.

»LO 6.3 🄴 Evaluate   What Does It Mean? What Do I Know?

Evaluation is a crucial step in reading. You need to be able to answer the seemingly simple question: "What does all this mean?"

But there's another aspect to evaluation. You need to evaluate, truthfully and honestly, your own level of understanding. What do you know as a result of your reading? Evaluation, then, consists of the following steps:

> **Identify the main ideas and themes and their value *to you personally*.** Try to determine the take-home message of the material you've read. For example, the take-home message of a chapter of an American history text might be, "Although Abraham Lincoln eventually called for the end of slavery, initially he was hesitant because of political considerations."
>
> Sometimes the main ideas and themes are spelled out, and at other times you will have to deduce them for yourself. Evaluating the main ideas and themes in terms of how they relate to you personally will help you understand and remember them more easily.

> **Prioritize the ideas.** Of all the information that is presented, which is the most crucial to the main message and which is the least crucial? Make a list of the main topics covered and try to rank them in order of importance.

> **Think critically about the arguments presented in the reading.** Do they seem to make sense? Are the author's assertions reasonable? Are there any flaws in the arguments? Would authors with a different point of view dispute what is being said? How would they build their own arguments?

> **Pretend you are explaining the material (talking—out loud!—about the material) to a fellow classmate who missed the assignment.** This is one time when talking out loud when no one is around is not only normal, but beneficial. Summarize the material aloud, as if you were talking to another person.
>
> Talking out loud does two things. First, it helps you identify weak spots in your understanding. Talking to yourself will help you nail down concepts that are still not clear in your own mind. Second, and equally important, because you are transforming the written word into the spoken word, you are thinking about the information in another way, which will help you remember it better.

> **Be honest with yourself.** Most of us are able to read with our minds on cruise control. But the net result is not much different from not reading the passage at all. If you have drifted off while you've been reading, go back and reread the passage.

> **Pat yourself on the back.** Just as you've done during each of your reading breaks, reward yourself for completing the reading passage. But keep in mind that there's one more step before you can really relax, and it's a crucial one: rethinking what you've read.

The Job of Reading

Memos. Annual reports. Instructions. Continuing education assignments. Professional journals.

Each of these items illustrates the importance of developing critical reading skills for on-the-job success. Virtually every job requires good reading expertise, and for some professions, reading is a central component. Polishing your reading skills now will pay big dividends when you enter the world of work. The better you are at absorbing written information, the better you'll be at carrying out your job.

For instance, in many corporations, vital information is transmitted through the written word, via e-mails, hard-copy memos, technical reports, or Web-based material. The person who repairs your broken washing machine or automobile has probably read numerous service manuals while attending continuing education classes required to master the complex computer diagnostic systems that are now standard equipment. The physician who gives you a physical may have taken an online distance learning class that required reading about the newest medical technologies. And every one of your college instructors probably spends hours each month reading about the newest developments in his or her field.

Furthermore, because not all supervisors are effective writers, you'll sometimes need to read between the lines and draw inferences and conclusions about what you need to do. You should also keep in mind that there are significant cultural differences in the way in which people write and the type of language they use. Being sensitive to the cultural background of colleagues will permit you to more accurately interpret and understand what you are reading.

In short, reading is a skill that's required in virtually every profession. Developing the habit of reading critically while you are in college will pave the road for future career success.

R Rethink ## Getting It the Second Time

You're human, so—like the rest of us—when you finish a reading assignment you'd probably like nothing more than to heave a sigh of relief and put the book away.

By now you know that there's a crucial step you should take that will assist you in cementing what you've learned into memory: rethinking what you've read. If you do it within 24 hours of first reading the assignment, it can save you hours of work later.

The best way to rethink an assignment is to reread it, along with any notes you've taken. "Yeah, right," you're probably thinking. "Like I have time for that." The goal, though, is not a literal rereading. In fact, it isn't necessary to reread word for word. You already know what's important and what's not important, so you can skim some of the less important material. But it is wise to reread the more difficult and important material carefully, making sure that you fully understand what is being discussed and why.

What's most critical, though, is that you think deeply about the material, considering the take-home message of what you've read. You need to be sure that your understanding is complete and that you're able to answer any questions that you had earlier about the material. Rethinking should be the central activity as you reread the passage and your notes.

> "Reading furnishes the mind only with materials of knowledge; it is thinking that makes what we read ours."
>
> John Locke, author, *Of the Conduct of the Understanding*, 1706

The benefits of rethinking the material can't be overstated. Rethinking transfers material from your short-term memory to your long-term memory. It solidifies information so that it will be remembered far better over the long haul.

The Concept Map as a Rethinking Tool

Concept mapping
A method of structuring written material by graphically grouping and connecting key ideas and themes

As we saw in Chapter 4, **concept mapping** is a method of structuring written material by graphically grouping and connecting key ideas and themes. Each key idea is placed in a different part of the map, and related ideas are placed near it—above, below, or beside it. A concept map looks similar to a graphic of the solar system, with the central idea (the sun) in the center, surrounded by related concepts (the planets).

Concept maps help you to rethink material you've read about, especially if you have used a more traditional outline earlier. Furthermore, once you have developed a concept map for a particular aspect of the material, you can create additional, expanded concept maps involving related information.

Concept maps are particularly useful for people with learning styles that depend on spatial relationships. Furthermore, students with certain kinds of learning disabilities—a topic we discussed earlier in this chapter—can also benefit from the use of concept maps.

An example of a concept map involving the material we've discussed so far is illustrated in **Figure 6.3.** Note how it summarizes the material and shows how it is related to the central topic of "Reading with Understanding."

figure 6.3
A Concept Map Illustrating the Key Ideas of Reading with Understanding

Speaking of **Success**

NAME: **John Irving**

SCHOOL: **University of New Hampshire**

The author of such novels as *The World According to Garp* and *The Cider House Rules,* John Irving is one of America's foremost storytellers. But his road to success was not always smooth, particularly because he suffers from the learning disability dyslexia, which makes both reading and writing difficult.

While attending Exeter Academy, his high school, Irving knew something was wrong. But in the 1950s, there was little known about learning disabilities. "I was a mediocre student—as it turned out, I was dyslexic, but no one knew this at the time,"[2] Irving noted. "To say that Exeter was hard for me is an understatement. I was the only student in my genetics class who failed to control his fruit-fly experiment. The Red Eyes and the White Eyes were interbreeding so rapidly that I lost track of the generations."

While at Exeter, Irving developed a love of wrestling, which became an important part of his life. As a member of the wrestling team, he learned from his coach how he could compensate for his shortcomings as an athlete: by being dedicated. "Talent is overrated," said his coach. "That you're not very talented needn't be the end of it. . . . An underdog is in a position to take a healthy bite."

Irving continued, "This was a concept of myself that I'd been lacking. I was an underdog; therefore, I had to control the pace—of everything. . . . The concept was applicable to my creative writing—to all my schoolwork, too.

"If my classmates could read our history assignments in an hour, I allowed myself two or three. If I couldn't learn to spell, I would keep a list of many most frequently misspelled words, and I kept the list with me; I had it handy even for unannounced quizzes," Irving said.

Irving's hard work and dedication permitted him to overcome his learning disability. Ultimately, he became one of the most prominent authors of our time. To what does he attribute his success? "Writing is one-eighth talent and seven-eighths discipline," he believes.

Looking Back

How do my reading styles and attention span affect my reading?

> The most important aspect of reading is understanding, not speed. People have different reading styles that can be modified to improve their ability to read with understanding.

> One problem people have with reading is a limited attention span. However, attention span can be increased with self-awareness and practice.

How can I improve my concentration and read more effectively?

> Reading should be approached with a clear sense of purpose and goals, which will vary from assignment to assignment. Examining the frontmatter of a book and creating advance organizers is also useful.

> Maintain focus by breaking down the reading into small chunks, taking breaks as needed, dealing with distractions, and writing while reading.

How can I best retain what I have read?

> Understanding of reading assignments can be cemented in memory by identifying the main ideas, prioritizing them, thinking critically about the arguments, and explaining the writer's ideas to someone else.

> Quickly rereading assignments and notes taken on them can greatly help in solidifying memories of what has been read. Concept maps that structure and relate ideas can also help.

[KEY TERMS AND CONCEPTS]

Advance organizers (p. 149)

Frontmatter (p. 149)

Attention span (p. 152)

Learning disabilities (p. 159)

Concept mapping (p. 164)

[RESOURCES]

ON CAMPUS

If you are experiencing unusual difficulties in reading, and the problem is one you encountered in high school, you may have a learning disability. If you suspect this is the case, take action. Many colleges have an office that deals specifically with learning disabilities. You can also talk to someone at your college's counseling center; he or she will arrange for you to be tested, which can determine whether you have a problem.

IN PRINT

The fourth edition of Joe Cortina and Janet Elder's book, *Opening Doors: Understanding College Reading* (McGraw-Hill, 2008), provides a complete set of guidelines for reading textbooks and other kinds of writing that you will encounter during college. Another useful volume is the seventh edition of *Breaking Through: College Reading* (Longman, 2009) by Brenda Smith.

ON THE WEB

The following sites on the World Wide Web provide the opportunity to extend your learning about the material in this chapter. (Although the Web addresses were accurate at the time the book was printed, check the *P.O.W.E.R. Learning* Web site [**www.mhhe.com/power**] for any changes that may have occurred.)

➤ The "Great Books Index: An Index to Online Great Books in English Translation" (**www.mirror.org/books/**): Check out this lengthy list of books. While it is one person's interpretation of what constitutes great books, it nevertheless contains a variety of 20th-century works, as well as older classics, written by a very diverse collection of writers.

➤ Increasing Textbook Reading Comprehension by Using SQ3R is the title of this site offered by Virginia Tech University (**www.ucc.vt.edu/lynch/TextbookReading.htm**). Offered here is a clear and detailed outline on how to use the SQ3R method as well as links to other reading comprehension aids such as critical reading, proofreading, and selective reading.

TAKING IT TO THE NET

1 Read a historical document. Choose a document that interests you by going to the Netscape search site (**www.netscape.com**) and conducting a search by entering the phrase "historical documents." After finding a document, read it, and summarize it in a short essay.

2 Go to a newspaper's Web site, such as that of *The New York Times* (**www.nyt .com**) or the *Atlanta Constitution* (**www.ajc.com**), and read one of the current editorials. Take notes on the editorial, concentrating on evaluating the strength of the argument(s). How persuasive was the editorial, and why?

The Case of . . .

War and Peace

One thousand four hundred eighty-four.

That's all Chenille Lawrence could think about when she got to the bookstore to purchase *War and Peace,* which her instructor said they'd be reading over the next four weeks. Sure, she thought to herself, it's great literature, as her instructor had said. It's undoubtedly a classic that every well-educated person should read some time in his or her life. Sure, maybe reading it would change her life in unimaginable ways, as her instructor had also argued (although she had strong doubts that its immediate effect would be anything but pain).

All she could think about, though, was its length—1,484 pages, not even counting the introduction. How would she ever get through such a giant book?

1. How would you advise Chenille to prepare for her reading of *War and Peace?* What sort of advance organizers would you suggest she create?

2. How would you suggest Chenille organize her time so that she could finish the book in the allotted four weeks?

3. How might Chenille stay focused on her reading? How might she most effectively use writing as a way to accomplish her task?

4. Why is evaluation important for effectively reading a long book such as *War and Peace?* How might Chenille evaluate the book and her understanding of it as she reads?

5. In what ways can Chenille use rethinking techniques to improve her understanding of the book?

Writing and Speaking

Learning Outcomes

By the time you finish this chapter you will be able to

>> LO **7.1**   Explain the best technique for getting started and writing a first draft.

>> LO **7.2**   Identify the process of moving from first draft to final draft.

>> LO **7.3**   Discuss how to conquer your fear of public speaking and make effective oral presentations.

Staring at the blank computer screen, Maria Ramos felt another surge of anxiety wash over her. She was beginning to panic.

The paper she was trying to get started on was due in two days, and she had not yet put a word down on paper. The problem was . . . well, that was just it: she didn't know what the problem was. The topic was completely hazy; she had no idea what her instructor was looking for.

As the minutes turned into hours, Maria was becoming increasingly desperate. Finally, for lack of a better idea, she decided to start writing down whatever came to mind, producing a flurry of stream-of-consciousness thoughts, recollections, and ideas.

Although most of the things that found their way to her computer screen had nothing to do with the paper topic, she was surprised to come up with a few thoughts that were relevant. And suddenly, she had an idea about how she could approach the assigned topic. Things gradually began to fall into place.

Maria had found her writing voice.

Looking Ahead

Few activities raise so many concerns and anxieties as writing and public speaking. Yet few skills are as important to your success, not only in college but also in the world outside the classroom. Taking time now to learn how to write well and speak well will not only increase your chances of success, but it will also improve your peace of mind!

This chapter focuses on writing and speaking. We begin by considering how to write, with a focus on composing college-level papers. We'll talk about how to get started and how you can move from a rough first draft to a final draft of which you can be proud.

The second part of the chapter looks at oral presentations. We'll discuss ways of getting over stage fright and how to engage listeners from the very start of your talk. We consider the importance of practicing neither too little nor too much.

P Prepare
Approach writing as a process

O Organize
Construct a scaffold by creating an outline and thesis statement

W Work
Get it down in the first draft; refine it in the second draft

E Evaluate
Be your own best critic: Fine-tune your work

R Rethink
Reflect on the writing process: what worked, what didn't

P.O.W.E.R. Plan

≫ LO 7.1 The Writing Process

What happens when you sit down to write? Does the sight of a blank page or blank screen leave your mind blank as well? Do your fingers, which move so quickly when you're playing a game on the computer, become sluggish when poised over a keyboard to write a paper?

Writing is not easy, and for many students, writing assignments raise more anxieties than any other academic task. There are many reasons for this anxiety. For one thing, papers often have a large impact on your final course grades. If you do all your writing at the last minute, with a deadline looming, writing is almost certainly a tense experience. Perhaps you've never really been taught how to write well. Or maybe you believe that there's some sort of special writing gene that you just weren't born with.

Stop! Delete from your memory any negative preconceptions you may have about writing. There is no mystery to writing; it's a skill that can be taught and a skill that, with practice, anybody can learn. Writing is not a product you read; it is a thinking and reasoning *process* that is the means of producing that product, a skill that can be learned like any other.

Using strategies based on *P.O.W.E.R. Learning* (summarized in the P.O.W.E.R. Plan), you will be able to achieve the goal of writing clearly and competently. These strategies will help you build upon your strengths and maximize your abilities. They will permit you to translate what's inside your head into words that communicate your experience or thoughts directly.

Journal Reflections

How I Feel about Writing

Reflect on the feelings you have about writing by answering the following questions:

1. When I receive a writing assignment, my initial reaction is . . .

2. Do you ever write for pleasure? When? Under what circumstances?

3. Which writing experiences are particularly pleasant for you? Which are unpleasant?

4. Are you particularly good at finding ways to put off writing tasks? Do you do anything to prevent this?

5. Writing experts believe that the very act of writing can help one think better. Why would this be true about writing? Have you ever experienced this phenomenon?

 Prepare

Confronting the Blank Page

There is nothing more intimidating than a blank piece of paper (or computer screen!). It is something that every writer faces, no matter how proficient. William Shakespeare, Jane Austen, Mark Twain, Anna Akhmatova, Ralph Ellison, and Sandra Cisneros all felt the challenge of having to fill that void with words.

Looked at another way, though, there is nothing more liberating than a blank page. It offers every possibility, and it gives you the freedom to say whatever you want to say. And therein lies one of the keys to good writing: deciding what it is you want to say.

Preparation will help you decide. Writing is a process, and preparation for it encompasses the following steps:

Deciding What Your Goal Is

To write successfully, you need to think about the end product. Is it a long research paper, based on information you must gather? An essay arguing a particular point of view? A

Nothing is more intimidating than a blank piece of paper—or a blank computer screen. On the other hand, it can also be liberating, offering you the freedom and opportunity to say what *you* want to say.

table 7.1	Major Types of College Writing
Research paper	A paper requiring abstract, critical thinking supported through the collection of existing information. Often requires analysis and synthesis of the material to develop a conclusion.
Essay	A paper written from an author's personal point of view and arguing a particular point. It may take the form of a review, criticism, or personal recollection or it may argue a political viewpoint.
Critical review	Criticism of an argument, article, musical piece, or other work.
Journal	Personal reflections on class readings or assignments.

fictional short story? A critique of someone else's work or argument? A book or movie review?

Most often, you'll be working to complete a class assignment that will explain what the goal is (see **Table 7.1**). But sometimes the assignment will provide you with several choices; it may even be vague or imprecise. If this is the case, your first step will have to be to decide what your goal is.

If there is a choice among different types of writing, decide which will make you most comfortable. If one choice is to prepare an essay, and you are creative and enjoy expressing your opinions, choose that option. If you enjoy gathering information and drawing a conclusion from your findings, a research paper might well be the best choice.

Choosing Your Topic

Once you've determined the specific type of writing you are going to do, the next step is to choose a topic. Although instructors often assign a particular topic, in some cases the choice will be left to you. However, the freedom to choose a topic does not come without a price. In fact, many students find that choosing what to write about is harder than actually writing the paper itself. Here are some things you can do to help pick an appropriate topic:

> **Use freewriting.** According to Peter Elbow, a writing expert who has revolutionized the teaching of writing, one of the reasons we find writing so hard is that we have a set of censors inside our heads.[1] Just as we set pen to paper, those censors are ready to spring up and whisper, "That's no good."

However, there is a way to keep these internal voices at bay. You can use a technique called **freewriting**. In freewriting, you write continuously for a fixed period of time—say, 5 or 10 minutes. The only rule that governs freewriting is to write continuously, without stopping. It doesn't matter whether the product is bad; it doesn't matter whether it's good. The only principle you must follow in freewriting is to get something—anything—down on paper.

Try it, and you'll see how liberating freewriting can be. Of course the product will not be perfect, but you'll most likely find that you've written something of value to you.

Suppose, for example, you are stuck for a topic. Through freewriting you can explore your feelings about the course you are going to be writing for, what you like and don't like, and from there go on to get some rough ideas down on paper. What's more, you'll probably form an "attitude" toward one or more potential topics, which can be used to add a personal voice and authenticity to your writing.

Freewriting

A technique involving continuous, nonstop writing, without self-criticism, for a fixed period of time

"How can I know what I think till I see what I say?"
Graham Wallas, author, *The Art of Thought*, 1926

Once the freewriting session is completed, you may want to write a single sentence that captures the main point of what you have written—the "center of gravity," Elbow calls it. You can then use this sentence as a springboard for further exploration of ideas the next time you write. (Test this method by completing **Try It 1** on page 174.)

> **Use brainstorming.** The oral equivalent of freewriting is **brainstorming**. While freewriting is done alone, brainstorming is most often done with others. In brainstorming, you say out loud as many ideas as you can think of in a fixed period of time. Although brainstorming works best when you do it with a group of friends or classmates, you can also do it by yourself. (This is one of those times when talking to yourself has its benefits.) Initially, the goal simply is to produce as many ideas as possible, no matter how implausible, silly, or irrelevant. Jot down the ideas that intrigue you as they come up, so you don't forget them.

As with freewriting, the point is to temporarily silence the censors that prevent us from saying whatever comes into our heads. In brainstorming, the initial goal is not to produce high-quality ideas but a high quantity of ideas. You can revisit and evaluate the ideas you've come up with later (see **Try It 2** on page 175).

Brainstorming
A technique for generating ideas by saying out loud as many ideas as can be thought of in a fixed period of time

Deciding Who Your Audience Is

That's easy, you may be thinking: It's my instructor. Not so fast. Although the instructor is the most obvious reader for what you write, you should think of your audience in terms of the ultimate purpose of the writing assignment. For example, if you're writing a paper about the dangers of global warming, are you directing it to a layperson who knows little about the issue? Or are you writing it for someone with a good understanding of science, someone who already knows about atmospheric pressure, *El Niño,* and the ozone layer? Clearly, the answer to this question will make a difference in how and what you write.

In short, it's crucial to know—and to keep in mind—the persons to whom you are writing. What is their level of knowledge about the topic? Are they already predisposed to a particular position? What do you think they would like to take away with them after reading what you've written?

Keeping an audience in mind serves another purpose: It personalizes your writing. Rather than targeting your writing to a nondescript group of individuals ("all the people who might be worried about global warming"), you individualize your audience. Think of the reader as your sister, or a friend, or your next-door neighbor. Think of how that individual would feel after reading what you've written, and what you would say to convince him or her.

Researching the Topic

To write most papers, you must do research, either in the library or on the World Wide Web (something we'll discuss further in Chapter 10). To put the information you find in a useable form, consider using a file-folder and note-card system, a proven technique that involves three steps:

1. **Assemble information folders.** Break down material you've found into subtopics by placing the raw information you've located (such as photocopies, computer printouts, and articles) into different multicolored file folders. Label each folder with a stick-on Post-It–type label, which will permit you to easily modify the topic of the folder if necessary in the future.

   This system can work on the computer, too: You can create a file-folder structure into which you put your notes and related material, assuming the

Try It!

1

Set Yourself Free: Freewriting

Use this space (or a separate sheet of paper) to practice freewriting for a 5-minute period. Optional guidance is offered below, but if you want to go ahead and "just do it," simply start writing. Be sure to keep your hand moving; stop controlling yourself. Write only for yourself; forget about what others might think.

If you need a little more guidance, you are not alone; most people need help the first time they try to freewrite. There are actually two kinds of freewriting: plain vanilla freewriting (like that above) and *focused* freewriting. Focused freewriting gives you a starting point.

Here are some starting points for focused freewriting:

Today I feel . . .

I remember . . .

I don't like . . .

I really like . . .

I get sick when . . .

I know . . .

I am . . .

I am not . . .

Using one of these lead-in phrases as a starting point, return to the blank space and begin your freewriting.

What is the main point of what you wrote? Was freewriting effective in helping you get something down on paper? Was it easy or difficult for you? Can you think of how the process of freewriting might help you when it's time to write a paper?

To Try It online, go to www.mhhe.com/power.

Try It! POWER

2

Get Your Brain Storming: Using Brainstorming to Generate Ideas

Your American history professor has asked you to come up with 10 ideas for a five-page paper on some aspect of the 1960s. Brainstorm in a group and come up with a list of possible topics, assigning one member of the group to record ideas below.

As you brainstorm, keep the length of the paper assigned and the sort of topic suited to American history generally in mind. Remember, the idea is to produce as many possibilities as you can, without evaluating how realistic or feasible they may be. Think quantity over quality.

After your group has concluded brainstorming, go back to your answers and circle each that you think is realistic for a paper topic. Did brainstorming work? Did you surprise yourself with the number of alternative possibilities you generated for each item?

To Try It online, go to www.mhhe.com/power.

information is in electronic form. For many of us this might not yet be completely practical—we still rely too heavily on handwritten notes and hard copies—but as more and more research material becomes available online, this will likely change. In addition, working on a computer allows you to easily save your work, something that you should be doing at every stage of the writing process. Saving your work in multiple formats (on hard drives, memory sticks, and printouts) is insurance against experiencing major headaches later on.

2. **Create note cards.** Taking notes on index cards is the best way of making information easy to use. *The key is to place no more than one major idea on each card.* If you stick to this rule, you will later find it easy to sort the cards and put them in logical order. It often helps to write the relevant subtopic (such as "Early Influences" or "Husband" or "Politics") at the top right-hand corner of the card for easy reference. (Once again, it is also possible to type notes directly into your computer and store them in a subfolder labeled "Early Influences," "Husband," "Politics," etc.)

   Be sure to write the ideas on the note card in your own words, unless you are directly quoting from a source—in which case you must remember to use quotation marks. It's also a good idea to mark a note card with the word "paraphrase" when you put someone else's unique idea in your own words, as in the sample note cards in **Figure 7.1** on page 176. (A **paraphrase** is a restatement of a passage using different words.) Using your own words will prevent you from accidentally copying others' words and passing them off as your own—which, as we'll discuss, is the gravest of academic sins.

Paraphrase
A restatement of a passage using different words

figure 7.1
Sample Note Cards

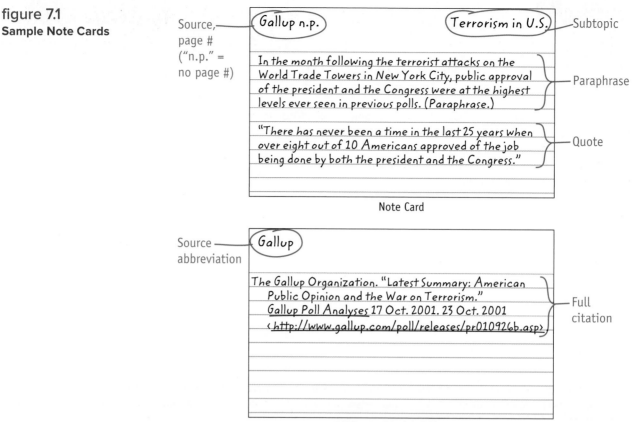

Note Card

Bibliographic (Source) Card

Keep in mind that even paraphrased material needs to be cited, unless it is what is called common knowledge. *Common knowledge* is information that is widely known, from multiple sources. For example, the September 11, 2001, terrorist attack on the United States is common knowledge and would not need to be cited. In contrast, one political scientist's explanation of *why* the terrorist attack occurred would need to be cited.

3. **Place source information on every note card.** Make sure every note card contains information that clearly identifies its source. It is extremely important that you know where the idea on the note card came from so you can credit this source when you write your paper. You do not need to include complete bibliographical information on every note card, but you must keep a master list—either on a separate set of note cards or in a computer file—with the full citation.

Table 7.2 illustrates examples of citations for different types of sources. For each source, the table shows citations using style guidelines of the Modern Language Association (MLA) or the American Psychological Association (APA), which are the two most frequently used styles. Courses in the humanities and arts usually use MLA style, while courses in the sciences typically use APA style (or, alternatively, the Council of Science Editors style). Your instructor will tell you which citation style he or she prefers.

Organize — Constructing a Scaffold

When builders begin construction on a building, they create a scaffold—a platform that is the framework allowing them to build the exterior of the building. In the

table 7.2		Sample Citations for Different Types of Sources[2]
Book with one author	MLA	Manning, Patrick. *The African Diaspora: A History through Culture*. New York: Oxford University Press, 2006.
	APA	Manning, P. (2006). *The African diaspora: A history through culture*. New York: Oxford University Press.
Book with more than one author	MLA	Skinner, Brain J., Porter, Stephen C., and Botkin, Daniel B. *The Blue Planet: An Introduction to Earth System Science*. New York: John Wiley & Sons, 2006.
	APA	Skinner, B. J., Porter, S. C., & Botkin, D. B. (2006). *The blue planet: An introduction to earth system science*. New York: John Wiley & Sons.
Magazine or newspaper article	MLA	Johnson, Steven, "The Long Zoom." *The New York Times Magazine* 8 October 2006: 50–56.
	APA	Johnson, S. (2006, October 8). The long zoom. *The New York Times Magazine*. pp. 50–56.
Scholarly journal article	MLA	Meininger, Herman P., "Narrating, Writing, Reading: Life Story Work as an Aid to (Self) Advocacy." *British Journal of Learning Disabilities* 34 (2006): 181–188.
	APA	Meininger, H. P. (2006). Narrating, writing, reading: Life story work as an aid to (self) advocacy. *British Journal of Learning Disabilities, 34*, 181–188.
Article with no author listed	MLA	"7th Inning Stretch: Roberto Clemente Award." *Baseball Digest* 2006: 69.
	APA	7th inning stretch: Roberto Clemente award. (2006). *Baseball Digest,* 69.
Article reproduced in CD-ROM database	MLA	Dahl, Eric."Two CPUs Too Slow? Try Four." *PC World* October 2006 (p. 28 in original publication). Retrieved October 12, 2006, from EBSCO Host CD-ROM database.
	APA	Dahl, E. (2006, October). Two CPUs Too Slow? Try Four. *PC World* (p. 28 in original publication). Retrieved October 12, 2006, from EBSCO Host CD-ROM database.
Article reproduced on Internet	MLA	Covarrubias, Amanda. "Warner Center Is at Development Crossroads." *Los Angeles Times* 12 October 2006 (p. C2 in original publication). Available on Internet (www.latimes.com/). Retrieved October 12, 2006.
	APA	Covarrubias, A. (2006, October 12). Warner Center is at development crossroads. *Los Angeles Times* (p. C2 in original publication). Retrieved October 12, 2006, from World Wide Web (www.latimes.com/).
Web document with author listed	MLA	Clark, Jessica. "Access to Usable Water: A Growing Global Concern." *Britannica*. (Internet site at www.britannica.com). Retrieved 12 October 2006.
	APA	Clark. J. Access to usable water: A growing global concern. *Britannica*. Retrieved October 12, 2006 from World Wide Web (www.britannica.com).
Web document with no author listed	MLA	"Getting the Most Out of Your Wellness Plan." *Wellness Junction* (Internet site at www.wellnessjunction.com). Retrieved 12 August 2006.
	APA	Getting the most out of your wellness plan. Retrieved August 12, 2006 from World Wide Web (www.wellnessjunction.com).

(continued)

table 7.2	Sample Citations for Different Types of Sources[2]		*(concluded)*
Newsgroup posting	MLA	Sobol, Steve. "Cell Phone Rudeness Backlash." On-line posting: alt.cellular (2 Aug. 2000). Retrieved on Deja.com (www.deja.com) 5 Feb. 2001.	
	APA	Sobol, S. (2000, August 2). Cell phone rudeness backlash. On-line posting (alt.cellular). Retrieved February 5, 2001, on World Wide Web (www.deja.com).	
E-mail	MLA	Gomez, Maria, curator. Brookridge Museum of Art. "Pre-Columbian Art," E-mail to Natalie Pellegrino. 14 Aug. 2000.	
	APA	Gomez, M., curator, Brookridge Museum of Art. (2000, August 12). Pre-Columbian art. E-mail to Natalie Pellegrino.	
Interview	MLA	Ahmed, Helen, M. D., pediatrician. Personal interview. 3 Aug. 2000.	
	APA	Ahmed, Helen, M. D., pediatrician. (2000, August 3). Personal interview.	
TV program	MLA	Roberts, Deborah, narrator, "Rachel Ray's Sizzling Success Story." *20/20*. ABC News. 19 Sept. 2006.	
	APA	Roberts, D., narrator. (2006, September 19). Rachel Ray's sizzling success story. *20/20*. ABC News.	
DVD	MLA	White, Terry. *Mac OS X Training for Windows Users*. DVD. Detroit, MI: Terry White Productions, 2005.	
	APA	White, T. (2005). *Mac OS X training for Windows users*. [DVD]. Detroit, MI: Terry White Productions.	

same way, when we read and listen to information, the author or speaker has (we hope!) already constructed an intellectual scaffold, or framework, for presenting the information to us. Our job as readers and listeners is to figure out what that organization is, like detectives following a trail of clues.

When we're writing, however, we're creating something new. Consequently, it's up to us to come up with the scaffolding for our written product.

Construct an Outline (and Be Ready to Change It!)

The key to organizing an extended piece of writing is the outline. Outlines provide a roadmap to follow when we're writing, a set of sequential steps that show us where we are heading and how we are going to get there.

The secret of successful outlining is flexibility: It is essential to keep an open mind about sequencing and to avoid getting "locked in" too early to a pattern that might later prove unworkable. The best approach is to write possible subtopics, based on your research, on index cards—or simply to type all of them into your computer. Then try to place them in a logical order. (If you use the computer, the program's outlining feature will even renumber the outline as you make changes.) Ask yourself how the subtopics build into a complete and convincing presentation. In doing so, always remember your audience: Consider what a reader would have to know already to understand a given fact or argument. Then try out several sequences and determine which order works best.

Develop the Paper's Structure

Although instructors sometimes provide a structure for a paper, you will ordinarily have to construct one yourself. One way to do this is to follow the **ABBCC structure.** "ABBCC" stands for the five parts of a typical research paper: *a*rgument, *b*ackground, *b*ody, *c*ounterarguments, and *c*onclusion. Each of these plays a specific role:

ABBCC structure
The structure of the typical research paper, consisting

- **Argument.** Just as we introduce ourselves when we meet someone for the first time, a writer needs to introduce a reader to the main argument being put forward in the paper. Every paper should have a main argument or **thesis,** a one- or two-sentence description of the main point of the paper. For instance, your thesis might make the argument that "Personal character does not matter in leaders; what matters is their effectiveness in accomplishing the goals for which they were elected."

  A thesis should be stated as an assertion ("People are their own worst enemies."). An effective thesis statement takes a position on some issue; many times this is signaled by use of an action verb ("The current technological revolution *requires* that people receive computer training") or the use of such keywords as "should" or "ought." For instance, "Smoking should be banned from restaurants and bars" presents a thesis statement. "This paper will discuss smoking in restaurants and bars," on the other hand, simply states the topic: we have no idea what stand the writer takes on smoking in restaurants and bars. **Try It 3** on page 180 will help you to turn ideas into thesis statements.

  The thesis or argument need not be the first sentence of the paper. In fact, it is usually wise to start off with something that grabs readers' attention. Begin with a controversial quote, an illustrative story, or a personal encounter—anything that is likely to make a reader sit up and take notice.

  In addition to presenting the main thesis of the paper, the first section should lay out the areas that you will cover and the general scope of the paper. You should use this section to present the paper's overall perspective and point of view. For example, "Taxpayers have every right to expect . . ." signals the writer's perspective on campaign finance reform—he or she is thinking about it as a taxpayer, as opposed to a legislator or political candidate.

- **Background.** You'll need to provide readers with a context in which to place your paper's arguments, and the background section is the place to do it. Provide a brief history of the topic, talking about different schools of thought on it. Introduce any unusual terms you might need to use. If the topic is highly controversial, discuss the reasons for the controversy. For example, if you are arguing that capital punishment should be abolished, you could briefly review the history of its use and of opposition to it.

- **Body.** The body makes up the bulk of most papers. In the paper's body, you provide evidence as to why your thesis is correct.

  This evidence should be presented in a logical order. Exactly what this means depends upon your topic. You may need to work chronologically if you are discussing a historical event. In other cases, you will want to start with the least controversial arguments and gradually move into the ones that are most debatable.

  When deciding on the order, keep your audience firmly in mind. For instance, a paper on the dangers of electromagnetic radiation written for a community law class would be very different from one written for a physics class.

Thesis
The main point of a paper, typically stating the writer's opinion about the topic of the paper

3

Make Your Point: Write a Thesis Statement

Write a thesis statement for each of the topics below. Remember that the thesis should be an *assertion*.

restricting access to particular World Wide Web pages in school libraries

the death penalty

same-sex marriage

cloning

global warming and modern technology

campaign finance reform

prayer in schools

stem-cell research

Evaluate each of the thesis statements that you wrote. Do they all contain an assertion? Is there a relationship between how controversial a topic is and how easy it is to write a thesis statement?

 WORKING IN A GROUP:

Each group member should generate three potential topics for a paper and compose a thesis statement for each. Then, as a group, evaluate each of the thesis statements.

To Try It online, go to www.mhhe.com/power.

- **Counterarguments.** You will also need to touch on the counterarguments to your position: Acknowledge them and then go on to systematically refute each one. This section need not be long, but it is crucial. By doing this you help reinforce your own position and strengthen your argument, showing that you have arrived at your point of view fully aware of—and unconvinced by—opposing views.

- **Conclusion.** A good ending to a paper is as important as a good beginning. It's where you pull everything together. And it is your last chance to drive home your thesis.

  The conclusion should summarize the thesis and the arguments that you have made regarding it. Do not introduce new information: The conclusion is a recap. Do make an effort to close with a flourish. You might cite a quotation, present an anecdote that is linked to one you presented at the start of the paper, or pose a rhetorical question ("If the government turns its back on welfare recipients, how can we claim to have a just society?"). However you choose to conclude the paper, make sure that it ties the various pieces together.

[W Work] Writing the Work

Now comes the moment that so many dread: It's time to face that blank page or screen and actually start writing. However, if you've followed the steps above and carefully prepared and organized, this phase is likely to be easier than you expect.

In fact, you should be so well prepared that you know just how to proceed: Your outline offers a clear roadmap, and your research notes will help you explain your ideas along the way. Your outline, if carefully composed, will actually provide you with the major headings of your paper. The job of writing the paper then becomes a matter of matching up the research to the appropriate outline heading. Looked at in this way, that blank page isn't so blank after all.

Don't try to do too much at one sitting. Professional authors writing a 500-page book don't think about the 500 pages they need to write; such thoughts are at best mind-numbing and at worst totally unproductive and paralyzing. Instead, professionals break their task down into smaller, more manageable pieces. They might decide that they'll write a certain number of pages in a given period of time—perhaps four or five pages a day. Or maybe they plan on writing one chapter per month.

You probably don't have as much time to devote to your writing as a professional writer, so the chunks you break your writing into should be shorter. For instance, if you have to write a 10-page paper, don't think of it as 10 pages. Instead, break it down into chunks of two pages a day, spread out over 5 days. Or think of it in terms of the major sections: an introduction, a description of the background of an issue, arguments in favor of a position, arguments against a position, and a conclusion. You could then schedule writing each of those five sections on a different day.

It's also helpful to divide the actual work of writing into two stages: writing the first draft and revising your draft.

» LO 7.2   Writing the First Draft

Starting a first draft is like diving into a cold lake. You know the initial plunge will be painful because the water is icy cold, but you know that once you're in, it won't feel so bad.

It's the same thing with writing a first draft. Getting started is often the hardest part. However, once you've put even a few words on paper, it gets easier.

When you set pen to paper or fingers to keyboard to begin writing, don't feel that you are carving your words in stone. Permit yourself to be less than perfect. Don't worry about word choice, grammar, sentence structure, spelling, or punctuation. That can come later. The first draft is meant to give you something to go on. The important thing is to fill up that blank space with *something*.

There are several strategies you can use to make writing the first draft less painful:

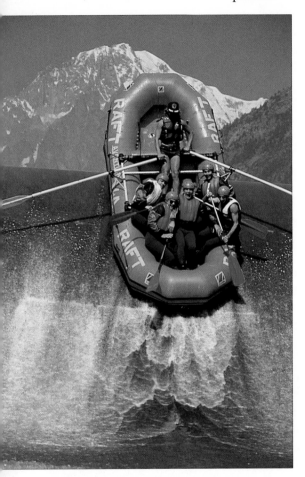

If you've ever gone whitewater rafting, you know that following the water's rhythm permits you to remain afloat. In the same way, on those occasions when you achieve a steady rhythm while writing and the words are coming rapidly, stick with it and go with the flow. Revising can come later.

> "I spend a great deal of my time thinking about the power of language—the way it can evoke an emotion, a visual image, a complex idea, or a simple truth."
>
> Amy Tan, author

> **Start where you like.** You need not follow the order of the outline when you write. For example, some writers start a paper by writing the conclusion first. By keeping the end in mind, they know just where they are headed, making the journey a little easier. Similarly, other writers save the beginning of the paper for last, reasoning that they'll be better able to tell their readers where the paper is going after it has actually gotten there.
>
> Write whatever part of the paper you feel most comfortable writing, because just having something on paper will encourage you to write the rest.

> **Turn off your inner critic.** If you're anything like most people, with every word you write, there's probably a voice somewhere in your head that's whispering, "Terrible sentence. Dumb idea. Forget it, you idiot, you'll never finish this paper." Your job is to turn off the voice of that inner critic, at least for now. (You'll want to use it later, when the nagging may come in handy as you revise your work.) While you're working on your first draft, you want to give yourself permission to be creative. As long as you write things down, you'll be able to go back later and make your paper better. But you can't revise what isn't there.

> **Go with the flow.** When you're writing your first draft, try to write quickly. Writing often takes on a rhythm, and you should try to write in sync with that rhythm. If you're on a roll, go with it: Don't stop (yet) to edit your work.
>
> On the other hand, if you're having trouble getting into a rhythm, and each word is like pulling teeth, take a break. Do something entirely different for a few minutes and then return with a fresh mind.
>
> If you're really having trouble, try rearranging your note cards (or scrambling your outline). Placing them in a new or even a random order may provide a fresh way of looking at your topic, and this may in turn free you enough to get your writing started.

> **Don't be afraid to modify your outline.** When you start writing, it's easy to fall into the trap of viewing an outline as a rigid, unbending framework. Your outline is a living document, and you should feel free to rearrange headings and to deviate from it as you're creating your first draft.
>
> Many writers find that their outlines need to be revised, and so might you. That's fine; that's why you're writing a first draft and not pretending to start with a final one.

> **Use your own voice.** Just as you have a distinctive speaking voice, each of us has a distinct *writing* voice. That voice represents our own unique style, a reflection of our outlook on life and of our past writing experiences. Novice writers sometimes get hung up trying to use a voice that isn't their own. For example, they may use words they would never normally use when speaking.

Avoid the temptation to write as if you were someone else. Instead, use your own natural voice and vocabulary, and don't use big words in an effort to impress your audience. If you'd feel foolish saying "heretofore" in a conversation, you shouldn't use it when you're writing a paper. Don't scan the thesaurus in search of unusual words to use in place of simple ones.

On the other hand, keep in mind that course papers use a more formal voice than you probably use in e-mails and instant messaging to close friends and family. You'll need to avoid the abbreviated and sometimes ungrammatical style of communicating you may be in the habit of writing in electronic messages.

> **Forget about it.** The last step in creating a first draft is the easiest: When you have finished your sketch of the entire paper, from introduction through conclusion, put it aside.

You need to let your mind idle in neutral for a while so that it will be at full strength when you move on to the next phase of writing: revision.

> **Voice**
> The unique style of a writer, expressing the writer's outlook on life and past writing experiences

Revising Your Draft

Remember that inner critic—that voice in your head—that you tuned out while you were writing the first draft? It's time to tune it back in.

The fact is that most of writing is *rewriting*. Sure, it's possible to hand in a first draft, and sometimes you'll even get a passable grade. But if you want to reach your own potential as a writer, you *must* revise.

Don't feel that revising is something that only students have to do. Professional writers may go through dozens of drafts—and still not be completely satisfied. Virtually no one has the ability to write a first-draft paper that is so lucid and compelling that it stands on its own.

Following several basic rules can make the revision process work smoothly for you:

> **Read the first draft out loud.** Read your paper out loud—to yourself, a friend, a pet, or your computer. It doesn't matter who's listening.

Reading out loud does several things. You'll more easily discover missing words, verbs that don't match the subject of the sentence, shifts in tense, missing transitions, and other things that you might have to fix. This is partly because speaking takes longer than silent reading; the slowed pace of reading out loud can help you identify problems that you'd otherwise miss.

> **Take the long view.** Start off by taking the broadest perspective possible and asking yourself a series of questions:

What is the purpose of my paper? Has that purpose been fulfilled?

Have I addressed every aspect of the assignment?

Does the paper tell its readers everything they need to know?

Will readers be able to follow its logic?

Does the paper make its points clearly?

Are the transitions between sections clear?

Reading the first draft of a paper aloud can help you identify problems that need to be addressed in a revised draft.

> **Be ruthless.** Words that we've put on paper tend to take on a life of their own—a life that we have created and so are often reluctant to change or part with.

It is natural to feel a bit parental toward our first draft, but it is important to fight this instinct. You need to be merciless and unforgiving with passages, paragraphs, phrases, and words that don't sound right or that do not ultimately add to your argument. Don't tear *yourself* down, but, like a coach demanding the best from his or her players, be demanding of your performance.

Start pruning at the paragraph level. Assess each paragraph to make sure that it adds to the final message, that it flows from the previous paragraph logically, and that it is consistent with what you are trying to accomplish.

Then move to the level of sentences and words. Evaluate each sentence, and then each word, to make sure that it adds to the clarity of your message.

By paring down your writing, you let your ideas shine through. If you are extremely fond of a phrase or a group of words that you suspect are unnecessary, write down or print out the sections and phrases, put them into an envelope, and toss the envelope into the top drawer of your dresser. You never know when you might need them. More important, knowing that you can save the cut material may make it easier to do the necessary cutting.

> **Check sequence and logic.** It's now time to reverse course. Whereas before the focus was on cutting extraneous material, you now need to check for what's *missing*.

For example, earlier cuts might have made it necessary to add or modify transitions between sections and paragraphs. You might also need to improve logic by reordering your ideas, reordering sentences within paragraphs, and reordering paragraphs within sections.

> **Check punctuation and spelling.** Check for the obvious stuff: Sentences should start with capital letters and end with the appropriate punctuation, commas should set off dependent clauses, and the like. Use a handbook or style manual if you're unsure.

Check your spelling carefully. This is one of the areas in which word processors earn their keep best. The spell-check feature will not only identify every misspelled word (that is, every word not in its dictionary), but it will also prompt you with alternative spellings.

Be careful not to rely completely on the spell-checker, however. Such programs can find only misspellings that do not form recognized words; if what you typed is a word, the spell-checker will ignore it, even if it is not the word you wanted to use. *Foe instants, know spelt-cheek pogrom wood fined eras inn thus sent-tense.* And yet every word in the preceding "sent-tense" is spelled incorrectly in this context.

> **Check that all quotes are cited and referenced correctly.** As we'll discuss in detail later, it is critical that you give proper credit to others' ideas and words. Make sure that you haven't directly quoted or paraphrased a source without acknowledging it.

> **Make it pleasing to the eye.** Instructors are human. They can't help but react differently to a paper that is neatly typed compared with one that is handwritten in a difficult-to-read scrawl.

"Wrestling with words gave me my moments of greatest meaning."

Richard Wright, author

Writing in Class: Strategies for Getting It Right

Your instructor pauses halfway through her lecture and says for the next 5 minutes you are to complete a short written assignment. Whether she calls it an in-class essay, a reaction paper, or a "pop paper," it calls for somewhat different strategies than an out-of-class writing assignment. Unlike traditional paper assignments—in which you have the luxury of time—an in-class writing assignment requires that you react immediately.

Here are some tips for completing in-class writing assignments:

- *Be prepared.* You should always come to class with pen and pencil, as well as knowing your student ID number (at least in big classes). Just as important, make sure you're up-to-date in the reading assignments.

- *Think first.* Before you start writing, spend a minute thinking about the assignment. What is its goal? How can you best approach it? What is it that you want to get across?

- *Make a quick outline.* Creating an outline—even a short one—will help you collect your thoughts and prepare for what you're going to say.

- *Timing is everything.* Assuming your instructor lets you know how much time you'll have (and ask how much, if he or she doesn't mention it), plan ahead appropriately. You don't want to run out of time before completing your assignment.

- *Be sure to answer every part of the question.* If your instructor asks for your opinion, be sure to give it but if he or she also wants to know *why* you feel the way you do, don't forget that part.

- *Neatness counts.* Be sure your answer is legible. If your handwriting is terrible, then print. The most brilliant of responses does you no good if your instructor can't read it.

A neat paper conveys a message: I'm proud of this paper. I've put time and effort into it. This is my best work.

A sloppy paper says something different.

Take the time, then, to make sure your paper looks good. This doesn't mean that you need to invest in a fancy plastic cover, or worry about the alignment of the staples, or spend a lot of time deciding which font to use on your word processor. But it does mean that the quality of the paper's appearance should match the quality of the writing.

E Evaluate Acting as Your Own Best Critic

Because you've already put so much work into your paper, you might be tempted to rush through the final stages of the P.O.W.E.R. process. Avoid the temptation. If you've carefully revised your paper, the last stages will not be time-consuming, and they may have a significant impact on your paper's ultimate quality—and your success.

Take these steps to *evaluate* what you've written:

▸ **Ask yourself if your paper accomplishes what you set out to do.** The beginning of your paper contains a thesis statement and the argument that you intended to make. Does your paper support the thesis? Is your argument upheld by the evidence you've reported? Would an impartial reader be convinced by what you've written?

- **Put yourself in your instructor's shoes.** Does the paper precisely fit the assignment requirements? Does it meet the instructor's underlying goals in giving the assignment?

- **Check the mechanical aspects of the paper.** The grammar and spelling must be correct; the paper should also look good. If your instructor requires that citations or references be reported in a certain style, make sure you've followed it. For example, your instructor might specify Modern Language Association style (used in the humanities), American Psychological Association style (used in the social sciences), or Council of Science Editors style (used in the sciences).

- **Have an objective reader take a look.** Many colleges have writing labs or centers that will help you with your writing. In many cases, their staff will take a look at a paper and provide feedback. You can also have a friend or family member read the paper, giving you comments.

If you've revised the paper with care, it will likely pass muster. If it doesn't, though, go back and work on it once again. By this point, it should require only minor tinkering to get it into shape.

R Rethink — Reflecting on Your Accomplishment

Rethinking is the homestretch of the writing process. It's a moment to savor, because it permits you to take a long view of what you've accomplished. You've gone from a blank page to words on paper that tell a story. You've turned nothing into something—an achievement in and of itself.

Rethinking occurs on several levels: rethinking the message, mechanics, and method. But don't address them until a little time has passed: Wait a day or so to reread the paper. Then, bringing your critical thinking skills to bear, reflect on the following:

- **Rethink the message.** Be sure that the overall message your paper conveys is appropriate. A paper can be like an advertisement. In most papers, you are seeking to communicate information to convince someone of a particular opinion. Make sure that the message is what you wish to communicate, and that ultimately the paper is successful in making the case.

- **Rethink the mechanics.** A television commercial filled with fuzzy images and annoyingly unsteady camera shots would not be very compelling, no matter how good the underlying product. In the same way, a paper with mechanical errors will not impress your readers or persuade them. Take another look at your writing style; look at grammar, punctuation, and word usage to make sure the choices you've made are appropriate.

- **Rethink the method.** Every time you finish a paper, you learn something—something about the topic of your writing and something about yourself. Ask yourself what you have learned to help you become a better writer in the future. What might you have done to improve the writing process? What could have gone better? What will you do differently the next time you write? Above all, remember what you've accomplished: You've transformed what's inside your head—your thoughts, your ideas, your values—into something that can potentially influence other people. You have exercised the ability to move others and get them to think in new ways. You've made a difference. That's the real power of writing.

Write Away

The first step in getting a job is putting pen to paper (or, probably more accurately, finger to keyboard). Whether you receive a lead for a job from a college career center, read an ad in the paper, or see a job listing on the Internet, you'll need to communicate in writing to the potential employer.

You are selling yourself in a letter of application. To be effective, keep these guidelines in mind:

- **Brief is better.** Employers are likely to get many letters, and long ones are least likely to be read.

- **State what you can do for the employer, not what the employer can do for you.** Don't tell a potential employer you really, really need a job to pay off your credit card bills. Instead, explain how your skills can help further an organization's goals.

- **Summarize your qualifications.** Respond specifically to the skills required for the job. List specific experiences you've had that are relevant to what the employer is looking for.

- **Enclose a résumé.** Your résumé should contain a detailed summary of your educational background and work experience, as well as other relevant qualifications.

- **Ask for an interview.** Close your letter with a request to meet and discuss the job. Provide your telephone number and e-mail address.

- **Proofread!** You must have zero tolerance for errors. Any mistake is likely to put you at the bottom of the pile of applications.

Career Connections

Acknowledging Others' Ideas: Academic Honesty and Plagiarism

As you move through the process of writing a paper, there are many temptations to cut corners. A friend may have written a paper the previous year on the same topic and offer to "lend" it to you . . . you may find a paper on the Web that addresses just what you intended to write . . . you and a friend may be enrolled in a very large class, and he may suggest that you each write part of the paper and "share" sections.

Don't yield to temptations such as these. Not only is honesty the best policy, but it's also the *only* policy in the world of academics. There's no greater academic sin than **plagiarism,** taking credit for someone else's words, thoughts, or ideas. In the academic world, plagiarism is about the same as stealing a stranger's car. Even if you just mean to "borrow" a passage, passing another person's work off as your own is totally wrong.

Furthermore, penalties for plagiarism are severe. In many colleges, plagiarism results in a comment on your transcript or can result in expulsion. You even could face legal charges, because almost all published material is copyrighted, which means that it is someone's *intellectual property*. If an author learns that you have used his or her writing as your own, the author has the right to take you to court and sue for damages.

If the moral and intellectual arguments against plagiarism don't convince you, here's the hard reality: It is likely you are going to get caught. Increasing numbers of instructors and colleges routinely use Web-based computer programs to check students' papers for plagiarism. The process is simple. Students turn in papers

Plagiarism

Taking credit for someone else's words, thoughts, or ideas

in electronic form, and they are passed through sophisticated programs such as *Turnitin* or *MyDropBox* that check submissions against sources on the Web. Alternatively, instructors may also type in passages that sound suspicious to them. These programs work extraordinarily well.

The bottom line: Plagiarism is wrong. Instructors hate it, and they often go to great lengths to identify it. Because the odds are that if you plagiarize, you are likely to be caught, *just don't do it.*

Avoiding Plagiarism

The best way to avoid plagiarism is to be very, very careful. Following these guidelines will help you:

> If you are writing a paper that requires the use of source materials from the library or the Web, *always* note the source, and distinguish between your ideas, quotations, and your paraphrases of others' ideas. If you've written something down without indicating the source, don't use it in your writing until you identify the source.

> Don't rely on a single source. It's too easy to make use of the same wording and terminology without being aware of it.

> When you quote directly from the work of another, use quotation marks, even in your notes.

> Be sure to keep accurate records as you are taking notes. When you paraphrase, be careful: It's not just a matter of rearranging the words and choosing synonyms for them. For instance, consider the following passage from the book *Nation of Nations*[3]:

> *In the 1860s they had come in a trickle; in the 1870s they became a torrent. They were farmers from the East and Midwest, black freedmen from the rural South, and peasant-born immigrants from Europe. What bound them together was a craving for land.**

> Here's one way of rephrasing the passage, but one that is so close to the original that it amounts to plagiarism:

> *In the 1860s they had come in a drizzle; in the 1870s, they became a deluge. There were crop-growers from the East and Midwest, former black slaves from the rural South, and common people from Europe. Holding them together was a hunger for land.*

> A more appropriate rewording of the original passage would be the following, which more clearly paraphrases the authors' ideas:

> *There was a great deal of growth in the number of settlers from 1860 to 1879. The settlers represented several groups, including farmers from the eastern and midwestern United States, former Southern slaves, and poor Europeans who had come to the United States to better their lives. They all shared a dream of obtaining land.*

> Even when paraphrasing, *it is necessary to cite the source* of the facts or ideas that you are using. In the example above, one way to cite here would be to add a footnote reference similar to the one at the bottom of this page (and those at the end of this book).

*Davidson, J.W., Gienapp, W.E., Heyrman, C.L., Lytle, M.H., & Stoff, M.B. (1996). *Nation of Nations: A Concise Narrative of the American Republic.* New York: McGraw-Hill.

Citation is necessary for two reasons: (1) to give credit where credit is due; and (2) to allow your readers to follow up for more information on a subject. Facts and ideas that are unique to a source or even those that are infrequently heard should be cited. It is probably advisable to cite too much rather than risk plagiarizing, but it is *not* necessary to have a citation after every sentence. Some facts are so basic ("Japan and Germany were the enemies of the United States in World War II") that no source is necessary.

› Keep in mind that you must cite material that you find on the World Wide Web. It was produced by someone else and that someone must be given credit. The rules for how to cite material found on the Web are still in flux, but you should at the very least include the site name, Web address (URL), and author, as well as the date you accessed the site.

And remember this: In your research on the Web, you might come across sites that offer to sell you term papers. Don't even think about it. The academic and legal consequences would be severe. In addition, the papers are often of low quality, and the same paper may be sold to dozens of students—potentially even to other students in your own class, making it easy for an instructor to identify plagiarized papers.

Try It 4 on page 190 will give you some practice in the proper use of other people's information and ideas. Before we turn to the topic of public speaking, which we consider next, make sure the distinction between summarization and plagiarism is clear in your mind.

» LO 7.3 Speaking Your Mind

Surveys find that most people are more afraid of public speaking than of dying! In a way, it's not surprising. How often are we so totally exposed to others' scrutiny? Not only do we have to worry about the message we're communicating—just as with our writing—but each of us also has to be concerned about nonverbal behavior and the impression we are making.... *Is my hair sticking out? ... This sweater was a big mistake. ... Are they bored? ... I wish my hands would stop shaking.*

Although you may be self-conscious about public speaking (complete **Try It 5** on page 192 to see where you stand), it's important to keep several points in mind:

› Audiences are generally sympathetic. They've all been where you are and probably share your fears about public speaking. They're on your side and are rooting for you to succeed.

› Being nervous is normal. Even accomplished entertainers like Bono and Meryl Streep report high levels of anxiety before and during performances.

› Once you start speaking, it will become easier. Anxiety tends to be highest *before* you start talking. Most people find that after they start to talk, their nervousness declines.

› Practice helps. Practice and preparation for the talk will go a long way toward easing your tension.

Keep in mind, too, that in many fundamental ways, speaking is like writing. You need to consider who your audience is, muster your arguments, and decide how to sequence those arguments.

The P.O.W.E.R. writing framework that we presented earlier in the chapter applies to speaking as well:

› **Prepare** what you will say and how you will say it. Think about your audience and the occasion on which you will speak, and try to be sure your words match both audience and occasion.

4

Summarize, Don't Plagiarize

Try to capture in your own words the meaning of the following quoted passages, without plagiarizing them in any way. Assume that you intend to reflect the main points of each author in a paper of your own, summarizing the arguments.

1. From *No Ordinary Time* by Doris Kearns Goodwin (New York: Simon & Schuster, 1995), pp. 628–629, on the political relationship between President Franklin D. Roosevelt and his wife, Eleanor.

   It was said jokingly in Washington during the war years that Roosevelt had a nightly prayer: "Dear God, please make Eleanor a little tired." But in the end, he often came around to her way of thinking. Labor advisor Anna Rosenberg had been one of those who criticized Eleanor's unceasing pressure on the President, but years later she changed her mind. "I remember him saying. 'We're not going to do that now. Tell Eleanor to keep away; I don't want to hear about that anymore.' And then 2–3 weeks later he would say, 'Do you remember that thing Eleanor brought up? Better look into it, maybe there's something to it—I heard something to indicate that maybe she's right.' I'm not sure she would have had the opportunity to bring things to his attention unless she pressured him—I mean he was so involved and in retrospect it was never anything for herself. . . . He would never have become the kind of President he was without her."

2. From "The Streak of Streaks" in *Bully for Brontosaurus* by Stephen Jay Gould (New York: W. W. Norton & Company, 1991), pp. 466–467, on baseball player Joe DiMaggio's 56-game hitting streak in 1941.

   Ed Purcell, Nobel laureate in physics but, for purposes of this subject, just another baseball fan, has done a comprehensive study of all baseball streak and slump records. His firm conclusion is easily and swiftly summarized. Nothing ever happened in baseball above and beyond the frequency predicted by coin-tossing models. The longest runs of wins or losses are as long as they should be, and occur about as often as they ought to. . . .

   But "treasure your exceptions," as the old motto goes. Purcell's rule has but one major exception, one sequence is so many standard deviations above the expected distribution that it should never have occurred at all: Joe DiMaggio's 56-game hitting streak in 1941. . . . Purcell calculated that to make it likely (probability greater than 50 percent) that a run of even 50 games will occur once in the history of baseball up to now (and

> **Organize** your thoughts, using notes to cue you to the main parts of your presentation and making logical connections for your audience to follow.

> **Work** carefully during your presentation by speaking clearly and calmly to your audience and avoiding distracting mannerisms or body language.

> **Evaluate** your performance after you finish your presentation and ask others to evaluate it, too. Take notes on the feedback.

> **Rethink** your entire approach when preparing for and delivering presentations each time you make one. Make the changes you feel you should make to improve your performance over time.

Meeting the Challenge of Public Speaking

Although speaking and writing share many features, speaking presents several unique challenges. Among the factors that you need to take into account when you are speaking are these:

> **The first minute counts—a lot.** If you can get your audience's attention, arouse their interest, and engage them in the first few minutes, you're on your way to a successful speech. On the other hand, let them drift off early on and you've lost them—potentially for good.

56 is a lot more than 50 in this kind of league), baseball's rosters would have to include either four lifetime .400 batters or 52 lifetime .350 batters over careers of 1,000 games. In actuality, only three men have lifetime batting averages in excess of .350, and no one is anywhere near .400 (Ty Cobb at .367, Rogers Hornsby at .358, and Shoeless Joe Jackson at .356). DiMaggio's streak is the most extraordinary thing that ever happened in American sports.

3. From "General Relativity" in *Who's Afraid of Schrodinger's Cat?* by Ian Marshall and Danah Zohar (New York: William Morrow and Company, 1997), pp. 170–171.

In 1916, Albert Einstein proposed an interaction between mass-energy and the structure of space-time. Mass-energy produces "curvature" in space-time—i.e., it deviates from flat, Euclidean space. Curved space-time in turn changes the paths of mass-energy through it. . . .

One test of the worth of any new scientific theory is whether it offers us additional predictions. How do the predictions of General Relativity differ from those of Newtonian gravity? One obvious one is that curved space will deflect not only matter but also light rays passing through it. Thus, light from a distant star should be deflected if it passes near the sun. Newtonian gravitation predicts a similar effect, but only half as much. During an eclipse of the sun in 1919, the measured deflection of light from a distant star won international acclaim for Einstein's theory. Given the technology of the time, one other experimental verification was possible, an explanation for an anomaly in the orbit of Mercury, and this, too, was achieved successfully.

WORKING IN A GROUP:
After you summarize the passages on your own, compare your answers to those of other classmates in your group. What different approaches did others in your group take? Which passages did people find particularly hard to summarize? Why? Did your group arrive at one best way to capture the authors' main points?

To Try It online, go to: www.mhhe.com/power.

How do you get them interested? There are several ways:

Begin with an anecdote. *"It was a scientist's dream, experienced as he dozed off in front of a fire, that led to one of the most important biological discoveries of all time."*

Start with a quotation. *"'I have seen the enemy, and he is us.' But are we really the enemy? I believe . . ."*

Arouse their curiosity. *"I have a secret, one that I've kept hidden for many years—until now."*

Talk about the significance of the topic. *"If you think that global warming is not a problem, take a look at what's happening to the beachfront up and down the Atlantic coast this year."*

Ask a question. *"Have you ever wondered how you could save enough money to buy a new car?"*

Use humor. *"My introduction to gardening was not promising: Seeking to surprise my mother, I 'weeded' her garden so enthusiastically that I pulled up all her flower seedlings."*

Try It 6 on page 193 will help get you started.

5

Determine Your Level of Self-Consciousness

One of the main reasons people feel nervous when speaking in public is their self-consciousness. To explore your own level of self-consciousness, answer the following questions,[4] choosing the phrase from the rating scale that is closest to your feelings.

0 = Extremely uncharacteristic

1 = Generally uncharacteristic

2 = Equally characteristic and uncharacteristic

3 = Generally characteristic

4 = Extremely characteristic

1. I'm concerned about my style of doing things. _____

2. I'm concerned about the way I present myself. _____

3. I'm self-conscious about the way I look. _____

4. I usually worry about making a good impression. _____

5. One of the last things I do before I leave the house is look in the mirror. _____

6. I'm concerned about what other people think of me. _____

7. I'm usually aware of my appearance. _____

Scoring: Add up the numbers to get a total score. If you score below 16, you are unusually low in self-consciousness, and public speaking should be less of a burden than it is for most other people. If you score between 16 and 22, you have a medium level of self-consciousness. Public speaking is not necessarily easy for you, but it does not provoke too many fears. If you score above 22, your level of self-consciousness is relatively high. Public speaking is likely to be particularly challenging for you.

To Try It online, go to www.mhhe.com/power.

> **Provide oral transition points.** When we're reading a textbook selection, we usually have the luxury of knowing exactly when a transition point occurs. It's marked by a title, section heading, or new paragraph. These markers help us construct a mental map that permits us to understand the overall structure of the piece we're reading.

Listeners don't have the same advantage. Unless the speaker orally signals that he or she is moving to a new part of a talk, listeners might get lost. However, there are several ways to erect verbal signposts throughout a speech. By using phrases such as the following, you can alert listeners that a twist in the journey lies ahead:

"To understand the problem, we need to consider . . ."

"The problems are clearly daunting. But there are solutions. Let's consider some of them . . ."

"Now that we've considered the solutions, we need to take a look at their costs . . ."

"Let's go back for a moment to an earlier point I made . . ."

"To sum up, the situation offers some unexpected advantages . . ."

> **Make your notes work for you, not against you.** A speaker is giving a talk, and suddenly she loses her place in her notes. She fumbles around, desperately trying to find her place and figure out what comes next.

Let's Talk

Devise a 1-minute opening to a talk about the thing you know most about in this world: you. The topic can be about one of your experiences or about anything that concerns you or reveals a little bit about your past, your feelings, or your opinions. Use any of the opening strategies that we've considered.

Which opening strategy are you going to employ?

Now write your opening:

Now try it out on a friend or classmate. Remember: Limit what you say to the 1-minute opening.

When you're finished, ask yourself how well you think your strategy worked. Why? Would another strategy have worked as well or better? What did your audience think of your opening? Why do you think it had the effect it did? Did your opening make your audience want to hear more? Did your opening make you want to *write* more?

To Try It online, go to www.mhhe.com/power.

It's a painful situation to watch—and even worse for the person experiencing the problem. How do you avoid finding yourself in such a predicament?

One way is by thoroughly acquainting yourself both with what you are going to say *and* with your notes. Once again, practice is your best friend. But the type of notes you have also makes a big difference.

Some speakers write out their entire talk in advance; others use no notes at all, counting on memorizing their talk. Avoid either extreme. If you write out your complete speech in advance, you'll experience an overwhelming urge to read it to your audience. Nothing could be more deadly. On the other hand, if you memorize your talk and have no notes at all, you'll be susceptible to a memory lapse that can make you feel completely foolish. Even if you can remember your talk successfully, you may end up sounding mechanical, like an amusement park guide who has given the same speech about the "jungle cruise" a thousand times.

Choose a middle ground. Develop an outline that includes the major points you wish to cover and have this outline in front of you when you speak. It might be written or typed on a sheet of paper, or you might use index cards (number them!). In addition, write out and memorize your opening and closing statements.

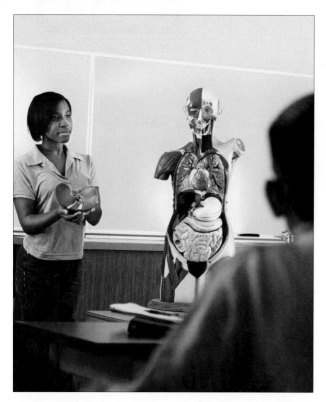

When used in a talk, visual aids help to keep an audience interested in what you are saying. They also take the focus away from you, making public speaking less nerve-wracking.

By memorizing the opening and closing statements, you'll have the opportunity to look your audience in the eye and engage them nonverbally at two of the most crucial junctures in your talk—the beginning and the end. Using an outline for most of your talk permits you to sound natural as you speak. You'll probably use slightly different words every time you give your talk, which is fine.

> **A picture can save you a thousand words.** Maps, charts, photos, drawings, figures, and other illustrations add another dimension to a presentation, helping to engage listeners. Computer programs, such as PowerPoint, permit you to create graphics relatively painlessly (as we'll discuss further in Chapter 10). Just be sure to give full credit to the source of anything you use that someone else created—the rules of plagiarism hold for talks you give, as much as for your writing.

You can even use props. For example, if you are talking about a series of Supreme Court rulings, you might incorporate a gavel into your talk. Effective visual aids make abstract concepts more concrete and immediate.

> **Use the right amount and kind of practice.** After you've written your opening and closing statements, constructed an outline, and decided what visual aids to use, it's time to practice. It's not just the amount of practice that is critical: How you practice is as important as how much you practice.

Running through your speech mentally will help you to familiarize yourself with your presentation, but you really need to give the speech out loud. Only by hearing yourself speak can you actually get a sense of how the presentation works as an oral presentation.

Use your "speaking voice" when you practice. When you practice, speak more loudly than your usual conversational voice, using the volume level that you'll want to use when you actually give the speech. Because your voice sounds different to you when you speak loudly, this tactic will help you get used to the sound of your voice at a louder-than-usual level.

Try to eliminate repeated, unnecessary phrases. We all have verbal "tics," such as the use of "umm," "ah," "you know," and "kind of." As you practice, avoid using them. In fact, it's a good idea to eliminate them from everyday speech as well. So each time you hear yourself using them, in any context, pause and remind yourself that you're trying to purge them from your speech.

Practice in front of a friend or classmate. It is only by actually trying your talk out in front of a warm body that you'll be able to approximate the experience of actually speaking in public, and your audience can provide you with feedback regarding what is working and what is not.

How much practice is enough practice? You've probably done enough when you do a good job giving a talk two or three times in a row. If you practice

"I could have been a big celebrity but for my fear of public speaking."

your talk two many times, you'll become so bored with it that the actual talk will sound canned and unconvincing.

▶ **Fight stage fright.** As you know, for many people, the mere thought of speaking in front of others causes a knot of fear to form deep in their gut. Even those who routinely speak in front of others experience some degree of anxiety. (Ask one or two of your course instructors if they ever feel nervous when teaching a class. Their answers may surprise you.)

Although you won't be able to alleviate your stage fright completely, several techniques can reduce the anxiety that public speaking produces. First, make sure you're wearing clothes that are comfortable and that make you feel pleased with your appearance. If you feel good about your appearance, you'll be more relaxed.

Five minutes before you get up to speak, take three slow, deep breaths. Concentrate on the feeling of the air going in and out of your body. If a particular part of your body feels tense, tighten it up even more and then relax it. Do it several times. Finally, visualize yourself giving the speech successfully and the relief that you'll feel afterward.

▶ **Monitor your nonverbal behavior.** Anxiety about public speaking can do strange things to people's bodies. Their hands may shake or feel icy cold. They may pace back and forth like a caged lion. They may sweat profusely. They may stand rigidly while speaking, looking like stiff toy soldiers. Or they may slump over a podium as if they wished they could dissolve into thin air.

To avoid appearing as if you were scared to death—even if you are—stand up straight and tall. Look directly at different members of your audience, shifting your gaze from one person to the next. Eye contact engages audience members, making them feel that your words are directed straight toward them.

If the thought of eye contact scares you, try a trick that some speakers use. Look directly at the *hairline* of different audience members; to your listeners, this is generally indistinguishable from eye contact.

Speaking Off-the-Cuff: Impromptu Speaking

What do you do when an instructor calls on you in class and asks, "What do you think the point of this poem is?" Just as anxiety-producing as giving a prepared talk (and probably a lot more common) is public speaking that is impromptu. **Impromptu talks** are unprepared presentations that require you to speak on a moment's notice.

Impromptu talk
Unprepared presentations that require speaking on a moment's notice

Impromptu speaking happens far more frequently than you may think: your professor asks you to explain why some historians consider Reconstruction a failed enterprise; a co-worker or classmate asks you to explain how a software program works; you visit your landlord to complain about the water heater that keeps breaking, and the landlord asks you for details. The response you give in each of these situations (and many others) is an exercise in impromptu speaking.

"PREPing" to Give an Impromptu Talk

Just because speaking impromptu is, by definition, unplanned, it does not have to be totally off the top of your head. There is a simple process that you can use when you're put on the spot. Known as the PREP formula,[5] it consists of breaking down an answer into four parts:

> **Point of view.** Initially provide your point of view or your stand on the issue.

> **Reasons.** Provide the chief reasons why you believe your position is correct.

> **Evidence or examples.** Give specific evidence to support your point of view.

> **Point of view, restated.** Restate your point of view.

Here's an example:

Professor Fiske: Who can tell me if racism is a uniquely American problem? Stephanie, why don't you take a stab at the question.

Stephanie: I don't believe racism is uniquely American at all. [**point of view**] *If we look at other times in history or other parts of the world today, we find all sorts of racial problems.* [**reasons**] *For example, consider Iraq and the Middle East. Or look at the difficulties that South Africa had. Or look at Nazi Germany.* [**evidence or examples**] *So it's hard for me to understand how anyone could contend that racism is uniquely American. Racism, unfortunately, is a universal fact of life.* [**point of view, restated**]

Although using the PREP system may seem awkward at first, you'll find it easy to learn. And with sufficient practice, it will become automatic, saving you lots of mental scrambling the next time you're called on in class (see **Try It 7**).

Remember: You're Already an Accomplished Public Speaker

Speaking in front of others is something you've done all your life. It might have been a heart-to-heart with a friend. It might have been with a group of friends deciding on what kind of pizza to order, with you arguing against anchovies and your friends arguing in favor. It might have been as a sports team member, with you shouting encouragement to your fellow athletes. The point is that you've already spoken in front of others—lots of times.

When you are faced with giving a formal presentation, give yourself credit for the times you've already spoken publicly. Let go of your fears and enjoy your moment in the spotlight. You may well find the experience satisfying and rewarding.

Put Yourself on the Spot

Each member of a class group should write two questions on separate note cards. Some examples: "Are basketball players paid too much?" "What's the best way to wash dishes?" "How can you get people to exercise more?"

Place the cards, face down, on a table. Have the first group member choose one of the cards at random, and immediately answer the question using the PREP system. Every person should take a turn answering a question.

After each person gives his or her extemporaneous speech, evaluate the responses by answering the following questions as a group:

Generally, how effective was the person's response to the question?

What were its greatest strengths?

What could have been done better?

To Try It online, go to www.mhhe.com/power.

speaking of success

Mesa
SAN DIEGO MESA COLLEGE

NAME: **Chuong Dang**

SCHOOL: **San Diego Mesa College, San Diego;**
University of California at San Diego

For students like Chuong Dang, who emigrated to the United States from Viet Nam, learning English was a major challenge. Dang struggled to adapt to his new language.

"My first encounter with English was in Viet Nam. But we learned mostly through listening, and it wasn't a good way," he explained. "When I arrived here I wasn't able to understand very well at all."

While in high school, Dang was able to improve his English skills considerably, but he faced new challenges when he entered San Diego Mesa College.

"I found English 101 quite difficult," he said. "I had to withdraw after the first class because I could not meet the requirements."

Dang explained that part of the problem was finding the right teacher, one who would take into consideration the challenges he faced in learning a new language.

"Later, I took another class where the teacher understood writing from an immigrant's perspective as opposed to that of a native English speaker," he explained. "Through rewriting essays and guidance from the teacher, I was able to improve my ability to speak and write in English."

One tactic Dang employed—and still uses today—was to use his school's writing workshop. It was there that he was able to polish both his writing and speaking skills.

"The writing workshop at Mesa was a big help. The instructors would go over my essays and help me to format my ideas in English and to rephrase what I was trying to say," he said.

"Every time I would go to the workshop I met with another person, and because of that I would learn different things each time," he added.

Hoping to continue on to graduate school and conduct research on cancer, Dang stresses the importance of reading and meeting new people as a way to learn not only about the language, but the culture as well.

"I would suggest to other students that they read and read," Dang suggests. "Read newspapers and books about recent events and history, as well as a variety of things about the United States. It was one of the ways that I was able to learn about American culture."

Looking Back

What are the best techniques for getting started and writing a first draft?

› Freewriting and brainstorming can help you choose a topic.

› Identifying the audience for writing is essential.

› Breaking down large writing tasks into smaller, more manageable pieces helps pave the way to completing a writing assignment.

› Good organization, which is essential to both writer and reader, often follows the ABBCC structure: *a*rgument, *b*ackground, *b*ody, *c*ounterarguments, and *c*onclusion.

How can I move from my first draft to my final draft?

› Use your outline as your roadmap.

› The best way to begin writing the first draft is to plunge in, starting anywhere in the paper.

› Revision is an essential part of writing: Most of writing is rewriting.

How can I conquer my fear of public speaking and make effective oral presentations?

› Although public speaking can be intimidating, audiences are generally sympathetic, speaking becomes easier once it is underway, and practice leads to success.

› The first minute of the presentation, oral transition points, visual aids, and having enough practice are important.

› Use the PREP system for giving impromptu (unrehearsed) talks.

[KEY TERMS AND CONCEPTS]

Freewriting (p. 172)

Brainstorming (p. 173)

Paraphrase (p. 175)

ABBCC structure (p. 179)

Thesis (p. 179)

Voice (p. 183)

Plagiarism (p. 187)

Impromptu talk (p. 195)

[RESOURCES]

ON CAMPUS

If you are having difficulties with writing, the first place to turn to is a cooperative classmate. Ask someone to read a draft of a writing assignment. He or she may be able to make enough constructive comments to allow subsequent drafts to come more easily. In addition, some colleges have writing clinics where you can bring a draft of your paper and work with a counselor. Finally, your instructors may be willing to read preliminary drafts of your work.

IN PRINT

John Langan's book *College Writing Skills* (McGraw-Hill, 2008, 6th ed.) presents a fine introduction to the art and practice of writing, with specific suggestions for how to get started and for editing and polishing first drafts.

Another excellent guide to writing is William Zinsser's classic, *On Writing Well: The Classic Guide to Writing Nonfiction* (HarperResource, 2006). A widely used guide to writing, Zinsser's book is helpful both for beginners and for more experienced writers.

Finally, Stephen Lucas's book *The Art of Public Speaking* (McGraw-Hill, 2008) provides an excellent introduction to public speaking. It is filled with tips for planning and delivering a talk.

ON THE WEB

The following sites on the World Wide Web provide the opportunity to extend your learning about the material in this chapter. (Although the Web addresses were accurate at the time the book was printed, check the *P.O.W.E.R. Learning* Web site [**www.mhhe.com/power**] for any changes that may have occurred.)

> The "Reference Shelf" from the Veterinary Education and Information Network (**vein. library.usyd.edu.au/elibrary/grammar.html**) offers a large collection of links to a variety of college sites providing information on utilization of grammar and effective writing.

> This site from the American College of Emergency Physicians (**www3.acep.org/ PrintFriendly.aspx?id=21766**) offers a comprehensive approach to not only preparing a speech, but delivering it as well. In addition there is a short outline on dealing with speaker apprehension.

> Bartleby.com offers William Strunk Jr. and E. B. White's *The Elements of Style* (**www. bartleby.com/141/**), the first edition of the classic text recommended by writing instructors for many years. This text is filled with helpful hints on word usage, punctuation, and avoiding common mistakes. It's a must for writers serious about improving their writing.

> "Plagiarism: What It Is and How to Recognize and Avoid It" at **www.indiana. edu/~wts/pamphlets/plagiarism.shtml** provides excellent advice and practice in avoiding plagiarism.

TAKING IT TO THE NET

1 Write a brief summary of a news story. Go to Yahoo! (**www.yahoo.com**) and scroll down to the "In the News." Click on and read one of the top stories. Summarize the news story, including only the most important facts.

2 Practice public speaking. Again, go to Yahoo! (**www.yahoo.com**) and scroll down to the "In the News." Read the two top stories and write brief notes for each on an index card. Now find a willing classmate or friend and explain the details of each story using your note cards for reference. Did your listener follow the story? Did he or she find it interesting? Were you able to answer any questions that your listener had?

The Case of . . .
The Reluctant Speaker

"No one," thought Erik Phillips, "could hate public speaking more than I do."

Erik was horrified at the thought of giving a presentation. Not only did he not like standing up in front of others, exposing himself to their scrutiny, but he was also embarrassed by his thick Louisiana accent, which his friends at the northern college he attended teased him about constantly.

He was sure he'd never be able to do it. Erik made up his mind to ask his instructor if he could write a paper instead of making the oral presentation. But before he could, one of his friends in the class told him that he had already asked for an alternative assignment and that the instructor had flatly refused, saying that it would be a "good experience" to give the talk.

Erik was stuck.

1. How would you advise Erik to prepare and organize for his talk?

2. Erik expressed a willingness to write a paper instead of giving a talk. Should he prepare the paper and read it for his presentation? Why or why not? How might he use the research for his paper to help with his talk?

3. Erik is especially nervous about speaking because he believes that his accent interferes with understanding. How might he deal with this particular anxiety? How could friends or classmates help him?

4. Do you think props would be helpful for Erik? What purpose might they serve?

5. What advice would you give Erik to reduce his anxiety?

Memory

Learning Outcomes

By the time you finish this chapter you will be able to

» **LO8.1** Explain what memory is and how it functions.

» **LO8.2** Identify problems with memory and develop strategies for dealing with those problems.

» **LO8.3** Utilize techniques for memorizing information.

The stack of note cards kept getting higher and higher. And as it grew, so did Rosa Carlozzi's sense of frustration. Taking a class on the biology of the human body, Rosa had described the functions of the major organs of the body on separate note cards, hoping that would help her to memorize them. But all that was happening was that the number of cards was increasing each week.

Rosa decided that drastic measures were called for. She began to take her stack of cards with her everywhere she went. Whenever she had a spare moment, she would shuffle through the cards, trying to memorize them. She sometimes felt a little silly walking around with her thick stack of cards. But as she spent more time going over them, she became more confident, and she began to recall more and more.

It worked! By the final, Rosa realized that she had succeeded in memorizing most of the information on the cards. She ended the semester with an A in the course.

Looking Ahead

Most of us have experienced the challenge of memorizing a seemingly impossible amount of information, and we tend to focus on our failures far more than on our successes. But the truth is that our memory capabilities are truly astounding. If you are like the average college student, your vocabulary contains some 50,000 words. You know hundreds of mathematical facts, and you can recall detailed images from scenes you saw years ago. You probably know the lyrics and music of dozens of songs. In fact, simply cataloging the memories you already have might well take a lifetime.

In this chapter, you'll learn how you can improve the memory skills you already have. We'll examine what memory is and why it sometimes fails us. Finally, you will become acquainted with specific ways to learn information so that you can recall it when you need to.

Retrieval
The process of finding information stored in memory

≫ LO 8.1 The Secret of Memory

Sure, sometimes you have trouble recalling information that you know you've learned. Or maybe you don't recall that you learned it, even though in fact you did. But this is not because information has disappeared from your head. The problem is one of *retrieval*. **Retrieval** entails finding information stored in memory and making it conscious so that it can be used. Every piece of information that you've ever learned is buried somewhere in your brain. The trick is to find it when you need it.

The proof of this assertion comes from the biology of memory. Consider what happens when you're exposed to some new information. Say your geometry instructor spends a class talking about the Pythagorean formula in geometry, which maintains that the square of the length of the hypotenuse of a right triangle is equal to the sum of the squares of the two other sides. (You may recall this formula as $a^2 + b^2 = c^2$.)

P Prepare
Determine what you need to remember

O Organize
Relate new material to what you already know

W Work
Use proven strategies to memorize new material

E Evaluate
Test your recall of new information

R Rethink
Consolidate memories through repeated review

P.O.W.E.R. Plan

When you first learn the formula, the wiring connecting a handful of the 70 trillion or so brain cells in your head is changed—forever. The information on the Pythagorean formula is etched into some tiny part of your brain, and unless that part of the brain is damaged in some way through injury or disease, it will stay there for the rest of your life.

The practical outgrowth of this biological process is straightforward: You already remember everything you need to know, and a lot more. With some effort, you could remember the names of everyone in your third-grade class. You know what you ate when you went to the eighth-grade dance. You remember the name of the body of water that borders Iraq. And you could even have remembered where you left your keys the last time you misplaced them.

The key to successful recall is to learn the material initially in a way that will allow you to recall it *easily* later. By using the strategies summarized in the P.O.W.E.R. Plan at the left, you'll be able to do that.

P Prepare ## Remembering the Right Stuff

Memorize what you need to memorize. Forget about the rest.

The average textbook chapter has something like 20,000 words. If you had to recall every word of the chapter, it would be nearly impossible. Furthermore, it would be a waste of time. Being able to spew out paragraphs of material is quite different from the more important ability to recall and deeply understand academic material in meaningful ways.

Within those 20,000 words, there may be only 20 different concepts that you need to learn. And perhaps there are only 10 keywords. *Those* are the pieces of information that should be the focus of your efforts to memorize.

How do you know what's so important that you need to recall it? One way is to use the guides built into most textbooks. Key concepts and terms are often highlighted or in boldface type. Chapters often have summaries that recap the most important information. Use such guideposts to understand what's most critical in a chapter.

Write down what you determine is important. Putting critical information in writing not only helps you manage what you need to remember, but the very act of writing it down makes it easier to memorize the information later.

In short, the first step in building a better memory is to determine just what it is that you wish to recall. By extracting what is important from what is less crucial, you'll be able to limit the amount and extent of the material that you need to recall. You'll be able to focus, laserlike, on what you need to remember.

It's not easy. We're all victims of information overload. We're exposed to more information in a year than our grandparents were exposed to in their entire lifetimes.

At the same time, new technologies such as smart phones and the availability of information on the Web have made us less practiced in using our memory in everyday life. It's no longer necessary to remember phone numbers, addresses, and other crucial bits of information that previously were routinely memorized.

In order to determine what is and is not important to remember, look at the big picture. Don't get lost in minute details. Instead, prepare yourself by taking a broad overview of material you wish to remember, and decide what your goal is going to be. (To begin testing your memory, complete **Try It 1.**)

> An education isn't how much you have committed to memory, or even how much you know. It's being able to differentiate between what you do know and what you don't.
>
> **Anatole France, French novelist (1844–1924)**

Remember This

Read the following story. Pay attention to the details, but don't take notes or make lists.

Demain entered the marketplace slowly, feeling his way. He had never seen such confusion.

Hundreds of wagons, caravans, booths, and carts were drawn up in a broad U, occupying three sides of the enormous town square, their awnings and curtains open and inviting. The colors and odors were a sensual assault; he perceived them not just through his eyes and nose, but as if they were pressing forcibly against his skin. And the sounds! He could scarcely keep himself from bolting back the way he had come, to the safety of the countryside.

A sense of wonder pushed him forward. He walked past gold merchants, with their gray cloaks and watchful eyes, and a potter, her shop filled three shelves high with vases, bottles, and jars of deep blues, reds, and yellows that Demain—accustomed to the brown clay that adorned his mother's kitchen—had never even imagined possible. Cloths were on sale in the booth next to the potter's—shamelessly long bolts of impossibly patterned prints, depicting herons, bulls, schools of fish, a field of wheat, great bowls of fruit, and men and women engaged in the pursuits he knew from stories: They danced in bold colors and graceful postures, harvested vast fields of bounty, fought battles of intricate strategy, and drank and courted in riotous taverns.

Past the dealers in rugs, chairs, hats, shoes, and wagons; past the blacksmith's huge muddy arms beating out rugged tools and fine weapons; past the fortune tellers and musicians, Demain at last came to the vendors of food and drink. Never had he felt so hungry. He was lifted off his feet—he swore he was floating—by the aroma of long lines of sausages, sides of beef, whole lambs, chickens on spits the length of spears, bacon and hams, fried potatoes, great vats of boiling vegetables, stewing tomatoes, and breads—all shapes and sizes of loaves, twisted into braids, curled into circles, flattened, puffed, elongated, pocketed, and glazed.

Demain felt the two coppers in his pocket—his holiday bounty—and hoped they would be enough.

Note: We'll return to the story of Demain later. For now, read on.
To Try It online, go to www.mhhe.com/power.

Thinking about the big picture also is important because it will help you move beyond sheer memorization. The point of improving your memory skills is not just to better recall a series of facts in order to spew them out on a test. Instead, the ultimate goal is to recall information in a way that allows you to understand it more fully, to think critically about it, and to be able to apply it to new situations.

>> LO 8.2 **○ Organize** Relating New Material to What You Already Know

Don't think of memorization as pumping gasoline (new information) into an almost-empty gas tank (your brain). You're not filling something that is empty. On the contrary, you are filling a container that already has a lot of things in it, that is infinitely expandable, and that never empties out.

If you approach each new memorization task as something entirely new and unrelated to your previous knowledge, you'll have enormous difficulty recalling it. On the other hand, if you connect it to what you already know, you'll be able to recall it far better. The way to get your brain to do this organizational work for you is by thinking about the associations the new material has with the old.

> "In the practical use of our intellect, forgetting is as important as remembering"
> **Psychologist William James**

> ▸ **Personalize information.** Suppose you need to remember information about the consequences of global warming, such

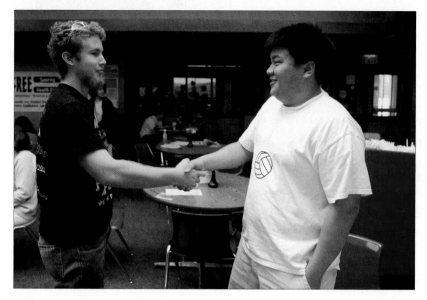

What would help you remember a person's name after you were introduced to him or her for the first time?

as the fact that the level of the oceans is predicted to rise. You might think about the rising level of the ocean as it relates to your personal memories of visits to the beach. You might think what a visit to the beach would be like with dramatically higher water levels, visualizing a shrunken shoreline with no room for sunbathing. Then whenever you think about global warming in the future, your mind is likely to associate this fairly abstract concept with its concrete consequences for beaches. The association you made while rehearsing the information makes it personal, long-lasting, and useful. (You can see this for yourself in **Try It 2** on page 208.)

▸ **Organize information by place.** *Where* you learn something makes a difference in how well you can recall it. Memory researchers have found that people actually remember things better in the place where they first studied and learned them. Consequently, one of the ways to jog your memory is to try to re-create the situation in which you first learned what you're trying to remember. If you memorized the colors that litmus paper turns when it is placed in acids and bases while you were in your campus science library, it might be helpful during a test to recall the correct colors by imagining yourself in the science library thinking about the colors.

Another effective place-related strategy is to introduce new data into your mind in the place that you know you're going to need to recall it at some future moment. For instance, suppose you know that you're going to be tested on certain material in the room in which your class is held. Try to do at least some of your studying in that same room.

≫ LO 8.3 · ⓦ Work · Using Proven Strategies to Memorize New Material

One of the good things about the work of memorization is that you have your choice of literally dozens of techniques. Depending on the kind of material you need to recall and how much you already know about the subject, you can turn to any number of methods.

As we sort through the various options, keep in mind that no one strategy works by itself. (And some strategies don't seem to work for example. Forget about supplements like ginko biloba—there's no clear scientific evidence that they are effective.[1]) Instead, try the following proven strategies and find those that work best for you. Feel free to devise your own strategies or add those that have worked for you in the past.

Rehearsal

Think it again: rehearsal. Say it aloud: rehearsal. Think of it in terms of the three syllables that make up the word: re—hear—sal. OK, one more time—say the word "rehearsal."

Journal Reflections

What Sort of Memory Do I Have— and Want?

1. What kinds of information do you remember best: faces, shapes, colors, smells, names, dates, or facts? Why do you think this is?

2. What kinds of information do you have the greatest difficulty remembering? Why do you think this type of information is hard for you to remember?

3. Is there any particular source of information about which you can remember exceptional amounts, such as baseball records or movie trivia? Why do you think you remember this information so effortlessly?

4. Do you use any memorization techniques now? Have you ever tried any in the past?

5. Suppose scientists devised a "memory drug" that would allow you to remember *everything* to which you were exposed. What would be the advantages and disadvantages of such a drug? Would you be likely to use it?

If you're scratching your head over the last paragraph, it's to illustrate the point of **rehearsal:** to transfer material that you encounter into memory. If you don't rehearse information in some way, it will end up like most of the information to which we're exposed: on the garbage heap of lost memory.

To test if you've succeeded in transferring the word "rehearsal" into your memory, put down this book and go off for a few minutes. Do something entirely unrelated to reading this book. Have a snack, catch up on the latest sports scores on ESPN, or read the front page of the newspaper.

Are you back? If the word "rehearsal" popped into your head when you picked up this book again, you've passed your first memory test. You can be assured that the word "rehearsal" has been transferred into your memory.

Rehearsal is the key strategy in remembering information. If you don't rehearse material, it will never make it into memory. Repeating the information, summarizing it, associating it with other memories, and above all thinking about it when you first come across it will ensure that rehearsal will be effective in pushing the material into memory.

Rehearsal
The process of practicing and learning material to transfer it into memory

Try It!

Organize Your Memory

As critical thinking expert Diane Halpern points out, having an organized memory is like having a neat bedroom: Its value is that you know you'll be able to find something when you need it. To prove the point, try this exercise she devised.[2]

Read the following 15 words at a rate of approximately one per second:

girl

heart

robin

purple

finger

flute

blue

organ

man

hawk

green

lung

eagle

child

piano

Now, cover the list, and write down as many of the words as you can on a separate sheet of paper. How many words are there on your list? _____

Mnemonics

Mnemonics

Formal techniques used to make material more readily remembered

Acronym

A word or phrase formed by the first letters of a series of terms

This odd word (pronounced in an equally odd fashion, with the "m" silent—"neh MON ix") describes formal techniques used to make material more readily remembered. **Mnemonics** are the tricks of the trade that professional memory experts use, and you too can use them to nail down the sort of information you will often need to recall for tests.

Among the most common mnemonics are the following:

> **Acronyms.** You're already well acquainted with **acronyms,** words or phrases formed by the first letters of a series of terms. For instance, although you may not have known it, the word "laser" is actually an acronym for "light amplification by stimulated emissions of radiation," and "radar" is an acronym for "radio detection and ranging."
>
> Acronyms can be a big help in remembering things. If you took music lessons, you may know that FACE spells out the names of the notes that appear in the spaces on the treble clef music staff ("F," "A," "C," and "E," starting at the bottom of the staff). Roy G. Biv is a favorite of physics students who must remember the colors of the spectrum (red, orange, yellow, green, blue, indigo, and

After you've done this, read the following list:

green

blue

purple

man

girl

child

piano

flute

organ

heart

lung

finger

eagle

hawk

robin

Now cover this second list and write down as many of the words as you can on the other side of the separate sheet of paper.

How many words did you remember this time? Did you notice that the words on both lists are identical? Did you remember more the second time? (Most people do.) Why do you think most people remember more when the words are organized as they are in the second list?

WORKING IN A GROUP:
Discuss with your classmates ways in which you can organize material from this book to make it easier to remember.

To Try It online, go to www.mhhe.com/power.

violet). And P.O.W.E.R. stands for—well, by this point in the book, you probably remember.

The benefit of acronyms is that they help us to recall a complete list of steps or items. The drawback, though, is that the acronym itself has to be remembered, and sometimes we may not recall it when we need it. For instance, Roy G. Biv is not exactly the sort of name that readily comes to mind. And even if we do remember Roy G. Biv, we might get stuck trying to recall what a particular letter stands for. (For example, we'd probably prefer not to spend a lot of time during a test trying to remember if the "B" stands for brown or beige or blue.)

▸ **Acrostics.** After learning to use the acronym "FACE" to remember the notes on the spaces of the music staff, many beginning musicians learn that the names of the lines on the staff form the acrostic, "Every Good Boy Deserves Fudge." **Acrostics** are sentences in which the first letters spell out something that needs to be recalled. The benefits—as well as the drawbacks—of acrostics are similar to those of acronyms. (You can explore acronyms and acrostics in **Try It 3** on page 210.)

Acrostic
A sentence in which the first letters of the words correspond to material that is to be remembered

Try It!

3 Do-It-Yourself Acronyms and Acrostics

In the first part of this **Try It,** work individually to create an acronym and an acrostic.

1. Figure out an acronym to remind you of the names of the five Great Lakes, using the first letters of their names (which are Erie, Huron, Michigan, Ontario, Superior).

2. Devise an acrostic for the nine planets in order of their average distance from the sun. Their names, in order, are Mercury, Venus, Earth, Mars, Jupiter, Saturn, Uranus, Neptune, Pluto. (Bonus question: Because many astronomers no longer believe Pluto is a planet, devise an acrostic that omits Pluto and just contains the first eight planets.)

After you've tried to create the acronym and acrostic, meet in a group and discuss these questions: How successful were you in devising effective acronyms and acrostics? Do some of the group members' creations seem more effective than others? Why? Is the act of creating them an important component of helping to remember what they represent, or would having them created by someone else be as helpful in recalling them? For your information, a common acronym for the Great Lakes is HOMES (**H**uron, **O**ntario, **M**ichigan, **E**rie, **S**uperior), and a traditional acrostic for the order of the planets is **M**y **V**ery **E**ducated **M**other **J**ust **S**erved **U**s **N**ine **P**izzas. (As for the bonus question that omits Pluto, future generations may use the acrostic My Very Educated Mother Just Served Us Noodles.)

To Try It online, go to www.mhhe.com/power.

> **Rhymes and jingles.** "Thirty days hath September, April, June, and November. . . ." If you know the rest of the rhyme, you're familiar with one of the most commonly used mnemonic jingles in the English language. Similarly, some of us learned the main theme of Schubert's Unfinished Symphony by singing the words "This is the symphony that Schubert wrote and never finished" when the theme first appears. For those who learned to recognize the symphony by using this mnemonic, it is virtually impossible to hear the symphony without recalling the words.

Although mnemonics are helpful, keep in mind that they have a number of significant shortcomings. First, they don't focus on the meaning of the items being remembered. Because information that is learned in terms of its surface characteristics—such as first letters that form a word—is less likely to be retained than information that is learned in terms of its meaning, mnemonic devices are an imperfect route to memorization.

There's another problem with mnemonics: Sometimes it takes as much effort to create a mnemonic device as it would to memorize the material in the first place. And because the mnemonic itself has no meaning, it can be forgotten.

Despite their drawbacks, mnemonics can be useful. They are particularly helpful when the material being memorized includes a list of items or a series of steps.

The Method of Loci and the Peg Method: Special Help for Recalling Sequences and Lists

The ancient Greeks had a way with words. Their orators could deliver speeches that went on for hours, without notes. How did they remember what they wanted to say?

They used a procedure called the **method of loci.** *Loci* (pronounced "low sigh") is the Latin word for "places," and it helps describe a procedure in which items in a sequence you wish to remember—such as the sections of a speech or a series of events—are thought of as "located" in a different place in a building.

Consider, for example, a speech that has three major sections: an introduction, a main body, and a conclusion. Each of the three sections has various points that you need to recall also.

To use the method of loci, you'd first visualize the living room, kitchen, and bedroom of a house with which you were familiar. Next, you'd mentally "place" the introduction of the speech into the living room of the house. You would mentally place each of the *parts* of the introduction on a different piece of furniture, following the way in which the furniture was laid out in the room (for example, you might proceed clockwise from the door). The easy chair might contain the first point of the introduction, the sofa the next point, and an end table the last point. Then you'd move into the kitchen and do the same thing with the body of the paper, laying out your arguments on different pieces of kitchen furniture or appliances. Finally, you'd end up in the bedroom, where you'd "place" the conclusion.

You can use the method of loci not only for public speaking, but for any situation in which you are trying to remember a series of steps. For example, if you wanted to recall the steps in the scientific method (e.g., develop a theory, form a hypothesis, conduct an experiment, etc.), you could think of each step as taking place in a different part of your apartment.

A close cousin of the method of loci is the **peg method.** The peg method uses a series of keywords tied to the digits one to ten to help you recall an important sequence of numbers. For instance, a set of "pegs" that you could use would link numbers with these words:

One is a sun.

Two is a zoo.

Three is me.

Four is a store.

Five is a dive.

Six are sticks.

Seven is heaven.

Eight is a gate.

Nine is a pine.

Ten is a den.

By thinking of exotic images using the peg words tied to the numbers, it becomes easier to recall a specific group of numbers that you need to memorize. For instance, suppose you had trouble remembering the value of *pi,* used to

Method of loci
A memory technique by which the elements in a list are visualized as occupying the parts of a familiar place

Peg method
A memory technique by which a series of memorized words is linked by images to a list of items to be remembered

Have you ever wondered how some waiters can remember what their customers have ordered without writing anything down? They use the same simple memory strategies that you can use to recall information you'll need to remember for tests.

calculate the circumference of a circle (3.14, in case you don't remember). Take the three relevant digits—3, 1, and 4—and translate them into the relevant peg words—me (3), sun (1), and store (4)—and think of an image linking the three.

For example, one possibility is to memorize the image of yourself wearing sunglasses, heading out to a store on a sunny day. Then, when you need to remember the value of *pi,* this image will pop into your head, and you'll be able to use the peg word system to figure out the number associated with each part of the image.

The peg method can also be used to memorize ordered lists of items, when the sequence in which they appear is important. For instance, you could use the peg system if you needed to recall the specific order in which bones of the foot and leg were connected to one another for your anatomy class. To use the peg system in this way, you link images of the ordered set of items to the 10 "numbers." The first item is linked with the sun, the second with a zoo, and so on.

Involve Multiple Senses

The more senses you can involve when you're trying to learn new material, the better you'll be able to remember. Here's why: Every time we encounter new information, all of our senses are potentially at work. For instance, if we witness a car crash, we receive sensory input from the sight of the two cars hitting each other, the sound of the impact, and perhaps the smell of burning rubber. Each piece of sensory information is stored in a separate location in the brain, and yet all the pieces are linked together in extraordinarily intricate ways.

What this means is that when we seek to remember the details of the crash, recalling a memory of one of the sensory experiences—such as what we heard—can trigger recall of the other types of memories. For example, thinking about the *sound* the two cars made when they hit can bring back memories of the way the scene looked.

In fact, just as we have preferred learning styles, many of us have a favorite memory style—one that we use most often when trying to recall information. Take a moment to learn about your own memory style by completing **Try It 4** on page 214.

You can make use of the fact that memories are stored in multiple ways by applying the following techniques:

> **When you learn something, use your body.** Don't sit passively at your desk. Instead, move around. Stand up; sit down. Touch the page. Trace figures with your fingers. Talk to yourself. Think out loud. It may seem strange, but doing this increases the number of ways in which the information is stored. By involving every part of your body, you've increased the number of potential ways to trigger a relevant memory later, when you need to recall it. And when one memory is triggered, other related memories may come tumbling back.

> **Draw and diagram the material.** We've already considered (in Chapter 4) the power of concept maps, the method of structuring written material by graphically grouping and connecting key ideas and themes. When we create a concept map, one of the things we're doing is expanding the modalities in which information can be stored in our minds.

Other types of drawing can be useful in aiding later recall. Creating drawings, sketches, and even cartoons can help us remember better. Your creations don't have to be great art or detailed, involved illustrations. Even rough sketches are effective, because creating them gets both the visual and tactile senses involved.

figure 8.1
Visualizing Memory

Recording of information

Storage of information in memory

Display of information retrieved from memory

> **Visualize.** Visualization is a technique by which images are formed to ensure that material is recalled. For instance, you now know that memory requires three basic steps: the initial recording of information, the storage of that information, and, ultimately, the retrieval of the stored information. As you read the three steps, you probably see them as logical and straightforward processes. But how do you remember them?

Visualization
A memory technique by which images are formed to help recall material

You might visualize a computer, with its keyboard, disks, and monitor (see **Figure 8.1**). The keyboard represents the initial recording of information. The disk represents the storage of information, and the monitor represents the display of information that has been retrieved from memory. If you can put these images in your mind, it will help you remember the three basic memory steps later.

Don't stop at visualizing images just in your mind's eye. Actually drawing what you visualize will help you remember the material even better.

Visualization is effective because it serves several purposes. It helps make abstract ideas concrete; it engages multiple senses; it permits us to link different bits of information together; and it provides us with a context for storing information.

What kind of visualization works best? There's a simple rule: Weird is good. The more extreme, outlandish, and eccentric the image you create, the more notable it will be and so the easier it will be to remember. And if you can remember the image, you'll probably remember the information that's attached to it (see **Try It 5** on page 216).

Think Positively

Emotions matter. If you're in a negative frame of mind when you try to memorize something, your negative feelings can become attached to the memory, making you less likely to recall it because you'll automatically tend to avoid those bad feelings. The opposite is also true: If you think positively about the process of memorization, those more positive feelings will end up being etched into your memory.

Of course, feelings can't be turned off in the same way we're able to turn off a light. If you feel nervous and scared about memorizing all the formulas you need to for your chemistry midterm, you can't just tell yourself it's great fun. But if you

4 Determine Your Memory Style

What's your dominant memory style? Do you most easily remember sounds, sights, or the way things feel? Read the statements below and circle the response choice that most closely describes your habits.

To help recall lectures, I . . .

V. Read the notes I took during class.

A. Close my eyes and try to hear what the instructor said.

K. Try to place myself back in the lecture room and feel what was going on at the time.

To remember a complex procedure, I . . .

V. Write down the steps I have to follow.

A. Listen carefully and repeatedly to the instructions.

K. Do it over and over again.

To learn sentences in a foreign language, I do best if I . . .

V. Read them on paper to see how they're written.

A. Hear them in my head until I can say them aloud.

K. See someone speaking them and then practice moving my mouth and hands the way the speaker did.

If I have to learn a dance move, I like . . .

V. To see a diagram of the steps before trying it.

A. Someone to coach me through it while I try it.

K. To watch it once and then give it a try.

When I recall a very happy moment, I tend to . . .

V. Visualize it in my head.

A. Hear the sounds that I heard when experiencing it.

K. Feel with my hands and body what I felt at the time.

When I have to remember driving directions, I usually . . .

V. See a map of the route in my mind.

A. Repeat the directions aloud to myself.

K. Feel my hands steering and the car driving along the correct route.

"Don't let those few Einsteins who can ace a test by never attending class and by sleeping on the textbook the night before trick you into using their study methods. My roommate tried to convince me that studying by osmosis was a proven method. Trust me, it isn't."

Keith Vernon, student, University of Puget Sound[3]

recognize your feelings, they lose much of their power to influence you and to block memories.

Overlearning

Think back to when you were learning your basic multiplication facts ($1 \times 1 = 1$; $2 \times 2 = 4$; and so forth). Let's suppose you had put each multiplication problem on a flash card, and you decided to go through your entire set of cards, trying to get every problem right.

The first time you went through the set of cards and answered all the problems correctly, would you feel as if you'd memorized them perfectly and that you'd never again make an error? You

ANSWER KEY:

If you chose mostly **V**s, your main memory style is visual; your preference is to remember things in terms of the way they appear. If you chose mostly **A**s, your main memory style is auditory; your preference is to recall material in terms of sound. If you chose mostly **K**s, your main memory style is kinesthetic; your preference is to remember using your sense of touch.

Keep in mind that this questionnaire only gives a rough idea of how we usually use our memories. Remember: All of us use all of the memory styles during the course of each day.

After completing the questionnaire, answer these questions:

How does your memory style affect the way you recall information?

How does your memory style affect the way you learn things initially?

How does your memory style relate to your preferred learning style?

How could you make greater use of your less-preferred memory style?

To Try It online, go to www.mhhe.com/power.

shouldn't. You would need several instances of perfect performance to be sure you had learned the multiplication facts completely.

Lasting learning doesn't come until you have over-learned the material. **Over-learning** consists of studying and rehearsing material past the point of initial mastery. Through overlearning, recall becomes automatic. Rather than searching for a fact and going through mental contortions until perhaps the information surfaces, overlearning permits us to recall the information without even thinking about it.

To put the principle of overlearning to work, don't stop studying at the point when you can say to yourself, "Well, I'll probably pass this test." You may be right, but that's all you'll do—pass. Instead, spend extra time learning the material until it becomes as familiar as an old pair of jeans.

Overlearning

Studying and rehearsing material past the point of initial mastery to the point at which recall becomes automatic

5

Visualize the Possibilities

You may have noticed how important visualization is to memory. In fact, many of the techniques we've discussed in this chapter rely in some measure on visualization, especially your visualization of extreme or absurd images.

Test the truth of this statement by drawing a concept map—itself a visual form of organizing material—of the concept of visualization. Start with the word "Visualization" in the center of the map and link as many other memory and mnemonic techniques to it as you can. For example, you might start by adding the concept of "drawing an image"—and then adding "weird image" to that. You may be surprised at the richness of your map.

Visualization

How well does the concept map reflect what you know about visualization? Is it a useful tool for you? Do you think that the act of creating a concept map itself is helpful in memorizing the material? Would using someone else's concept map be less helpful than creating your own?

 WORKING IN A GROUP:

Compare your concept map with those of your classmates. What are the major similarities and differences? How do you account for them? Are some of the participants' concept maps more likely to help recall information than others?

To Try It online, go to **www.mhhe.com/power**.

Special Memorization Strategies for Special Courses

Foreign language courses, as well as those in math and science, often pose particular memorization challenges. Here are some special strategies you can use to attack these subject areas:

For foreign language courses:

- When memorizing vocabulary, don't just read words silently—say them aloud and write them out.
- Using Post-It notes, write the name of objects around your living space in the foreign language.
- Practice speaking in the language lab.
- When others are called on in class, give answers silently to every question.
- Don't be afraid to make mistakes—you probably occasionally mispronounce words in your native language, without dire consequences.

For math and science courses:

- Memorize formulas by learning how to derive them.
- Practice formulating problems, not just solving them.
- Don't memorize problems—memorize concepts. Once you fully understand a concept and know how to apply it, there's often little left to memorize.
- Memorize in an organized way, starting with the most simple concepts and moving to more complex ones. Think about how the concepts build on one another.

E Evaluate

Testing Your Recall of New Information

The memory strategies just described can bring you to a point where you probably feel comfortable in your ability to remember the material you've been learning. Once you've used one or more of them to help you, it's time to test yourself—to evaluate whether you'll be able to recall the material when you need it. There are several ways to evaluate your memory:

> **Use in-text review questions and tests.** Many textbook chapters end with a quiz or a set of review questions about the material. Some have questions scattered throughout the chapter. Don't ignore them! Not only do such questions indicate what the writer of the book thought was important for you to learn and memorize, but they can also provide an excellent opportunity for evaluating your memory.

> Even if you've answered the review questions earlier, while you were first reading the material (which is always a good idea), answer them again later as you study for the test and then the final.

> **Test yourself.** Temporarily transform yourself into your instructor, and prioritize what you're most likely to be tested on. Then create your own test, writing out some questions.

> Later, after as little as a few hours, take the test, and then grade it. How have you done? If you've achieved a grade that you're satisfied with, then fine. If, on the other hand, you've missed some key pieces of information, then you'll want to return to work and spend more time on memorization.

Memory On the Job

- Military genius Julius Caesar could dictate as many as seven letters at a time to his secretaries.

- Conductor Arturo Toscanini memorized every note of 400 different musical pieces. When a musician told him, just before a concert, that his instrument had just broken and he was unable to play a particular note, Toscanini paused a moment, but then told him not to worry, because that note was not in the piece they were about to play.

- Warren Buffett, one of the world's most successful investors, could recall sales figures from companies in which he had invested dozens of years earlier.[4]

Improving your memory is not only something that will help you do better in college. Whatever your future job—be it military general, musician, business tycoon, or anything else—a good memory will further your career success.

Not all professionals need the same kind of memory skills, of course. A camera operator at a television network must remember lighting combinations; lawyers need to recall the details of witness testimony; elementary school teachers must remember what kinds of exercises work best for certain students; physicians need to keep track of a host of medical conditions and medicines. But in each of these professions, memory abilities are an important aspect of job performance.

Memory is also important in terms of keeping track of people's names and functions. Being able to recall the names of those with whom you work, professional colleagues from other companies, and clients is an important skill. People are flattered when you remember their names. It says you think they are important and worth noticing.

In short, remember this: The strategies that you learn in college to improve your memory will pay big dividends in the world of work.

> **Team up with a friend or use a study group.** When it comes to evaluating your memory, two heads (or more!) are often better than one. Working with a classmate or study group—especially others who may have a different preferred learning style from your own—can help you test the limits of your memory and assess areas in which you need work.
>
> For instance, you and a friend can take turns testing yourselves, switching back and forth between asking and answering questions. Turn it into a contest: One of you can be Alex Trebek of *Jeopardy,* and the other, a contestant. Or work with several people, forming a study group. The important thing is to switch who's asking and who's answering the questions. Even when you're directing questions to others—evaluating their memory—you're giving your own memory a workout. (Put your memory to the test in **Try It 6.**)

R Rethink ## Consolidating Memories

Memory consolidation
The process by which the physical links between brain cells that represent memory become fixed and stable over time

Like fine wines, memories need time to age. Psychologists talk about this as the process of **memory consolidation.** What this means is that the physical links between brain cells that represent memory in the brain need time to become fixed and stable. This process explains why information is not suddenly and permanently established in memory the first time we're exposed to it. In fact, the process of consolidation may continue for days and even—in some cases—for years.[5]

Remember Demain

Remember the passage earlier in this chapter (**Try It 1**) about Demain, who found himself in the midst of a colorful, aromatic bazaar of booths and shops? Without turning back to the passage, write down everything you can remember about what Demain experienced in the marketplace—the shops, sights, and foods.

Now reread the passage, trying to remember its details by using one or more techniques from this chapter. You might use the method of loci, the peg method, the method of organizing ideas into chunks, or other techniques. Then answer these questions about the passage:

1. What scenes were depicted on the cloths?

2. What were the gold merchants wearing?

3. After the cloth shop, what businesses did Demain pass to arrive at the vendors of food and drink?

4. What foods did Demain see and smell at the fair?

How would you assess your performance on these questions? Do you think you would have remembered more initially if you had used some of the memory techniques in this chapter? Do you see how you could employ these techniques in your own studying? Did one seem to work better for you than others?

To Try It online, go to www.mhhe.com/power.

Players of games such as *Trivial Pursuit*® know the value of having a teammate to help dredge up obscure facts from memory. In the same way, studying with others can help you test and expand you own memory and uncover areas that need improvement.

Obviously you don't have years to wait. But it does pay to try to memorize material in advance of the time that you'll really need to use it. Then, when you go back to reconsider it, it will become even more well-established in your mind.

The phenomenon of memory consolidation explains why cramming is not a great idea. As we discussed in the chapter on taking tests, cramming is the process of spending the preceding evening or even the hours just before a test trying to memorize as much as possible. The memories that come from cramming simply don't last, because they aren't rehearsed and processed sufficiently. It's far more effective to distribute studying over many shorter sessions.

The best way to ensure good recall is to return to the material even after your personal evaluation tells you that you've got it down. Wait several days, if possible, and then review it again. You'll be able to identify the aspects of the material that you know well, as well as the things that just haven't jelled yet in memory. Rethinking the material, then, not only permits you to consolidate memory but also helps you identify where you need more work.

Speaking of Success

NAME: **Jordan M. Miller**

SCHOOL: **Surry Community College, Dobson, North Carolina**

For Jordan Miller, there were three keys to academic success that permitted him to make a successful transition to college: developing good organizational skills, learning new reading strategies, and learning to speak up in class and ask the right questions. Until he mastered those skills, academic success was elusive.

"I was struggling in my junior year at high school," he recalled, "and noticed that my peers were preparing to go on to college and realized that I wasn't where I wanted to be at the time."

One immediate solution was to find a personal place to study, which helped him organize his studying.

"Everyone has different study habits," he noted, "but for me, I had to find a place where I could always go to study. Before that, I was studying all over the house. But after I got more organized, I found a specific place to study and saw I could concentrate better, and things would go faster."

Miller's pursuit of new study habits and approaches were further expanded when he enrolled in Surry Community College and took a reading class.

"I noticed that when I would read something, by the time I reached the end of the page I forgot what I had read," he said. "Through a reading class at Surry, I began to slow my reading. I started to highlight

sections and annotate important bits of information such as names and dates in the margins. This helped a lot.

"As a result I didn't have to go back and re-read the book. Instead, I could just review my notes and annotations," Miller added. "In addition, I noticed that I, as well as other students, would often skip over graphs and figures. But I came to the conclusion that they were very important."

Miller, who plans to continue his education at the University of North Carolina at Wilmington, also overcame his fear of speaking up in class and asking questions, which proved to be a key skill.

"I always sat in the back of the class, but I found there were too many distractions. Just about anything would sidetrack me," he said. "As soon as I moved to the front, things changed.

"But I was scared to ask questions, fearing the other students would think I wasn't smart enough," Miller added. "It was only after I started asking questions that I realized that all my classmates had the same questions."

"I would urge all students to ask questions and seek out the teacher for explanations. And remember, if you have a question about the material, others probably have the same question, too," he said.

Looking Back

What is memory and how does it function?

> Information we actively process is permanently etched into the brain, but it is not always readily available for retrieval.

> The challenge is to recall information when we need it, and the key to effective recall is learning material in a way that makes recall easy.

Why might I have problems with memory, and how can I deal with those problems?

> The problems we have with memory are mostly related to the inability to recall or retrieve information when it is needed. However, if information is rehearsed carefully, you can usually recall it more easily.

> Memory can be improved through careful preparation, by selecting in advance the pieces of information that are worthy of memorization and rehearsal.

> Another key to effective memorization is linking new information to information that is already in memory.

What are some techniques I can use for memorizing information?

> Many memory techniques are available to improve memorization. Rehearsal is a primary one, as is the use of mnemonics such as acronyms, acrostics, and rhymes.

> Other memory techniques are the method of loci, the peg method, visualization, and the use of multiple senses while learning new material.

> Overlearning is a basic principle of memorization.

> Memory takes some time—days or even longer—to reach the point of consolidation, when the physical links between brain cells that represent memory become stable. The need for consolidation explains why cramming is ineffective for long-term recall.

[KEY TERMS AND CONCEPTS]

Retrieval (p. 203)

Rehearsal (p. 207)

Mnemonics (p. 208)

Acronym (p. 208)

Acrostic (p. 209)

Method of loci (p. 211)

Peg method (p. 211)

Visualization (p. 213)

Overlearning (p. 215)

Memory consolidation (p. 218)

[RESOURCES]

ON CAMPUS

If you have considerably more difficulty memorizing material than your classmates, it's possible that you might have a learning disability. If you suspect this, visit the college learning disabilities office or counseling center.

IN PRINT

In *Improving Your Memory* (Johns Hopkins, 2005), Janet Fogler and Lynn Stern provide an overview of practical tips on maximizing your memory. Barry Gordon and Lisa Berger provide insight into the functioning of memory and how to improve it in *Intelligent Memory* (Penguin, 2004). Finally, *The Memory Doctor* by Douglas Mason and Spencer Smith (New Harbinger Publications, 2005) offers simple techniques for improving memory.

ON THE WEB

The following sites on the World Wide Web provide the opportunity to extend your learning about the material in this chapter. (Although the Web addresses were accurate at the time the book was printed, check the *P.O.W.E.R. Learning* Web site [**www.mhhe.com/power**] for any changes that may have occurred.)

> "Concept Mapping" (**www.coun.uvic.ca/learning/critical-thinking/concept-mapping.html**), an online handout from the University of Victoria's Learning Skills Program, outlines this memory aid, which improves recall by building meaning structures around key concepts.

> Need a mnemonic? Have one you'd like to share? Then just go to **www.mnemonic-device.com/,** a new site devoted entirely to mnemonics. This fun and educational site covers a variety of subjects from astronomy to weather.

> Mind Tools, a bookstore specializing in works on memory, offers a number of free online articles (**www.mindtools.com/memory.html**) detailing methods for improving memory. It includes examples of how each technique can be applied to such topics as remembering lists and foreign languages.

TAKING IT TO THE NET

1 Practice the rehearsal technique for storing information in memory. Go to Yahoo! (**dir.yahoo.com**) and click on "Regional" and again on "U.S. States." Click on your state, then on "Government," and finally on "Elected and Appointed Officials" to find the names of your state's U.S. Senators. Repeat the names several times. Now explore another, unrelated site on the Web. After a few minutes, write down the names of your state's U.S. Senators from memory. How did you do?

2 Practice the visualization memory technique. Go to MovieWeb's site listing the top 1,000 all-time highest grossing movies (**www.movieweb.com/movies/box-office/alltime.php**). Try to memorize the top 10 movies by creating weird visual images based on the titles.

The Case of . . .
Remember the Alamo

For Kyle Binder, history had always been a hard subject. Although he had no trouble learning general historical trends and concepts, he had difficulty keeping names, dates, and places sorted out.

Consequently, when his American history instructor, Ms. Teeler, announced that a major history exam was scheduled for the following week, Kyle panicked. He hadn't finished 100 pages of the assigned reading (300 pages altogether!), and here he was expected to learn what seemed to be virtually everything there was to know about the United States' western expansion during the 1800s. Ms. Teeler had said that the test would focus in particular on the Battle of the Alamo and its significance in U.S. history. When Kyle couldn't even recall where the Alamo was located, he knew he'd better get started memorizing. But where to begin?

1. How should Kyle prepare for the history exam? Should he simply get the history text and start reading? Why or why not?

2. How can Kyle prevent the facts of history from appearing to be a jumble of random words and numbers? How should he use his existing knowledge to structure historical information? Why might this become easier the more often Kyle does it?

3. Suppose Kyle is expected to remember the names of several officers in the two armies involved in the Battle of the Alamo, names that seem unusual to him and very hard to remember. Which memory technique is likely to be most effective? How would it work?

4. To remember lists of events in the western expansion movement, what technique would you recommend that Kyle use? How would it work?

5. How could Kyle use multiple senses while learning about the western expansion and the Battle of the Alamo?

Choosing Your Courses and Major

Learning Outcomes

By the time you finish this chapter you will be able to

» **LO9.1** Create a plan to prepare for the academic choices that college demands.

» **LO9.2** Outline a strategy for choosing courses that ensure you are getting the most out of your studies.

» **LO9.3** Explain how participation in service learning can improve your college experience.

» **LO9.4** Explain the criteria for choosing a major.

"Physics for Poets." The course title jumped out at Gwen Izell. She had never liked science much, but she was intrigued by this title. Here was a class that seemed designed with her in mind. "Physics for Poets," the description began, "is designed for nonscience majors. It presents the links between physics and the arts." Gwen decided to take a chance and enroll in the class.

It turned out to be one of the best decisions she ever made. She loved the course. The instructor was terrific, making physics fascinating. Not only did she begin to like the subject matter but she was also good at it.

Gwen was hooked. She took several other science courses over the next semesters. And during her senior year she found herself in an interview with a middle school principal, telling him—a bit to her surprise—that she'd be glad to teach seventh-grade physical science.

Looking Ahead

Our academic and professional careers are propelled by many forces, not the least of which is chance. Gwen Izell, like many other students, found a new direction while leafing through her course list. Although she never would have predicted at the start of college that she would end up taking a variety of science courses and teaching physics, her willingness to take a chance in selecting a course led to a new passion and to a career opportunity.

In this chapter we focus on choosing an academic course of study, one of the central challenges of college life. Not only do the choices we make color our entire college experience, but they also may determine the path we follow once we graduate.

This chapter begins by considering the many choices that you'll have to make as a routine part of attending college, including the choice of courses, instructors, and especially majors—each of which has long-term implications. You'll learn ways to select courses each term that meet your personal needs and maximize your chances of getting the courses you want.

Ultimately, the degree to which your college education benefits you is in your hands. By learning various strategies, you can act decisively to get the most out of your college experience.

Making Academic Choices

It's a moment filled with promise.

A list of courses for the upcoming term lies on the table in front of you. Many of them sound interesting. Each offers the possibilities of new knowledge and therefore has the potential to change your life in significant ways.

As you leaf through the course catalog and begin to make your decisions, you will likely be feeling a wide range of emotions: anticipation over what you'll learn; hope that the course can bring you closer to your dreams; fear that you won't be able to do well; and excitement that you're proceeding with your college career, taking another of the many small steps that will eventually add up to a complete journey through college.

Choosing what courses to take can be intimidating. But if you approach the problem thoughtfully, your final choices will make the best of the possibilities offered. Let's consider how to proceed, using the P.O.W.E.R. Plan on the right as a guide.

P.O.W.E.R Plan

>> LO **9.1** **P Prepare**

Becoming Familiar with Your Options and Requirements

Choosing which courses to take requires that you take several significant preparatory steps before you jump in. These include the following:

Familiarize Yourself with Your College Catalog

Your college catalog—which may be published as an actual booklet, be located entirely online, or both—is similar in some ways to a catalog published by, say, a clothing manufacturer. Like a clothing catalog, a college catalog provides you with information about the merchandise that's offered, its cost, and the steps you need to take in placing an order. In this case, though, instead of a new pair of pants, the merchandise offered in the catalog is a college degree.

College catalogs are actually legal documents that offer you a contract. If you are admitted to the college and you fulfill certain requirements (such as taking a particular set of courses, maintaining a certain level of grades, and—let us not forget—paying your tuition bills on time), you'll get something in return. That something is a college degree.

Because they outline contractual obligations, college catalogs are important documents. They provide a summary of what your institution expects and offers in a number of areas:

1. **Academic regulations.** Every college has strict rules, requirements, and policies; these are all spelled out in the college catalog. For example, to graduate you need a certain number of courses or course credits. Similarly, if you wish to add or drop a course, you must do so by a certain date.

   In addition, colleges often require that you maintain a certain grade point average. A **grade point average** (or **GPA;** also known as a *quality point average*) is a numeric average in which letter grades are transformed into numbers. Most colleges use a four-point scale in which A = 4, B = 3, C = 2, D = 1, and F = 0. In such a system, a 3.0 GPA is equivalent to a B average, while a 3.5 would be halfway between an A and B.

   For example, if your five grades for a term were A, A, B, B, and C, and all the courses had the same number of credits, you would translate your grades into 4, 4, 3, 3, and 2. Next, you would sum the numbers and divide by the number of courses to find the average. That works out to [(4 + 4 + 3 + 3 + 2) ÷ 5], or a 3.2 GPA. In addition, if you have access to your transcript online, your college may calculate your GPA for you each semester. (You can also calculate your GPA online at the P.O.W.E.R. Learning Website, **www.mhhe.com/power.**)

2. **Academic programs.** Most of the college catalog is a description of the school's academic departments and its **majors**—specializations in a particular subject area, each requiring a set course of study.

Grade point average (GPA)
(Also known as *quality point average.*) A numeric average in which letter grades are transformed into numbers

Major
A specialization in a particular subject area, requiring a set course of study

Requirements for majors generally fall into two or three categories. First, typically, are collegewide requirements that every student enrolled in the college must fulfill. Second are specific requirements for each particular major; to major in an area, you must take a specified number of courses or credits in that area. Finally, if the major falls within a broader academic unit (such as a school of education), that broader entity may have its own requirements for a degree.

For instance, a psychology major might be required to fulfill collegewide requirements that apply to all students enrolled in the college, such as a specified number of English, writing, math, and science courses. The Department of Psychology will have its own separate requirements for its majors to complete, such as taking no fewer than six psychology courses. Finally, because the Department of Psychology may be housed in a more general Division of Social Sciences, there may be divisional requirements to fulfill (perhaps a course in social science methodology or a foreign language requirement).

The college catalog also provides information for students who have transferred from another college. For instance, transfer students may receive credit for only a certain number of courses or credits earned at their first institution. Or they may be required to take particular courses even if they already took them at their previous school.

If you attend a two-year community college, your college catalog also may provide information on transferring to a four-year school. For instance, two-year colleges often have formal agreements (known as *articulation agreements*) with particular four-year colleges that will automatically accept certain courses or credits taken at your current institution. Articulation agreements may even spell out what groups or blocks of courses will be accepted, as a set, by a four-year college. Knowing what courses will automatically be counted at other colleges is crucial if you are thinking about transferring later. (To learn more about transferring, go to the *P.O.W.E.R. Learning* Web site at **www.mhhe.com/power** and select Chapter T.)

3. **Course listings.** The college catalog usually lists all the courses the school offers, even though not all of them may be offered every term. Courses are listed by department, and the descriptions typically include the course name, the number of credits the course provides, and a short description.

Some courses have **prerequisites**—requirements that must be fulfilled before one can enroll. If the course has a prerequisite, this will be stated. Take these prerequisites seriously, because you will not be permitted to enroll in a course if you haven't completed the prerequisite for it. In addition, the prerequisite course may not be offered every term, so you may have to wait a year (or more!) before getting into the course you want.

Sometimes course descriptions also name the instructors who teach the course and the time and place the class meets. However, this information may also be published separately.

Make an Appointment with Your College Advisor

The job of a **college advisor** (sometimes called **college counselor**) is to give you good, clear-headed advice. Your advisor will be someone who knows the ins and outs of the college's regulations, and whose experience in working with other students provides a good deal of knowledge in other areas as well. Advisors can help you figure out what classes to take, how to overcome academic bureaucracies,

Prerequisites
Requirements that must be fulfilled before a student may enroll in a course or discipline

College advisor
An individual who provides students with advice about their academic careers

whom to go to about a problem, and generally how to prepare yourself for graduation and beyond. They can even provide information on extracurricular activities, volunteer opportunities, and part-time jobs.

Advisors are particularly busy at the beginning of each term (as well as when the course schedule comes out). Consequently, find out their office hours, schedule an appointment early, and be sure to keep your scheduled appointment. Don't go unprepared when you do go. **Figure 9.1** provides a checklist you should go through before your appointment.

Advisors can be tremendously valuable resources. Take some time to get to know your advisor as a person—and to let him or her get to know you. To get a better sense of who your own advisor is, complete **Try It 1,** "Get to Know Your College Advisor" on page 230.

If you find that you and your advisor aren't a good match and you know of another advisor who is willing and qualified to advise you, you might consider making a switch. Just be sure you have given your original advisor a chance. It is not your advisor's fault, for example, that you missed your only chance this year to take astronomy. Similarly, even though you may not like your advisor's message ("You still need to take a science course"), this doesn't mean that he or she doesn't have your best interests at heart. If you feel you can trust and speak with your advisor frankly, you and your college career will have gained a valuable ally.

College advisors can play an important role in your academic career, providing valuable advice, helping you overcome problems, and making sure that you meet all the requirements needed to graduate.

"It can be no dishonor to learn from others when they speak good sense."
Sophocles, author, *Antigone*

———	Check the college catalog for information about the advisor, noting any potential links or conversational topics that might be used to open the meeting.
———	Be on time, be aware of how much time is scheduled for your appointment, and check the time frequently during the appointment.
———	Summarize who you are (e.g., hometown, high school, grades in high school, interests, high school or community activities, etc.) to begin the more formal part of the meeting.
———	List some or all of the courses you plan to take in the next term.
———	Prepare some questions about your course choices (e.g., difficulty of the courses, whether they match your interests, whether they will fulfill your requirements, what future courses or career choices they might lead to, personality of the instructors, etc.).
———	List the extracurricular activities you're considering.
———	Prepare some questions about these activities (e.g., how time-consuming, how interesting, what sorts of students participate in them, etc.).
———	Be prepared to ask about the advisor's impressions of the college.
———	Be prepared to ask the advisor to recommend activities, events, and the like on campus or off, and which to avoid.
———	List any other issues you would like to raise (e.g., impressions of the college so far, roommate issues, personal issues, etc.).
———	Be prepared to ask about the availability of the advisor in the future (e.g., office hours, policy on calling outside office hours, etc.).
———	Remember to thank the advisor before leaving.

figure 9.1
Advisor Visit Checklist
(You can also also complete this checklist online at **www.mhhe.com/power.**)

1

Get to Know Your College Advisor

It is helpful to get a feel for who your advisor is, so schedule a 15- to 30-minute appointment with him or her. Before you meet with your advisor, do some background research by looking at your college catalog. College catalogs usually provide information on the background of faculty and staff, listing their titles, where they went to college and graduate school, what departments they teach in, and what their areas of academic interest are. In addition, you can search the Web; some instructors have their own home pages that describe their background.

To learn more about your advisor, cover some of these topics when you meet:

Philosophy of college advising:

Words of advice:

Things to try at the college:

Things to avoid at the college:

After you have met with your advisor, consider the following questions: Do you have a better sense of your advisor as an individual? What things did you learn that can help you? How can you use your advisor's responses to take better advantage of what your college has to offer?

To Try It online, go to www.mhhe.com/power.

No matter how helpful your advisor is (or unsupportive, for that matter), remember that ultimately *you* are responsible for your academic career. Advisors provide guidance, but you need to take charge of your own college experience.

Organize

Examining What You Have Done and What You Need to Do

Where Are You?

If you've prepared well, you have a basic understanding of how the courses you are taking now or have already taken fulfill your college requirements. To figure out what you still need to do, you should organize a complete list of the requirements you need to fulfill to graduate.

Try It 2, "Create a List of Required Courses" on page 232 provides a form that you can complete. (Sometimes colleges will offer such a list—known as a *degree audit*—online. If yours does, you should check it frequently to make sure you are moving ahead in the right direction.)

Even if you have yet to decide on a major, you might now be taking courses to satisfy requirements for a major you are considering. Noting this on your list will help you make decisions and plan for the future.

If this is just the start of your college career, you'll probably have completed only a few of the requirements. Don't let the blank spaces on the form overwhelm you; the credits have a way of adding up quickly.

If you are further along in your college career and have trouble remembering what courses you've taken, get a copy of your transcript from the registrar, or—if you have online access—print out a copy. The **registrar** is the official designated to oversee the scheduling of courses, the maintenance of transcripts, and the creation and retention of other official documents. (A **transcript** is the official record of the courses you've taken and the grades you received in them.)

It's also a good idea to check your transcript periodically to make sure it's accurate and to keep a record of course descriptions from your college catalog. (You can simply save a copy of each year's catalog, or if it is online, print out copies.) You might need the course descriptions if you apply for graduate school or must be certified for a particular occupation.

As you're recording the courses you've taken, remember that meeting graduation requirements may not be the same as meeting your major's requirements. For instance, some schools not only require that you take and pass certain courses, but sometimes you also have to achieve a certain minimum grade in your courses as a whole. Or you may have to get a grade of C or better in a course for it to be counted toward your major. In this case, if you received a C- in the course, you'd still get credit toward graduation, but the course wouldn't count toward the number of credits you need in your major.

Confusing? You bet. That's why it's important to keep track of where you stand from the very start of your college career. (It's a good idea to keep all relevant information together on your computer, in a file folder, or even in a shoebox.) There's no worse surprise than finding out a month before you thought you'd be graduating that you lack some critical requirement. Don't count on others to keep track of this information for you. No one knows more about what you've done than you do.

> "Choosing courses can make or break you in college. The better you are at it, the better your grades and the less your aggravation."
>
> **Student, University of Colorado[1]**

Registrar

The college official designated to oversee the scheduling of courses, the maintenance of grades and transcripts, and the creation and retention of other official documents

Transcript

A college's official record of courses taken and grades received by students

CHAPTER NINE Choosing Your Courses and Major

POWER

Try It!

2

Create a List of Required Courses

Use the form below to list all of your required courses. The form covers both prerequisite courses (i.e., courses you must take before you can take other courses) and requirements imposed by your college, the division of which your department is a part, and your department. In addition, the form allows you to indicate both credit requirements and grade requirements.

Type of Course	Credits Required	Credits Completed	Grade Required	Grade Achieved	Whose Requirement?		
					College	Division	Department
I. Prerequisite Courses							
Total Prerequisite Courses							
II. Required Courses							
Total Required Courses							

What does the information in the chart tell you? How can you use it to plan your future course selections? What courses do you wish to take that are not requirements? How much leeway do you have to take nonrequired courses?

To Try It online, go to www.mhhe.com/power.

Where Are You Going?

You should also use the information you have recorded to help determine which courses you should take in the upcoming term. Once you have declared a major, you can add those requirements to your record.

Now that you know where you are and where you are going, you are ready to start selecting courses to take you there.

W Work | Choosing the Next Term's Courses

The course listings for the next term are published online or in print in a *course schedule*. It is typically organized by department, with each course in the department having a number, such as "History 204: The French Revolution." Generally, the higher the number, the more advanced the course. The course schedule will tell you when and where the class meets and whether there are any prerequisites for the course.

Go with What You Know

Chances are, you already know of at least one or two courses you need to take in a given term. Perhaps this is the term you plan to fulfill your natural science or your foreign language requirement. There may be some courses you have been waiting to take, since some courses are only taught once a year. A good place to begin is to find out when these courses are given and where.

Draft a Personal Schedule for the Term

First, write down when the courses you absolutely have to take are scheduled. If, as is the case for many introductory courses in large colleges, you have a choice of times, choose one you prefer. In choosing times, take into consideration whether you are a "morning person," at your best first thing in the morning, or whether you usually drag yourself out of bed in the morning and don't fully function until noon. This will be the beginning of your time management for the upcoming term.

Next, choose **electives**—courses that are not required. Keep in mind broad considerations about the kinds of courses you need to take for your major and for graduation. But also explore courses that simply sound interesting to you. College offers the opportunity to discover who you are and what you like and do best, but the only way that can happen is by taking intellectual risks.

Electives
Courses that are not required

Try to balance easier and more difficult courses for a particular term. You don't want to load up on all highly challenging courses. In addition, signing up for too many courses in a single term—beyond the norm for you—can be self-defeating. (For more on choosing courses, see the *Course Connections* feature.)

To get started in deciding which courses to take for the upcoming term, complete **Try It 3** on page 235, "Choose Your Courses."

Register for Courses

The rest of the work of choosing courses consists of **registering,** or completing the college's paperwork to become formally enrolled in your chosen classes.

Register
To enroll formally in courses

Meeting with your advisor is an essential step. Sometimes, in fact, it's mandatory, and you won't be allowed to register without your advisor's signature. But even if it's not required, it's a good idea to go over your proposed course of studies. You may have overlooked something, or your advisor may be able to suggest some alternative courses that will work better for you.

What Are Courses *Really* Like?
The Covert College Catalog

Although the official college catalog is the place to start to identify courses that you need to take, there's a wealth of other sorts of unofficial information about courses that you can make use of. Tapping into this often-hidden body of knowledge can help you make informed judgments about which courses are best for you.

Among the sources of information about courses you're considering:

- **Current instructors.** Your current instructors know their colleagues and their reputations and may be willing to provide you with off-the-record suggestions.

- **Your classmates.** Ask your classmates for advice and experiences in particular classes, knowing it is colored by their own performance in the class. In addition, students have their own biases, and they are not always objective in their evaluations of instructors. For some, "easy course" equals "good course." That's why you should be extremely wary of material on such online evaluation sites as "Rate My Professor." Sometimes the students who provide comments have a dispute with the instructor, and the students who bother to provide comments often do not represent a fair sampling of views.

- **Instructor evaluations.** Sometimes schools permit access to instructor evaluations from previous terms. If these are available, they can be used to get an idea of how other students have reacted to a class you're considering taking.

- **Previous course syllabus.** An instructor may post a class syllabus online or may keep it on file in a departmental office. By examining the syllabus, you'll see exactly what a course covers (and how it compares to the official course description in the catalog).

- **Course instructors themselves.** Sit in on a class that you're thinking about taking, or talk with instructors during their office hours. There's nothing more direct than what you'll learn from the person who will be teaching the course in the upcoming term.

Remember, though, that the ultimate responsibility for taking the right courses rests with you. Advisors sometimes make mistakes and overlook a requirement; ultimately, you know best what's right for you.

After meeting with your advisor, your next step will be to register. Course registration varies significantly from one school to another. In some cases, it's a matter of listing course numbers on a form, along with some alternatives.

In an increasing number of schools, you will be expected to register for your courses using an automated system, online or over the telephone. If your college uses online registration, you will be prompted to enter course information on a Web form, and your registration will be accomplished completely online.

If your college uses a telephone registration system, you will probably be given a specific time period in which to call. When you do call, you'll receive voice prompts to enter your course choices using your telephone's touch-tone key pad (see **Figure 9.2** on page 236).

E Evaluate | ## Deciding Whether You Are in the Classes You Need

Picture this horror story:

You receive your grade report from the previous term. You're excited because you know you've done well. You're especially looking forward to seeing your Spanish grade because you know you were on the

Choose Your Courses

Use the form below to make your course selections for the coming term. The form will allow you to verify that you are meeting course requirements, avoiding schedule conflicts, and signing up for instructors you want.

Course Selections

Term: _____

Course Name and Number	Credits	Required Course or Just for Fun?	Pre-requisites Met?	Meeting Grade Required	Days Class Meets	Times Class Meets	Instructor Name	Instructor Permission Required?

After completing the chart, answer these questions: How does the next semester seem to be shaping up? Will you be able to take courses you *want* to take, as opposed to those you *need* to take? Have you encountered any conflicts and considered ways to deal with them? Have you made any choices that open you to new intellectual possibilities?

To Try It online, go to www.mhhe.com/power.

borderline between an A– and a B+. Instead you're astounded to see that there is no grade listed for the Spanish class, but you've received an F in a French class that you didn't even take. That F pulls down your grade point average, and at the bottom of your grade report is an announcement that you are on academic probation.

Here's the explanation: Because of an error during registration, you were never formally enrolled in the Spanish course, even though

Before you go online, fill in this entire worksheet, listing all courses you wish to add, drop, or change including laboratory and discussion sections, and the appropriate "action codes" you will enter. Be sure to fill in all boxed areas properly.

1. Call the system at (555) 444-3214 (From On-Campus, call 4-3214)

2. Enter your student ID number [1][2][6] - [0][4] - [9][8][1][1]

3. Enter your branch code [1]   (Undergraduate = 1, Graduate = 2)

4. Enter your personal ID number (PIN) [6][7][7][5]

5. If the Schedule Confirmation you receive in the mail instructs you to get from your advisor a Registration Approval Code before add/drop, enter that code [ ][ ][ ][ ]

6. For each add, drop, or change you want to make, enter the appropriate action code from the list below and the schedule number for the course you want affected by that action.

Action Code*	Schedule Number of Course Requested	Dept	Course #	Section #	Crd	Day/Time
[1][0]	[7][8][2][8][4][0]	Psych	102	1	3	T-T 11:15-12:30
[1][0]	[6][7][2][9][4][7]	Engl	231	1	3	M-W-F 9:05-9:55
[1][0]	[2][6][0][4][6][3]	Phed	102	2	1	M 4:00-4:50
[1][0]	[1][2][0][3][0][9]	Latn	124	1	3	T-T 9:00-10:15
[1][0]	[8][8][0][1][8][1]	Hist	102	1	3	M-W-F 10:10-11:05
[1][0]	[7][2][4][9][6][2]	Phys	101	3	3	T-T 2:30-3:45
[ ][ ]	[ ][ ][ ][ ][ ][ ]					
[ ][ ]	[ ][ ][ ][ ][ ][ ]					
[ ][ ]	[ ][ ][ ][ ][ ][ ]					
[ ][ ]	[ ][ ][ ][ ][ ][ ]					

7. After completing the form, enter the online registration system at www.umass.edu/virtual-registrar and enter your username and password.

*Action Code	Action
10	ADD a course or Swap between sections of a course (To SWAP, simply add the new section; the old section will automatically be dropped from your schedule.)
30	ADD a course with Pass/Fail option or CHANGE existing course to Pass/Fail
90	DROP a course
80	REMOVE Pass/Fail or Audit option from existing course
50	CHANGE variable credit for an existing variable credit course
40	ADD a course with AUDIT grading option or CHANGE existing course to AUDIT grading
60	LIST your course schedule

Note: Action Codes 30 and 80 are not available to graduate students.
40 is not available to undergraduates.

figure 9.2
A Sample Telephone/Web Course Registration Worksheet

you actually spent the entire term attending classes in the course. To compound the mistake, your instructor never noticed that you weren't on her class roster. At the end of the term, when she was filling out her grade report, she didn't notice that your name wasn't listed. So no grade was reported for Spanish.

At the same time, the instructor of the French class in which you were erroneously enrolled had to give you a grade at the end of the semester. Because you never completed any assignments or took any tests, your average for the semester was 0—warranting an F for the term. That F is what appeared on your grade report.

The situation—which is far more likely to occur at a large university than a small college—might be seen as a comedy of errors if it weren't so painful. Fortunately, if this were actually your story, it would most likely have a happy ending—eventually. You would go to your college registrar, who would be able to tell you what to do to get the F erased and the appropriate grade added. Still, undoing the cascade of errors would take time and a considerable amount of effort.

Difficulties such as these are encountered by a surprising number of students every term. Many problems, however, can be avoided with a bit of "due diligence" on the part of the student. One key is to evaluate your success in registering.

First, be sure you are registered for the courses you think you are. In many schools, you can determine on the Web whether you have successfully enrolled in the courses you want. If your college doesn't use an online registration system, you will be given a list of courses in which you are enrolled for the upcoming term.

Second, whether you have online access or a hard copy, carefully look over the courses in which you are enrolled. Use the following checklist to determine how successful your efforts to register have been:

> Are the courses in which you are enrolled the ones you wanted?

> Are the times accurate? Are there any conflicts?

> Have any substitutions been made?

> Are you registered for the number of credits that you wanted to be registered for?

Third, if there are any problems, try to correct the situation immediately. If there has been a clerical or computer error, you should pay a visit to the registrar's office. Sometimes, though, you'll find that there was no mistake. Class sizes are almost always limited, and not every student who wants to enroll can do so, either because of physical limitations (the room can hold only a certain number of students) or because of educational considerations (learning may be maximized when only a small number of students are in the class).

When a course is overbooked, you have several alternatives. One is to sign up for another section of the course that is not overbooked. Another is to attempt to register for an entirely different course.

Finally, you may appeal directly to the course instructor. Instructors sometimes will permit particularly interested or motivated students to enroll in the class, even if the official capacity has been reached. You may find that approaching an instructor with a polite request may yield you a slot in the course after all.

If none of these alternatives works, you will have to add a course to the ones you have already registered for. How do you add courses after the registration period has ended? Often, you'll need to complete a special form. Depending on the timing of your request, the form may require the signature of the instructor whose course you are adding. In other cases, you may be able to add and drop courses online, depending on the course registration system your college uses.

Also keep in mind that if you drop a class during a term, you must do it officially, through the registrar and course registration system. Simply ceasing to attend doesn't mean you'll be dropped from the class list. Instead, you'll probably end up with a failing grade in the course unless you complete the necessary paperwork to officially drop the course.

"Help—I Can't Get into the Courses That I Need to Graduate!"

For some students, their efforts to register result in utter disaster. Sometimes most or all of their first choices are unavailable, and they end up enrolled in only a few of the courses they had requested. Or perhaps they cannot get into the one crucial course required for graduation.

Whatever the problem, there are several steps you can take to improve the situation:

> **Don't despair—act!** There is virtually no academic problem that can't be solved in some way. Focus your energies on finding a creative solution to the problem.

> **Identify classes that are still available and enroll in them.** There are probably many classes offered at your college that are still available. Registrars or departments often maintain lists of classes that have many openings.

> **Talk with your advisor.** Perhaps what you think of as an absolute requirement can be waived or appealed. Or maybe some other course can substitute for a particular required course.

> **Speak with individual course instructors.** It may be that the instructor of the course you need will make an exception and permit you to enroll; it can't hurt to ask.

> **Consider taking a must-have, required course at another college.** If you live in an area where there are other schools in the vicinity, it may be possible to enroll in a course that you simply must take at another school. It also may be possible to take the course using distance learning. As we'll discuss further in Chapter 10, **distance learning** courses are taught at some other institution, and students participate via either video technology or the World Wide Web.

Before you take a course offered by a college other than your own, make sure that you'll receive credit for the course at your school. Also keep in mind that you'll probably have to pay for courses offered by other schools over and above what you've already spent for your own school's tuition.

Distance learning
The teaching of courses at another institution, with student participation via video technology or the Web

R Rethink

Learning What You Love and Loving What You Learn

Take one step back. No, make that two steps back.

Stepping back and taking stock of where you are in your course of studies and where you're headed are absolutely essential tasks. In fact, they are among the most important things you can do during your college career. They can mean the difference between plodding through your courses, focused only on day-to-day deadlines and tribulations, and, alternatively, gaining a sense of satisfaction as you progress toward your own goals and see yourself growing as a person.

Taking stock of your course of studies is not something you need to do every day, or once a week, or even once a month. But you should do it, without fail, at least once every term. Circle a date on your calendar so you'll be sure to do it, and treat it no differently than any other deadline you simply can't miss.

When you do take stock, answer the questions in **Try It 4.** If you're satisfied with your answers, feel affirmed in the choices you've made. You're on the right track, and you should feel secure in the knowledge that you're getting from college what you want to.

On the other hand, if you're less than satisfied with the answers you come up with, take action. Choose courses in the future that better match your goals. Consider changing your major to one that more closely reflects what you want to get

Reflect on Your College Experience

As you proceed in college, take a few moments at regular intervals (e.g., once a semester, once a year) to rethink your entire college experience. With a small group of classmates, discuss your reactions to the following topics and questions:

COURSE WORK

- Are my courses moving me toward my educational, career, and personal goals?
- Are the classes I'm taking helping me to meet my short- and long-term goals?
- Are the classes I'm taking meeting my expectations?

PERSONAL COMMITMENT

- Am I working hard to get the most out of the classes I'm taking?
- Am I doing my best in every class?
- Am I keeping the goal of learning—apart from doing well in classes—in mind as I progress through my classes?

PERSONAL GROWTH

- What personal growth am I experiencing?
- Am I becoming closer to the person I want to be?
- Are my critical thinking abilities growing?

COLLEGE

- Is my school providing me with the best educational experience possible?
- Am I learning not only in the classroom but outside the classroom?
- Am I learning from my fellow students as well as my instructors?

CHANGES

- Is there anything (my course selections, my major, or my college) that I should consider changing?
- Have I made the best choices in the past? How can I remedy mistakes that I have made?

To Try It online, go to www.mhhe.com/power.

out of college. And, if you're truly unhappy with the way your college career is proceeding, consider changing colleges.

Whichever option you choose, don't simply accept dissatisfaction with your college career. There are few times in our lives when we have the opportunity to partake of an experience that has the potential to raise us to new intellectual and emotional heights. College should be intellectually enlightening and exciting. We should be able to see how our education is preparing us for the rest of our lives. The worst thing we can do is let the time slip away without being confident that our college experience is the best experience possible.

»LO 9.3 Service Learning: Helping Yourself by Helping Others

Service-learning

Courses that allow a student to engage in community service activities while getting course credit for the experience

As you make decisions about what courses to take, you should be sure to consider those that involve service learning. In courses with **service learning,** you engage in community service activities—while getting course credit for the experience.

Service learning is a win–win activity. It links classroom education to real-world community needs. As a student, you are able to gain valuable experience and knowledge that can give you greater insight into a subject area. You can build on the material that you are learning in class and apply that information outside the classroom to real-world situations. Students in a class can share their service-learning experiences, thereby expanding their understanding of the subject matter.

In addition, you can learn useful skills that can be helpful in your future career. Working outside the classroom can give you experience that will make you a more desirable job candidate. Finally, service learning can help you learn more about yourself and what your strengths and weaknesses are.

Your community is a winner, too. It receives critical support that immediately can improve the quality of life for its citizens. In fact, your efforts can have an impact that echoes for years.

Community service activities span a vast range. For instance, you might tutor an elementary school child in an after-school program as part of a course in elementary education. You'll learn firsthand about the reading process, while the skills (and perhaps motivation) of the child being tutored improve.

Or you might enroll in an abnormal psychology class and volunteer at a halfway house for patients with severe psychological disorders. You'll gain a firsthand understanding of disorders that would be impossible to gain simply from reading a textbook, while the patient may benefit from the social interaction you provide. Other examples of service-learning activities are shown in **Table 9.1**.

table 9.1   Service-Learning Possibilities
Here are just a few possibilities for service-learning activities:
• Develop a Web site for a social service agency.
• Participate in a "Big Brother" or "Big Sister" program.
• Raise funds for a local food bank.
• Register voters for the next election.
• Volunteer at a local government office.
• Help organize a Special Olympics for people with mental retardation.
• Participate in an educational program to protect the environment.
• Help staff a shelter for battered women.
• Volunteer to feed the homeless.
• Organize a blood drive.
To learn of more service-learning opportunities, go to the Web site of the National Clearinghouse for Service-Learning Organizations, Networks, and Resources at **www.servicelearning.org.**

Whatever service-learning activity you do, there are several basic principles to keep in mind:

- **Ask questions.** Don't feel shy about asking for clarification of your responsibilities. It's the best way to maximize your learning. Remember, though, that the staff may be overworked and may not have time to immediately respond.

- **Maintain a positive outlook.** You may face challenges unlike those you've encountered before. You may see things that are upsetting and depressing. Keep your own good fortunes in mind, and be grateful for the opportunity for growth that the experience is providing you.

- **Go with the flow.** You may not agree with everything that is being done at your placement site, but don't think that your ideas are necessarily better than those of the professionals who work there. Voice your concerns, but remember that you're at the site to help, not to make the rules.

- **Keep your commitments.** The staff depends on you. If you don't complete a task or show up, you are leaving someone in a lurch and shirking your responsibilities.

- **If you have concerns, discuss them with your supervisor and faculty sponsor.** Don't let your concerns fester. If you're asked to do things that you believe are inappropriate, discuss them with the appropriate person.

- **Keep a journal.** You'll probably be required to keep a journal of your experiences for the academic class attached to your service-learning experience. Even if you're not, keep a journal anyway. Writing in a journal offers a way of reflecting on the meaning of your experiences, as well as providing an enduring record of what you've accomplished.

Many students point to service learning as the high point of their college career. And for most, it's not because of what they have gained personally—even though that's a significant part of it—but because of the difference they made in improving the lives of others. To consider service learning further, complete **Try It 5** on page 242.

≫ LO 9.4 Choosing Your Major

You attend a family gathering and encounter relatives you haven't seen for a while. What's the first question they ask when you say you're attending college? You can bet on it: "What's your major?"

Although one could argue that there are lots of other important questions that you could be asked—"What interesting things have you learned?" comes to mind—having a major focus of study is an important part of college. A major is important because it focuses what we study, leading us to become experts in a specific area.

If you're having trouble choosing a major, one strategy is to consider the kinds of activities you most like doing outside the academic arena. For example, if you've enjoyed coaching a youth soccer team, you might want to consider an education major.

Try It!

Explore Service-Learning Opportunities

To find out about the service-learning opportunities available to you, complete the following activities:

A. Examine the courses offered at your college and identify three that contain service-learning components.

1. Course number and name ———————————————————————
What is the service-learning activity?

2. Course number and name ———————————————————————
What is the service-learning activity?

3. Course number and name ———————————————————————
What is the service-learning activity?

B. Identify three potential service-learning activities in your community by contacting social service agencies, food banks, the Red Cross, or religious organizations. You can also do research on the Web.

1. Organization name ———————————————————————————
What is the service-learning activity you might conduct?

2. Organization name ———————————————————————————
What is the service-learning activity you might conduct?

3. Organization name ———————————————————————————
What is the service-learning activity you might conduct?

 WORKING IN A GROUP:

Compare your findings with other students in your class. What opportunities did you find? What service-learning opportunities might you seek out in the future? Discuss what you see as the advantages and disadvantages of service learning.

To Try It online, go to www.mhhe.com/power.

Some students know what they want to major in when they begin college; some don't have a clue. That's fine. No one says you should know right away.

In fact, some educators feel that it's better to delay choosing a major. Waiting gives you the opportunity to explore a range of possibilities and gain a more rounded education. Exposure to subjects such as history, art, and literature provides people with a common background and critical thinking skills that are useful no matter what they eventually study and choose as a career.

Furthermore, taking a variety of classes in a broad range of courses can lead to quite practical outcomes. Look at **Table 9.2**, which shows areas that employers want emphasized in colleges. The skill areas in which employers are interested can only be attained by taking a broad array of courses.

In addition, taking a variety of classes in a broad range of subjects can help you identify a major that you're really interested in. You might find after taking a civics course that you have a passion for legal studies. Or a physics class may lead you to consider a major in engineering. College is meant to be a time of exploration, and leaving yourself open to the future—and the unknown—is a completely reasonable thing to do. (To begin your own exploration of majors, complete **Try It 6,** "Identify Major Attractions" on page 244.)

table 9.2 What Skills Do Employers Want?	
Knowledge of Human Cultures and the Physical and Natural World	
• Science and technology	82%
• Global issues	72%
• The role of the United States in the world	60%
• Cultural values and traditions (U.S./global)	53%
Intellectual and Practical Skills	
• Teamwork skills in diverse groups	76%
• Critical thinking and analytic reasoning	73%
• Written and oral communication	73%
• Information literacy	70%
• Creativity and innovation	70%
• Complex problem solving	64%
• Quantitative reasoning	60%
Personal and Social Responsibility	
• Intercultural competence (teamwork in diverse groups)	76%
• Intercultural knowledge (global issues)	72%
• Ethics and values	56%
• Cultural values/traditions—U.S./global	53%
Integrative Learning	
• Applied knowledge in real-world settings	73%
The percentages in the table refer to the percentage of employers that want colleges to "place more emphasis" on these essential learning outcomes.	
Source: These findings are taken from a survey of employers commissioned by the Association of American Colleges and Universities 2006.	

Try It!

6

Identify Major Attractions

To complete this assessment, check off each of the characteristics that applies to you. Then use the pattern of results to determine how closely your interests and personality style match with the characteristics of others who are already in a particular field of study.

Characteristic	Is This Me?	Possible Field of Study
• High interest in creative expression. • Appreciation of nonverbal communication. • Understanding of aesthetics. • Commitment to perfection. • Ability to manipulate form and shape.		Arts (e.g., dance, drama, music, art, creative writing)
• Interest in organization and order. • Ability to lead and manage people. • Interest in practical problem solving. • Ambition and interest in financial incentives. • Can-do attitude. • Ability to simplify complexity.		Business
• Intense interest in solving real problems. • "Tinkerer" mentality a plus. • Extreme ability to focus on minute details. • Commitment to exactness and perfection. • Strong logical ability. • Ability to work alone for long stretches.		Engineering sciences (e.g., engineering, computer science)
• Interest in people. • Desire to solve real human problems. • Commitment to people more than money. • Tolerance of "messy" situations with multiple, partial solutions. • Insight and creativity. • Ability to work with people.		Helping professions (e.g., nursing, counseling, teaching, many areas of medicine)
• Interest in human emotions and motivations. • Interest in cultural phenomena. • Ability to integrate broad areas of study and inquiry. • Good skills of human observation. • Interest in the panorama of human life.		Humanities (e.g., English literature, history, theater, film)

Characteristic	Is This Me?	Possible Field of Study
• Interest in words, word origins, and speech. • View of language as a science. • View of literature as human expression. • Appreciation of cultural differences as scientific phenomena.	_____ _____ _____ _____	Languages and linguistics
• Interest in physical performance. • Enjoyment of sports and athletics. • Commitment to helping others appreciate physicality. • Patience and perseverance. • Commitment to perfection through practice.	_____ _____ _____ _____ _____	Physical education
• Enjoyment of research questions; high level of curiosity about natural phenomena. • Quantitative thinking a requirement; high comfort level with mathematics and statistics. • Minute problem-solving skills; attention at great level of detail. • Strong logical ability. • Ability to work with others.	_____ _____ _____ _____	Physical, biological, and natural sciences (e.g., physics, astronomy, chemistry, biology, some areas of medicine)
• Interest in people as individuals or groups. • Ability to think quantitatively and qualitatively. • High comfort level with mathematics and statistics. • High level of creativity and curiosity. • Ability to work with others. • Interest in theory as much as problem solving.	_____ _____ _____ _____ _____ _____	Social sciences (e.g., psychology, communication, sociology, education, political science, economics)
• Interest in the inner life. • Interest in highly theoretical questions. • Ability to think rigorously about abstract matters. • Appreciation of the human search for meaning.	_____ _____ _____ _____	Spiritual and philosophical studies

Use the results to focus on the kinds of courses and educational experiences that are involved in potential fields of study. Examining your responses may lead you toward some unexplored territory.

After you complete the chart, consider how you can use the information. Did you learn anything new about yourself or about various courses of study? Do your responses direct you toward a particular major? Do they direct you away from any major?

To Try It online, go to **www.mhhe.com/power**.

But what if you don't have any idea which major you wish to pursue? If you are still in your first year of college, you have plenty of time to make up your mind. But here are some approaches that should help. You may also want to look ahead to the discussion of decision making in Chapter 11 as the time to declare a major (usually by the end of your second year) draws nearer.

1. **Celebrate your indecision.** If you don't have to make a decision for some time, take advantage of the situation. Enjoy the fact that you're uncommitted and that you have an uncommon degree of freedom. In addition, remember that there are a lot of others in the position of not knowing what to major in. Many students struggle to identify a major, and some change majors a number of times, just as most people change careers several times.

2. **Focus on your interests.** Take a long look inward, paying attention to what your interests are. What do you most like to do in life? What are your strengths and weaknesses? What do you want to get out of life? The more you know about yourself, the easier it will become to narrow down the choices for a major. Completing the **Journal Reflections,** "Focusing on Your Interests," is a good place to start.

3. **Seek the help of others.** College campuses provide many resources to help their students choose a major (and also to help narrow the choices for potential careers). Talk to other students majoring in areas that interest you. Find out what they like and don't like about the field and its requirements. You will probably find your interest in the major grows or diminishes depending on how you feel about the issues they mention.

   Speak with your advisor. If you've gotten to know your advisor, he or she can often provide reasonable, helpful information. For instance, you may be able to find out about the strengths and weaknesses of various departments.

   You can also turn to your college counseling or career center. Most colleges have offices that can provide information about the different majors, including information about career opportunities typically available to graduates with the various majors. Sometimes it's possible to take tests that will help focus your choices, pinpointing how your interests, values, and personality type fit with particular careers.

4. **Consider double-majoring—or inventing your own major.** Although it's not easy, there are paths you can take if you know clearly what you want to do, but find it doesn't fit a single existing major.

   A **double major** is a course of study that fulfills all the requirements for each of two majors. If you can't decide between two majors, or if you are interested in a career that overlaps two majors, this is a reasonable solution. The downside: It can be an awful lot of work. Because both majors usually carry a number of their own requirements, you may have very little freedom to pick courses other than those directly relating to one of the two majors.

   Another option that some, although not all, colleges permit is the creation of a **unique major** geared to your own needs. Again, this is not an easy road to take because you must put together a cohesive set of courses that centers upon a discipline not normally offered through a major. Furthermore, you must also get the support of a faculty member or a committee of faculty members to oversee the process.

   If double-majoring or inventing a major seems too daunting, there's another option that may resolve the difficulty of choosing between two

Double major
A course of study that fulfills all the requirements for two majors

Unique major
Specialization in a particular subject area that is geared to the student's own needs. Not offered by all colleges, and generally requires the support of faculty to oversee the process

Journal Reflections

Focusing on Your Interests

The following questions are intended to lead you to explore areas of personal preference and interest that should inform your choice of a major. These questions are informal and designed to be answered briefly; more extended and formal "interest inventories" are available in your college's counseling office.

1. Do you think you would enjoy being told precisely what to do and how to do it, or would you rather work things out by yourself, without extensive instructions or supervision? What implications might your answer have for a choice of majors?

2. Are you ambitious and success-oriented and not ashamed to admit that you'd like to earn a lot of money, or are success and money of secondary importance to you? What implications might your answer have for a choice of majors?

3. Are you the artistic type and do you enjoy performing, creating, and viewing/listening to artistic works, or is art of relatively little interest to you? What implications might your answer have for a choice of majors?

4. Do you enjoy working with others, or do you prefer to work on your own? What implications might your answer have for a choice of majors?

majors: majoring in one field and minoring in another. A **minor** is a secondary specialization in a discipline different from one's major. Typically students must take at least four courses in a discipline for their study to qualify as a minor.

Minor
A secondary specialization in a discipline different from one's major

5. **Be career-oriented, but not too career-oriented.** If you have a good idea about what career you wish to embark upon once you graduate, you can easily find out which skills are required to be successful in that field. Knowing what you'll need to gain entry into a field can help you determine a good major that will set you on the road toward your desired profession.

   Don't narrow your options too much, however. Students sometimes fear signing up for classes that don't seem to lead directly toward a career. Or they may avoid courses that seem to point them in the direction of a career that would be "unacceptable" to their parents or friends. One of the greatest sources of indecision in choosing a major stems from the mistaken notion that when you choose your major, you're also choosing a career.

Choosing a Job That's Right for You

It's a question no family member can resist asking, and one that you've probably asked yourself: What kind of work are you going to do when you graduate?

Happily, it's a question you don't have to answer, at least not yet. Although some students know from their first day in college what they want to do (and actually choose their college on that basis), many—perhaps most—don't decide on a career path until late in their academic career.

And that's fine. After all, one of the reasons you are in college is to expose yourself to the universe of knowledge. In one sense, keeping your options open is a wise course. You don't want to prematurely narrow your options and discard possibilities too early. And even if you're quite sure in your choice of careers, it doesn't hurt to explore new possibilities.

In the Career Connections features in previous chapters, we've discussed various strategies for exploring future professions. Here, in summary, are some steps to take to identify a career:

1. **Clarify the goal of your search.** There's no single perfect career choice. Some people search for the ideal career, assuming that they need to identify the one, and only one, career for which they have been destined. The reality is, though, that there are many careers that they could choose that would make them equally happy and satisfied.

   Start with what you already know about yourself. You've already done a lot of mental work toward narrowing down a profession. Do you hate the sight of blood? Then you're probably well aware you're not cut out to be a surgeon or a veterinarian. Does the sight of a column of numbers bring an immediate yawn? Count out accounting and statistics.

   Awareness of your likes and dislikes already puts you on the road to identifying a future career. Knowing what you don't want to do helps to identify what you do want to do and to narrow down the kinds of occupations for which you're more suited.

2. **Gather information.** The more you know about potential careers, the better. Examine career-planning materials, read industry profiles, and visit relevant Web sites (such as the excellent Department of Labor site at **www.bls.gov/oco/**). Talk with career counselors. Discuss your options with people who work in professions in which you're interested. Find out how they chose their career, how they got their current job, and what advice they have for you.

   In addition, consider participating in an internship in a profession that you think might be attractive. *Internships* are off-campus, temporary work situations that permit you to obtain experience in a particular field. They are not always paid, but in many cases can substitute for a course. For example, you might be able to receive three college credits for spending 10 hours a week at a work site during the course of a term.

   Internships are an excellent way to learn about a profession, up close and personal. Working as an intern will let you know the kinds of things employees do on a day-to-day basis and the responsibilities and duties of the profession you're interested in. You can gain experiences that you would not be able to get on campus.

3. **Narrow down your choices.** Once you've gathered enough information to give yourself a reasonable comfort level, narrow down the choices. If it's early in your college career, you don't need to make up your mind. If it's late and you feel the pressure to choose, then make the decision. Just do it. Remember, there's no single, absolutely correct decision; there are many right decisions.

   Whatever it is you ultimately choose as a career, think of it only as a first step. As the average life span continues to lengthen due to advances in medical technology, most people will pass through several careers during the course of their life. By periodically taking stock of where you are and considering your goals, you'll be in a position to make career changes that bring you closer to your ideal.

   (To learn much more about career choices, go to the *P.O.W.E.R. Learning* Web site at **www.mhhe.com/power** and select Chapter C.)

Don't fall into that trap. Follow your heart—not always your head—and pursue courses without regard to how they may broaden or narrow your future job opportunities. You may discover a passion, and an aptitude, that you never knew you had. Even if you oriented toward a specific profession, remember that employers often prefer well-rounded employees over ones who are narrowly focused on a particular subject area.

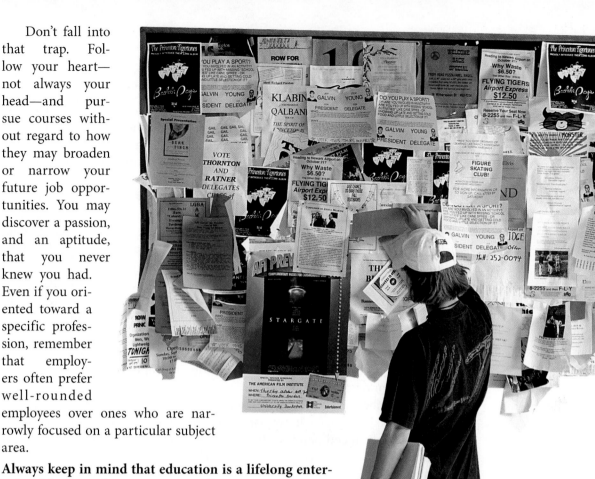

6. **Always keep in mind that education is a lifelong enterprise.** Educational opportunities will continue to present themselves not just through the undergraduate years, but for the rest of your life.

Consequently, no matter what your choice of major, you're not precluding the possibility of taking courses in other areas in the future. You may eventually end up in a graduate school pursuing a masters degree, a doctorate, or an MD. You also may take courses periodically at local colleges even after you graduate, enrolling in them because they will help you advance in your career or simply because they interest you.

In addition, choosing a major is not an irreversible choice. Many students change their major to a new one at some point during college—just as most people change their careers several times over the course of their lifetimes.

In short, choosing a major is not a decision that places your life on a set, unchangeable course. Instead, it's one step in what can be a lifetime of learning.

College counseling and career centers are excellent sources of information on potential majors and occupations.

"Far and away the best prize that life offers is the chance to work hard at work worth doing."

President Theodore Roosevelt

Accepting Responsibility for Your Academic Performance

You received the highest grade in your class . . . you received an A on a paper . . . your instructor tells you your class participation was the best in the course.

Take pride in your success, and reflect on what you did to achieve it. If you're doing well academically, it's not an accident. It's because you've worked hard and put your intellectual capacities to full use.

On the other hand, each of us has moments of academic disappointment. When you get a poor grade in a course, it hurts. But even if you feel tempted to shrug it off publicly, don't make that mistake privately. It's just as important to take responsibility for and reflect on your academic disappointments as it is to accept your successes.

There is, of course, a great difference between reflecting on what has happened and blaming ourselves. When things go wrong, it's reasonable to reflect to understand what went wrong. It is not useful, however, to spend time and energy blaming ourselves.

Learn from your mistakes. Consider why something went wrong, analyze what you could have done—or avoided doing—to prevent it, and seek ways of preventing a similar outcome in the future.

Remember, success occurs because we want it to and because we've worked hard to make it happen. It can happen every day if we allow it. And success is not just reaching an end point, such as when we're handed our diploma. Success is a process. Any achievement that brings us closer to fulfilling our goals and dreams is a success.

"Actually, I'm hoping what I'm going to be when I grow up hasn't been invented yet."

Speaking of Success

NAME: **Alexandria Guttman**

SCHOOL: **University of Arizona, Tucson**

When Alexandria Guttman began her freshman year at the University of Arizona, she planned to study architecture. However, after only one semester of architecture classes, she realized that her interests had changed. During the next few years at college, Guttman changed her major several times.

"After pre-architecture, I changed to graphic design, then to political science, and then to psychology," said Guttman. "At that point, I still really had no idea what I wanted to do."

It turned out that taking classes in a wide range of topics helped her narrow down her interests. She also took a class that provided an overview of all potential majors, which helped give her career ideas she might not have considered otherwise. In addition, Guttman worked as an intern for a stockbroker for two years while she was in college, which gave her hands-on experience that helped her rule out a career in the financial industry. Guttman ultimately decided to major in marketing, saying it was a "perfect major for me as it fit my personality and my strengths."

Guttman graduated from the University of Arizona with a degree in marketing. She used her educational background to get a job in the entertainment business as a coordinator, where she ultimately worked her way up to Associate Manager of Retail Marketing and Strategy of a major entertainment company in Los Angeles, California.

Guttman is currently a Senior Brand Analyst at Mattel, and she credits her experiences in college (and her initial indecision) with pointing her in the right direction. She learned that it is just as important to learn what you don't want to do as it is to figure out what you do want to do.

Looking Back

How can I prepare for the academic choices that college demands?

➤ Making course choices involves finding out as much as possible about what your college has to offer. The college catalog is the best initial source of this information.

➤ An important source of information and personal guidance in college is your college advisor, who has training and experience in advising students on courses, instructors, requirements, and regulations.

What is the best way to choose courses and ensure I'm getting the most out of my studies?

➤ In choosing courses, check out your selections with your academic advisor and then register for the courses. You should be prepared to choose different courses or course sections if your initial selections are unavailable.

➤ Verify that you have received your chosen courses, that the schedule of courses makes sense, and that your course schedule will help provide the number of credits needed to graduate.

➤ Be prepared to deal with errors during registration or to cope with the unavailability of courses that you need to take.

➤ Reflect on your college experience regularly, verifying that course choices, academic performance, personal growth, choice of major, and your overall educational experience are satisfactory.

How can participation in service learning improve my college experience?

➤ In service-learning courses, students engage in community service activities while receiving course credit.

➤ Service learning benefits both students and the community.

How can I choose a major?

➤ Choosing a major first involves accepting a period of indecision, finding out more about yourself, seeking the help and advice of others, considering going beyond the traditional structure of your college major, trying out unusual courses, and taking career plans into account.

[KEY TERMS AND CONCEPTS]

Grade point average (GPA) (p. 227)

Major (p. 227)

Prerequisites (p. 228)

College advisor (p. 228)

Registrar (p. 231)

Transcript (p. 231)

Electives (p. 233)

Register (p. 233)

Distance learning (p. 238)

Service learning (p. 240)

Double major (p. 246)

Unique major (p. 246)

Minor (p. 247)

[RESOURCES]

ON CAMPUS

The obvious choice for information about courses is your advisor. Sometimes your advisor will be associated with a general program, such as liberal arts; sometimes with a particular department, such as English or Sociology; or sometimes with a collegewide academic advising center. Your course instructors also can often give good advice about what future courses to sign up for. Finally, don't forget about your fellow students; they can be an excellent source of information about the most interesting and exciting courses. If you'd like advice about future careers, visit your college career center. Not only will it have pamphlets and books on different jobs, but the staff also can often provide tests that can help you see how your personal strengths fit with potential majors and careers.

IN PRINT

The *Guide to College Majors* published by the Princeton Review (2008) provides a good overview of college majors, as does *College Majors That Work* by Michael Viollt (Octameron Associates, 2004).

Probably the most popular guide to careers is *What Color Is Your Parachute 2009?* (Ten Speed Press, 2008). In it you'll find ways to make decisions about choosing (and changing) professions, as well as ways to obtain a job.

ON THE WEB

Many sites on the World Wide Web provide the opportunity to extend your learning about the material in this chapter. (Although the Web addresses were accurate at the time the book was printed, check the *P.O.W.E.R. Learning* Web site [**www. mhhe.com/power**] for any changes that may have occurred.)

> "Selecting College Courses" (**www.advising.wayne.edu/hndbk/courses.php**), a guide offered by the Advising Center at Wayne State University, provides a solid list of questions to ask yourself when choosing your courses.

> Wesleyan University offers "A Guide to Choosing a Major" (**www.wesleyan.edu/ deans/major_declaration/guide.html**) online. Though some of the information is tailored specifically to Wesleyan, many of the ideas are helpful for students at any college or university. Even if you've already decided on a major, this site can help you to examine and reevaluate your academic priorities.

> Major Resource Kits are listed at the University of Delaware's Career Services Center (**www.udel.edu/CSC/mrk.html**). Dozens of majors are listed, ranging from Apparel Design to Women's Studies. Each major has a sample of job titles, types of employers, and resources for finding employment. This is a great site for getting ideas for future careers.

TAKING IT TO THE NET

1 Colleges usually have a set of core courses that each student must take to fulfill the liberal arts education requirement. Visit a college Web site (not your own) and see if you can determine the core requirements for that school. How many science courses are required? How many math courses? Are any other types of courses required?

2 Use different search engines to help locate information about selecting classes or majors. Go to Excite (**www.excite.com**), Yahoo! (**www.yahoo.com**), and AltaVista (**www.altavista.com**) and type in the phrase "choosing college classes." Look over the first few pages in each search. Did they offer any helpful information on choosing classes or majors? Are there any common tips that are offered by most or all of the sites?

The Case of . . .

Major Problems

As Chen Lee began his junior year, he still was unsure which major to choose. He had come to college as an "undeclared major" and that was still his official designation—although he thought "clueless major" would be a more accurate label.

Chen had thought seriously about several possibilities, including communications and marketing, but none seemed to offer just what he was looking for. Part of the trouble was, of course, that he really didn't know what he was looking for. In fact, he was a lot clearer about what he didn't want to major in than what he did want to major in.

The clock was ticking away, and he felt lost. His parents offered many suggestions, but that just seemed to increase the pressure. And now he was getting warnings from the school that he had to make a decision.

1. What seems to be Chen's main problem in coming to grips with the choice of a major?

2. How can Chen's prior consideration of majors such as communications and marketing help him move closer to a decision?

3. How would you advise Chen to make use of his understanding of what he doesn't want to major in?

4. How can Chen find out more about himself? Why is this important in choosing a major?

5. Do you think Chen is taking this decision too seriously or not seriously enough? What advice would you give him about the importance of the choice of a major?

Learning Outcomes

By the time you finish this chapter you will be able to

» LO **10.1**   Explain the educational uses of technology.

» LO **10.2**   Describe what is available on the Web.

» LO **10.3**   Explain distance learning.

» LO **10.4**   Outline a strategy for developing information competency.

» LO **10.5**   List criteria for gathering information from the Web.

Technology and Information Competency

Brian Sullivan didn't remember much about the auto accident that left him with two badly broken legs. But the aftermath of the accident, which occurred in August just before his second year of college, was all too clear. He was in terrible pain, and his physicians said there was no way he could return to college in the fall.

At first, Brian was dejected, because he didn't want to lose a term of study. But after a series of e-mail conversations with his campus advisor, he learned he did have an option: Enroll in distance learning classes taught entirely online. He could participate fully and receive course credit for the classes without ever stepping foot on campus. He decided to give it a shot and signed up for three online courses.

The beginning of the term was tough, as Brian acclimated himself to the online course system. But he soon got the hang of it. Within a few weeks he became adept at participating in online discussions, sending in assignments, and chatting with his fellow classmates and his instructor.

He also found he could stay in touch with his friends on campus, who texted and emailed him frequently and whose lives he could follow on Facebook.

What Brian feared would be a lost term turned into something quite different: a term that brought him both academic success and with his friends—all thanks to technology.

Looking Ahead

The technology that permitted Brian to keep up with his classes and friends didn't even exist a few decades ago. Education is changing, especially as it takes increasing advantage of "virtual" resources—e-mail, the Web, and other evolving technologies. In fact, you might already be taking a distance learning course entirely on the Web, never setting foot in the same room as your instructor or your classmates.

Technology also is making a profound difference in how we are taught, the ways we study and carry out our work, and how we communicate with our professors and other students. It is changing the way you can access the vast quantities of information published each year—tens of thousands of books, journals, and other print materials, and literally billions of Web pages. But successfully wading through all that information requires significant new skills in information competence that weren't necessary in the past.

In this chapter we discuss how technological advances increase your opportunities to achieve success in college.

We'll first consider the basic educational uses of technology. We'll also talk about distance learning, an approach to education that involves studying with an instructor who may be thousands of miles away. Finally, we'll consider how you can use technology to develop information competency—locating and using both the information traditionally held in libraries *and* information created for and in the virtual world of cyberspace.

» LO 10.1 You and Technology

It's a great tool that can help you achieve success in your classes. It can save you hours of time. At the same time, it can be extremely frustrating, annoying, and maddening. And sometimes instead of saving time, it can eat up hours of your time.

"It," of course, is technology. Today, it is as much a necessity to use technology as as it was for you to learn to write using pen and paper earlier in your schooling. No one facing the job market in the 21st century will want to leave college without a strong working knowledge of a variety of technologies and what they can do for you.

Journal Reflections

Could I Live without Technology?

1. What do you use technology for most? Texting? E-mail? Surfing the Web? Classwork?

2. How much time do you spend using technology? How does it affect your social relationships?

3. What technological devices could you live without? What devices could you not live without?

4. How much and what kinds of technology do you like to have in your courses? Why?

If you are not yet at ease with technology, relax. No one is born with technology skills. With practice, however, using a broad range of technologies will become second nature.

And if using technology is as familiar to you as brushing your teeth in the morning, be patient with those who are less at ease with it. A "digital divide"—often reflecting socioeconomic disparities—separates students who have had considerable and easy access to computers and technology prior to college from those for whom access to computers was difficult. Many students grow up in homes without computers, and even those who had computers at home may not have had access to high speed Internet connections. (To explore your feelings about the role technology plays in your life, complete the *Journal Reflections*.)

Technology and Your Academic Life

Even if you don't feel particularly proficient with technology in general, it already plays a big role in your life. Computers run your car's engine, make your digital camera work, allow you to record iPod tunes, and make sure the bus you're waiting for runs on time.

Technology also has revolutionized academic life. Here are some of the ways you may encounter technology in your classes:

> **Course Web sites.** Many college courses have a Web site associated with them. The Web site may reside in a nationally developed course management software system (such as Blackboard, desire2learn, or eCollege) with which your college has a licensing agreement. In other cases, colleges develop their own course management systems.

Whatever course management system is used, the Web site will probably contain basic information about the course, such as a copy of the syllabus. Or it may provide important emergency updates, such as class cancellations or changes in paper due dates.

In other classes, the Web site may be much more elaborate and play a central role in the class. For instance, class Web sites that require a username and password for access may contain exercises and quizzes to be completed (and scored) online. All your grades for the class may be stored on the Web site, accessible to you at any time of the day or night.

In some classes, you may electronically deposit papers and essays onto the class Web site. Later, your instructor can read them online, post comments on your submissions, and return them to you on the Web site. You may carry out group projects on the Web site, or hold virtual discussions on the site. You may even be required to take your major tests and final exams on the Web site.

> **CD-ROMs.** Textbooks frequently come with a CD that contains exercises, demonstrations, and other interactive media. For example, a psychology textbook might come with a CD that includes activities that allow you to participate in simulations of famous experiments, such as training Pavlov's dogs. Or a music class may have a CD that includes musical selections.

> **Textbook Online Learning Centers and Companion Web sites.** Most textbooks have a Web site that is tied to the book. The Web site typically includes chapter summaries, interactive reviews, flash cards, and practice tests. These resources, which are usually described in the Preface to most textbooks, can be extremely valuable study tools. (The Online Learning Center for *P.O.W.E.R. Learning* can be found at **www.mhhe.com/power.**)

> **Podcasts.** In some classes, instructors sometimes produce audio or video recordings, called **podcasts,** of lectures or other instructional material relevant to the class. You can either access them on the Web or download them to a mobile device (such as an iPod) that permits you to listen and view them outside of class whenever you want.

> **Blogs.** Some instructors maintain blogs of their own. A **blog** is a kind of Web-based public diary in which a writer offers ideas, thoughts, short essays, and commentary. If your instructor has a blog and tells you to read it, get in the habit of checking it routinely. It not only will contain information relevant to the course that you'll need to know, but it also may reveal personal insights that can help you know your instructor better.

Some instructors ask students to create their own blogs and share them with other students in the class. For instance, a political science instructor might ask students to keep a record of their reactions to an ongoing election campaign.

If you are asked to create your own blog, your instructor will provide you with directions regarding what to write and how to post your blog on the Web. Remember to follow the guidelines carefully. And never forget: Once you post your blog on the Web, it becomes a public document with the potential for virtually anyone to view.

> **Wikis.** A **wiki** is a public document, posted on the Web, that permits others to add or edit the document collectively. The philosophy behind wikis is that "many heads are better than one" and that the joint efforts of many ultimately create information that is better than any one individual, working alone, could create.

An instructor who assigns wikis might ask that you create an article as a class or group. You also might be asked to contribute to an existing wiki by adding information, verifying material, and making corrections. Sometimes

Podcast
An audio or video recording that can be accessed on the Internet and viewed on a computer or downloaded to a mobile device

Blog
A Web-based public diary in which a writer provides commentary, ideas, thoughts, and short essays

Wiki
A public document, posted on the Web, that permits others to add or edit the document collectively

Getting the Most Out of Instructors' PowerPoint Presentations

Traditional "chalk-and-talk" lectures are a thing of the past in many classes. Instead, increasing numbers of instructors are using presentation programs such as PowerPoint to project material in their classes.

This newer technology calls for fresh strategies for taking notes and absorbing the information. Here are some tips:

- **Listening is more important than seeing.** The information that your instructor projects on screen, while important, ultimately is less critical than what he or she is saying. Pay primary attention to the spoken word and secondary attention to the screen.

- **Don't copy everything that is on every slide.** Instructors can present far more information on their slides than they would if they were writing on a blackboard. Oftentimes there is so much information that it's impossible to copy it all down. Don't even try. Instead, concentrate on taking down the key points.

- **Remember that key points on slides are . . . key points.** The key points (often indicated by bullets) often relate to central concepts. Use these points to help organize your studying for tests, and don't be surprised if test questions directly assess the bulleted items on slides.

- **Check to see if the presentation slides are available online.** Some instructors make their class presentations available on the Web to their students, either before or after class time. If they do this before class, print them out and bring them to class. Then you can make notes on your copy, clarifying important points. If they are not available until after a class is over, you can still make good use of them when it comes time to study the material for tests.

- **Remember that presentation slides are not the same as good notes for a class.** If you miss a class, don't assume that getting a copy of the slides is sufficient. Studying the notes of a classmate who is a good notetaker will be far more beneficial than studying only the slides.

---

projects stretch across the entire term, and you can observe the changes in the wiki as the class becomes more knowledgeable about the subject matter.

> **Classroom presentation programs.** Many instructors use technology during class itself. For example, rather than using transparencies and overhead projectors, an increasing number of instructors present material electronically using PowerPoint slides or some other presentation program. Presentation programs help instructors to create professional-looking slides that contain not only text but also often graphics such as photos, charts, maps, and animations.

If you are lucky, your instructor might later place the slides projected in class onto the class Web site, where they can be reviewed after class. Sometimes instructors even put the slides on Web sites before class. That gives you the chance to print them out and bring them to class, writing class notes on them. (For tips on making best use of instructors' presentation programs in class, see the **Course Connections.**)

> **Individual response technology ("clickers"). Individual response technology** is a method used to involve students more actively during class. If you are in a class using IRT, you will receive or be asked to purchase a wireless personal handset, similar to a television remote control; usually called a clicker. The clicker is used to transmit answers to multiple-choice or true-false questions

Individual response technology
This method uses a wireless handset to transmit students' answers to the instructor's computer, resulting in more classroom interactivity

posed by your instructor. After you answer the question by pressing the appropriate button on the clicker, it transmits a signal to a receiver attached to the instructor's computer.

As answers are received, the computer records and combines the input from everyone in the class. The combined results are then displayed and projected to the class, providing an opportunity to discuss the class responses. One of the best things about clicker technology is that it gives you immediate insight into how well you understand the material being discussed in class. It also allows you to see how your own personal results compare with those of your classmates.

» LO 10.2 Using the Internet and the Web

The Internet and the Web have revolutionized communication. And we haven't seen anything yet: Visionaries say it won't be too long before they will allow our refrigerators to order milk when supplies are running low or permit our physicians to constantly monitor our vital organs.

Although many people use the two terms interchangeably, the Internet and the Web are actually different, if related, concepts. The **Internet** is the electronic network that connects millions of computers together. Hooking up to this network permits a user to share information with virtually anyone else who has a computer. The **Web** (or, as it was originally called, the *World Wide Web*), provides a graphical means of locating and accessing information on the Internet. Using the Web has become the standard way to find and use such information. The Web provides a way to transmit typewritten text, visual material, and auditory information—graphics, photos, music, soundbites, video clips, and much more.

The Internet provides the backbone of virtual communication. Among its most common uses are the following:

> **E-mail. E-mail,** short for "electronic mail," offers a way for people to send and receive messages with incredible speed. On most college campuses, e-mail is the most common form of communication among students and faculty.

>> **Text messaging (or texting). Text messaging** (or **texting**) permits you to send short messages from mobile phones to other phones or e-mail accounts. They are typically limited to 160 characters or less. Using text messaging, you can communicate with others in real time. You can also sign up to receive automatic text messages, such as receiving information whenever there are breaking news events.

>> **Instant messaging (IM).** Instant messaging allows you to communicate in real time with friends and instructors. With **instant messaging,** you create a list of other users with whom you wish to keep in touch. If others on your list are online at the same time you are, you'll know instantly, and you'll be able to send messages back and forth. Instructors sometimes hold virtual office hours using instant messaging, and businesses increasingly use instant messaging to facilitate employee communication.

>> **Listservs. A listserv** is a subscription service that automatically e-mails messages on general topics of shared interest to people who have added their names to its mailing list. Members can respond to messages by replying to the listserv, and their responses will be distributed automatically to

---

Internet
A vast network of interconnected computers that share information around the world

Web
A highly graphical interface between users and the Internet that permits users to transmit and receive not only text, but also pictorial, video, and audio information

E-mail
Electronic mail, a system of communication that permits users to send and receive messages via the Internet

Text messaging (texting)
Short messages sent from mobile phone to other phones or e-mail accounts

Instant messaging
A system that allows one to use a computer to communicate in real time with friends and instructors

Listserv
A subscription service through which members can post and receive messages via e-mail on general topics of shared interest

everyone on the mailing list. (In most cases it's also possible to respond directly to an individual who posts a message of interest, without sending that response to all members of the listserv.) Among the thousands of listservs online are those relating to jazz, tourism, privacy issues, and libertarianism.

> **RSS feeds.** RSS, which stands for both "Really Simple Syndication" or "Rich Site Summary," permits you to subscribe to your favorite Web site, which feeds you new information without you having to visit the site. RSS feeds provide news, listings of events, and scientific discoveries. To use RSS feeds, you need a news reader, software that will check feeds and allows you to read new material.

Using E-Mail Effectively

Although e-mail (illustrated in **Figure 10.1**) has become the preferred means of written communication for many of us, you may be unaware of some of the basics of how it works. For example, every e-mail address contains three basic elements:

> **Mailbox name.** The mailbox name—the name assigned to your account on an e-mail system—is often some variant of your own name (e.g., conan_ obrien), though it may also be totally fictitious (e.g., hepcat9).

> **@.** The "at" sign.

> **Domain name.** The domain name is the name of the organization that hosts the e-mail "post office" to which the user subscribes—often an institution (e.g., umass.edu or mcgraw-hill.com), an Internet service provider (e.g., aol. com or earthlink.net), or a multifaceted system such as yahoo.com or hotmail.com. *Host computers* are connected directly to the Internet. You can usually tell what kind of an organization hosts an e-mail account by the last part of the address (the *extension*): for example, *.edu* is an educational organization, *.com* is a commercial organization, *.org* is a nonprofit or charitable organization, *.mil* is the military, and *.gov* is a governmental organization (see **Table 10.1** on page 262).

Many e-mail providers (e.g., Gmail or Yahoo! Mail) have their own, unique e-mail systems on which e-mail can be retrieved anywhere you have access to the Web. Others use particular software programs such as Microsoft's Outlook or

figure 10.1
E-Mail
E-mail sent via Google's G-mail.

table 10.1	Domain Extensions		
E-Mail Address	**Extension**	**Type of Organization**	
jasper.johns@asu.edu	.EDU	Arizona State University—Educational	
dowd@nytimes.com	.COM	The New York Times—Commercial	
send.help@redcross.org	.ORG	American Red Cross—Charitable or nonprofit	
general@army.mil	.MIL	United States Army—Military	
head.counter@census.gov	.GOV	U.S. Census Bureau—Government	

Outlook Express to send and receive mail; you must have that software installed on your computer to retrieve your e-mail. Sometimes colleges have their own unique e-mail system that you can access through your college Web site.

Many colleges require that you establish a college e-mail account to which they can send official communications. In such cases, even if you already have an e-mail account, you'll need to check mail coming to your official college address. One way to simplify matters is to have mail automatically forwarded from your college e-mail account to your original account.

Even better, start using your college e-mail account routinely, and have your messages forwarded to it from your original account. Not only will you be sure to receive essential college e-mails, you will avoid having to write your instructors using a return e-mail address that, while amusing to your friends ("stoned_mindless@gmail.com"), may be less appropriate for instructor e-mails.

Writing Effective E-mail Messages

Even if you are an experienced e-mail user, there are several things you can do to improve the effectiveness of the messages you send. Among the most important to keep in mind when writing formal e-mail messages:

> **Use an informative subject line.** Don't say "IMPORTANT" or "meeting" or "question." None of those help recipients sort out your message from the dozens of others that may be clogging their inboxes. Instead, something like "Reminder: resident advisor applications due 5:00 pm 10/11" is considerably more useful. In addition, *always* use a subject line: Some recipients routinely delete messages without a subject line, fearing they contain viruses.

> **Make sure the recipient knows who you are.** If you are writing someone you know only casually, jog their memory with a bit of information about yourself. If you don't know them at all, identify yourself early in the message ("I am a college student who is interested in an internship . . .").

> **Keep messages short and focused.** E-mail messages are most effective when they are short and direct. If at all possible, keep your message short enough that it fits on one screen without scrolling down to see the rest. The reason is

simple: Recipients sometimes don't read beyond the beginning of a message. If you do need to include a good deal of material, number each point or set them off by bullets so recipients will know to read down.

> **Try to include only one major topic per e-mail.** It's often better to write separate e-mails rather than including a hodgepodge of unrelated points in an e-mail. This is especially true if you want a response to each of the different points.

> **Put requests near the beginning of the e-mail.** If you want the recipient to do something in response to your message, respectfully put the request at the very beginning of your message. Be explicit, while being polite.

> **Keep attachments to a minimum.** If possible, include all relevant information in the body of your e-mail. Large attachments clog people's e-mail accounts and may be slow to download. In addition, recipients who don't know you personally may fear your attachment contains a virus and will not open it.

> **Avoid abbreviations and emoticons in formal e-mails.** When writing informal e-mails to friends, abbreviations such as AFAIK ("as far as I know"), BTW ("by the way"), CYA ("see ya"), OIC ("oh, I see"), and WTG ("way to go") are fine. So are **emoticons (or smileys),** which signal the emotion that you are trying to convey. However, they should be avoided in formal e-mails. Recipients may not be familiar with them, and they may make your e-mail seem overly casual.

> **Above all, always be respectful and courteous.** It always pays to be polite. In fact, as we discuss next, there are certain guiding principles that govern civility on the Web and which you should always keep in mind when writing e-mail.

Emoticons (or smileys)
Symbols used in e-mail messages that provide information on the emotion that the writer is trying to convey. Emoticons usually look like faces on their side, with facial expressions related to the intended emotion or tone

Netiquette: Showing Civility on the Web

Although e-mail and text communication is usually less formal than a letter, it is essential to maintain civility and demonstrate good etiquette, which in the e-mail world is known as *netiquette,* especially when communicating with your instructors. Here are some rules:

> **Don't write anything in an e-mail or text message that you'll regret seeing on the front page of the campus newspaper.** Yes, e-mail and texts are usually private, but the private message you write can easily be forwarded by the recipient to another person or even scores of other people. Worse yet, it's fairly easy to hit "reply all" in e-mail when you mean simply to "reply": In this case, you might think that you are responding to an individual when in fact the e-mail will go to everyone who received the message along with you.

> **Be careful of the tone you convey.** It is harder in e-mail and texts to express the same kind of personality, and often the same degree of subtlety, that our voice, our handwriting, or even our stationery can add to other forms of communication. This limitation means that attempts at humor and especially sarcasm can backfire. If you're using humor, consider adding an emoticon to clarify the intent of your message.

> **Never write anything in an e-mail or text that you wouldn't say in person.** If you wouldn't say something in a face-to-face conversation, don't say it electronically.

- **Don't use all capital letters.** Using all caps MAKES IT LOOK AS IF YOU'RE SHOUTING.

- **Never send an e-mail or text when you are angry.** No matter how annoyed you are about something someone has written in a message, don't respond in kind—or at least wait until you've cooled down. Take a deep breath, and wait for your anger to pass.

- **Be especially polite and professional when writing to instructors.** Instructors often get dozens, and sometimes hundreds, of e-mails and texts from students each week, and they are especially sensitive to messages that are inappropriate. Follow these guidelines to be sure your e-mail will receive maximum attention:

  - Always use the subject line in e-mail messages, identifying the class you are in and describing the general topic of the e-mail (e.g., "Psych 100, Lec 3, exam query").

  - Address instructors politely (as in "Dear Professor xx," as opposed to, say, "Yo, Prof!" or "Hey!").

  - Be concise. Make your point quickly, and try not to write more than a few paragraphs.

  - Avoid emoticons, non-standard abbreviations, and slang; you're writing an instructor, not a friend.

  - Don't tell your instructor that you need to hear from him or her immediately. It's fine to convey that your concerns are urgent, but don't make demands. If there is a deadline involved—for instance, if you are facing a registration deadline—respectfully ask for a response before that date.

  - At the end of every message, thank the instructor and be sure to sign your complete name.

  - Finally, proofread what you've written and make sure your spell-check tool is on.

  To consider e-mail and text message netiquette more, complete **Try It 1**.

Classroom Netiquette: Using Technology Appropriately

Many instructors have guidelines about the appropriate use of technology while in their classrooms. Even if they don't explicitly provide rules, you can be sure they would want you to follow these guidelines:

- **Turn off your cell phone.** Most instructors ask that you keep your cell phones off (or set on "vibrate" mode) while in class. Cell phones ringing at random times are distracting and annoying, both to your fellow students and your instructor.

- **Don't send texts or make calls while in class.** It's obvious that you should be paying attention to what's going on in class rather than what's going on in the outside world.

- **If you use your laptop to take notes, stay on task.** No matter how tempting it is to check your e-mail messages, IM with a friend, or surf the Web, avoid the temptation. Use your laptop to take notes, and nothing else.

- **Don't use headphones connected to your computer.**

- **Never use your cell phone to text answers to problems in class.** Cheating is cheating, whether done using high-tech or low-tech methods. Don't do it.

Using E-Mail Netiquette

Read the e-mail below, written by a student to his instructor, and respond to the questions that follow.

```
●  ●  ●                          Class                                    ⬭
   ◁       ◯      ✐       ▣      A      ◯        🗎
 Send     Chat   Attach  Address  Fonts  Colors  Save As Draft

        To: Professor@ketchum.edu

        Cc:

 ≡▾  Subject: Class

Yo, Professor!!!

    I'm in your class, and I couldn't come yesterday because I had something I had to do.
Did I miss anything important? Can u send me any assignments u gave out AS SOON AS
POSSIBLE so I can work on it?

    I'm attaching the worksheet that was do. Hope it doesn't fill up your mailbox too
much   :-) !!
         BTW, when is ur next test?
            BJ
```

1. What rules of "netiquette" does the e-mail violate?

2. If you were the instructor to whom the e-mail message was sent, how do you think you would react to receiving it? What questions would you have about the message?

3. Based on the e-mail, what opinion might you have of the student who wrote it?

4. Rewrite the e-mail so that it is consistent with good netiquette.

To Try It online, got to **www.mhhe.com/power**.

Protecting Yourself: Spam Management and Safety

The downside of e-mail is *spam*, the virtual equivalent of junk mail. Spam may range from get-rich-quick schemes to advertisements for body enhancements or pornography. Spam is more than a nuisance; it takes up valuable transmission resources ("bandwidth"), disk space, and computer time.

Some e-mail systems apply a filter that uses a few simple rules to separate the wheat (e-mail you actually want to read) from the chaff (spam). Unfortunately, these systems are not perfect: They sometimes let junk through and can even at times dispose of messages you want. The only absolutely reliable way to deal with spam is to delete it yourself as quickly as possible.

Here are a few tips for dealing with spam:

> Consider using two e-mail addresses—one for personal messages and one you use when you visit newsgroups and chat rooms.

> Don't use anything similar to your actual name as your username or screen name.

> *Never* give anyone your password, and change your password frequently.

> *Never* respond to e-mails that ask for personal or financial information, even if it appears to be legitimate. Such requests may originate in *crimeware,* programs that steal personal financial information. For instance, in a practice called *phishing,* spam or pop-up messages are used to trick you into disclosing bank account or credit card numbers, passwords, or other personal information.

> In a phishing scam, the e-mail appears to be from a legitimate source and asks you to update or validate information by providing account information. In reality, such messages are from con artists seeking to steal your identity. If you think such a request may be legitimate, call the organization from which it appears to come.

> *Do not click* on any links in the e-mail message until you're sure it's real. Not only can such links lead to the disclosure of personal information about you, but it may lead to the secret installation of software that can spy on you.

> *Never* open an attachment from someone you don't know. Computer viruses, which can ruin everything on your hard drive, are often spread through e-mail attachments.

> Finally, if your e-mail program has a span filter, periodically check your spam folder to make sure no legitimate e-mails may have been directed there by mistake.

KEEPING SAFE

There's an even darker side to the Web than financial criminals looking to steal from you. Specifically, you need to be wary of sexual predators who use the Web to identify potential victims. To help protect yourself, use these guidelines:

1. Don't give out personal information to strangers, such as your name, phone number, address, hometown, or your future schedule—anything that can be used to identify you.

2. Never send photos of yourself or friends or family to someone you don't know.

3. Don't reply to e-mails that are offensive, weird, or distressing in any way.

4. Don't arrange to meet anyone that you've only met on the Web.

5. If you do have problems with someone over e-mail, immediately contact your college or local police.

SOCIAL NETWORKING WEB SITES

Many college students use social networking Web sites such as MySpace.com or Facebook.com to stay in touch with their friends and to make new acquaintances. In fact, Facebook has more than 150 million active users.

Although social networking Web sites offer many possibilities for interacting with friends and making new acquaintances, they need to be used appropriately. Don't post information about yourself or photos that you wouldn't want your instructors, parents, or future employers seeing. For instance, faculty at colleges can—and sometimes do—open accounts on Facebook.com and read students' postings. Furthermore, employers increasingly are using Facebook and MySpace in hiring decisions. In short, be thoughtful of what you post about yourself.

At the same time, be an informed consumer of material you encounter on social networking Web sites. Some of the profiles contain bogus material or are entirely false. Individuals sometimes disguise their identities or make up false ones. It's important to verify whom you are communicating with before exchanging personal information.

Distance learning
The teaching of courses entirely online with student participation via the Web

» LO 10.3 Distance Learning: Classes without Walls

Do you find that your schedule changes so much from one day to the next that it's hard to fit in a course that meets at a regularly scheduled time? Interested in an unusual course topic that your own college doesn't offer? Want to take a class during the summer but find yourself summering too far from a college campus?

The solution to your problem may be to enroll in a **distance learning** course. Distance learning is a form of education in which students participate via the Web or other kinds of technology. Although most distance learning courses are taught via the Web, some use teleconferencing, fax, and/or express mail.

The key feature of distance learning courses is the nature of interaction between instructor and students. Rather than meeting in a traditional classroom, where the instructor, you, and the other students are physically present, distance learning classes are most often virtual. Although some schools use "Webcasts" of lectures with virtual discussion rooms or employ lectures on videotape or CDs, most students in distance learning courses will never sit through a lecture or even participate in a real-time conversation with students in the class. They may never even know what their instructor or classmates look like or hear their voices.

If you take a distance learning course, you may read lecture notes posted on the Web, search and browse Web sites, write papers, post replies to discussion topics on a *message board,* and take online quizzes and exams. You will see your instructor's and classmates' responses through

In distance learning, you can take classes at another institution without physically having to be on that campus. Although taking courses online can help you fulfill graduation requirements, make sure before you register that your own college will accept the course credits. What do you think the future of distance learning will be?

comments they post on the Web. You may be expected to read a textbook entirely on your own.

You may already be familiar with the kinds of technologies used in distance learning courses, because many traditional, face-to-face courses already contain elements of distance learning. In **blended** (or **hybrid**) **courses,** instruction is a combination of the traditional, face-to-face classroom interaction and a significant amount of online learning. Students in blended courses spend more time working alone or in collaboration with others online. Students in blended courses also may spend less time in face-to-face classroom settings and more time working independently online.

In contrast to blended courses, all instruction takes place online in distance learning classes. However, distance learning is not for everyone. Whether you're a good candidate for it or not depends on your preferred style of course taking. Complete **Try It! 2** to see whether you are suited to learn at a distance.

Distance learning classes have both advantages and disadvantages. On the plus side, distance learning courses offer the following:

> **You can take a Web-based distance learning course anywhere that you have access to the Web.** You can be at home, at the college library, or on vacation at the beach and still participate.

> **Distance learning classes are more flexible than traditional classes.** You can participate in a course any time of the day or night. You set your own schedule.

> **Distance learning classes are self-paced.** You may be able to spread out your work over the course of a week, or you may do the work in a concentrated manner on one day.

> **You may have more contact with your instructor than you do with a traditional class.** Even though you may not have face-to-face contact, you may have greater access to your instructor, via e-mail and the Web, than in traditional classes. You can leave messages for your instructor any time of the night or day; most instructors of distance learning classes respond in a timely way.

> **Shy students may find it easier to "speak up" in a distance learning class.** You can think through your responses to make sure you are communicating just what you wish to say. You don't have to worry about speaking in front of other people. For many people, distance learning is liberating.

> **You can become a better writer.** Because distance learning usually involves more writing than traditional courses, you receive more practice writing—and more feedback for it—than in traditional classes.

On the other hand, distance learning has disadvantages that you should keep in mind:

> **You are a prisoner of technology.** If you lose access to a computer and the Web, you won't be able to participate in the class until the problem is fixed.

> **You won't have direct, face-to-face contact with your instructor or other students.** Distance learning can be isolating, and students sometimes feel alone and lost in cyberspace.

> **You won't get immediate feedback.** In a distance learning class, it may be hours, or sometimes days, before you receive feedback on what you have posted to a message board, depending on how well the pace of other students matches your own.

Blended (hybrid) courses
Courses in which instruction is a combination of traditional, face-to-face and online methods

Try It! POWER

Assess Your Course-Taking Style

2

Your preferred course-taking style—how you participate in classes, work with your classmates, interact with your teachers, and complete your assignments—may make you more or less suitable for distance learning. Read the following statements and indicate whether you agree or disagree with them to see if you have what it takes to be a distance learner.

	Agree	Disagree
1. I need the stimulation of other students to learn well.		
2. I need to see my teacher's face, expressions, and body language to interpret what is being said.		
3. I participate a lot in class discussions.		
4. I prefer to hear information presented orally rather than reading it in a book or article.		
5. I'm not very good at keeping up with reading assignments.		
6. I'm basically pretty easily distracted.		
7. I'm not very well organized.		
8. Keeping track of time and holding to schedules is NOT a strength of mine.		
9. I need a lot of "hand-holding" while I work on long assignments.		
10. I need a close social network to share my feelings, ideas, and complaints.		
11. I'm not very good at writing.		
12. Basically, I'm not very patient.		

The more you disagree with these statements, the more your course-taking style is suited to distance learning. Interpret your style according to this informal scale:

Disagreed with 10–12 statements = Excellent candidate for distance learning

Disagreed with 7–9 statements = Good candidate for distance learning

Agreed with 6–9 statements = Probably better taking classes on campus

Agreed with 10–12 statements = Avoid distance learning

To Try It online, go to www.mhhe.com/power.

‣ **Distance learning classes require significant discipline, personal responsibility, and time management skills.** You won't have a set time to attend class as you do in traditional courses. Instead, you must carve out the time yourself. Although instructors provide a schedule of when things are due, you have to work out the timing of getting them done.

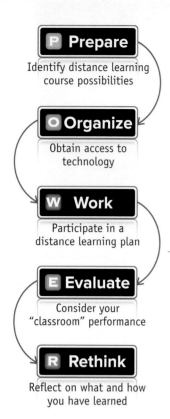

P **Prepare**

Identify distance learning course possibilities

O **Organize**

Obtain access to technology

W **Work**

Participate in a distance learning plan

E **Evaluate**

Consider your "classroom" performance

R **Rethink**

Reflect on what and how you have learned

P.O.W.E.R. Plan

Consequently, many students believe that distance learning courses are more difficult than traditional classes. You must be focused and committed to keeping up with the course. You need to be prepared to work hard on your own for a substantial number of hours each week.

Despite these potential challenges to distance learning courses, they are becoming increasingly popular. More and more colleges are offering them. Many companies encourage employees with crowded schedules to take distance learning as a way of providing continuing education.

If you are considering taking a distance learning course, follow these steps, which are summarized in the P.O.W.E.R. Plan on the left.

P **Prepare**

Identify Distance Learning Course Possibilities

How do you find a distance learning course? In some cases, your own college may offer courses on the Web and list them in your course catalog. In other cases, you'll have to find courses on your own.

The best place to look is on the Web itself. By searching the Web, you can find distance learning courses ranging from agronomy to zoology. Don't be deterred by the physical location of the institution that offers the course. It doesn't matter where the college is located, because for most distance learning classes, you'll never have to go to the campus itself.

But before you sign up for a potential course that you would like to count toward your degree, *make sure that your own college will give you credit for it.* Check with your advisor and registrar's office to be certain.

You should also find out what the requirements of a course are before you actually sign up for it. Check the syllabus carefully and see how it meshes with your schedule. If it is a summer course and you are going to be away from your computer for a week, you may not be able to make up the work you miss.

Finally, try to talk with someone who has taken the course before. Was the instructor responsive, providing feedback rapidly? If necessary, could you speak with the instructor by phone? Was the course load reasonable? (**Try It 3** will help you to work through the process.)

O **Organize**

Obtaining Access to Technology

Although you don't need to be a computer expert, you will need some minimal e-mail and Web skills to take a distance learning course. If you don't have sufficient technological expertise, beef up your computer skills by taking a computer course or workshop *before* you actually sign up for the course.

You'll also need access to a computer connected to the Internet. It doesn't have to be your own computer, but you will certainly need regular and convenient access to one. Make sure that the computer you plan to use has sufficient internal resources to quickly connect to the Internet; a very slow connection is frustrating.

Be sure to make all your arrangements for computer access prior to the start of a course. It can take several weeks to set up Internet service on a home computer if you don't have it already.

Get Some Distance on the Problem

3

Working by yourself initially, see if you can find distance learning courses of interest to you. Start by checking your school's course catalog to see what might be offered there. If you're already comfortable online, you might also try the following:

- *The Chronicle of Higher Education's* Distance Education: Daily Updates (**chronicle.com**).
- The World Lecture Hall (**www.utexas.edu/world/lecture/index.html**), hosted by the University of Texas, which provides a list of distance learning courses offered worldwide.

Try to find five courses you would be interested in and list them below. After you have completed your list, share your list with others in a group.

1. How diverse were the courses you were able to find?

2. Were particular subject areas better represented than others?

3. Why?

To Try It online, go to **www.mhhe.com/power**.

 Work

Participating in a Distance Learning Class

Successfully participating in a distance learning course involves several skills that are distinct from those needed for traditional classes. To get the most out of a distance learning course, you'll need to do the following:

> **Manage your time carefully.** You won't have the luxury of a regular schedule of class lectures, so you'll have to manage your time carefully. No one is going to remind you that you need to sit down at a computer and work. You will need every bit of self-discipline to be successful in a distance learning course.

- **Check in frequently.** Instructors may make crucial changes in the course requirements. Make sure to check for any changes in due dates or class expectations.

- **Find a cyberbuddy.** At the start of the semester, try to make personal contact with at least one other student in the class. You can do this by e-mailing, phoning, or actually meeting the student if he or she is geographically nearby. You can share study strategies, form a study group, and share notes. Connecting with another student can help you avoid feelings of isolation that may interfere with your success.

- **Make copies of everything.** Don't assume everything will go well in cyberspace. Make a printed copy of everything you submit, or alternatively have a backup stored on another computer.

- **Have a technology backup plan.** Computers crash, your connection to the Internet may go down, or an e-mailed assignment may be mysteriously delayed or sent back to you. Don't wait until the last minute to work on and submit assignments, and have a plan in place if your primary computer is unavailable.

E Evaluate Considering Your "Classroom" Performance

As with any class, you'll be receiving feedback from your instructor. But unlike many courses, in which almost all the feedback comes from the instructor, much of the feedback in a distance learning course may come from your fellow students. What can you learn from their comments?

At the same time you'll be receiving feedback, you will likely be providing feedback to your classmates. Consider the nature of feedback you provide, and be sure that you use the basic principles of classroom civility.

R Rethink Reflecting on What and How You Have Learned

Distance learning is not for everyone. If your preferred learning style involves extensive, face-to-face interaction with others, you may find that your experience is less than satisfying. On the other hand, if you are at ease with computers and enjoy working on your own, you may find distance learning highly effective.

As you reflect on your distance learning experience, go beyond the technology and think about the learning outcomes. Ask yourself whether you learned as much as you would have in a traditional class. You should also consider ways that the experience could have been more effective for you. And think about whether you were so absorbed by the technology that you lost sight of the real goal of the course: learning new material.

Most educational experts believe that distance learning will play an increasingly important role in higher education. Furthermore, because it offers an efficient way of educating people in far-flung locales, it is a natural means of promoting lifelong learning experiences. In short, the first distance learning class you take is likely not to be your last.

»LO 10.4 Finding Facts: Developing Information Competency

One of the greatest advances brought about by technology involves the area of research. More than ever, people require **information competency,** the ability to determine what information is necessary, and then to locate, evaluate, and effectively use that information. The sheer abundance of material available today makes information competency a critical skill.

We'll consider the ways in which you can use the two primary storehouses of information available today to boost your own level of information competency. One you can walk or drive to—the library. The other—the Web—doesn't have a physical location. Both are indispensable in anyone's quest for information.

Information competency
The ability to determine what information is necessary, and then to locate, evaluate, and effectively use that information

Libraries

No matter how imposing or humble their physical appearance, whether they contain only a few hundred volumes or hundreds of thousands of them, libraries are a good place to focus your efforts as you seek out and gather information. Although every library is different, all share two key elements: the material they hold—their basic collections—and tools to help you locate the material you need.

What Can Be Found in a Library's Basic Collection?

Libraries obviously contain books, but they typically have a lot more than that, including some or all of the following:

- **Periodicals.** *Periodicals* include magazines published for general audiences, specialized journals for professionals in a field, and newspapers. Magazines and journals are often bound and stored by year; newspapers are usually kept in *microform,* in which documents have been photographed and stored on either microfilm (reels of film) or microfiche (plastic sheets).

- **Indexes and online databases.** An index provides a listing of periodical articles by title, author, and subject. Some indexes also provide a short summary, or *abstract*, of the contents of each article.

> "Knowledge is of two kinds: we know a subject ourselves, or we know where we can find information upon it."
> **Samuel Johnson**

  Most indexes come in both print and electronic form. In their electronic form, they are known as an **online database,** an organized body of information on a related topic. For example, the National Center for Biotechnology Information (NCBI) maintains *Medline,* an online public database that provides information on medical research. The advantage of online databases over traditional, print-based indexes is that the database sometimes provides the full text of material they identify in a search.

Online database
An index in electronic form composed of an organized body of information on a related topic

- **Encyclopedias.** Some encyclopedias, such as the *Encyclopedia Britannica* or *World Book Encyclopedia*, attempt to cover the entire range of knowledge, and they may take up many volumes. Others are more specialized, covering only a particular field, such as the *Encyclopedia of Human Behavior* or the *Encyclopedia of Religion*. Most are printed as multivolume sets of books, although an increasing number are available electronically, on CD-ROM or online. Encyclopedias provide a good general view of a topic, but they lack depth: Use them at the earliest stage of your hunt for information for an overview of key issues, and move from there to more specific and current sources.

> **Government documents.** Census records, laws, and tax codes are some of the millions of government documents that are stored in libraries.

> **Musical scores.** The music to *Rent*, the Brahms *Alto Rhapsody*, and The Beatles' greatest hits are among the musical scores you can find in libraries.

> **Reserve collections.** Reserve collections hold heavily used items that instructors assign for a class. Sometimes reserve material can be checked out for only an hour or two and used in the same room; in other cases the material can be used overnight or for a few days.

Locating Information in a Library

The place to begin searching for information in a library is the library catalog. Catalogs list all materials that are held in the library and provide their location. Most library catalogs are computerized, though a few still use name cards filed in drawers or microform (microfiche or microfilm). You are usually able to access computerized catalogs from home or residence hall rooms as well as from computers housed in the library itself.

Library catalogs traditionally allow searches by title, author name, and subject; electronic catalogs also typically allow searching by keyword. Individual catalog entries generally include additional information about the material, such as the publisher, date of publication, number of pages, and similar information.

Say, for example, you're writing a paper on Ernest Hemingway. To find books he *wrote* in an electronic catalog, you would enter his name in the "author" field. You may be presented with the listing shown in **Figure 10.2.**

Of course, you could also search on "Hemingway" as the subject, which would yield a list of books *about* him and his work; if you entered his name in a "keyword" search, the catalog would return a more comprehensive list of books both by *and* about him.

figure 10.2
Online Catalog Entry

Online catalog entry for a book called *The Old Man and the Sea*. Note especially the call number and due date these will tell you where the book is to be found and whether it is on the shelves or is checked out.

The key piece of information in a catalog entry is the book's **call number,** a code that tells you exactly where to find it. Most college libraries use the Library of Congress classification system, which assigns to each book a unique combination of letters and numbers.

Because the record illustrated in **Figure 10.2** is from an electronic search, it contains further helpful information. The word "Available" under "Due Date" tells you that one copy the book has not been checked out by another patron and should be sitting on the shelf. You'll need to familiarize yourself with your library's particular system to know precisely how you can make most efficient use of the catalog. Chances are there's a handout or posted set of instructions nearby.

Once you have identified the material you need and where it is located, you'll need to go find it. In all but the biggest libraries, you can simply go into the **stacks,** the place containing shelves where the books and other materials are kept, and—using the call number—hunt for it. In libraries with closed stacks, you must fill out a form with the call numbers of the books you want. A library aide will find and deliver the material to a central location.

What if you go to the location in the stacks where the material is supposed to be and you can't find it? The material may be checked out, in use by someone else at that time, incorrectly shelved, or simply lost. Whatever the reason, *don't give up.* If the material is checked out to another user, ask a librarian if you can **recall** the material, a process by which the library contacts the person who has the book and asks him or her to return it.

If the librarian informs you that the material is not checked out, wait a few days and see if it appears on the shelf. Someone may have been using it while you were looking for it. If it was misshelved, the librarian may be able to find it. If the material is truly lost, you may be able to get it from another library through **interlibrary loan,** a system by which libraries share resources.

Finally, even if you do find exactly what you were looking for, take a moment to scan the shelves. Because books and other materials are generally grouped by topic, you may find other useful titles in the same place. One of the pleasures of libraries is the possibility of finding an unexpected treasure—material that your catalog search did not initially identify but that may provide you with exactly what you need.

Finding Information on the Web

The Web is vast—sometimes frustratingly so. In fact, no one knows how much material exists on the Web. Not only is more information added to the Web every day, but the information also resides on thousands of individual computers. Anyone with minimal Web savvy and access to a *server* (a computer with a permanent Internet connection) can set up a personal Web site.

The fact that anyone can put information on the Web is both the biggest asset and greatest disadvantage of using the Web as an information source. Because minimal computer skill is the only expertise a person needs to set up a Web page, there may be as much misinformation on the Web as there is information. Consequently, keep the usual consumer rule in mind: Buyer beware. Unless the Web site has been

Call number
A unique classification number assigned to every book (or other resource) in a library. Call numbers are used for ease of location

Stacks
The shelves on which books and other materials are stored in a library

Searching for materials in the library stacks can be frustrating if they are not on the shelves. However, you may unexpectedly find relevant and interesting material while browsing.

Recall
A way to request library materials from another person who has them

Interlibrary loan
A system by which libraries share resources, making them available to patrons of different libraries

Browser

A program that provides a
way of navigating around the
information on the Web

established and is maintained by a reliable organization, the information it contains may not be accurate.

There are a number of key factors involved in each Web search. They include a browser, Web pages, links, and search engines.

> **Browsers.** To use the Web, your computer has to have a browser. A **browser,** as its name implies, is a program that provides a way of looking at the information on the Web. Among the major browsers are Microsoft's Internet Explorer and Firefox's Mozilla (see **Figure 10.3**).

Using a browser is a bit like taking a taxi: Once you get in, you get to where you want to go by providing an address. The address, also known as a URL (Uniform Resource Locator), identifies a unique location on the Web, a *Web site* or a *Web page* (one of the parts of a site).

Web addresses are combinations of letters and symbols. They typically start off with "**www.[domain_name].[xxx]**"—the address of the hosting Web site (e.g., **www.iastate.edu,** the home page for Iowa State University). If you're looking for a subsite or a particular page on the site, the address becomes increasingly specific: **www.iastate. edu/visitors/** will take you to a "visitors" site—a collection of pages—hosted by **iastate.edu.** A *page* on that site—for example, **www.iastate.edu/visitors/directions.shtml,** which offers directions to campus—ends with a specific name, usually followed by ".htm," ".html," or ".shtml." Because most addresses begin with "http://," this part of the address is often dropped in references to a site.

You can often get a decent idea of what kind of site you're going to by taking a careful look at the Web address: You can tell that **www.mhhe.com/power,** for example, is a site that has something to do with "power" and is hosted by a commercial entity (which you might or might not recognize as McGraw-Hill Higher Education). (Hmm, might be worth checking out. . . .)

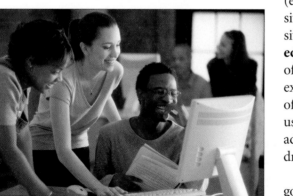

It is becoming increasingly easy for anyone to put material on the Web, and many students are creating their own personal Web pages containing information and photos about their lives.

> **Web pages.** Web pages are the heart of the Web. A **Web page** is a document that presents you with information. The information may appear as text on the screen, to be read like a book (or more accurately, like an ancient scroll). It might include a video clip, an audio clip, a photo, a portrait, a graph, or a figure. It might offer a news service photo of the president of the United States or a backyard snapshot of someone's family reunion.

> **Links.** Web sites typically provide you with **links**—embedded addresses to other sites or documents that, at a click, cause your browser automatically to "jump" there. Just as an encyclopedia article on forests might say at the end, "See also Trees," Web pages often refer to other sites on the Web—only it's easier than with a book. You just have to click on the link with your mouse and—*poof!*—you're there.

> **Search engines.** A **search engine** is simply a computerized index to information on the Web. When you know what information you want to find but don't have an address for it, a search engine can often steer you toward relevant sites.

The various parts of the Web are similar to the components of traditional libraries, as illustrated in **Figure 10.4.** A Web browser is equivalent to a library card; it gives you access to vast quantities of material. Web sites are like the books of a library; Web pages are the book pages, where the content resides. Links are analogous to "see also" portions of books that suggest related information. And search engines are like a library's card catalog, directing you to specific locations.

Web page
A location (or site) on the Web housing information from a single source and (typically) links to other pages

Link
A means of "jumping" automatically from one Web page to another

Search engine
A computerized index to information on the Web

Traditional Library   **Web**

Library card   Web browser

Book   Web site

"See Also" pages   Web links

http://www.nbcnews.com
http://www.whitehouse.gov
http://www.umass.edu
http://www.ama-assn.org

Library catalog   Search engine

figure 10.4
Comparison of Library and Web
The various parts of the Web are similar to the components of a traditional library.

"Go ask your search engine."

Locating Information on the Web

There is no central catalog of the contents of the Web: instead, there are a number of different search engines. Furthermore, depending on the search engine you use and the type of search you do, you'll identify different information.

Search engines themselves are located on the Web, so you have to know their addresses. After you reach the "home" address of a search engine, you enter your search terms. The search engine then provides a list of Web sites that may contain information relevant to your search.

Some search engines, such as Yahoo!, specialize in organizing information by subject, making it easy to search for information on, say, different dog breeds, the Islamic religion, or car repair. Using Yahoo! for its subject directories is like searching for information using the subject entries in a library catalog (see **Figure 10.5**).

Other search engines, such as Google or AltaVista, catalog many more pages than Yahoo! but don't group them by subject. Due to the breadth of their coverage, they might be more useful when you are looking for obscure pieces of information or for numerous sources for different perspectives on a topic. Using Google or AltaVista is like performing a keyword search in a library catalog.

> "Don't let that little glowing screen become an adversary. If you plan correctly, the computer can become your most useful tool at college—next to your brain."
>
> Greg Gottesman, author

Finally, a third type of search engine is exemplified by Ask.com and AlltheWeb.com. Known as metasearch tools, these sites send your search commands to other search engines, compiling the results into a single, unified list.

There's no single search engine that works best. Most people develop their own preferences based on their experience. The best advice: Try out several of them (some features are summarized in **Table 10.2** on page 279) and see which works best for you. To get started, work through **Try It 4,** "Work the Web: Information, Please!" on page 280.

figure 10.5
Starting a Search
This search on Google on How do I use the Web? identified more than 2.8 billion sites.

table 10.2 Major Search Sites on the Web[2]

Search Site	Comments
A9 www.a9.com	Amazon product that offers search results from Google along with a number of additional features, including search results from Amazon's "Search Inside the Book." A9 also saves your search history and tracks the click history of sites you have viewed from your search results.
Open Directory www.dmoz.org	The Open Directory Project is the largest, most comprehensive human-edited directory of the Web. It is constructed and maintained by a vast, global community of volunteer editors.
Google www.google.com	Most popular search site. Ranks pages by tracking the links from pages ranked high by the service. Google offers a number of services and tools that are worth exploring.
Ask.com www.ask.com	Formerly known as Ask Jeeves, this site allows submission of questions in plain English and suggests relevant sites.
Alltheweb www.alltheweb.com	Returns results quickly from an extremely large database gathered by the Yahoo! crawler; offers multimedia and news searches; has a good advanced search interface.
Alta Vista www.altavista.com	Searches Web sites and Usenet newsgroups with advanced search options.
Windows Live www.live.com	Microsoft's search engine that offers searches of the general Web as well as some deep Web sources; includes a Search Builder that includes an option to retrieve results based on recent updates, popularity, and exact or approximate match.
SearchEdu.com www.searchedu.com	Service that limits results to the .edu domain; also offers to search well-known dictionaries, encyclopedias, almanacs, etc.
Yahoo! Search search.yahoo.com	Offers easy access to dictionaries, patents, and encylopedias, as well as a huge database.
Lycos www.lycos.com	Emphasizes search results from the Open Directory and offers Web sites from the Fast Search index.
Answers.com www.answers.com	This site is able to access more than 4 million subjects from more than 100 dictionaries, almanacs, and encyclopedias. Includes a directory that contains dozens of subcategories for searching.

Becoming a Savvy Surfer

The process you use to search the Web couldn't be easier—or more difficult. The vast amounts of material online and the relative ease of navigation afforded by the Web make finding information quite simple: What is hard is finding appropriate information.

Consider the search illustrated in **Figure 10.5** on page 278. It is the result of entering How do I use the Web? into the home page of Google. The search identified over 2.8 *billion* Web sites related to the topic.

Using the list of sites generated by the search is simple. With the mouse, click on the site address of the relevant document, and the home page of the site will (eventually) appear on your computer screen. You can then take notes on the material, in the same way you'd take notes on material in a book.

Many of the million sites Google returned, however, may well be of little use. It's easy in such a search to end up in a virtual dead end, in which the information

"First, they do an online search."

Try It!

Work the Web: Information, Please!

Try to find the answer to the first question below on Yahoo! (**www.yahoo.com**), Google (**www.google.com**), *and* Dogpile (**www.dogpile.com**). Then use whichever search engine you prefer to find answers to the remaining questions.

1. What was the French Revolution and when did it occur?

2. Who is Keyser Soze?

3. What are the words to Dr. Martin Luther King Jr.'s "I Have a Dream" speech?

4. Is the birthrate in the United States higher or lower than that in Brazil?

5. What is the ecu?

How easy was it for you to find the answers to the questions? Which search engine(s) did you prefer, and why?

To Try It online, go to www.mhhe.com/power.

you have found is only minimally related to the topic you're researching. If you do find yourself at a site that's of no use to you, simply hit the "back" button on your browser until you return to where you started.

How can you limit your search in the first place, so that you find sites more directly relevant? The following tips can help you to get the most from a search[1]:

1. **Before you type anything into your computer, phrase your search as a question.**

2. **Identify the important words in that question.** Then think of words that are related to the important words. Write all the words down.

3. **Go to your favorite search engine.** Google is the most popular today, but preferences vary.

4. **Type in two or three words from your list,** making sure they are spelled correctly, then search. Note: You can do a few things here to limit the number of results returned, thus making your search more efficient. Most search engines allow you to use the following:

   - *Quotation marks*, to denote a phrase—words that should appear together, in a specific order (e.g., "animal rights").

- *Plus signs,* used before terms that must appear in all results returned (+ "animal rights" + experimentation).
- *Minus signs,* before terms you do not want to appear in results (+ "animal rights" + experimentation − fur).
- *Boolean operators*—words like AND, OR, AND NOT, and NEAR (e.g., "animal rights" AND experimentation NOT fur).

Check the "Help" section of your preferred search engine for more precise information on limiting your searches.

5. **Open a new window,** type in a different arrangement of your terms, and search again.

6. **Identify the common links between the two searches.** Read the very brief summaries provided.

7. **When you choose a Web site, open the page in a new window** so that you can go back to your list of hits.

8. **Open a text editor window.** Copy and paste the site's address into that window and follow it with an annotation of your own. Do that for five sites.

9. **See if you have found the answer you were looking for.** If not, reformulate your question to come up with new key words.

10. **Resist the temptation to simply cut and paste the material into a new document,** once you've found the information you're looking for. It's too easy to succumb to plagiarism if you simply copy material. Instead, take notes on the material using the critical thinking and note-taking skills you've developed for use with other, more traditional information sources.

    Then save your notes. You can save your notes on a computer's hard drive, a flash drive, or a network drive (if you have space on one). You can also print out hard copies of what you create virtually.

    However you do it, *make sure you save material frequently and make backup copies.* Nothing is more frustrating than laboring over a document for hours and having it disappear into cyberspace.

Evaluating the Information You Find on the Web

In most instances, you'll find more information than you need, and you'll have to evaluate the information you have found. Some of the important questions you must address before you can feel confident about what you've found include the following:

"On the Internet, nobody knows you're a dog."

> **How authoritative is the information?** It is absolutely essential to consider the source of the material. Approach every piece of information with a critical eye, trying to determine what the author's biases might be. The best approach is to use multiple sources of information. If one source diverges radically from the others, you may reasonably question the reliability of that source.

Another approach is to consider the publisher of the material or sponsoring institution. For instance, sites established by well-known publishers and organizations are more likely to contain accurate information than those created by unknown (and sometimes anonymous) authors. Remember, the Web is completely unregulated: *anyone* can put *anything* on the Web. One way of evaluating Web information is to consider a site's host. Commercial Web pages (whose address includes the letters *.com*, short for commercial) often tend to include the least objective material. On the other hand, addresses including the letters *.gov* (government), *.org* (nonprofit organization), *.mil* (military), and *.edu* (educational and research institutions) generally include more objective information.

But not always. For example, some instructors place student papers on the Web, giving them an *.edu* address. Such papers vary considerably in their authoritativeness. Similarly, some nonprofit organizations with a *.org* address hold extreme positions. Furthermore, *blogs,* those personal Web sites that contain personal diaries, are pervasive on the Web. Because they are not subject to any editorial scrutiny before they are published, they are of questionable authoritativeness. In short, any Web content must be evaluated on its merits.

> **How current is the information?** No matter what the discipline, information is changing at a rapid rate. Even a field like Chaucerian English, which concentrates on poetry written in the 14th century, advances significantly year by year as scholars make new discoveries, come to new insights, and reach new conclusions.

Consequently, don't assume that, because you're researching a historical topic, old sources will suffice. Consider whether what you've found is the most recent and up-to-date approach. Compare older sources to newer ones to identify changes in the ways in which the topic is considered.

> **How well are claims documented?** Are there references and citations to support the information? Are specific studies identified?

> **Is anything missing?** One of the hardest questions to answer is whether your research is complete. Have you found all the relevant sources? Have you missed anything that is important?

Although there is no way to answer these questions definitively, you can do a couple of things. One way to ensure that you haven't missed anything important is to check out the sources that you have found. Many will have bibliographies and lists of suggested additional readings. By carefully considering this information, you'll be able to get a good sense of the important work in your topic area and verify that you haven't overlooked some critical source.

You can also talk to your course instructor, describing generally what you've found. Probably the best person to turn to, however, is a reference librarian.

The stereotype of a librarian as someone whose main job is to stop people from talking in the library is dead. Librarians today are masters at information management and technology. They are people who can help you find your way through a huge range of data sources—both in the library and on the Web—and steer you to the right material.

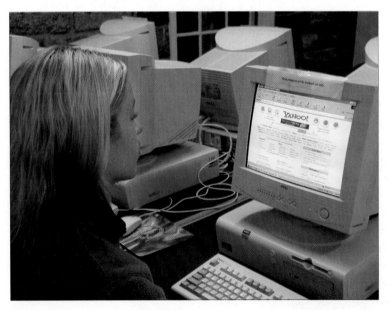
Being familiar with a variety of search engines is a useful skill.

Exploring Careers on the Web

The Web is one of the newest ways to explore careers that may interest you. You can begin to gather information by going to a Web site devoted to jobs, such as **www.monster.com** or **www. jobweb.com.** Both sites present a variety of career-related information. You can also find other sites using the various search engines we've been discussing.

In addition, you can find postings for many jobs on the Web. In fact, it is possible to apply for jobs using the Web. Some firms advertise their job needs on their company sites, and you can e-mail a cover letter and a résumé listing your education and experience. An increasing number of jobs are obtained in this way.

Keep this in mind, too: The technological expertise you develop during college will later help you in your professional life. Already, more and more jobs require computer skills, and every projection of the future suggests that technology will become a central facet of the workplace.

Make use of librarians—but do it properly. If your library offers regular orientations, sign up for one. Then try looking for material yourself. If you're having trouble sorting through what you've found (or can't find material in the first place), ask for help.

The better the question, the better the answer. Don't ask vague, unfocused questions (e.g., "Where are the books about nuclear power?"). Instead, sharpen your question, being as precise as possible ("I'm writing a paper on the environmental effects of using nuclear power to generate electricity. I've found two books and several Web sites, but they're not quite right. I wonder if you have any ideas about where I might find additional material?").

Don't be afraid to ask. Think of librarians as highly trained guides who can save you hours of aimless wandering in an increasingly dense forest of information.

A Final Word

The Information Age presents us with great promise and opportunity. Through the use of media such as e-mail and the Internet, we have at our fingertips the ability to communicate with others around the world. We can break the bounds of our physical location and reach across geography to learn about others. The computer keyboard truly can be said to contain keys to the entire earth and its peoples.

speaking of success

NAME: **Francine Sanchez**

SCHOOL: **Lehman College, New York, NY, BA; University of Pennsylvania, MA in Social Work**

In her senior year of high school, Francine Sanchez suddenly found herself as the oldest of four siblings in what had become a single-parent family. As a result, she was forced to take on a more significant role in her household, helping care for her three younger brothers and sisters.

With these unexpected demands thrust upon her, Sanchez realized that time management was crucial to meet the challenges she faced. Despite the circumstances, she committed herself to pursue a college education full time.

"I was determined not to go into debt for college, and I knew that my family could not afford to provide me with financial assistance," said Sanchez, who is now Education Program Development Coordinator for the New York City Administration for Children's Services. "At one point I juggled three part-time jobs," she added.

"I learned a lot about myself in college, and learned my own strengths that have helped me," said Sanchez, who went on to graduate with honors from Lehman College. She eventually completed a masters degree in Social Work at the University of Pennsylvania.

Through her years of undergraduate and graduate school, Sanchez was always involved in many activities outside of academics, requiring her to manage her time carefully.

"During my first year as an undergraduate, I learned a lot of things through academic experiences, and one was to be able to say 'no' when I felt I had a lot on my plate," said Sanchez. "There came a point where I realized my limitations." Sanchez also said that it was very important to make time for herself, especially when weighed down with work.

"If ever I got to the point where I felt overwhelmed or stressed out, I would just stop and take a short break," she added. "For me it was watching something light on TV. For someone else it could be taking a walk, working out, or talking to a friend. It's important to learn to do that and decompress."

Looking Back

What are the educational uses of technology?

▸ Course Web sites, CD-ROMs, textbook Web sites, podcasts, blogs, wikis, classroom presentation programs, and individual response technology (IRT) are among the major educational uses of computers.

What is available on the Web?

▸ The Internet is a vast network that connects millions of computers. It has numerous useful features, including e-mail, instant messaging, newsgroups, listservs, and the Web.

▸ E-mail and the Web are the most frequently used features of the Internet.

▸ E-mail permits instant communication across the world. Users can reply to messages, forward them, and include attachments.

What is distance learning?

▸ Distance learning is a form of education that does not require the physical presence of a student in a classroom. It is usually conducted over the Web.

▸ Distance learning requires some adjustments for students, but it is likely to increase in popularity in future years.

How can I develop information competency?

▸ There are two main sources of information today: libraries and the Web.

▸ Information in libraries is available in print form, electronic form, and microform.

▸ Library resources can be found through the use of the library catalog, which may be print-based but is increasingly likely to be computerized.

▸ The Web is another major source of information. Web users access Web pages (or sites) by using a browser, locate information by using search engines, and move from site to site by following links on each Web page.

What do I need to keep in mind as I use the Web to gather information?

▸ Using the Web effectively to find information can be tricky. It has many dead ends, false trails, and distractions, and the accuracy of the information presented as fact can be difficult to assess.

▸ Information on the Web must be carefully evaluated by considering how reliable the source is, how current the information is, how well the source's claims are documented, and how complete the information is.

[KEY TERMS AND CONCEPTS]

[R E S O U R C E S]

ON CAMPUS

If you are having difficulty connecting or surfing the Web, the first place to turn is your college's computer center. Most campuses have consultants who can help you with the technical aspects of computer usage.

If you need access to computers, most colleges have computer labs. Typically, these labs provide computers with Web access, as well as printers. It's important to check their hours, as they usually are not open 24/7. In addition, you may have to wait in line for a computer, so it is a good idea to bring some other work to the lab so you have something to do while waiting. You may also need to provide printer paper if you want to print something out.

The librarians at your college library are the people to whom you should turn first if you need help in locating information. In recent years, librarians—most of whom hold advanced degrees—have undergone a significant change in what they do, and most are equally at home using traditional print material and searching electronic information storehouses.

IN PRINT

A good introductory guide to computers is Michael Miller's *Absolute Beginner's Guide to Computer Basics* (Que, 2007). *Web Search Savvy: Strategies and Shortcuts for Online Research* by Barbara Friedman (Lawrence Erlbaum, 2004) provides a step-by-step guide to locating information of all sorts. Finally, *Peterson's Guide to Online Learning* (Peterson's, 2005) offers clear instruction on becoming an effective online learner.

ON THE WEB

Many sites on the Web provide the opportunity to extend your learning about the material in this chapter. (Although the Web addresses were accurate at the time the book was printed, check the *P.O.W.E.R. Learning* Web site [**www.mhhe.com/power**] for any changes that may have occurred.)

> Imperial College's (London) Department of Computing offers FOLDOC (Free Online Dictionary of Computing) at **foldoc.org.** If you're having a hard time trying to figure out some computer jargon, this site—a dictionary of computer terminology—might help. Topics are listed alphabetically, and a search engine helps locate specific information.

> The WWW Virtual Library (**www.vlib.org/**) is one of the oldest catalogs of the Web, providing useful links to thousands of subjects.

> Yahoo! (**www.yahoo.com**) is a very popular Internet search engine and subject directory. Unlike Google and Alta Vista, as a subject directory, Yahoo! allows browsing through prearranged categories (e.g., education, health, social science, and more). It also offers easy access to news, weather, maps, the Yellow Pages, and much more.

1   Using the search engine of your choice, find the address for the Web site of the libraries of the University of California at Berkeley. Once there, try to find "Finding Information on the Internet: A Tutorial." Try the tutorial, which will help you understand many of the basic skills needed to use the Internet effectively. (Would taking the tutorial *first* have helped you find it?)

2   To see for yourself how the Web can be a great resource for locating information on important issues, try to find the answer to this question: "What are the effects of media violence on children?" Go to a search engine (try **www.google.com**) and type in the phrase: "media violence and children" (being sure to include the quotation marks). Look over the first page of documents that the search engine turns up. Are they in fact about the effects of media violence on children? Do they answer the question you are asking? What is the answer to the question?

The Case of . . .
The Missing File

Katrisha was almost done with her paper. She'd been working in a marathon session, sitting in front of her computer screen with only a couple of breaks over the course of an afternoon.

She'd begun work just after noon, when the sky was bright and clear. By now, some 4 hours later, it was dark and gray and she heard thunder in the distance. But who cared about the weather? The main thing was that she was almost done.

She didn't usually put things off, but this time she'd gotten behind and was forced to do the work at the last minute. She was writing a report on software that blocks "adult" sites from home computers. Luckily she'd been able to find what she needed using various search engines and incorporating the information into her paper.

The assignment was due by 5:00 P.M., but the professor accepted papers submitted via e-mail. As long as the message was sent before 5:00, she would be OK. She still had an hour to put the final touches on the paper and send it off.

Suddenly, there was a bright flash of lightning, followed by a clap of thunder. At the same moment, her computer screen went black as the electricity was cut.

Much to Katrisha's relief, the outage lasted only a few seconds. Her computer began to reboot, and the screen powered up again. In a few moments, she figured, she could continue her work.

But when the computer had fully restarted, the file with the paper that she'd been working on all day was nowhere to be found. She searched frantically through the various files on the computer, but to no avail. Her heart sinking, she realized that everything she had done over the afternoon was lost.

1. How well did Katrisha use her time to work on her paper? What advice would you give her about the preparation stage of working on a paper?

2. Did Katrisha organize her work well? What would you tell her to do next time?

3. Clearly, Katrisha should have saved her work frequently while she was working. What else should she have done while working on her paper to help her recover from such a catastrophe?

4. What should Katrisha do first to start solving her immediate problem with her professor?

5. What should she do next to begin reconstructing her paper and recovering as much of her work as possible?

CHAPTER 11

Making Good Decisions

Learning Outcomes

By the time you finish this chapter you will be able to

» LO **11.1**   Identify strategies for improving the quality of your decisions.

» LO **11.2**   Implement plans to use for problem solving.

» LO **11.3**   Recognize and correct problems that affect critical thinking.

For Rich Rinkowski, the moment of truth was fast approaching. He had to make up his mind and decide what he was going to do when he graduated. Throughout his college career he had intended to go to law school, and he had majored in criminal justice. He'd already been accepted to law school by the middle of his senior year, and it seemed that his future was well in hand.

Except for one thing: He was no longer sure he wanted to be a lawyer.

The reason for his indecision was an internship he held working for a film director during the summer between his junior and senior years. Although Rich spent a good deal of his time photocopying and making coffee, he learned a lot about the film industry. In fact, after talking several times at length with the director, Rich began to wonder seriously if he might build a career in the movie industry.

Rich's girlfriend and family were dead set against it: They argued that law was a far safer choice.

As his final term went by, Rich knew he had to make up his mind. But how?

Looking Ahead

Like Rich, all of us face important decisions in our lives at one time or another. How can we make the right decisions? The best way is to employ some basic techniques that can help improve the quality of our decision making.

This chapter will give you a sense of what decision making is and is not, and it discusses a structured process that can help make your decisions the right ones. We'll also consider the related issue of problem solving. You'll confront a variety of problems as you proceed through college. We'll look at a number of proven techniques that will help you solve them.

Neither making decisions nor solving problems is easy. Sometimes the best decision or solution to a problem is one that we don't see at first; we all have mental blind spots. The best problem solvers and decision makers have learned how to use critical thinking to see around these blind spots. To help you improve your critical thinking skills, we'll examine some common problems that can affect our thinking and discuss several biases that can make us jump too quickly to conclusions.

» LO 11.1 Making Good Decisions: A Framework

Decision making
The process of deciding among various alternatives

Decision making is the process of deciding among various alternatives. Whether you are trying to decide between a Ford or a Honda; between an apartment that is close to your job or one that is close to campus; or simply between a hamburger or pizza—every one of these choices requires a decision. Some decisions are easily made and have few consequences, but others, such as whether to major in music composition or follow a pre-med course of study, can involve the deepest examination of our beliefs and values.

Whatever you're deciding, you need to think critically to make a reasoned decision. You need to apply your past knowledge, synthesize and evaluate alternatives, and reason and reflect on a course of action. The greater your depth of thinking about the components of the decision, the more likely it is that you'll come up with the best choice.

To make a good decision, map out a strategy for making the choice that is best for you. Every decision can benefit from your effort to systematically think through the options involved, based on the P.O.W.E.R. Plan illustrated below.

P Prepare Identifying Your Goals

Every decision starts with the end you have in mind: the goals you wish to accomplish by making the decision.

> "Nothing is more difficult, and therefore more precious, than to be able to decide."
>
> Napoleon I, *Maxims*, 1804–15

For example, suppose you are trying to decide between enrolling in one of two classes next term, neither of which is required: swimming or psychology. To decide, you need to consider both your short- and long-term goals. For instance, the swimming class may raise your level of fitness, and you'll end up with a certificate that will allow you to be a lifeguard during the summer. The psychology class may provide you with some useful information—perhaps information you can use in other classes, perhaps techniques that will help you learn and remember better—but this is by no means certain. In terms of short-term goals, then, the swimming class may be the better choice. On the other hand, while the psychology class may not provide as clear-cut an immediate payoff, it may help you meet your longer-term goal of graduating with honors and becoming a successful teacher.

In short, every decision should start with a consideration of what our short- and long-term goals are. Identifying the goals that underlie decisions ensures that we make decisions in the context of our entire lives and not just to provide short-term answers to immediate problems.

O Organize Considering and Assessing the Alternatives

Every decision is based on weighing various alternatives. Determining what those alternatives are, and their possible consequences, is often the most difficult part of decision making.

Develop a List of Flexible Alternatives

It's important not only to think thoroughly about the obvious alternatives but also to consider those that are less obvious. For instance, if you are trying to obtain additional funds to support your college theater group, you might consider raising ticket prices for productions, holding a raffle to raise funds, or asking for sponsorship from a local business. After additional thought, though, you might reframe the issue, considering how best to place pressure on the college administration to increase funding for your group.

In short, the way you develop and frame alternatives is critical to the solution that you ultimately reach. The more alternatives you have, the better able you will be to come to a good solution.

How can you be sure that you've considered all the alternatives? You can't. But using the freewriting technique described in Chapter 7 can help you maximize your efforts.

In *freewriting,* one writes continuously for a fixed period of time, perhaps 5 or 10 minutes. During this period, the idea is to write as many different ideas as possible, without stopping. It makes no difference whether the alternatives are good or bad or even whether they make sense. All that matters is that you let yourself brainstorm about the topic for a while and get it down on paper.

P Prepare
Identify your goals to help make decisions

O Organize
Consider and assess the alternatives

W Work
Make and carry out the decision

E Evaluate
Consider the outcomes

R Rethink
Reconsider your goals and options

P.O.W.E.R. Plan

We've all been there: facing a mind-boggling array of similar choices. However, by systematically assessing the alternatives, we can make informed decisions that will satisfy us.

With freewriting, evaluating the worth of the ideas you've generated comes later. After you have produced as many possibilities as you can, then you go back and sift out the reasonable ones from those that are truly unlikely or just plain wacky. It's OK if you have to delete quite a few alternatives from your list; the process is likely to have liberated some truly reasonable alternatives that you might not otherwise have come up with. (Try the technique in the "Use Freewriting" exercise—see **Try It 1.**)

Assess Alternatives

Once you have generated as extensive a list of alternatives as possible, assess them. You need to follow three key steps when assessing each alternative:

1. *Determine the possible outcomes for each alternative.* Some outcomes are positive, some negative. Consider as many as you can think of. If you are considering ways of solving transportation problems, one alternative might be to purchase a car. That alternative produces several potential outcomes. You know that it will be easier to get wherever you want to go, and you might even have a better social life—clearly positive outcomes. But it is also true that buying and owning a car will be expensive, or it may be difficult to find convenient parking—both significant negative outcomes.

2. *Determine the probability that those outcomes will take place.* Some outcomes are far more likely than others. To take this into account, make a rough estimate of the likelihood that an outcome will come to pass, ranging from 100 percent (it is certain that it will occur) to 0 percent (it is certain that it will never occur). For instance, consider the possible outcomes of buying a car illustrated in **Figure 11.1.**

   Obviously, the probabilities are just guesses, but going through the exercise of estimating them will make the outcomes more real and will permit you to compare the various alternatives against one another more easily.

3. *Compare the alternatives, taking into account the potential outcomes of each.* Systematically compare each of the alternatives as illustrated in **Figure 11.1.** Then ask yourself the key question: Which alternative, on balance, provides the most positive (and most likely) outcomes?

Obviously, not every decision requires such an elaborate process. In fact, most won't. But when it comes to major decisions, those that could have a large impact upon you and your life, it's worthwhile to follow a systematic process.

figure 11.1

Outcomes of Buying a Car

Making a rough estimate of the positive and negative outcomes of buying a car, and how likely each of those outcomes will be, can help illuminate the consequences of a decision.

Alternatives	Probability
Outcomes in favor of purchasing a car	
Easier transportation	100%
Greater opportunities for part-time job	75%
Improvement in social life	30%
Outcomes against purchasing a car	
Increase in expenses for gas and maintenance	100%
Difficulty/time spent looking for parking	40%

Use Freewriting

Use freewriting to think of as many answers as you can to each of the following questions. The ground rules are that you should spend three minutes on each question, generating as many ideas as possible—regardless of whether they are feasible. To give yourself maximum freedom, write each answer on a separate page.

1. How can you make room in your schedule to take one more course next term than you're taking this term?
2. How can someone get from the 3rd floor to the 20th floor of a building?
3. What should you do if you suspect that one of your instructors is a space alien?
4. What would happen if humans' average life span were extended to 125 years?

After generating ideas, go back and evaluate them. How many were actually feasible or realistic? Do you think freewriting fed to the production of more or fewer ideas than you would have come up with if you hadn't used the process? Did the quality of ideas change?

 WORKING IN A GROUP:

After you have answered the questions above, form a group of classmates and compare your answers to those of others. As a group, try to identify the best answers to each question.

To Try It online, go to www.mhhe.com/power.

Take a look at **Career Connections** on page 294 for another process that you can follow to help you make a career decision.

| **W** Work |

Making and Carrying Out the Decision

Working through the previous steps will lead you to the point of decision: choosing one of the alternatives you've identified. Having carried out the steps will make the actual decision easier, but not necessarily easy.

Choosing among Alternatives

The reason that important decisions are difficult is that the alternatives you have to choose from carry both benefits and costs. Choosing one alternative means that you have to accept the costs of that choice and give up the benefits of the other alternatives.

What if, after going through the steps of the process laid out here, you still can't make up your mind? Try these strategies:

▸ **Give the decision time.** Sometimes waiting helps. Time can give you a chance to think of additional alternatives. Sometimes the situation will change, or you'll have a change in viewpoint.

If all else fails, toss a coin to decide what alternative to follow. Tossing a coin at least brings you to a decision. Then, if you find you're unhappy with the result, you'll have gained important information about how you really feel regarding a particular choice.

Career Connections

Weighing Career Possibilities

One of the most important decisions you'll ever make is choosing a career. Here's one method that can help you:

- Generate a selection of choices to consider after graduation. Make a list of possibilities—including work (e.g., computer programming, banking, teaching, law, business, insurance, computer software development, etc.), further study (e.g., graduate school, business school, law school, etc.), and even some pie-in-the-sky possibilities (e.g., jazz musician, circus performer).

- Determine life-satisfaction considerations that are important to you. Generate a list of criteria to use in weighing these postgraduation possibilities. For instance, you might want to consider the following:

  Benefit to society
  Income
  Parents' opinions
  Friends' opinions
  Interest in the activity
  Prestige

  Job security/job openings
  Benefits (vacation, health insurance, etc.)
  Time off
  Practicality/attainability
  Everyday working conditions

- Determine how well a particular option fulfills each of the life-satisfaction factors you consider important. By systematically considering how a potential postgraduation path fulfills each of the criteria you use, you'll be able to compare different options. One easy way to do this is to create a chart like the one in **Table 11.1** (which shows an example of how computer programming might fulfill the various criteria).

- Compare different choices. Using the chart, evaluate your possibilities. Keep in mind that this is just a rough guide and that it's only as accurate as (a) the effort you put into completing it and (b) your understanding of a given choice. Use the results in conjunction with other things you find out about careers—and yourself.

table 11.1   Making Career Decisions

Life-Satisfaction Considerations	Possible Choice #1 *Computer programming*	Possible Choice #2	Possible Choice #3	Possible Choice #4
Benefit society	√			
Income	√			
Parents' opinions	√			
Friends' opinions				
Interest in the activity	√			
Prestige				
Job security/job openings	√			
Benefits	√			
Time off				
Practicality/attainability	√			
Everyday working conditions				
Other				
Other				
Other				
Other				
Other				

Journal Reflections

My Decision Crossroads

Have you ever made a decision that proved to be of great importance in terms of the direction your life would take? For example, perhaps you broke off a romantic relationship, or decided to quit a sports team because practice took up so much time, or participated in an act of civil disobedience during a protest rally. Reflect on that decision by answering these questions.

1. What was an important decision that you made that had significant effects on your life?

2. What have been the main benefits and disadvantages that you derived from the decision?

3. Every decision to do something is also a decision not to do other things. What did your decision keep you from doing?

4. Considering both the benefits and disadvantages of the decision, would you say that you made a good decision?

5. Thinking critically about the approach you used to make the decision, what alternative approaches might you have used to make it? Could these alternatives have produced a different decision? How?

> **Make a mental movie, acting out the various alternatives.** Many of us have difficulty seeing ourselves in the future and envisioning how various options would play out. One way to get around this difficulty is to cast yourself into a series of "mental movies" that have different endings depending on the decision you make. Working through the different scripts in your head makes potential outcomes far more real and less abstract than they would be if you simply left them as items on a list of various options.

> **Toss a coin.** This isn't as crazy as it sounds. If each alternative seems equally positive or negative to you, pull out a coin—make option A "heads" and B "tails." Then flip it.

> The real power of the coin-toss strategy is that it might help you discover your true feelings. It may happen while the coin is in the air, or it may be that when you see the result of the coin toss, you won't like the outcome and will say to yourself, "No way." In such a case, you've just found out how you really feel.

> **Ask for advice.** Although Western society teaches the virtues of rugged individualism, asking others for their advice is often an excellent strategy. A friend, instructor, parent, or counselor can provide

helpful recommendations—sometimes because they've had to make similar decisions themselves. You don't have to take their advice, but it can help to listen to what they have to say.

> **Learn to view indecision as a decision.** Sometimes we spend so much time making a decision that our indecision becomes a decision. It works like this: Suppose a friend asks you to help her work on a student government task force that is studying the use of alcohol on campus. You'd like to participate, but, because you'll have to commit to a term-long series of meetings, you're worried about the amount of time it will take up.

Because the first meeting isn't going to occur for a few weeks, you have some time to make up your mind. But you just can't seem to decide. Finally, it's the day of the meeting, and you still don't know what to do.

The truth is, you've made the decision: You don't really want to be on the committee. Your indecision is telling you that—bottom line—you don't have sufficient interest to make the commitment.

> **Go with your gut feeling.** Call it what you like—gut feeling, intuition, hunch, superstition—but sometimes we need to go with our hearts and not our minds. If you've thought rationally about a decision and have been unable to determine the best course of action but have a gut feeling that one choice is better than another, follow your feelings.

Following a gut feeling does not mean that you don't need to consider the pros and cons of a decision rationally and carefully. In fact, generally our "intuitions" are best when informed by the thoughtfulness of a more rational process.

> "In any moment of decision, the best thing you can do is the right thing, the next best thing is the wrong thing, and the worst thing you can do is nothing."
> **President Theodore Roosevelt**

Carrying Out the Decision

Ultimately, decisions must move from thought to action—they have to be carried out. Consequently, the final stage in making a decision is to act upon it. You need to turn your decision into behavior.

E Evaluate Considering the Outcomes

Did you make the right decision?

Even if you've spent time and mental effort in thinking through a decision, you still need to consider the results. Even well-considered decisions can end up being wrong, either because you neglected to consider something or because something has changed: either you or the situation.

For instance, suppose you were trying to decide between a major in management or one in biology. If you decide to go into management, it means that you'll be taking more courses related to finance and economics. As you take these courses, you will find out whether you're enjoying them. If you find you are consistently unhappy with them, you should allow yourself to reevaluate your decision to major in management and reconsider the alternatives. It's not too late to change your mind.

In fact, even major life decisions are often reversible. That's why it's so important to evaluate your choices. If you chose the wrong alternative, reverse course and reconsider your options.

Remember: It's not a bad thing to change your mind. In fact, admitting that a decision was a mistake is often the wisest and most courageous course of action. You don't want to be so rigidly committed to a decision that you're unable to evaluate the consequences objectively. Give yourself permission to be wrong.

Reconsidering Your Goals and Options

We can get to most places by multiple routes. There's the fastest and most direct route, which will get us to our destination in the least amount of time. Then there's the longer, more scenic route, where the trip itself provides pleasure. You can "take the long way home," as the song goes.

Is one route better than the other? Often not. Both take us to our destination. However, the experience of reaching our goal will have been very different.

Decisions about how to achieve a goal are similar to traveling down different routes. There's often no single decision that is best, just as there's often no single road to a particular place. Consequently, it's important to periodically reconsider the major decisions that we've made about our lives.

Ask yourself these questions:

> Are my decisions still producing the desired consequences?

> Are my decisions still appropriate, given my circumstances and changes in my life?

> Are my decisions consistent with what I want to get out of life?

> Do my decisions fit with my mission statement (a written, guiding philosophy of life, discussed in Chapter 3)?

Periodically taking stock like this is the best way to make sure that your decisions are taking you where you want to go. Taking stock also helps you be more effective in making future decisions.

Deciding to Change Colleges

One of the biggest decisions you'll potentially face involves changing colleges, or **transferring.** You may be changing from a two-year to a four-year school. Or you may find that your current school doesn't offer the course of study you want or meet some other important need. Whatever the reason, there are several questions to keep in mind when making such an important decision:

Transferring
Changing colleges

> **Do I meet the minimum requirements for admission?** Every college has its own requirements for admission. For example, you'll probably be required to have a minimum grade point average for admission.

> **What new requirements will I have to meet at another school?** Because every school has its own particular set of requirements, you'll want to know the courses you'll have to take to graduate.

> **What courses have I taken that the other school will accept as meeting its requirements?** You'll need to determine the degree of *course equivalency,* in which courses you've already taken substitute for courses at another college.

> **Is there an articulation agreement between my current school and the school I'm considering transferring to?** *Articulation agreements* are official pacts between schools that set out course equivalency.

Keep in mind that although your current school may smooth the way for a transfer, it's the school to which you are transferring that determines how successful the transfer process will be. (You'll find additional information on transferring to another college at the *P.O.W.E.R. Learning* Web site at **www.mhhe.com/ power.**)

Problem Solving: Applying Critical Thinking to Find Solutions

Two trains are approaching one another, each moving at 60 miles an hour. If the trains continue moving at the same speed, how long will it be before . . .

If this is what comes to mind when you think of problem solving, think again. **Problem solving** encompasses more than the abstract, often unrealistic situations portrayed in math texts. It involves everyday, commonplace situations: How do we divide the grocery bill so that each person pays a fair share? How do I keep my 1-year-old from tumbling down the stairs when there seems to be no way to fasten a gate at the top? How can I stop a faucet from dripping? How do I manage to study for a test and complete a paper the same evening?

While decision making is most focused on choosing among various alternatives, the central issue in problem solving is *generating* alternatives. Since many problems require that decisions be made regarding alternatives, decision making and problem solving are often related.

Problem solving
The process of generating alternatives to work on

What's the Problem?

The first step in solving any problem is to be as clear as you can about what the problem is. This may sound easy, but often it isn't. In fact, it may take some time to figure out just what is at stake. The reason is that some problems are big and hard to define, while others are quite precise, such as mathematical equations or the solution to a jigsaw puzzle. Determining how to stop terrorism or finding peace in the Middle East are big, ill-defined problems. Simply determining what information is required to solve such problems can be a major undertaking.

To determine what the problem is and set yourself on a course for finding a solution, ask yourself these questions:

> What is the initial set of facts?

> What is it that you need to solve?

> Which parts of the problem appear to be most critical to finding a solution?

> Is there some information that can be ignored?

The more systematically you approach a problem, the better. For instance, you can apply the five P.O.W.E.R. steps to problems, similar to how they can be used to make decisions. By considering a problem systematically and thinking through your options, your choices will become clearer to you.

As you clarify what the problem is, you may find that you have encountered similar problems before. Your experience with them may suggest the means to the solution of the current problem. For example, consider the problem of the trains rushing toward each other. If you have worked on this kind of problem before, you might know a fairly simple equation you can write to determine how long it will take before they meet. If someone asks you about the problem they have keeping their toddler from tumbling down the stairs, you might offer your experience in keeping your puppy from visiting an off-limits area of your house.

"Problems are only opportunities in work clothes."
Henry J. Kaiser (1882–1967), entrepeneur, *Maxim*

On the other hand, to solve many of the problems we face in our daily lives, we have to do more than reach into our memories of prior situations. Instead, we need to devise novel approaches. How do you do this? There are several strategies you might use.

Strategies for Solving Life's Messier Problems

> **Break the problem down into smaller, more manageable pieces.** Break a problem down into a series of subgoals. As you reach each subgoal, you get closer to your overall goal of solving the problem. For example, if your goal is to spend your junior year in your school's program in St. Petersburg, a subgoal would probably be to learn some basic Russian. By reaching this subgoal, you move closer to reaching your ultimate goal—a year abroad in a country that interests you.

> **Work backward.** Sometimes you know the answer to the problem, but not how to get there. Then it's best to work backward. A **working backward** strategy starts at the desired solution or goal and works backward, moving away from the goal. For example, consider this problem:

> *Water lilies on a certain lake double in area every 24 hours. From the time the first water lily appears until the lake is completely covered takes 60 days. On what day is the lake half covered?*

> Most people solve this problem readily if they work backward. Here's how: If the pond is fully covered on day 60, how much is it covered the day before? Because the water lilies double each day, there had to be half as many the day before day 60. The answer, then, is that half the lake is covered on day 59. Only by moving backward could one see the solution clearly.

> Some kinds of academic problems can be solved using the same strategy. For example, if you know what courses you must have completed to graduate, it's sometimes easiest to work backward from that point, determining the courses you need to take each year.

> **Use a graph, chart, or drawing to redefine the problem.** Transforming words into pictures often can help us to devise solutions that otherwise would elude us. One good example is this problem:

> *A hiker climbs a mountain on Saturday, leaving at sunrise and arriving at the top near sunset. He spends the night at the top. The next day, Sunday, he leaves at daybreak and heads down the mountain, following the same path that he climbed the day before. The question is this: Will there be any time during the second day when the hiker will be at exactly the same point on the mountain as he was at exactly the same time on the first day?*

> Trying to solve the problem through the use of math or words is quite difficult. However, there's a simpler way: drawing the two paths. As you can see from **Figure 11.2,** the drawing helps provide a solution.

> **Consider the opposite.** Problems can sometimes be solved by considering the opposite of the problem you're seeking to solve. For example, to define "good mental health" you might try to define "bad mental health."

> **Use analogies.** Some problems can be solved through the use of **analogies,** comparisons between concepts or objects that are alike in some respects but

Working backward
The strategy of starting at the desired solution or goal and working toward the starting point of the problem

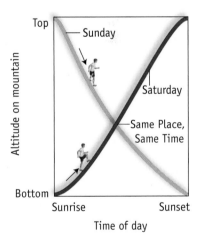

figure 11.2
Up and Down the Mountain: The Paths to a Solution

Analogy
A comparison between concepts or objects that are alike in some respects but dissimilar in most others

dissimilar in most others. For instance, if you liken a disastrous experience attending summer camp to a voyage on the *Titanic,* you're using an analogy.

Analogies may help us gain additional insight into the problem at hand, and they may provide an alternative framework for interpreting the information that is provided. For instance, the manufacturers of Pringles potato chips found that they could cut packaging costs if they slightly moistened the chips before packaging them—an idea that came when researchers noticed that dry tree leaves, which normally crumble easily, could be packed together tightly when they were wet.

> **Take another's perspective.** By viewing a problem from another person's point of view, it is often possible to obtain a new perspective on the problem that will make the problem easier to solve.

> **Forget about it.** Just as with decision making, sometimes it's best simply to walk away from a problem for a while. Just a few hours or days away from a problem may give us enough of a break to jar some hidden solutions from the recesses of our minds. The idea of "sleeping on it" also sometimes works; we may wake up refreshed and filled with new ideas.

Test these problem-solving strategies in **Try It 2.**

Assessing Your Potential Solutions

If a problem clearly has only one answer, such as a math problem, this step in problem solving is relatively easy. You should be able to work the problem and figure out whether you've been successful. In contrast, messier problems have several possible solutions, some of which may be more involved and costly than others. In these cases, it's necessary to compare alternative solutions and choose the best one. For example, suppose you want to surprise your best friend on her birthday. She is working in Omaha, about 90 miles from you, and you need to find a way to get there. Perhaps you could rent a car, take a bus, or find some other way. Money is an issue. You will want to figure out how much each alternative costs before choosing

Exercise Your Problem-Solving Skills

2

Working in a group, try to solve these problems.[1] To help you devise solutions, a hint regarding the best strategy to use is included after each problem.

1. One cold, dark, and rainy night, a college student has a flat tire on a deserted stretch of country road. He pulls onto the shoulder to change it. After removing the four lug nuts and placing them into the hub cap, he removes the flat tire and takes his spare out of the trunk. As he is moving the spare tire into position, his hand slips and he upsets the hub cap with the lug nuts, which tumble off into the night where he can't find them. What should he do? (*Hint:* Instead of asking how he might find the lug nuts, reframe the problem and ask where else he might find lug nuts.)

2. Cheryl, who is a construction worker, is paving a walk, and she needs to add water quickly to the concrete she has just poured. She reaches for her pail to get water from a spigot in the front of the house, but suddenly realizes the pail has a large rust hole in it and cannot be used. As the concrete dries prematurely, she fumbles through her toolbox for tools and materials with which to repair the pail. She finds many tools, but nothing that would serve to patch the pail. The house is locked and no one is home. What should she do? (*Hint:* When is a pail not a pail?)

3. What day follows the day before yesterday if two days from now will be Sunday? (*Hint:* Break it up or draw a diagram.)

4. A caterpillar has to climb up the muddy wall of a well that is 12 feet deep. Each day the caterpillar advances 4 feet, but each night as he sleeps, he slips back 2 feet. How many days will it take him to get out? (*Hint:* Draw it.)

5. Carrie has four chains, each three links long. She wants to join the four chains into a single, closed chain. Having a link opened costs 2 cents and having a link closed costs 3 cents. How can Carrie have the chains joined for 15 cents? (*Hint:* Can only end links be opened?)

6. What is two-thirds of one-half? (*Hint:* Reverse course.)

7. Juan has three separate large boxes. Inside each large box are two separate medium-sized boxes, and inside each of the medium boxes are four small boxes. How many boxes does Juan have altogether? (*Hint:* Draw it.)

After working to solve these problems, consider these questions: Which problems were the easiest to solve, and which were more difficult? Why? Were the hints helpful? Do you think there was more than one solution to any of the problems? Did your initial assumptions about the problem help or hinder your efforts to solve it? (*Note:* Answers to the problems are found on page 310.)

To Try It online, go to www.mhhe.com/power.

one as your solution to the problem. Since every penny you spend getting there is a penny less that you will have to celebrate, you will want to weigh the options carefully.

Finally, spend a bit of time seeing whether there is a way to refine the solution. Is the solution you've devised adequate? Does it address all aspects of the problem? Are there alternative approaches that might be superior? Answering these questions, and refining your solution to address them, can give you confidence that the solution you've come up with is the best. For example, if you're trying to get to Omaha, you might decide to use the ride board at your school to try to find a ride with someone going to Omaha that day. Maybe your friend's family is going to be driving in and could pick you up or could even lend you a car for the trip.

Remember that not every problem has a clear-cut solution. Sometimes we need to be satisfied with a degree of uncertainty and ambiguity. For some of us, such a lack of clarity is difficult, making us uneasy, and it may push us to choose solutions—any solution—that seems to solve the problem. Others of us feel more

Using Critical Thinking in Your Classes

Nowhere is critical thinking more important to use—and demonstrate to your instructors—than when you're in your classes. Here are some strategies to foster your skills as a critical thinker when you are in class:

- **Ask questions.** Most instructors welcome questions. Even if an instructor doesn't have time to provide a full response, the very act of formulating a question will help you think more critically about the course material.

- **Accept that some questions have no right or wrong answers.** Understanding that some questions have no simple answer is a sign of cognitive sophistication. Sometimes the best an instructor can do is present competing theories. Although you may want to know which theory is right, accept that sometimes no one knows the answer to that question—that's why they're theories, not facts!

- **Keep an open mind.** Your instructor and classmates have their own perspectives and opinions. Even if you disagree with them, try to figure out why they hold their views. It will help you to see the multiple sides of different issues.

- **Don't deny your emotional reactions—manage them.** There may be times that an instructor or classmate says something that is bothersome or even makes you angry. That's OK. But be sure to manage your emotions so that they don't overwhelm your rational self. And use your emotional reactions to gain self-understanding into what's important to you.

- **Try to think like a professional in the discipline you're studying.** If you're in a biology class, try to think like a biologist. If you're taking an art history course, put yourself in the shoes of an art historian. Professionals in various disciplines have different perspectives regarding what's important and what's not, and you should try to temporarily adopt those perspectives when you're in a particular class.

- **Don't be afraid of looking unintelligent.** No one wants to look foolish, especially in front of a roomful of classmates. But don't let self-defeating feelings prevent you from expressing your concerns. Take intellectual risks!

comfortable with ambiguity, but this may lead us to let problems ride, without resolving the situation.

Either way, it's important to consider what your own problem-solving style is when you seek to identify solutions. And keep in mind that often there is no perfect solution to a problem—only some solutions that are better than others. (To find out whether you have a high need for clarity in problem solving or whether you tolerate ambiguity more easily, complete **Try It 3.**)

Reflect on the Process of Problem Solving

It's natural to step back and bask in the satisfaction of solving a tough problem. That's fine—but take a moment to consider your success. Each time we solve a problem we end up a couple steps ahead, but only if we've thought about the process we went through to solve it.

Go back and consider what it took to solve the problem. Can the means you used to come up with your solution be applied to more complex kinds of problems? If you arrived at a solution by drawing a chart, would this work on similar problems in the future? Taking a moment to rethink your solution can provide you with an opportunity to become an expert problem solver and, more generally, to improve your critical thinking skills. Don't let the opportunity slip away.

Find Your Problem-Solving Style

To get a sense of how much you prefer ambiguity versus clarity in the problems you face, rate how much you agree with each of the statements in the questionnaire[2] below. Use this rating scale:

1 = Strongly disagree
2 = Disagree
3 = Not sure, but probably disagree

4 = Not sure, but probably agree
5 = Agree
6 = Strongly agree

1. An expert who doesn't come up with a definite answer probably doesn't know too much. _____
2. There is really no such thing as a problem that can't be solved. _____
3. A good job is one where what is to be done and how it is to be done are always clear. _____
4. In the long run, it is possible to get more done by tackling small, simple problems than large and complicated ones. _____
5. What we are used to is always preferable to what is unfamiliar. _____
6. A person who leads a well-organized, routine life in which few surprises or unexpected happenings arise really has a lot to be grateful for. _____
7. I like parties where I know most of the people more than ones where all or most of the people are complete strangers. _____
8. The sooner we all acquire similar values and ideals, the better. _____
9. I would like to live in a foreign country for a while. _____
10. People who fit their lives to a schedule probably miss most of the joy of living. _____
11. It is more fun to tackle a complicated problem than to solve a simple one. _____
12. Often the most interesting and stimulating people are those who don't mind being different and original. _____
13. People who insist upon a yes or no answer just don't know how complicated things really are. _____
14. Many of our most important decisions are based upon insufficient information. _____
15. Teachers or supervisors who hand out vague assignments give opportunities for individuals to show initiative and originality. _____
16. A good teacher is one who makes you wonder about your way of looking at things. _____

To score this questionnaire, you'll first need to change the numbers you have in items 9 to 16 in this way: If you've put a 1, change it to a 6; change 2 to 5; change 3 to 4; change 4 to 3; change 5 to 2; and change 6 to 1. (Items 1 to 8 don't need to be changed.) Now add up your total score.

If you scored below 30, you have a low tolerance for ambiguity in problem solving. You prefer problems to be clear-cut and dislike uncertainty.

If you scored between 30 and 60, you have an average tolerance for ambiguity. Most of the time problems that are vague don't present you with any particular difficulty, although you generally prefer things to be fairly concrete.

If you scored above 60, you have a high tolerance for ambiguous problems. You don't mind—and in fact prefer—problems that are unclear.

To Try It online, go to www.mhhe.com/power.

Don't Fool Yourself: Avoiding Everyday Problems in Critical Thinking

Being able to think clearly and without bias is the basis for critical thinking. As you have probably noticed already, the quality of the thinking you do regarding problems and decisions plays a crucial role in determining how successful you are.

Unfortunately, it is sometimes the alternative you *didn't* think of that can end up being the most satisfactory decision or solution. So how can we learn to think critically and avoid blind spots that hinder us in our decision making and problem solving? We can start by considering the common obstacles to critical thinking.

Here are some of the decision-making and problem-solving pitfalls to look out for. Avoiding them will improve your critical thinking greatly.

> **Don't assume that giving something a name explains it.** The mere fact that we can give an idea or problem a name doesn't mean we can explain it. Yet we often confuse the two.

For instance, consider the following sequences of questions and answers:

Q. *Why do I have so much trouble falling asleep?*
A. *Because you have insomnia.*

Q. *Why is he so unsociable?*
A. *Because he's an introvert.*

Q. *Why did the defendant shoot those people?*
A. *Because he's insane.*

Q. *How do you know he's insane?*
A. *Because only someone who was insane would shoot people in that way.*[3]

It's clear that none of these answers is satisfactory. All use circular reasoning, in which the alleged explanation for the behavior is simply the use of a label.

> **Don't accept vague generalities dressed up as definitive statements.** Read the following personality analysis and think about how well it applies to you:

You have a need for other people to like and admire you and a tendency to be critical of yourself. You also have a great deal of unused potential that you have not turned to your advantage, and although you have some personality weaknesses, you are generally able to compensate for them. Nonetheless, relating to members of the opposite sex has presented problems to you, and while you appear to be disciplined and self-controlled to others, you tend to be anxious and insecure inside.

If you believe that these statements provide an amazingly accurate description of your unique qualities, you're not alone: Most college students believe that the descriptions are tailored specifically to them.[4] But how is that possible? It isn't. The reality is that the statements are so vague that they are virtually meaningless. The acceptance of vague but seemingly useful and significant statements about oneself and others has been called the *Barnum Effect,* after showman and circus master P. T. Barnum, who coined the phrase "there's a sucker born every minute."

Distinguish Fact from Opinion

Read the following statements and try to determine which are facts and which are opinions.

1. College students should get at least 7 hours of sleep every night. _____
2. The average college student sleeps less than 7 hours a night. _____
3. Nikes offer better styling and comfort than any other brand of shoe. _____
4. Two out of five sports figures surveyed preferred Nikes over Converse shoes. _____
5. The U.S. government spends too much money on guns and missiles and not enough money on education. _____
6. Government figures show spending is much higher for guns and missiles than for education. _____
7. In general, U.S. high school students receive less classroom instruction in foreign languages than their counterparts in Europe and Asia. _____
8. No student in the United States should graduate without having studied a language other than English for at least 4 years. _____
9. Michael Jordan is the most outstanding, most exciting, and certainly most successful basketball player who ever stepped onto a court. _____

Items 1, 3, 5, 8, and 9 are opinions; the rest are facts. What are the main differences between opinion and fact?

To Try It online, go to www.mhhe.com/power.

> **Don't confuse opinion with fact.** Opinions are not fact. Although we may be aware of this simple formula, almost all of us can be fooled into thinking that someone's opinion is the same as a fact.

A fact is information that is proven to be true. In contrast, an opinion represents judgments, reasoning, beliefs, inferences, or conclusions. If we accept some bit of information as a fact, we can use it to build our opinions. But if we are presented with an opinion, we need to determine the facts on which it is built to judge its reliability.

The difference between fact and opinion can sometimes be subtle. For instance, compare these two statements:

1. Every college student needs to take a writing course during the first term of college.
2. Many college students need to take a writing course during the first term of college.

The first statement is most likely an opinion, because it is so absolute and unqualified. Words such as "every," "all," and "always" are often evidence of opinion. On the other hand, the second statement is more likely a fact, since it contains the qualifier "many." In general, statements that are qualified in some way are more likely to be facts.

Complete **Try It 4** to see the difficulties sometimes involved in distinguishing between fact and opinion.

One impediment to critical thinking is difficulty in distinguishing fact from opinion. For example, although many people are of the opinion that older people have a hard time learning new material, age need not be a deterrent to learning.

Even though two events are related to each other, it doesn't mean that one causes the other. Instead, there is often some other factor that is the actual cause of the relationship.

To see this for yourself, consider each of the following (actual!) findings. What might be a plausible explanation for each one?

1. Ice cream sales and the timing of shark attacks are highly related. Why?

2. The number of cavities children have and the size of their vocabulary are closely related. Why?

3. Skirt hemlines tend to rise as stock prices rise. Why?

4. Women with breast implants have a higher rate of suicide than those without breast implants. Why?

> **Avoid jumping to conclusions.**

> *When Ellen Philips, an African-American student at a small, largely white college in Alabama, stopped by a fraternity house to visit a friend, the student who answered the door asked if she was there to apply for the position of cook.*

People jump to conclusions, sometimes based on racial bias, sometimes because they are misinformed, or sometimes because they make the wrong assumptions.

Why is it so easy to jump to conclusions? One reason is that we sometimes aren't aware of the assumptions that underlie our thinking. Another is our reliance on "common sense."

> **Be skeptical of "common sense."** Much of what we call common sense makes contradictory claims. For example, if you believe in the notion "Absence makes the heart grow fonder," you may assume that your high school girlfriend, now in college across the country from you, will arrive home at Christmas even more in love with you than before. But what about "Out of sight, out of mind," which suggests a less positive outcome? Common sense often presents us with contradictory advice, making it a less than useful guide to decision making and problem solving.

5. People who own washing machines are more likely to die in car accidents than those who don't. Why?

6. Men who carry their cell phones in their front pants pockets have a lower sperm count than those who don't carry them in their front pants pockets. Why?

Once you've completed this **Try It,** look at the possible explanations listed below. Keep in mind that these are simply theories; we don't know for sure if they're correct:

6. Men with high-stress jobs may be more likely to have cell phones, and it is the stress that produces the low sperm count—not the placement of a phone in their pocket.

5. People who own washing machines are more likely to own cars, and therefore, they stand a higher risk of dying in a car crash.

4. Having breast implants and committing suicide both may be a result of unhappiness or a poor self-image.

3. Skirt hemlines go up, as does the stock market, when people are feeling less conservative and more optimistic.

2. Both the number of cavities children have and the size of their vocabularies are related to their age.

1. The actual cause is probably an increase in temperatures during summertime, which causes both sales of ice cream and ocean swimming to increase.

To Try It online, go to **www.mhhe.com/power**.

> **Don't assume that just because two events occur together one causes the other.** Just because two events appear to be associated with each other—or, in the language of social science, are *correlated* with each other—we cannot conclude that one event has caused the other to occur. It's a basic rule: *Correlation does not prove causation.*

For example, suppose you read that a study showed that 89 percent of juvenile delinquents use marijuana. Does this mean that smoking marijuana *causes* juvenile delinquency?

No, it doesn't. It is pretty safe to say that 100 percent of juvenile delinquents grew up drinking milk. Would you feel comfortable saying that milk causes delinquency? With correlations such as marijuana use and delinquent behavior, it is very likely that there's some third factor—such as influence of peers—that causes people both to (a) try drugs and (b) engage in delinquent behavior. The bottom line: We do not know the cause of the correlation.

In short, we need to be careful in assuming causality. Even if two events or other kinds of variables occur together, it does not mean that one causes the other. To see this for yourself, take a look at the statements in **Try It 5,** "What's the Real Explanation?"

NAME: **Dr. Ben Carson**

SCHOOL: **Yale University, B.A.;**
University of Michigan Medical School, M.D.

Few who knew Ben Carson as a fifth grader would have guessed that he would become a surgeon whose skills would save the lives of hundreds of patients.

Dr. Carson grew up in a poor, single-parent household in Detroit. His mother, who had only a third-grade education, worked two jobs cleaning bathrooms.

To his classmates—and even to his teachers—he was "the dumbest kid in the class," according to his own not-so-fond memories. He had a terrible temper and once tried to stab another child.

Dr. Carson was headed down a path of self-destruction until a critical moment in his youth: His mother, convinced that she had to do something dramatic to prevent him from leading a life of failure, laid down some rules. He could not watch television except for two programs a week, could not play with his friends after school until he finished his homework, and had to read two books a week and write book reports about them.

His mother's strategy worked. As he wrote his weekly book reports for his mother, worlds opened to him.

"Of course, we didn't know she couldn't read, so there we were submitting these reports," he said. "She would put check marks on them like she had been reading them. As I began to read about scientists, economists, and philosophers, I started imagining myself in their shoes."[5]

As he got in the habit of hard work, his grades began to soar. Ultimately, he received a scholarship to attend Yale University, and later he was admitted to the University of Michigan Medical School. He is now head of pediatric neurosurgery at Johns Hopkins University, one of the most prestigious medical schools in the world; he is also the author of three books.

Dr. Carson tries to pass on to others the lessons he learned as a child. He has established a fund for students in grades 4 through 12 who maintain a 3.75 grade point average. Each month, 800 children come to his hospital, where he underscores the importance of education. As he says, "There is absolutely nothing in this world that you can't become simply through the acquisition of knowledge, because knowledge creates power and you make yourself into a more valuable person."[6]

Looking Back

How can I improve the quality of my decisions?

➤ A structured process of decision making can clarify the issues involved, expand our options, and improve the quality of our choices.

➤ Good decision making begins with understanding your short- and long-term goals.

➤ Decision making is improved if you have a large number of alternatives.

➤ For difficult decisions, strategies include giving the decision time, acting out alternatives, tossing a coin to test your feelings, understanding that indecision is often a decision itself, and acting on gut feelings.

What strategies can I use for problem solving?

➤ Problem solving entails the generation of alternatives to consider.

➤ We need to first understand and define the problem and to determine the important elements in coming to a solution to a problem.

➤ Approaches to generating solutions include breaking problems into pieces, working backward, using pictures, considering the opposite, using analogies, taking another's perspective, and "forgetting" the problem.

➤ Problem solving ultimately requires the evaluation and refinement of the solutions that have been generated.

What are some problems that affect critical thinking, and how can I avoid them?

➤ Labeling, using vague generalities, accepting opinion as fact, jumping to conclusions, mistaking common sense, and assuming correlation all pose threats to critical thinking.

➤ Awareness of the biases that may affect our thinking can help us avoid them.

[KEY TERMS AND CONCEPTS]

Decision making (p. 290)   Problem solving (p. 298)   Analogy (p. 299)
Transferring (p. 297)   Working backward (p. 299)

[RESOURCES]

ON CAMPUS

Some colleges offer courses in critical thinking, and they are a good bet to help increase decision-making and problem-solving skills. In addition, courses in logic and philosophy will help improve critical thinking skills.

If you are having a personal problem that is difficult to solve, don't hesitate to turn to staff at the campus counseling center, mental health center, or residential life office. Trained counselors and therapists can help sort through the different options in an objective manner. They may identify possibilities for solutions that you didn't even know existed. Even if the person with whom you speak initially is not the right one, he or she can direct you to someone who can help.

IN PRINT

If you have trouble making good decisions, *Learning to Think Things Through: A Guide to Critical Thinking Across the Curriculum,* by Gerald M. Nosich (Prentice Hall, 2008), is an excellent, concise guide to increasing your decision-making skills.

Asking the Right Questions: A Guide to Critical Thinking, 8th edition (Prentice Hall, 2006) teaches readers how to effectively consider alternate points of view while making personal choices.

For a general overview of critical thinking skills, read Richard Paul and Linda Elder's *Critical Thinking: Tools for Taking Charge of Your Learning and Your Life* (Prentice Hall, 2006).

ON THE WEB

The following sites on the Web provide the opportunity to extend your learning about the material in this chapter. (Although the Web addresses were accurate at the time the book was printed, check the *P.O.W.E.R. Learning* Web site [**www.mhhe.com/power**] for any changes that may have occurred.)

> Mind Tools, Ltd. (**www.psychwww.com/mtsite/index.html**) offers links to other sites that can help with setting goals, time management, and stress control and to numerous other helpful sites. It also includes shareware for setting up life plans.

> "Basic Guidelines to Problem Solving and Decision Making" (**www.managementhelp.org/prsn_prd/prob_slv.htm**) by Carter McNamara, Ph.D., provides basic guidelines to problem solving and decision making in seven steps. This site is rich in links to comprehensive approaches to decision making, critical and creative thinking, time management, and organization.

> "Critical Thinking Core Concepts" (**http://mcckc.edu/longview/ctac/point.htm**), by Lauren Miller and Michael Connelly of Longview Community College, presents principles of critical thinking with exercises and examples. The site contains a short history of logic and answers the question: "What is the point of studying critical thinking?"

[ANSWERS TO TRY IT 2 PROBLEMS]

1. Remove one lug nut from each of the other three tires on the car and use these three to attach the spare tire. This will hold until four more lug nuts can be purchased.
2. Dump the tools out of the toolbox and use it as a pail.
3. Thursday.
4. Five days; on the fifth day the caterpillar will reach the top and will not have to slide down again.
5. Open all three links on one chain (cost = 6 cents) and use them to fasten the other three chains together (cost = 9 cents; total cost = 15 cents).
6. It is the same as one-half of two-thirds, or one-third.
7. 33 boxes (3 large, 6 medium, 24 small).

1 Making good decisions can depend on distinguishing legitimate appeals (good reasons) from fallacious appeals (bad reasons). Go to San Jose State University's "Mission: Critical," an interactive tutorial in critical thinking (**www.sjsu.edu/depts/itl/graphics/adhom/appeal.html**). After reading the description of the different kinds of fallacious appeals, do the related exercises.

2 Locate three problem-solving strategies on the Internet. Possible strategy: Go to Yahoo! (**www.yahoo.com**) or AltaVista (**www.altavista.com**), and enter the key phrase "problem solving." Search the results until you find at least three different problem-solving strategies. Are these strategies similar to the ones described in the book? If not, how are they different?

The Case of . . .
Left Holding the Lease

Erica had a problem.

In the spring of her first year of college, she and her friend Shira had found a two-bedroom apartment to share for the upcoming school year. The apartment was on the expensive side, but they had decided that it was worth it because it was so close to campus. She and Shira had jointly paid the security deposit on the apartment. However, because Shira hadn't been around when it came time to sign the lease, only Erica had signed it. Consequently, Erica was legally responsible for fulfilling the terms of the lease.

Now, only two weeks before the start of the fall term, Shira told Erica that she had realized she couldn't afford the rent and that she had decided she had to live with her parents. Erica was simultaneously furious with Shira and panicky at the thought of having to pay the rent by herself.

How was she going to deal with the problem?

1. Is the problem a purely financial and legal one, or are there personal and social considerations that should be taken into account in solving the problem?

2. Is the problem solely Erica's problem, or should Shira take responsibility for solving it as well?

3. What alternatives does Erica have for dealing with the situation?

4. How should Erica go about evaluating the outcomes for each alternative?

5. Based on your analysis of the problem, what advice would you give Erica for dealing with the situation?

Learning Outcomes

By the time you finish this chapter you will be able to

>> LO **12.1** Discuss why the increasingly racial, ethnic, and cultural diversity of society is important to you.

>> LO **12.2** Utilize strategies to become more at ease with differences and diversity.

>> LO **12.3** Build lasting relationships and deal with conflict.

Diversity and Your Relationships with Others

He was born in the Kapi'olani Maternity and Gynecological Hospital in Honolulu, Hawaii. His mother was an American of primarily English descent from Wichita, Kansas. His father was born in Africa, in Nyang'oma Kogelo, Nyanza Province, Kenya. His parents met while taking a Russian language class. He spent most of his childhood in Hawaii, except for a few years in Indonesia.

In describing his childhood, he later said, "The opportunity that Hawaii offered—to experience a variety of cultures in a climate of mutual respect—became an integral part of my world view, and a basis for the values that I hold most dear."

He is Barack Obama, who grew up to be President of the United States.

Looking Ahead

Whether you have skin that is black or white or brown, are Jewish or Muslim or Greek Orthodox, were born in Cuba or Vietnam or Boise, are able-bodied or physically challenged, college presents a world of new opportunities. Because almost every college draws students from a wider sphere than the average high school, college permits you to encounter people with very different backgrounds from your own. If you take the opportunity to form relationships with a variety of individuals, you will increase your understanding of the human experience and enrich your life.

In this chapter, we consider how social diversity and relationships affect your college experience. We examine the increasing diversity of college campuses, which reflects that of society at large, and consider the meanings and social effects of race, ethnicity, and culture. We look at practical strategies for acknowledging—and shedding—prejudice and stereotypes and being receptive to others on their own merits.

We next discuss relationships from a broader perspective, exploring ways that you can build lasting friendships with others. Finally, the chapter discusses the conflicts that can arise between people and what you can do to resolve them.

≫ LO 12.1 Living in a World of Diversity

No matter where we live, our contacts with others who are racially, ethnically, and physically different from us are increasing. The Web is bringing people from across the globe into our homes, as close to us as the computer sitting on our desk. Businesses now operate globally, so co-workers are likely to come from many different countries and cultures. Being comfortable with people whose backgrounds and beliefs may differ from our own is not only a social necessity, but it is virtually a requirement for career success.

By the mid-21st century, the percentage of people in the United States of African, Latin American, Asian, and Arabic ancestry will be greater than the percentage of those of Western European ancestry—a profound statistical, and social, shift. College enrollments will mirror these changes, as populations that were minority become the majority.

Furthermore, it's not just racial and ethnic characteristics that comprise diversity. As you can see in the Diversity Wheel in **Figure 12.1**, diversity encompasses characteristics such as gender, sexual orientation, age, and mental and physical

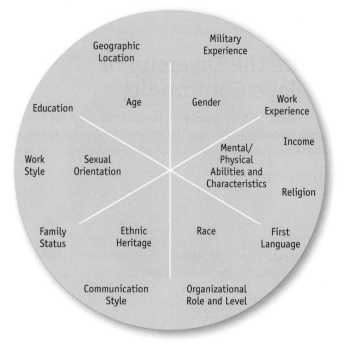

characteristics. Layer on top of that factors such as education, religion, and income level, and the complexity of others—and ourselves—becomes apparent. (You can examine the diversity of your own campus by completing **Try It 1** on page 316.)

Race, Ethnicity, and Culture

Are you African-American or Black? Caucasian or white or Euro-American? Hispanic or Latino? American Indian or Native American?

The language we use to describe our ethnic and racial group membership, and those of other people, is in constant flux. And what we call people matters. The subtleties of language affect how people think about members of particular groups, and how they think about themselves.

Our cultural heritage plays an important role in shaping who we are.

Try It

1

Determine the Diversity of Your College Community

Assess the degree of diversity that exists at your college, and the overall attitude toward diversity on your campus, by answering these questions. When thinking of diversity, remember to include the many different ways in which people can be different from one another, including race, ethnicity, culture, sexual orientation, physical challenges, and so on.

1. Overall, what is your sense of how diverse your campus is?

2. What is the nature of your college's *student* diversity in terms of statistics for membership in different racial, ethnic, or cultural groups? (You may be able to find these statistics on your college's Web site.)

3. What is the nature of your college's *faculty* diversity in terms of statistics for membership in different racial, ethnic, or cultural groups?

4. What courses are available that directly address diversity as an issue? (A good place to check is your college catalog listing of courses in the social sciences and humanities.)

To Try It online, go to www.mhhe.com/power.

Race
Traditionally, biologically determined physical characteristics that set one group apart from others

Ethnicity
Shared national origins or cultural patterns

Culture
The learned behaviors, beliefs, and attitudes that are characteristic of an individual society or population, and the products that people create

One of the difficulties in understanding diversity is that many of the terms we use are ill-defined and often overlapping. The term **race** is generally used to refer to obvious physical differences that set one group apart from others. According to such a definition, whites, Blacks, and Asian Americans are typically thought of as belonging to different races, determined largely by biological factors.

Ethnicity refers to shared national origins or cultural patterns. In the United States, for example, Puerto Ricans, Irish, and Italian Americans are categorized as ethnic groups. However, ethnicity—like race—is very much in the eye of the beholder. For instance, a Cuban American who is a third-generation citizen of the United States may feel few ties or associations to Cuba. Yet whites may view her as "Hispanic," and Blacks may view her as "white."

Finally, **culture** comprises the learned behaviors, beliefs, and attitudes that are characteristic of an individual society or population. But it's more than that: Culture also encompasses the products that people create, such as architecture, music, art, and literature. Culture is created and shaped by people, but at the same time it creates and shapes people's behavior.

Race, ethnicity, and culture shape each of us to an enormous degree. They profoundly influence our view of others, as well as who we are. They affect how others treat us and how we treat them in turn. They determine whether we look people in the eye when we meet them, how early we arrive when we're invited to dinner at a friend's house, and even, sometimes, how well we do in school.

Because many of us grow up in neighborhoods that are not ethnically diverse, we may have little or even no experience interacting with people who are different from us. In fact, some college campuses don't have much diversity, and consequently even in college your exposure to people who have different backgrounds may be limited.

At some time, though, that will change. As the United States becomes increasingly diverse, it's not a matter of "if" but "when" you will be exposed to people who have profoundly different backgrounds from your own. Whether in the workplace or the neighborhood in which you reside, living in a diverse environment will be part of your life.

» LO 12.2 Building Cultural Competence

We're not born knowing how to drive a car or cook. We have to learn how to do these things. The same is true of developing a basic understanding of other races, ethnic groups, and cultures. Called **cultural competence,** this knowledge of others' customs, perspectives, background, and history can teach us a great deal about others, as well as ourselves. Cultural competence also provides a basis for civic engagement, permitting us to act with civility toward others and to make the most of our contributions to society.

Building cultural competence proceeds in several steps, outlined in the P.O.W.E.R. Plan on the right.

Cultural competence
Knowledge and understanding about other races, ethnic groups, cultures, and minority groups

P Prepare
Accept diversity as a valued part of your life

O Organize
Explore your own prejudices and stereotypes

W Work
Develop cultural competence

E Evaluate
Check your progress in attaining cultural competence

R Rethink
Understand how your own racial, ethnic, and cultural background affects others

P.O.W.E.R. Plan

P Prepare Accepting Diversity as a Valued Part of Your Life

In the title of her book on social diversity, psychologist Beverly Tatum asks, *Why Are All the Black Kids Sitting Together in the Cafeteria?*[2] She might just as well have asked a similar question about the white kids, the Asian-American kids, and so forth. It often appears as if the world comes already divided into separate racial, ethnic, and cultural groups.

It's more than appearances: We form relationships more easily with others who are similar to us than with those who are different. It's easier to interact with others who look the same as we do, who come from similar backgrounds, and who share our race, ethnicity, and culture because we can take for granted certain shared cultural assumptions and views of the world.

But that doesn't mean that "easy" and "comfortable" translate into "good" or "right." We can learn a great deal more, and grow and be challenged, if we seek out people who are different from us. If you look beyond surface differences and find out what motivates other people, you can become aware of new ways of thinking about family, relationships, earning a living, and the value of education. It can be liberating to realize that others may hold very different perspectives from your own and that there are many ways to lead your life.

Journal Reflections

Thinking about Race, Ethnicity, and Culture

1. Were race and ethnicity discussed in your family as you were growing up? In what ways?

2. Do you demonstrate—through your behavior, attitudes, and/or beliefs—your own ethnic background? How?

3. Are there cultural differences between you and members of other races or ethnicities? What are they?

4. Are you proud of your ethnicity? Why?

5. Think what it would be like to be a member of a racial group or ethnicity other than your own. In what ways would your childhood and adolescence have been different? How would you view the world differently?

Letting diversity into your own life also has very practical implications: As we discuss in **Career Connections,** learning to accept and work with people who are different from you is a crucial skill that will help you in whatever job you hold.

 Organize

Exploring Your Own Prejudices and Stereotypes

Arab. Gay. African American. Hispanic. Female. Disabled. Overweight.

Quick: What comes into your mind when you think about each of these labels? If you're like most people, you don't draw a blank. Instead, a collection of images and feelings comes into your mind, based on what you know, have been told, or assume about the group.

The fact that we don't draw a blank when thinking about each of these terms means that we already have a set of attitudes and beliefs about them and the groups they represent. Acknowledging and then examining these preexisting assumptions is a first step toward developing cultural competence: We need to explore our own prejudices and stereotypes.

Prejudice refers to evaluations or judgments of members of a group that are based primarily on their membership in the group rather than on their individual

Prejudice
Evaluations or judgments of members of a group that are based primarily on membership in the group and not on the particular characteristics of individuals

Diversity in the Workplace

Diversity, and issues relating to it, are a part of today's workplace. For example, in one California computer assembly company with several thousand employees, 40 different languages and dialects are spoken among people representing 30 nationalities.[3] Furthermore, employers must deal with issues ranging from whether time off for religious holidays should count as vacation time to whether the partner of a gay or lesbian worker should be covered by the worker's medical insurance.

The gulf in the workplace between people with different cultural backgrounds may be wide. For instance, an immigrant from Japan might consider it the height of immodesty to outline his or her accomplishments in a job interview. The explanation? In Japan, the general cultural expectation is that people should stress their incompetence; to do otherwise would be considered highly immodest.

The increasing diversity of the workplace means that increasing your cultural competence will serve you well. It will help you perform on work teams that are composed of people of different races and ethnic backgrounds; it will help you supervise people whose native language and customs may be different from yours; and it will help you to work for a boss from another country and cultural background.

Equally important, gaining cultural competence will help you respond to the legal issues that surround diversity. It is illegal for employers to discriminate on the basis of race, ethnic background, age, gender, and physical disability. Cultural competence will help you not only to deal with the letter of the law but also to understand why embracing diversity is so important to getting along with others in the workplace.

characteristics. For example, the auto mechanic who doesn't expect a woman to understand auto repair or a job supervisor who finds it unthinkable that a father might want to take a leave for child care are engaging in gender prejudice. *Gender prejudice* is evaluating individuals on the basis of their being a male or female and not on their own specific characteristics or abilities. Similarly, prejudice can be directed toward individuals because of their race, ethnic origin, sexual orientation, age, physical disability, or even physical attractiveness.

Prejudice leads to discrimination. **Discrimination** is behavior directed toward individuals on the basis of their membership in a particular group. Discrimination can result in exclusion from jobs and educational opportunities. It also may result in members of particular groups receiving lower salaries and benefits.

Prejudice and discrimination are maintained by **stereotypes** beliefs and expectations about members of a group. For example, do you think that women don't drive as well as men? Do you agree that "white men can't jump"? Do you believe that people raised in the jungles of South America are less intelligent than those raised in a Western society? Do you think that people on welfare are lazy? If you answered yes to any of these questions, you hold stereotypes about the group being referred to. It is the degree of generalization involved that makes stereotypes inaccurate. Some white men can't jump. But the fact is, many can—and do—and stereotypes ignore this diversity.

To develop cultural competence, it's important to identify our prejudices and stereotypes and to fight them. Sometimes they are quite subtle and difficult to detect. For instance, a wealth of data taken from observation of elementary school classrooms shows that teachers are often more responsive to boys than to girls. The teachers don't know they're doing it; it's a subtle, but very real, bias.

Why does this happen? In part it's because we're exposed to stereotypes from a very young age. Parents and relatives teach them to us, sometimes unwittingly, sometimes deliberately. The media illustrate them constantly and often in very subtle ways. For instance, African Americans and Latinos are often portrayed

Discrimination

Behavior directed toward individuals on the basis of their membership in a particular group

Stereotypes

Beliefs and expectations about members of a group that are held simply because of their membership in the group as unemployed or as criminals, women are less likely than men to be shown as employed, and gay men are frequently depicted as effeminate.

But it's not only stereotypes that lead us to view members of other groups differently from those of our own. For many people, their own membership in a cultural or racial or ethnic group is a source of pride and self-worth. There's nothing wrong with this. However, these feelings can lead to a less desirable outcome: the belief that their own group is superior to others. As a result, people inflate the positive aspects of their own group and belittle groups to which they do not belong. The bottom line is continuing prejudice.

> "Prejudice is the child of ignorance."
> **William Hazlitt, essayist**

To overcome stereotypes and to develop cultural competence, we must first explore and identify our prejudices. To begin that process, complete **Try It 2,** "Check Your Stereotype Quotient."

W Work

Developing Cultural Competence

Although it's neither easy nor simple to increase your understanding of and sensitivity to other cultures, it can be done. Several strategies are effective:

> **Study other cultures and customs.** Take an anthropology course, study religion, or learn history. If you understand the purposes behind different cultural customs, attitudes, and beliefs, you will be able to understand the richness and meaning of other people's cultural heritage.
>
> Many colleges offer workshops on diversity and prejudice reduction. These can help too. The important point is that understanding comes from knowledge, and you won't be able to fully appreciate others without learning about their background.

> **Travel.** There is no better way to learn about people from other cultures than to see those cultures firsthand. College vacations offer you the time to travel, and relatively inexpensive charter flights can take you to Europe, Asia, and other places around the globe. Sometimes, in fact, it's cheaper to take a trans-oceanic flight than to travel to closer locations in the United States.
>
> If you can't afford airfare, take a car or bus ride to Mexico or Canada. In many parts of Canada, French is spoken and the culture is decidedly different from that in the United States (or the rest of Canada, for that matter).
>
> Travel needn't be international, however. If you are from the northern states, head south. If you are from California, consider heading east. If you live in a large metropolitan area, travel to a different area from ones you're familiar with. No matter where you go, simply finding yourself in a new context can aid your efforts to learn about other cultures.

> **Participate in service learning.** Sometimes you can learn about people who are different from you in your own backyard—or, more precisely, the backyard of your college. By becoming involved in community service, such as tutoring middle school students, volunteering to work with the homeless, or working on an environmental cleanup, you get the opportunity to interact with people who may be very different from those you're accustomed to.

> **Don't ignore people's backgrounds.** None of us is color blind. Or blind to ethnicity. Or to culture. It's impossible to be completely

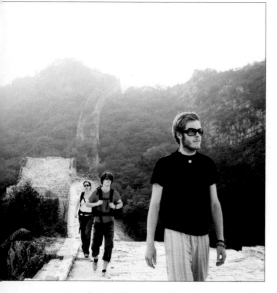

Travel provides us with an opportunity to become immersed in very different cultures and to see the world—and ourselves—through different eyes.

Check Your Stereotype Quotient

Do you hold stereotypes about other people? How pervasive do you think they are? Respond to the following informal questionnaire to get a sense of your susceptibility to stereotyping.

1. When you see five African-American students sitting together in a cafeteria, do you think that they are exhibiting racism? Do you think the same thing when you see five white students sitting together in a cafeteria?

2. When you are speaking with a person who has a speech-related disorder such as stuttering, are you likely to conclude that the person is less intelligent than a fluent speaker?

3. When an elderly woman can't remember something, do you assume her forgetfulness is because she is old or perhaps has Alzheimer's disease?

4. When an attractive blonde female student states an opinion in class, are you surprised if the opinion is intelligent and well expressed?

5. If a person with a mobility disorder turns down your offer for assistance, would you be offended and resentful?

6. If you found out that a star professional football player is gay, would you be surprised?

What do you think your answers tell you about yourself and your views of others?

 WORKING IN A GROUP:

Compare your answers with those of your classmates. What do you think causes the similarities and differences in responses?

To Try It online, go to www.mhhe.com/power.

POWER

Try It

3

Contemplate a Questionnaire

Read and consider each of the following questions[4]:

1. What do you think caused your heterosexuality?
2. When and how did you decide you were heterosexual?
3. Is it possible that heterosexuality is just a phase you may grow out of?
4. Is it possible your heterosexuality stems from a neurotic fear of others of the same sex?
5. To whom have you disclosed your heterosexual tendencies?
6. Why do you insist on showing off your heterosexuality?
7. Why do heterosexuals place so much emphasis on sex?
8. There seem to be many unhappy heterosexuals. Techniques have been developed that might enable you to change your sexual orientation. Have you considered changing?
9. Considering the menace of hunger and overpopulation, can the human race survive if everyone were heterosexual like yourself?

What are your reactions to this questionnaire?

What do your reactions tell you about the assumptions you hold about what others are like?

Substitute the label "homosexual" for each occurrence of "heterosexual" in the questionnaire and read through it again. How have your reactions changed?

To Try It online, go to www.mhhe.com/power.

unaffected by people's racial, ethnic, and cultural backgrounds. So why pretend to be? Cultural heritage is an important part of other people's identity, and to pretend that their background doesn't exist and has no impact on them is unrealistic at best, and insulting at worst. It's important, though, to distinguish between accepting the fact that other people's backgrounds affect them and pigeon-holing people and expecting them to behave in particular ways.

➤ **Don't make assumptions about who people are.** Don't assume that someone is heterosexual just because most people are heterosexual. Don't assume that someone with an Italian-sounding last name is Italian. Don't assume that a Black person has two Black parents. (To get a sense of how our assumptions color our thinking, think about the questions in **Try It 3.**)

➤ **Accept differences.** Different does not mean better. Different does not mean worse. Different just means not looking, acting, or believing exactly the same as you. We shouldn't attach any kind of value to being different; it's neither better nor worse than being similar.

In fact, even people who seem obviously different on the surface probably share many similarities with you. Like you, they are students; they have fears and anxieties like yours; and they have aspirations and dreams, just as you do.

The important point about differences is that we need to accept and embrace them. Think about some differences you may have with people who are similar to you. Perhaps you really can't stand classical music, yet one of your childhood friends has taken piano lessons since he was five and loves it. Chances are you both accept that you have different tastes and see this difference as part of who each of you is.

E Evaluate Checking Your Progress in Attaining Cultural Competence

Because cultural groups are constantly changing, developing cultural competence is an ongoing process. To evaluate where you stand, ask yourself the following questions:

> Do I make judgments about others based on external features, such as skin color, ethnic background, cultural customs, gender, weight, or physical appearance?

> Who are my friends? Do they represent diversity or are they generally similar to me?

> Do I openly express positive values relating to diversity? Do I sit back passively when others express stereotypes and prejudices, or do I actively question their remarks?

> Am I educating myself about the history and varying experiences of different racial, ethnic, and cultural groups?

> Do I give special treatment to members of particular groups, or am I even-handed in my relationships?

> Do I recognize that, despite surface differences, all people have the same basic needs?

> Do I feel so much pride in my own racial, ethnic, and cultural heritage that it leads me to look less favorably upon members of other groups?

> Do I seek to understand events and situations through the perspectives of others and not just my own?

R Rethink Understanding How Your Own Racial, Ethnic, and Cultural Background Affects Others

If you are a member of a group that traditionally has been the target of prejudice and discrimination, you probably don't need to be told that your race, ethnicity, and cultural background affect the way that others treat you. But even if you are a member of a traditionally dominant group in society, the way in which others respond to you is, in part, a result of others' assumptions about the groups of which you are a part.

Diversity in the Classroom

The increasing diversity of classrooms presents both opportunity and challenge. The opportunity comes from the possibility of learning on a firsthand basis about others and their experiences. The challenge comes when people who may be very different from us call into question some of our most fundamental beliefs and convictions.

Here are some ways that you can be better equipped to deal with the classroom challenges involved in diversity:

- **Present your opinions in a respectful manner.** Don't get annoyed or angry when others disagree with your point of view. Be tolerant of others' perspectives and their thinking.

- **Don't assume you can understand what it's like to be a member of another race, ethnicity, cultural group, or gender.** Talk about your own experiences, and don't assume you know what others have experienced.

- **Don't treat people as representatives of the groups to which they belong.** Don't ask someone how members of his or her racial, ethnic, or cultural group think, feel, or behave with respect to a particular issue. No single individual can speak for an entire group. Furthermore, group members are likely to display little uniformity on most issues and in most behaviors. Consequently, this type of question is ultimately impossible to answer.

- **Seek out students who are different from you.** If you are assigned a group project, volunteer to work with others who are different from you. You may learn more working with others who are dissimilar than those who are like you.

- **Don't be afraid to offer your opinion out of concerns for "political correctness."** If you offer an opinion in a respectful, thoughtful, and tolerant manner, you should feel free to voice your opinion. Even if your views are minority opinions, they deserve to be considered.

In short, both how we view others and how we ourselves are viewed are affected by the groups to which we—and others—belong. But keep this in mind: No matter how different other students are from you in terms of their race, ethnicity, and cultural background, they undoubtedly share many of the same concerns you do. Like all of us, they question themselves, wonder whether they will be successful, and fret about what they will do for the rest of their lives. Bridging the surface difference between you and others can result in the development of close, lasting social ties—a topic we consider next.

Building Lasting Relationships

> "I have met the most amazing individuals and made the most incredible friends in such a short amount of time."
>
> **Student, Wittenberg University[5]**

Few of us lead our lives in isolation. There's a reason for this: Relationships with others are a critical aspect of our sense of well-being. The support of friends and relatives helps us feel good about ourselves. In fact, studies have found that our physical and psychological health may suffer without friendships. The social support of others acts as a guard against stress and illness. And if we do get sick, we recover more quickly if we have a supportive network of friends.

Our relationships with others also help us understand who we are. To understand our own abilities and achievements, we compare them with those of others who are similar to ourselves. Our attitudes, beliefs, and values are influenced—and shaped—by others. We are who we are largely because of the people with whom we come in contact.

Making Friends

Although some of us naturally make friends with ease, for others making friends is more difficult. But building relationships is not a mystery. Here are several ways to go about it:

- **Invest time in others.** There's no better way to demonstrate that you are interested in being friends than investing time. Relationships need to be nourished by the commitment of time. You can't expect friendships to flourish unless you spend time with people.

- **Reveal yourself.** Good friends understand each other. The best way to make that happen is to let others get to know you. Be open and honest about the things you like and dislike. Talk about where you come from, what your family is like. Find out about the other person. Having a deeper understanding of where someone comes from not only helps build bridges between people of different racial and ethnic backgrounds, but it also helps build friendships. By honestly communicating your beliefs and attitudes, you give others the chance to learn those things you have in common.

- **Let others know you like them.** It may seem scary, but don't be coy and try to pretend you are uninterested in the friendships of others. Take the risk of being rebuffed. You don't have to announce outright that you like someone. Instead, reveal your interest in a friendship by inviting the person to do something with you or simply by engaging in conversation, sharing something about your life. Your actions will speak louder than words.

- **Accept others as they are, not as you would like them to be.** One mark of friendship is acceptance of people the way they are, warts and all, and not the way you would like them to be. Do not impose conditions on accepting others. Keep in mind that no one is perfect and that everyone has both good and bad qualities.

- **Show concern and caring.** This is really the substance of friendship and the basis for the trust that develops between friends. Don't be afraid to show your interest in the fortunes of others and to share the sadness when they suffer some setback or loss.

- **Be open to friendships with people who are very different from you.** Don't assume that the only "appropriate" friends are your peers who are similar to you, such as other college students. Open yourself to friends who are older, who are younger, who work at your school, and who are different from you in fundamental ways.

- **Not everyone makes a good friend.** People who put you down, consistently make you feel bad, or behave in ways that violate your own personal standards are not friends. Choose your friends based on the good feelings you have when you are with them and the concern and care they show for you. Friendship is a two-way street.

≫ LO 12.3   The R-Word: Relationships

Relationships move beyond friendship. They occur when two people feel emotionally attached, fulfill each other's needs, and generally feel interdependent. When a true relationship exists, several components are present:

- **Trust.** Relationships must be built on a foundation of trust. We need to be able to count on others and feel that they will be open with us.

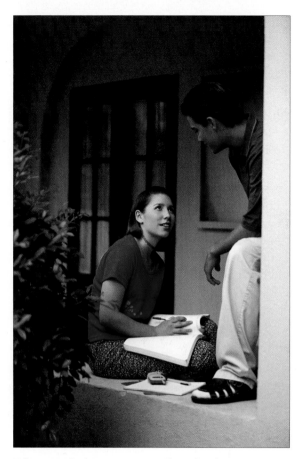

What you *don't* say matters. Close, lasting relationships are often built on good listening skills.

> **Honesty.** No relationship can survive if the partners are not honest with one another. Each partner must share a commitment to the truth. Your life does not have to be a completely open book—it's the rare individual who has no secrets whatsoever—but it is important to be honest about your fundamental beliefs, values, and attitudes. Those in good relationships accept one another, blemishes and all. A relationship based on untruths or even half-truths lacks depth and meaning.

> **Mutual support.** Healthy relationships are characterized by mutual support. A partner's well-being should have an impact on you, and your well-being should affect your partner. In good relationships, the partners seek out what is best for both, and they act as advocates for and defend each other.

> **Loyalty.** The mark of a good relationship is loyalty. Loyalty implies that relationship partners are supportive of each other, even in times of adversity and difficulty.

> **Acceptance.** Your best friend develops a love for the Dave Matthews Band and listens to their CDs seemingly without interruption. You can't stand to listen to them. Do you decide that you can no longer be friends? Of course not.

In good relationships small annoyances don't get in the way of the deeper connection between you and another person. We don't have to like everything others do to maintain relationships with them. We don't even have to appreciate or approve of every aspect of their personality. What is crucial is the willingness to accept others as they are, without constantly yearning for changes. All of us wish to be accepted by others as we are, not as they'd like us to be; we should offer the same approval to those with whom we maintain relationships.

> **Willingness to embrace change.** Change is part of everyone's life. As people grow and develop, they change. So do relationships.

We need to accept change as a fundamental part of relationships and build upon that change. In fact, we need to welcome change. Although change brings challenges with it, it also helps us understand ourselves and our own place in the world more accurately.

It is only natural that some relationships will fade over time. People do outgrow one another. That's inevitable. What's important is not to live in fear that your relationship is so fragile that you have to avoid or ignore changes in who you and a partner are. Instead, both partners in a relationship should do their best to accept transformations in the relationship as a part of life. (To learn more about your views of close relationships, complete **Try It 4.**)

Communicating in Relationships

Communicating well in personal relationships is a blend of talking and listening. Not only does it help to do both well, but it is also important to know when it's time to listen and when it's time to speak up. Listening is an often overlooked skill in personal relationships. We may be so busy trying to communicate our feelings and interests that we overlook the need of the other person to be heard. As friendships

Understand Your Relationship Style

Each of us has a general manner in which we approach close relationships with others. Read the three statements below, and determine which best describes you[6]:

1. I find it relatively easy to get close to others and am comfortable depending on them and having them depend on me. I don't often worry about being abandoned or about someone getting too close to me.

2. I am somewhat uncomfortable being close to others; I find it difficult to trust them completely and to allow myself to depend on them. I am nervous when anyone gets too close, and often love partners want me to be more intimate than I feel comfortable being.

3. I find that others are reluctant to get as close as I would like. I often worry that my partner doesn't really love me or won't want to stay with me. I want to merge completely with another person, and this desire sometimes scares people away.

The choice you make suggests the general style of emotional bonds that you develop with others.

If you thought the first statement described you best, it is probably easy for you to develop close ties with others. Around 55 percent of people describe themselves in this way.

If statement 2 describes you best, you probably have a more difficult time getting close to others, and you may have to work harder to develop close ties with other people. About 25 percent of people place themselves in this category.

Finally, if statement 3 describes you best, you, along with the 20 percent of people who describe themselves in this way, aggressively seek out close relationships. However, they probably present a source of concern to you.

Keep in mind that this is an inexact assessment and presents only a very rough estimate of your general approach to close relationships. But your response can be helpful in answering these questions: Are you generally satisfied with your relationships? Would you like to change them in some way?

To Try It online, go to www.mhhe.com/power.

---

develop into personal relationships, simply talking isn't enough. How you express yourself, especially in moments of difficulty, can be very important to getting your message across.

Being a Good Listener: The Power of Supportive Silence

When it comes to building relationships, how you listen is sometimes more important than what you say. The silence involved in listening is a powerful force, one that can bind us more closely to others.

We've already discussed the art and science of listening as it applies to academic success in Chapter 4. The same principles that promote learning about lecture topics also promote learning about our friends. You can't call yourself a good friend without knowing what others are like and what they are thinking. Good listening is one of the ways to enhance your understanding of others.

When we are heard, we appreciate it because we get the message that our listeners care about us, not just about themselves. Similarly, when we listen, we show that we have respect for those who are speaking, are interested in their ideas and beliefs, and are willing to take the time to pay attention to them.

There are several ways you can improve your ability to listen:

1. **Stop talking!** Are you the kind of person who revels in telling stories about what happened to you? Do you wait eagerly for others to finish what they are saying so that you can jump in with a response? Do you accidentally cut other people off or finish their sentences while they are speaking?

> "The reason why we have two ears and only one mouth is that we may listen the more and talk the less."
>
> **Zeno of Citium, philosopher**

No one likes to be interrupted, even in casual conversation. In more personal relationships, it is a sign of not respecting what the other person has to say and is hurtful.

2. **Demonstrate that you are listening.** Linguists call them "conversational markers"—those nonverbal indications that we're listening. They consist of head nods, uh-huhs, OKs, and other signs that we're keeping up with the conversation. Eye contact is important too. Listening this way shows that we're paying attention and are interested in what the other person is saying.

In addition, don't multitask. If you're having a serious conversation, turn off your cell phone. If it does ring, don't look at caller ID. Even glancing at your phone for a moment shows you're not paying full attention.

3. **Use reflective feedback.** Carl Rogers, a respected therapist, developed a very useful way to lend support to someone and draw him or her out. In **reflective feedback,** a listener rephrases what a speaker has said, trying to echo the speaker's meaning. For example, a listener might say, "as I understand what you're saying . . . ," or "you seem to feel that . . . ," or "in other words, you believe that . . ."

In each case, the summary statement doesn't just "play back" the speaker's statements literally. Instead, it is a rephrasing that captures the essence of the message in different words.

Reflective feedback has two big benefits. First, it provides speakers with a clear indication that you are listening and taking what they're saying seriously. Second, and equally important, it helps ensure that you have an accurate understanding of what the speaker is saying.

4. **Ask questions.** Asking questions shows that you are paying attention to a speaker's comments. Questions permit you to clarify what the speaker has said, and they can move the conversation forward. Further, people feel valued when others ask them about themselves.

5. **Admit when you're distracted.** We've all had those moments: Something is bothering you and you can't get it out of your mind, or you've simply got to finish something and don't really have time to chat. If at the same time someone wants to engage you in conversation, your distraction will undoubtedly show, making the other person feel you are not interested in her or him.

The way to deal with this situation is to admit that you're distracted. Simply saying, "I'd love to talk, but I've got to finish reading a chapter," is enough to explain the situation to a classmate who wants to talk about his date.

Reflective feedback

A technique of verbal listening in which a listener rephrases what a speaker has said, trying to echo the speaker's meaning

Loneliness

Loneliness

A subjective state in which people do not experience the level of connection with others that they desire

Loneliness is a subjective state: We can be totally alone and not feel lonely, or we can be in the midst of a crowd and feel lonely. Loneliness occurs when we don't experience the level of connection with others that we desire. There are also different types of loneliness. Some of us feel lonely if we lack a deep emotional attachment to a single person, which can occur even if we have many friends. Others feel loneliness because they believe they don't have enough friends.

The reality is that there is no standard that indicates the "right" number of relationships. There's no standard against which to measure yourself and the number, and kind, of relationships that you have. It's something you need to decide. It is clear, though, that first-year college students almost always report higher degrees of loneliness than students in subsequent years of study.

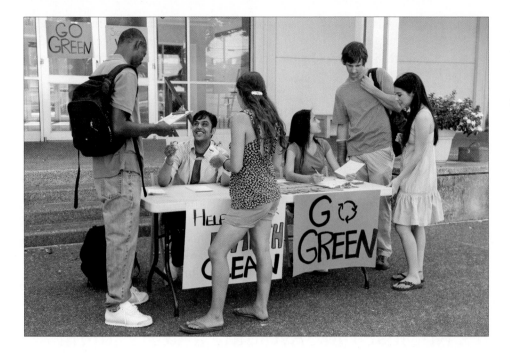

On the other hand, loneliness is not inevitable. Several strategies for dealing with loneliness follow:

> **Become involved in campus activities.** Join a club. Volunteer to help some social organization. Try out for a play. You'll soon get to know others who have similar interests.

> **Find a study partner.** Ask one of your classmates to study with you. You can review your class notes, work together on a project, or study for tests together. Working together will not only help you master the class material, but it will also help you make what can become an important social connection.

> **Know that you're not alone in your loneliness.** If you're feeling lonely, you may find yourself looking at your classmates and noticing groups of people engaged in social activities. This can make you feel even more isolated. Don't be fooled by such social illusions into believing that you are the only one experiencing loneliness. Remember that for every person you notice who is socializing, there are others who are not doing so.

> **Take advantage of orientation and first-year student social events.** Even if you don't consider yourself particularly good at socializing, it's important to make the effort. If you're shy—and even if you're not—consider it a social success if you meet just one new person at such an event.

> **Take a job on campus.** Campus jobs provide not only income but social connections as well. Through work you can meet members of the college staff and make connections with other students.

> **Remember that loneliness is a subjective—and typically temporary—state.** If you interpret your feelings of isolation as due to your personal failings ("I'm alone because I'm not a very likable or interesting person"), you'll experience loneliness. On the other hand, if you view your isolation as a consequence of temporary, short-term factors ("Everyone has a lot of work this semester and there are few opportunities to socialize"), you're less likely to feel loneliness. In short, don't blame yourself for your sense of loneliness.

What if your feelings of loneliness are extreme and you experience a sense of complete isolation and alienation from your classmates? If the feeling persists, it's wise to talk to someone at your college counseling center, a health service provider, or your advisor. Although everyone feels isolated at times, such feelings shouldn't be extreme. Counselors can help you deal with them.

Lonely in a Crowd: Dealing with Too Many People

For some students, it's not a lack of social companionship that is difficult. Instead, juggling too many obligations leads to social overload and, in fact, a kind of loneliness. This is particularly true for nontraditional, older students who may be managing classes, jobs, and families.

For those who feel they never have a moment to themselves, it is important to carve out time for solitude. Write in breaks in your weekly schedule every once in while where you can get away from it all. Just taking a lunch break, eating by yourself on a park bench, can be rejuvenating if you're not interrupted. That means turning off your cell phone and not telling others where you'll be. Just 30 minutes of quality "alone time" can make a difference.

It's Not Just Talk: Avoiding and Handling Conflicts in Relationships

Listening communicates a great deal in personal relationships, but as discussed previously, it is also important to put yourself forward. Generally, close relationships are built on good communication, so day to day there may be no problem in this regard. But when misunderstandings or conflicts occur—as they definitely will from time to time—communication can fall apart. In these situations your ability to communicate in words is tested, and more sensitive listening and more careful ways of saying what you think and feel are needed.

The Subject Is "I" and Not "You"

Suppose a close friend says something with which you disagree: "All you guys are the same—you expect to get everything your way!" You might respond by directing anger at the other person, directly or indirectly accusing the person of some imperfection. "You're always looking for something to complain about!" Such responses (and, as you will notice, the initial statement) typically include the word *you*. For instance, consider these possible responses to indicate disagreement: "*You* really don't understand"; "*You're* being stubborn"; and "How can *you* say that?"

These types of statements cast blame, make accusations, express criticism, and make assumptions about what's inside the other person's head. And they lead to defensive replies that will probably do little to move the conversation forward: "I am *not!*"; "I do so understand"; "I'm not being stubborn"; and "I can say that because that's the way I feel."

"I" statements

Statements that cast responses in terms of oneself and one's individual interpretation

A far more reasonable tactic is to use "I" statements. **"I" statements** cast responses in terms of yourself and your individual interpretation. Instead of saying, for example, "You really don't understand," a more appropriate response would be, "I think we're misunderstanding each other." "You're being stubborn" could be rephrased as "I feel like you're not really listening." And "Why don't you call when you're going to be late?" becomes "I worry that something has happened to you when you don't call if you are going to be late." In each case, "I" statements permit you to state your reaction in terms of your perception or understanding, rather than as a critical judgment about the other person. (Practice using "I" statements in **Try It 5**.)

Switch "You" to "I"

Working in a group or in pairs, turn the following "you" statements into less aggressive "I" statements. For example, a possible "I" statement alternative to "You just don't get it, do you?" would be "I don't feel I'm making my feelings clear."

1. You just don't get it, do you?

2. You never listen to what I say.

3. You don't see where I'm coming from.

4. You don't really believe that, do you?

5. You never try to see my point of view.

6. Please stop interrupting me and listen to what I'm saying for a change.

7. Stop changing the subject!

8. You're not making sense.

9. You keep distorting what I say until I don't even know what point I'm trying to make.

10. You use too many "you" statements. Use more "I" statements when you're talking to others.

To Try It online, go to **www.mhhe.com/power.**

Resolving Conflict: A Win–Win Proposition

Even with careful attention to putting our own feelings forward instead of making accusations, whenever two people share their thoughts, concerns, fears, and honest reactions with each other, the chances are that sooner or later some sort of conflict will arise.

Conflict is not necessarily bad.

Often, people are upset simply by the fact that they are having a conflict. It is as though they believe conflicts don't occur in "good" relationships. In fact, however, conflict is helpful in some very important ways. It can force us to say what is really on our minds. It can allow us to clear up misconceptions and miscommunications before they begin to undermine the relationship. It can even give us practice at resolving conflicts with others with whom we might not share such good relations.

Like anything else, though, there are good ways to resolve conflict, and there are bad ways. Good ways move people forward, defining the problem and promoting creative problem solving. Bad ways make the situation worse, driving people apart rather than bringing them together. The following are some fundamental principles of conflict resolution that you can use when conflict occurs in personal and professional relationships:

> **Stop, look, and listen.** In the heat of an argument, all sorts of things that otherwise would go unsaid get said. If you find yourself making rash or hurtful statements, stop, look at yourself, and listen to what you and the other person are saying.
>
> Stopping works like a circuit breaker that prevents a short circuit from causing a deadly fire. You've probably heard about counting to 10 to cool off when you're angry. Do it. Take a break and count to 10 . . . or 20 . . . or more. Whether you count to 10 or 100, stopping gives you time to think and not react rashly.

> **Defuse the argument.** Anger is not an emotion that encourages rational discourse. When you're angry and annoyed with someone, you're not in the best position to evaluate logically the merits of various arguments others may offer. It may feel exhilarating to get our fury off our chests in the heat of an argument, but you can bet it isn't taking anyone any closer to resolving the problem.
>
> Don't assume that you are 100 percent right and the other person is 100 percent wrong. Make your goal *solving the problem* rather than winning an argument.

> **Get personal.** Perhaps you've heard others suggest that you shouldn't get personal in an argument. In one sense that's true: Accusing people you're arguing with of having character flaws does nothing to resolve real issues.
>
> At the same time, you should be willing to admit personal *responsibility* for at least part of the conflict. The conflict would not exist without you, so you need to accept that the argument has two sides and that you are not automatically blameless. This creates some solid ground from which you and the other person can begin to work on the problem.

> **Listen to the real message.** When people argue, what they say is often not the real message. There's typically an underlying communication—a subtext—that is the source of the conflict.
>
> It's important, then, to dig beneath what you're hearing. If someone accuses you of being selfish, the real meaning hidden in the accusation may be that you don't give anyone else a chance to make decisions. Remember, arguments are usually about behavior, not underlying character and personality. What people *do* is not necessarily synonymous with what they *are*.

If you rephrase the person's statement in your own mind, it moves from an insult ("You're a bad person") to a request for a change of behavior ("Let me participate in decision making"). You're much more likely to respond reasonably when you don't feel that the essence of your being is under attack.

> **Show that you're listening.** It's not enough only to listen to the underlying message that someone is conveying. You also need to acknowledge the *explicit* message. For example, saying something like, "OK. I can tell you are concerned about sharing the burden on our group project, and I think we should talk about it" acknowledges that you see the issue and admit that it is worthy of discussion. This is a far more successful strategy than firing back a countercharge each time your partner makes a complaint.

> **If you are angry, acknowledge it.** Don't pretend that everything is fine if it isn't. Ultimately, relationships in which the partners bottle up their anger may suffer more than those in which the partners express their true feelings. If you're angry, say so.

> **Ask for clarification.** As you're listening to another person's arguments, check out your understanding of what is being said. Don't assume that you know what's intended. Saying something like "Are you saying . . ." or "Do you mean that . . ." is a way of verifying that what you *think* someone means is really what is meant.

> **Make your requests explicit.** If you're upset that your roommate leaves clothes lying around your apartment or dorm room, remarking that he or she is a "pig" shows more than that you are angry. It also shows that your intent is to hurt rather than to solve the problem.
>
> It's far better to be explicit in your concerns. Say something like "It would make me feel better if you would pick up your clothes from the floor." Couching your concern in this way changes the focus of the message from your roommate's personality to a specific behavior that can be changed.

> **Always remember that life is not a zero-sum game.** Many of us act as if life were a **zero-sum game,** a situation in which when one person wins, the other person automatically loses. It's what happens when you make a bet: If one person wins the bet, the other person loses.
>
> Life is not like that. If one person wins an argument, it doesn't mean that others automatically have to lose it. And if someone loses an argument, it doesn't mean that others have automatically won. In fact, all too often conflict escalates so much that the argument turns into a lose–lose situation, where everyone ends up a loser.
>
> However, life can be a win–win situation. The best resolution of conflict occurs when both parties walk away with something they want. Each may not have achieved *every* goal but will at least have enough to feel satisfied.

> **Finally, if a relationship involves emotional or physical abuse, you must seek help or decide to end the relationship immediately.** If a partner is emotionally or physically abusive to you, seek assistance from trained counselors. Don't wait. It is virtually impossible to deal with abuse on your own. Your college counseling center, mental health center, or medical center can offer you help. If you are physically threatened or injured, call 911.

Zero-sum game

A situation in which when one person wins, the other person automatically loses

When Relationships Are Over: Dealing with Endings

Not all relationships last a lifetime. Sometimes they just wind down, as the two people involved slowly lose interest in maintaining their partnership. At other times, they break apart, as disagreements build and there is not a strong enough bond to hold the two parties together. Or there may be an abrupt rupture if some event occurs that destroys one partner's feeling of trust.

Caring for others is rewarding, but risky. When relationships don't work out, their endings can be painful, even devastating, for a time. Even when relationships evolve naturally and change is expected, the transformation in a relationship may not be easy. Parents die. Children grow up and move away from home. Siblings get new jobs on the other side of the country.

There is one sure cure for the heartache of a lost relationship: time. There are some other things you can do, however, as you wait for time to pass and for the pain to ease:

1. **Do something—anything.** Mow the lawn, clean out the closets, go for a run, see a movie. It won't completely get your mind off your loss, but it beats languishing on your bed, thinking about what you might have done differently or what could have been.

2. **Accept that you feel bad.** If you're not experiencing unhappiness over the end of a relationship, it means that the relationship wasn't terribly meaningful in the first place. Understand that unhappiness normally accompanies the end of a relationship, and allow yourself some satisfaction over the fact that you'd been able to maintain a relationship that, at least at one point, was meaningful.

3. **Talk to a friend or relative.** Talking about your sadness will help you to deal with it better. Other people can help you feel better about yourself, offer different perspectives, and simply support you by listening. Make use of your network of existing relationships to get you through a difficult period.

4. **Write about the relationship.** If you have a journal, writing about the relationship and its aftermath can be therapeutic. You can say whatever you want without fear of being contradicted.

5. **Talk to a professional.** If your sadness over a relationship feels totally overwhelming or continues for what you perceive to be too long a time, talk to a counselor or other professional. He or she can help you gain a better understanding of the situation and perhaps help you understand why you are taking it so hard. And remember that, ultimately, the pain will disappear: Time does heal virtually all wounds.

Speaking of **Success**

NAME: **Lindsey Beck**

SCHOOL: **Three Rivers Community College, Norwich, Connecticut**

Although many students who start college face a variety of obstacles, Lindsey Beck faced unusual challenges. Not only was she a single mother beginning classes shortly after her son Kevin was born, but she also had just ended an abusive relationship that had sapped her self-confidence.

To her own surprise, one of the ways Beck was able to move on and ultimately succeed was by developing her writing skills.

"I learned about strategies to deal with my situation from exercises where we confront ourselves in our writing," Beck explained. "By being honest with my writing and looking at myself and saying 'this is who I am and where I am,' I was able for the first time to understand my relationship with my abuser."

As a result, Beck used writing both as a way to deal with her relationships and to push herself toward academic excellence.

"Through writing, I realized I needed to stop blaming others for what was happening to me. I needed to take control and become a role model for my son. As a result, I became very passionate about writing."

Beck credits her English instructors for getting her involved in writing.

"Although my English classes were the hardest ones for me, I looked up to my instructors because they challenged me and were able to lead me and act as mentors," Beck said.

As Beck became more confident in her abilities, she made it her goal to learn something from every class and takes her education very seriously.

"I love school and am humbled by the fact that I can go," said Beck, who plans to pursue her education in the fields of microbiology and genetics.

"Every assignment you do is for yourself. It's not just for a grade, but reflects on the person you are.

"Overall, if you can sit down and make it something you are proud of, you can push yourself and have a sense of accomplishment," she said. "In the end it goes beyond the class and grade."

Looking Back

Why is the increasing racial, ethnic, and cultural diversity of society important to me?

▸ The diversity of the United States—and of U.S. college campuses—is increasing rapidly, and the world is becoming smaller as television, radio, the Internet, the Web, and international commerce bring people and cultures closer together.

▸ Being aware of diversity can allow you to accept the challenge and opportunity of living and working with others who are very different.

How can I become more at ease with differences and diversity?

▸ Cultural competence begins with accepting diversity by seeking out others who are different, as well as exploring your own prejudices and stereotypes.

▸ You can learn about other cultures by traveling to other countries and geographic areas. It also helps to accept differences simply as differences.

How can I build lasting relationships and deal with conflict?

▸ Relationships not only provide social support and companionship, but they also help people understand themselves.

▸ The central components of good relationships are trust, honesty, mutual support, loyalty, acceptance, and a willingness to embrace change.

▸ Listening is an important skill for relationship building, demonstrating that the listener really cares about the other person.

▸ Conflict is inevitable in relationships, and sometimes it is useful because it permits us to clear up misconceptions and miscommunications before they escalate.

▸ Although the end of a relationship can be very painful, the pain does subside over time.

[KEY TERMS AND CONCEPTS]

Race (p. 316)
Ethnicity (p. 316)
Culture (p. 316)
Cultural competence (p. 317)

Prejudice (p. 318)
Discrimination (p. 319)
Stereotypes (p. 319)
Reflective feedback (p. 328)

Loneliness (p. 328)
"I" statements (p. 330)
Zero-sum game (p. 333)

[RESOURCES]

ON CAMPUS

For students who reside on campus, one of the most frequent sources of difficulties for first-year students involves roommate problems. If you and your roommate are having problems getting along, begin by speaking with your resident advisor or residence hall director. If the problem persists, talk with a member of the residential life office. You can also speak with a counselor at the college counseling office.

Anyone who feels he or she is facing discrimination based on race, gender, ethnic status, sexual orientation, or national origin should contact a university official *immediately*. Often there is a specific office that handles such complaints. If you don't know which campus official to contact, speak to your academic advisor or someone in the dean's office and you'll be directed to the appropriate person. The important thing is to act and not to suffer in silence. Discrimination is not only immoral, but it is against the law.

IN PRINT

Beverly Tatum's *Why Are All the Black Kids Sitting Together in the Cafeteria? And Other Conversations about Race* (HarperCollins, 2003 rev. ed.) explores race, racism, and the everyday impact of prejudice.

In *Affirming Diversity* (Allyn & Bacon, 2007), Sonia Nieto examines how ethnic and cultural factors affect student success.

Finally, Joseph Folger, Marshall Poole, and Randall Stutman's *Working through Conflict: Strategies for Relationships, Groups, and Organizations* (Allyn & Bacon, 2008) suggests a variety of practical approaches to resolving conflict.

ON THE WEB

The following sites on the Web provide the opportunity to extend your learning about the material in this chapter. (Although the Web addresses were accurate at the time the book was printed, check the *P.O.W.E.R. Learning* Web site [**www.mhhe.com/power**] for any changes that may have occurred.)

▸ "Communication Improvement" (**www.colorado.edu/conflict/peace/treatment/ commimp.htm**) is an outline posted by the Confliction Research Consortium at the University of Colorado. It includes a lengthy section on improving communications, with added links to improving listening skills and conflict resolution.

▸ "Language and Culture" (**www.ncela.gwu.edu/resabout/culture/**), a site from George Washington University's National Clearinghouse for English Language Acquisition & Language Instruction Educational Programs, provides links dealing with culture, diversity, and multiculturalism, connecting to everything from the American Folk Life Center to worldwide ethnology resources.

▸ Understanding "Race Relations" (**racerelations.about.com**), a comprehensive site on About.com, discusses topics ranging from affirmative action to white privilege. Hundreds of links are provided for more in-depth discussions and background on a variety of subjects, including race relations, hate crimes, gay/lesbian issues, and many other topics.

TAKING IT TO THE NET

1 Explore cultural differences using the Internet. Go to Yahoo! (**dir.yahoo.com**), choose "Society and Culture," and then "Cultures and Groups." Click on "Cultures" and type a topic that you find interesting into the search field. Make sure to limit your search to just this category. How many pages did you find? Read and compare the information from different cultural groups.

2 Use the Internet to help find a volunteer organization that sounds interesting to you. Using either Yahoo! (**www.yahoo.com**) or AltaVista (**www.altavista.com**), enter "volunteer organizations" into the search field. Examine the volunteer organizations listed and write down the ones that you find interesting. Consider contacting one or more to explore possibilities of participating in the organization that will mesh with your other responsibilities.

The Case of . . .

Answering for All

Jace Kinkaid stood out in any crowd. With his six-foot-eight height, he towered above most of his classmates. Even when he was seated at a desk, he looked huge. And since he was an African American, his skin color set him apart from his classmates, almost all of whom were white.

Although, by and large, people were polite and nice enough to him, Jace felt isolated from most of his peers and instructors. While he had one or two good friends from high school with whom he kept in touch, he was not close to many people on campus. His isolation came to a head, however, in the most public of places: his English literature class. It happened when his instructor, a white man, was leading a discussion on *The Fire Next Time,* a novel by noted Black writer James Baldwin. The instructor turned to Jace and asked him to comment on a passage from the novel.

"Does it ring true to you, Jace, as an African American?" asked his instructor, who then went on to inquire, "What do African Americans think about the perspective that Baldwin is taking?"

Jace was taken aback. What was he supposed to say? He hardly felt like a representative of every black person. He barely knew how he felt, let alone everyone else who was African American. What an absurd situation to be placed in—his instructor asking him to answer for millions of other people. He felt awful—embarrassed, upset, and angry at his instructor for putting him on the spot.

1. Why was the instructor's question so troubling to Jace? If the instructor really wanted Jace's opinion about the passage, what should he have said?

2. Would the question have had a different effect if the instructor had also been African American? Why or why not?

3. What are some cultural assumptions that the instructor is making about Jace? About African Americans? About white people?

4. What response might Jace make in this situation to make his feelings clear without causing excessive conflict?

Money Matters

Learning Outcomes

By the time you finish this chapter you will be able to

» LO **13.1** Explain the purpose of a budget and outline how to prepare and stick to one.

» LO **13.2** Discuss the help available to pay for your college education.

» LO **13.3** Analyze the value of a college education.

eah Flores's college career depended on the contents of the envelope she held in her hands.

The letter inside from the financial aid office spelled out her school's offer of aid for the upcoming term. As she tore open the envelope, Leah wondered whether it would be enough. She knew that without a substantial amount of support, she would have to drop out. She couldn't stand the thought, particularly because she had been doing so well.

As she looked at the numbers on the form, Leah's heart soared. Not only had she been given a loan, but also most of her aid was in the form of a direct scholarship.

Things would still be tight, but she could manage. Her financial worries were over—at least for one more term.

Looking Ahead

Money problems aren't always solved as happily as they were for Leah Flores. Even under the best of circumstances, our finances present us with many challenges. Money often plays a large role in where we go to college, where we live, and what jobs we take. It is the source of many of our problems and stress, forcing us to find a balance between what we need and what we want.

This chapter will show you how to manage your money. It begins by discussing the process of preparing a budget and identifying your financial goals—the basis for money management. The chapter goes on to examine ways you can keep track of your spending and estimate your financial needs and resources, and it discusses ways to control your spending habits and save money.

Education is one of the largest financial expenditures anyone encounters in life. Knowing the best ways to meet the costs of a college education—finding loans, grants, and scholarships—can give your finances a big boost and help you avoid graduating with thousands of dollars of debt. You will also learn what to do if your personal finances get out of control and discover how to stop the downward spiral of unpaid bills, defaulted loans, and unfavorable credit ratings. The chapter ends by suggesting ways to develop a financial philosophy.

≫ LO 13.1 Managing Your Money

Do you know where your money goes? Do you spend more than you think you should? Do you never have quite enough cash to buy the things you want?

Answering these questions and understanding the role money plays in your life is the first step of wise money management. To begin getting a grip on your finances, answer the questions in the **Journal Reflections** exercise.

If you have money problems—and there's virtually no one who doesn't have some concerns about finances—the solution is to develop a budget. A **budget** is a formal plan that accounts and plans for expenditures and income. Taking your goals into account, a budget helps determine how much money you should be spending each month, based on your income and your other financial resources. Budgets also help prepare for the unexpected, such as the loss of a job or an illness that would reduce your income, or for sudden, unanticipated expenses, such as a major car repair.

Although all budgets are based on an uncomplicated premise—expenditures should not exceed income—budgeting is not simple, particularly when you are a student. There are several times during the year that require especially large

Budget
A formal plan that accounts for expenditures and income

Journal Reflections

My Sense of Cents

Answer the following questions about your financial sense.

1. How much money do you now have in your pockets and wallet? (Guess first, then look.) How close did you come?

2. Do you know how much money you typically spend in a month, including money spent on food, lodging, and other items?

3. How good a sense of your finances do you think you have? How secure do you feel in your understanding of where your money goes?

4. How important is money to you? Why?

5. Research shows that although winning the lottery or other large sums of money brings an initial surge in happiness, a year later the winners' level of happiness returns to what it was before.[1] Why do you think this is true in general, and would it be true for you?

expenditures, such as the start of a semester, when you must pay your tuition and purchase books. Furthermore, your income is usually erratic; it may be lower during the school year and higher during the summer. But a budget will help you deal with the ups and downs in your finances, smoothing the curves and extending your view toward the horizon. Learning budgeting skills also helps prepare you for the world of work, as discussed in this chapter's **Career Connections** on page 342.

Most of all, a budget provides security. It will let you take control of your money, permitting you to spend it as you need to without guilt, because you have planned for the expenditure. It also makes it easier to put money aside because you know that your current financial sacrifice will be rewarded later, when you can make a purchase that you've been planning for.

Budgeting is very personal: What is appropriate for one person doesn't work for another. For a few people, keeping track of their spending comes naturally; they enjoy accounting for every dollar that passes through their hands. For most people, though, developing a budget—and sticking to it—does not come easily.

> "There was a time when a fool and his money were soon parted, but now it happens to everybody."
> **Adlai Stevenson, politician**

Budgeting on the Job

If you've ever held a job, the salary you received was determined, in part, by your employer's budget.

Although they may not always be accessible to every employee, budgets are part of the world of work. Regardless of who the employer is—be it a small dry cleaning business or the massive federal government—there is a budget outlining anticipated income and expenditures. Managers are expected to keep to the budget, and if their expenditures exceed what is budgeted, they are held accountable.

For this reason, the ability to create and live within a budget is an important skill to acquire. Not only will it help keep your own finances under control, but it will also prepare you to be financially responsible and savvy on the job—qualities that are highly valued by employers.

However, if you follow several basic steps—illustrated in the P.O.W.E.R. Plan—the process of budgeting is straightforward.

P Prepare
Identify financial goals

O Organize
Determine expenditures and income

W Work
Make a budget that adds up

E Evaluate
Review the budget

R Rethink
Rethink financial options

P.O.W.E.R. Plan

P Prepare — Identifying Your Financial Goals

Your first reaction when asked to identify your financial goals may be that the question is a no-brainer: You want to have more money to spend. But it's not that simple. You need to ask yourself *why* you want more money. What would you spend it on? What would bring you the most satisfaction? Purchasing a DVD player? Paying off your debt? Saving money for a vacation? Starting a business? Paying for college rather than taking out loans?

You won't be able to develop a budget that will work for you until you determine your short- and long-term financial goals. To determine them, use **Try It 1,** "Identify Your Financial Goals" on page 344.

O Organize — Determining Your Expenditures and Income

Do you open your wallet for the $10 that was there yesterday and find only a dollar? Spending money without realizing it is a common affliction.

There's only one way to get a handle on where your money is going: Keep track of it. To get an overview of your expenditures, go through any records you've kept to identify where you've spent money for the last year—old checks, rent and utility receipts, and previous college bills can help you.

In addition, keep track of everything you spend for a week. *Everything.* When you spend 75 cents for a candy bar from a vending machine, write it down. When you buy lunch for $3.99 at a fast-food restaurant, write it down. When you buy a 44-cent stamp, write it down.

Record your expenditures in a small notebook that you carry with you all the time. It may be tedious, but you're doing it for only a week. And it will be eye-opening: People are usually surprised at how much they spend on little items without thinking about it.

Make a list of everything you think you'll need to spend over the next year. Some items are easy to think of, such as rent and tuition payments, because they occur regularly and the amount you pay is fixed. Others are harder to budget for because they can vary substantially. For example, the price of gasoline changes frequently. If you have a long commute, the changing price of gasoline can cause

Keeping to a budget is a constant balancing act. For example, even though you know you'll need to purchase books at the start of each semester, you can't predict exactly how much they'll cost.

substantial variation in what you pay each month. Similarly, the cost of books varies considerably from one term to another. (Use **Table 13.1** on page 346 to estimate your expenditures for the coming year. You can also prepare a monthly budget online at the *P.O.W.E.R. Learning* Web site at www.mhhe.com/power).

When you are listing your upcoming expenditures, be sure to include an amount that you will routinely put aside into a savings account that pays you interest. It's important to get into the habit of saving money. Even if you start off small—putting aside just a few dollars a week—the practice of regularly putting aside some amount of your income is central to good financial management.

Determine Your Income Sources

You probably have a pretty good idea of how much money you have each month. But it's as important to list each source of income as it is to account for everything you spend.

Add up what you make from any jobs you hold. Also list any support you receive from family members, including occasional gifts you might get from relatives. Finally, include any financial aid (such as tuition reductions, loan payments, or scholarships) you receive from your college. Use **Table 13.2** on page 347 to record this information. When you do, be sure to list the amounts you receive in terms of after-tax income.

W Work

Making a Budget That Adds Up

If you've prepared and organized your budget, actually constructing your budget is as easy as adding 2 + 2. Well, not exactly; the numbers will be larger. But all you need to do is add up your list of expenses, and then add up your sources of income. In a perfect world, the two numbers will be equal.

TRADITION · COMPETITION · TUITION

Try It!

Identify Your Financial Goals

Determining your financial goals will help set you on the path to securing your financial future. Use this **Try It** to get started.

Step 1. Use the planning tool below to identify and organize your financial goals.

SHORT-TERM GOALS

What would you like to have money for in the short term (over the next 3 months)? Consider these categories:

Personal necessities (such as food, shelter, clothes, household supplies, transportation, loan and credit card payments, medical or child care expenses):

Educational necessities (such as tuition, fees, books, school supplies, computer expenses):

Social needs (e.g., getting together with family, friends, and others; charitable contributions; clubs and teams):

Entertainment (e.g., movies and shows, trips, recreation, and sports):

Other:

MID-RANGE GOALS

What would you like to have money for soon (3 months from now to a year from now), but not immediately? Use the same categories:

Personal necessities:

Educational necessities:

Social needs:

Entertainment:

Other:

LONG-RANGE GOALS

What would you like to have money for 1 to 3 years from now? Use the same categories:

Personal necessities:

Educational necessities:

Social needs:

Entertainment:

Other:

Step 2. Now put each of your lists in **priority** order.

Short-Term Priorities:

Mid-Range Priorities:

Long-Range Priorities:

What does the list tell you about what is important to you? Did you find any surprises? Would you classify yourself as a financial risk-taker or someone who values financial security?

 WORKING IN A GROUP:

Consider these questions: Compare your priorities with those of your classmates. What similarities and differences do you find, and what can you learn from others' priorities?

To Try It online, go to **www.mhhe.com/power.**

table 13.1 Estimated Expenditures, Next 12 Months

Category	Now to 3 Months from now	3–6 Months from now	6–9 Months from now	9–12 Months from now
Personal Necessities				
Food				
Shelter (rent, utilities, etc.)				
Clothing				
Household supplies				
Transportation (car payments, gas, repairs, bus tickets, etc.)				
Loan and credit card payments				
Medical expenses				
Child care expenses				
Other				
Educational Necessities				
Tuition and fees				
Books				
School supplies				
Computer expenses				
Other				
Social Needs				
Relationships				
Clubs and teams				
Charitable contributions				
Other				
Entertainment				
Movies and shows				
Trips				
Recreation and sports				
Other				
TOTAL				

table 13.2 Estimated Income, Next 12 Months

Category	Now to 3 Months from now	3–6 Months from now	6–9 Months from now	9–12 Months from now
Wages				
Family Support				
Financial Aid				
Tuition reductions				
Loan income				
Scholarship payments				
Other				
Interest and Dividends				
Gifts				
Other				
TOTAL				

But most of the time, the world is not perfect: Most of us find that expenditures are larger than our income. After all, if we had plenty of excess cash, we probably wouldn't be bothering to make a budget in the first place.

If you find you spend more than you make, there are only two things to do: decrease your spending or increase your income. It's often easiest to decrease expenditures, because your expenses tend to be more under your control. For instance, there are many things you can do to save money, including the following:

> **Control impulse buying.** If you shop for your groceries, always take a list with you, and don't shop when you're hungry.

> **Make and take your own lunch.** Brown-bag lunches can save you a substantial amount of money over purchasing your lunches, even if you go to a fast-food restaurant or snack bar.

> **Read the daily newspaper and magazines at the library or online.** Not only do college libraries subscribe to many daily newspapers and magazines, but major newspapers and magazines are also online.

> **Check bills for errors.** Computers make mistakes, and so do the people who enter the data into them. So make sure that your charges on any bill are accurate.

> **Cut up your credit cards and pay cash.** Using a credit card is seductive; when you take out your plastic, it's

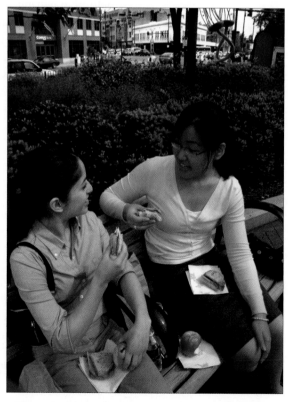

Bag it! One way to cut down on expenditures is to reduce everyday expenses, such as by making your own lunch, rather than grabbing a bite at a campus snack bar. Even small savings like this can add up fast.

easy to feel as if you're not really spending money. If you use cash for purchases instead, you'll see the money going out.

> **Make major purchases only during sales.** Plan major purchases so they coincide with sales.

> **Share and trade.** Pool your resources with friends. Car pool, share resources such as computers, and trade CDs.

> **Live more simply.** Is cable TV an absolute necessity? Is it really necessary to eat out once a week? Do you buy clothes because you need them or because you want them? Do you really need to send so many text messages?

There are as many ways to save money as there are people looking to save it. But keep in mind that saving money should not necessarily be an end in itself. Don't spend hours thinking of ways to save a dime, and don't get upset about situations where you are forced to spend money. The goal is to bring your budget into balance, not to become a tightwad who keeps track of every penny and feels that spending money is a personal failure. To help you get started, get a sense of your current style of saving money in **Try It 2.**

Finally, it's important to remember that budgets may be brought into balance not only by decreasing expenditures but also by increasing income. The most direct way to increase income is to get a part-time job if you don't already have one.

Many students work during college. Although working adds to the time-management challenges you will face, it does not necessarily mean that your grades will suffer. In fact, some students who work do better in school than those who don't work, because those with jobs need to be more disciplined and focused. In addition, a part-time job in an area related to your future career may prove to be helpful in getting a job after you graduate.

On the other hand, working too much can be harmful. Jobs not only take their toll in hours away from your studies, but also in added stress. Consequently, it's sometimes better to take out a student loan to cover college costs than to work excessive amounts. Obviously you don't want to thoughtlessly get into debt, because you don't want to burden your future with loan payments. But the well-thought-out use of loans, if they allow you to focus on your studies, may be a good investment in your future.

🄴 Evaluate Reviewing Your Budget

Budgets are not meant to be set in stone. You should review where you stand financially each month. Only by monitoring how closely actual expenditures and income match your budget projections will you be able to maintain control of your finances.

You don't need to continually keep track of every penny you spend to evaluate your success in budgeting. As you gain more experience with your budget, you'll begin to get a better sense of your finances. You'll know when it may be possible to consider splurging on a gift for a friend, and when you need to operate in penny-pinching mode.

The important thing is to keep your expenditures under control. Review, and if necessary revise, your budget to fit any changes in circumstances. Maybe you receive a raise in a part-time job. Maybe the financial aid office gives you more support than you expected. Or maybe you face a reduction in income. Whatever the change in circumstances, evaluate how it affects your budget, and revise the budget accordingly.

Try It! **POWER**

2

Determine Your Saving Style

Read each of the following statements and rate how well it describes you, using this scale:

1 = That's me

2 = Sometimes

3 = That's not me

	1	2	3
1. I count the change I'm given by cashiers in stores and restaurants.			
2. I always pick up all the change I receive from a transaction in a store, even if it's only a few cents.			
3. I don't buy something right away if I'm pretty sure it will go on sale soon.			
4. I feel a real sense of accomplishment if I buy something on sale.			
5. I always remember how much I paid for something.			
6. If something goes on sale soon after I've bought it, I feel cheated.			
7. I have money in at least one interest-bearing bank account.			
8. I rarely lend people money.			
9. If I lend money to someone repeatedly without getting it back, I stop lending it to that person.			
10. I share resources (e.g., CDs, books, magazines) with other people to save money.			
11. I'm good at putting money away for big items that I really want.			
12. I believe most generic or off-brand items are just as good as name brands.			

Add up your ratings. Interpret your total score according to this informal guide:

12–15: Very aggressive saving style

16–20: Careful saving style

21–27: Fairly loose saving style

28–32: Loose saving style

33–36: Nonexistent saving style

What are the advantages and disadvantages of your saving style? How do you think your saving style would affect your ability to keep to a budget? If you are dissatisfied with your saving style, how might you be able to change it?

To Try It online, go to www.mhhe.com/power.

R Rethink Reconsidering Your Financial Options

If all goes well, the process of budgeting will put you in control of your financial life. Your expenditures will match your income, and you won't face major money worries.

In the real world, of course, events have a way of inflicting disaster on even the best-laid plans:

> You lose your job and can't afford to pay next semester's tuition.

> Your roommate moves out and leaves you with a $300 cable bill. You don't have $300.

> Your parents, who have promised to pay for your education, run into financial difficulties and say they can't afford to pay your college costs any longer.

> Your car breaks down, and repairing it will cost $1,500. If you don't have a car, you can't get to campus. But if you pay for repairs, you can't afford tuition.

All of us face financial difficulties at one time or another. Sometimes it happens suddenly and without warning. Other times people sink more gradually into financial problems, each month accumulating more debt until they reach a point at which they can't pay their bills.

However it happens, finding yourself with too little money to pay your bills requires action. You need to confront the situation and take steps to solve the problem. The worst thing to do is nothing. Hiding from those to whom you owe money makes the situation worse. Your creditors—the institutions and people to whom you owe money—will assume that you don't care, and they'll be spurred on to take harsher actions.

These are the steps to take if you do find yourself with financial difficulties (also see **Table 13.3**).

> **Assess the problem.** Make a list of what you owe and to whom. Look at the bottom line and figure out a reasonable amount you can put toward each debt. Work out a specific plan that can lead you out of the situation.

> **Contact each of your creditors.** Start with your bank, credit card companies, and landlord, and continue through each creditor. It's best to visit personally, but a phone call will do.

> When you speak with them, explain the situation. If the problem is due to illness or unemployment, let them know. If it's due to overspending, let them know that. Tell them what you plan to do to pay off your debt, and show them your plan. The fact that you have a plan demonstrates not only what you intend to do but also that you are serious about your situation and capable of financial planning.

> If you've had a clean financial record in the past, your creditors may be willing to agree to your plan. Ultimately, it is cheaper for them to accept smaller payments over a longer time than to hire a collection agency.

> **See a credit counselor.** If you can't work out a repayment plan on your own, visit a credit counseling service. These are nonprofit organizations that help people who find themselves in financial trouble. Your bank or a creditor can help you identify one, or you can call the National Foundation for Credit Counseling at 1–800–388–2227 or visit their Web site at **www.nfcc.org.**

> **Stick to the plan.** Once you have a plan to get yourself out of debt, follow it. Unless you diligently make the payments you commit to, you'll find your debt spiraling out of control once again. It's essential, then, to regard your plan as a firm commitment and stick to it.

table 13.3 Steps in Dealing with Financial Difficulties

Assess the Problem	Make a list of what you owe and to whom.
	Figure out a reasonable amount you can put toward each debt.
	Work out a specific plan.
Contact Each of Your Creditors	Start with your bank, credit card companies, and landlord.
	Explain the situation.
	Show them your plan to pay off debt.
See a Credit Counselor	If you cannot work out a repayment plan on your own, visit a credit counseling service.
Stick to the Plan	Once you have a plan, make a commitment to stick to it.
	Your bank or creditor can help you identify a credit counselor.

Credit Cards

"Congratulations! You've been preapproved for a Gold card! Just send us your signature on the enclosed authorization form, and we'll rush you your card."

Have you ever gotten such a letter in the mail? If so, you're far from the only one: Millions of people in the United States are regularly enticed to receive credit cards in just such a manner, and college students are especially attractive targets. In many cases, it doesn't even matter if you have income; the mere fact that you're a college student is sufficient to win you approval to receive a card.

Credit cards are not necessarily bad. In fact, used appropriately, they can help get you through brief periods when you must make a purchase—such as replacing a tire for your car—but temporarily don't have enough money to do so. But it's easy to fall into debt. That's why the average credit card debt owed by college students is over $2,700. And about 10 percent of college students owe more than $7,000.

You don't want to be years past your college graduation and still paying for a slice of pizza you purchased in your first month on campus. That's why it's important to consider the use of credit cards very carefully.

There are several questions you should ask when deciding whether to get and use a credit card:

1. **Is there an annual fee?** Many cards charge an annual fee, ranging from $20 a year to $100 a year. You need to determine whether the advantages of the card are worth the cost of an annual fee.

2. **What is the interest rate?** Interest rates—the percentage of the unpaid balance you are charged on credit cards—vary substantially. Some interest rates are as low as 12 percent per year, while some are as high as 25 percent per year. If the rate is 25 percent, you will

> "It is difficult to learn the meaning of fiscal responsibility, especially when you've got a new VISA and there's a great-looking sweater in the shop window. It's even harder when the sweater is on sale."
>
> **Lauren Pass, student, Grossmont Community College[2]**

It's easy for most college students to get credit cards, and even easier to use them once they have them. The hard part comes later—paying the bills.

be charged an additional $250 each year if you owe an average of $1,000. Furthermore, although some interest rates are *fixed,* meaning that they don't vary from month to month, others are *variable,* which means they change each month. How much they change is tied to various factors in the overall economy. To get a better sense of how interest rates add up, try "Maintain Your Interest" (**Try It 3**).

3. **Do I need a credit card?** There are good reasons for getting a credit card, and bad ones:

THE PLUSES OF CREDIT CARDS:

> **Establishing a good credit history.** If you've ever owed money to a bank or your college, a computer file exists describing your payment history. If you have never missed a loan payment and always pay on time, you have a good credit history. If you haven't paid on time or have missed payments, your history will reflect this. Negative information can stay in a file for 7 years, and it can keep you from getting future loans, so it's important to establish and keep a clear credit history. (To get a copy of your credit report, complete **Try It 4**, on page 354, "Learn What Your Credit History Shows.")

> **Emergency use.** Few of us carry around enough cash to deal with emergencies. A credit card can be a life saver if we're on a trip and the car breaks down and needs emergency repairs.

"Graduates, faculty, parents, creditors . . ."

> **Convenience.** Sometimes it's just easier to make purchases using a credit card. For instance, we can make purchases over the telephone or online if we have a credit card. Furthermore, credit cards not only provide a record of purchases, but they also give us limited consumer protection should a product prove to be defective.

THE MINUSES OF CREDIT CARDS:

On the other hand, there can be significant drawbacks to the use of credit cards. Potential problems include the following:

> **Interest costs can be high.** As you saw in **Try It 3,** the interest rate on credit card purchases can be significant. Unless you pay off your entire balance each month, your account will be charged interest, which can add up rapidly.

> **It's too easy to spend money.** Credit cards are so convenient to use that you may not realize how much you're spending in a given period. Furthermore, spending can become addictive. Unless you're careful, you can end up exceeding your budget by a significant amount.

> **If you're late in making your payments or exceed your credit limit, your credit rating will be damaged.** Credit card companies have long memories, and any mistakes you make will be reflected in your credit record for close to a decade. That may prevent you from buying a car or house in the future and jeopardize your ability to take out student loans.

> **You become susceptible to identity theft.** *Identity theft* occurs when your credit card number (or Social Security number) and name are used by someone fraudulently. Identity thieves may use your credit card number to make purchases, open new credit card accounts in your name, open new phone accounts, or even rent a house in your name. They can change the address on existing accounts so you don't even know that they are running up bills in

Maintain Your Interest

Suppose you saw a $275 television set on sale "for a limited time" for $240. The $35 discount tempts you. The trouble is you don't have $240 to spare. But you *do* have a credit card—and you decide to buy the TV with the card and pay it off over time.

The advantages of this strategy are that you get the discount and have immediate use of the television set. The main disadvantage is that you will end up paying more than the $240 figure that you have in mind as the bargain price for the TV. In fact, depending on how high your credit card's interest rate is, how long you take to pay your bill in full, and how large each monthly payment is, you may wipe out most or all of the $35 savings that caused you to make the purchase in the first place. The more slowly you pay off the loan, the more money you pay for the television set.

For example, suppose you use a card with an annual interest rate of 12 percent, compounded monthly, meaning that the interest charge is applied each month, rather than at the end of the year—making the true annual rate 12.68 percent. (Some cards even compound on a *daily* basis, resulting in a real interest rate that is even higher.) At the end of a year, assuming you pay $10 per month toward the $240 purchase, you will have paid $120 and still have $143.61 to pay. At the end of 2 years, you would end up paying $35 in interest on top of the $240 purchase price.

The 12-month calculation is illustrated in the first table below. To see how much of a factor the interest rate is, complete the second table, which shows the same purchase on a credit card with a 20 percent annual (approximately 1.67 percent monthly) interest rate, compounded monthly. (These calculations can also be figured automatically on several Web sites, including **www.bankrate.com** and **www.quicken.com.**)

Credit Card Payments: 12% Interest, Compounded Monthly (1% per month)

	Month 1	2	3	4	5	6	7	8	9	10	11	12
Unpaid Balance	$240.00	$232.40	$224.72	$216.97	$209.14	$201.23	$193.24	$185.18	$177.03	$168.80	$160.49	$152.09
Plus Interest of	2.40	2.32	2.25	2.17	2.09	2.01	1.93	1.85	1.77	1.69	1.60	1.52
Minus Payment of	10.00	10.00	10.00	10.00	10.00	10.00	10.00	10.00	10.00	10.00	10.00	10.00
Balance Due	$232.40	$224.72	$216.97	$209.14	$201.23	$193.24	$185.18	$177.03	$168.80	$160.49	$152.09	$143.61

Credit Card Payments: 20% Interest, Compounded Monthly (approx. 1.67% per month)

	Month 1	2	3	4	5	6	7	8	9	10	11	12
Unpaid Balance	$240.00	$234.01	$227.92	$221.72	$215.42							
Plus Interest of	4.01	3.91	3.81	3.70								
Minus Payment of	10.00	10.00	10.00	10.00	10.00	10.00	10.00	10.00	10.00	10.00	10.00	10.00
Balance Due	$234.01	$227.92	$221.72	$215.42								

How much would the $240 TV set cost if you bought it with this higher-rate card, paying $10 per month for 12 months and then paying the remaining balance by check? How does this compare with the nondiscounted purchase price of $275?

To Try It online, go to **www.mhhe.com/power.**

4

Learn What Your Credit History Shows

Big Brother is alive and well, at least in terms of your credit history. If you've ever had a credit card in your own name, taken out a student loan, or simply received an unsolicited offer for credit in the mail, there's probably a computer file describing who you are, where you live, and your financial history. It shows how high your credit lines are on every credit card you have, if you've ever been late on a payment, and a considerable amount of additional information.

Even worse: Many people's credit histories are riddled with errors. That's why it's important to check the record periodically. To get a complimentary copy of your credit report, go to the Web site maintained by the three major credit companies (Transunion, Experian, and Equifax): **www.annualcreditreport.com.**

Be prepared: You will be asked for a variety of information, including your name, address, Social Security number, birth date, prior addresses for the past 5 years, and other names (like a maiden name) you may have been known by. In addition, you may be asked to sign up for future reports for a fee; if you don't want them, say "no." Eventually, you will receive an online copy of your credit report.

Once you get your credit report, check it carefully. If you find any mistakes, contact the credit bureau and explain the error. They are legally responsible for investigating the report and correcting the file. It's a good idea to check your file once a year.

To Try It online, go to www.mhhe.com/power.

your name. Detecting identity theft is one of the reasons you should examine your credit card statements—in fact all your financial statements, such as bank accounts—very carefully every month.

» LO 13.2 Paying for College

Tuition costs vary greatly from one school to another, but they are substantial everywhere. The average public community college costs $2,500 per year in tuition; the average four-year public college costs $7,000; and the average private college costs $26,300.[3] If you live on campus, count on another five or six thousand dollars for room and board.

Nothing about college is cheap. It takes enormous expenditures of three often scarce commodities: energy, time, and money. Perhaps surprisingly, many students find money the easiest of them to find. While it's not simple to get financial aid and no one is going to walk up to you and offer you an all-expenses-paid scholarship, you can find many sources of funding for your education if you are persistent.

To find this money, however, you will need to spend ample amounts of the other two scarce commodities: time and energy. The entire process of securing financial aid takes a considerable amount of preparation, because you need to identify potential sources of funds and then apply for them. You should assume the process will take somewhere between several weeks and several months, depending on the type of aid you're applying for.

Identifying the Different Types of Funding Available

Funding for college comes in three basic categories: loans, grants, and scholarships. Although each supplies you with funds for college, they do so in very different ways.

Getting the Most Out of Your Classes: How Cutting Classes Costs

Think about how much college costs you each term. Go ahead and add it up: tuition, books, transportation, housing, food, supplies, etc., etc. It's a pretty hefty sum.

Now count the number of hours you're in class during the term. If you divide the number of hours into the amount you spend on college, you'll come up with a dollar value that shows how much every hour of the courses in which you're enrolled is worth.

What you'll immediately see is that every class is worth a great deal. For most students, missing a day's worth of classes is the equivalent of giving up $50 at the very minimum. Students attending expensive private colleges may be losing hundreds of dollars.

If all the other reasons for not missing a class aren't convincing enough, then think in these economic terms. Giving away something you've paid for is irrational. It's really no different than buying thousands of dollars' worth of CDs and then throwing them away, one by one, over the course of the semester. Only in the case of your college courses, what you're giving is far more precious—your education.

Consequently, resolve to get your money's worth out of your courses by attending them faithfully. Not only will you benefit economically, but you'll maximize your chances for learning the material and ultimately being successful in your college career and beyond.

▸ **Loans.** When you receive a **loan,** a bank, credit union, or other agency provides funds that must be repaid after a specified period of time. A loan carries a particular interest rate, which is stated as an annual percentage rate. Think of a loan as renting money: As long as you have the use of someone else's money, you have to pay them "rent" for the privilege. Banks and other lending agencies make money through the interest they charge on loans, just as they do with credit cards.

For example, suppose a bank gives you a $5,000 loan that has an interest rate of 8 percent per year. Not only must you pay back the $5,000 over a specified period, but you must pay the bank interest of 8 percent on the balance that you owe on the loan. Obviously, the higher the interest rate, the more you are paying for the privilege of borrowing the bank's money.

Three factors must be considered when you receive a loan: the stated amount of the loan (called the **principal**), the interest rate (stated as a percentage), and the length of the loan (referred to as the **term** of the loan). All three factors are important, because they determine how much your payments will be when you pay the loan back.

Many loans for college have an enormous advantage over loans you'll take out for other purchases, such as a car or house, because payments on college loans are *deferred* until you graduate and (presumably!) begin to earn an income—that is, it is often not necessary to start paying back the loan until you graduate. Depending on the type of loan you take out, interest on the loan is either paid for by the government while you are enrolled in college or is deferred until you graduate.

There are several national loan programs, sponsored by the federal government, that lend money to students. The major ones include the following:

• **Stafford loans.** Stafford loans are available to any student who is registered at least half-time and is a U.S. citizen or permanent resident. They provide from just over $2,600 to $10,000 a year.

Loan
Funds provided by a bank, credit union, or other agency that must be repaid after a specified period of time

Principal
The stated amount of a loan

Term
The length of time for which money is lent

"If you would be wealthy, think of saving as well as getting."
—Benjamin Franklin

Stafford loans come in two types: subsidized and unsubsidized. *Subsidized Stafford loans* are awarded through colleges on the basis of student financial need. For subsidized loans, the government pays interest until repayment begins, typically after the student graduates. *Unsubsidized Stafford loans* do not require demonstration of financial need. Interest is not paid by the government; instead it accumulates while the student is in college. However, the student doesn't have to make any payments until after graduation, when both principal and accumulated interest must be repaid over a specified period, which is up to 10 years.

- **PLUS loans.** If your parents support you and claim you as a deduction on their income tax return, they may take out a PLUS loan. PLUS loans can cover up to the full amount of a student's cost of college attendance and can be paid back over a 10-year period.

- **Perkins loans.** Perkins loans have a low interest rate. They are awarded on the basis of exceptional financial need, as determined by a student's college. The loans are made by a school's financial aid office.

College loans like these are relatively easy to get, though more difficult in the wake of the 2008 stock market crash. It is also important to remember that someday you'll need to pay them back. And many students are paying back a great deal. For instance, the average indebtedness is almost $9,000 for community college students and $22,700 for 4-year college students.[4]

Because college graduates often start off earning less than they thought they would after graduation, high levels of debt can lead to difficulties. More than half of graduates feel burdened by their debt, and a quarter report having significant problems paying back their loans. Consequently, think hard when taking out a loan and consider how much you'll have to pay back each month after you graduate.

Grant
An award of money that does not have to be repaid

> **Grants.** A **grant** is money that does not have to be repaid. Obviously, it's more advantageous to receive a grant than a loan. And not surprisingly, it's harder to qualify for grants than loans—harder, but not impossible. Several grant programs exist that can help reduce the amount you'll need to pay for college. They include the following:

- **Pell grants.** Based on need, Pell grants are provided to undergraduate students who have earned no previous degrees. They are awarded by college financial aid offices, which follow a formula provided by the federal government. Every student who meets certain need criteria is eligible for a Pell grant, ensuring that the neediest students receive some support.

- **Federal Supplemental Educational Opportunity Grants (FSEOG).** The government supplies a limited number of FSEOGs to every college, which can provide these grants to needy students. Unlike Pell grants, which are guaranteed to every eligible student, FSEOGs are in limited supply. Once a college awards its allotment for a given year, no other awards are possible.

- **Work-study grants.** Work-study grants provide jobs for undergraduates with financial needs. The jobs are typically related to a student's course of study or involve community service work, and part of the salary is paid by the government. Because a work-study position is often part of a student's total package of financial aid, it is generally considered a grant, even though work is required.

Scholarship
An award of money to a student based on need or merit

> **Scholarships.** **Scholarships** are support awarded by colleges, organizations, and companies. Like a grant, a scholarship is money that does not have to be

repaid. Most scholarships are based primarily on a student's financial need, although some are based on merit. For instance, students with exceptional academic or athletic abilities may receive a scholarship even though they wouldn't necessarily qualify under typical need-based measures.

The most frequent source of scholarships is one's own college, which may give money to reduce tuition and fees. But there are literally thousands of organizations that provide scholarships, ranging from companies such as Microsoft to nonprofit groups, such as the Boy Scouts and Girl Scouts.

The federal government also provides some scholarships to students whose family income does not rise above certain levels. These include the following:

- **Hope scholarship.** The Hope scholarship is a tax credit that helps free up funds for college. Students receive a 100 percent tax credit for the first $1,000 of tuition and required fees, and a 50 percent credit on the second $1,000.

- **Lifetime learning tax credit.** This tax credit is targeted to older students who are going back to school, changing careers, or taking courses to upgrade their skills, as well as to juniors and seniors in 4-year colleges. Families can receive a 20 percent tax credit for the first $5,000 of tuition and fees, and the amount will increase in future years.

Researching Possible Sources of Financial Aid

As you can see, there are many sources of financial aid. The biggest problem often is finding them.

Your first stop on your search for sources of financial aid should be your college's financial aid office. Every college has one, and it tends to be one of the busiest places on campus.

Most student aid offices contain a great deal of information about possible sources of aid. But that's only a starting point. The library and the Web also contain many types of information that can direct you to specific possibilities. One place to get started is the Federal Student Aid Information Center in Washington, which can be reached at 1-800-4-FED-AID (1-800-433-3243) or on the Web at **studentaid.ed.gov/students/publications/ student_guide/index.html.** The center will send you "The Student Guide," which describes programs that account for almost three-fourths of all financial aid awarded to students.

Keep in mind, however, that where money is involved, there are scams. Do not pay money to someone who offers to identify obscure scholarships that will yield you thousands of dollars. It's unlikely that anyone could find sources that you couldn't find yourself through careful research. Be especially wary of Web sites that ask for a credit card number to provide you with online information. The results are likely to be disappointing. (The Web sites we provide at the end of the chapter are completely reputable.)

Whatever the potential source of financial aid, you'll be asked to bare your financial soul. There will also be forms galore. Before actually completing the forms, it will be important to gather the information you will need. If you are being supported by your parents, they will have to complete some of the forms.

"Good day, Madam. I'm working my son's way through college."

Keep track of deadlines! If you miss a deadline for applying for financial aid, you'll be out of luck; no exceptions are made. You'll just have to wait for another aid cycle.

Finally, make sure you know what your needs are. The typical costs of college include not only tuition but also fees, books, and supplies, as well as associated costs, such as transportation, housing, food, and child care.

Apply for Financial Aid

It may seem that for every dollar in aid you get, there is a different line to complete on a complicated form. Prepare yourself for a blizzard of paperwork.

Following are the steps in applying for financial aid:

> **Speak with a financial aid counselor at your school.** Because the best source of financial aid is your own college, make an appointment to discuss your needs with a campus financial aid counselor or officer. In addition to giving you the most up-to-date information about possible sources of aid, the college financial aid officer can provide you with the forms you need to fill out and a list of the deadlines you need to meet.

> **Decide how much aid you need.** It's important to ask for just the right amount of aid, neither too little nor too much. If you ask for too little aid, you may be strapped for funds during the school term. It's much more difficult to get aid in the middle of a term than during the normal application period.

> At the same time, don't apply for more financial aid than you actually need. First, there is an issue of equity: What you get in aid may reduce the pool for others, and if you receive surplus aid you may be preventing other students from getting their fair share. Second, you don't want to load yourself up with unnecessary debt. Most graduates pay from $150 to $175 a month to pay off their student loans; you don't want to end up with so much debt that your loan payments are even higher than this.

> **Fill out your college's application for financial aid.** Colleges have their own forms to apply for financial aid. Carefully fill the form out, making sure you file it before the required deadline. In fact, the earlier you get the form in, the better: Most schools have a limited pool of funds, and the earlier you get your application in, the higher your chances of getting an appropriate share of the financial aid pie.

> **Write a personal letter to accompany your application.** If you think there are factors that affect your ability to pay for college which are not adequately reflected in the application—such as a recent job loss—write a letter to the financial aid officer describing them.

> **Complete a Free Application for Federal Student Aid (FAFSA) and Financial Aid PROFILE.** The FAFSA and PROFILE are standard forms used to assess a student's financial capabilities and determine how much the student and family can be expected to contribute toward college expenses. One or both of the forms are used by almost every college. They require a great deal of information, including past, present, and expected income from all sources. Copies of several tax returns from prior years are also required.

> Be scrupulously honest when you complete the forms, which you can do on the Web at **www.fafsa.ed.gov** (for the FAFSA) and **profileonline.collegeboard.com** (for the PROFILE). If you fail to include a source of income that is later discovered by a financial aid provider, you may be required to repay immediately any aid that you have received. In addition, you may face

disciplinary measures that put your education in jeopardy; in the worst case, you may even face legal charges.

> **Wait.** It takes time for loan applications to be processed and financial aid decisions to be made. Be prepared to wait, and consider contingency plans for various possibilities.

Evaluate Your Financial Aid Package

Sometime later, when the college has had time to consider your application for aid, you will receive an official response. This is most likely to be in the form of a "package"—a combination of loans, grants, scholarships, and, perhaps, an offer of an on-campus job. This is the time for a thorough evaluation of the offer. Consider the various elements of the package carefully to determine whether, taken together, they will fully meet your financial needs.

Keep in mind that you may not have to accept every element of the package that is offered to you. For instance, you may decide to accept a scholarship but turn down a loan. That decision may mean that you'll have less debt after you graduate, but that you'll have to work more hours at a part-time job—a tradeoff that you may or may not wish to make.

What if the package doesn't seem sufficient? The most important thing is not to give up. A polite visit or call to the financial aid office is in order.

When you speak to someone from financial aid, lay out your difficulty with the package. If the aid is so low that you won't be able to attend college, let the financial aid office know. If you had noted special circumstances in a letter, ask if they were taken into account. (Sometimes letters and other vital pieces of information get overlooked.) Ask if there is a formal appeal process and, if there is, ask how to begin it.

Your main goal is to get the financial aid office to take a second look at your application. By being polite and to-the-point in your dealings with the office staff, you stand a better chance of having them reevaluate your application.

Having good grades will help your chances of getting the financial aid office to take a second look, and poor grades will hurt: If you are not doing well in your classes, you have less bargaining power.

What if the school is unable to come up with a greater level of support? The first step is to ask the staff of the financial aid office for advice. They may be able to suggest an approach that you initially overlooked. The second step is to redouble your research efforts. You may be able to take out a loan to make up the deficit. Finally, consider alternatives to full-time college attendance. It may be preferable to attend school part-time while working than to give up college altogether or to get so much into debt that it will be hard to pay off your loans.

Above all, don't give up! If it's important enough to you, you will be able to find some way to afford an education.

Show Me the Money: Building a Financial Philosophy

There's a famous line from *Jerry Maguire*, the 1996 Tom Cruise movie about a sports agent, in which an athlete claims his family motto is "Show me the money." That blunt statement might be used to illustrate one financial philosophy—that life revolves around money.

Many would disagree. For instance, authors Vicki Robin and Joe Dominguez argue in their book *Your Money or Your Life*[5] that most people find that money

5 Discover Your Personal Financial Philosophy

Begin to create a personal financial philosophy by completing this exercise. Start by completing this Attitudes Toward Money questionnaire.

	Strongly Disagree	Disagree	Neutral	Agree	Strongly Agree
1. Money is essential for happiness.					
2. Having money guarantees happiness.					
3. Money makes no difference to one's happiness.					
4. More money equals more happiness.					
5. Beyond having enough to live modestly on, money doesn't make much of a difference.					
6. I frequently worry about money.					
7. I frequently daydream about having a lot of money.					
8. If I suddenly had to live on very little money, I could adjust easily.					
9. If I suddenly won a lot of money, I would go on a spending spree.					
10. If I suddenly won a lot of money, I would share it with my relatives.					
11. If I suddenly won a lot of money, I would give a large percentage to charity.					
12. If I found a substantial amount of cash in a bag, I would try hard to find its rightful owner.					
13. If I could carry only a briefcase full of $100 bills out of a burning building or my pet dog, I would take the dog.					
14. I plan to make a lot of money in my career.					
15. I plan to make only enough money to live in reasonable comfort.					
16. It's great to have money.					
17. Money is a necessary evil.					
18. Money is the root of all evil.					

is a controlling force in their lives and, consequently, their major source of stress. Acquiring and spending money becomes an obsession, and the simple pleasures of life are lost. They outline an alternative approach in which we reprioritize our values, live frugally, and ultimately achieve financial independence.

Whether you choose to follow the path of Jerry Maguire or that of Vicki Robin and Joe Dominguez, the important thing is to develop your own personal

After completing the questionnaire, answer these questions about your sources of satisfaction.

1. Which activities that you engaged in over the last 5 years have given you the greatest satisfaction?

2. How much money did those activities cost?

3. How would you spend your time if you could do anything you chose?

4. How much money would this cost each year?

PERSONAL FINANCIAL PHILOSOPHY

Based on the results of your Attitudes Toward Money questionnaire and the sources of your satisfaction, sum up your personal financial philosophy here in a short paragraph:

To Try It online, go to www.mhhe.com/power.

financial philosophy. Consider the role that money plays in your life. How much does money motivate what you do? Are you interested in becoming rich, or do you tend to think more in terms of simply having enough to have a comfortable life, without lots of luxuries? What activities bring you the greatest satisfaction in life? Do those activities require a certain level of income? Explore these questions further in **Try It 5.**

College is one of the biggest investments that you'll ever make. If you only think of it in terms of its eventual financial payoff—getting a better job and leading a more affluent life—you'll be missing some central aspects of the process of educating yourself.

» LO 13.3 Keeping in Mind the Value of a College Education

Our present focus on paying for college has led us, of necessity, to focus on the dollars-and-cents of education. Without a doubt, college is expensive. On the other side of the equation, there's no question that having a college education has vast financial value: People who are college graduates earn nearly twice as much money each year as those with only a high school degree.

But the money we spend on education buys us far more than a better salary. It gives us a better understanding of the world and its people, insight into who we are, better job opportunities, and a chance to befriend people who share the common goal of becoming well-educated citizens of a global society.

It would be terribly shortsighted to put a price tag on education, deciding, in effect, that if you must pay a lot you won't bother with an education. You may need to choose your school according to the tuition it charges and the financial aid package it offers you, but that's not the same as choosing to skip college altogether because it is going to be financially stressful. An experience that will permit us to reach our potential is worth *everything*.

Speaking of Success

NAME: **Edmund Fixico**

SCHOOL: **Fort Berthold Community College,
New Town, North Dakota**

Although he always had thoughts about going to college, until recently circumstances and opportunities were not right for Edmund Fixico.

"I had always planned to go to college, but I dropped out of high school in the eleventh grade," said Fixico. Two years later, he completed high school work, but higher education remained a distant dream.

Fixico started work as a bricklayer at age 19 and continued for more than two decades before finally enrolling in college. His job and starting a family took much of his time and energy.

"I had to work, but also I knew I had to go back to school someday," he said. "My wife encouraged me, and finally—at the age of 42—I enrolled at Fort Berthold Community College."

Fixico, who is pursuing a degree in Human Services, had apprehensions about his return to school.

"I was concerned that everyone would be younger than me. But the average age at Fort Berthold is about 31, which made me feel more comfortable. I also wasn't sure I could still do many basic things, like math and writing. I felt I would have to learn everything over again in a short span of time," he added.

Fixico puts in long hours of studying, staying up late after the rest of his family has gone to bed. He also learned to ask for assistance from faculty and advisors.

"I'm pretty much a shy person, so it was hard for me to ask for help," he noted. "But the classes are small, and you have more time with the instructor. You can get to know them well, and they offered a lot of support."

One of the courses that proved to be a tremendous help was a class in study strategies. "One of my first classes had a writing assignment that asked us to describe what is going on in our lives, and so I wrote about starting college," said Fixico. "I also learned how to schedule my time because I work full time."

Fixico is determined to succeed, and he is making good progress toward his degree. A member of the Cheyenne-Arapo tribe of Oklahoma, he is motivated by a desire to show future generations of American Indians the value of a college education.

Looking Back

What purpose does a budget serve and how can I prepare and stick to one?

▸ Concerns about money can be significantly reduced through the creation of a budget by which spending and income can be planned, accounted for, and aligned with your goals.

▸ Budgets provide security by helping you control your finances and avoid surprises.

▸ The process of budgeting involves identifying your financial goals, keeping track of current expenses and estimating future expenses, and making the necessary adjustments to keep income and spending in balance.

▸ If financial difficulties arise, contact your creditors and arrange a plan for paying off the debt. If you need help in designing a repayment plan, nonprofit credit counselors can help.

What help is available to pay for my college education?

▸ Loans for education are available with reasonable interest rates and conditions, especially the ability to defer paying the loans back until after graduation. Several federal programs offer loan guarantees, interest subsidies, and lower interest rates.

▸ Grants offer money without requiring repayment. They are harder to receive than loans because they are typically reserved for people with exceptional financial need.

▸ Scholarships are usually awarded by colleges and other institutions based on either financial need or academic, athletic, or other abilities.

What is the value of a college education?

▸ A college degree leads to a significantly higher salary (college graduates earn nearly twice as much as those with only a high school degree).

▸ In addition, a college education offers a better understanding of the world, insight into ourselves, better job opportunities, and a chance to befriend people in a global society.

[KEY TERMS AND CONCEPTS]

Budget (p. 340)

Loan (p. 355)

Principal (p. 355)

Term (p. 355)

Grant (p. 356)

Scholarship (p. 356)

[RESOURCES]

ON CAMPUS

The bursar's or treasurer's office handles money affairs. Not only does it collect money owed for tuition, but it also may perform other services such as cashing checks.

If you are receiving financial aid, there is usually a particular office devoted to the complexities of scholarships, loan processing, and other forms of aid. The personnel in the office can be very helpful in maximizing your financial aid package as well as in solving financial problems related to your schooling. If you have a problem with your finances, see them sooner rather than later.

IN PRINT

Paying for College without Going Broke 2009 by Kalman Chany and Geoff Martz (Princeton Review, 2008) includes many practical tips for finding ways to finance a college education.

Fred Rewey's *Winning the Cash Flow War* (Wiley, 2005) offers a clear path to getting all your finances under control.

ON THE WEB

The following Web sites provide additional information about money matters. (Although the Web addresses were accurate at the time the book was printed, check the *P.O.W.E.R. Learning* Web site [**www.mhhe.com/power**] for any changes that may have occurred.)

‣ College Answer (**www.collegeanswer.com/index.jsp**) is a valuable, time-saving tool for students and their parents who are trying to identify sources of funds to pay for college. Through this service you can receive information about scholarships, fellowships, grants, work study, loan programs, tuition waivers, internships, competitions, and work co-operative programs.

‣ "FinAid: The SmartStudent Guide to College Financial Aid" (**www.finaid.org**) provides a free, comprehensive, independent, and objective guide to student financial aid. It was created by Mark Kantrowitz, author of *The Prentice Hall Guide to Scholarships and Fellowships for Math and Science Students*. The site's "calculators" page (**www.finaid.org/calculators/**) offers loads of online calculators including: College Cost Projector, Savings Plan Designer, Expected Family Contribution and Financial Aid Calculator, Loan Payment Calculator, and Student Loan Advisor (undergraduate).

‣ "Managing Your Money" (**www.nd.edu/%7Efinaid/managing_money/**), sponsored by the Office of Financial Aid at Notre Dame University, offers eight links covering everything from responsible borrowing to tips on developing credit card smarts.

‣ *Funding Education Beyond High School: The Guide to Federal Student Aid* is a comprehensive resource on the types of student financial aid from the U.S. Department of Education. It provides information on how to apply for grants, loans, and work-study through the Federal Student Aid office. This publication is available in pdf form on the U.S. Department of Education's Web site at **http://studentaid.ed.gov/students/publications/student_guide/index.html**.

] TAKING IT TO THE NET

1 Find four sources of financial aid. One possible strategy: Go to Yahoo! (**dir.yahoo.com**) and choose "Education," "Financial aid," then "Grants" or "Scholarship programs." What is available? What are the differences between scholarships and grants?

2 Discover three new ways to save money. Possible strategy: Using the search engine of your choice, enter the phrase "saving money." Examine the sites for tips and tricks to help you hold on to what you earn.

The case of . . .

Overdrawn, Overwrought, and Over Her Head

Her life was a house of cards, and someone had just pulled one out from the bottom.

At least that's what it felt like to Tara Kenko. The month had started out badly when Tara found that she had made a mistake in her checking account balance and had only $439, instead of the $939 she thought she had. After paying her share of the rent—$210—she didn't have enough money left to make her car payment. So she just put the bill aside, figuring that she'd take care of it later in the month when she got paid.

Things went from bad to worse 2 days later when her car refused to start. She had to have it towed to a mechanic, who told her that it would cost about $350 to get it fixed. She didn't have that either, but she figured she could put it on her credit card. But later, when she went to pick up her car and pay for the repair, which turned out to be closer to $400 than $350, her card was rejected. She called the credit card company from the repair shop and was told that she had exceeded her authorized credit limit. The mechanic wouldn't let her take her car until she paid for the repairs, so she was forced to leave it and catch a bus to campus.

The final straw came in her chemistry class. The instructor announced that students in the class would have to buy yet another textbook to help them with a particular set of experiments. Having already spent $150 for books in that class alone, Tara was both angry and dismayed. She had no idea how she was going to find the money to pay for the book, let alone her regular car payment and the car repairs. She was in deep financial trouble, and she didn't know what to do.

1. What should Tara do now to start addressing her problem? What steps should she take immediately?

2. Can you suggest some approaches Tara can take to deal with the problem of the new book for her chemistry class?

3. How do you think the mistake may have occurred in Tara's checking account? What advice would you give her to avoid a similar mistake in the future?

4. Given that Tara does not have a lot of leeway in her finances for multiple disasters such as the ones that befell her this month, what general course would you advise her to take as a way to plan her expenditures more effectively?

5. What steps might Tara take to decrease her expenses? What might she do to increase her income?

Stress, Health, and Wellness

Learning Outcomes

By the time you finish this chapter you will be able to

>> **LO 14.1** Explain what stress is and how to control it.

>> **LO 14.2** Discuss what is involved in keeping fit and healthy, and why this is important to do.

>> **LO 14.3** Identify the main threats to health and well-being.

>> **LO 14.4** Analyze the components of sexual health.

ouisa Denby's day began badly: She slept through her alarm and had to skip breakfast to catch the bus to campus. Then, when she went to the library to catch up on the reading she had to do before taking a test the next day, the one article she needed was missing. The librarian told her that replacing it would take 24 hours. Feeling frustrated, she walked to the computer lab to print out the paper she had completed at home the night before.

The computer wouldn't read her flash drive. She searched for someone to help her, but she was unable to find anyone who knew any more about computers than she did.

It was only 9:42 A.M., and Louisa had a wracking headache. Apart from that pain, she was conscious of only one feeling: stress.

Looking Ahead

Have you had days like Louisa's? Are most of your days like hers? Then you're no stranger to stress. It's something that all college students experience to varying degrees throughout their college careers. In fact, almost a one-third of first-year college students report feeling frequently overwhelmed with all they need to do.[1]

Coping with stress is one of the challenges that college students face. The many demands on your time can make you feel that you'll never finish what needs to get done. This pressure produces wear and tear on your body and mind, and it's easy to fall prey to ill health as a result.

However, stress and poor health are not inevitable outcomes of college. In fact, by following simple guidelines and deciding to make health a conscious priority, you can maintain good physical and mental health.

This chapter covers the ways you can keep fit and healthy during—and beyond—college. It offers suggestions on how you can cope with stress, improve your diet, get enough exercise, and sleep better. It also will help you consider particular threats to mental and physical health that you're likely to face while you are in college, including alcohol and drugs, pregnancy, sexually transmitted infections, and rape.

» LO 14.1 Living with Stress

Stressed out? Tests, papers, reading assignments, job demands, roommate problems, volunteer activities, committee work. . . . It's no surprise that these can produce stress. But it may be a surprise to know that so can graduating from high school, starting your dream job, falling in love, getting married, and even winning the lottery.

Virtually *anything*—good or bad—is capable of producing stress if it presents us with a challenge. **Stress** is the physical and emotional response we have to events that threaten or challenge us. It is rooted in the primitive "fight or flight" response wired into all animals—human and nonhuman. You see it in cats, for instance, when confronted by a dog or other threat: Their backs go up, their fur stands on end, their eyes widen, and, ultimately, they either take off or attack. The challenge stimulating this revved-up response is called a *stressor*. For humans, stressors can range from a first date to losing our chemistry notes to facing a flash flood.

Because our everyday lives are filled with events that can be interpreted as threatening or challenging, stress is commonplace in most people's lives. There are three main types of stressors:

1. **Cataclysmic events** are events that occur suddenly and affect many people simultaneously. Tornadoes, hurricanes, and plane crashes are examples of

Stress

The physical and emotional response to events that threaten or challenge us

Cataclysmic events

Sudden, powerful events that occur quickly and affect many people simultaneously cataclysmic events. Although they may produce powerful immediate consequences, ironically they produce less stress than other types of stressors. The reason? Cataclysmic events have a clear end point, which can make them more manageable. Furthermore, because they affect many people simultaneously, their consequences are shared with others, and no individual feels singled out.

2. **Personal stressors** are major life events that produce a negative physical and psychological reaction. Failing a course, losing a job, and ending a relationship are all examples of personal stressors. Sometimes positive events—such as getting married or starting a new job—can act as personal stressors. Although the short-term impact of a personal stressor can be difficult, the long-term consequences may decline as people learn to adapt to the situation.

3. **Daily hassles** are the minor irritants of life that, singly, produce relatively little stress. Waiting in a traffic jam, receiving a tuition bill riddled with mistakes, and being interrupted by noises of major construction while trying to study are examples of such minor irritants. However, daily hassles add up, and cumulatively they can produce even more stress than a single larger-scale event. (**Figure 14.1** indicates the most common daily hassles in people's lives.[2])

Personal stressors
Major life events that produce stress

Daily hassles
The minor irritants of life that, by themselves, produce little stress, but which can add up and produce more stress than a single larger-scale event

What Is Happening When We Are Stressed?

Stress does more than make us feel anxious, upset, and fearful. Beneath those responses, we are experiencing many different physical reactions, each placing a high demand on our body's resources. Our hearts beat faster, our breathing becomes more rapid and shallow, and we produce more sweat. Our internal organs churn out a variety of hormones. In the long run, these physical responses wear down our immune system, our body's defense against disease. We become more susceptible to a variety of diseases, ranging from the common cold and headaches to strokes and heart disease. In fact, surveys have found that the greater the number of stressful events a person experiences over the course of a year, the more likely it is that he or she will have a major illness (see **Try It 1** on page 370, "Assess Your Susceptibility to Stress-Related Illness").

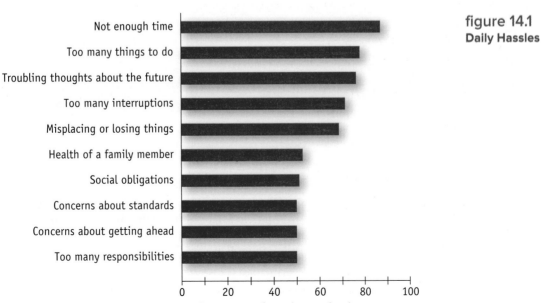

figure 14.1
Daily Hassles

Try It!

1

Assess Your Susceptibility to Stress-Related Illness

Are you susceptible to a stress-related illness? The more stress in your life, the more likely it is that you will experience a major illness.

To determine the stress in your life, take the stressor value given beside each event you have experienced and multiply it by the number of occurrences over the past year (up to a maximum of four), and then add up these scores.[3]

87 Experienced the death of a spouse

77 Got married

77 Experienced the death of a close family member

76 Were divorced

74 Experienced a marital separation

68 Experienced the death of a close friend

68 Experienced pregnancy or fathered a pregnancy

65 Had a major personal injury or illness

62 Were fired from work

60 Ended a marital engagement or a steady relationship

58 Had sexual difficulties

58 Experienced a marital reconciliation

57 Had a major change in self-concept or self-awareness

56 Experienced a major change in the health or behavior of a family member

54 Became engaged to be married

53 Had a major change in financial status

52 Took on a mortgage or loan of more than $10,000

52 Had a major change in use of drugs

50 Had a major conflict or change in values

50 Had a major change in the number of arguments with your spouse

50 Gained a new family member

50 Entered college

50 Changed to a new school

50 Changed to a different line of work

49 Had a major change in amount of independence and responsibility

47 Had a major change in responsibilities at work

Handling Stress

Stress is an inevitable part of life. In fact, a life with no stress at all would be so boring, so uneventful, that you'd quickly miss the stress that had been removed.

That doesn't mean, though, that we have to sit back and accept stress when it does arise. **Coping** is the effort to control, reduce, or tolerate the threats that lead to stress. Using the P.O.W.E.R. principles (illustrated in the P.O.W.E.R. Plan on page 372) can help you ward off stress and actively deal with it.

Coping
The effort to control, reduce, or learn to tolerate the threats that lead to stress

46 Experienced a major change in use of alcohol

45 Revised personal habits

44 Had trouble with school administration

43 Held a job while attending school

43 Had a major change in social activities

42 Had trouble with in-laws

42 Had a major change in working hours or conditions

42 Changed residence or living conditions

41 Had your spouse begin or cease work outside the home

41 Changed your choice of major field of study

41 Changed dating habits

40 Had an outstanding personal achievement

38 Had trouble with your boss

38 Had a major change in amount of participation in school activities

37 Had a major change in type and/or amount of recreation

36 Had a major change in religious activities

34 Had a major change of sleeping habits

33 Took a trip or vacation

30 Had a major change in eating habits

26 Had a major change in the number of family get-togethers

22 Were found guilty of minor violations of the law

Scoring: If your total score is above 1,435, you are in a high-stress category and therefore more at risk for experiencing a stress-related illness.

But keep in mind the limitations of this questionnaire. There may be factors in your life that produce high stress that are not listed. In addition, a high score does not mean that you are sure to get sick. Many other factors determine ill health, and high stress is only one cause. Other positive factors in your life, such as getting enough sleep and exercise, may prevent illness.

Still, having an unusually high amount of stress in your life is a cause for concern. If you do score high, you may want to take steps to reduce it.

To Try It online, go to www.mhhe.com/power.

P Prepare ## Readying Yourself Physically

Being in good physical condition is the primary way to prepare for future stress. Stress takes its toll on your body, so it makes sense that the stronger and fitter you are, the less negative impact stress will have on you. For example, a regular exercise program reduces heart rate, respiration rate, and blood pressure at times when the body is at rest—making us better able to withstand the negative consequences of stress. Furthermore, vigorous exercise produces endorphins, natural painkilling

Prepare
Ready yourself physically

Organize
Identify what is causing you stress

Work
Develop effective coping strategies

Evaluate
Ask yourself if your strategies for dealing with stress are effective

Rethink
Place stress in perspective

P.O.W.E.R. Plan

chemicals in the brain. Endorphins produce feelings of happiness—even euphoria—and may be responsible for the "runner's high," the positive feelings often reported by long-distance runners following long runs. Through the production of endorphins then, exercise can help our bodies produce a natural coping response to stress.

If you now drink a lot of coffee or soda, a change in your diet may be enough to bring about a reduction in stress. Coffee, soda, chocolate, and a surprising number of other foods contain caffeine, which can make you feel jittery and anxious even without stress; add a stressor, and the reaction can be very intense and unpleasant.

Eating right can alleviate another problem: obesity. Around one-third of people in the United States are obese, defined as having body weight more than 20 percent above the average weight for a person of a given height. In addition, students often gain weight during the first year of college, averaging an increase of 5 to 7 pounds. One in six students gains 10 pounds or more.

Being overweight can bring on stress for several reasons. For one thing, the extra pounds drag down the functioning of the body. This can lead to fatigue and a reduced ability to bounce back when we encounter challenges to our well-being. In addition, feeling heavy in a society that acclaims the virtues of slimness can be stressful in and of itself.

Organize Identifying What Is Causing You Stress

You can't cope effectively with stress until you know what's causing it. In some cases, it's obvious—a series of bad test grades in a course, a roommate problem that keeps getting worse, a job supervisor who seems to delight in making things difficult. In other cases, however, the causes of stress may be more subtle. Perhaps your relationship with your boyfriend or girlfriend is rocky, and you have a nagging feeling that something is wrong.

Whatever the source of stress, you can't deal with it unless you know what it is. To organize your assault on stress, take a piece of paper and list the major circumstances that are causing you stress. Just listing them will help put you in control, and you'll be better able to figure out strategies for coping with them.

> ### Sources of Stress
> 1. Government professor talks so fast that notetaking is nearly impossible
> 2. Difficulty paying rent this month.
> 3. Not enough time to study for Tuesday's psych test

Work Developing Effective Coping Strategies

A wide variety of tactics can help you deal with stress. Among the most effective approaches to coping are these:

- **Take charge of the situation.** Stress is most apt to arise when we are faced with situations over which we have little or no control. If you take charge of the situation, you'll reduce the experience of stress. For example, if several assignments are all due on the same day, you might try negotiating with one of your instructors for a later due date.

- **Don't waste energy trying to change the unchangeable.** There are some situations that you simply can't control. You can't change the fact that you have come down with a case of mono, and you can't change your performance on a test you took last week. Don't hit your head against a brick wall and try to modify things that can't be changed. Use your energy to improve the situation, not to rewrite history.

- **Look for the silver lining.** Stress arises when we perceive a situation as threatening. If we can change how we perceive that situation, we can change our reactions to it. For instance, if your computer science instructor requires you to learn a difficult spreadsheet program in a very short time, the saving grace is that you may be able to use the skill to your advantage in getting a high-paying temporary job during school vacation. (You can practice finding the silver lining in **Try It 2** on page 374.)

- **Talk to friends and family. Social support,** assistance and comfort supplied by others, can help us through stressful periods. Turning to our friends and family and simply talking about the stress we're under can help us tolerate it more effectively. Even anonymous telephone hotlines can provide us with social support. (The U.S. Department of Health and Human Services maintains a master toll-free number that can provide telephone numbers and addresses of many national helplines and support groups. You can reach it by calling 1-800-336-4797.)

- **Relax.** Because stress produces constant wear and tear on the body, it seems possible that practices that lead to the relaxation of the body might lead to a reduction in stress. And that's just what happens. Using any one of several techniques for producing physical relaxation can prevent stress. Among the best relaxation techniques:

  Meditation. Though often associated with its roots in the ancient Eastern religion of Zen Buddhism, meditation, a technique for refocusing attention and producing bodily relaxation, is practiced in some form by members of virtually every major religion. Meditation reduces blood pressure, slows respiration, and in general reduces bodily tension.

  How do you meditate? The process is actually rather simple. As summarized in **Table 14.1** on page 375, it includes sitting in a quiet room with eyes closed or focused on a point about 6 feet away from you and paying attention to your breathing. Though the specifics of what you do may vary, meditation works by helping you concentrate on breathing deeply and rhythmically, sometimes murmuring a word or sound repeatedly.

  Progressive relaxation. Progressive relaxation does some of the same things that meditation does, but in a more direct way. To use progressive relaxation, you systematically tense and then relax different groups of muscles. For example, you might start with your lower arm, tensing it for 5 seconds and then relaxing it for a similar amount of time. By doing the same thing throughout the parts of

"A smooth sea never made a skillful mariner."
English proverb

Social support
Assistance and comfort supplied by others in times of stress

CHAPTER FOURTEEN Stress, Health, and Wellness

Try It!

Look for the Silver Lining

Consider the following list of potentially stressful situations. Try to find something positive—a silver lining—in each of them. The first two are completed to get you started.

Situation	Silver Lining
1. Your car just broke down and repairing it is more than you can afford right now.	1. This is the perfect time to begin exercising by walking and using your bicycle.
2. Your boss just yelled at you and threatened to fire you.	2. Either this is a good time to open an honest discussion with your boss about your job situation, OR this is a good time to get a more interesting job.
3. You have two papers due on Monday and there's a great concert you wanted to go to on Saturday night.	3.
4. You just failed an important test.	4.
5. You're flat broke, you have a date to go to a play on Saturday night, and you can't afford the tickets.	5.
6. Your last date went poorly and you think your girlfriend/boyfriend was hinting that it was time to break up.	6.
7. You just found out you missed the due date for your student loan application.	7.
8. You just got cut from a sports team you loved.	8.
9. Your best friend is starting to turn weird and seems not to enjoy being with you as much as before.	9.
10. You just realized you don't really like your academic major, and you're not even sure you like your college much anymore.	10.

 WORKING IN A GROUP:

After you have considered each of these situations individually, discuss each of them in a group. What similarities and differences in others' responses did you find? Evaluate the different responses, and consider whether—and why—some ways of reframing the situations were better than others.

To Try It online, go to www.mhhe.com/power.

your body, you'll be able to learn the "feel" of bodily relaxation. You can use the technique when you feel that stress is getting the better of you. (Use **Try It 3** on page 376 to experience progressive relaxation for yourself.)

> **Remember that wimping out doesn't work—so keep your commitments.** Suppose you've promised a friend that you'll help him move, and you've

table 14.1 Methods of Meditation

Step 1. Pick a focus word or short phrase that's firmly rooted in your personal belief system. For example, a nonreligious individual might choose a neutral word like *one* or *peace* or *love*. A Christian person desiring to use a prayer could pick the opening words of Psalm 23, *The Lord is my shepherd;* a Jewish person could choose *Shalom.*

Step 2. Sit quietly in a comfortable position.

Step 3. Close your eyes.

Step 4. Relax your muscles.

Step 5. Breathe slowly and naturally, repeating your focus word or phrase silently as you exhale.

Step 6. Throughout, assume a passive attitude. Don't worry about how well you're doing. When other thoughts come to mind, simply say to yourself. "Oh, well," and gently return to the repetition.

Step 7. Continue for 10 to 20 minutes. You may open your eyes to check the time, but do not use an alarm. When you finish, sit quietly for a minute or so, at first with your eyes closed and later with your eyes open. Then do not stand for one or two minutes.

Step 8. Practice the technique once or twice a day.

promised yourself that you'll spend more time with your children. You've also been elected to the student body governing board, and you've made a commitment to bring more speakers to campus. Now you are facing all the demands connected to these commitments and feeling stressed.

You may be tempted to cope with the feeling by breaking some or all of your commitments, thinking, "I just need to sit at home and relax in front of the television!" This is not coping. It is escaping, and it doesn't reduce stress. Ducking out of commitments, whether to yourself or to others, will make you feel guilty and anxious and will be another source of stress—one without the satisfaction of having accomplished what you set out to do. Keep your promises.

E Evaluate Asking If Your Strategies for Dealing with Stress Are Effective

Just as the experience of stress depends on how we interpret circumstances, the strategies for dealing with stress also vary in effectiveness depending on who we are. So if your efforts at coping aren't working, it's time to reconsider your approach. If talking to friends hasn't helped ease your stress response, maybe you need a different approach. Maybe you need to see the silver lining or cut back on some of your commitments.

If one coping strategy doesn't work for you, try another. What's critical is that you not become paralyzed, unable to deal with a situation. Instead, try something different until you find the right combination of strategies to improve the situation.

Try It!

3

Try Progressive Relaxation

You can undertake progressive relaxation almost anywhere, including the library, a sports field, or a classroom, because tensing and relaxing muscles is quiet and unobtrusive. Although the following exercise suggests you lie down, you can use parts of it no matter where you are.

1. Lie flat on your back, get comfortable, and focus on your toes.
2. Become aware of your left toes. Bunch them up into a tight ball, then let them go. Then let them relax even further.
3. Now work on your left foot, from the toes to the heel. Without tensing your toes, tighten up the rest of your foot and then let it relax. Then relax it more.
4. Work your way up your left leg, first tensing and then relaxing each part. You may move up as slowly or as quickly as you wish, using big leaps (e.g., the entire lower leg) or small steps (e.g., the ankle, the calf, the front of the lower leg, the knee, etc.).
5. Repeat the process for the right leg.
6. Now tense and relax progressively your groin, buttocks, abdomen, lower back, ribs, upper back, and shoulders.
7. Work your way down each arm, one at a time, until you reach the fingers.
8. Return to the neck, then the jaw, cheeks, nose, eyes, ears, forehead, and skull.

By now you should be completely relaxed. In fact, you may even be asleep—this technique works well as a sleep-induction strategy.

To vary the routine, play with it. Try going from top to bottom, or from your extremities in and ending with your groin. Or target any other part of your body to end up at, and take the most circuitous route you can think of.

To Try It online, go to www.mhhe.com/power.

R Rethink   ## Placing Stress in Perspective

It's easy to think of stress as an enemy. In fact, the coping steps outlined in the P.O.W.E.R. Plan are geared to overcoming its negative consequences. But consider the following two principles, which in the end may help you more than any others in dealing with stress:

> **Don't sweat the small stuff . . . and it's all small stuff.** Stress expert Richard Carlson[4] emphasizes the importance of putting the circumstances we encounter into the proper perspective. He argues that we frequently let ourselves get upset about situations that are actually minor.
>
> So what if someone cuts us off in traffic, or does less than his or her share on a group project, or unfairly criticizes us? It's hardly the end of the world. If an unpleasant event has no long-term consequences, it's often best to let it go. One of the best ways to reduce stress, consequently, is to maintain an appropriate perspective on the events of your life.

> **Make peace with stress.** Think of what it would be like to have no stress—none at all—in your life. Would you really be happier, better adjusted, and more successful? The answer is "probably not." A life that presented no challenges would probably be, in a word, boring. So think about stress as an exciting, although admittedly sometimes difficult, friend. Welcome it, because its presence indicates that your life is stimulating, challenging, and exciting—and who would want it any other way?

Anticipating Job Stress

Students are not the only ones who have to cope with stress. It's also one of the prime hazards of the world of work. Illnesses related to job stress result in costs of $150 billion each year.

Consequently, taking potential stress into account should be an important consideration when choosing a profession. Asking yourself the following questions can help you identify the factors that may induce stress on the job:

- How much control over working conditions will I have? (The more control an employee has in day-to-day decision making, the lower the level of stress.)

- What are the demands of the job? Will I face constant demands to do more work and to work more quickly? (Higher work demands create a more stressful work environment.)

- What is the tolerance for error? (Some occupations, such as air traffic controller, have no margin for error, while others, such as many white-collar professions, give workers a second chance if they make a mistake.)

- How closely do my abilities and strengths match the requirements of the job? (A good match between one's abilities and the demands of a job is the best insurance against an unduly stressful work environment.)

- How well do I cope with stress?

If your coping skills are good, you may be suited for entering a high-stress occupation. But if you have difficulty dealing with stress, choosing a career in a field that produces less stress makes more sense.

Career Connections

Depression and Suicide

Almost no student passes through college without at least occasionally feeling depressed. The stress of college life can lead to feeling sadness, unhappiness, and even hopelessness on occasion.

Most of the time, depression is a normal reaction to distressing circumstances. It may occur in response to the death of a loved one, the end of a relationship, failure at an important task, or any number of events. Usually, the depression is temporary, and people return to their normal emotional state.

For some students, however, depression is more than fleeting. Around 3 percent of people suffer from *major depression,* a psychological disorder in which depression is severe and lasts more than two weeks. Major depression can occur without any obvious cause, and students who suffer from it feel extremely sad, hopeless, tired, and worthless.

Major depression ultimately can lead to suicide. But suicide occurs for other reasons. For instance, those who commit suicide may be perfectionists, inhibited socially, or prone to extreme anxiety when they face any social or academic challenge.

Several warning signs indicate when a student's problems may be severe enough to justify concern about the possibility of a suicide attempt. They include:

- School problems, such as missing classes and a sudden change in grades

- Frequent incidents of self-destructive behavior, such as careless accidents

- Loss of appetite or excessive eating

- Withdrawal from friends and peers

- Sleeping problems

- Signs of depression, tearfulness, or overt indications of psychological difficulties, such as hallucinations

- A preoccupation with death, an afterlife, or what would happen "if I died"
- Putting affairs in order, such as giving away prized possessions or making arrangements for the care of a pet
- An explicit announcement of suicidal thoughts

If you know someone who shows signs that he or she is suicidal, urge that person to seek professional help. You may need to take assertive action, such as enlisting the assistance of family members, counselors, or instructors. This requirement is especially true if people say they feel urges to harm not only themselves but others. Talk of hurting oneself or others is a serious signal for help, not a confidence to be kept.

For immediate help with a suicide-related problem, you can call the following national hotlines that are staffed with trained counselors: 800-784-2433 or 800-448-3000.

Responding to Death and Grief

One of the most stressful experiences that one can endure is the death of a loved one. Even if the death is not unexpected, as with an elderly grandparent, the finality and sense of loss can be immense. When it is a surprise—as when a friend commits suicide, a family member is killed in war, or a parent unexpectedly succumbs to a heart attack—the pain can be overwhelming.

Although everyone's grief is different, people's reactions usually follow a pattern. Initially, people feel shock and numbness, and they may even deny the death. Reality soon sets in, however, and people experience the pain of the death. They typically feel enormous sadness, depression, and yearning for the dead individual.

In time, however, people accept the death and move on with their lives. Although intense feelings of grief may occur, people usually are able to pick up their lives, and their happiness returns to its previous level.

If you experience the death of a loved one, there are several things you can do to maintain your mental health and your academic standing:

- Expect that your grief will be intense and painful—but understand that it will not always be so painful. With time, feelings of sadness begin to subside.
- Talk to others about your feelings. Family and friends, some of whom may also be experiencing the grief, can help you sort out your reactions and bring you comfort.
- Don't hesitate to voice your recollections of the person who has died. Talking about the person who has died can be therapeutic.
- Be sure to let your college officials know about your situation. If you have to leave campus to attend a funeral, tell someone in your Dean's Office, and they can contact your instructors. When you return to campus, get in touch with each of your instructors to catch up on the work you missed.

≫ LO 14.2 Keeping Well

Eat right. Exercise. Get plenty of sleep.

Pretty simple, isn't it? We learn the fundamentals of fitness and health in the first years of elementary school.

Yet for millions of us, wellness is an elusive goal. We eat on the fly, stopping for a bite at the drive-in window of a fast-food restaurant. Most of us don't exercise enough, either because we feel we don't have enough time or because it's not much fun for us. And as for sleep, we're a nation in which getting by with as little sleep as possible is seen as a badge of honor.

You can buck the trends, however; you can begin to eat more properly, exercise effectively, and sleep better by following several basic rules. They include the following:

> "The first wealth is health."
> Ralph Waldo Emerson, author and poet

Eating Right

> **Eat a variety of "whole" foods, including fruits, vegetables, and grain products.** Strive to eat a range of different foods. If you make variety your goal, you will end up eating the right foods. You can learn more about maintaining variety in your diet by visiting the government Web site (**www.mypyramid .gov**) that describes the food guide "pyramid" and allows you to construct a personalized eating plan.

> **Avoid processed foods.** Make an effort to choose "whole" foods, or foods in a state as close as possible to their natural state: Brown rice is better than white rice, and both are better than a preservative-filled, packaged "rice casserole" mix.

> **Avoid foods that are high in sugar and salt content.** Read labels on product packages carefully and beware of hidden sugars and salts. Many ingredients that end in -ose (such as dextrose, sucrose, maltose, and fructose) are actually sugars; salt can lurk within any number of compounds beginning with the word *sodium*.

> **Seek a diet low in fat and cholesterol.** The fat that is to be especially avoided is saturated fat—the most difficult for your body to rid itself of.

> **Remember: Less is more.** You don't need to walk away stuffed from every meal. Moderation is the key. To be sure you don't eat more than your body is telling you to eat, pay attention to internal hunger cues.

> **Schedule three regular meals a day.** Eating should be a priority—a definite part of your daily schedule. Avoid skipping any meals. Breakfast is particularly important; get up early enough to eat a full meal.

> **Be sensitive to the hidden contents of various foods.** Soda and chocolate can contain substantial quantities of caffeine, which can disrupt your sleep and, along with coffee, become addictive. Many cereals—even those labeled "low fat"—contain a considerable amount of sugar or salt. Pay attention to labels. And watch out for fast foods: Research finds that eating fast foods just a few times a week leads to significant weight gains over the long run.[5]

> **If you want to loss weight, follow a sensible diet.** There's really only one proven way to lose weight: Control your food portions, eat a well-balanced diet, and increase the amount of exercise you get. Fad, quick-fix diets are ineffective.

> **Beware of eating disorders.** Between 1 and 4 percent of college-age women, and a smaller percentage of

The lure of fast food is difficult to resist, and eating a balanced, nutritious diet is a challenge for most college students.

men, suffer from an eating disorder. Those with *anorexia nervosa* may refuse to eat, while denying that there is anything unusual in their behavior and appearance—which can become skeletal. Some 15 to 20 percent of those with anorexia literally starve themselves to death. *Bulimia* is a disorder in which individuals binge on incredibly large quantities of food, such as a gallon of ice cream and a whole pie, but later feel so much guilt and depression that they induce vomiting or take laxatives to rid themselves of the food. Eating disorders represent serious threats to health and require aggressive medical intervention. (If you need advice or help with an eating problem, contact the National Eating Disorders Association at **www.nationaleatingdisorders.org** or call 800-931-2237.)

Making Exercise a Part of Your Life

Exercise produces a variety of benefits. Your body will run more efficiently, you'll have more energy, your heart and circulatory system will run more smoothly, and you'll be able to bounce back from stress and illness more quickly.

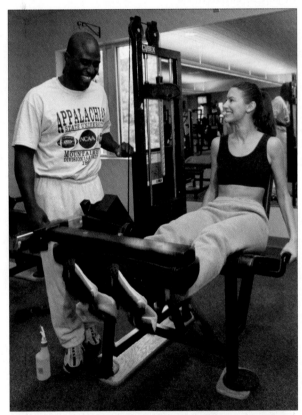

To maintain the habit of exercising, you need to choose an activity you enjoy doing. In addition, working out with others turns exercise into a social activity and gives you social support, increasing the chances you'll stick with an exercise regimen.

> **Choose a type of exercise that you like.** Exercising will be a chore that you end up avoiding if you don't enjoy what you're doing.

> **Incorporate exercise into your life.** Take the stairs instead of elevators. Leave your car at home and walk to campus or work. When you're on campus, take the longer way to reach your destination.

> **Make exercise a group activity.** Exercising with others brings you social support and turns exercise into a social activity. You'll be more likely to stick to a program if you have a regular "exercise date" with a friend.

> **Vary your routine.** You don't need to do the same kind of exercise day after day. Choose different sorts of activities that will involve different parts of your body and keep you from getting bored. For example, for cardiovascular fitness, you might alternate between running, swimming, biking, or using a cardio training machine.

One note of caution: Before you begin an exercise program, it is a good idea to have a physical checkup, even if you feel you're in the peak of health. This is especially true if you're starting an exercise program after years of inactivity. You also might consult a personal trainer at the gym to set up a program that gradually builds you up to more vigorous exercise.

Getting a Good Night's Sleep

Do you feel as if you don't get enough sleep? You probably don't. Most college students are sleep-deprived, a condition that causes them to feel fatigued, short-tempered, and tense. Sleep deprivation makes staying alert in class nearly impossible (see the **Course Connections** feature).

Staying Alert in Class

If you're having trouble staying alert and—even worse—staying awake in class, the best solution is to get more sleep. Short of that, there are several strategies you can try to help stay awake:

- Throw yourself into the class. Pay close attention, take notes, ask questions, and generally be fully engaged in the class. You should do this anyway, but making a special effort when you're exhausted can get you through a period of fatigue.

- Sit up straight. Pinch yourself. Stretch your muscles in different parts of your body. Fidget. Any activity will help you thwart fatigue and feel more alert.

- Eat or drink something cold in class. If your instructor permits it, the mere activity of eating a snack or drinking can help you stay awake.

- Avoid heavy meals before class. Your body's natural reaction to a full stomach is to call for a nap, the opposite of what you want to achieve.

- Stay cool. Take off your coat or jacket and sit by an open window. If it's warm, ask your instructor if there's a way to make the classroom cooler.

- Take off *one* shoe. This creates a temperature difference, which can be helpful in keeping you awake.

Ultimately, insufficient sleep leads to declines in academic and physical performance. You can't do your best at anything if you're exhausted—or even tired.

Often the solution to the problem is simply to allow yourself more time to sleep. Most people need around eight hours of sleep each night, although there are wide individual differences. In addition to sleeping more, there are also some relatively simple changes you can make in your behavior that will help you to sleep better. They include the following:

- **Exercise more.** Regular exercise will help you sleep more soundly at night, as well as help you cope with stress that might otherwise keep you awake.

- **Have a regular bedtime.** By going to bed at pretty much the same time each night, you give your body a regular rhythm and make sleep a habit.

- **Use your bed for sleeping and not as an all-purpose area.** Don't use your bed as a place to study, read, eat, or watch TV. Let your bed be a trigger for sleep.

- **Avoid caffeine after lunch.** The stimulant effects of caffeine (found in coffee, tea, and some soft drinks) may last as long as 8 to 12 hours after it's consumed.

- **Drink a glass of milk at bedtime.** Your mom was right: Drinking a glass of milk before you go to bed will help you get to sleep. The reason: Milk contains a natural chemical that makes you drowsy.

- **Avoid sleeping pills.** Steer clear of sleeping pills. Although they may be temporarily effective, in the long run they impair your ability to sleep because they disrupt your natural sleep cycles.

- **Don't try to force sleep on yourself.** Although this advice sounds odd, it turns out that one of the reasons that we have trouble sleeping is that we try too hard. Consequently, when you go to bed, just relax, and don't even attempt to go to sleep. If you're awake after 10 minutes or so, get up and do something else. Only go back to bed when you feel tired. Do this as often as necessary. If you follow this regimen for several weeks—and don't take naps or rest during the day—eventually getting into your bed will trigger sleep.

Drug Use and Abuse

For better or worse, drugs—ranging from legal drugs such as vitamins, cold-relief medicine, and the nicotine in cigarettes to illegal drugs such as marijuana and methamphetamines—are common in contemporary society. Because patterns of drug use or avoidance are often established in college, it is a good idea to learn what you can do now, before negative patterns of use, and in some cases, abuse, take hold.

Nicotine

Despite the clear evidence of its dangers, smoking remains a significant health problem. Smoking causes lung damage and increases the risks of developing cancer, emphysema, and a host of other diseases.

Why do people smoke, when the evidence is so clear about its risks? They start to smoke for a variety of reasons. Smoking is sometimes viewed as a kind of initiation into adulthood, a sign of growing up. In other cases, teenagers see smoking as "cool," a view promoted by movies and television.

The problem is that, no matter what reason persuades a person to try out a few cigarettes, smoking can quickly become a habit, because a major ingredient of tobacco—nicotine—is an addictive drug. An addictive drug produces a biological or psychological dependence. The absence of the drug leads to a craving for it that may be nearly irresistible.

Smoking is one of the hardest addictions to break. Among the suggestions for quitting are the following:

> **Remain smoke-free one day at a time.** Don't think about not smoking tomorrow, or next week, or for the rest of your life. Instead, think of not smoking for the rest of the day. You can worry about tomorrow . . . tomorrow.

> **Visualize the consequences of smoking.** Visualize blackened, rotting lungs filled with smoke. Then think about the fresh, pink lungs that you'll have after you've stopped smoking.

> **Exercise.** The all-purpose antidote, exercise, will make you feel better physically and take your mind off smoking.

> **Use nicotine patches or nicotine gum.** "The Patch" and nicotine gum can provide enough nicotine to satisfy your craving for the drug, while permitting you to stop smoking. Physicians can also sometimes prescribe drugs that help reduce the craving for nicotine.

> **Avoid people when they're smoking.** It's nearly impossible to avoid the urge to smoke when others are lighting up. If you're trying to quit, stay away from people who are smoking.

> **Enlist the social support of family and friends.** Tell others that you're trying to quit, and accept their encouragement and praise.

> **Reward yourself.** Every few days, give yourself some kind of reinforcement for spending a period of time smoke-free. Go to a movie; buy a CD. Think about how you can afford these more easily since you aren't buying cigarettes anymore.

> **Join a quit-smoking program.** Many college health services hold periodic programs to help students who want to stop smoking. By enrolling in one, you'll receive the support of others who are in the same boat as you are.

> **Keep trying.** If after quitting you start smoking again, just consider that lapse as part of the process of quitting. Many people quit several times before they manage to quit for good.

Alcohol

The drug most likely to be found on college campuses is alcohol. It may surprise you to know that though it initially seems to raise your spirits, alcohol is actually a depressant. As the amount of alcohol one consumes increases, its depressive effects become more obvious. You've probably seen its other negative effects: Drinkers show poor judgment and less impulse control. As judgment is impaired, drinkers may engage in casual or risky sexual behavior or act aggressively. Memory is impaired, and speech becomes slurred and eventually incoherent. As they drink more, people become less coordinated and their reaction time slows. If you drink enough, you'll pass out. And as some well-publicized cases in the news illustrate, if you consume enough alcohol in a short period, you can die. It's that simple.

The potential negative consequences of drinking have done little to prevent the use of alcohol on college campuses. Although a not insignificant number of students drink little or no alcohol, more than 75 percent of college students say they've had a drink within the last 30 days. Some drink a great deal: 17 percent of female students and 31 percent of male students admitted drinking on 10 or more occasions during the past 30 days.[6]

Some students drink even more, and the extent of alcohol consumption can reach astonishing levels. Half of all male college students and 40 percent of all female college students have engaged in **binge drinking,** defined as having at least four (for females) or five (for males) drinks in a single sitting. Such heavy drinking doesn't just affect the drinker. Most college students report having had their studying or sleep disturbed by drunk students. Further, around one-third of students have been insulted or humiliated by a drunk student, and 25 percent of women have been the target of an unwanted sexual advance by a drunk classmate.

Close to 20 million people in the United States are alcoholics, and college students make up their fair share of the total. **Alcoholics,** individuals with serious alcohol-abuse problems, become dependent on alcohol, experiencing a physical craving for it. They continue to drink despite serious consequences. Furthermore, they develop a tolerance for alcohol and must drink increasing amounts to experience the initially positive effects that alcohol brings about.

The long-term consequences of high levels of alcohol consumption are severe. Heavy drinking damages the liver and digestive system and can even affect brain cells. In fact, virtually every part of the body is eventually affected by heavy alcohol use.

To examine your own use of alcohol, complete **Try It 4** on page 385.

Binge drinking
Having at least four (for females) or five (for males) drinks in a single sitting

Alcoholics
Individuals with serious alcohol-abuse problems who become dependent on alcohol and continue to drink despite serious consequences

Illegal Drugs

"Just say 'no.'"

If it were only so easy. Decisions about drugs are quite a bit more complicated than simplistic antidrug slogans would have you believe. Using or not using drugs involves, at a minimum, peer pressure, your values, and the effects they have on your body, your behavior, and your self-image.

Several things are clear, however. Despite the prevalence of illicit drug use among college students—surveys show that around one-third of college students report having used an illegal drug at least once in the previous year—the benefits of drug use are difficult to enumerate. Apart from a temporary high, the advantages of using drugs are nil, and the use of illegal drugs is among the riskiest activities in which people can engage. Not only does drug use make you vulnerable to arrest, but it also poses short- and long-term health risks. The escape from one's

Journal Reflections

College Drinking Experiences

Examine your own feelings about alcohol use by answering these questions.

1. Why do you think people use alcohol?

2. What do you think the minimum age to legally drink alcohol should be, and why?

3. Do you know people who drink only to get drunk?

4. Have you ever suspected any of your friends or acquaintances of being alcoholics? Why? Did you do anything about it?

5. Efforts to alter one's states of consciousness through the use of alcohol or other drugs are found in almost every culture. Why do you think this is the case?

responsibilities that drugs provide is likely to make it even harder to later deal with those responsibilities—which aren't going to go away.

Not all illegal drugs are the same, and they produce widely varying effects and consequences (see **Table 14.2** on page 386). But they all share a common result: a reduction in awareness of and engagement with what is happening around you.

People often fall into drug use without much thought. But doing so is still a choice. Preaching and slogans are not going to help you to make a sensible decision. You need to employ every critical thinking skill you can to determine exactly what you wish—and don't wish—to introduce into your body. Give some thought to why escape is attractive and consider seeking counseling instead. Allow yourself to consider the long- and short-term effects of drug use—both the physical effects as well as the potential effects on your own aspirations and dreams. Think about the legal consequences of drug use: A drug conviction can lead to expulsion from college and refusal by many employers to hire you. Furthermore, random drug tests are increasingly a part of corporate life, and your ability to qualify for and keep a job may be placed at risk if you use drugs—even only occasionally.

Drugs that produce addiction, such as cocaine and heroin, present a further set of problems. The lives of people with drug addictions become centered on the drug. They enter into a pattern of alternating highs—when on the drug—and lows. During their lows, much of their thinking is centered on obtaining the drug and looking forward to their next high.

Drug addiction and abuse is not confined to illegal drugs. An increasing number of people use over-the-counter drugs for the high they produce. For example, cold and cough medications containing dextromethorphan (DXM) are among the

Try It! POWER

Consider Your Drinking Style

4

If you drink alcohol, do you have a style of use that is safe and responsible? Read the statements below and rate the extent to which you agree with them, using the following scale:

1 = Strongly disagree

2 = Disagree

3 = Neutral

4 = Agree

5 = Strongly agree

	1	2	3	4	5
1. I usually drink alcohol a few times a week.					
2. I sometimes go to class after I've been drinking alcohol.					
3. I frequently drink when I'm alone.					
4. I have driven while under the influence of alcohol.					
5. I've used a fake ID card to purchase alcohol.					
6. I'm a totally different person when I'm drinking alcohol.					
7. I often drink so much that I feel drunk.					
8. I wouldn't want to go to a party where alcohol wasn't being served.					
9. I avoid people who don't like to drink alcohol.					
10. I sometimes urge others to drink more alcohol.					

The lower your score (i.e., the more 1s and 2s), the better able you are to control your alcohol consumption and the more likely it is that your alcohol use is responsible. The higher your score (i.e., the more 4s and 5s), the greater is your use and reliance on alcohol, and the more likely it is that your alcohol consumption may be reckless. If your score is over 40, you may have an alcohol problem and should seek professional help to control your alcohol usage.

To Try It online, go to www.mhhe.com/power.

most commonly abused over-the-counter drugs. Taken in the large quantities that produce a high, they put users at risk for vomiting, hallucinations, seizures, brain damage, and even death.

Addiction's Warning Signs

Addictions to drugs—including alcohol—can begin subtly, and you may not be aware of the extent of the problem. Here are some signs that indicate when use becomes abuse:

▸ Feeling you need to be high to have a good time.

▸ Being high more often than not.

▸ Getting high to "get yourself going."

table 14.2 Illegal Drugs

Drug	Street Name	Effects	Withdrawal Symptoms/ Health Hazards
Stimulants			
Cocaine **Amphetamines** Benzedrine Dexedrine Methamphetamine	Coke, blow, snow, lady, crack Speed Speed Meth	Increased confidence, mood elevation, sense of energy and alertness, decreased appetite, anxiety, irritability, insomnia, transient drowsiness, delayed orgasm	Apathy, general fatigue, prolonged sleep, depression, disorientation, suicidal thoughts, agitated motor activity, irritability, bizarre dreams
Depressants **Alcohol** **Barbiturates** Nembutal Seconal Phenobarbital	Booze Yellowjackets, yellows Reds	Anxiety reduction, impulsiveness, dramatic mood swings, bizarre thoughts, suicidal behavior, slurred speech, disorientation, slowed mental and physical functioning, limited attention span	Weakness, restlessness, nausea and vomiting, headaches, nightmares, irritability, depression, acute anxiety, hallucinations, seizures, possible death
Rohypnol	Roofies, rope, "date-rape drug"	Muscle relaxation, amnesia, sleep	Seizures
Narcotics **Heroin** **Morphine**	H, hombre, junk, smack, dope, crap, horse Drugstore dope, cube, first line, mud	Anxiety and pain reduction, apathy, difficulty in concentration, slowed speech, decreased physical activity, drooling, itching, euphoria, nausea	Anxiety, vomiting, sneezing, diarrhea, lower back pain, watery eyes, runny nose, yawning, irritability, tremors, panic, chills and sweating, cramps
Hallucinogens **Cannabis** Marijuana Hashish Hash oil	Bhang, kit, ganja, dope, grass, pot, smoke, hemp, joint, weed, bone, Mary Jane, herb, tea	Euphoria, relaxed inhibitions, increased appetite, disoriented behavior	Hyperactivity, insomnia, decreased appetite, anxiety
MDMA	Ecstasy	Heightened sense of oneself and insight, feelings of peace, empathy, energy	Depression, anxiety, panic attacks
LSD	Acid, quasey, microdot, white lightning	Heightened aesthetic responses, vision and depth distortion, heightened sensitivity to faces and gestures, magnified feelings, paranoia, panic, euphoria	Anxiety, depression, flashbacks

> Going to class or work high.

> Missing class or work because you are high.

> Being unprepared for class because you were high.

> Feeling regret over something you did while you were high.

- Driving while high.
- Having a legal problem due to being high.
- Behaving, while high, in a way you wouldn't otherwise.
- Being high in nonsocial, solitary situations.
- Thinking about drugs or alcohol much of the time.
- Avoiding family or friends while using alcohol or drugs.
- Hiding drug or alcohol use from others.

Any one of these symptoms indicates that you have a drug or alcohol problem. If you do have a problem, seek professional help. Addictions to illegal drugs or alcohol are extremely difficult to deal with on your own. No matter how good your intentions, almost no one can overcome the cravings brought about by an addiction to a particular substance without help.

Here are some places to which you can turn:

1. **College health services, counseling centers, and mental health centers.** Most colleges provide services to help you overcome an addiction. They can evaluate the extent of the problem and refer you to the proper place for further help. (To learn about your own campus resources, complete **Try It 5** on page 388.)

2. **Drug treatment centers and clinics.** Sometimes located in hospitals and sometimes independently run, drug treatment centers or clinics can provide help. You can also check your telephone book for a local listing of Alcoholics Anonymous or Narcotics Anonymous.

3. **Government hotlines.** The federal government provides extensive information about drug and alcohol use. For starters, call the National Clearinghouse on Alcohol and Drug Information at 1-800-729-6686. For alcohol difficulties in particular, call the National Council on Alcoholism and Drug Dependence at 1-800-622-2255. For drug problems, you can call the National Institute on Drug Abuse at 1-800-662-4357. Finally, you can visit the National Council on Alcoholism and Drug Dependence Web site at **www.ncadd.org** for help with alcohol and drug problems.

»LO14.4 Sexual Health and Decision Making

Relationships. Contraception. AIDS. Rape.

Sexual health includes a host of issues, involving not just your body, but your heart and mind as well. In fact, it is often said that our most important sexual organ is our brain. It determines what we view as sexually arousing, and it's what we use to make decisions and choices about our sexuality.

Although the focus of the brief discussion of sexual health here is on strategies for protecting yourself (from sexually transmitted infections, pregnancy, and rape), sexual decisions are also a reflection of your basic values. You can't make responsible decisions about sex without knowing what is important to you and how you view yourself. So you don't want to wait until a sexual encounter begins before thinking through your views of sexuality and what is and is not right for you. Deciding to have—or not to have—sex should be a

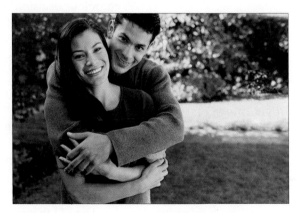

Relationships and sexuality raise substantial issues, involving your attitudes, beliefs, values, and emotions, as well as your body, in a complex intermix. Making responsible decisions requires that you know who you are and what's important to you.

Tap Into Campus Resources

Complete the following chart to identify the campus office locations and their services that deal with alcohol and drug problems.

Campus Resource	Where Is It?	What Service Does It Provide?	How Do You Get in Touch?
Health Center			
Mental Health Center			
Campus Chaplain			
Drug and Alcohol Education Center(s)			
Counseling Center			
Residential Life Office			
Ombudsman			
Campus Security Services			
(add other offices here)			
(add other offices here)			
(add other offices here)			
(add other offices here)			

To Try It online, go to **www.mhhe.com/power**.

conscious decision between two individuals that must be made with great responsibility and thoughtfulness.

Avoiding Sexually Transmitted Infections

Sexually transmitted infections (STIs)
Infections acquired through sexual contact

Acquired immune deficiency syndrome (AIDS)
A potentially lethal, sexually transmitted disease that causes the destruction of the body's immune system

Right now, one out of five people in the United States is infected with one of the many types of **sexually transmitted infections (STIs)**—infections acquired through sexual contact. At least one out of four will eventually contract an STI at some point in life.

There are many varieties of STIs, although all share a similar origin: sexual contact. Depending on the type of infection, symptoms may include warts in the genital area, pelvic infection, painful urination, infertility, blindness, and even death.

The STI that has had the greatest impact in the last decade is **acquired immune deficiency syndrome (AIDS).** Although in the United States it initially most often affected homosexuals, AIDS quickly spread among heterosexuals. Some populations are particularly affected, such as intravenous drug users. Worldwide, more than 25 million people have already died from the disease. Some estimates suggest that 40 million people now carry the AIDS virus. Despite new treatments, AIDS remains incurable. In the United States, AIDS is the leading cause of death among men 25 to 44 years of age and the third leading cause of death among women in that age range.

Although AIDS is the best-known STI, the most common is chlamydia, an infection that if left untreated can cause sterility in some sufferers. Genital herpes is a virus that appears as small blisters or sores around the genitals. Although the sores heal after several weeks, the infection can remain dormant and reappear periodically. Other STIs, although somewhat less common, afflict millions of people. (See **Table 14.3** on page 390 for a summary of the common STIs.)

The only completely effective way to avoid sexual transmission of these infections is through avoiding sexual activity. However, many people are unwilling to make such a choice. Several alternative approaches, called "smart sex" or "safe sex" practices, reduce the risk of contracting STIs. They include the following:

> **Know your sexual partner—well.** You should not have sexual contact with a person who is only a casual acquaintance. You want to know the person well enough to have a discussion with him or her in which you both talk about your sexual histories.

> **Prevent the exchange of bodily fluids during all sex acts.** Avoid unprotected intercourse (vaginal or anal) and oral sex.

> **Use condoms.** Condoms not only prevent the spread of AIDS and other STIs, but they also prevent pregnancy.

> **Be faithful to a single partner.** People in long-term relationships with only one other individual are less likely to contract AIDS and other STIs than those with multiple sexual partners.

Preventing Unwanted Pregnancy

There is one and only one totally effective means of preventing pregnancy: Not having sexual intercourse. **Abstinence,** refraining from intercourse, only works, however, if you practice it with absolute consistency—something that many people find difficult. But it certainly is possible. Despite the folklore that insists "everybody's doing it," they're not. In fact, if you think critically about what others say about their sexual activity, you'll probably conclude that what they say is more boasting (and outright lying) than straight talk.

Those who do want to have a sexual relationship can still avoid pregnancy. Methods of contraception include the following:

> **Birth control pills.** Composed of artificial hormones, birth control pills are among the most effective ways of preventing pregnancy—as long as they are taken as prescribed. Except for women with certain medical conditions, the side effects are minimal.

> **Implants.** One of the newest forms of birth control, implants work through a simple surgical procedure in which a small capsule is inserted into a woman's arm. Implants last for 5 years, preventing pregnancy for the entire period. With few side effects, implants are highly effective, but they are only practical for women who wish to avoid pregnancy for extended periods.

> **Intrauterine device, or IUD.** IUDs are small pieces of plastic or copper inserted by a medical practitioner into a woman's uterus. Although highly effective, some have been found to produce unacceptable side effects, including infections and scarring that can make it impossible for a woman to get pregnant when she wants to.

Abstinence
The avoidance of sexual contact

table 14.3 Commonly Sexually Transmitted Infections

	Cause	Transmission	Symptoms
AIDS—HIV	Human immuno-deficiency virus (HIV)	Coming in direct contact with infected blood, semen, or vaginal secretions. Anal or vaginal intercourse, being born to an infected female, receiving infected blood or blood products, or sharing needles and syringes with someone infected with the HIV virus.	In early stages of infection with HIV there typically are no symptoms. As the disease progresses the following are usual symptoms: Chronic or swollen glands. Weight loss of more than 10 pounds. Flu-like symptoms that persist. Purple spots on the skin and inside the mouth, nose, or rectum. Unusual susceptibility to parasitic, fungal, bacterial, and viral infections or certain cancers.
Chlamydia	Bacteria	Vaginal or anal intercourse or oral sex with someone who is infected.	Many infected people have no symptoms, but when present the most common are the following: Pain, burning or "itching" sensations with urination. Vaginal infections may be associated with abnormal discharge. Oral infections may be exhibited by a sore throat but usually have no symptoms. Penile infections may be associated with a discharge.
Gonorrhea	Bacteria	Vaginal or anal intercourse or oral sex with someone who is infected.	Many infected people have no symptoms but are still contagious. Most common symptoms are the following: Pain, burning or "itching" sensations with urination. Vaginal infections may be associated with abnormal discharge, or vaginal bleeding between periods. Penile infections may be associated with a yellowish discharge.
Hepatitis A	Virus	Spread through contaminated feces and anal–oral contact during sexual activity.	Symptoms for hepatitis A and B will be similar: nausea, vomiting, diarrhea, fatigue, lack of appetite, dark urine, light stools, and/or abdominal tenderness.
Hepatitis B	Virus	Spread via blood by sexual contact or via an injection with a contaminated needle.	Symptoms for hepatitis A and B will be similar: nausea, vomiting, diarrhea, fatigue, lack of appetite, dark urine, light stools, and/or abdominal tenderness.
Genital herpes	Herpes simplex virus (HSV)	Contact with virus in infected blisters or virus being shed from the site of previous infections that may have no symptoms.	Cluster of tender, painful blisters, ulcers, or sores typically on or around the lips, mouth, genitals, or anus. Symptoms may be very mild or not present at all, but people are still infected and contagious. Blisters, ulcers, and sores last one to three weeks during initial outbreaks. Lesions heal, but person still has herpes. Lesions commonly recur without being re-exposed to the disease.
Genital warts	Human papilloma virus (HPV)	Vaginal or anal intercourse or oral sex with someone who has the virus.	Small bumpy "cauliflower" looking warts that are usually painless and appear on or around the genitals or anus. Itching and burning around the lesions may occur, but such symptoms are rare. Infections without symptoms are common.

- **Diaphragms and cervical caps.** Diaphragms and cervical caps are circular, dome-shaped pieces of thin rubber that a woman inserts into her vagina to cover the cervix. A sperm-killing (spermicidal) cream or jelly must be used simultaneously, and the diaphragm or cervical cap must be removed after sexual intercourse. Although side effects are few, the risk of pregnancy is somewhat higher than with the other forms of birth control we've discussed; some 18 percent of women using them become pregnant.

- **Condoms.** Condoms are thin sheaths that fit over the penis and prevent sperm from entering the vagina. When used with a contraceptive jelly that kills sperm and positioned properly, condoms are highly effective, with 2 pregnancies per 100 users per year. But with condoms used as they typically are, there are 15 pregnancies per 100 users per year.

- **Injections.** Progestin, administered as an injection every three months, provides excellent protection, but it cannot be used for more than two years.

- **Ring.** A polymer ring with hormones is worn in the vagina for three weeks, and then removed for one week. It provides excellent protection when used properly.

- **Contraceptive sponge.** The sponge, shaped like a large mushroom cap, is inserted into the vagina. It can be left in place for 24 hours, during which time it can be used for multiple acts of intercourse. Although it has few side effects, it has a failure rate of between 17 and 25 percent.

- **Periodic abstinence.** The only form of birth control that involves no chemical or mechanical intervention, periodic abstinence (also known as the rhythm method) consists of refraining from intercourse during times in a woman's menstrual cycle when pregnancy is possible. With a failure rate of 20 percent, periodic abstinence requires close scrutiny of calendars, body temperature, and cervical mucus—all of which can be indicators of the time of the month to avoid intercourse.

- **Sterilization.** Sterilization is a surgical procedure that causes a person (either a man or a woman) to become permanently incapable of having children.

- **Emergency contraception.** Several forms of birth control can prevent pregnancy after unprotected intercourse. These involve using increased doses of certain oral contraceptive pills within 72 hours or insertion of a copper intrauterine device (IUD) within 5 to 7 days following unprotected sex.

- **Withdrawal and douching (*ineffective* birth control).** Withdrawal, in which a man removes his penis from a woman's vagina before ejaculating, and douching, flushing the vagina with a liquid *after* the man has ejaculated, just don't work. *They should not be used for birth control* because they are so ineffective.

Date Rape

We usually think of rape as a rare crime, committed by strangers. Unfortunately, rape is surprisingly common and rapists usually know their victims. In a national survey conducted on college campuses, one out of eight women reported having been raped. In about half the reported cases, the rapists were first dates, casual dates, or romantic acquaintances—situations categorized as **date rape.** Overall, women are far more likely to be raped by someone they know than by a stranger. There is a 14 to 25 percent chance that a woman will be the victim of rape during her lifetime.[7] Although date rape is the more common type on campus, it is only different from any other form of rape in that the victim is acquainted with the rapist.

Date rape
Forced sex in which the rapist is a date or romantic acquaintance

What leads to rape? Most often, rape has less to do with sex than with power and anger. Rapists use forced sex to demonstrate their power and control over the victim. The rapist's pleasure comes not so much from sex as from forcing someone to submit. Sometimes sexual behavior is a demonstration of the rapist's rage at women in general.

In addition, rapes sometimes are brought about by the common—but untrue—belief that when women offer resistance to sex, they don't really mean it. If a man holds the view that when a woman says no to sex, she really means yes, he is likely to ignore a woman's protests, and the encounter may end in rape. Some men may even believe that it is unmasculine to accept no for an answer.

Some rapists employ the illegal drug rohypnol, which has come to be known as the "date rape drug." When it is mixed with alcohol, it can prevent victims from resisting sexual assault. People who are unknowingly given the drug don't even remember the rape, so it's important to keep a careful eye on anything one drinks at a party.

Whatever the causes, rape is devastating to the victim. Victims experience extreme anxiety, disbelief, fear, and shock. These reactions may linger for years, and rape victims may experience a long-lasting fear of entering into relationships. (Victims of rape and other sexual assaults can call a 24-hour hotline at 1-800-656-HOPE or visit the Rape, Abuse, and Incest National Network Web site at **www. rainn.org.**)

Both men and women must be sensitive to the issue of date rape. Among the suggestions for reducing its incidence are the following:

> **Set limits.** You have the right to set firm limits, and these should be communicated clearly, firmly, and early on.

> **No means no.** When a partner says no, it means no—nothing else.

> **Be assertive.** You should never passively accept being pressured into an activity in which you don't want to engage. Remember that passivity may be interpreted as consent.

> **Communicate.** Women and men should talk about their views of sexual behavior and what is and is not permissible.

> **Be vigilant.** Women should keep close tabs on what they are given to drink in social situations; victims of date rape have sometimes been given mind-altering drugs.

> **Avoid assumptions.** Don't assume that certain kinds of dress or flirtatious behavior are an invitation to sex.

> **Keep in mind that alcohol and drugs cloud judgment.** Nothing hinders communication more than alcohol and drugs.

Speaking of **Success**

NAME: **Shorena Kalandaris**

SCHOOL: **Smith College, Northampton, Massachusetts**

Shorena Kalandaris spent her high school years preparing to leave her native Republic of Georgia, located where Europe and Asia meet. She knew that she wanted to pursue college in the United States, and after graduation from high school, she enrolled in Smith College in Massachusetts.

Studying in the United States was not easy for Kalandaris. She was separated from her family in Georgia for long months at a time, and she had to quickly learn the skills necessary to take care of herself while away from her family.

"I have always had many interests and activities, but being alone here, I had to manage my time myself. I participate in competitive ballroom dance and had to balance that with my studies," noted Kalandaris.

Cultural differences proved challenging, and Kalandaris sought out other international students to cope with the unique challenges of her situation. She became involved in campus organizations that support international students, and she was active in organizing activities for the international student community.

Kalandaris excelled at Smith, and she was nominated to be a candidate for the Goldman Sachs Global Leaders program. Young leaders from across the United States were chosen to attend leadership training in from current global leaders, and they met with other students who had the same passion to make changes to their world.

Kalandaris plans to attend the London School of Economics for her junior year abroad, and she intends to return to Georgia after earning a graduate degree in economics. Ultimately, her goal is to work for the National Bank of Georgia to help improve the Georgian economy.

Says Kalandaris, "I would encourage students to have diverse interests, but to aim for quality experiences. Have a goal, because it is very easy to get distracted. Once you have a goal, the rest of your plan will fall into place."

Looking
Back

What is stress and how can I control it?

▸ Stress is a common experience, appearing in three main forms: cataclysmic events, personal stressors, and daily hassles. Excessive stress is not only unpleasant and upsetting, but it also has negative effects on the body and mind.

▸ Coping with stress involves becoming prepared for future stress through proper diet and exercise, identifying the causes of stress in one's life, taking control of stress, seeking social support, practicing relaxation techniques, training oneself to redefine and reinterpret stressful situations, and keeping one's promises.

What is involved in keeping fit and healthy, and why is it important for me to do so?

▸ For all people, keeping fit and healthy is both essential and challenging. It is vital to learn to eat properly, especially by eating a variety of foods on a regular schedule and by restricting your intake of fat, cholesterol, and salt.

▸ Exercise is valuable because it improves health and well-being. Choosing exercises that we like, making everyday activities a part of exercise, and exercising with others can help form the habit of exercise.

▸ The third key element of good health is sleeping properly. Good exercise and eating habits can contribute to sound sleep, as can the development of regular sleeping habits and the use of sleep-assisting practices.

What are the main threats to my health and well-being?

▸ One of the major threats that college students (and others) face is the improper use of drugs. The most commonly abused drug is alcohol, which is a depressant (despite an initial reduction of inhibitions and feeling of euphoria) and can lead to a physical or psychological dependence. Nicotine is the second most commonly abused drug.

▸ The use of illegal drugs presents not only potential dangers related to law-breaking and prosecution but short- and long-term health risks as well. Drugs cause a reduction in awareness and involvement in life, and some drugs can be dangerously addictive.

What are the components of sexual health?

▸ Sexual health is as important as other forms of health. People must make their own individual decisions about their sexuality and how they will express it.

▸ Many forms of contraception are available, ranging from abstinence to surgical implants. Each form has different procedures, risks, and effectiveness.

▸ The incidence of sexually transmitted infections (STIs) is high in the United States, with about 25 percent of the population contracting an STI at some point in life.

▸ Rape is a surprisingly common crime, with most victims knowing the rapist—often in a circumstance known as date rape.

[KEY TERMS AND CONCEPTS]

Stress (p. 368)

Cataclysmic events (p. 368)

Personal stressors (p. 369)

Daily hassles (p. 369)

Coping (p. 370)

Social support (p. 373)

Binge drinking (p. 383)

Alcoholics (p. 383)

Sexually transmitted
    infections (STIs) (p. 388)

Acquired immune deficiency
    syndrome (AIDS) (p. 388)

Abstinence (p. 389)

Date rape (p. 391)

[RESOURCES]

ON CAMPUS

Your college health service/medical provider is the first line of defense if you become ill. The staff can provide you with advice and often medical care and can give help if you are the victim of rape or in other emergencies. Furthermore, colleges often have health education offices that help educate students on safer sex practices, on how to eat in healthier ways, and generally on how to increase wellness. Colleges sometimes offer stress reduction workshops to help students cope more effectively.

Finally, many colleges have mental health counselors that can help you deal with emotional problems. If you are depressed, have trouble sleeping, or face other problems coping with the problems of life, speaking with a counselor can be extremely helpful. Check with your school's counseling center or health center to identify someone appropriate with whom to speak.

IN PRINT

10 Simple Solutions to Stress: How to Tame Tension and Start Enjoying Your Life (New Harbinger Publications 2007) provides 10 simple techniques for coping with stress and its effects on your health and in your life.

YOU: The Owner's Manual, Updated and Expanded Edition: An Insider's Guide to the Body That Will Make You Healthier and Younger (Collins Living, 2008) is an engaging and comprehensive book that not only provides practical information on how the body works but also offers hundreds of pointers on how to live healthier, resist disease, and maintain a high quality of life.

Deborah Schoeberlein's *EveryBody: Preventing HIV and Other Sexually Transmitted Infections, Revised Edition* (RAD, 2001) offers clearheaded and accurate advice on decisions relating to sexual behavior.

ON THE WEB

The following sites on the Web provide the opportunity to extend your learning about stress, health, and wellness. (Although the Web addresses were accurate at the time the book was printed, check the *P.O.W.E.R. Learning* Web site [**www.mhhe.com/power**] for any changes that may have occurred.)

▸ The American Dietetic Association's Web site not only provides information for its professional members, but it also includes updated consumer tips and articles (**www.eatright.org/Public/**). Features include strategies for smart grocery shopping, discussion of the latest fad diets, and guidelines for healthy eating.

▸ "Stress Management" (**stress.about.com/od/copingskills/**), on About.com, offers in-depth and comprehensive information on coping with stress. Dozens of links cover teens through the elderly, self-assessment, psychotherapy and relaxation techniques.

▸ "Eating Disorders: Mirror, Mirror" (**www.mirror-mirror.org/eatdis.htm**) is a guide to eating disorders offering definitions, coping strategies, links to related organizations, and personal messages from survivors.

- "Healthy Women" (**www.healthywomen.org/healthtopics**), from the National Women's Health Resource Center, offers a number of good articles on health issues, including a concise presentation and discussion of various methods of contraception.

- The Massachusetts Department of Public Health (**www.mass.gov/dph/cdc/bcdc.htm**) offers information on the prevention and control of sexually transmitted infections, including links to fact sheets and publications containing further information. Also discussed are tuberculosis and the West Nile virus.

TAKING IT TO THE NET

1 Find two stress reduction techniques. One possible strategy: Go to AltaVista (**www.altavista.com**) and enter the phrase "stress reduction techniques" into the search field. Examine the sites located until you find two stress reduction techniques. Try each of the techniques. Do you feel less stressed and more relaxed? Which of the techniques works best for you?

2 Locate the most-recent statistics on drug use by U.S. students. One possible approach: Go to Yahoo! (**www.yahoo.com**) and enter the phrase "drug statistics government." Examine the results and consider how they compare to your own perceptions of the extent of drug use.

The Case of . . .
The Opposing Perspectives

It started out innocently, as a date to study for an exam. And then it turned wrong.

Here's what Bob had to say:

Patty and I were in the same statistics class. She usually sat near me and was always very friendly. I liked her and thought maybe she liked me, too.

Last Thursday after class I suggested that she come to my place so we could study for midterms together. She agreed immediately.

That night everything seemed to go perfectly. We studied for awhile and then took a break. I could tell that she liked me, and I was attracted to her. I started kissing her. I could tell that she really liked it.

We started touching each other and it felt really good. All of a sudden she pulled away and said "stop." I figured she didn't want me to think that she was "easy" or "loose." . . .

I just ignored her protests and eventually she stopped struggling. I think she liked it but afterwards she acted bummed out and cold.

Patty, on the other hand, had a very different view of their encounter:

I knew Bob from my statistics class. He's cute and we are both good at statistics, so when a tough midterm was scheduled, I was glad that he suggested we study together. It never occurred to me that it was anything except a study date.

That night everything went fine at first. We got a lot of studying done in a short amount of time, so when he suggested we take a break, I thought we deserved it.

Well, all of a sudden he started acting really romantic and started kissing me. I liked the kissing, but then he started touching me below the waist. I pulled away and tried to stop him but he didn't listen. After a while I stopped struggling; he was hurting me and I was scared. He was so much bigger and stronger than me. I couldn't believe it was happening to me. I didn't know what to do.

He actually forced me to have sex with him. I guess looking back on it I should have screamed or done something besides trying to reason with him, but it was so unexpected. I couldn't believe it was happening.[8]

1. Was Bob being dishonest in setting up the study date? Was he dishonest during the sexual encounter?

2. What could Patty have done when Bob began acting "romantic"?

3. Was Bob right to interpret Patty's initial responsiveness to his advances as acceptance of a sexual relationship? Was Patty "leading him on"?

4. Did Patty's initial responsiveness justify Bob's pursuing sex beyond the point at which she said "stop"?

A Final Word

Throughout this book you've seen how the principles of *P.O.W.E.R. Learning* can be applied to a variety of situations, ranging from reading and writing to coping with stress. You can use the framework in any situation where you need to organize your thinking and behavior in a systematic way. It's a tool you can call on throughout your lifetime.

College is the beginning of a journey that leads to your future. This book has been designed to help you with the demands and challenges of college, but at the same time to prepare you for life after school. It has tried to show you that it is *you* who must make things happen to fulfill your goals and aspirations.

Ultimately, however, there are some key ingredients to success that no book can teach you and that only you can provide: integrity and honesty, intellectual curiosity, and love. I hope this book will help you as you consider what your contribution to the world will be and as you work to make that contribution.

Glossary

ABBCC structure: The structure of the typical research paper, consisting of *a*rgument, *b*ackground, *b*ody, *c*ounter-arguments, and *c*onclusion.

Abstinence: The avoidance of sexual contact.

Academic honesty: Completing and turning in only one's own work under one's own name.

Acquired immune deficiency syndrome (AIDS): A potentially lethal, sexually transmitted disease that causes the destruction of the body's immune system.

Acronym: A word or phrase formed by the first letters of a series of terms.

Acrostic: A sentence in which the first letters of the words correspond to material that is to be remembered.

Active listening: The voluntary act of focusing on what is being said, making sense of it, and thinking about it in a way that permits it to be recalled accurately.

Advance organizers: Broad, general ideas related to material that is to be read or heard, which pave the way for subsequent learning.

Alcoholics: Individuals with serious alcohol-abuse problems who become dependent on alcohol and continue to drink despite serious consequences.

Analogy: A comparison between concepts or objects that are alike in some respects, but dissimilar in most others.

Attention span: The length of time that attention is typically sustained.

Auditory/verbal learning styles: A style that favors listening as the best approach to learning.

Binge drinking: Having at least four (for females) or five (for males) drinks in a single sitting.

Blended (hybrid) courses: Courses in which instruction is a combination of traditional, face-to-face and online methods.

Blog: A Web-based public diary in which a writer provides commentary, ideas, thoughts, and short essays.

Brainstorming: A technique for generating ideas by saying out loud as many ideas as can be thought of in a fixed period of time.

Browser: A program that provides a way of navigating around the information on the Web.

Budget: A formal plan that accounts for expenditures and income.

Call number: A unique classification number assigned to every book (or other resource) in a library. Call numbers are used for ease of location.

Cataclysmic events: Sudden, powerful events that occur quickly and affect many people simultaneously.

College advisor: An individual who provides students with advice about their academic careers.

Community service: Making contributions to the society and community in which you live.

Concept mapping: A method of structuring written material by graphically grouping and connecting key ideas and themes.

Coping: The effort to control, reduce, or learn to tolerate the threats that lead to stress.

Cramming: Hurried, last-minute studying.

Critical thinking: A process involving reanalysis, questioning, and challenge of underlying assumptions.

Cultural competence: Knowledge and understanding about other races, ethnic groups, cultures, and minority groups.

Culture: The learned behaviors, beliefs, and attitudes that are characteristic of an individual society or population, and the products that people create.

Daily hassles: The minor irritants of life that, by themselves, produce little stress, but which can add up and produce more stress than a single larger-scale event.

Daily to-do list: A schedule showing the tasks, activities, and appointments due to occur during the day.

Date rape: Forced sex in which the rapist is a date or romantic acquaintance.

Decision making: The process of deciding among various alternatives.

Discrimination: Behavior directed toward individuals on the basis of their membership in a particular group.

Distance learning: The teaching of courses at another institution, with student participation via video technology or the Web.

Double major: A course of study that fulfills all the requirements for two majors.

Educated guessing: The practice of eliminating obviously false multiple-choice answers and selecting the most likely answer from the remaining choices.

Electives: Courses that are not required.

E-mail: Electronic mail, a system of communication that permits users to send and receive messages via the Internet.

Emoticons(or smileys): Symbols used in e-mail messages that provide information on the emotion that the writer is trying to convey. Emoticons usually look like faces on their side, with facial expressions related to the intended emotion or tone.

Ethnicity: Shared national origins or cultural patterns.

Evaluation: An assessment of the match between a product or activity and the goals it was intended to meet.

Flash cards: Index cards that contain key pieces of information to be remembered.

Freewriting: A technique involving continuous, nonstop writing, without self-criticism, for a fixed period of time.

Frontmatter: The preface, introduction, and table of contents of a book.

Grade point average (GPA): Also known as *quality point average*. A numeric average in which letter grades are transformed into numbers.

Grant: An award of money that does not have to be repaid.

Hearing: The involuntary act of sensing sounds.

"I" statements: Statements that cast responses in terms of oneself and one's individual interpretation.

Impromptu talk: Unprepared presentations that require speaking on a moment's notice.

Individual response technology: This method uses a wireless handset to transmit students' answers to the instructor's computer, resulting in more classroom interactivity.

Information competency: The ability to determine what information is necessary, and then to locate, evaluate, and effectively use that information.

Instant messaging: A system that allows one to use a computer to communicate in real time with friends and instructors.

Interlibrary loan: A system by which libraries share resources, making them available to patrons of different libraries.

Internet: A vast network of interconnected computers that share information around the world.

Learning disabilities: Difficulties in processing information when listening, speaking, reading, or writing, characterized by a discrepancy between learning potential and actual academic achievement.

Learning style: One's preferred manner of acquiring, using, and thinking about knowledge.

Left-brain processing: Information processing primarily performed by the left hemisphere of the brain, focusing on tasks requiring verbal competence, such as speaking, reading, thinking, and reasoning; information is processed sequentially, one bit at a time.

Link: A means of "jumping" automatically from one Web page to another.

Listserv: A subscription service through which members can post and receive messages via e-mail on general topics of shared interest.

Loan: Funds provided by a bank, credit union, or other agency that must be repaid after a specified period of time.

Loneliness: A subjective state in which people do not experience the level of connection with others that they desire.

Long-term goals: Aims relating to major accomplishments that take some time to achieve.

Major: A specialization in a particular subject area, requiring a set course of study.

Master calendar: A schedule showing the weeks of a longer time period, such as a college term, with all assignments and important activities noted on it.

Memory consolidation: The process by which the physical links between brain cells that represent memory become fixed and stable over time.

Meta-message: The underlying main ideas that a speaker is seeking to convey; the meaning behind the overt message.

Method of loci: A memory technique by which the elements in a list are visualized as occupying the parts of a familiar place.

Minor: A secondary specialization in a discipline different from one's major.

Mnemonics: Formal techniques used to make material more readily remembered.

Motivation: The inner power and psychological energy that directs and fuels behavior.

Online database: An index in electronic form composed of an organized body of information on a related topic.

Overlearning: Studying and rehearsing material past the point of initial mastery to the point at which recall becomes automatic.

Paraphrase: A restatement of a passage using different words.

Peg method: A memory technique by which a series of memorized words is linked by images to a list of items to be remembered.

Personal Mission Statement: A formal statement regarding what a person hopes to achieve during his or her lifetime.

Personal stressors: Major life events that produce stress.

Plagiarism: Taking credit for someone else's words, thoughts, or ideas.

Podcast: An audio or video recording that can be accessed on the Internet and viewed on a computer or downloaded to a mobile device.

P.O.W.E.R. Learning: A system designed to help people achieve their goals, based on five steps: *Prepare, Organize, Work, Evaluate,* and *Rethink.*

Prejudice: Evaluations or judgments of members of a group that are based primarily on membership in the group and not on the particular characteristics of individuals.

Prerequisites: Requirements that must be fulfilled before a student may enroll in a course or discipline.

Principal: The stated amount of a loan.

Priorities: The tasks and activities that one needs and wants to do, rank-ordered from most important to least important.

Problem solving: The process of generating alternatives to work on.

Procrastination: The habit of putting off and delaying tasks that need to be accomplished.

Race: Traditionally, biologically determined physical characteristics that set one group apart from others.

Read/write learning style: A style that involves a preference for written material, favoring reading over hearing and touching.

Recall: A way to request library materials from another person who has them.

Receptive learning style: The way in which we initially receive information.

Reflective feedback: A technique of verbal listening in which a listener rephrases what a speaker has said, trying to echo the speaker's meaning.

Register: To enroll formally in courses.

Registrar: The college official designated to oversee the scheduling of courses, the maintenance of grades and transcripts, and the creation and retention of other official documents.

Rehearsal: The process of practicing and learning material.

Retrieval: The process of finding information stored in memory and returning it to consciousness for further use.

Right-brain processing: Information processing primarily performed by the right hemisphere of the brain, focusing on information in nonverbal domains, such as the understanding of spatial relationships and recognition of patterns and drawings, music, and emotional expression.

Scholarship: An award of money to a student based on need or merit.

Search engine: A computerized index to information on the Web.

Self-actualization: A state of self-fulfillment in which people realize their highest potential in their own unique way.

Self-concept: People's view of themselves that forms over time, comprising three components: the physical self, the social self, and the personal self.

Self-efficacy: The expectation that one is capable of achieving one's goals in many different kinds of situations.

Self-esteem: The overall evaluation we give ourselves as individuals.

Self-fulfilling prophecy: A phenomenon that occurs when we hold a belief or expectation that affects our behavior, thereby increasing the likelihood that our beliefs or expectations *will* come true.

Service learning: Courses that allow a student to engage in community service activities while getting course credit for the experience.

Sexually transmitted infections (STIs): Infections acquired through sexual contact.

Short-term goals: Relatively limited steps toward the accomplishment of long-term goals.

Social support: Assistance and comfort supplied by others in times of stress.

Stacks: The shelves on which books and other materials are stored in a library.

Stereotypes: Beliefs and expectations about members of a group that are held simply because of their membership in the group.

Stress: The physical and emotional response to events that threaten or challenge us.

Study groups: Small, informal groups of students whose purpose is to help members work together and study for a test.

Study notes: Notes taken for the purpose of reviewing material.

Tactile/kinesthetic learning style: A style that involves learning by touching, manipulating objects, and doing things.

Term: The length of time for which money is lent.

Test anxiety: A temporary condition characterized by fears and concerns about test-taking.

Text messaging (texting): Short messages sent from mobile phones to other phones or e-mail accounts.

Thesis: The main point of a paper, typically stating the writer's opinion about the topic of the paper.

Time log: A record of how one spends one's time.

Transcript: A college's official record of courses taken and grades received by students.

Transferring: Changing colleges.

Unique major: Specialization in a particular subject area that is geared to the student's own needs. Not offered by all colleges, and generally requires the support of faculty to oversee the process.

Values: The qualities we see as desirable and most important.

Visual/graphic learning style: A style that favors material presented visually in a diagram or picture.

Visualization: A memory technique by which images are formed to help recall material.

Voice: The unique style of a writer, expressing the writer's outlook on life and past writing experiences.

Web: A highly graphical interface between users and the Internet that permits users to transmit and receive not only text but also pictorial, video, and audio information.

Web page: A location (or site) on the Web housing information from a single source and (typically) links to other pages.

Weekly timetable: A schedule showing all regular, prescheduled activities due to occur in the week, together with one-time events and commitments.

Wiki: A public document, posted on the Web, that permits others to add or edit the document collectively.

Working backward: The strategy of starting at the desired solution or goal and working toward the starting point of the problem.

Zero-sum game: A situation in which when one person wins, the other person automatically loses.

Endnotes

Chapter 1

1. Gottesman, G. (1994). *College survival.* NY: Macmillan. P. 70.
2. "The American Freshman: National Norms for 2006" Published by American Council on Education and University of California at Los Angeles Higher Education Research Institute.
3. Gottesman, G. (1994). *College survival.* NY: Macmillan. P. 70.
4. Adapted from "How Is College Different from High School?" Web site at Southern Methodist University Altshuler Learning Enhancement Center, **www.smu.edu/alec/transition.html**.
5. Ibid.

Chapter 2

1. Adapted from Ferner, J.D. (1980). *Successful time management.* NY: Wiley. P. 33.
2. National Survey of Student Engagement: 2004 Annual Report.
3. Adapted from Ferner, J.D. (1980). *Successful time management.* NY: Wiley. P. 33.
4. Gottesman, G.(1994). *College survival.* NY: MacMillan.

Chapter 3

1. Adapted from Lazear, D. (1999). *The intelligent curriculum: Using MI to develop your students' full potential.* Tucson, AZ: Zephyr Press.
2. Rosenberg, M. (1979). *Conceiving the self.* NY: Basic Books.
3. Maslow, A.H. (1987). *Motivation and personality* (3rd ed.). NY: Harper & Row.
4. www.benjerry.com/our_company/our_mission/index.cfm.
5. Bolles, R.N. (2008). *The 2008 what color is your parachute?* Berkeley, CA: Ten Speed Press.
6. Roberts, S.V., Auster, B.B., & Barone, M. (1993, September 20). Colin Powell, superstar: Will America's top general trade his uniform for a future in politics? *U.S. News & World Report.*

Chapter 4

1. Pauk, W. (2004). *How to study in college* (8th ed.). Boston: Houghton Mifflin.
2. Tyler, S. (1997). *Been there, should've done that.* Haslett, MI: Front Porch Press. P. 117.
3. Adapted from Johnson, G. (2000). *The living world* (2nd ed.). New York: McGraw-Hill.
4. Tyler, S. (1997). *Been there, should've done that.* Haslett, MI: Front Porch Press. P. 114.

Chapter 5

1. Tyler, S. (1997). *Been there, should've done that.* Haslett, MI: Front Porch Press. P. 126.
2. Tobias, S. (1995). *Overcoming math anxiety.* NY: W. W. Norton & Company.
3. Tyler, S. (1997). *Been there, should've done that.* Haslett, MI: Front Porch Press. P. 128.

Chapter 6

1. Bransford, J.D., & Johnson, M.K. (1972). Contextual prerequisites for understanding: Some investigations of comprehension and recall. *Journal of Verbal Learning and Verbal Behavior,* 11, p. 722.
2. Quotes from Irving, J. (December 11, 1995). Slipped away: At fifty-three, the novelist remembers his first love: wrestling.

The New Yorker, pp. 70–77; and Gussow, M. (April 28, 1998). John Irving: A novelist builds out from fact to reach the truth. *The New York Times* on the Web. **www.nytimes.com/library/books/042898irving-novel.html.**

Chapter 7

1. Elbow, P. (2001). *A community of writers.* NewYork: McGraw-Hill.
2. Adapted from Gregory, H. (2002). *Public speaking for college and career.* New York: McGraw-Hill.
3. Davidson, J.W., Gienapp, W.E., Heyrman, C.L., Lytle, M.H., & Stoff, M.B. (1996). *Nation of nations: A concise narrative of the American republic.* NewYork: McGraw-Hill. P. 540.
4. Scale items are adapted from Fenigstein, A., Scheier, & Buss, A. (1975). Public and private self-consciousness, assessment and theory. *Journal of Consulting and Clinical Psychology,* 43, Table 1, p. 324.
5. Wydro, K. (1985). *Thinking on your feet: The art of thinking and speaking under pressure.* Englewood Cliffs, NJ: Prentice Hall.

Chapter 8

1. Gold, P.E., Cahill, L., & Wenk, G.L. (2003, April) The low-down on ginkgo biloba. *Scientific American,* pp. 86–91.
2. Halpern, D.F. (1996). *Thought and knowledge: An introduction to critical thinking.* Mahwah, NJ: Erlbaum. P. 48.
3. Gottesman, G. (1994). *College survival.* NY: Macmillan. P. 59.
4. Greenberg, J., & Baron, R.A. *Behavior in organizations* (6th ed.). Upper Saddle River, NJ: Prentice Hall.
5. Kandel, E.R. (1995). Steps toward a molecular definition of memory consolidation. In D.L. Schacter (Ed.), *Memory distortions: How minds, brains, and societies reconstruct the past.* Cambridge, MA: Harvard University Press.

Chapter 9

1. Tyler, S. (1997). *Been there, should've done that.* Haslett, MI: Front Porch Press.
2. Ibid.

Chapter 10

1. Liebovich, L. (2000, August 10). Choosing quick hits over the card catalog. *The New York Times,* pp. 1, 6. Based on material from Eliot Soloway, University of Michigan, School of Education.
2. Adapted from Internet Search Engines. State University of New York, Albany, Libraries. February 1, 2005. **library.albany.edu/internet/engines.html.**
3. Schibsted, E. (June 1999). The legends: Jerry Yang and David Filo. *Business,* 20 June 1999.
4. Ibid.

Chapter 11

1. Adapted from Haplern, D.F. (1996). *Thought and knowledge: An introduction to critical thinking* (3rd ed.). Mahwah, NJ: Erlbaum; and Bransford, J.D. & Stein, B.S. (1993). *The ideal problem solver* (2nd ed.). New York: W. H. Freeman.
2. Table 1, "The scale of tolerance-intolerance of ambiguity," p. 34, in Budner, S. (1962). Intolerance of ambiguity as a personality variable. *Journal of Personality,* 30(7), pp. 29–50. Copyright © Duke University Press, 1962.

3. Forer, B. (1949). The fallacy of personal validation: A classroom demonstration of gullibility. *Journal of Abnormal and Social Psychology,* 44, pp. 118–123.

4. Byrne, D., & Kelley, L. (1981). *An introduction to personality* (3rd ed.). Englewood Cliffs, NJ: Prentice Hall. P. 304.

5. *21st century lives: Neurosurgeon Ben Carson.* (Accessed September 8, 2000). **www.abcnews.go.com/onair/WorldNewsTonight/ wnt000908_21st_carson_feature.html.** ABC News.

6. Ibid.

Chapter 12

1. Nolan, M.F. (1997, April 26). Tiger's racial multiplicity. *The Boston Globe,* p. A11.

2. Tatum, B.D. (1997). *"Why are all the black kids sitting together in the cafeteria?" And other conversations about race.* New York: Basic Books.

3. Malone, M.S. (1993, July 18). Translating diversity into high-tech gains. *The New York Times,* p. B2.

4. Adapted from *Working it out: The newsletter for gay and lesbian employment issues,* 1992.

5. Sponholz, M., & Sponholz, J. (1996). *The Princeton Review college companion.* New York: Random House. P. 24.

6. Adapted from Hazan, C., & Shaver, P. (1987). Romantic love conceptualized as an attachment process. *Journal of Personality and Social Psychology,* 52, pp. 511–524.

Chapter 13

1. Diener, E., & Biswas-Diener, R. (2002). Will money increase subjective well-being? *Social Indicators Research,* 57, pp. 119–169.

2. Gottesman, G. (1994). *College survival.* New York: Macmillan. P. 206.

3. The College Board, "Annual Survey of Colleges, 2009."

4. *College on credit: How borrowers perceive their education debt: Results of the 2002 national student loan survey* by Dr. Sandy Baum and Marie O'Malley, Nellie Mae Corporation; The College Board, "Trends in Student Aid, 2008."

5. Dominguez, J., & Robin, V. (1993). *Your money or your life: Transforming your relationship with money and achieving financial independence.* New York: Penguin USA.

Chapter 14

1. Sax, L.J., Astin, A.W., Korn, W.S., & Mahoney, K. (1999). *The American freshman: National norms for fall 1999.* Los Angeles: Higher Education Research Institute, UCLA.

2. Chamberlain, K., & Zika, S. (1990). The minor events approach to stress: Support for use of daily hassles. *British Journal of Psychology,* 81, pp. 469–481.

3. Source of table: Marx, M.B., Garrity, T.F., & Bowers, F.R. (1975). The influence of recent life experience on the health of college freshman. *Journal of Psychosomatic Research,* 19, pp. 87–98.

4. Carlson, R. (1997). *Don't sweat the small stuff . . . and it's all small stuff.* New York: Hyperion.

5. Pereira, M., Kartashov, A.I., Ebbeling, C.B., Van Horn, L., Slattery, M.L., Jacobs, Jr., D.R., & Ludwig, D.S. (2005, January 1.) Fast-food habits, weight gain, and insulin resistance (The CARDIA Study): 15-year prospective analysis. *The Lancet,* 365, pp. 36–42.

6. Wechsler, H., Lee, J.E., Nelson, T.F., & Kuo, M. (2002). Underage college students' drinking behavior, access to alcohol, and the influence of deterrence policies. *Journal of American College Health,* 50, pp. 223–236.

7. Koss, M.P. (1993). Rape: Scope, impact, interventions, and public policy responses. *American Psychologist,* 48, pp. 1062–1069.

8. Adapted from Hughes, J.O., & Sandler, B.R. (1987). *"Friends" raping friends: Could it happen to you?* Washington, DC: Association of American Colleges.

Credits

Photo Credits

Page 1, rubberball/Getty Images

Page 2, Photodisc/Getty Images

Page 8, Purestock/Getty Images

Page 15, (t) CORBIS, (b) NASA/Photo Researchers

Page 23, Courtesy of Robert S. Feldman

Page 28, Digital Vision/Getty Images

Page 29, Photodisc/Getty Images

Page 42, Ingram Publishing/Alamy

Page 46, BananaStock/Jupiterimages

Page 51, Ed Bock/CORBIS

Page 52, (l) Courtesy of Robert S. Feldman, (r) Logo of Vassar College. Reprinted with permission of Vassar College

Page 56, image100 Ltd

Page 57, Royalty-free/CORBIS

Page 58, Rick Smolan/Stock Boston

Page 59, Photodisc/Getty Images

Page 76, ASSOCIATED PRESS

Page 84, (l) Reuters/CORBIS, (r) Logo of George Washington University. Reprinted with permission of the George Washington University

Page 89, Phil Boorman/Taxi/Getty Images

Page 90, PhotoLink/Getty Images

Page 91, ColorBlind Images/Iconica/Getty Images

Page 95, David R. Frazier Photolibrary, Inc./Alamy

Page 99, Jose Luis Pelaez, Inc./CORBIS

Page 100, Michael Doolittle/Alamy

Page 116, rubberball/Getty Images

Page 117, Jeffrey Coolidge/CORBIS

Page 125, Pando Hall/Getty Images

Page 127, Royalty-free/CORBIS

Page 134, Commercial Eye/Iconica/Getty Images

Page 140, (l) Courtesy of Robert S. Feldman, (r) Logo of Columbia College. Reprinted with permission of Columbia College

Page 145, Ken Banks/CORBIS

Page 146, Siede Preis/Getty Images

Page 155, Ian Shaw/Alamy

Page 161, Sonda Dawes/Image Works

Page 165, (l) Getty Images, (r) Logo of University of New Hampshire. Reprinted with permission of the University of New Hampshire

Page 169, ColorBlind Images/Iconica/Getty Images

Page 170, Stockbyte

Page 171, Duane Osborn/Somos Images/CORBIS

Page 182, Didier Givois/Vandystadt/Photo Researchers, Inc.

Page 183, Martin Poole/Riser/Getty Images

Page 194, image 100 LTD

Page 198, (l) Courtesy of Robert S. Feldman, (r) Logo of San Diego Mesa College. Reprinted with permission of San Diego Mesa College

Page 202, Digital Vision

Page 203, Photodisc/Getty Images

Page 206, Spencer Grant/PhotoEdit

Page 212, Heide Benser/CORBIS

Page 220, John Touscany/Index Stock

Page 221, (l) Courtesy of Robert S. Feldman, (r) Logo of Surry Community College. Reprinted with permission of Surry Community College

Page 225, Ant Strack/CORBIS

Page 226, Lucidio Studio, Inc./CORBIS

Page 229, CORBIS

Page 241, Alistair Berg/Digital Vision/Getty Images

Page 249, Photodisc/Getty Images

Page 251, Courtesy of Robert S. Feldman

Page 255, Mango Productions/CORBIS

Page 256, Creatas Images/Jupiter Images

Page 260, Getty Images

Page 267, Brand X Pictures/PunchStock

Page 275, John Giustina/Riser/Getty Images

Page 276, Jose Luis Pelaez, Inc./CORBIS

Page 282, Susan Van Etten/PhotoEdit

Page 284, (l) Courtesy of Robert S. Feldman, (r) Logo of Lehman College. Reprinted with permission of Lehman College

Page 289, Lester Lefkowitz/Stone/Getty Images

Page 290, Royalty-free/CORBIS

Page 292, The McGraw-Hill Companies/Gary He Photographer

Page 293, Colin Anderson/CORBIS

Page 305, Royalty-free/CORBIS

Page 308, (l) Courtesy of Carson Scholars Fund, Inc., (r) Logo of Yale University. Reprinted with permission of Yale University

Page 313, Photodisc Red/Getty Images

Page 314, Digital Vision/Getty Images

Page 315, Jupiterimages/Comstock Images/Getty Images

Page 320, Pulp Photography/CORBIS

Page 326, Royalty-free/CORBIS

Page 329, Yellow Dog Productions/Lifesize/Getty Images

Page 335, (l) Courtesy of Robert S. Feldman, (r) Logo of Three Rivers Community College. Reprinted with permission of Three Rivers Community College

Page 339, Lawrence Manning/CORBIS

Page 340, Nikreates/Alamy

Page 343, ASSOCIATED PRESS

Page 347, Don Smetzer/Alamy

Page 351, ICP/Alamy

Page 363, (l) Courtesy of Robert S. Feldman, (r) Logo of Fort Berthold Community College. Reprinted with permission of Fort Berthold Community College

Page 367, Ryan McVay/Getty Images

Page 368, Photodisc/Getty Images

Page 379, Steve Prezant/CORBIS

Page 380, Mike Rominger/Courtesy Appalachian State University

Page 387, Digital Vision/Getty Images

Page 393, Courtesy of Robert S. Feldman.

Text Credits

Page 4, Figure 1.1: © 2008 The Regents of the University of California. All rights reserved.

Page 46, Cartoon–Procrastination: © 2009 Michael Maslin from cartoonbank.com. All Rights Reserved.

Page 71, Cartoon–Good Dog Never Great Dog: © The New Yorker Collection 2000 Alex Gregory from cartoonbank.com. All Rights Reserved.

Page 73, Cartoon–doing homework?: Calvin and Hobbes © 1992 Watterson. Distributed by Universal Press Syndicate. Reprinted with permission. All rights reserved.

Page 133, Peanuts cartoon–is life a multiple choice test?:Peanuts by Charles Schultz © United Feature Syndicate, Inc. Reprinted by permission.

Page 154, Peanuts cartoon–about this book: Peanuts by Charles Schultz © United Feature Syndicate, Inc. Reprinted by permission.

Page 194, Cartoon–Fear of Public Speaking: © 2009 Leo Cullum from cartoonbank.com. All Rights Reserved.

Page 208, Try It! #2: Adapted in part from Halpern. D.F. (2003) *Thought and Knowledge: An Introduction to Critical Thinking*, 4th ed. Mahwah, N.J. pg. 65. Used by permission of Erlbaum Associates, Inc. and Diane Halpern.

Page 243, Table 9.2: Peter D. Hart Research Associates. 2007. *How should colleges prepare students to succeed in today's global economy?* Washington, DC: Peter D. Hart Research Associates.

Page 250, Cartoon–What I'm going to be when I grow up: © The New Yorker Collection 1999 Barbara Smaller from cartoonbank .com. All Rights Reserved.

Page 278, Cartoon–As Your Search Engine: © The New Yorker Collection 2000 John Caldwell from cartoonbank.com. All Rights Reserved.

Page 279, Cartoon–First They do an Online Search: © The New Yorker Collection 1998 Arnie Levin from cartoonbank.com. All Rights Reserved.

Page 281, Cartoon–Nobody Knows You're a Dog: © The New Yorker Collection 1993 Peter Steiner from cartoonbank.com. All Rights Reserved.

Page 294, Table 11-1: "The scale of tolerance-intolerance of ambiguity," Table 1 p.34, in Budner, Stanley (1962). "Intolerance of ambiguity as a personal variable." *Journal of Personality*, Vol. 30, No. 7, pp. 29–50. Used by permission of Wiley-Blackwell, UK.

Page 295, Cartoon–No, Yes, Maybe: © 2009 Charles Barsotti from cartoonbank.com. All Rights Reserved.

Page 300, Cartoon–FoxTrot: FoxTrot © 2009 Bill Amend. Reprinted by permission of Universal Press Syndicate. All Rights Reserved.

Page 315, Fig. 12-1 Diversity Wheel: Loden: *Implementing Diversity, Best Practices for Making Diversity Work in Your Organization.* Used by permission of The McGraw-Hill Co., Inc.

Page 327, Try It #4: Copyright © 1987 by the American Psychological Association. Adapted with permission. Hazan, C., & Shaver, P., Romantic love conceptualized as an attachment process. *Journal of Personality and Social Psychology*, 52, 511–524. No further reproduction or distribution is permitted without written permission from the American Psychological Association.

Page 343, Cartoon–Tradition, Competition, Tuition: © 2009 Michael Maslin from cartoonbank.com. All Rights Reserved

Page 352, Cartoon–Graduates, faculty, parents: © The New Yorker Collection 1993 Arnie Levin from cartoonbank.com. All rights reserved.

Page 357, Cartoon–working my son's way through college: © The New Yorker Collection 1974 J.B. Handelsman from cartoonbank .com. All Rights Reserved.

Page 370, Try It #1: Reprinted from *Journal of Psychosomatic Research,* Volume 19, Issue 1, Martin B. Marx, Thomas F. Garrity and Frank R. Bowers, *The influence of recent life experience on the health of college freshmen*, pp. 87–98. Used with permission from Elsevier, Inc.

Index

A page number followed by 'f' indicates a figure; 't' indicates a table.

Strategies for Success for Student Athletes

A

Learning Outcomes

By the time you finish this chapter you will be able to

>> LO **A.1**   Identify the special advantages of being a student athlete that help meet challenges in college.

>> LO **A.2**   Explain how to deal most effectively with course instructors and time management issues.

>> LO **A.3**   Discuss the best ways to seek and use help.

>> LO **A.4**   Analyze strategies for dealing with pain, injury, and the potential of burnout.

It was two days before the basketball game with Kansas State, and Lucas Givens had just found out that the coach had rescheduled practice. Usually this wouldn't have been a problem, but the time of the practice overlapped with an exam review session that his biology class instructor was offering.

Lucas hadn't done as well as he'd hoped on his last exam, and he really needed to do well on this test in order to get a decent grade in the course. He knew his biology instructor would notice if he missed the review session, because Lucas had been forced to take a makeup exam the last time because of another game. He understood that the instructor didn't like giving what she called "special privileges" to athletes, and Lucas felt like his every move was being scrutinized. If he missed the review session, he knew the instructor would be unwilling to cut him any slack in the future.

To top it off, Lucas's arm wouldn't stop hurting. He'd hurt it a few weeks before, and despite hours of physical therapy, it didn't seem to be getting any better. The dull, aching pain was a constant reminder of the demands—both academic and athletic—that Lucas faced.

Looking Ahead

If you are a student athlete, you may find yourself in a situation similar to that of Lucas. Many student athletes at times feel overwhelmed by the day-to-day challenges that confront them as they navigate the demands of college life.

The good news is that your status as an athlete provides you with special strengths in meeting the challenges of college. You already know the importance of hard work and perseverance. You are aware of how to seek the best from yourself.

Most of all, as an athlete, you know the value of training. You realize that there are skills that you have learned that have made you a better athlete, regardless of your natural abilities. You know that the way you have developed these skills is by practicing them, over and over, until they have become a natural part of who you are.

Ultimately, you understand the equation that *hard work = success*. You recognize that good athletes are made, not born. Although certainly an athlete's natural talents are important, it is how he or she builds on those talents that determines the athlete's ultimate success.

In the same way, good students are made, not born. While academic success comes easier to some and is more difficult for others, the way that we build on our natural talents shapes how successful we will be academically. Just as with athletics, we need to study, learn, and practice the strategies that lead to success.

In this chapter, we examine the special challenges that student athletes face. We will show you how to use the attributes and values you probably already have as an athlete to help maximize your academic success. In addition, we will discuss strategies for juggling the demands on your time and taking advantage of help that is available to you.

»LO A.1 Your Special Strengths in Meeting the Challenges of College

There is no doubt that your status as a student athlete brings with it certain advantages. For example, the strong work ethic and high expectations you need to succeed as an athlete also will help you succeed as a student.

However, at the same time each of those advantages has a downside. Specifically, consider these benefits—and their related drawbacks—to being a student athlete:

Your Work Ethic

▸ *The upside.* As an athlete, you know the value of hard work. You know that success in sports is unattainable unless you put in sufficient practice. This work ethic, when applied to academics, can help you maximize your own success.

▸ *The downside.* The long hours of work that you devote to athletics may prevent you from putting in as much time as you would like—and need—into academic endeavors. You may experience stress and unhappiness over this lack of time.

Expectations

▸ *The upside.* You are almost certainly the recipient of other people's high expectations for you, and you probably hold high expectations for yourself. High expectations help you maintain your motivation, and they put you in the proper frame of mind to succeed. Holding positive expectations can help you do your best.

▸ *The downside.* If your expectations are unrealistically high, you may be setting yourself up for disappointment. It's unlikely that you'll do equally well in every domain of your life, and you need to be realistic about what you can and cannot expect to do. Your expectations need to be realistic in order for them to be helpful. In addition, if you don't meet the expectations of others, you may feel that you have disappointed them. Such negative feelings may hinder your abilities to rebound from failure.

Availability of Student Services

▸ *The upside.* Colleges and universities often provide athletes with special student services to help them navigate college life. These services can range from help with registering for classes to keeping tabs on your academic progress.

▸ *The downside.* You may have so many demands on your time that making use of the special services may be difficult or impossible. Alternatively, you may become so dependent on student services that you lose valuable opportunities to solve problems on your own.

Social Networks

▸ *The upside.* You have a built-in social network. One of the greatest challenges students face when they begin college is building a network of friends. Because you are playing a sport, your teammates provide a ready-made group of people who are probably similar to you in many ways.

▸ *The downside.* Although it is usually easy to make friends among your teammates, it may be more difficult to make friends who are not athletes. You may have limited time available to socialize and to expand your social network. Furthermore, because your teammates are having experiences similar to yours, they may not be able to provide the objective advice and support that you might be able to get from a friend who is not part of your athletic network.

Journal Reflections

On Being a Student Athlete

1. What do you enjoy most about your participation in college athletics?

2. As an athlete, have your course instructors treated you differently from nonathletes? How?

3. What academic difficulties have you faced because of your participation in college athletics?

4. What academic advantages have you experienced because of your participation in college athletics?

Physical Health

› *The upside.* As an athlete, you are probably at the peak of physical conditioning. The hours of practice you put in help keep your body in excellent shape.

› *The downside.* Your health may be compromised by the wear and tear on your body that you suffer during training. You may experience persistent pain, and you are subject to physical injuries. There may also be restrictions on what you can and cannot do, and if you are injured, it may take a long time to heal and regain your physical strength.

Public Visibility

› *The upside.* If you play in a highly visible sport on campus, you may be a role model for others. Being a role model is a real responsibility, but it can provide significant benefits if you handle it wisely. Others may seek out your opinion and ask your advice. You may influence how campus issues are resolved, and you may have the opportunity to participate in fund-raising for causes you support. You may inspire disadvantaged children and adolescents to become more involved in academics and to attend college.

› *The downside.* There's a downside to being highly visible: Your every move may be scrutinized. Each word you utter in class, every object that you pick up while browsing in a store, even what you order at a fast-food restaurant may be analyzed and dissected because of your celebrity. That means you must be on your best behavior—literally all of the time. Use this test: If you wouldn't want

Building Networks That Can Lead to a Job

As a college athlete, you will likely be invited to more than your share of dinners, lunches, banquets, and a range of events that mark a variety of occasions. Although you may look at your attendance at some of these events as an obligation that you would like to avoid, they are actually golden opportunities. The opportunity comes from the potential to network with people—people who just may be able to help you get your first job.

When you go to ceremonial events, take the time to talk with attendees other than your teammates and other students. The community members who are present are people who appreciate what you do. In fact, they may have been involved in athletics themselves when they were in college. This gives you a common bond that will make conversation flow more easily. In addition, attendees are often community leaders—the kind of people who are likely to have many connections that can help you get an internship or, eventually, a job.

If socializing doesn't come easily to you, push yourself. Give yourself the goal of meeting a certain number of strangers. At first, set your goal low, such as meeting only two new people. As you become more comfortable with networking, you can set your sights higher. The important thing is to make the connections.

Ultimately, *who* you know is less important than *what* you know. Still, the reality is that developing a network of people in the world outside of college can only help you get the job you want.

to have something you do on the front page of your college newspaper, then don't do it.

Financial Issues

- ▸ *The upside.* For many athletes, the only reason that they are able to attend college may be athletic scholarships. Scholarship aid offers a wonderful opportunity to attend a college or university that otherwise would be financially out of reach.

- ▸ *The downside.* Athletic scholarships come with many strings attached. It is not easy to supplement one's income, because NCAA rules allow athletes to work for only a limited number of hours each term. In addition, if you are injured or you stop participating in athletics, there is the possibility that you may lose your scholarship. Finally, an athletic scholarship may require you to maintain a certain minimum grade point average, adding to the pressure and stress you face.

NCAA Oversight

- ▸ *The upside.* The NCAA (as well as the NAIA or NJCAA) offers a broad range of support services. For example, many schools make use of the CHAMPS/Life Skills program to help student athletes achieve academic, athletic, career, and general personal development success. (You can learn more about this program at the NCAA Web site at **www.ncaa.org** under "Education Programs.")

- ▸ *The downside.* The regulatory bodies are strict, and if you break the rules, the consequences could be severe. You must become acquainted with a variety of regulations (involving such topics as the total prohibition of gambling and maintaining eligibility).

» LO A.2 Time Management for Student Athletes

Student athletes have no more than the 168 hours in a week that every other student has, but the demands on those hours are often greater for athletes. Perhaps the biggest difficulty is the lack of flexibility in scheduling activities. Games are scheduled months, and sometimes years, in advance, and practices are scheduled at the beginning of the season, sometimes even before classes begin. Still, there may be changes in practice times, rescheduled games, and—if you're lucky—playoff games at the end of the season that can't be anticipated in advance.

> "You can practice shooting eight hours a day, but if your technique is wrong, then all you get is very good at shooting the wrong way. Get the fundamentals down and the level of everything you do will rise."
>
> Michael Jordan, basketball star[2]

All these demands make effective time management particularly crucial for student athletes. Detailed time management strategies are laid out in the full chapter on time management, but there are some lines of attack that are especially relevant to athletes. Among the most important tips for effective time management that especially apply to student athletes are the following:

> **Be sure of your priorities**. Only you can know what is most important to you as you navigate your way through college. Take the time to determine what is most important to you by asking yourself several key questions:
>
> 1. What are the most important reasons I am in college?
> 2. What are my most important long-term goals?
> 3. How can I best achieve those goals?
> 4. How does managing my time bring me closer to my goals? (For help in determining your priorities, use **Try It 1** on page A–8.)

> **Use your traveling time well.** Traveling to away games and meets can eat up big chunks of time. Make use of that time wisely. You can read, study, make and go through flash cards, or write outlines. The more you do while traveling, the less there is to do when you get back to campus.

> **Use a PDA (personal digital assistant) or a traditional calendar.** Think using a BlackBerry, iTouch, or some other type of hand-size personal digital assistant is too, well, geeky for you? Think again. PDAs are widely used in business, and many companies purchase them for their employees and require their use.
>
> PDAs are replacements for traditional schedule books and calendars. PDAs have all the features of a traditional book, but offer several significant advantages. For one, entering an event into the daily schedule makes it also appear in a weekly, monthly, and annual calendar. Recurring events, like classes, can be entered once and then repeated across the term. The information can also be synchronized with a computer, so your schedule is stored in more than one place.
>
> But if you don't want to go high tech and use a PDA, that's fine. Just be absolutely sure to use some kind of traditional calendar.

> **Be flexible.** Although the goal of time management is to schedule your time in advance, it's important to remain flexible. If you slip behind on a project that has a high priority, allocate more time to it. Think of schedules as living, breathing documents that can be revised.

> **Don't let short-term goals overshadow your long-term goals.** You should not let your short-term goals make you forget your long-term goals. It is tempting to place all your energies into activities that can bring about a clear-cut and immediate outcome, such as winning the next game you play.

However, don't let your desire to win make you forget your long-term goals. For the vast majority of your life you will not be a student athlete but a wage earner, family member, and world citizen. Keep that in mind as you make choices about how to expend your time.

‣ **Make use of the off-season.** One thing you do know for sure: Every sport has an off-season. Try to budget your time in a way that allows you to take advantage of terms in which the demands on your time are lower. Schedule more, and harder, classes during the off-season.

‣ **Learn the art of saying "no."** A key to effective time management is knowing when to say "no"—no to that after-game party, that spur-of-the-moment movie, that trip to get a burger. There will be times when you can participate in those things, but there are other times when you will just have to postpone the fun. Knowing when to say no (and yes) is a key aspect of time management for student athletes. (To learn strategies for saying no, complete **Try It 2** on page A-10.)

≫LO A.3 Getting Help

You're facing your nightmare scenario. You haven't had enough time to study for the first few tests in several of your classes, and you are falling further and further behind. Although things are going well on the field, you feel as if your academic life is heading for a giant collision with reality. If you don't start doing better academically, you'll be ineligible to play. And if you don't play, you might lose your athletic scholarship.

You need help ... and you need it fast.

If you ever find yourself in such a situation, you know the feeling of desperation that can come over you. But there are steps you can take to salvage the situation. The worse thing you can do is to do nothing. Act! Use the following steps (which are summarized in the P.O.W.E.R. Plan) to obtain and then make effective use of the resources that are available to you.

P **Prepare**
Decide you need help

O **Organize**
Determine the kind of help you need and where to get it

W **Work**
Make effective use of help

E **Evaluate**
Assess your progress

R **Rethink**
Reconsider your views of receiving help

P.O.W.E.R. Plan

P **Prepare** Deciding You Need Help

Coming to the realization that you are in trouble and need help is the first step in improving the situation. As an athlete, you've been trained to be self-reliant, so you may feel that even asking for help is a failure.

Quite the contrary: Seeking out help is an indication that you are aware of the situation. Realizing that the situation has moved beyond your own abilities to resolve it is a sign of maturity.

O **Organize** Determining the Kind of Help You Need, and Where to Get It

Realizing that you need help is just the first step. You also need to get straight in your own mind the kind of help that you need and to identify where you can find that help. In order to do that, ask yourself these questions:

‣ *What are the specific courses in which I am having trouble?* You're probably not having the same level of difficulty in all of your courses. Choose the ones that are most troublesome and focus on those.

Try It!

1

Determining Your Priorities

Use this **Try It** to consider your priorities and assess how well your current activities relate to your goals and reasons for being in college.

REASONS FOR ATTENDING COLLEGE:

What are the two main reasons that you are in college? Answer this question in terms of your future, not your past (i.e., avoid answers like "My parents made me attend").

R1:

R2:

GOALS:

What are your two most important long-term goals in life?

G1:

G2:

PRIORITIES:

Think about your main college-related activities during the current academic term, as listed in column 1. Indicate in the second column the reason for attending college and/or the goal to which each activity relates. Then, in the third column, set a priority for each activity, from a high of 1 to a low of 5. (Many activities will have the same priority level, but try to spread your priority assignments as much as possible.)

Activities	Related to Reason/ Goal Number:	Priority
Academic Activities		
Attending classes		
Doing daily (short-term) homework assignments		
Doing long-term assignments (e.g., papers)		
Studying each day		
Studying for major examinations		
Other—specify:		
Athletic Activities		
Attending practices, strategy sessions, etc.		

Activities	Related to Reason/ Goal Number:	Priority
Attending games		
Training/exercising outside of formal practices		
Attending athletic events for fund-raising, publicity, alumni relations, etc.		
Attending other athletics-related meetings		
Studying strategies, plays, defenses, etc.		
Other—specify:		
Social/Personal Activities		
Attending school events (including athletic and other events)		
Being with friends		
Dating, partying		
Watching television		
Playing video/computer games		
Reading		
Internet surfing		
Reading/writing e-mail, instant messaging, etc.		
Other—specify:		
Other		
Traveling, visiting family and friends		
Necessities: eating, sleeping		
Maintenance: laundry, shopping, hygiene		
Other—specify:		

WRAP-UP:

How well do your priorities match your reasons for being in college and your goals for when you finish college? Should you make any adjustments?

Saying No to Temptation

You will often face difficult choices during your college career. Among the most difficult (and most frequent) are choices between fun and work. Use this **Try It** to plan ahead for making such choices wisely.

Consider each choice that does NOT relate to your goals in college and does NOT fit into your priorities as a "temptation." Write down below the most common temptations that you are likely to face during the next few months. Then consider the WORST reason to say Yes to that temptation and the BEST reason to say No. Fill in the table below to prepare yourself. (The table has been started for you to show you how to proceed.)

Temptation	Worst Reason to Say Yes	Best Reason to Say No
Let's go see that great new movie tonight.	I can probably finish studying for the big exam tomorrow morning, just before class.	Who am I kidding? I'll never study tomorrow morning, and there's no way I'm going to fail an exam for a movie I can see later.
What a bummer—a 2-point loss. Let's go out and drown our sorrows.	Why not? I'm too bummed to write this paper anyway.	I'm not going to make one loss the excuse for another. I'm going to knuckle down and finish my paper.
Wow! A 1-point win at the final buzzer! Party! Party!		I'll party a little later, after I finish reading this assignment. Go ahead without me, and I'll try to catch up with you.
Hey, this TV show is going to be great! We're all going to watch it at Joe's place. Come on.	If I don't show up, people will think I'm a jerk.	
Your girlfriend/boyfriend called and would really like to see you tonight— but you've got a paper to do.		

> *What is the specific difficulty I am encountering?* Are you doing badly on the tests in one or more courses? Are you having trouble producing satisfactory papers? Is the problem class participation? First determine specifically what the problem is, and then you can figure out what you need to do to address it.

> *What kind of help do I need?* If you don't perform well on the multiple-choice exams in a class, perhaps tutoring in the course content would be helpful. Or perhaps your problems stem from difficulties in taking multiple-choice tests in general, and you would benefit from learning effective strategies for taking such exams. Sometimes using publisher-generated material can help. For example, many textbooks are accompanied by a *Student Study Guide* or have an online Web site with practice tests.

> *Can a study group help?* Sometimes the simplest route for receiving help is to organize a study group with other students in a class. It doesn't need to be a group. In fact, just meeting regularly with another student in the class to go over assignments and study for tests can be beneficial. Whether it consists of only you and another student, or is made up of a larger number of students, a study group can help you pinpoint difficult issues and make sure you are

on the right track when studying. It can also give you extra motivation to tackle the more challenging aspects of a class.

> *Have I discussed the problem with my course instructor?* The individuals who are in the best position to determine the help you need are the instructors of the courses in which you need help. They can provide guidance about the specific areas in which you need help. In addition, some instructors may be willing to go over material with you and provide personalized instruction. (Don't expect this to happen very often; most instructors simply don't have the time to provide extensive tutoring on class material to individual students.)

In some cases, individual classes will have a support system built into the course. For example, if the class is large, teaching assistants may be able to provide support and perhaps even individual tutoring for students who are having problems with the course content.

Discussing your difficulties with your course instructor serves another purpose beyond simply getting information: It shows that you are concerned about your class performance. Instructors will be more likely to go the extra mile for students who are genuinely concerned about how they are doing than for those who appear to ignore the problem.

If you find yourself struggling in your academic work, don't wait until it's too late for help. There are a number of resources available to help you succeed in class, but you must make the first move.

> *Where can I get help?* If you are lucky, finding help will not be difficult. Colleges want their students to be successful, and they try to provide the resources students need in order to make that success a reality. In some cases, though, you may have to dig through a college bureaucracy to find the appropriate person who can help you.

As a student athlete, your first point of contact should be your academic advisor. Many athletic departments offer academic support to athletes, and that's the person you should speak with first. If the athletic department doesn't provide an advisor, then you most likely will have been assigned an advisor in some other unit of the college. Make an appointment with your advisor to discuss the situation and get advice about where to go next.

If you don't have an advisor, there are sure to be other offices on campus where you can seek help. Try your campus Office of Student Services or Student Affairs or your campus Counseling Center. With persistence, you will eventually reach a person who can help you—or at least lead you in the right direction.

Complete **Try It 3** on page A-12 to identify the resources on your own campus that are available to student athletes.

W Work   Making Effective Use of Help

You've identified the kind of help you need and found someone to help you. Now the real work begins.

As a recipient of aid, it's easy to think of yourself as being in a passive role, assuming that the person who is helping you is responsible for making sure you make progress. However, that's just not true. *You* have the responsibility for ensuring that the help you receive is effective. It will take your effort and hard work to

Try It!

3

Identifying Campus Resources

As an athlete and a member of a college community, you have many resources you can turn to when things get tough. The key is to find them in time. Do some legwork in advance to identify good resources for a range of academic challenges you may face in the future. Be creative: Consider teachers, coaches, academic advisors, counselors, library staff, friends, classmates, academic support services—anyone who might help. List the best resources in the second column and information on how to contact them (phone number, office location, e-mail address, etc.) in the last column.

Use this **Try It** table to find and list the resources in advance of your need for them. Update it as you continue your college career.

If I Need Help with:	I Can Go to:	Contact Information
A specific course (list courses):		
Understanding a homework or paper assignment		
Coming up with a good paper topic		
Understanding how to write a paper		
Finding articles or books as background for a research paper		
Learning to take tests		
Writing more effectively		
Basic math concepts and skills		
Basic grammar skills		
Reading better		
Studying more effectively		
Managing my time better		
Overcoming my anxiety about getting everything done on time		
Other:		

produce the desired outcome, in the same way that it is the effort and hard work of players that make a coach's guidance effective.

How can you make best use of the help you are receiving? Here are some guidelines:

> **Treat tutoring sessions as a regular class.** Even though the help you are receiving is personalized, you shouldn't treat your tutor as an employee whose job description can change on a whim. Treat your tutor with respect. Arrive

at tutoring sessions on time, and don't leave early. If you must miss a session, notify the tutor as far in advance as possible.

> **Coordinate your tutoring with your course instructor.** Let instructors of courses in which you are receiving help know about the assistance you are getting. They may be able to suggest particular areas on which you should concentrate. They also may be able to suggest specific study materials (such as a *Student Study Guide* that accompanies your textbook) that would be helpful. Finally, letting your instructor know that you are seeking help demonstrates your effort and motivation.

> **Don't expect your tutor to do your work.** You should not expect your tutor to write papers for you, to complete assignments, or to supply you with test questions. There are limits—both practical and ethical—that constrain just what a tutor can do, and you need to keep those limits in mind.

> **Learn the process of studying a subject area, as well as its content.** A good tutor will teach you not only course content but also ways of studying the material effectively. The study strategies you use for an English class are different from those you will use for a math class. The more you learn strategies for dealing with new material, the better the ultimate outcome.

> **If it's not working out, discuss the situation with your tutor.** Tutors are no more alike than college instructors. Some work hard and go the extra mile, while others may behave in a mechanical, unsympathetic manner. If you find the help you are receiving is inadequate or problematic, discuss the problem with your tutor. If you can't find an acceptable solution, try to identify another tutor.

E Evaluate   Assessing Your Progress

It's important to check out whether the help you are receiving is beneficial. Keep track of how you perform on tests, papers, and other assignments. Get feedback from your instructors after each graded assignment to check your progress. If you are still dissatisfied with your grade, consider how it might be improved. Ask yourself these questions:

> Is my tutor providing the help I most need?

> Am I making the most of each tutoring session?

> Have I focused on the right areas of study?

> Do I need more practice in certain areas?

> Am I putting in sufficient work outside of tutoring sessions?

Remember, ultimately it is you who is responsible for your success in school—not your tutor. Your successes and failures are due to the amount of hard work that you invest in your studies.

R Rethink   Reconsidering Your Views of Receiving Help

One central value of North American society is self-reliance. While this independent streak motivates people to "make it on their own," it also makes many feel reluctant to seek out much-needed help. When help is provided, it may be accepted with hesitation.

Dealing with Course Instructors

Behind the faces of the course instructors that you see in class are human beings— human beings with particular beliefs, attitudes, values, and even prejudices about the students in their classes. Some instructors may hold student athletes in high esteem, particularly if they themselves participated in athletics when they were in college.

On the other hand, some instructors may harbor negative feelings about student athletes, believing that they receive special privileges from the college or that the athletics program receives too much emphasis or requires too big a budget. In some cases, instructors simply may be unaware of the particular challenges that student athletes face.

What should you do if you encounter an unsympathetic instructor? How can you avoid alienating an instructor in the first place? Consider using one of these strategies to win over instructors and make them more likely to be your ally:

- *Know the class policies and syllabus.* Before you ask an instructor for something special, be sure you already have studied the class syllabus and know the instructor's policies on makeup exams and paper extensions. The class policy may already provide for makeups and extensions, and you want to stay within the normal guidelines as much as possible. Instructors do not like to reexplain things that they've already talked about in class or have included on the course syllabus.

- *Ask for exceptions well in advance.* You have a much better chance of receiving an extension on a paper or rescheduling an exam if you ask in advance. In most cases, you will know your schedule months ahead. Check out the course schedule to see if there are any conflicts. Instructors tend to be more sympathetic if they see you actively planning in advance, rather than waiting until the last minute to make a special request.

- *Be flexible.* If you are asking to reschedule a test or get an extension on a paper, be as flexible as you possibly can when asking for the change. If an instructor agrees to give you a makeup test, for example, make a real and visible effort to schedule the makeup at a time convenient for the instructor, even if you are inconvenienced. Remember that it is the instructor who is doing you a favor, not the other way around.

- *Give 100 percent to the class.* You can't expect to receive special consideration if your instructor does not view you as a motivated, hard-working student. Do your best, and make it apparent that you are doing your best.

- *Never act as if you deserve special consideration because you are a student athlete.* You should never convey the impression that you think you warrant special privileges that are unavailable to other students. All students have their own unique, personal set of challenges and demands. Any request that you make is just one of many that an instructor receives during the course of the term, and you should not act as if yours are somehow more important.

- *Seek the intervention of others in dealing with very difficult instructors.* What if you are unable to win the cooperation of an unsympathetic instructor, and your academic success in the course is jeopardized? If all else fails, you might consider asking for the intervention of someone in the athletic department.

   However, this is an extreme measure. Be aware that there is a chance that your situation may go from bad to worse if your instructor views the intervention as a personal attack. Instructors who are unsympathetic to student athletes in their classes may be just as unsympathetic to a call from a representative of the athletic department.

Consequently, it is important to understand the dynamics of receiving help. It is important to be aware that those who provide help are doing so with your best interests in mind. There is nothing wrong with seeking out help—and there is a problem if you actively avoid making use of assistance that is available to you.

As a student athlete, you face challenges that nonathletes don't confront. Make use of the academic opportunities that are available to you as much as you make use of the athletic opportunities you find in college.

»LO A.4 Pain and Injury: The Special Challenge to the Student Athlete

You hurt. You hurt a lot. Practices have been tough; the coach is pushing you hard; and your knee, which you injured in high school and has always been your weak point, is throbbing five minutes after you run onto the court. The pain doesn't even let up after practice. It's there all the time. You sometimes awake in the middle of the night in agony. Even just sitting at your desk and twisting your knee in a certain way can produce shooting pain.

Now you're supposed to be studying for two tests tomorrow. All you can think about is the pain.

The pain that comes from an injury can be overwhelming, focusing your attention on little else but the pain itself. How can you deal with such pain? There are several things you can do to respond effectively to pain and the sports injuries that cause it, including the following:

> **Understand what pain is.** Pain is a symptom of something else. It is your body's way of alerting you to an injury to some cells that make up the body.
>
> However, pain is not only a direct physical reaction to something that is wrong. The way that we react to an injury influences how much pain we experience. Even a minor stimulus can produce the experience of strong pain if it is accompanied by anxiety. (That's why even minor dental procedures sometimes produce great pain.) Consequently, the amount of pain we experience reflects our emotions and thoughts.
>
> In addition, pain is an important warning sign. If we never experienced pain, we wouldn't be aware of situations in our bodies that required attention.

> **Deal with the source of the pain.** Under no circumstances should you ignore pain. Pain is a warning that something is wrong. Don't "suck it up" and pretend that everything is fine. Instead, use pain as the warning it is meant to be, and act on it. Consult your team trainer, a physician, or another health practitioner. Visit your student health center. Even if you have experienced similar pain in the past, you cannot make a self-diagnosis. Go to a professional, even if you are apprehensive about what you may find out.

> "The will to win is important, but the will to prepare is vital."
>
> Joe Paterno,[3] football coach

> **Follow through on treatment for the pain.** Once you know what is causing your pain, follow through on the advice you receive about how to treat the pain. Don't decide that you know better and things will improve on their own. If it is recommended that you do physical therapy, follow through. Put as much effort into the therapy as you would into a team practice.

> **Use drug therapies to reduce pain with exceptional care.** Drugs work: They can reduce pain significantly. Furthermore, by reducing the pain, they can make the body relax, which in turn makes the natural healing process proceed more rapidly.

However, there's a potential price to be paid for the habitual use of drugs: They can be addictive. Even superstar athletes like NFL quarterback Brett Favre, developed a dependency on the painkiller Vicodin. It took six weeks in rehab to overcome the drug habit.

To avoid drug problems, follow prescriptions *precisely*. If a drug seems ineffective, go back to the person who prescribed it and ask for a change. There are many potentially effective drugs, and if one doesn't work, an alternative can be tried.

Furthermore, avoid the use of steroids. Although they can increase muscle mass and strength and decrease body fat, they also can lead to heart attacks, strokes, cancer, depression, and even violent behavior. They are dangerous, and their side effects outweigh any possible benefits.

In any case, **never** use illegal drugs or drugs that have been prescribed for someone else. Not only are you playing Russian roulette with your body, but such drugs may have side effects that produce depression, anxiety, and social withdrawal. If you are caught using illegal drugs, this can lead to expulsion from school or legal action.

▶ **Use stress-reduction techniques.** Because stress makes pain worse, use stress-reduction techniques. For example, you might try to reduce the things that are causing you stress. If a relationship is causing you stress, consider ending it. If you are overwhelmed with course work, seek out help from your instructors or a teaching assistant, or consider working with a tutor.

You can also use relaxation techniques, such as progressive relaxation or meditation, that can help you deal with the physiological reactions that accompany stress. Finally, try *self-talk,* in which you either think or say to yourself affirmations that you have the ability to deal with a situation. Such self-talk can be in the form of action words ("You can do it!") or mood words ("Relax!").

▶ **Understand the side benefits of recovering from injury.** It seems obvious that recovering from an athletic injury is beneficial. But awareness of the side benefits of recovery can at the least be comforting and, at most, can actually be psychologically beneficial, thereby speeding recovery time.

What are the side benefits of recovery? You may gain a broader perspective, be able to focus on other areas of your life while recovering, and learn better time management strategies. In addition, physical therapy for the injury may improve your overall fitness level. Finally, as with facing and overcoming any adversity, recovering from an injury may give you a kind of mental toughness that will help you deal with future challenges.

Hazing

When Jean-François Caudron came to training camp on a hockey scholarship, he knew he had to prove himself to his coaches. But it wasn't only his coaches that he felt he had an obligation to, it was to his teammates as well. So he willingly participated in an initiation ritual called "Rookie Night." It involved shaving his body, painting his toenails, and tossing back enough warm beer to make him vomit.[4]

Hazing
An activity that humiliates or degrades a person joining a team or other group

In some ways, Caudron was lucky. There are instances in which hazing has led to severe injury and even death.

Hazing is an activity designed to humiliate or degrade a person who is joining a team or other group. It encompasses a wide variety of abusive behaviors, including yelling, making people wear embarrassing clothing, forcing them to drink large quantities of alcohol or foul-tasting liquids, tattooing and piercing, beatings, paddling, bondage, and confining someone in a small space.

Although it is universally banned on college campuses (and is illegal in most states), four out of five athletes say they have participated in some form of a hazing ritual.[5] In most cases, it is fairly benign, but in others it can lead to terrible consequences.

Hazing is a difficult practice from which to escape, because teammates may exert enormous peer pressure to go along with the ritual. However, keep these facts in mind:

> You don't need to accept hazing. It is your decision. You do have a choice.

> No one should be allowed to do something that harms you. Period.

> You don't owe it to anyone to allow yourself to be hazed. You can be accepted by your teammates and not be hazed.

> Your first allegiance is to your family and friends—not your team. Family members and real friends don't make you suffer indignity and pain.

It's important to keep in mind that your job as a team member is to do your best at your sport. That's where your responsibility as a teammate lies, and not as a participant in an illegal practice that can harm you.

Burnout: When Athletics No Longer Matter

When I was sixteen, I was swimming worse than when I was thirteen, and I felt like I was never going to come out of it. I really wasn't enjoying the sport anymore because I was doing so poorly, and that time was really tough. . . . I'd done it for over ten years, and it's hard to give up something after that long. . . . I guess I realized that you have to make it fun. If you're so serious about it all the time and it starts going bad, then it's really going to destroy you.

Leslie Hoh, University of Missouri–Columbia, swimmer[6]

Have you ever felt that you'd reached the end of your rope, that sports competition was bringing you no pleasure, and that you would welcome the opportunity to drop out of athletic activity altogether? If so, you may have been suffering from burnout. **Burnout** is a condition in which an athlete feels dissatisfaction, physical or emotional exhaustion, disillusionment, and frustration. In burnout, sports are devalued, and athletic accomplishment may decline.

There are many reasons why athletes experience burnout. One is feeling chronic stress. Student athletes may feel torn by the athletic, academic, and social demands of college. They may feel they have too much to do and not enough time to do it in.

Furthermore, the special demands of athletics may be particularly difficult to surmount. Athletes face constant pressure to win, and their successes and failures are extremely public. They may have to spend excessive amounts of time in practice, and then the payoff—in terms of actual playing time—may be relatively low. In addition, student athletes may feel that they have relatively little control over their lives. Each moment may seem scheduled, and in such situations it is hard to develop a sense of independence and self-sufficiency. (To see if you have the symptoms of burnout, complete **Try It 4** on page A–18.)

Burnout

A condition in which an athlete feels dissatisfaction, physical or emotional exhaustion, disillusionment, and frustration

Try It!

4 Are You Burning Out?

Consider the symptoms below that may indicate burnout and note whether you have experienced each symptom often, sometimes, or never. If you have a pattern of four or more "sometimes" answers and three or more "often" answers, talk to a friend or go to your campus counseling center and ask for some help from a professional.

	Never	Sometimes	Often
1. I'm tired for days at a time without being able to figure out why.			
2. My friends and teammates tell me that I'm moody.			
3. I experience periods when my mood is bad and stays bad no matter what I do.			
4. I can't even get happy about winning.			
5. Nothing seems to give me pleasure.			
6. Others tell me to cheer up and quit acting so sad.			
7. I go through periods when I can hardly think.			
8. I have way too much to do and no time to do it in.			
9. I just can't seem to pay attention in class.			
10. I can't even pay attention to my coaches.			
11. I keep making stupid mental mistakes.			
12. I have times when it's hard even to get out of bed.			
13. I go through periods when I can't sleep well.			
14. I'm not getting enough playing time and respect from my coaches.			
15. I have serious doubts about my athletic abilities.			
16. I wonder what I'm even doing in college.			
17. I think I'm really a fake and that my incompetence will soon be found out.			
18. People tell me I'm no fun to be with.			
19. I get into arguments with people for no real reason.			
20. I think I'm letting everyone down—my team, my coaches, and my parents.			

Burnout may lead student athletes to be less effective physically. Your performance can suffer, and you may lose your motivation to succeed. If burnout is not addressed, it can ultimately cause you to drop out of athletics completely. In the worst case, it can have a negative impact on your academic success, too.

You can use several strategies to avoid burnout. They are:

> **Be sensitive to the early warning signs of burnout, and take steps to prevent it.** Know the symptoms of burnout. If you begin to experience them, talk to someone about it—a family member or friend, an instructor, or a counselor at your college's counseling center. Think hard about changes you can make in your life to make burnout less likely.

> **Be clear in your own mind as to why you are playing.** Play for yourself, not for others. You should not be on a team only to make others feel proud of you or because others expect it of you. If it's not enjoyable in and of itself, then you shouldn't be doing it.

> **Hold realistic expectations.** You may not always play as well as you want; you may not always receive all the playing time you'd like; you may be asked to do more than you think you can do and may not always receive support from all your instructors. These are the facts of life for student athletes. Being aware that you may face tough times, and that things will not always proceed as you'd like them to, can help you confront the problems more effectively when they do occur.

> **Manage your time more effectively.** As we discussed, time management is one of the keys to avoiding burnout. If you use effective time management techniques, you'll be better prepared to face the multiple demands on your time.

> **Take time off.** If you're experiencing the symptoms of burnout, take some time off every once in a while. Relax and do something entirely different from what you usually do.

> **Give it up.** What if you are profoundly unhappy about your participation in athletics? If you are honest with yourself and you are truly unhappy, then it is not unreasonable to end your sports participation, at least for a while.

> Of course, leaving sports should be your last response to burnout, not your first. It is a momentous decision, and it will have implications that reverberate throughout every aspect of your college life. You certainly shouldn't end your team participation without talking it through with a coach, academic advisor, friend, or some other person who can provide you with good advice. Ultimately, though, you may come to the conclusion that the most reasonable course for you might be to end your participation on a team.

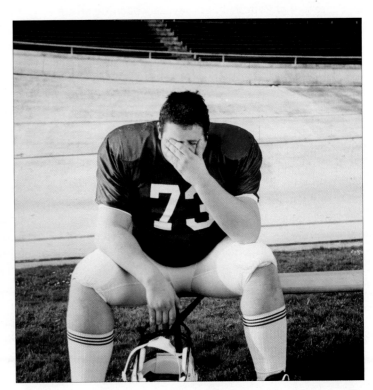

Athletes can be under so much pressure that they can succumb to burnout.

speaking of success

NAME: **Dr. Rod Paige, former U.S. Secretary of Education**

SCHOOL: **Jackson State University, Jackson, Mississippi**

From his earliest years, Rod Paige had two loves: education and football. He excelled at both, ultimately becoming the U.S. teacher-in-chief as Secretary of Education via several coaching stints at a number of colleges.

Paige has come a long way from his poor roots in rural Mississippi. His father was a barber and high school principal, and his mother was a librarian. "My parents told us the solution to the world's problems was education," said Paige, and he took those words to heart.

Paige attended Jackson State University, a historically black college that was segregated at the time. There he played end on the football team and became an honor student. Said his college roommate, Walter Reed, "If there was a test and somebody had made a 98, we knew it had to be Rod." On the field, Paige was known as a hard-hitting, dogged player.

Sports were critical to Paige's success. He credits football coach Harrison Wilson for motivating him to look ahead and to be aggressive. "He was always looking forward, preparing and planning. He would say, 'I'm going to own a house like that one day,' or 'I'm going to be a president of a university one day.'

That kind of rubbed off on me. . . . He created the ambition in my life," said Paige.

After graduating from college, Paige became a teacher and college football coach. He also pursued his education, receiving a masters and a doctoral degree from Indiana University. It wasn't easy. Because he had attended a segregated, underfunded college as an undergraduate, his academic preparation did not equal that of many of his graduate school classmates. Nevertheless, through hard work and determination, he succeeded. "I adopted a philosophy that if you can do this in an hour, I'll do it in three. When we come to class, I'm not going to take a backseat," he said.

Paige went on to become athletic director and then dean of Texas Southern University's education school. He eventually was hired as superintendent of the Houston school system, which led to his appointment as the U.S. Secretary of Education.

Athletics remains an important part of who Paige is, and the values he learned as a student athlete are a central part of his life. "The game of football has left an indelible mark on my heart and on my life," says Paige.[7]

Looking Back

What are the special advantages of being a student athlete that help meet the challenges of college?

▸ The special advantages include having a strong work ethic, holding high expectations, the availability of special services, a strong social network, good health, the possibility of acting as a role model, and financial support.

▸ At the same time, each of those advantages is accompanied by potential disadvantages of being a student athlete.

How can I deal most effectively with course instructors and time management issues?

▸ Among the strategies for dealing effectively with course instructors is knowing the class policies and syllabus well, asking for exceptions in advance, being flexible, giving 100 percent to a class, never demanding special consideration, and seeking the intervention of others.

▸ Effective time management depends on being certain of one's priorities, using a PDA (personal digital assistant), or calendar, being flexible, keeping long-term goals in mind, making use of the off-season, and just saying "no."

What are the best ways to seek and use help?

▸ Effective help-seeking involves determining the kind of help that is needed and identifying potential resources.

▸ To use help effectively, student athletes should be active recipients of the aid, taking responsibility for their own progress.

How do I best deal with pain, injury, and the potential of burnout?

▸ Pain and injury can be dealt with by seeking treatment and following medical advice carefully, following through with treatment, and not ignoring pain.

▸ Burnout, in which an athlete may be physically and psychologically exhausted, can be addressed by being sensitive to the early warning signs, understanding why one is playing, holding realistic expectations, managing time effectively, and taking time off.

[KEY TERMS AND CONCEPTS]

Hazing (p. A-16)   Burnout (p. A-17)

[RESOURCES]

ON CAMPUS

As a student athlete, your college's athletic department usually provides support ranging from physical therapy to tutoring. If you are unsure of the resources that are available to you, ask your coach.

IN PRINT

Hilary Abramson's *Student Athlete's Guide to College* (Princeton Review, 1999) provides a wealth of information on the advantages of athletic participation, including a clear summary of NCAA, NAIA, and NJCAA eligibility rules. *Student-Athlete Success: Meeting Challenges of College Life* (Jones & Bartlett Publishers, 2008) is an accessible guide for student athletes, parents, and coaches. It gives current information about the challenges surrounding student athletes, and offers clear strategies and techniques for coping with the unique pressures faced. Finally, Becky Bell's *If I Knew Then What I Know Now* (Game of Life, 2003) offers advice and strategies from student athlete leaders.

ON THE WEB

The following sites on the World Wide Web provide the opportunity to extend your learning about the material in this chapter. (Although the Web addresses were accurate at the time the book was printed, check the *P.O.W.E.R. Learning* Web site [**www.mhhe.com/power**] for any changes that may have occurred.)

➤ This link (**www.marquette.edu/cof/SAA/athletes-report-final.htm**) provides an in-depth discussion of the issues confronting student athletes, and is an interesting look at how a university is attempting to deal with the issues of athletes and academics.

➤ This interview with a Purdue University football player, at **www.purdueexponent.org/2001/12/03/features/**, will give you an inside look at the demands faced by a college athlete and the importance of time management.

➤ The National Collegiate Athletic Association (NCAA) site (**www.ncaa.org**) offers a number of features designed for promoting optimal health (beyond peak athletic performance). At this site, click on "Academics & Athletes" and then "Personal Welfare" to link to a number of resources for making healthy choices.

TAKING IT TO THE NET

1 Are athletes exceptionally healthy—or do they have more health problems than nonathletes? Locate one or more sites on the Web with information about the health issues that athletes face, including both advantages and risks of being a college athlete. Write down any information that appears helpful or interesting.

2 What stereotypes do athletes have to deal with in college? Use a search engine to locate on the Web five or more stereotypes about college athletes (e.g., "the dumb jock"). Try to find factual information about these stereotypes. Write down a summary of what you find.

[NOTES]

1. Quoted in Bell, B. (2003). *If I knew then what I know now.* Tucson, AZ: Game of Life.
2. Quoted in Isenberg, M., & Rhoads, R. (2001). *The student athlete survival guide.* Camden, ME: Ragged Mountain Press/McGraw-Hill.
3. Palestini, R. (2008). *A game plan for effective leadership: Lessons from 10 successful coaches in moving theory to practice.* Lanham, MD: Rowman & Littlefield Education.
4. O'Hara, J. (2000, March 6). "The hell of hazing." *Maclean's*, p. 50.
5. Hoover, N.C. (1999, August 30). National survey: Initiation rites and athletics for NCAA sports teams. Alfred University.
6. Quoted in Quitmeir, L. (2000, November 16). Olympic trial and error. *Columbia Missourian*, pp. B1, B3.

7. Paige quotes from Fields-Meyer, T., & Kramer, L. (2001, November 19). Class act. pp. 151–155; Winters, R. (2001, February 5). Teacher in chief. **www.cnn.com/allpolitics/ time/2001/02/12/teacher.html**; Chappell, K. (2001, October). Rod Paige: America's education chief; America's coach. USA Football site. **www.usafootball.com/features/ rodPaige.html**.

[PHOTO CREDITS]

Page A-1: © Digital Vision/Getty Images
Page A-2: © Nick Koudis/Getty Images
Page A-11: © Veer
Page A-19: © B. Bird/Zefa/CORBIS
Page A-20: © Reuters/CORBIS

The Case of . . .

The Icy Pressure

There was pressure on Gino Criswell. He hadn't been a starter on the hockey team at the beginning of the season, but one of his teammates had been severely injured. He was out for the season, leaving a starting position open for Gino.

Although starting was a dream come true, it brought enormous pressures that Gino hadn't anticipated. The coach pushed him mercilessly during practice, trying to raise his level of play. Furthermore, the team was having a winning season, which brought even more pressure as the team edged nearer to a playoff berth. The coach was constantly extending practice and even adding some additional ones to the schedule. The hockey games, which usually drew small crowds, were playing to a full rink. He felt that his every move on the ice was being watched—and criticized—by the fans.

To add to the pressure, Gino was devoting so much time to the hockey team that he barely could keep up with his classes. Even when he found time to study, he was usually so exhausted that he couldn't concentrate effectively. The professor in his hardest class, macroeconomics, was no help. In fact, he acted downright hostile when Gino asked if he could postpone a paper that was due the following week. The professor said that he would grant no favors to any student, but particularly to athletes.

Gino didn't know what to do. His grades were slipping, and he wasn't even playing that well on the ice. He didn't think he could handle the pressure.

1. What advice might you give Gino?

2. Is there anything Gino could have done in advance to prevent getting into a situation like this one?

3. What specific strategies could Gino use to deal with his professors?

4. Is there anything Gino can do in terms of his participation on the hockey team that would help the situation?

5. What advice could you give Gino to prevent a situation like this from occurring again in the future?

Taking Charge of Your Career

Learning Outcomes

By the time you finish this chapter you will be able to

» LO **C.1**   Identify your ideal career and job.

» LO **C.2**   Analyze strategies for finding and getting a job.

» LO **C.3**   Discuss how to maximize job interviewing skills.

Darla Ketcham thought she was ready for the job interview.

She'd spent quite a bit of time thinking about her upcoming interview for the product manager's position at a Pepperidge Farm frozen food processing subsidiary, readying answer after answer for the position. She'd carefully researched the company online, reviewed her own experience, and had even gone so far as to purchase and try a sampling of Pepperidge Farm products (which proved to be not much of a sacrifice, actually).

But when the interviewer, seemingly out of the blue, asked her, "Why are manhole covers round?" she was clueless. How should she know? What did that question have to do with frozen cheesecake?

Looking Ahead

Luckily for Darla, what she later called the "manhole incident" was a turning point. Once she got beyond her initial shock, she realized that the aim of the question was to test not her knowledge of manhole covers but her problem-solving skills. After first noting that not all manhole covers are round, she then came up with a few creative possibilities. The interviewer, clearly satisfied, moved on to other, more predictable questions.

Job interviews can be anxiety-producing events. But they are just one of a series of challenging activities that are part of the process of choosing a career and finding a job. In this chapter, we address strategies for identifying your career goals and planning to achieve them. We consider the things you need to know to find the right career path and examine ways to get the job you want.

≫ LO C.1 Career Planning

P Prepare
Identify your ideal job, skills, and career goals

O Organize
Find career opportunities

W Work
Create a career portfolio

E Evaluate
Get feedback on your résumé and cover letter

R Rethink
Reconsider your career choices

P.O.W.E.R. Plan

You're just beginning college. How are you supposed to know for sure what you want to do professionally for the rest of your life?

Happily, you're *not* supposed to know for sure. You're not even expected to have a clue about what you're going to do professionally. That's what college, and some thoughtful career planning, are all about. Your college years are a time to find out who you are, identify your strengths and weaknesses, and gain more understanding of your likes and dislikes.

Furthermore, career planning is not about preparing yourself for a rest-of-your-life job. Sure, there are people who know that they want to be an airline pilot from the fifth grade on, and they train for that career single-mindedly and stick with it for their entire working lives. Those people are the exception.

For most of us, career planning is an ongoing process. You're planning for your *next* job, not the job that has to last a lifetime. In fact, most people will have three to five different professions during their working lives. Some of those professions probably don't exist now.

P Prepare

Identifying Your Ideal Job, Skills, and Career Goals

The first step in career planning is to forget about specific jobs and occupations. Instead, think about what your values are and what it is you enjoy doing. Consider how you'd like to spend your time, even if you didn't get paid for it. Are you mechanically inclined, easily able to take things apart and put them back together? Do you like to spend time outdoors? Do you enjoy numbers, or crossword puzzles, or surfing the Web? Do you like to participate in service activities, helping others?

Use your likes and dislikes as a start to making your ideal job description. Complete **Try It 1** on page C-4 to get a sense of what your dream job would be like.

It's also important to consider the skills that you have. For example, you may dream of playing professional baseball, but unless you have certain physical skills, it's unlikely you'll be the next Derek Jeter. As you think about your skills, don't limit yourself to specific areas. For instance, you should consider not only your natural abilities, those skills you've inherited from your parents and other relatives, but also skills involving intellectual, academic, and social domains.

Once you've reflected on the activities involved in your ideal job and the skills that you have, use that information to help determine your specific career goals. Apart from what you might do during the day, do you want a job that helps others? A job that pays very well? One with flexible hours? Is having an impact on future generations important to you? Use **Try It 2** on page C-6 to identify your long-term career goals.

> "If a man is called to be a street sweeper, he should sweep streets even as Michelangelo painted, or Beethoven composed music, or Shakespeare wrote poetry. He should sweep streets so well that all the hosts of heaven and earth will pause to say, here lived a great street sweeper who did his job well."
> **Martin Luther King, Jr.**

≫ LO C.2   Finding Career Opportunities

Research, research, research.

That's the name of the game when it comes to identifying possible careers. There are literally thousands of different occupations, and the number—and variety—of jobs are constantly shifting.

There's no way anyone can keep track of every option. Fortunately, there are several classification systems that can help you organize information about career possibilities and make your research manageable.

However you decide to carry out your search for information about careers, be sure to keep notes about what you find. Your notes don't have to be elaborately written or suitable for handing in to an instructor. Just keep them simple, legible, and organized, and make sure that they include the source of the information you're describing.

Books and Web Sites

A good first step in obtaining career information is the U.S. Department of Labor's *Occupational Outlook Handbook (OOH)*. The *OOH*, published every two years, categorizes occupations into 11 broad groupings. It provides information on kinds of work, working conditions, job outlook, earnings, education and training requirements, and expected job prospects.

You can also visit the Department of Labor Web site at **www.bls.gov/oco/**, which provides a wealth of additional information. Among the most interesting features of the Web site is a compilation of the most up-to-date information on the hottest professions, in terms of projected future growth. (This information, summarized in **Table C.1,** must be used with care: The mere fact that a job is expanding rapidly doesn't necessarily mean that there are huge numbers of openings. A quickly growing profession may have only a few openings, and even with rapid growth, the absolute number of jobs may still be relatively small in coming years.)

POWER Try It!

Discovering Your Ideal Job

PART I:

The first column of the table below contains questions about your personal preferences, focusing on *what* you like to do and *how* you like to do it. Briefly answer the questions, using the space in the second column.

Questions	Your Preferences
When you have some time on your hands, what do you find yourself doing?	
Have you ever gotten so engrossed in something that you completely lost track of time? What were you doing?	
At school, what classes have you enjoyed most?	
After or outside of school, what activities have you found most enjoyable?	
Have you ever watched someone doing something and thought you would really like to try it? What was it?	
What would you willingly get out of bed early to do?	
What sort of problem would you willingly stay up all night to solve?	
What jobs have you seen or read about that made you wonder how a person learns to do them?	
Have you ever thought, *"Now, that's a cool job. I wonder how you get to do that?"* What was that job?	
Do you like working alone or with others? Why?	

You are likely to find the *OOH,* and a wealth of other information, either in the career center of your college or in its library. In addition, almost every public library has a reference section on careers, and state employment centers often have extensive materials to help identify careers.

In addition to books, you may find CD-ROMs, pamphlets, and other helpful material at career centers, libraries, and employment centers. These resources also may offer on-site computers with software that can help you gather job-related information. For example, the *Discover Career Guidance and Information System* and *SIGI PLUS (System of Interactive Guidance and Information)* are widely used computer programs that have proven helpful to college students engaged in career searches.

Interest and Personality Assessments

In many cases, college career centers can administer occupational assessments that will systematically assess your interests and personality. These standardized tests, for which there is sometimes a charge, take about an hour to complete. They provide

Do you prefer indoor or outdoor work?	
Do you prefer sitting or moving around while working?	
Do you like a fairly formal setting or a completely informal one?	
When you are in a group, do you prefer to lead or to be led?	
Do you prefer continually doing tasks with which you are completely familiar, or learning new tasks all the time?	
Do you prefer to use your muscles, your brain, or your other talents?	
Are you good at explaining complex tasks so that others can perform them, or do you prefer to take direction from others?	
Do you enjoy persuading people that your views or ways of doing things are right?	
Do you enjoy solving problems? If so, do you prefer to work alone or with others?	

PART II:

Now use your work preferences to write a description of your ideal job in the space below. Be as brief as you can, and in no case exceed four lines.

MY IDEAL JOB WOULD INVOLVE:

detailed feedback on who you are and the kinds of professions for which you seem to be most suited. Among the most widely available assessment inventories are:

> **Campbell Interest and Skill Survey (CISS).** In this inventory, people are asked to identify their interests and skills. Based on their results, test takers receive suggestions regarding whether they should pursue—or avoid—particular professions.

> **Kuder Occupational Interest Survey.** The Kuder test assesses your interests and compares them to the interests of others already in the field. The test assumes that if you have similar interests to people in a profession, you are particularly well suited to that line of work. (It also provides advice on appropriate majors.)

> **Strong Interest Inventory (SII).** The SII measures your likes and dislikes to get a sense of your personality. It uses your personality type to match you with professions that are populated with people who have similar personality types.

Try It!

2 Identifying Your Long-Term Career Goals

Consider each of these areas as you determine your long-term goals:

- Achievement
- Advancement opportunities
- Challenge
- Contribution to society
- Control, power
- Creativity

- Financial
- Friendships with co-workers
- Helping others
- Independence
- Leadership
- Learning new things

- Loyalty
- Prestige
- Recognition from others
- Security
- Variety
- Working with others

Using this list, create a set of your three most important occupational goals. For example, three primary goals might be to (1) be challenged to reach my potential, (2) work with others in a cooperative environment, and (3) make a lasting contribution to society. However, don't be influenced by these examples—choose goals that are your own.

MY PRIMARY CAREER GOALS ARE TO:

1.

2.

3.

Stating your career goals up front, even before you know the range of careers that exists, is important. Identifying your goals helps you know what it is that *you* want out of work. Future employers are more interested in what you bring to your job rather than how well a job fulfills your important goals. It's crucial that you consider what has significance to you before making career decisions. If an occupation doesn't fulfill your major goals, it will not be a good choice for you.

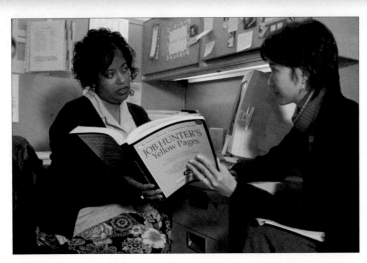

Visit the career center at your school to learn of job opportunities and available resources. Schedule a meeting with one of the career counselors who can help you with choosing a career, creating a portfolio, and preparing for the job interview process.

Personal Interviews

To get a close-up-and-personal look at a profession, another strategy is to talk with people who are already in it. People love to talk about their jobs, whether they love them or hate them, so don't be afraid to ask for an interview. You don't need a lot of their time—just enough to get an inside view of what it's like to work in their profession. Some questions you might want to ask:

- What's your typical day like?
- How did you find your job?
- What are the best and worst aspects of being in your profession?
- What do you look for in someone who wants to enter your field?

table C.1 Fastest Growing Occupations, 2006–2016

Occupation	2006	2016	Percent Increase from 2006 to 2016	Education and Training Category
Network systems and data communications analysts	262	402	53.4	Bachelor's degree
Personal and home care aides	767	1,156	50.6	Short-term on-the-job training
Home health aides	787	1,171	48.7	Short-term on-the-job training
Computer software engineers, applications	507	733	44.6	Bachelor's degree
Veterinary technologists and technicians	71	100	41.0	Associate degree
Personal financial advisors	176	248	41.0	Bachelor's degree
Makeup artists, theatrical and performance	2	3	39.8	Postsecondary vocational award
Medical assistants	417	565	35.4	Moderate-term on-the-job training
Veterinarians	62	84	35.0	First professional degree
Substance abuse and behavioral disorder counselors	83	112	34.3	Bachelor's degree
Skin care specialists	38	51	34.3	Postsecondary vocational award
Financial analysts	221	295	33.8	Bachelor's degree
Social and human service assistants	339	453	33.6	Moderate-term on-the-job training
Gaming surveillance officers and gaming investigators	9	12	33.6	Moderate-term on-the-job training
Physical therapist assistants	60	80	32.4	Associate degree
Pharmacy technicians	285	376	32.0	Moderate-term on-the-job training
Forensic science technicians	13	17	30.7	Bachelor's degree
Dental hygienists	167	217	30.1	Associate degree
Mental health counselors	100	130	30.0	Master's degree
Mental health and substance abuse social workers	122	159	29.9	Master's degree
Marriage and family therapists	25	32	29.8	Master's degree
Dental assistants	280	362	29.2	Moderate-term on-the-job training
Computer systems analysts	504	650	29.0	Bachelor's degree
Database administrators	119	154	28.6	Bachelor's degree
Computer software engineers, systems software	350	449	28.2	Bachelor's degree
Gaming and sports book writers and runners	18	24	28.0	Short-term on-the-job training
Environmental science and protection technicians, including health	36	47	28.0	Associate's degree
Manicurists and pedicurists	78	100	27.6	Postsecondary vocational award
Physical therapist	173	220	27.1	Master's degree
Physician assistants	66	83	27.0	Master's degree

Note: Numbers are in thousands of jobs.
Source: From Table 2, Fastest Growing Occupations, 2006–2016, in "Occupational employment projections to 2016," published in the November 2007 *Monthly Labor Review.*

Instructors as Career Guides

Each of your instructors has a job—that of college instructor. But despite the similarity in job title, each got that job in a different way, using different tactics and strategies. Each followed his or her own particular career path and has a distinct educational background. Furthermore, your instructors may have had a variety of positions, and possibly a number of previous careers, prior to becoming a college instructor.

You can learn a great deal about career opportunities and the process of getting a job by talking to your course instructors about their own careers. Set up an appointment with each of your course instructors, and ask questions such as these:

- What is your educational and professional background?
- How did you get your current job?
- What students have you had that have been particularly successful careerwise? What qualities did they have that set them apart from other students of yours?
- What general advice do you have for someone seeking to identify careers and looking for a job?
- Knowing me from your course, what skills would you encourage me to work on and develop in order to increase my chances of successfully getting a job?

You can gain valuable insights into careers and job searches from your course instructors. Furthermore, talking with your course instructors can help you get to know them better, and it may eventually pave the way for your course instructors to provide letters of recommendation. Instructors also sometimes get leads on jobs, and if they know your career plans, they may pass them on to you. Finally, if you build a relationship with your instructor, it may help you do better academically in your course—no small benefit!

Keep in mind, of course, that the answers you get will be the opinions of one individual, reflecting his or her unique, personal experience. That's why it is a good idea to talk to several practitioners of a particular occupation and to consider what they say in the context of other research that you have conducted about the profession.

Be sure to write a thank-you note following an interview. Not only is it a common courtesy, but it also serves the additional purpose of reinforcing who you are and your interest in their profession. You never know: One day, they might have a job opening, and you might want to ask them for a job!

Work — Creating a Career Portfolio

Career Portfolio

A dynamic record that documents your skills, capabilities, achievements, and goals, as well as provides a place to keep notes, ideas, and research findings related to careers

The research you've done on careers forms the foundation for creating a Career Development Portfolio. A **Career Portfolio** is a dynamic record that documents your skills, capabilities, achievements, and goals, as well as provides a place to keep notes, ideas, and research findings related to careers. Such a portfolio will provide an easy-to-access history of your job-related activities, and it will include material that will be helpful for you and, later, for potential employers. You'll want to keep and update your Career Portfolio as long as you are pursuing a career.

A Career Portfolio consists of a number of key components, which will vary depending on your year in college and—later—the stage you have reached in your career. No matter where you are in career planning, though, your Career Portfolio will consist of two main parts. The first part, background information, will hold

Journal Reflections

Thinking about Work

At some point in your life, you've almost surely had a job. Maybe it was a summer position delivering mail, working in a factory, painting houses, or entering data. Or maybe it was selling lemonade when you were a kid or raking leaves for the neighbor next door. Or maybe it was unpaid community service in which you volunteered your time.

Whatever your specific experiences, you no doubt have developed some ideas about what it's like to work. Here's a chance to explore your thinking about work.

1. What was most rewarding about the work you did: the ability to earn money, social aspects involving your fellow employees, or enjoyment of the work itself?

2. What would you see as the positive and negative aspects of supervising other people? Would you like to supervise others at some point in your career?

3. How important is the amount of money that you're paid for the work you do?

4. Do you see work as something you must do in order to earn a living, or something that is a central and important aspect of life in and of itself?

5. How important is variety in what you do? How important is stability in what you do?

information to help you keep track of your accomplishments and notes on your career research; the second part, which includes your résumé and cover letter, will be material that you share with potential employers.

Your Career Portfolio can either be in the form of a traditional, hard-copy version, or you can create an e-Portfolio online. Some colleges provide online templates or "wizards" that guide you through the process of creating a Career Portfolio. E-Portfolios have the advantage of being easily modified, and—since they reside on the Web—they are accessible any place you have access to the Web.

Career Portfolio Part I: Background Information

The information in this section of your Portfolio is meant to help you make career-related decisions and record your thinking about careers. This part is for your eyes only. Although you will draw on the material for the "public" part of your Portfolio that potential employers will see, think of it as your own, private repository of information.

> **Basic personal data.** Keep a record of data and identification numbers that you think you'll never forget—but, even with the best intentions, you probably will not remember at the least opportune moment. For example, include your social security number, addresses (home and college), college ID number, and telephone numbers. If you're a renter, keep a record of your landlord's name and address; you might need a credit reference one day.

> **Career research notes.** Whether you have notes collected from book- or Web-based research, results of personality and interest assessments, or interviews with people in a particular occupation, they belong in your Career Portfolio. They will provide a record of your career-related activities.

> **Syllabus and outline from courses you have taken.** Include a copy of the syllabus and course outline of every course you take, along with the grade you received in the course. The information contained in a course syllabus and outline will serve to jog your memory about the material the course covered. Without these materials, you're at the mercy of your memory when you're trying to recall the content of a course you may have taken several years earlier.

> For further documentation relating to your courses, you could include a copy of the course description from the college catalog and, if the class had a list of competencies that students were to attain, a copy of these as well.

> **Transcripts.** Include the most recent version of your transcript, listing the courses that you took, credits earned, and grades you received in your classes.

> **Your personal history.** If someone were to write your biography, what are the key events that you'd want him or her to know about?

> The events that would be included in your biography can form the core of a list that you should make of every significant experience you've had. Although the list should include every employment-related experience you've had, such as last summer's job with a landscape service, don't limit yourself only to job experiences. Also include other accomplishments, such as the community service you performed in a battered women's shelter. Personal events that have had a major impact on who you are should also earn a place in your personal history, such as the car accident you had and the six months of physical rehabilitation that followed. Use **Try It 3** to help make this list, which you'll use later to create a résumé.

> **Description of your ideal job.** Include a copy of the ideal job description you created in **Try It 1.**

> **Long-term career goals.** Your Career Portfolio should have the statement of your long-term career goals that you developed in **Try It 2** on page C-6.

> **Writing samples.** Add examples of your best writing. These can be papers that you've handed in for classes or other writing you have done on your own. The idea is to have a sample of your writing easily available should a potential employer ask for one.

> **Credentials.** Include copies of any credentials you have earned. For example, place in the Portfolio a copy of diplomas you have earned, certificates of workshop or training participation you have received, proof of noncredit continuing education courses you have taken, and the like. You never know when an employer might want to see documentation of your accomplishments.

Cataloging Your Personal History

3

	Activity or Event	When Activity or Event Took Place	Where Event Occurred (e.g., company, hospital, social agency)	Responsibilities or Actions Performed	Skills or Talents Used	Achievements, Results, or Insights
Did you work for pay or not, during or before high school?						
Were you a member of any clubs or other organizations in high school?						
Have you held any paid jobs since high school?						
Have you performed any community service?						
Have you provided any services to a religious institution?						
Are you working, either on campus or off campus, while at college?						
Are you in any clubs or organizations at college?						
Have you had any personally significant life experiences?						
Have you ever been called upon to exercise skills or talents you didn't know you had?						
Have you ever solved a tough problem and felt great satisfaction?						
Have you ever worked in a group to solve a problem?						
Have you ever organized a complex task on your own?						
Have you ever led a group in the performance of a large task?						
What is the best thing you have ever done?						

WORKING IN A GROUP:

Compare your responses to those of other students in the group. What are the unique capabilities that you have, the things that set you apart from others in the group? How could you take advantage of those unique capabilities when you are seeking a job?

Career Portfolio Part II: Résumé and Cover Letter

This section of your Career Portfolio encompasses information that you will share with potential employers. Whereas the material in the first part of your Portfolio provides the background for your career planning, this is the public face of your Portfolio.

Think of the components of the first part as the equivalent of the backstage of a play, with a director and crew working behind the scenes to pull things together. In contrast, this second part of the Portfolio is the play the audience sees, the part that should proceed flawlessly. You want the critics to offer nothing less than two thumbs up for your production.

You may wonder: If you're not going to use your résumé and cover letter until you're actually looking for a job, why should you prepare it now? The answer is that it's much easier to prepare job-search materials when you're not under time pressure to produce them than when you're in the middle of looking for a job. You'll be able to create several drafts, rewrite them, receive feedback from others, and incorporate their suggestions.

By taking the opportunity to write a résumé and cover letter under (relatively!) leisurely conditions, you'll be better able to perfect what you produce. When you actually do begin your job search, your task will be updating rather than starting from scratch. Consequently, the work you put in now will pay big dividends later.

The two primary elements that belong in the second part of your Career Portfolio are your résumé and your cover letter.

RESUME

A résumé (pronounced res-oo-may) is a brief summary of your qualifications for a job. It is the first thing that potential employers see and should serve to arouse their interest. Actually, a human may not even initially see it: An increasing number of employers use computers to screen résumés. The computers look for key skills, and if they are lacking, they send an automatic rejection.

Consequently, the résumé must be crafted with great precision and care. If you've created a personal history statement earlier for Part I of your Career Portfolio, use it to get started.

The key elements of a résumé include the following and are illustrated in a sample résumé in **Figure C.1**.

> **Contact information.** Include your name, address (current and permanent if they're different), phone number(s), and e-mail address. *Don't* include your sex, age, race, or marital status. Not only are they irrelevant, but employers who take them into consideration are breaking antidiscrimination laws.

> **Job objective.** If you are targeting a specific job, include a specific objective (such as, "to obtain a position as a buyer for a major retail department store"). However, if you're willing to be flexible, provide a more general job objective (for example, "to obtain an entry-level position in retail sales").

> **Education.** Include the colleges you've attended or are currently attending, with the actual or anticipated year of graduation and degree earned.

> **Awards and honors.** If you've won any awards or honors (such as membership in an honors program or inclusion on the Dean's List) mention them. If you have none that you want to include, leave this category off your résumé.

> **Campus and community activities.** Include activities in which you've participated, and indicate any in which you've had a leadership role. You

Catherine M. Diaz

Present Address
5327 Meridian St.
Kansas City, MO 64110
816 555-1212

Permanent Address
47 Franklin Lane
Springfield, MA
413 555-7711

JOB OBJECTIVE—To obtain a position as entry-level news reporter

WORK EXPERIENCE
The University News, University of Missouri–Kansas City campus newspaper
Campus News Editor/Reporter

- Shared position of Campus News Editor; was responsible for assigning, coordinating, and editing of news stories and features relating to UMKC campus two times a week.
- Occasionally reported on issues of student housing, tuition, and diversity.
- Member of editorial board responsible for editorials.
- Wrote musical reviews on everything from local rock bands to Kansas Symphony Orchestra.

Kansas City Star, Kansas City, Missouri
News Intern
- Contributed background and library research for both feature and human interest stories.
- Aided in putting together special insert on Kansas Symphony Orchestra 2005 season.

EDUCATION
University of Missouri–Kansas City
BA English, June 2007

HONORS AND AWARDS
Academic Dean's List
The University News 2005 Award for Best Feature News Story on shortage of student housing

CAMPUS AND COMMUNITY ACTIVITIES
Women International Student Organization
Association of Latin American Students, Secretary

PROFESSIONAL MEMBERSHIP
Associated Collegiate Press

PARTICULAR SKILLS
Play piano and flute in local band
Speak fluent Spanish

REFERENCES
Available upon request

figure C.1
Sample Résumé

want to demonstrate that you are an involved, contributing member of your community.

> **Professional memberships.** Do you belong to any professional organizations that are relevant to the job you'll be seeking? If so, include them.

> **Work experience.** List your experience, starting with your most recent job and working backward. Include the job title, dates, and your major on-the-job responsibilities.

Don't feel you need to include every job you're ever held (for example, leave out the occasional pet sitting). Instead, focus on the key positions that illustrate your ability to hold a job and to carry out responsibilities. Furthermore, as you present your work experience, always remember that the focus should be on how your past work can get you a job in the profession you want in the future.

› **Particular skills.** Do you know how to program in Linux? Can you speak Spanish fluently? Are you a certified lifeguard? Can you use an Excel spreadsheet or PowerPoint?

Include a brief list of the special skills you have. Once again, make sure that the skills you list are related to the job you're seeking. For example, if you're seeking a job as an emergency medical services technician, lifeguard training is relevant, but it may not be if you're looking for a programming job.

› **References.** A "reference" category is optional, but if you include it simply say "References available upon request." Don't list specific names, but have them available should you be asked for them. (We'll discuss who to ask and how to obtain references later in the chapter.)

As you create a résumé, keep in mind some general rules. First, keep it short. In a résumé, less is more. Generally, résumés should be no longer than one page.

Second, make it look good. Your résumé should appear professional. Use plenty of white space, with one-inch margins on every side. Use strong action words, such as those in **Table C.2.** Avoid articles (such as "the," "a," and "an") and pronouns (such as "I" or "we"); don't write in full sentences.

Finally, proofread, proofread, proofread. You want to be sure that no typographical errors or misspellings find their way into your résumé.

The same rules hold for the second element of Part II of your Career Portfolio, your cover letter, which we discuss next. Before moving on, though, get a start on creating a résumé by completing **Try It 4** on page C-16.

COVER LETTER

Although your résumé is the centerpiece of your presentation to potential employers, your cover letter is no less important. It shows that you can string words together into well-crafted sentences, and it gives you the opportunity to bring life to the list of qualifications on your résumé. It also gives you the opportunity to say how enthusiastic you are about the job for which you're applying and to illustrate how well your qualifications match the job requirements.

In writing a cover letter, keep in mind the perspective of the person who is reading it. Potential employers have a problem that they need to solve: identifying someone to do work that they need done so much that they're willing to pay someone to do it. The better you can provide them with a solution to this problem, the more attractive you will be.

What this means is that your cover letter should be oriented toward helping employers solve *their* problem, not toward how the job will solve *your* problems. Consequently, don't talk about how you think the job will fulfill you as a person or how much you need it to pay your bills. Instead, orient your letter toward describing how well your own unique qualifications match the specific job requirements.

table C.2   Action Words

Using strong action words and making sentences short will help you prepare a professional and eye-catching résumé. Here is a list of action words to get you started. Use words that best describe what you do and who you are.

Achieved	Directed	Investigated
Administered	Discovered	Launched
Advised	Drafted	Led
Aided	Edited	Managed
Approved	Educated	Moderated
Arranged	Enabled	Monitored
Archived	Established	Negotiated
Assigned	Evaluated	Operated
Assisted	Examined	Organized
Authored	Expanded	Oversaw
Budgeted	Expedited	Performed
Built	Extracted	Recommended
Calculated	Facilitated	Recruited
Cataloged	Fashioned	Regulated
Chaired	Granted	Remodeled
Classified	Forecasted	Reported
Coached	Formulated	Restored
Collected	Founded	Reversed
Compiled	Generated	Reviewed
Computed	Guided	Saved
Conducted	Identified	Scheduled
Contracted	Illustrated	Solved
Controlled	Improved	Strengthened
Coordinated	Increased	Summarized
Counseled	Influenced	Supervised
Created	Informed	Supported
Critiqued	Initiated	Trained
Delegated	Inspected	Translated
Demonstrated	Installed	Trimmed
Designated	Instituted	Tutored
Designed	Instructed	Upgraded
Developed	Integrated	Validated
Devised	Interviewed	Worked
Diagnosed	Invented	Wrote

POWER Try It!

4

Creating a Résumé

It's time to use some of the pieces you have been thinking about and working on to create a résumé. You have explored your ideas about your ideal job (**Try It 1**) and your occupational goals (**Try It 2**), and you have gathered important elements of your personal history (**Try It 3**). Now put the pieces together by filling in the worksheet below. Then use the worksheet to create a clean, one-page résumé that you can have reviewed and proofread.

Contact Information:
Your name, address, phone number(s), and e-mail address.

Job Objective:
Use your ideas about your ideal job and your list of occupational goals. Write one statement, beginning with the word "To," that sums up your goals. Be specific ONLY if you are applying for a job you understand and want to focus on; otherwise, state your goals broadly and generally.

Education:
List any colleges attended, including your current college, starting with the most recent. If you have taken college courses without being formally enrolled, list those too.

Awards and Honors (Optional):
List any honors you have received. Academic honors are of primary importance, but honors and awards from social, religious, and community groups (e.g., 4-H, Red Cross, Rotary Club) may be worth including if they testify to personal characteristics that may help you gain employment, such as leadership, perseverance, or a sense of civic duty.

Campus and Community Activities (Optional):
List any clubs, teams, or activities in which you participated in college. Include high school activities only if they were significant and are related to your career goals. Also list community activities in which you have participated, especially those in which you had a leadership role.

Although every cover letter should be tailor-written to a specific position (see the two sample letters in **Figure C.2** on pp. C-18 and C-19), they typically contain the following elements:

> **Introduction: Catching the reader.** Describe why you are writing, how you learned about the job, and why you are interested in it. Emphasize the connection between the position requirements and your qualifications.

Professional Memberships (Optional):

List any professional organizations related to your career goals of which you are or have been a member. Professional organizations are groups such as the Modern Language Association; any of a number of national honor societies; the National Student Speech, Language, and Hearing Association; National Art Education Association; Student Sports Medicine Association; and the like.

Work Experience (If You've Had Any):

List all jobs you have had, including paid jobs (on campus and off), apprenticeships, internships, and similar "real" jobs. List your most recent work experience first and work backward through time. Include the title of the job, organization for which you worked, dates of work, and major responsibilities. Understand that you may be asked about any of the jobs you list, including your reasons for moving to the next job.

Particular Skills (Optional):

List anything you are particularly good at that might transfer to a work setting, including academic skills (e.g., excellent writing ability, ability to speak Russian), work skills (e.g., ability to fix computer hardware problems, write and debug software programs, repair engines, create Web sites, speak publicly), and even recreational skills and hobbies (e.g., unusual ability to complete or write crossword puzzles; proven ability to write creatively—meaning you have been published; ability to build and program robots, etc.).

References:

Available on request.

> ▸ **Letter body: Drawing in the reader.** Here's where you describe, in very brief terms, who you are and what makes you unique. Highlight major accomplishments and qualifications from your personal history, making the argument that your skills are a close match to the job. Show enthusiasm!
>
> You can also include information that does not appear on your résumé; for instance, if you paid for your education entirely on your own, mention that fact. In addition, you can write about what you hope to accomplish on the job.

July 29, 2010

Mr. Reginald Pelly
Assistant Vice President
WorldWide Publishing Corp
New York, NY 10011

Dear Mr. Pelly:

Jennifer Windsor, Director of Editorial Development at WorldWide Publishing, advised me of an opening in your company for an entry-level trade book editor. From my enclosed résumé, you will find that both my experience and my education fully meet the requirements you have outlined for the position.

My current position as a copy editor at a medium-sized daily newspaper has given me experience in dealing with deadlines and working closely with others. Having served as a reporter for six years, I can relate to the needs of writers as well. My colleagues consider me both outgoing and diplomatic, traits that have served me well in my work as an editor.

I will contact you Monday to learn when we can meet for an interview.

Sincerely,

Martina L. Veschova

Enclosure: Résumé

figure C.2
Two Sample Cover Letters

Finally, show that you know something about the organization to which you are applying. Do some homework to learn about the employer, and state specifically what you find attractive about them.

> **Conclusion: A call for action.** End the letter by restating your interest in the position and suggesting that you would like to discuss the position further. State that you are available to meet for an interview. Thank the employer for considering your application.

Martin L. Chen

14A Orchard Street
Boise, Idaho 83702   email: marlchen@mrnr.com   Phone: 207 889-3763

July 29, 2010

Ms. Arlene Washington
Director, Human Services
Mercy General Hospital
18 Medical Plaza
Chicago, IL 60604

Dear Ms. Washington:

I am writing in response to the position advertised July 22, 2007, in the *Chicago Tribune* seeking a Lead Cost Analyst Accountant. My professional experience and education match well with the position requirements listed. Enclosed is my résumé.

In addition to being self-motivated, I work well under pressure and welcome new challenges and opportunities. Among some of my accomplishments are the following:

- Analyzed, defined, and produced appropriate budgets for wages and salary costs, materials, expenses, and workload.
- Provided extensive, timely, and appropriate reporting for all aspects of the various budgets.
- Investigated variations from budget.
- Performed cost benefit analyses and assisted with capital expenditure proposals.

My experience in supervising a team of four co-workers has taught me patience and has strengthened my organizational skills. My greatest satisfaction in a job comes from selecting, training, and motivating personnel. I believe I have the qualities that can help a department become more efficient and productive.

I am familiar with Mercy General Hospital from news stories on breakthrough cancer research conducted there, and I have further researched your hospital and its contributions to medicine. I feel there is a good fit between my career goals and your needs. I welcome the opportunity to discuss the position further, and look forward to hearing from you soon. Thank you for your consideration.

Yours truly,

Martin L. Chen

Enclosure

figure C.2
Two Sample Cover Letters *(concluded)*

Like your résumé, the letter should read well and look good. Before you send it, be sure to proofread it carefully.

The point of including a sample cover letter in your Career Portfolio is to be ready at a moment's notice to revise the sample and send it off. Job opportunities sometimes appear unexpectedly, and it will be much easier for you to respond quickly, and respond well, if you already have a sample letter on file.

Unless you are certain of the job you'll be seeking in the future, you might want to prepare several cover letters, targeted at the different job possibilities you are considering. In addition, the act of writing cover letters for a variety of professions may actually help you come to a decision regarding the path you ultimately choose to follow.

One final note about your Career Portfolio: Keep in mind that it is a work in progress, a living document that is meant to be revised as your interests and aspirations change. That's why it may be a good idea to keep your Career Portfolio in virtual form, rather than as a hard copy. By creating an e-Portfolio, you will be able to make revisions easily. An e-Portfolio also simplifies the process of producing your résumé and cover letter for an actual job opening.

E Evaluate — Getting Feedback on Your Résumé and Cover Letter

After you have created the key elements of your Career Portfolio—your résumé and cover letter—it's time to evaluate their effectiveness. Start by asking a trusted person, such as one of your course instructors or someone on the staff of your college's career center, to review what you've created. Ask them to provide honest and concrete suggestions, because the more feedback you receive, the better the finished product will be.

Once you've received an initial review, one of the best strategies is to ask individuals working in the field in which you're interested to review your résumé and cover letter. Requesting feedback from one or two people who are already working in your desired profession, particularly if they have hired people in the past, serves several purposes. First, your reviewers will be in the best position to know what employers are looking for, and they can tell you how to present yourself most effectively. Not only can they help you say the right things, but they can also help you avoid saying the wrong thing.

But there's an extra bonus from seeking advice from someone currently working in the field: You become a known quantity to them, and at some point in the future they may have a job opening and you may spring to mind. Or if you contact them in the future, they may be able to steer you to a job opening.

R Rethink — Reconsidering Your Career Choices

Going through the process of identifying your skills and resources, researching careers, and building a Career Portfolio may lead you to solidify your ideas about which occupation you'd like to pursue. That's great—that's the point of career exploration.

But even if you are sure about what you intend to do professionally, it's important to take some time to reconsider your choices. Consider these questions:

> Does the occupation you've chosen take advantage of your skills and strengths?

> Have you been diligent in carrying out research about alternative careers?

> Are you excited about your choice?

> Does the job fit closely with your values and aspirations?

The most important thing is to avoid what psychologists call "foreclosure." Foreclosure is making a premature decision and sticking with it so persistently that you ignore other possibilities, even ones that hold considerable promise. Keeping an open mind by reconsidering your choices will help you be sure that you've made the best decisions.

What if you haven't been able to narrow things down? What if you're still completely up in the air about what career you'd like to pursue? First, realize that often it is absolutely fine to delay making a decision. If you're just starting college and don't know what you want to do, you're similar to millions of other first-year students who have no idea about their future careers. As you move through college and become exposed to new ideas and subject areas, you may move in professional directions that you can't even contemplate now. So relax for the moment, and don't feel pressured into making a decision.

On the other hand, if you're close to the point where you need to start work, and you still don't have a clue about what you want to do, then maybe you need to rethink your approach. Assuming you've considered various possibilities, you may want to reconsider the career-planning strategies you've been using. Ask yourself these questions:

▸ Have you been too restrictive or too selective in considering possibilities?

▸ Have you done sufficient research?

▸ Have you rejected professions that seem somewhat interesting without carefully considering what they have to offer?

▸ Have you underestimated (or overestimated) your skills?

▸ Have you taken full advantage of all the resources your college offers in terms of career planning?

By retracing the steps you took when you began the career process (see the P.O.W.E.R. Plan), you may find there are things that you could do to bring you closer to a decision. Finally, don't despair if you haven't identified something that you want to do for the rest of your life. Remember that most people change jobs multiple times during their working lives. If your first job doesn't work out, you've got many years to find something that works better for you. Like career planning itself, your career is an unfolding process.

> "Your true pilot cares nothing about anything on earth but the river, and his pride in his occupation surpasses the pride of kings."
> Mark Twain, author, *Life on the Mississippi*, 1883

Your References: Who Says What about You

Getting the job you want sometimes can hinge less on what you say about yourself and more on what others say about you. A good reference can make the difference between getting a job and getting passed over. A bad reference can destroy your chances of being offered a position.

That's why finding just the right people to supply potential employers with a reference can be the key to obtaining the job you want. That's why it's critical to identify people who are willing to speak on your behalf well before you face a deadline.

Identifying People to Provide References

Several categories of individuals can provide you references, including:

▸ Former job supervisors

▸ Colleagues in previous positions

▸ Class instructors

▸ Community service supervisors

Starting Over: Once You Have a Job You Want

What's the best time to start looking for a job? When you already have one and don't need to find a new position.

Even if you feel happy and secure in your job, it makes sense to be prepared for the unexpected. Perhaps you'll get a new boss whom you can't work with, or your current job's activities and requirements change for the worse. Or maybe the company will downsize or be merged with another corporation, causing widespread layoffs.

For a variety of reasons, then, you'll want to keep your résumé and Career Portfolio updated, even if you've just started a new job. You will want to stay in contact with the people who have provided you with references in the past.

Above all, take every opportunity to learn new skills. As the economy and technology change, you'll want to have cutting-edge skills that will allow you to compete effectively.

In short: Be prepared!

> Coaches, club advisors, or heads of professional groups to which you belong
> People who can provide character references (e.g., clergy)

The most effective references come from people who know you well—very well—and can speak to your skills, abilities, accomplishments, motivation, and character. In addition, people who can speak to the specific requirements of the job you're seeking (especially those who have worked with you in environments similar to that of the potential job) are highly effective.

The least effective references are those from family members or friends or, even worse, friends of friends. For instance, a reference from someone famous who happens to play tennis occasionally with your uncle will rarely be helpful, unless that person knows you well. Remember a key rule of references: The ability of a reference provider to describe in detail *your* strengths and *your* accomplishments is considerably more important than the identity of the reference provider, whatever *his or her* strengths and accomplishments.

What if you're seeking a position straight out of college, and you have no relevant work experience? That's fine. Potential employers understand that you've been in school, and they don't expect you to provide a reference from someone in a field in which you've never worked.

The necessity of having people to act as references points out the importance of networking. Even while you're in college, it's critical to build up a network of people who can vouch for you. To network effectively, be sure to keep in touch with people who know you and like you. And try to expand your network of contacts. For example, whenever you're at a social event, talk to people you don't know and don't just hang out with people you're familiar with.

Asking for a Reference

When choosing someone to be a reference, **always ask permission.** Never give out the names of people who you think will provide references without asking them beforehand. Not only is seeking permission common courtesy, but asking first avoids violating another rule of references: *No reference is better than a bad reference.* You need to check that the reference someone provides will be an explicitly positive one.

Although you can't directly ask someone if they can provide a positive reference (it's very hard for someone to tell you straight out that they can't), you can approach the issue indirectly. When asking someone to serve as a reference, ask them if they have any reservations. If they do, no matter how minor, turn to someone else to provide the recommendation.

You should also offer some guidelines for those providing recommendations. Let them know why you're asking them in particular, and remind them of the context in which they've known you. If there is something you'd like them to specifically address in providing you with a reference—such as, for example, the unusual creativity you showed in a previous position or the fact that you wrote exceptionally good research papers in a class—let them know. The more explicit information you can provide them, the better.

The best time to request references from people is when their experience with you is fresh in their minds. For example, you should ask for a reference from an instructor at the end of a course or from an internship advisor when the internship is completed. Request a general letter, and add it to your Career Portfolio.

In addition, your college may have a career center that can maintain a file of letters of recommendation for you. These letters can then be sent to potential employers upon your request. The advantage is that such letters can be confidential—you won't get to see them—and potential employers may place greater weight on them because they'll be viewed as potentially more candid than nonconfidential letters.

Using the Web in Your Job Hunt

The Web has changed some of the rules for conducting a job search. It permits you to post your résumé and have the potential for thousands of possible employers to screen it. It also permits employers to post their job needs and have the potential for thousands of possible employees to see them. You can even apply for jobs online. Internet services can help you to conduct automated searches, exposing you to job listings in your chosen field and receiving e-mails containing job postings that fit your skills.

The advantages of electronic job searches— such as the potentially wide exposure of your résumé—come at some potential costs. First, your résumé quite likely will be "read" by a computer. That means you must be extremely precise and follow some specific stylistic rules to avoid its being misread or ignored. Second, there are security issues, since you never know who may be reading your résumé.

In using the Web for a job search, you need to cast your net widely. Although general interest job sites such as **monster.com** and **careerbuilder.com** post millions of jobs each year, there are more focused boards that can help you identify possible jobs in specific industries (see **Table C.3** on page C-24). In addition, most large companies post job openings on their own Web sites.

There are several general guidelines to follow when posting your résumé on an online employment site:

> Be very precise in the words you employ. For example, use action verbs and other words that are standard within an industry.

> Use simple type styles, such as Arial or Times New Roman.

> Avoid elaborate formatting, such as tabs or italics.

table C.3	Finding the Right Site on the Web[1]
Specific Sites	
www.HigherEdJobs.com	Teaching
www.EngineerJobs.com	Engineering
www.ShowBizJobs.com	Acting
www.Medzilla.com	Doctors, nurses
www.RXCareerCenter.com	Pharmaceuticals
www.HR.com	Human resources
www.dice.com	Information technology
www.LegalStaff.com	Legal
www.AgCareers.com	Agriculture

> Use a standard 80 characters per line.

> As always, proofread, proofread, proofread. A typographical error is more than embarrassing: Computers screening your résumé may reject your application before a human ever sees it because they do not recognize a misspelled word.

»LO C.3 Job Interviews: Putting Your Best Foot Forward

For a potential employer who has never met you, a job interview puts a face to what has previously been an impression based on mere words written on a page. The interview is your chance to show who you are, to demonstrate your enthusiasm for a potential position, and to exhibit what you can bring to a position.

The fact that interviews are so important may make them seem intimidating and overwhelming. However, remember that the mere fact that you've been invited to an interview means you've overcome some of the highest hurdles already. Furthermore, there are a variety of concrete strategies you can follow to ensure that you maximize the opportunity an interview presents. Among the most important are the following.

Before the Interview

> **Learn about the potential employer.** It's important to learn as much as you can about the position and the company that is offering it. Go to the potential employer's Web site and find out as much as you can about the organization's management style and company culture. Then try to find magazine and newspaper articles to gain a sense of the success and effectiveness of the organization. The bottom line: If an interviewer asks, "What do you know about our organization" be prepared to answer, "Quite a bit, because I've researched it thoroughly."

> **Prepare with questions.** Come to the interview prepared with questions. Think up a set of questions and write them down so you can remember them—it's perfectly fine to refer to them during the interview. Having targeted questions shows that you've spent time thinking about the position. (Don't ask about salary during the interview; salary issues are usually addressed if you get an actual job offer.)

> **Prepare answers.** Finally, come prepared with answers to likely questions. For instance, it shouldn't be a surprise if an interviewer asks you to "tell me about yourself." So have an answer ready, a two- or three-minute response that touches on these aspects of who you are:

1. Your career goals and interests, and what led you to develop them.

2. Your intellectual and people skills, such as your problem-solving capabilities and ability to relate to a variety of people.

3. Your previous experiences that are relevant to the job, including major accomplishments.

4. Your personality traits and values. For example, employers are interested in your dependability, motivation, ability to adapt to new situations, willingness to take direction, and—often—your ability to work in teams.

5. Something personal about you, such as a hobby or unusual skill, that may be irrelevant to the job but gives the interviewer a sense of you as a person.

Obviously, this is a lot to cover in just a few minutes, so practice it until you can do it comfortably within that short time frame. Going longer than three minutes runs the risk of boring your interviewer. Furthermore, don't just practice it by yourself. Have someone else listen to it and give you feedback.

Other favorite interview questions include "What are your major strengths and weaknesses?" "Why do you want to leave your current position?" "What are your major qualifications?" "What are your short-term and long-range goals?" and "Why should I hire you?" Although you can't prepare for every possible question in advance, thinking through some of the most likely possibilities will help you feel more confident and ready to deliver polished responses.

During the Interview

Arrive at your interview on time, prepared, and confident. Do your homework and find out as much as you can about the company. Bring questions that demonstrate you are knowledgeable about the organization and are highly interested in the position.

- **Be punctual.** Allow yourself enough time to arrive well ahead of the scheduled interview. That will help you find a parking space, locate the building and room, and generally get composed.

- **Dress appropriately.** Wear the right clothes for the interview. Stop by beforehand to see how people dress. If you're unsure of how formal to be, keep in mind that it's almost always better to be overdressed than to be underdressed. This is not the time to make a fashion statement. You want to look professional.

- **Use your social skills effectively.** Shake hands firmly, and look the interviewer in the eye. Show that you're interested in the interviewer as a fellow human being, not just as someone who might give you a job. Listen attentively to what he or she has to say, and be responsive. Above all, try to think confidently. Thinking positive, confident thoughts will help you appear positive and confident.

- **Ask questions.** If you have prepared for the interview, you've got some questions to ask about the organization with which you're looking for a job. Be sure to ask them. Interviewers almost always ask if you have any questions, but if they don't, try to work them in when you sense that the interview is almost over. It's also a good idea to ask about the hiring process the employer is using. Ask how long it will be before they will be making a decision and when you will be hearing from them again.

Rule No. 1: Just be yourself. Unless, of course, you're sloppy, lazy, or otherwise undesirable, in which case, be someone else. Be ready to humbly sell yourself, and if someone asks about your weak points, say, 'Occasionally I just work too hard.'

Rainbow Rowell, the *Daily Nebraskan*[2]

Try It!

Interviewing

5

Nothing will prepare you better for an upcoming interview than a number of prior interviews. To get practice interviewing, ask an instructor, a person who has had experience in hiring, or even a fellow student to role-play an interview with you in which they will interview you, the potential job applicant. Tell them that you will prepare for your role carefully and that you will treat the practice interview seriously.

Follow these steps:

- Choose a company or organization that you would like to work for, and provide the person who will interview you with some details about it, such as information from the company Web site.

- You should also research your chosen company as a potential interviewee would, to gain enough knowledge to answer potential interview questions well.

- Hold the interview. You should be serious and try to play your role well. If you like, you can "dress the part" to help you set the right tone. You may also want to tape-record the session.

- After you've concluded the interview, ask your interviewer for a critique of your performance. Ask the interviewer to make as candid a judgment as he or she can as to which category you would fit into based solely on the interview: (A) Offer a job; (B) Don't offer a job; or (C) Call back for another interview to follow up with additional questions.

After you've completed the steps outlined above, answer the following questions:

1. What did you learn from the interview?

2. Critically assess your performance as an interviewee. What was your greatest strength as an interviewee? Your greatest weakness?

3. What would you do differently during an actual interview?

4. How can you better prepare for an actual interview in the future?

> **Above all, be yourself and be honest.** You do yourself no favor by pretending to be someone other than who you are. Getting a job under false pretenses virtually guarantees that neither you nor your employer ultimately will be satisfied with your job performance. You may end up doing things you don't like to do and may not be very good at, and neither you nor your employer will find that acceptable for very long. (To get experience interviewing, complete **Try It 5**.)

After the Interview

You may heave a sigh of relief at the end of your interview, but the interviewing process is not over yet. In fact, what you do after the interview is as important as what you do during the interview.

Interview follow-up consists of several steps, each of which can make the difference between whether you get the job or not:

> **Evaluate your interview performance.** Are you pleased with how you presented yourself in the interview? What did you do particularly well? What things could you have done better? Are there things you forgot to say? Were there out-of-the-ordinary questions that surprised you? Did you prepare sufficiently for the interview? What could you have done to be better prepared before you walked in the door?
>
> Jot down your impressions of the interview while they're still fresh in your mind and place them in your Career Portfolio. These notes will be valuable when you prepare for future interviews.

> **Consider if you still want the position.** Suppose, for a moment, you were actually offered the job. Do you really want it?
>
> It's important to ask yourself whether, given what you learned about the position, you would accept it if it were actually offered to you. You probably found out things about the position that interested you, and others that may be worrisome. Evaluate the job, and if there are too many negatives, rethink whether you'd actually want it.
>
> However, unless there are so many negatives that you're certain that under no circumstances would you take the job, don't withdraw your application. It may be that if you are offered the job, you could negotiate with your potential employer to eliminate the factors that you find undesirable.

> **Write a thank-you note.** It's common courtesy to thank someone for giving you his or her time during an interview.
>
> It's also strategically important. It shows that you are polite and can be counted on to do the right thing. It demonstrates your interest in the job. And it gives you one more opportunity to show you have the "right stuff."
>
> Although you shouldn't turn your thank-you note into a sales pitch, do indicate your continued interest in the position. Write about the aspects of the job that were of particular interest to you and explain how you can see yourself fitting in well with the company.
>
> It doesn't hurt to write two thank-you notes, one sent via e-mail right after the interview and one that is a more traditional written note, mailed (via regular mail) to arrive about a week after the interview.

> **Follow up.** If you haven't heard from the employer in a few weeks, and it's past the point where you were told you'd be contacted, it's perfectly reasonable to e-mail or call. The purpose is not to badger the employer into hiring you—that's not going to work—but to simply check up on where the process stands. Of course, it also serves another purpose: to remind a potential employer of your continued interest in the position. You can also use the opportunity to provide additional information or to inform the employer of another job offer.

Phone Interviews

Sometimes the first interview you have will be a telephone interview. Employers may use phone interviews to do an initial screening before determining which applicants to actually invite for an onsite interview.

Although all the tips we've discussed about interviewing effectively hold, there are some additional strategies to keep in mind:

> **Be prepared.** You may get no notice of a telephone interview; an employer may simply call you out of the blue. So be prepared to speak about your background and accomplishments. If you are caught totally off guard, tell the interviewer that you can't talk at that moment, and arrange a later time to speak.

> **Keep your résumé and list of accomplishments in clear view in front of you.** Don't depend on your memory.

> **Take notes on the conversation.** Be sure to have a pen and paper handy.

> **Avoid distractions.** Turn off call waiting, banish others from the room, and make sure there is no music or television in the backround.

> **Avoid saying "um," "er," "you know," and other verbal "tics."** These are especially apparent on the phone, so practice not saying them.

> **Don't eat or drink during the phone interview.** Interviewers will know that you're doing it, and it is distracting.

> **Practice being interviewed on the phone.** Have a friend call you, and practice speaking on the phone. It's harder than you think, especially if it's a conference call and there are several people on the other end of the phone asking questions.

Speaking of Success

The Art Institute of Houston®

NAME: **James S. Cook**

SCHOOL: **Art Institute of Houston, Houston, Texas**

James Cook readily admits he wasn't a very diligent student when in high school, skipping classes and not working very hard. He felt he would never make it to college.

His outlook would have almost become a reality if it were not for his love of art.

"I've always been an artistic person and had an eye for design," Cook said. "I started out doing graffiti on buildings, but I knew that I had to put my skills into an actual profession where I could succeed and not be the starving artist."

To further his education, he enrolled in the Art Institute of Houston, pursing a degree in graphic design. But he was not able to focus on his studies.

"I still had fuzzy goals, and I was stuck in trying to be social, instead of academic," he noted. "I wanted to succeed, but I wasn't fully engaged. If a class met three days a week, I'd be there for two and a half days."

He fell further and further behind, and became involved in activities that eventually led to a run-in with the law, causing Cook to drop out of college temporarily. However, it led Cook to turn his life around.

"I grew up and put away my childish ways," Cook said. "I hoped to return to the Art Institute, but I wasn't sure if they would let me back in."

Through the efforts of two administrators who saw his promise, Cook did return, with a new major in multimedia and Web design and, more important, with a new set of goals. "The major thing I did was set a goal," he explained. "I said to myself that I'm going to graduate, and I'm going to do it on time. I also set little goals for myself along the way, helping me to know that I was on the right path.

"One of my main goals is to bring up my grade point average, which is now 3.1, to where I will qualify for the National Vocational Technical Honor Society, and I expect to do that the next quarter," he added. "Another goal is to use my hardheadedness within the system instead of against it."

Cook has kept busy. To support himself financially he has waited tables and has started a business designing Web sites and producing multimedia presentations. For spiritual support, he has become a youth leader in his church's youth ministry—in addition to carrying close to a full load of courses.

"Once I got back into school, my goals and focus were clear," Cook said. "I saw I could reach those goals. I knew I had to study and work hard in class."

Looking Back

How do I identify my ideal career and job?

> Careful and systematic research is the key to identifying possible careers.

> Books, Web sites, interest and personality assessments, and informational interviews provide useful information about careers.

> A Career Portfolio can document a person's skills, capabilities, achievements, and goals, as well as provide a place to keep notes and research findings relating to jobs. It also includes one's résumé and cover letter.

What are the best strategies for finding and getting a job?

> It is important to find appropriate references.

> The Internet not only provides substantial information about potential jobs and companies, but also can play an important role in getting a job.

How can I maximize my job interviewing skills?

> Job interviews require a significant amount of preparation.

> Useful interview strategies include being punctual, dressing appropriately, using social skills effectively, asking questions, being oneself, and being honest.

> After an interview, follow up with the interviewer.

[KEY TERMS AND CONCEPTS]

Career Portfolio (p. C-8)

[RESOURCES]

ON CAMPUS

Your campus almost certainly has an office devoted to career planning. In addition, your college library, as well as any public library, will surely have books that can help you decide on a career and find a job.

IN PRINT

There are thousands of books that can help you with career planning. One classic is Richard Bolles's *What Color Is Your Parachute* (Ten Speed Press, 2008), which comes out in a new edition almost every year.

Another useful guide is Frank Satterthwaite and Gary D'Orsi's *The Career Portfolio Workbook* (McGraw-Hill, 2003).

Finally, *Acing the Interview: How to Ask and Answer the Questions That Will Get You the Job* (AMACOM, 2008) offers a great variety of pointers that will help you prepare for interviews more effectively.

ON THE WEB

The following sites on the Web provide opportunities to extend your learning about the material in this chapter. (Although the Web addresses were accurate at the time the book was printed, check the *P.O.W.E.R. Learning* Web site [**www.mhhe.com/power**] for any changes that may have occurred.)

▸ The Planning a Career section of Mapping Your Future's Web site (**www.mapping-your-future.org/planning/**) discusses everything from developing a career plan to writing a résumé. It offers an abundance of other information related to students and schooling as well.

▸ Welcome to Resumania (**www.resumania.com/**)—a fun but practical look at those things you shouldn't put into a résumé. The term "Resumania" was coined by Robert Half, founder of the specialized staffing firm Robert Half International Inc. (RHI), to describe errors made by job seekers on résumés, applications, and cover letters.

▸ From the University of Texas at Austin (**www.gslis.utexas.edu/careers/resume_assistance.php**), this site provides dozens of tips on various topics, including how-to articles on résumé writing, behavioral interviewing, and how to dress for an interview.

TAKING IT TO THE NET

1 Use the Internet to identify two companies that work in one field that is of potential career interest to you (e.g., using the HotJobs section of **www.yahoo.com**). Find out what you can about the companies, trying to go beyond the public relations statements that you will find on their Web sites. Write down your impressions about such features as their location, current financial situation, history, work setting and atmosphere, dress code, and benefits, as well as your need for prior experience in the field, your chances for advancement, and anything else of interest to you. Note similarities and differences between the two companies. Can you tell enough about the two companies to prefer one over the other? Would your preparation for an interview with each company be different?

2 Explore at least two Web sites that offer advice about interviewing. See if you can find sample questions that are often asked at interviews (including both traditional questions and brainteasers), tips on what to do and not do at an interview, hints for making a good impression and improving your chances of success, and other advice. Write down the names of the Web sites you found helpful and take notes on the advice they offer.

[NOTES]

1. Farquharson, L. (2003, September 15). Find a job. *The Wall Street Journal,* p. R8.
2. Combs, P. (1998). *Major success.* Berkeley, CA: Ten Speed Press, p. 103.

[PHOTO CREDITS]

The Case of . . .
The Job That Got Away

It should have been a slam-dunk interview.

At least that's what AJ Watts thought the day before he was scheduled to talk with a senior manager at the Luce Company. He felt he was perfect for the sales position Luce had been advertising on their Web site—he was good with people and certainly could talk a good game. Sure, he had no experience except for the painting jobs he held in college. But he figured what he lacked in experience he could make up in charm—it was sales, after all. Even though he didn't really know all that much about the company because the ad hadn't said much, the salary and benefits were terrific. It had all the makings of a dream job.

However, the day of the interview, everything went wrong. First his car wouldn't start, and he had to borrow a friend's, setting him back a half hour. Then he got lost getting to the Luce headquarters.

By the time he arrived, he was 20 minutes late. He ran into the building from the parking lot, and because it was a hot day, he was short of breath and sweating profusely when he finally found the correct office.

Although he thought things couldn't get much worse, they did. The interviewer was visibly annoyed at AJ's tardiness, and he showed his anger by asking a series of tough questions. AJ, after trying his best to calm down, eventually began to get angry himself. When the interviewer asked AJ if he had any questions about the position, AJ couldn't think of one. The interview ended on a chilly note, with the interviewer snapping that if the company were interested in pursuing AJ as an employee, he'd let him know in the next few weeks.

So much for my dream job, thought AJ, as he made his way back to the parking lot.

1. Was AJ adequately prepared for the interview? What steps could he have taken before the interview to ready himself?

2. Is there anything AJ could have done to avoid being late? Once he realized he was going to be late, what could AJ have done to minimize the effects of his tardiness?

3. After the interview, what could AJ have done to try to remedy the situation? What steps should he take immediately? What could he do later?

4. Can you suggest ways that AJ could have prevented the interview from going so badly?

Transfer Strategies: Making the Leap from Community College to a Four-Year School

Learning Outcomes

By the time you finish this chapter you will be able to

》 LO T.1   Discuss the strategies for choosing a specific college or university to transfer to.

》 LO T.2   Explain how to transfer credits.

》 LO T.3   Identify ways to adjust to a new college.

Alicia Martinez's campus visit had not gotten off to a great start. After driving two hours from home just to get to the Florida State campus, she drove around for another 10 minutes looking for a parking space. Compared to her community college campus, which had only a few buildings, the State campus was huge.

By the time she finally parked and found the Admissions office, her scheduled campus tour had already left, but the secretary in the office told her she could catch up with the tour. Alicia sprinted out of the office, looking for the tour group. To her relief, she soon found it and began walking around campus with the group.

As soon as she calmed down, Alicia found herself enjoying the tour. The library was amazing, and the campus student center looked like an upscale hotel. The large lecture hall they visited—so big the professor needed a microphone to be heard—was intimidating, but she figured she could manage.

In fact, as she saw more and more of the campus, she became more convinced that this was the right move for her. It would be a big transition from a small community college to a large university, but she was prepared for the challenge.

Looking Ahead

The transition that Alicia was contemplating—transferring from a two-year community college to a four-year college or university—is one that millions of students make each year. That doesn't make it any easier, though. Transferring from one school to another is challenging, no less challenging than the move from high school to college.

But it's a challenge that can be met. With careful thought, preparation, and work, transferring can produce benefits that will help you for the rest of your life, both personally and professionally.

In this chapter we consider the transfer process. We address strategies for maximizing the credit you'll receive from your prior educational experiences. In addition we consider the application process and how to make choices among different educational institutions. Finally, we discuss ways of avoiding "transfer shock" when you move to a new college or university.

≫ LO T.1 Mastering the Transfer Process

Transferring from one school to another is not just a matter of credits, units, and courses. It is a process that will have an impact on your life in significant ways.

Although it is a complicated process, transferring can be broken down into a series of steps that will help you navigate your way in the P.O.W.E.R. Plan.

 Prepare ### Making the Decision to Transfer

Deciding whether to continue your education should not be taken lightly. You'll need to consider a variety of factors, including academic, financial, and social considerations. However, in some ways the most important part of the process is considering the reasons why you may be thinking of transferring in the first place.

Why Transfer?

There are many good reasons to transfer—and some not so good ones. Let's start with the advantages of continuing your college education at a four-year institution:

> **You will have more career opportunities.** As we discuss in the Career Connections box, graduates of four-year schools have more opportunities in the job market and are more likely to get jobs that require sophisticated skills.

> **Your salary will be higher.** Graduates of four-year schools make on average $8,400 more annually than graduates of two-year schools (see **Figure T.1**). Over your lifetime, that's a big difference. In addition, unemployment rates differ: The unemployment rate for people with a bachelor's degree is lower by more than half a percentage point than for those with only an associate's degree.[1]

> **You will be better educated, understanding more about the world around you.** At its most basic level, college is about gaining an education, and the more college courses you take, the better educated you'll be. Don't underestimate the value of the knowledge you will gain if you continue your education. You will be better informed about the world, have more basic knowledge, and have the opportunity to specialize in different areas.

> **You'll have more options .** By enrolling in a new school you may find a program of study that is not available at your present, two-year school. This will open new options and directions for your education. You may have more opportunities to take advantage of an internship, study abroad, or even put together your own program of study. In short, the school to which you transfer may meet your own needs more effectively than your current college.

Ultimately, once you graduate from a four-year college, you'll have more options available to you. As a graduate of a four-year school, you'll have gained more knowledge, skills, and experiences to be better able to fit into and profit from a changing world—both professionally and socially. You'll be better able to adjust to the changes that will inevitably occur during your lifetime.

On the other hand, there are reasons for transferring that may not be so good. Wanting to transfer because you don't know what else to do, because your parents won't let you live at home anymore unless you enroll, or because your boyfriend or girlfriend is enrolling and you don't want to be away from them are all questionable reasons for transferring.

P Prepare
Make the decision to transfer

O Organize
Get it together: Determine where you should transfer to

W Work
Apply to four-year schools

E Evaluate
Assess your options

R Rethink
Reconsider your choices

P.O.W.E.R. Plan

Educational Degree Attained	Median Weekly Earnings in 2005 (Dollars)	Unemployment Rate in 2005
Some high school, no diploma	$409	7.6%
High school graduate	$583	4.7%
Some college, no degree	$653	4.2%
Associate's degree	$699	3.3%
Bachelor's degree	$937	2.6%
Master's degree	$1,129	2.1%
Professional degree	$1,370	1.1%
Doctoral degree	$1,421	1.6%
Source: U.S. Department of Labor, Bureau of Labor Statistics, July 26, 2006.		

figure T.1
Those Who Learn More Earn More: Earnings by Educational Level, and Unemployment Rate

The Career Benefits of Transferring

A decision to transfer to a four-year college and continue your college education is sure to produce benefits to your career that extend across your lifetime. More education translates into more career options, more income, and ultimately more career satisfaction.

For instance, many employers require that workers have, at a minimum, a bachelor's degree. They welcome the range of knowledge and skills that potential employees obtain during four years of education, compared to two. In some cases, you won't even be considered for a position without a four-year college degree, regardless of the skills you may have. Consequently, transferring opens up a variety of career choices that you would not have otherwise.

Similarly, transferring can lead to a higher salary. The average salaries of those with a bachelor's degree are nearly $10,000 a year higher than for graduates of two-year colleges. Furthermore, in some cases, salaries increase more rapidly for those with a bachelor's degree. Promotion opportunities may also be greater for those with more education.

Finally, your general satisfaction with your career may be higher with more education under your belt. By furthering your education, you are more likely to attain the benefits of college that we spoke of in the first chapter, including having a better understanding of the world, a greater ability to deal with rapid societal changes, and more understanding of others from different cultures and backgrounds. Such capabilities not only will make your work life more rewarding and enriching, they also are likely to increase your general satisfaction with your life outside of work.

However, even these less-than-optimal reasons may have value if they at least get you thinking about the possibility of continuing your education. To delve into the reasons—pro and con—for transferring, complete **Try It 1** on page T-6.

Choosing Not to Transfer

In some cases, choosing *not* to continue your education is the right choice. For example, if you have had considerable academic difficulties, you may think twice about moving to a four-year school, where often the academic challenges are even greater than you're currently experiencing. Furthermore, if you have little academic motivation and continually have to force yourself to be academically engaged, transferring to a four-year institution may not be the right choice.

Also, depending on your area of study (such as a trade profession), a two-year program may be the wisest choice. You may also need a more flexible schedule, which may be more difficult to obtain at a four-year institution.

Keep in mind that choosing *not* to continue your education is not an irreversible decision. You could work for a few years and then go back to college. "It's never too late to learn" is an accurate statement, and you may later decide that the time is right.

Whatever choice you make, be sure that it is *your* choice—a thoughtful, reasoned, and logical decision that takes account of your needs and preferences. Don't just do something because everyone else is doing it. The more you think about your choices—which you can explore further in the *Journal Reflections*—the more committed you will be about your ultimate decision.

O Organize

Getting It Together: Determining Where You Should Transfer To

Once you've made the decision to transfer to a four-year institution, you'll need to determine *how* to do it and decide what schools you're interested in applying to.

Journal Reflections

Should I Transfer?

Contemplate the reasons why you might want to transfer by considering the pluses and minuses of your current college.

1. What are the things you like best about your current college experience?

2. What aspects of your current college experience do you like least?

3. What are the things that you would miss most if you complete your schooling at your current school?

4. What might you gain if you transfer to a new college to continue your education?

5. What would be the drawbacks of transferring to a new college?

Although it's never simple to transfer—you're dealing not just with the bureaucracy of your current institution but also with the one that you're seeking to transfer to—there are things you can do to simplify the process.

Begin with your own campus advisor. Almost all two-year colleges have a designated transfer advisor who can provide guidance. Even if there is no specific individual charged with providing transfer help, you can be sure that you'll find written material, on the Web and in brochures and catalogs, that can help you out.

A transfer advisor can help you identify four-year institutions with which your present college has existing relationships. Those institutions are the schools that should be at the top of your list of most likely transfer possibilities. Why? Because agreements between colleges will make the most of what you've already accomplished, giving you academic credit for more, or even most, of the courses you've already taken. (We'll talk more about the specific types of agreements later in the chapter.)

Transferring to Four-Year Institutions that Don't Have Formal Arrangements

Don't limit your choices of transfer schools only to those with formal arrangements. Although it clearly will be easier to transfer to a four-year institution that has a formal agreement with your current school, almost every four-year school

1

Why Consider a Transfer?

Examine your reasons for considering a transfer at this time by answering the questions below. Jot down notes in response to each question. Some reasons may seem more serious than others, but the purpose of this exercise is not to judge yourself, but to know yourself.

You may want to complete this exercise with the help of other people whose opinions you respect (such as fellow students, friends, parents, siblings, other relatives). If you are comfortable with this approach, you may find that varied ideas, suggestions, and feedback can really help you sharpen your focus and identify your strongest reasons for considering a transfer.

I. ACADEMICS:

- Does your current institution offer enough courses that you are interested in?
- Are there specific courses that you would like to look for elsewhere?
- Is there an entire area of study (i.e., a major) that you would like to pursue in another institution?
- Do the courses you have taken seem too limiting or too easy?
- Have you not done well academically and think you might do better or find better teachers at another institution?
- Have the courses you've taken sparked an interest that you would like to pursue in a four-year college?
- Have you discovered that you are a more serious student and more interested in learning than you thought you were?

II. EXTRACURRICULAR ACTIVITIES:

- Does your current institution offer enough extracurricular activities?
- Are there particular sports, clubs, organizations, or other activities that you would like to try, whether at a competitive level or a less formal level, that are not offered at your current institution?
- Are you interested in experiencing, even just as a spectator, a higher level of student sports or performances?

accepts community college transfers. It may be harder, and you may be forced to take some extra courses, but the trade-offs may be well worth it. Why should you consider transferring to a school that lacks an agreement with your current community college? There are several good reasons:

> **You may be seeking a specialized major that only certain colleges offer.** If you have well-established career goals that involve specific course work or a specialized course of study, you may be limited in the four-year institutions that provide what you want.

> **You may wish to continue your education in another state or geographic locality.** Because formal agreements are usually arranged between state-supported institutions within the same state, you're unlikely to find four-year colleges with agreements in locations that are distant from your current school.

> **You are seeking new academic challenges.** Perhaps you have done well in your current school, but you feel you haven't been challenged. Transferring to an institution that is highly selective in its admissions requirements may give you the opportunity to take on more academic challenges.

III. CAREER REASONS:

- Are you thinking of a career that is different from (e.g., more demanding or stimulating) the ones that a two-year degree will enable you to pursue?
- Have you identified a specific career that you can't pursue any further at your current institution?
- Are you interested in a career that promises to pay better than the ones available with a two-year degree?
- Have you been looking for a job and found nothing that is right for you?
- Are you simply not ready to start a career, but don't yet know what you want to do?
- Are you trying to expand your career choices by educating yourself further?

IV. SOCIAL REASONS:

- Do you feel that you have "used up" or exhausted the social possibilities available at your current institution?
- Do you want a more active, campus-centered social experience than what's found at your current institution?
- Are you interested in meeting a greater number of students from different states, regions, countries, and/or cultural backgrounds?
- Do you simply feel that you need a "bigger pond" to swim in?

V. OTHER REASONS:

- Are you simply looking to make a fresh start in a different place?
- Are you considering a change for geographical reasons (e.g., different climate, different region)?
- Are you considering a change to a different setting (e.g., a switch from an urban environment to a more rural one, or vice versa)?
- Are you trying to get away from someone or something in your current school or neighborhood?
- Are you pursuing someone who is at the institution you are considering transferring to?
- Are you being pressured (e.g., by parents) to transfer to a four-year college?
- Can you identify any other reasons why you are considering a transfer?

> **You are seeking a college that is very different from your current institution.** You may currently be attending a small school, with a student body that is not very diverse and classes where you know everyone. Maybe, though, for the rest of your college career, you'd like to experience a much larger campus, with a more diverse student body and classes in which you hear a broader range of opinions.

Narrowing the Choices

Once you've done the background research on which four-year schools best fit your academic needs, you may have a fairly long list of possibilities. How do you narrow that list to a manageable few to which you will actually apply? Here are some things to take into consideration:

> **Does the college have the program you want?** Be sure that the school offers the program that you want and that there's a strong likelihood that you'll be able to get into the program. Sometimes certain majors have their own admissions standards. You want to be confident that you'll be accepted into the program of your choice.

Location and setting of a new school may be important factors to you. You may be looking for something entirely different than your current surroundings. Available housing or commuting time might also weigh heavily on your decision.

➤ **What is the philosophy and mission of the college?** Although every school has the basic goal of educating students, there are other aspects to the mission that differ significantly from one college to the next. You'll find a statement of the philosophy and mission of most schools on the Web or in a catalog. Use it to get a sense of what is important: Is the school oriented more to research than to teaching? Is there a religious affiliation? Is there an emphasis on student choice and freedom, or are there so many requirements that there is little room for experimentation?

➤ **How large is the college or university? Schools vary significantly in size.** The smallest four-year institutions have fewer than 1,000 students, and the largest over 50,000. Size matters: It sets the tone of the institution. Smaller schools offer more individual attention, and often classes are smaller than at larger schools.

At smaller schools, courses are typically taught only by faculty, but in larger universities with graduate programs, graduate students may do much of the teaching.

On the other hand, larger institutions may offer more courses in a greater variety of disciplines and often provide more services. Furthermore, even if their classes tend to be larger—and sometimes huge—the classes may break down into smaller sections with individual attention.

➤ **Where do you want to live?** There are four-year colleges and universities throughout the United States and Canada that can provide you with a fine education. You need to ask yourself whether location is an important consideration. How close to your family and friends do you want to be? Do you enjoy large cities, with their great cultural resources and sense of excitement, or do you prefer quieter, more rural areas where you can more easily enjoy natural resources? Do you intend to live at home and commute, or do you wish to live in a residence hall?

➤ **What is the student body like?** There are vast differences in the makeup of the student body of different colleges. You might want to consider the male–female ratio, the ethnic and racial composition of the students who attend, the number of foreign students, and the proportion of out-of-state to in-state students. You'll also want to check out the number of transfer students on campus and the number accepted each year. Finally, especially if you're an older student, you should check out the average age of the undergraduate student body on campus.

➤ **What extracurricular activities can you participate in?** Even if you haven't been a regular participant in activities outside the classroom at your current institution, you may wish to get more involved after you transfer. Consequently, determine what extracurricular activities are available at the schools you are considering. The possibilities can be staggering, including intramural sports, service organizations, student government, religious groups, theater and other arts groups, and campus publications.

"'Tis education forms the common mind, Just as the twig is bent, the tree's inclined."

Alexander Pope, author (1688–1744)

> **Is student housing available?** One of the primary questions you need to ask yourself is where you intend to live. If you are thinking about living on campus, you'll need to know the options available to you. In addition to traditional residence halls, where you will probably have a double or triple room with the bathroom down the hall, many schools also have suites and apartments that you can share with only a few other students.

> **How much will it cost?** There are vast differences in the costs of different four-year schools. Public, state-supported schools are almost always less expensive than private colleges. However, even public four-year schools are usually more expensive than public two-year schools. Although financial aid packages at four-year schools may ease the sticker shock, you are still likely to end up paying more at a four-year college than you pay at a two-year school.

> **What is the school's reputation?** Although you won't find it in the school's promotional literature, try to find out something about the school's reputation. Among questions to ask: Are graduates highly regarded by employers? Are graduates readily admitted to graduate schools?

The only way to find answers to such questions is by asking as many knowledgeable people as possible. For example, your community college transfer counselor will have a good idea of the reputation of nearby four-year schools. Your instructors might also have some suggestions. Finally, you can consult college guidebooks (such as the *Fiske Guide to Colleges*) or the *U.S. News & World Report* annual rankings of colleges, which usually provide a fairly accurate picture of the strengths and weaknesses of four-year schools.

> **What is your own personal take on the school?** There is nothing like a campus visit to get a sense of what a college is like. If you can, take the time to visit the schools in which you are interested. Take a tour, talk to students, and get a general feel for the campus.

Don't be swayed by first impressions and irrelevant aspects of the visit—potential students tend to be less enthusiastic about a school if they visit on a cloudy, rainy day than if it's sunny and bright. At the same time, listen to your gut feelings. If you end up feeling that a school just isn't right for you, it probably isn't.

> **Will the four-year school accept me?** In making your decision about which schools to apply to, be sure to consider whether it is likely that you'll be accepted. Although some four-year colleges have formal agreements that they will accept every graduate of certain two-year schools who are in good academic standing and have a certain number of credits, most schools do not have such an arrangement.

Every college will evaluate your academic credentials before they accept you. You need to examine a college's degree of selectivity and realistically consider your chances of getting in. Some colleges have minimum standards for prior academic performance which they state up front; others apply some type of standards but don't explicitly say what they are. In any case, your prior academic performance (including your high school grades) will be taken into consideration.

Does this mean you should avoid taking a risk and rule out applying to a school that you'd really like to attend? Absolutely not. You lose nothing—except the application fee—by applying to a college even if you believe it's a toss-up as to whether you'll be accepted. The important thing is to apply to other schools as well, ranging from those where you're nearly certain you'll be accepted to those that are a stretch.

Try It!

2

Your Transfer Preferences

The questions below should help you define your preferences and narrow your options.

1. What are the two or three main reasons why you are considering a transfer? (Use the list of reasons you generated as part of **Try It 1** on page T-6.)
2. Where do you want to live? What country, region, state, city, or area?
3. What type of setting do you prefer (i.e., urban, suburban, rural)?
4. How large a school do you want to attend (e.g., fewer than 5,000 students, between 5,000 and 10,000 students, or more than 10,000 students)?
5. What sort of student body do you prefer in terms of diversity, gender mix, geographical origins, etc.?
6. What potential major(s) are you considering?
7. What sort of academic standards and difficulty level do you want in a four-year college (high, moderate, relaxed)?
8. How much money are you prepared to pay each year? How large a loan are you willing to carry?
9. What other needs do you have (e.g., sports programs, religious affiliation, art or performance opportunities, student housing, handicapped accessibility, laboratory facilities, library, etc.)?

Use your answers to these questions to find four-year colleges that will meet your needs. You can do this by discussing your needs with a counselor at your current institution and/or by using a Web-based college search tool, such as the one at **furtheryoureducation.com** or **collegeboard.com.** If you find a school in your immediate area (i.e., commuting distance) or in your state, remember to find out if it has any kind of transfer arrangement with your current institution.

After you've examined the options, try to narrow down your choices to no more than five. If you pick a range of schools—some relatively sure bets, some that are good possibilities, and perhaps a "stretch" school—you should be in good shape when admissions letters are sent out.

It's also important to create a backup plan in the event that none of your applications are successful. Be prepared to take action by rethinking your choices of schools. In addition, you might consider working for a year and reapplying or taking an additional class or two to improve your academic record. Preparing in advance for any eventuality is important.

To help you decide on the four-year school that you'd like to apply to, complete **Try It 2.**

W Work | Applying to Four-Year Schools

If you've prepared and organized yourself adequately, you're now ready to apply. In some ways, applying is the easiest part of the process of transferring, since in essence all you're doing is filling in the blanks on a variety of forms. Still, it's not simple, because there are quite a few steps you'll need to follow:

1. **Obtain an application from the colleges to which you are applying.** Sometimes you can download the forms from the Web, while in other cases you will have to ask the school to mail you an application. It is even possible that your current college may have applications available.
2. **Make a list of the application deadlines.** Schools have deadlines for receiving all your materials. Sometimes there is a priority period, during which your

Documenting Your Courses

While you are gathering the information that you need to send to the colleges to which you are applying, there's one more step in the process: Gather documentation for every course that you have taken. What that means is to collect as full a description as possible of each course that you have completed (or in which you are currently enrolled).

There are several good reasons for documenting your courses. Some time in the future, you may wish to take a course at your new institution that requires that you've already taken a prerequisite (a particular course that must be completed before one can enroll in the new course). For instance, you may want to take an abnormal psychology class that requires that you've already had an introductory psychology class. You may need to provide evidence not just that you've taken a course called "Introductory Psychology" but what the course consisted of.

In other cases, there may be a required course at the college to which you transfer that you've already taken. Having full documentation of the course content will make getting excused from the required course at your new institution considerably easier.

To document your prior courses, put together a separate folder for every course you've taken. At the very least, it should contain a syllabus for the course showing the course description and goals, textbook name, and topics covered. You can also include in the folder any papers or tests you've completed in the course.

Think of your course documentation in the same way you think of a medical insurance policy. You may never need to use it, but if you do need to, you'll be awfully glad you have it.

---

application will get preferential treatment. Miss the priority period, and you may lose your preference. In other cases, schools have a "rolling" admissions process, which means the earlier you get your application in, the earlier you will learn about whether you have been accepted.

3. **Identify individuals who can provide you with a recommendation.** Because most schools require several recommendations, you will need to identify several people who can provide you with strong references. Look back over your academic career and think of the courses in which your performance was strongest or the classes in which an instructor took special notice of your talents. You can also ask counselors, employers, or members of the clergy who know you well to write a letter. Good recommendations can also be provided by high school teachers who knew you.

   Be sure to ask people if they are willing to write a recommendation well before any deadlines, and give them any forms provided by the college to which you are applying. Also include a stamped, addressed envelope to make it easy for them to return the recommendation.

4. **Arrange for transcripts and test scores to be sent .** You will need to send an official college transcript, listing the courses you have taken and your grades, to the colleges and universities to which you are applying (also see the **Course Connections** feature). In some cases they may also want a copy of your high school transcript.

   You also may need to send a copy of your standardized test scores, such as the SAT or ACT. You won't need to retake these examinations if you have already taken them; just arrange for the testing service to have them sent directly to the schools to which you are applying.

5. **Complete the applications .** Filling out forms is not fun. It takes effort and concentration. But it is important to complete the application carefully and legibly. You are providing a first impression that can make an impact, even in a small way, on the person deciding on your admission.

The application will undoubtedly ask for a variety of information, including your name, social security number, addresses, educational history, residency status, languages spoken, and so forth. Not only should you be clear in your answers, but you must follow the cardinal rules of applications: Be yourself, and be honest.

If an application requires an essay, leave yourself plenty of time to write it. After you compose a first draft of the essay, it is perfectly acceptable to run it by others who are good writers to get their feedback. Use their comments to improve your essay. Remember that the essays are less a test of writing mechanics—although they do matter a lot—and more a way for the college to get a sense of who you are. Let your personality show through.

The last three steps in completing your applications are proofread, proofread, and proofread. You need to be sure that you have answered all the questions, that you've checked your spelling, and that everything is legible. Don't forget to sign the application, and then send it off—and wait!

Use the checklist in **Try It 3** to keep track of your work.

E Evaluate Assessing Your Options

At some point down the road—it may be as soon as a month or so, or as long as six months later—you will know how successful you have been. Whatever the outcome, you'll need to deal with your options.

If you've been accepted by most, or even all, of the schools to which you have applied, consider yourself lucky. But you still face some tough decisions, because each school will have specific benefits and drawbacks.

Although you probably considered the pros and cons of the colleges before applying, you are likely to have gained some new information from your letter of admission. Specifically, you may have learned how many of your prior credits will be accepted for transfer. Comparing what the different schools will permit you to transfer can help you make an informed decision.

Financial Aid Packages

Your acceptance letter may have brought another piece of information, this in the form of a number: the amount of financial support you are being offered. If financial aid makes a difference to you—and it most likely will—you must then carefully evaluate the different financial packages.

Financial aid packages are not written in stone. You have nothing to lose by attempting to negotiate a better package, and there are two strong reasons for trying. First, financial aid is generally made up of several components, including direct scholarships, loans, and campus job earnings. The greater the direct scholarship offered, the better, since there is no payback or work required. Second, the overall size of the financial aid package can make the difference between whether you can afford to attend the school or not. Thus, it makes sense to try to ask for a larger overall package.

Although negotiating may seem daunting, it's important to make the effort. Here are the steps to follow:

> Call to make an appointment to speak with a financial aid officer.

> Prepare a case that shows why you need a better package. Remember that you can ask for a larger package overall and/or ask for a change in the specific components of the package. Justify what you are asking for by showing how the current financial aid offer is too small to allow you to afford attending the college.

Following the Application Trail

Use the running checklist below to keep track of the steps you will take in applying for admission to four-year colleges.

Application Step	Notes	Step Begun (date)	In Progress	Step Completed (date)
1. Obtain applications (enter college names)	Enter application deadlines below			
College 1:				
College 2:				
College 3:				
College 4:				
College 5:				
College 6:				
2. Identify and ask for references (enter name of each reference below)	Enter addresses, phone numbers, e-mail addresses below			
Reference 1:				
Reference 2:				
Reference 3:				
Reference 4:				
Reference 5:				
3. Follow up on references	Enter a check (✓) if letter of recommendation has been sent			
Reference 1:				
Reference 2:				
Reference 3:				
Reference 4:				
Reference 5:				
4. Arrange transcript(s)	Enter contact information to obtain transcript (usually Registrar's Office)			
Transcript 1:				
Transcript 2:				
Transcript 3:				
5. Complete applications (fill out form, complete essay, proofread, mail)	Enter F for form, E for essay, P for proofread, and M for mail			
College 1:				
College 2:				
College 3:				
College 4:				
College 5:				
College 6:				
6. Keep track of results	Accepted? Financial aid?			
College 1:				
College 2:				
College 3:				
College 4:				
College 5:				
College 6:				

- If your desired school's offer is smaller than that of another college, mention that. A college that knows you will definitely attend if they can provide a better offer has a greater incentive to provide more aid.

- Be polite as you present your case. Heavy-handed tactics will not work. You want the financial aid officer to do everything possible to permit you to attend the college.

To help you assess your options among several colleges that have accepted you for enrollment, complete **Try It 4** on page T-16.

R Rethink   Reconsidering Your Choices

If you've been accepted to a four-year school, the decision to attend takes on a life of its own. Before you enroll, though, take a moment to reassess your decision. Are you continuing your education for the right reasons? Are you doing it for yourself or to please someone else? Does the thought of taking more classes, spending late nights writing papers, and studying for tests fill you with dread and anxiety?

Unless you are fully committed to attending college, you should reconsider your decision to transfer. In most cases, you'll probably conclude that your decision to pursue a transfer to a four-year school was the right one. But if you are not sure, then systematically review your choices. For instance, you might want to work for a period before continuing your schooling. Many colleges will permit you to defer admission for a year, and that might be the right option for you to take at that point in time.

(To review the steps in transferring, see the **P.O.W.E.R. Plan** on page T-3.)

» LO T.2 Making the Most of Your Transfer Credits

Perhaps you are moving straight from a two-year college to a four-year school. Or perhaps your route has been a little more roundabout, and your earlier educational progress has come in fits and starts. Maybe you've had to suddenly leave college because of a business transfer or the need to take care of an ailing relative, and you have accumulated college credits from a number of schools.

Whether the route has been straight or winding, having your college credits evaluated to determine how many will be accepted for transfer to a four-year college is central to transferring. The outcome of this process is crucial, and it can determine how many and what courses you will need to take in the future. It can also save—or cost—you thousands of dollars.

Getting Credit Where Credit Is Due

The process of determining how much credit you will receive is complicated and the outcome can be affected by several factors, including:

- **Where you earned the credits.** Unless a school is accredited (approved) by the appropriate state or regional authorities, courses will not be accepted for transfer. Although most two-year schools are accredited, if you have any doubts, you should check before beginning the process of transferring. Similarly, if you took a course through a continuing education program, the credits you earned may not count as college-level work (even if you received "continuing education credit" for them).

- **The grades you received in the course.** Many four-year colleges require a grade of C or better in order to accept a course.

- **When the credits were earned.** If the credits were earned many years earlier, some colleges will not accept them. This is especially true of programs in which there have been significant advances, such as computer technology and genetics.

- **The level of the courses.** In order to graduate from a four-year program, you will need to take a variety of lower- and higher-level courses. Some four-year programs will accept only a limited number of lower-level courses and will require you to take more upper-level courses when you transfer.

- **Residency requirements.** Virtually all schools require that you earn a certain number of credits on their campus. Consequently, the need to fit in the required number of courses at the new college may cause some previous credits to be disallowed.

All these factors, and many more depending on a particular college's regulations, enter into decisions about whether your prior credits can be transferred. Happily, though, matters can be much simpler if the college you wish to transfer to has a special arrangement with your current school. As we discuss next, such agreements can ease the transition significantly.

Transfer Agreements

In some cases, schools have done much of the work of transferring credits for you by entering into transfer agreements. Among the most common arrangements are the following:

- **Articulation agreements.** Most community colleges have **articulation agreements,** formal arrangements with selected four-year colleges that will automatically accept certain courses or credits taken at your current institution. Articulation agreements may even spell out what groups or blocks of courses will be accepted, as a set, by a four-year college to which you're considering applying.

  For example, an articulation agreement might specify that English 1 at a community college is the equivalent of English 100 at a particular college covered by the agreement, and that History 2 is the equivalent of History 101. If you have taken one of the courses covered by the articulation agreement and achieved some specified minimum grade, credit for that course will automatically transfer to the four-year college.

  Articulation agreements are often complicated and difficult to understand, but it's worth the time and effort to decipher what they say. They can save you literally hundreds of hours, permitting you to avoid repeating courses similar to ones you have already taken or scrambling to complete requirements at your new college.

  In most cases, articulation agreements cover basic, general education courses. They typically do not cover the more specialized, advanced courses counted toward a future major at the four-year institution to which you are transferring. There is an exception to this general rule, however: 2 + 2 plans.

- **2 + 2 plans.** Many state higher education systems have what are called 2 + 2 plans. A **2 + 2 plan** is a formal agreement between a community college and a four-year institution that permits students to transfer courses into a specific major or specialty program.

Articulation agreements
Formal arrangements with four-year colleges that will automatically accept certain courses or credits taken at your current institution

2 + 2 plans
A formal agreement between a community college and a four-year institution that permits students to transfer courses into a specific major or specialty program

Try It!

Assessing Your Options

If you have several options to consider, complete this **Try It** to organize your thoughts and weigh the options.

1. How closely does each college match the preferences you identified in **Try It 2** on page T-10? Use a scale of 1 to 4 to rate each college, where "1" = Not a close match and "4" = A very close match. Then add the ratings in each column.

Your Preferences	Ratings (1 to 4, Higher Is Better)		
	College 1	College 2	College 3
1. Your main reasons for transferring:			
Reason 1			
Reason 2			
Reason 3			
2. Where you want to live			
3. Setting of school			
4. Size of school			
5. Student body			
6. Major(s)			
7. Academic standards			
8. Cost			
9. Other needs			
Total Preference Rating (highest possible rating is 44)			

2. Now look more closely at the cost of attending each college. Use the categories below to estimate what it would cost **per year** to attend each one. Then, in the last row, enter a "3" for the highest cost college, a "2" for the next lowest, and a "1" for the lowest (assuming you are rating three colleges).

Your Preferences	College 1	College 2	College 3
Estimated Costs			
Tuition			
Room and board			
Textbooks and supplies			
Transportation			
Other expenses			
Total costs			

Your Preferences	College 1	College 2	College 3
Estimated Available Funds			
Savings or help from home			
Scholarships			
Loans			
College work programs			
Other work			
Other income			
Total funds available			
Costs minus funds			
Cost Rating (1 to 3, assuming three colleges; higher number corresponds to lower cost)			

3. Next consider how many credits from your current institution you will be permitted to transfer to each college. In the last row enter a "3" for the greatest number of transferable credits, a "2" for the next lowest, and a "1" for the lowest (assuming you are rating three colleges).

Your Preferences	College 1	College 2	College 3
Number of credits transferable			
Credit Transfer Rating (1 to 3, assuming three colleges; higher number corresponds to more credits transferable)			

4. Now consider your overall impression of each college, based on visits you have made or on other information. Rate each college on a scale from 1 to 4, where "1" = very unfavorable impression and "4" = very favorable impression.

Your Preferences	College 1	College 2	College 3
Overall Impression Rating (1 to 4, higher is better)			

5. Finally add up your four separate ratings to produce a Total Rating for each college.

Your Preferences	College 1	College 2	College 3
Total Rating (= Total Preference Rating + Cost Rating + Credit Transfer Rating + Overall Impression Rating. Higher is better; highest possible rating is 54.)			

While you may use these ratings any way you want, or even ignore them, they may help you decide among your options.

Courses a student takes at the community college level are applied not only to general education requirements at the new institution but also to a major or other specific program. In most cases, 2 + 2 plans are restricted to only a few selected majors, such as human services, nursing, computer technology, or engineering.

The main advantage of 2 + 2 plans is clear: They can provide you with a real head start after your transfer. The downside of a 2 + 2 plan is that it may tie you to a specific major earlier than you may want. Unless you are quite sure of what you want to specialize in, 2 + 2 plans may lead you to make a choice before you are ready to make it.

> **Priority enrollment plans.** Even if there is no formal agreement between a community college and a four-year state school to accept particular courses, some state four-year colleges have priority enrollment plans. In a **priority enrollment plan,** a four-year school gives preference to students from community colleges within the state when it considers which students to admit as junior-year transfers. Although priority enrollment does not guarantee admission, it provides potential transfer students from state community colleges with an advantage over other applicants.

Priority enrollment plan

A plan that gives preference to students from community colleges within the state when it considers which students to admit as junior-year transfers

The Appeal Process: When No May Not Mean No

You've completed Psychology 1, "Introduction to Psychology," at your community college, but the university to which you are transferring hasn't given you credit for it. What should you do?

Although you may think your hands are tied, you generally do have some options. Remember, transfer credit decisions are not made by a college but by a person who works for that college. That person can be rushed, can make a bad decision, or may just plain be in a bad mood when evaluating your previous courses.

If you feel that a mistake has been made, you probably have the right to appeal the decision. Don't appeal it lightly or without considerable deliberation, but also don't be reluctant. You won't be seen as a troublemaker but as a serious student who wants to right a possible academic wrong.

The first thing to do is to try for an informal resolution. E-mail or call the office where the decision was made, contacting the person who made the initial decision. Ask if the decision can be reviewed, and be ready to show why you should be granted the credit.

If the informal route is ineffective, then you may be able to file a formal appeal. An appeal may consist of a form, or it may be a letter stating your case. Find out what the specific process is, and be prepared for a lengthy procedure. Your appeal may be evaluated by a committee of faculty and administrators. Keep it brief and to the point and, as always, be sure you carefully proofread the document before you send it.

What arguments are most persuasive? The best is to clearly demonstrate that the course you have taken is, in fact, very similar to the one offered at your new institution. You can demonstrate the similarity by showing that the course syllabus and textbooks used in the two courses cover similar material. If the syllabus from the course you took does not show a significant course component that was actually included in the course, enclose additional handouts from the course, or ask the original course instructor to provide a "To Whom It May Concern" letter that states that the seemingly missing component was, in fact, covered in the course.

> "Knowledge comes, but wisdom lingers."
> **Alfred Tennyson, author (1809–1892)**

≫LO T.3 Making the Move: Mastering the Transition from Old to New College

You've done it!

You've made the move from your previous school to your new one. However, your feelings of elation at being accepted may turn to anxiety and concern as you face the prospect of starting over. How you manage the transition can have repercussions for the rest of your college career.

Transfer Shock

Many students experience what has been called *transfer shock*, the feeling that their new college is so different from their old one that they will be unable to adjust. Students experiencing transfer shock may feel lonely and unhappy, and they may question their decision to transfer.

Why might you face transfer shock? There are a number of challenges posed by a transfer to a new college, including these:

> **Time management issues.** Every college operates on a slightly different schedule and time frame. Your old college may have started the term in August and finished before the end-of-year holidays. Your new college may start later and finish the term after the first of the year.
>
> The two schools may even have different term lengths. You might be changing from a semester system, in which the term consisted of 15 weeks, to a quarter system, in which terms last 10 weeks. What that means is the rhythm of the terms will be completely different. For example, in a quarter system, the term is nearly over at the same point in a semester system where you've just reached the midpoint of the course. Such changes in the timing of a course can be disorienting, and you need to prepare yourself for them by paying special attention to time management strategies.

> **Academic requirements may be more stringent.** Your courses may be more rigorous, requiring greater effort. You may be reading and writing more than you were used to. Assignments may call for more higher-order thinking, and courses may present concepts that are more abstract. You also may have to take classes in technical subject areas in which you have little interest or natural ability.
>
> If your classes are large, you may have to take multiple-choice exams, bubbling in your answers on machine-scored forms just like you did when you took the SAT or ACT standardized tests.
>
> In addition, your classes may require the use of technology in significant ways. Course assignments may be posted on a course Web site, and you may do homework online. You will need to develop new technology skills and have access to a computer.

> **Financial demands.** Four-year institutions are often more expensive than two-year colleges. Even if you have received a generous financial package from your new school, you still may face difficulties in making ends meet. In addition, if the courses are more challenging than you've previously faced, you may have less time to work at a part-time job to help support yourself.

> **Roommate challenges.** If you previously lived at home and commuted to college, becoming a residential student will offer a stark contrast. You may live

in a small room with two, three, or sometimes even four other students with whom you may have little in common. You'll share a bathroom with people you don't know and whose concerns about cleanliness and neatness may be very different from your own.

> **Commuting issues.** If you are a nonresidential commuter, you will have your own set of challenges that residential students don't need to worry about. For example, your new college may be farther away from home than your old one, requiring a longer commute. In addition, once you arrive on campus, you may encounter parking problems. On some campuses, finding a parking space close to where your classes are will be a challenge.

If you are commuting to a school where most other students live on campus, you'll face other issues, as well. For example, scheduling times to work on a group project will be more difficult. If you forget to pick up a book at the library, it may mean you need to make a long trek back to campus.

> **College size differences.** If your new school is larger than your old one, you'll face other challenges. Bigger colleges mean more students, larger classes, and a bigger library. You will probably have to stand in longer lines. In large classes, there may be hundreds more students sitting with you in a huge lecture room than you've experienced before. The only thing smaller will be your view of the professor, who may be so far away from where you are sitting that you can barely see him or her.

On the other hand, that doesn't mean that the skills you have developed in your earlier years of college are suddenly useless. If you have learned to use a computerized library catalog and find a book in the stacks at your old school, you'll undoubtedly quickly manage to do the same thing at your new school. Similarly, taking lecture notes in large classes requires much the same set of skills as taking notes in small ones.

> **Diversity issues.** The student body of your community college might have been relatively homogeneous, consisting of students who grew up in the same geographic area and having little ethnic and racial diversity. Moving to a new four-year school may mean a more diverse student body, which can be challenging but can also be a great learning experience.

For example, you may find yourself uncomfortable with the political attitudes advocated by classmates in your courses. You may hear speeches by people whose views you find puzzling or even objectionable. You may be assigned a residence hall roommate whose habits and customs you don't understand. Other classmates may practice religions that you've never even heard of.

All this means is that you have to be open to people who are different from you. Realize that they have had experiences that are very different from the ones you've had, and that their perspective on the world may be quite dissimilar from yours. However, opening yourself to people who are different from you will enrich both your college experience and your education as a whole.

In addition to facing these challenges, you will undoubtedly encounter challenges that are specific to your own situation. Use **Try It 5** on page T-22 to consider the factors that might have the most impact on you.

Overcoming Transfer Shock

Although there are clearly many challenges in a successful transfer experience, there are several strategies you can use to diminish and even avoid the consequences of transfer shock. Consider these:

> **Knowledge is power.** Find out as much as you can about your new college before you get there. Read the information on the school Web site and in the

catalog. Understand what is expected of you academically and the kinds of courses you need to take. Learn about the extracurricular activities and campus organizations that are available to you. Understand the technology resources that are available, such as where you can have access to a computer and how the library functions. The more you know about your school, the less anxiety you'll have.

> **Attend orientation.** Virtually all schools have an orientation program for new students. Don't ignore it even though you probably went through an orientation at your previous school. You'll receive valuable information, and you will meet transfer counselors who can give you advice on which courses to take. You will be introduced to the college's resources, and you'll find out how to sign up for courses. If you're living on campus, you'll also receive information about your residence hall.

> **Meet with your advisor.** At some point after you are accepted into your new college, you will be assigned an advisor. Meet this person as soon as possible, because he or she holds several keys to your academic future.

Your advisor will help you navigate through the maze of requirements that you will need to fulfill. He or she will help you choose courses, assist you in filling any gaps in your background, and generally advise you on the things you need to do to have a successful academic career. Good advisors can not only help you understand the things you need to do but also give guidance on the things you *shouldn't* do.

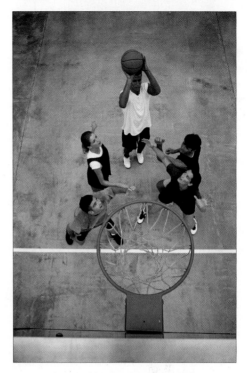

Getting involved in extracurricular activities, such as intramural sports, can help alleviate transfer shock by providing opportunities to meet people with similar interests.

> **Seek out other transfer students .** Having friends who are going through the same thing you are can make the transfer experience much more manageable. Seek out other transfer students, because they will provide a sounding board for what you are going through and can also be a source of information you may have missed.

> **Find a mentor.** Get to know your instructors. Remember, they went into teaching because they enjoy interacting with and getting to know students. Even if you are in a large class with hundreds of other students, your instructor will enjoy meeting you. Choose an instructor who seems most approachable and likable, and stop by his or her office at the beginning of the term. Periodically drop in, just to say hello or to discuss an academic issue. You'll soon find yourself building a relationship with that individual. If you do that every term, you will develop a valuable network of instructors who will keep you feeling like you are a part of the academic community of the school.

> **Remember that you have done it before.** Keep in mind that this is not the first time you have started college. You did it several years earlier, and you were successful enough to be accepted by your current school. You're also older than most typical beginning students, so you probably have a degree of maturity not seen in the average first-year college student. You know what college is like.

Your prior experiences and successes put you several steps ahead of most beginning students on the campus to which you have transferred. That doesn't mean the transition will be easy or stress-free. It does mean, though, that you can be more confident that you will master this new transition and be successful.

POWER Try It!

5 Absorbing the Shock of a Transfer

Once you have decided to transfer to a four-year college, you can expect to feel some degree of transfer shock. A good way to lessen the effects of transfer shock is to prepare in advance for the shocks that you are most likely to experience and to be ready to do something about them. Use this **Try It** to consider likely shocks and prepare to absorb them.

In the first column, consider the most likely sources of discomfort under each category that applies to you. If you don't think you will experience any shock in that category, move on to the next. Then in the second column, try to come up with creative ways to deal with each possible shock.

This is an exercise that you may want to complete with a group of friends. It helps to put a lot of creativity and imagination from more than one mind to work in thinking up effective "shock absorbers" to call on in your first months at your new school.

Source of Potential Shock	What Can I Do about It?
Time management issues: • Different term schedule at new college? • Courses meet at different times of day? • Assignments due on shorter time line? • Need to do part-time work to afford new college? • Less time structure and more responsibility to manage own time? • Other time issues?	
Academic issues: • Harder courses at new college? • Courses move at faster pace? • More reading and writing? • Need to spend more time in library? • Different types of tests? • Greater use of technology? • Other academic issues?	
Financial issues: • Hard to pay tuition and fees? • Worries about student loans? • Higher transportation costs? • More expensive books, and more of them? • Higher entertainment costs? • Higher cost for clothing and food? • Other financial issues?	

Roommate issues: • Not used to living with others? • Worried about not liking roommates? • Pressure to spend money and time to fit in with roommates' lifestyle? • Different standards of cleanliness, privacy, noise, and so forth? • Other roommate issues?	
Commuting issues: • Longer commuting time? • Parking problems? • Feeling left out of campus life? • Hard to make good friends? • Hard to schedule group study time with others? • Other commuting issues?	
College size issues: • Hard to find things? • Longer lines and waits? • Hard to pay attention or ask questions in large classes? • Large library hard to understand? • Confusing array of entertainment and social events? • Generally feeling lost and ignored? • Other size issues?	
Diversity issues: • Hard to understand other people's ideas, dress, habits? • Hard to relate to different backgrounds and experiences? • Hard to accept unusual ideas and practices? • Feeling that others are looking down on you? • Other diversity issues?	

UNIVERSITY OF
WASHINGTON

NAME: **Elese Washines**

SCHOOL: **University of Washington at Seattle; double major in Mathematics and American Indian Studies**

After having excelled at Yakima Valley Community College, a two-year school in the state of Washington, Elese Washines had the opportunity to transfer to some of the best colleges in the country, including Harvard, Purdue, and Dartmouth. However, after much thought, she decided to stay much closer to home and enrolled at the University of Washington in Seattle.

Washines, a member of the Yakama Nation, felt that the offer of a full academic scholarship, a strong mathematics department, and a strong diverse student population at the University of Washington made her decision easier.

Another important factor in her decision was meeting with members of the school's Student Outreach Ambassadors program, a group of diverse students who work to recruit new students.

"I really liked the message they gave. And when one student introduced himself to me in his native language and described being a Pacific Islander, I knew I could be involved with my culture and still pursue the education I wanted," she added. Making the decision to attend the University of Washington, which was almost 10 times larger than her community college, was easier than actually going there.

"I had traveled a lot, and I thought I was experienced in being away from home," Washines noted, "but once I got to the University of Washington, I was homesick a lot. I really missed being around my tribe and family, and I even considered dropping out."

One of the things that helped her overcome the homesickness was to become more involved with other native students.

"All the native students found each other in the student groups and it became our family away from home," she added.

Ultimately, transferring to a much larger institution worked out well for Washines, who plans to teach at the Yakama Nation Tribal School. "I didn't find it intimidating. I just saw it as offering more options. It becomes what you make of it."

Looking Back

What are the strategies for choosing a specific college or university to transfer to?

➤ To *prepare* to transfer, consider the reasons why you should (or shouldn't) transfer.

➤ The *organization* step in the transfer process involves identifying schools to which you might consider transferring.

➤ The *work* of transferring involves the actual application process.

➤ To *evaluate* your options, consider the positive and negative aspects of schools to which you have been accepted, including the amount of financial aid that has been offered.

➤ It's also important to *rethink* your choices to ensure you've made the right decisions.

How do I transfer credits?

➤ Determining which credits will transfer is a central issue for transferring students.

➤ Many schools have articulation agreements, formal arrangements that determine which courses or credits will automatically transfer.

➤ Many states have 2 + 2 plans that permit students to transfer into specific majors or programs.

How can I adjust to a new college?

➤ Some students face transfer shock, which impedes the transition to their new college.

➤ Among the steps to combat transfer shock are getting as much information as possible, attending orientation, seeking out other transfer students, and finding a mentor.

[KEY TERMS AND CONCEPTS]

Articulation agreements (p. T-15)

2 + 2 plans (p. T-15)

Priority enrollment plan (p. T-18)

[RESOURCES]

ON CAMPUS

To help plan a transfer from a two-year college to a four-year school, seek out your transfer advising office. Staff in that office will be well equipped to give you advice and information about the schools to which most students transfer. In addition, you can call or visit the transfer office at the schools to which you are thinking about transferring.

IN PRINT

A variety of books provide useful information about the transfer process. Nadine Koch and K. William Wasson's *The Transfer Student's Guide to the College Experience* (Houghton Mifflin, 2002) is a good place to start.

In addition, Eric Freedman's *How to Transfer to the College of Your Choice* (Ten Speed Press, 2001) and Susan B. Weir's *Transitions: A Guide for the Transfer Student* (Wadsworth Publishing, 2007) provide a variety of strategies to help master the transfer process.

ON THE WEB

The following sites on the Web provide opportunities to extend your learning about the material in this chapter. (Although the Web addresses were accurate at the time the book was printed, check the *P.O.W.E.R. Learning* Web site [**www.mhhe.com/power**] for any changes that may have occurred.)

> The benefits of transferring to a four-year college are explored at **www.intstudy. com/study_abroad/livfiles/saww6a14.htm.** From the International Education Site, this link provides an in-depth feature on how the advantages of transferring to a four-year institution far outweigh the difficulties of the potentially lengthy and sometimes confusing transfer process.

> **collegetransfer.net** is a free Web site that provides extensive information on transferring to four-year institutions, with information on over 4,000 institutions across the country, including information on how courses will transfer from one school to another.

> Most state university systems offer a transfer guide to students who wish to move from a two-year institution to a four-year university. This site (**www.ribghe.org/ transferguide.htm**) from the state of Rhode Island gives a detailed account of the transfer process.

> At **www.ccc.edu/admissions/articulation.shtml#** you will find a comprehensive look at the articulation agreements of City Colleges of Chicago that encompass 209 programs at 52 senior institutions. This example is followed by hundreds of other institutions of higher learning across the country.

TAKING IT TO THE NET

1 Finances are often one of the main considerations students face when transferring from a community college to a four-year school. In order to explore this issue, visit several college Web sites and learn about their financial aid policies. Review the approaches used by different colleges offering aid. Do most offer scholarships? What about work-study? Are low-interest loans an option?

2 Use the Internet to find information on the steps to follow and issues to consider when transferring to a four-year school. Go to Google (**www. google.com**) and Yahoo! (**www.yahoo.com**) and enter "transferring to a four year college." Many of the sites are for community colleges that offer a multitude of tips and suggestions on preparing for a transfer. Review a number of them and consider the strategies that you might use.

[NOTES]

1. Based on data from the Bureau of Labor Statistics, 2003.

[PHOTO CREDITS]

The Case of . . .

Perry's Poor Credit

Three courses at Foothill Community College, one of which produced a grade of F. A course started, but then dropped, at Nassau Community College. Two online courses from eArmyU while in the military service. Finally—and more recently—a semester's worth of courses at Holyoke Community College.

Not a very coherent picture, thought Perry Washington. It's not that he set out to build such a checkered record. It's just that his military service, his marriage and subsequent divorce, and his job kept him moving around.

Despite his past, Perry was actually quite proud of his current stint at Holyoke Community College. He was doing well, with a solid B average. This time, he thought, he would stick it out and earn his associate's degree.

Still, Perry was surprised when one of his instructors asked him if he intended to transfer once he completed his associate's degree. With such a blemished academic record, was it even possible to think of transferring to a four-year school? Could he overcome his background? Was it even worth thinking about obtaining a bachelor's degree?

1. What advice would you give Perry about the possibility of transferring to a four-year school?

2. What would be the advantages of continuing his education beyond an associate's degree?

3. What are the first steps Perry should take to consider transferring?

4. What should Perry do to determine if his credits might transfer?

5. How should Perry identify schools he might transfer to?

Instructor's Annotations

P.O.W.E.R. Learning: Becoming a Successful Student

Learning Outcomes

» **LO 1.1** Explain the benefits of a college education.

» **LO 1.2** Identify the basic principles of the P.O.W.E.R. Plan.

» **LO 1.3** Discuss how expert students use P.O.W.E.R. Learning to achieve college success.

Chapter Opening Example   page 1

Jessie's story at the beginning of the chapter should be instantly relatable to many of your students. The balancing act between their personal and academic lives is a constant source of stress for many new students. During the opening of this course, it is important to keep students focused on the long-term goal, even if their short-term struggles create roadblocks.

Ask your students to write down their greatest hopes and biggest fears for academic success. Tell them that this list will be for their own personal reflection and possibly class discussion. Many students will be encouraged to discover that while their goals and motivations may differ, the fears associated with their academic careers are truly universal.

» LO 1.1 Explain the benefits of a college education   page 2

TEACHING TIP   page 2

During the first days, you will be in a position in which you need to ask students to discuss personal information. Set the stage for students to respect one another. One way to encourage confidentiality and respect is to shut the classroom door.

TEACHING TIP   page 2

Ask your students to identify their expectations for respectful discussion within your classroom.

DISCUSSION PROMPT   page 4

Ask your students how many of the courses they are taking have a service learning component.

» LO 1.2 Identify the basic principles of the P.O.W.E.R. Plan   page 5

TEACHING TIP   page 6

The faculty who have taught with this book believe that the use of the P.O.W.E.R. plan is one of the greatest strengths of this text. Encourage your students to make a commitment to using this concept now. A great place to start is with the P.O.W.E.R. Profile.

Prepare
Organize
Work
Evaluate
Rethink

1

P.O.W.E.R. Learning:
Becoming a Successful Student

STUDENT ALERT   **page 6**

Some of your students will report that they have done goal-setting exercises before. Encourage them to plan anew as they begin college. Suggest that they consider goals specifically aligned with their reasons for being in school. Also, many students may struggle with writing specific goals. Give them direct feedback on their goals.

TEACHING TIP   **page 8**

Students will begin to discover differences in each classmate's learning styles as they share the way they set goals.

STUDENT ALERT   **page 8**

Many students have difficulty writing specific, measurable goals. Give them direct feedback about their goals.

DISCUSSION PROMPT   **page 10**

Ask students to give an example of their own organizational tools and methods.

TEACHING TIP   **page 10**

Share with students how you organize for class.

TEACHING TIP   **page 11**

Using $3'' \times 5''$ cards, have your students answer the question: "If I could get more motivated, I'd do so much better with my _____" (insert schoolwork, diet, exercising, or the like). Have students work in pairs to come up with possible solutions for each other.

TEACHING TIP   **page 12**

Have students use "I" statement in their goals to reinforce their personal responsibility.

DISCUSSION PROMPT   **page 14**

Ask students to share their best ideas for staying motivated.

TEACHING TIP   **page 15**

Ask students to bring in all of their course syllabi and identify the different ways they will be evaluated in all of their classes.

DISCUSSION PROMPT   **page 16**

When have students seen the idea of "rethinking" used by their family or friends? By their local, state, or national government?

» LO 1.3 Discuss how expert students use P.O.W.E.R. Learning to achieve college success   **page 17**

TEACHING TIP   **page 17**

Successful students know their faculty members' names by the second week of class. Challenge your students to know all of their faculty by name.

TEACHING TIP   **page 17**

Understanding why students are in college and what skills they believe they have are crucial to academic success.

DISCUSSION PROMPT   **page 18**

Striving to be perfect: When does it help, and when does it hurt?

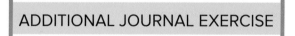

[**ADDITIONAL JOURNAL EXERCISE**]

A Letter to Myself

Have students write a letter to themselves to be read on graduation day. In it, they should outline their greatest fears and their ultimate goals. Encourage students to revisit this letter during the course of their academic careers and on their actual graduation days. The experience of visualizing the end product of their education can be profound.

P.O.W.E.R. Learning: Becoming a Successful Student

ADDITIONAL JOURNAL EXERCISE

Journal Writing, Reflection Cards, and Reaction Cards

Processing personal experiences through written reflection is an important part of thinking and learning. Most student success course faculty use some form of written communication to keep in touch with students about events and self-discovery. These writings are a way to create a private conversation between you and your students and to assess the integration of experiences in your student's understanding of your course goals.

There are several factors to consider regarding these writings and there are a variety of ways to manage them. Here are a few examples:

> Semester-long notebooks with multiple entries (usually weekly) that are evaluated quarterly.

> End-of-class reaction cards where students spend the last five minutes of class summarizing the topics discussed during that class meeting.

> A sequence of papers guided by the assigned prompts and assembled into a portfolio.

> Weekly reaction cards and e-mail entries that respond to self-discovery prompts and goals.

It is important that these writings be evaluated regularly and that personalized feedback is given to the students.

IN-CLASS ACTIVITY

Forced Choice

"Thinking on your feet" is a skill that is valued in many environments; the forced choice exercise allows this skill to happen naturally. Create a list of eight to ten statements or questions about a prompt. Label one end of the room "Agree" and the other end "Disagree." Pose the statement or question and have students move to the appropriate side of the room. Allow individuals to explain their choice, without creating an opportunity for discussion. Then, quickly move on to the next question. This activity allows students to move around the room, to speak, and to listen.

Making the Most of Your Time

Learning Outcomes

» LO **2.1**   Discuss strategies to manage your time effectively.

» LO **2.2**   Identify ways to deal with surprises and distractions.

» LO **2.3**   Explain ways to balance competing priorities.

Chapter Opening Example   page 28

Like Meadow in the chapter opening example, many students will be overextended. The purpose of this chapter is to provide them with strategies for using the time they do have in the most effective manner possible.

» LO **2.1**   Discuss strategies to manage your time effectively   page 29

P.O.W.E.R. UP   page 30

Ask students to bring all their class syllabi and a calendar with them to class. Have them predict the busiest weeks in their first semester on campus using these tools. How can they use this knowledge?

DISCUSSION PROMPT   page 30

Ask students to share the phrases that they associate with the use of time (e.g., "24/7"; "time flies when you are having fun") and discuss how these words shape our understanding of time.

» LO **2.2**   Identify ways to deal with surprises and distractions   page 32

TEACHING TIP   page 33

To teach time management effectively, have students bring calendars, PDAs, and other electronic devices regularly to class and make time for students to use them.

STUDENT ALERT   page 33

Students need assistance moving between daily calendars and a semester or long-term plan. There are more ways than ever to distract us from doing what we have planned. Help them make the connection between small steps and major accomplishments.

STUDENT ALERT   page 34

This chapter is so full of charts and attention to the details needed for planning that your students might reject the work and call it tedious. Assure them that an understanding of the process will provide them with choices in planning their personal and academic lives.

» LO **2.3**   Explain ways to balance competing priorities   page 34

STUDENT ALERT   page 34

The issue of "balance" is introduced here. Many students will challenge you to tell them "one right way" to manage time and then come up with lots of reasons why *that* particular way will not work for them. Emphasize that effective time management is based on identifying priorities, making appropriate choices, and understanding one's learning style preference.

Instructor's Annotations

TEACHING TIP page 41

Have students make copies of Figure 2.3 or place it on their personal computers or PDAs.

DISCUSSION PROMPT page 43

After they complete the exercise outlined in Figure 2.4, have your students exchange charts and look at life from someone else's perspective.

TEACHING TIP page 44

Ask students to make a daily to-do list for two weeks. Check for it at the beginning of each class. This routine is how new habits are created.

TEACHING TIP page 44

Encourage your students to mark or check items off their lists. This is a visual reminder of "getting things done" and can create a sense of accomplishment when the list seems overwhelming.

DISCUSSION PROMPT page 44

Saying "no" is a perfect example of being able to accept personal responsibility for one's actions. Choices and consequences are a theme you should discuss throughout this course.

STUDENT ALERT page 46

Sometimes students (and teachers) are so busy handling the *urgent* priorities that making time for *important* priorities is difficult.

TEACHING TIP page 46

Students will admit that procrastination is a problem. Ask them about their use of electronic devices, such as mobile phones, text messaging, iPods, mp3 players, e-mail, Facebook, and so on. Discuss the magic of an e-break.

TEACHING TIP page 48

Have students generate a list of ways that they allow others to misuse their time and brainstorm solutions to the problem.

DISCUSSION PROMPT page 50

Ask your students how many have jobs outside of class. You might be surprised at how many hours they are working and how little time they believe they have free for studying.

TEACHING TIP page 51

Refer back to the "168 Hours in a Week" activity done earlier to assess whether there is time to do more. Just as important, discuss the differences between engagement and simply scheduling activities. The energy needed for success is entirely different.

ADDITIONAL JOURNAL EXERCISE

Writing Down Goals

Ask your students to consider what they want to accomplish in the next five years. What kinds of relationships, jobs, skills, and talents do they want to have? Then ask them to work backward and consider what they hope to accomplish within one year. Finally, ask them to make a list of the things they want to accomplish tomorrow. Do they see any correlations between tomorrow's tasks and their "hoped for" accomplishments at the end of the year? At the end of five years? The relationship between "the activities I participate in today and the abilities I have in the future" is fundamental for students to grasp. Have them write an intention or reflection statement about this idea.

Making the Most of Your Time

GROUP ACTIVITY

How Much Is 168?

Collect coins prior to class (everyone has them lurking in their couch cushions, center driving consol, etc). Make sure that you fill a clear container with exactly 168 coins. Have students guess how many total coins are in the jar. Reveal the total number and highlight the connection that this is equivalent to the number of hours in a given week. Discuss whether students think this number is large or small. The visual display may help put into perspective exactly how big (or small) 168 can be.

IN-CLASS ACTIVITY

168 Hours in a Week

This activity helps you understand how you use your time each week. Everyone has the same amount of time, and knowing how you choose to use your time will give you the power to change your behaviors.

STEP 1: List the amount of time per week for each activity (arrive at a daily average and multiply by 7); also account for weekend differences:

a. Class time (# of hours in class each week)

b. Job/work

c. Studying

d. Commuting/transportation time

e. Non–school-related interests

f. Family responsibilities

g. Sleeping

h. Eating

i. Personal grooming

STEP 2: Add together a–i for a subtotal. Then subtract your subtotal from 168 for the total.

If the number in your TOTAL line is negative, you have committed to more time than there is in a week. YOU ARE IN TROUBLE. If you have time left over, ask yourself what choices you have for your time. Do you have time for more sleep? Volunteering? Friends?

For a printable version of this activity, please see the Instructor's Manual.

Discovering Your Learning Styles, Self-Concept, and Values

Learning Outcomes

≫ LO**3.1**   Identify your learning style and how it affects your academic success.

≫ LO**3.2**   Explain self-concept and how it affects you.

≫ LO**3.3**   Create a personal mission statement.

≫ LO**3.4**   Recognize strategies for making wise personal decisions.

Chapter Opening Example   page 56

Shaniqua's "light bulb" moment highlights a very real situation for many students. Illustrate the concept of preferences using the P.O.W.E.R. Up exercise.

≫ LO**3.1**   Identify your learning style and how it affects your academic success   page 57

P.O.W.E.R. UP   page 58

Illustrate the concept of preferences by asking students to write their name on a sheet of paper. Then ask them to write their name again but this time use their other hand. Ask the students to discuss their observation about this activity.

STUDENT ALERT   page 58

This chapter provides multiple ways to discuss the same information with your students; begin to agree on a common language for discussing learning issues. You will return to this topic repeatedly throughout the semester.

TEACHING TIP   page 58

Every college campus has someone who understands and works with this information. Call on your colleagues to help you.

TEACHING TIP   page 62

Ask students to circle all the words and phrases that best describe their own learning styles and preferences. Ask them to write a paper or talk with a classmate about the words they selected to describe themselves.

TEACHING TIP   page 62

The combination of individual personality and learning is a captivating concept for students. Tap into this interest.

STUDENT ALERT   page 63

Reassure your students that they may possess or use all of these learning traits. The MBTI provides information about how we prefer to learn and interact with the world.

TEACHING TIP   page 68

Refer back to the P.O.W.E.R. Up exercise of writing your name.

DISCUSSION PROMPT   page 68

If your students are in a learning community, this is a great environment for discussing different teaching styles. Encourage students to use the TRY IT 3 model with other courses, without referring to instructors by name.

STUDENT ALERT   page 68

Remind your students to make a direct connection between what faculty members value and what they choose to focus on.

Discovering Your Learning Styles, Self-Concept, and Values

» LO 3.2 Explain self-concept and how it affects you _____ **page 68**

STUDENT ALERT **page 69**

Real learning and personal growth are hard. It is not in our nature to seek out discomfort, but it is in moments of struggle that life-altering reflection occurs.

DISCUSSION PROMPT **page 71**

Expect your students to take over the class with their need to spend time talking about self-concept and self-esteem issues. Let them! It will be time well spent.

» LO 3.3 Create a personal mission statement _____ **page 73**

DISCUSSION PROMPT **page 75**

Ask students to think about how this information is relevant to their own lives. Have they ever experienced a *cycle of failure* with activities or courses? How did they break the cycle?

TEACHING TIP **page 76**

Look for opportunities to extend this discussion beyond the classroom: guest speakers, campus counseling services, films, and other media presentations.

TEACHING TIP **page 77**

The P.O.W.E.R. process in this chapter culminates with TRY IT 5, which will be a personal mission statement and reference point for each student that you should refer back to throughout the semester.

TEACHING TIP **page 78**

Don't forget to constantly link the information about values, motivation, self-concept, etc. to learning preferences and the goal of academic success.

DISCUSSION PROMPT **page 78**

Connect a discussion on motivation to the goals that students set for themselves in Chapter 1, that is, "Why am I going to college?"

TEACHING TIP **page 81**

Assign TRY IT 5 as a formal writing assignment, which includes composition, editing, conferencing, and rewriting.

» LO 3.4 Recognize strategies for making wise personal decisions _____ **page 82**

DISCUSSION PROMPT **page 82**

Recreate a childhood moment. Have students share a dream for the future. Ask them to respond to the prompt, "if I could be anything I want to be," or write a speech they might give in 10–20 years as an honored graduation speaker.

[**ADDITIONAL JOURNAL EXERCISE**]

Journal to Your Learning Style

Ask students to journal on their college experience thus far, but do not limit them simply to pen and paper. Offer students the opportunity to journal in a way the feel matches their learning style. Encourage students to consider how they learn and to come up with creative ways of journaling "outside the box." This journal entry is great for students to share with their peers!

IN-CLASS ACTIVITY

Learning Pyramid

The Learning Pyramid is a wonderful teaching/learning activity. Pair up students and ask one person from each pair to volunteer to be the teacher; the other will be the learner. Ask each of the teachers to step outside the room with you. Once outside the room, provide each of them with a copy of the Learning Pyramid. The task of each teacher is to find a way to communicate the information on the page without showing the sheet to the student or using the word pyramid to describe how the information is organized on the sheet. Give your teachers a full five minutes to study the information and determine their strategy for teaching it. You may choose to let them work on a similar strategy together or separately; there is merit to both approaches. During the five-minute preparation period, you may go back the classroom and discuss something else with the students who are in the classroom. At the end of the preparation period, take up all copies of the pyramid and tell the teachers they have five minutes to teach the information to their students. Inform everyone that at the end of the teaching session, a test will be given to see if the students know the information. When the five minutes are up, ask everyone to recreate the information that was on the sheet. They should then share their pictures.

PROCESSING THE EXERCISE

Ask everyone to answer the following question: Who was the learner, and who was the teacher? Why? What implication does this have for studying? For teaching? For learning?

Taking Notes

Learning Outcomes

» LO **4.1**   Explain methods for effective note taking.

» LO **4.2**   Explain methods for taking notes in class.

» LO **4.3**   Apply techniques for taking notes from written materials.

Chapter Opening Examples
page 89

Students will tell you they need to learn new study skills, but they will not easily change familiar habits, such as how they take notes. Encourage them to adopt the strategies in this chapter systematically for a month before they decide to return to their old ways.

» LO **4.1**   Explain methods for effective note taking   page 90

» LO **4.2**   Explain methods for taking notes in class   page 90

Because Learning Outcomes 4.1 and 4.2 cover a lot of the same material, they are grouped together. While both outcomes stand on their own, you cannot have a serious discussion of what effective notes are without also explaining the methodology behind effective notes. Be sure to use both Learning Outcomes to enhance each other but also note to students that these should be stand-alone concepts.

TEACHING TIP
page 90

Ask students to bring their syllabus to class every time. Suggest that students ask if their faculty members update their syllabus on a Web site or through some other format.

TEACHING TIP
page 91

First-year students often do not realize that faculty members do not always announce textbook reading assignments; the faculty often assumes that students will do this without being told. The material needs to be read prior to discussion about that prompt in class, not afterward!

DISCUSSION PROMPT
page 92

Ask students to create a list of distracting behaviors of faculty. Then, share a list of distracting behaviors by students. Use these lists to illustrate that despite our biases, we still have to find a way to accomplish the goal of classroom time–LEARNING!

STUDENT ALERT
page 92

Remind students that they need to be rested and alert when they come to class.

TEACHING TIP
page 92

Invite students to create an ideal note taking toolbox that includes the best of all the tools available. Leave it in the room as a visual reminder of the information in this chapter.

TEACHING TIP
page 92

Point out that not needing the text during class does not mean that students are not expected to read it prior to class.

STUDENT ALERT
page 94

First-year students may assume that it is the faculty member's responsibility to provide technical support so that they may take notes with emerging technologies. This assumption might be something to discuss with your students.

DISCUSSION PROMPT
page 95

Ask students to discuss how they determine what to write down in their notes.

DISCUSSION PROMPT   page 97

Remind students to keep their abbreviations consistent in all of their notes. Text messaging has increased the use of abbreviations. How can students use these new abbreviations in class?

TEACHING TIP   page 98

The outline form works best with instructors who use it to create their lectures. It is generally not a useful format for discussion classes. Consider doing a short lecture on a prompt that lends itself to outline note taking to provide students with an opportunity to practice.

DISCUSSION PROMPT   page 98

What do your students do about information presented on an overhead or through a PowerPoint presentation that they missed? Can they request copies of the information from their faculty members? Why or why not?

TEACHING TIP   page 99

Ask students to take notes on a chapter of this text using the outline format.

TEACHING TIP   page 100

It is a good policy to encourage students to discuss the behaviors of challenging instructors without using specific names.

TEACHING TIP   page 105

Make it a practice to have students verbally recount the main points of your class during the last 2-3 minutes of each meeting.

STUDENT ALERT   page 107

Many students believe that reading their notes is the same as actively studying them. Demonstrate the process of rewriting notes, creating questions from notes,

summarizing notes, and discussing notes as more active ways to study and "rethink" one's notes.

STUDENT ALERT   page 107

Note taking is like time management. There are daily notes that support the overall course goals, just like daily to-do lists support the semester (and lifetime) plan. Help students make the connection between daily habits and "the bigger picture."

» LO 4.3 Apply techniques for taking notes from written materials   page 108

TEACHING TIP   page 108

Encourage students to argue with the author, create questions, circle new or important words, and/or write their own ideas as they read. Point out that it is important to own the books they are studying.

TEACHING TIP   page 109

Encourage students to review their notes each day before class.

STUDENT ALERT   page 110

Make certain that your students understand that notes can and should be taken on print materials as well as lectures.

ADDITIONAL JOURNAL EXERCISE

Why Do We Take Notes?

Ask students why it is important to take notes. Have them write a journal response to that question, and then encourage the class to share their ideas. This exercise will help generate a frank discussion of note taking biases and rationales.

Taking Notes

ADDITIONAL JOURNAL EXERCISE

Have students bring notes from another class and ask them to write a paragraph or two on the prompt outlined in their notes. Are they able to formulate the main ideas of the lecture back into a one- to two-paragraph essay? If so, what aspects of their notes did they find most helpful? If not, what valuable pieces of information were they missing?

IN-CLASS ACTIVITY

Films are extremely appropriate to use in college classrooms and can often illustrate a point better than your words and actions. Consider using films for any of the following reasons.

> To promote discussion about a value or theme relevant to college life and your course.

> To provide a source of information for your students to practice listening skills, concentration skills, note-taking skills, test-taking skills, or other study skills.

> To accommodate students with different learning styles.

> To appeal to students who have grown up in a film- and video-based culture.

Films provide students with yet another way to sharpen their understanding of how they recall information. They may begin to recognize that facts are easier to recall if presented with multiple images of an idea—visually, auditory, verbally, etc.

For this class, you may consider choosing a short video or segment of a longer video. Have students practice note taking skills while watching the video. You may also want to provide similar information in a written format to give students the opportunity to compare and contrast the same informational notes taken from two different sources.

Taking Tests

Learning Outcomes

》LO 5.1 Identify kinds of tests you will encounter in college.

》LO 5.2 Explain the best ways to prepare for and take various kinds of tests.

》LO 5.3 Analyze the best strategies for answering specific kinds of test questions.

Chapter Opening Example   page 116

Earlier in the term students, should have noted in their planners when all of their tests, projects, and so on were scheduled for the entire term. Now is a good time to do this activity, if you have not assigned it yet. Extend the activity during the opening class discussion about taking tests by asking your students to include a prediction about what type of test will be given, next to each date that they have a test scheduled.

》LO 5.1 Identify kinds of tests you will encounter in college   page 117

DISCUSSION PROMPT   page 119

After reviewing Table 5.1, ask students to identify which types of questions they believe are most effective for each of their courses during this term.

》LO 5.2 Explain the best ways to prepare for and take various kinds of tests   page 119

DISCUSSION PROMPT   page 120

Do your students agree with the Notre Dame student's quote, or do they believe their high school provided more rigorous preparation for college? Do they have other life experiences they feel helped prepare them?

STUDENT ALERT   page 121

Some high schools do not use essay questions as a way of evaluating students. Find out how familiar your students are with writing essays on exams.

DISCUSSION PROMPT   page 121

Ask your students to share their preparation styles for different types of questions. Do they see any connections between the way they prepare for a test and their individual learning styles?

TEACHING TIP   page 123

Visualization is used more and more, in a variety of areas, such as athletics and wellness. Model this activity with your class.

TEACHING TIP   page 124

Test anxiety is a good topic for guest speakers to address. Many campuses have experts in this area, and because you test and evaluate your students, someone outside that relationship can provide a valuable, and possibly different, perspective.

TEACHING TIP   page 126

A student's ability to focus and work productively in a study group has a lot to do with his or her learning style. Refer to the work you did in Chapter 3. Encourage students who want to use a study group to complete the TRY IT 3 activity.

TEACHING TIP   page 127

Ask your students to share their thoughts about cramming. If they are firmly convinced that cramming is effective, you will have to work harder to teach this chapter.

TEACHING TIP   page 128

This is a good time to mention the physical aspects of test preparation, from sleep and nutrition to techniques for dealing with sweaty palms and fluttering stomachs, to the actual location where the test is given and how your students may need to adapt to that setting to be successful.

STUDENT ALERT   page 128

Students often miss the importance of this information. Emphasize the importance of skimming the entire exam, with the main purpose of balancing items and point to totals for each section of the test.

TEACHING TIP   page 129

Really emphasize the importance of skimming the entire exam with the main purpose of balancing time and point totals for each section of the test.

» LO 5.3 Analyze the best strategies for answering specific kinds of test questions   **page 130**

DISCUSSION PROMPT   page 130

Ask students to share their test-taking experiences. What testing principles have worked for them?

DISCUSSION PROMPT   page 133

The Peanuts cartoon poses an interesting question. Do your students agree? Encourage your students to place the specific techniques presented in the chapter in the context of a bigger picture; namely, what is higher education all about?

TEACHING TIP   page 134

Tests are *really* stressful for many students. Don't forget to remind students that it is okay to reward themselves after a test—especially if they earned a good grade!

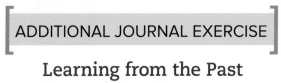

ADDITIONAL JOURNAL EXERCISE

Tests Are Everywhere

Ask your students to identify the different ways they have been tested, evaluated, and assessed in their lives. Tell them to think "outside the box" of academic life. What values, actions, behaviors, and beliefs are tested by life?

GROUP ACTIVITY

Failure and Success

In small groups, discuss the concepts of failure and success. How do they recognize failure and success that is not associated with a grade? How will they know if they are successful or failing in the workforce?

IN-CLASS ACTIVITY

Using Your Notes to Take a Test

If you did the In-Class Activity for Chapter 4 and had students take notes from a short video in class, prepare a test on the same prompt. Have students refer to their notes to study for the test. This exercise will give them valuable practice taking tests and reinforce the importance of good notes for test success.

ADDITIONAL JOURNAL EXERCISE

Learning from the Past

Have students think of a time that they did not perform well on a test or quiz. Have them outline how they prepared for that test. If they knew then what they know now, how would their preparations have been different?

Building Your Reading Skills

Learning Outcomes

» **LO 6.1**   Explain how reading style and attention span affect reading.

» **LO 6.2**   Identify how to improve concentration and read more effectively.

» **LO 6.3**   Discuss how best to retain what you have read.

Chapter Opening Example

page 145

Consider requiring a common reading assignment for your class as you teach this chapter, preferably a short story or article. Bring it to class the first day you discuss reading. If students are in a linked course or learning community, then ask them to bring a common reading from their other class.

» LO 6.1   Explain how reading style and attention span affect reading
page 146

TEACHING TIP **page 146**

Students often do not know that they are struggling with reading. Encourage them to approach the concept of successful reading with fresh eyes.

TEACHING TIP **page 147**

Have students read a section of this text's frontmatter. See if the experience provides any added insight into the text or the course.

STUDENT ALERT **page 150**

Some students in your class will be excellent readers, some weak. Let the strong readers share their methods and model them in small group settings or in pairs.

DISCUSSION PROMPT **page 151**

With this chapter, you are almost halfway through the text. Use TRY IT 3 as a midterm evaluation of this text: Are your students learning what the author (and you) want to teach? Are they learning what they want to learn?

STUDENT ALERT **page 152**

A sense of place is critically important when considering reading assignments and attention span. Making the transition from private spaces to public spaces, such as libraries and dorm rooms, can be difficult for students.

» LO 6.2   Identify how to improve concentration and read more effectively
page 154

STUDENT ALERT **page 154**

Few students are aware of their attention span. Make sure that conversations and TRY IT 5 are really focused on how attention span can influence success in college.

DISCUSSION PROMPT **page 155**

For a humorous aside, allow a few minutes for the class to share some of their favorite excuses for not reading. What is your own best example of being distracted?

STUDENT ALERT **page 156**

Remind students that we each have to decide which reading techniques work best for us. At the same time, encourage them to be open to trying new techniques.

TEACHING TIP **page 157**

Bring in copies of college texts or other books in which you have written or taken notes. Discuss with your students the importance of buying their texts so that they can be active readers.

Building Your Reading Skills

TEACHING TIP   **page 158**

Spend a few minutes connecting this information to ideas in Chapter 8 on memory.

DISCUSSION PROMPT   **page 159**

Take a moment to discuss disabilities. Developing sensitivities to differences of all kinds should be a theme throughout this course.

» LO **6.3**   Discuss how best to retain what you have read   **page 162**

TEACHING TIP   **page 163**

Encourage students to think of evaluation in another way. How directly do their reading skills determine how they will be evaluated (graded) in their other classes?

TEACHING TIP   **page 164**

Connect the Concept Map information in Chapter 4 to taking notes.

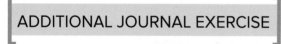

ADDITIONAL JOURNAL EXERCISE

Reading in Real Life

Take an international incident and have students read about it in state, national, and international newspapers. Are the stories different? How so? How do these differences shape their thinking about the event?

OUT-OF-CLASS ACTIVITY

Faculty Reading Interview

Students do not readily communicate with faculty members outside of the classroom. Encouraging students to develop relationships with faculty members is one of the single most important goals you can pursue in a student success course.

Require students to consider thoughtfully which faculty member they would like to know more about, though discourage them from interviewing you, because you will have ample opportunity for talking with and listening to your students in class and through other activities. Remind them to follow basic courtesies, such as requesting an appointment for the interview and being on time. The student should make certain that the faculty member knows beforehand what the appointment is about; he or she might even want to provide a copy of the questionnaire for the faculty member to read prior to the interview.

For more information and the full questionnaire, please see the Instructor's Manual.

Writing and Speaking

Learning Outcomes

» **LO 7.1** Explain the best technique for getting started and writing a first draft.

» **LO 7.2** Identify the process of moving from first draft to final draft.

» **LO 7.3** Discuss how to conquer fear of public speaking and make effective oral presentations.

Chapter Opening Example   page 169

Writer's block is going to happen to every student (probably multiple times) in his or her college career. This chapter should help students develop strategies for handling it when it inevitably happens.

» **LO 7.1** Explain the best technique for getting started and writing a first draft   **page 170**

TEACHING TIP   **page 172**

Assign the task of writing a paper that relates to this course, or allow students to bring in an assignment from another course—especially if this course is linked to a course in a learning community—to practice the processes discussed in this chapter.

TEACHING TIP   **page 173**

Teach this chapter with the expectation that students will take a written assignment and turn it into an oral presentation.

DISCUSSION PROMPT   **page 173**

Ask your students to make a list of the characteristics (vocabulary, graphics, voice) that would distinguish a paper written for an instructor from one written for a classmate, a friend, or a family member.

STUDENT ALERT   **page 173**

Help your students distinguish between gathering information and processing it.

DISCUSSION PROMPT   **page 175**

Ask students to generate a list of all of the "10-minute tasks" associated with writing a 10-page paper.

TEACHING TIP   **page 175**

Primary sources are much easier to identify and reference when they are available in the library than on the Web. Take time to explain this point as you discuss the importance of citations.

STUDENT ALERT   **page 176**

Many students have written research papers. Have them share organizational methods they know. Are they willing to try out new strategies?

TEACHING TIP   **page 178**

There are many organizational structures for preparing papers other than AABBCC. Ask your students which ones they know about.

STUDENT ALERT   **page 179**

Ambiguity is frustrating to many first-year students. They want to know the "one right way," and of course, there isn't just one.

TEACHING TIP   **page 179**

Objectivity is often a skill that must be taught; it does not come naturally for many of us! Use this topic to teach what objectivity means, and bring it to play often in your classroom. It is a key ingredient to all problem solving.

TEACHING TIP   **page 181**

Ask students to recall their learning styles inventory. Which learning style preferences influence their approach to a writing project?

» LO 7.2 Identify the process of moving from first draft to final draft   **page 181**

TEACHING TIP   **page 182**

Requiring journals provides an opportunity for students to organize and express their thoughts in writing on a regular basis.

TEACHING TIP   **page 183**

Ask students to bring in a favorite novel and to identify an actor whose voice would sound right reading it. Can they tell you why? Ask them to analyze the characteristics of "their own voice."

TEACHING TIP   **page 184**

Ask students to read one another's papers and provide feedback.

DISCUSSION PROMPT   **page 184**

Rather than spending time trying to convince students about the importance of good spelling, ask them to tell you why correct spelling matters.

TEACHING TIP   **page 184**

Bring in examples of appropriate "final" products.

STUDENT ALERT   **page 185**

Students may resist the idea that they can predict an instructor's evaluation. Help them to see why it's important to make the effort to do so.

DISCUSSION PROMPT   **page 186**

Pair up students and have them talk about rethinking the message and the mechanics.

TEACHING TIP   **page 186**

Ask students to attach a page to the end of every paper they turn in to you with responses to the "rethink" prompts on page xx.

DISCUSSION PROMPT   **page 187**

Plagiarism is but one form of cheating. Many sources tell us that cheating of all kinds is on the rise in colleges today. Have students discuss this topic using examples from their personal experience.

TEACHING TIP   **page 188**

Read and discuss your institution's academic integrity code.

STUDENT ALERT   **page 189**

Many college campuses use student judicial boards to handle issues involving academic integrity. Invite one of the students from this board to speak to your class.

» LO 7.3 Discuss how to conquer fear of public speaking and make effective oral presentations   **page 189**

TEACHING TIP   **page 189**

Connect this information to the learning styles information in Chapter 3. Ask students to identify strategies for speaking in public, even when it is not their strong suit.

DISCUSSION PROMPT   **page 190**

Ask students to share some effective opening statements or strategies they have used or observed.

TEACHING TIP   **page 192**

Have students generate a list of transition phrases or verbal messages that lead listeners through an oral presentation.

Writing and Speaking

DISCUSSION PROMPT   **page 192**

Ask students to discuss the advantages and disadvantages of giving a presentation using paper (8½ × 11 sheets), note cards (3 × 5), overhead transparencies, slides, computers, videos, etc.

TEACHING TIP   **page 195**

Videotape your students and allow them to take the video home to watch in private. Ask them to provide you with a written critique of their performance.

DISCUSSION PROMPT   **page 196**

Ask students to list several occasions when they have spoken in public. Why did they speak? What were the results?

ADDITIONAL JOURNAL EXERCISE

Overcoming Fears

Have students reflect on their greatest fears with respect to both writing and giving presentations. Have them write down every aspect of the experience that causes panic or unease. Sometimes naming your fears can lessen them. If students are comfortable, consider using this exercise as a springboard for an in-class discussion. They may be surprised to find that many of their own anxieties are reflected in their classmates.

IN-CLASS ACTIVITY

Fishbowl

This classroom discussion technique promotes a stimulating class discussion. It can stir spirited discussions on almost any topic, but it is particularly effective for issues regarding gender, diversity, values, stereotypes, and behaviors.

PROCEDURE

Divide the class by gender (or some other criterion) and place one of the groups on the floor in a small circle facing inward. The other group (e.g., men, women) sits in desks or chairs, arranged concentrically around the inner circle (also facing inward). Instruct the members of the inner circle to share their answers, opinions, or ideas about the issue being discussed. Members of the outer circle are to listen carefully but *may not speak*. If members of the outer circle want to make a contribution to the conversation, they must tap someone in the inside on the shoulder and ask them to change places (i.e., the inner member shifts to the outer listening circle). The person tapped may decline if he or she still has ideas to share, but in most cases someone will be willing to swap places to allow the person from the outer circle to join the conversation. Swapping often goes on continuously in a lively discourse.

ADVANTAGE:

This kind of focused conversation keeps everyone attentive to the task, gives everyone with something to say a chance, and allows those who want to listen to be observers.

CONCLUSION

To wind up the fishbowl, ask students to summarize the main points of the discussion, list one new viewpoint they heard, and comment on what surprised them the most.

Memory

Learning Outcomes

» LO 8.1 Explain what memory is and how it functions.

» LO 8.2 Identify problems with memory and develop strategies for dealing with memory problems.

» LO 8.3 Utilize techniques for memorizing information.

Chapter Opening Example   page 202

Many students have less experience with memorization than they may think. Memory is a skill that can be honed. Be sure students understand that the strategies in this chapter will grow stronger with practice.

» LO 8.1 Explain what memory is and how it functions   page 203

TEACHING TIP   **page 203**

Invite a colleague from the Biology or Psychology department to talk about the physiological and psychological aspects of memory.

STUDENT ALERT   **page 204**

Memory skills can be enhanced. Good recall of facts enhances thinking but is not a substitute for intelligent thought.

STUDENT ALERT   **page 205**

Often students have difficulty discriminating between what's important and what actually can be done. Spend time talking about how to make this distinction.

» LO 8.2 Identify problems with memory and develop strategies for dealing with memory problems page 205

DISCUSSION PROMPT   **page 205**

There are indicators that a protein is released during repetitive activities that allow for this "etching in the brain" to take place. What do your students believe is involved in the process of memory?

» LO 8.3 Utilize techniques for memorizing information   page 206

DISCUSSION PROMPT   **page 208**

Ask students to share their favorite mnemonic devices, such as ways they remember how to spell words ("i" before "e" except after "c"; a PIEce of PIE; "a rat" in separate; I will love you truly in JULY). They probably have several clever tricks of their own.

DISCUSSION PROMPT   **page 210**

Start a well-known advertising jingle or slogan and ask your students to finish it. Can they? Does it surprise anyone that so many people can "know" the same thing? What implications does this knowing have for society? For memory? For learning?

STUDENT ALERT   **page 211**

The method of loci is complex, and some students will reject working with it because of the level of thinking involved. Remind them that finding meaningful ways to put information together can help them improve their memory. The complexity of this approach simply requires that they spend more time on it.

TEACHING TIP   **page 211**

Encourage students to create stories or images that bring life to difficult ideas.

DISCUSSION PROMPT　　　　**page 212**

Can your students attach powerful emotions to information they can remember?

TEACHING TIP　　　　**page 213**

Visualization is a powerful tool. Most athletes will have used this skill in their sport; if you have any athletes or former athletes in your class, ask them to speak about their use of this important skill.

DISCUSSION PROMPT　　　　**page 214**

What influence can reading and writing about mathematical problems and graphing results have on students'
ability to understand and thus remember and learn math?

TEACHING TIP　　　　**page 217**

Ask students to report which of their class texts contain review questions.

DISCUSSION PROMPT　　　　**page 218**

Ask students if they can remember a time they were totally immersed in an activity. Do they worry about their memory during those intensely focused times? Why or why not?

Choosing Your Courses and Major

9

Learning Outcomes

» LO **9.1** Create a plan to prepare for the academic choices that college demands.

» LO **9.2** Outline a strategy for choosing courses that ensure you are getting the most out of your studies.

» LO **9.3** Explain how participation in service learning can improve your college experience.

» LO **9.4** Explain the criteria for choosing a major.

Chapter Opening Example
page 225

Students may not always be focused on the ultimate result of their education. This is okay, but this chapter should serve as a wake-up call that the decisions will need to be made sooner rather than later. Be open to students' ideas and make sure to really listen to what they are saying. This is one chapter that lends itself particularly well to conversations and connections!

» LO **9.1** Create a plan to prepare for the academic choices that college demands
page 227

STUDENT ALERT
page 227

Most students do not realize how much valuable information can be found in a college catalog. Have students bring it to class and give them assignments or ask questions that will ensure that they read it.

TEACHING TIP
page 228

A critical part of academic planning is teaching your students about academic policy. Be sure you include information about calculating GPA, understanding academic "good standing," repeat policies, and every institutional rule that pertains to academic progress and retention.

STUDENT ALERT
page 228

If you have first-generation college students or international students in your class, be particularly mindful of the vocabulary of higher education. As faculty, we are immersed in this language and may take for granted that students know what we are talking about.

» LO **9.2** Outline a strategy for choosing courses that ensure you are getting the most out of your studies
page 231

TEACHING TIP
page 231

Your institution may have forms, such as the one in TRY IT 2 and specifically designed for particular majors, that can be picked up at an advising center, department, or on the university Web site. Have your students bring a copy to class.

STUDENT ALERT
page 233

Remind students to consider their learning styles when planning their schedules. Have they scheduled their hardest classes when they learn best?

DISCUSSION PROMPT
page 237

Online faculty rating sources are common, and students are likely to consider these when registering for classes. Discuss the pros and cons of using this information.

CHAPTER 9

Choosing Your Courses and Major

TEACHING TIP   **page 237**

Although academic planning usually focuses on what courses students need to take for graduation, we need to encourage students to consider taking a few courses just for fun that may enrich their lives but don't fall into any required category.

STUDENT ALERT   **page 238**

Course availability is an issue on most college campuses. Encourage students to plan ahead and meet with an advisor early. Students should get answers to all of their questions well in advance of registration time and always have a back-up plan!

DISCUSSION PROMPT   **page 238**

So much emphasis is placed on academic planning and career choice—moving through life expeditiously, making a good living—that we often lose sight of the value of loving what we do. Have your students share their dreams for the future with their classmates.

» LO 9.3   Explain how participation in service learning can improve your college experience   **page 240**

TEACHING TIP   **page 240**

Service learning is an excellent way to help students focus on potential majors. You may want to do a service project as a class activity. Remember that it is important to assign and evaluate students' written reflections of the experience.

» LO 9.4   Explain the criteria for choosing a major   **page 241**

DISCUSSION PROMPT   **page 246**

Ask your students to create a list of skills that they would like to have when they graduate. Have them look for courses that teach those skills. Does this lead to a major?

TEACHING TIP   **page 247**

Visit the career center or check out your institution's career services Web site.

TEACHING TIP   **page 249**

This is an excellent place to discuss international study. Invite a speaker to class or visit the international program office on your campus.

TEACHING TIP   **page 249**

Visit the alumni office on your campus. Connect the "life-long learning" experiences and support that your campus offers its students and alumni.

STUDENT ALERT   **page 250**

Accepting responsibility and not blaming others is a key first-year student issue. You need to reinforce the idea of "ownership of choices" throughout the semester.

IN-CLASS ACTIVITY

Higher Education Game*

What is it all about? What is higher education, and what does it represent to my parent(s), my community, my employer, and about me? This activity promotes creativity and inspires a different type of conversation about the purpose of college, the curriculum, and decisions about a major.

PROCEDURE:

STEP 1: Provide large sheets of paper or poster board and colored markers for each student. Tell them to think about the meaning of higher education and its value in their lives.

STEP 2: Give them 15 minutes to brainstorm and represent their ideas in pictorial form.

*Adapted from Katy Murphy's "Gaming: A Faculty Primer," presented at the FYE Conference in Columbia, South Carolina, February 1995.

STEP 3: Provide 15 minutes for your students to discuss their ideas and share their images.

IN-CLASS ACTIVITY

The Four-Year Plan

Graduation doesn't just happen. There are many important choices that students need to make *at the right time* if they want to find themselves happily wearing a cap and gown, receiving a diploma, and moving on to the next phase of their lives. One of the best activities for doing so is making out a four-year plan.

PROCEDURE:

STEP 1: This exercise does not require anything special—just a copy of your institution's course catalog or other program of study and some paper. If your students already know what major they will declare, tell them to create a four-year course plan for that major. They should be certain to observe all prerequisites and the course offering limitations that might exist.

If some students are uncertain or have more than one major they would like to consider, simply assign them to a specific major or tell them to choose one for the purposes of this exercise.

STEP 2: Once students have created a four-year course plan, ask them to identify the extracurricular experiences that might support this particular major. Experiences your students should consider include: study abroad, internships, co-op experiences, service learning, summer jobs, volunteer activities, clubs or organizations, and research and teaching opportunities. Ask them to find room in their four-year plan for at least three of these experiences.

STEP 3: Have the students "test out" their four-year plan with their academic advisor, departmental faculty member, or other appropriate representative for that major. What did they learn? Is theirs a realistic plan? Could they repeat this process if they changed their mind about their major? Ask them to turn in the final drafts to you.

Technology and Information Competency

Learning Outcomes

>> LO **10.1** Explain the educational uses of technology.

>> LO **10.2** Describe what is available on the Web.

>> LO **10.3** Explain distance learning.

>> LO **10.4** Outline a strategy for developing information competency.

>> LO **10.5** List criteria for gathering information from the Web.

Chapter Opening Example   page 255

Like Tara in the opening example, you will have students who are intimidated by technology. It is a common mistake to assume a level of technological savvy when dealing with any audience; this goes double for first-year students. It is important to establish that there is nothing wrong with a lack of technology education and that these are all lessons that any student can master.

>> LO **10.1** Explain the educational uses of technology   page 256

STUDENT ALERT   page 257

How have your students used technology and computers? Has it been for fun only or for academic purposes? They may want to share their experiences. What are some similarities and differences between using technology for entertainment or for education?

TEACHING TIP   page 257

Try to schedule this class in a computer lab or smart classroom. It makes teaching and learning this material more effective.

TEACHING TIP   page 258

Technology can be both a burden and a benefit to learning. Ask your students to be discerning users of the tools they have at their disposal.

TEACHING TIP   page 259

Incorporate this information with the speaking skills lesson in Chapter 7. Combining technology and presentations will bring out the best in your students.

>> LO **10.2** Describe what is available on the Web   page 260

TEACHING TIP   page 260

Use this opportunity to share your institution's policies on electronic communication and use of university resources. Student honor codes may be relevant as well in explaining personal responsibility in the technological world.

DISCUSSION PROMPT   page 260

Should the Internet and Web be regulated? Has the lack of regulation led to more harm than good? How has our world been fundamentally changed as a result of this technology? Give your students an opportunity to reflect on the magnitude of changes in their lives.

DISCUSSION PROMPT   page 261

In how many college classes has the use of e-mail been a course requirement? Has it enhanced or detracted from the learning process?

DISCUSSION PROMPT   page 266

Why do electronic media allow us to feel an anonymity that we should not? Does this anonymity encourage uncivil behavior?

» LO 10.3 Explain distance learning page 267

STUDENT ALERT   **page 267**

You might be surprised to find a number of preconceptions that students have about distance learning. It might be helpful to preface this learning outcome with a simple show of hands survey regarding whether students think distance learning is easier or harder than learning in a traditional classroom. This simple gauge, which may change from one class to the next, will help you determine how comfortable your students are with the concept of distance learning.

STUDENT ALERT   **page 268**

Can your students apply the information in TRY IT 2 to their learning style? How closely related are "course taking styles" and "learning styles"?

DISCUSSION PROMPT   **page 270**

Have students brainstorm what courses and situations would encourage distance learning. Are they interested in exploring this option? Can they see where it would be expedient in their futures?

TEACHING TIP   **page 272**

Having (or not having) a back-up plan is a constant problem for students. A back-up plan is critical to academic success. Students need to be aware of the "time stamped" nature of many assignments, which assures the instructor of submission deadlines.

» LO 10.4 Outline a strategy for developing information competency page 273

TEACHING TIP   **page 273**

Many libraries are now referred to as "information commons." Be sure to know the terminology used at your school so students will not be confused by references you make.

TEACHING TIP   **page 274**

Most libraries have staff members who conduct informative tours and demonstrate how to use all the resources of the library. Scheduling a tour makes the library less intimidating for your students.

TEACHING TIP   **page 274**

An information search, done in teams, is a fun way to introduce students to the physical space in the library. This can be equally effective with an online catalog search in class.

» LO 10.5 List criteria for gathering information from the Web page 275

STUDENT ALERT   **page 276**

Many first-year students have done research in high school or for personal reasons using the Internet, but that does not mean they have done good research. Check with your students about their experience in this area.

TEACHING TIP   **page 278**

If your campus has learning communities, or any form of co-curricular academic programming, consider teaching these skills in this context.

DISCUSSION NOTE   **page 281**

How do you and your students determine what information is important, credible, and useful?

OUT-OF-CLASS ACTIVITY

Connect to the Global Society

Ask students to find information about distance learning courses at an academic institution outside the United States or in a different area of the country. Require them to bring the information to class for a

Technology and Information Competency

discussion about the advantages and disadvantages of attending a school they have never actually seen.

IN-CLASS/OUT-OF-CLASS ACTIVITY

Library Information Search

In the Instructor's Manual, you will find a worksheet for students to complete that has them use library resources to find specific information. Have students use both physical and online library resources to answer certain questions posed in the worksheet.

IN-CLASS/OUT-OF-CLASS ACTIVITY

Search Engine Compare & Contrast

Depending on your classroom setup, either have students do searches in class or out of class and create printouts of their results. Compare the results from one search engine versus another. Foster a classroom discussion by outlining why certain sites appear on multiple engines' first pages while others do not. Have students look at sites that appear on both search engines to indentify which traits the site has that makes it so popular.

ADDITIONAL JOURNAL EXERCISE

Have students write their technology biography. Encourage students to think back on significant technological moments in their lives. Challenge them to identify when they sent their first e-mail, conducted their first search engine search, etc. You may find, if you have older students in your class, that they remember technological advances that other students do not. This difference can foster a great conversation about evolving technologies.

Making Good Decisions

Learning Outcomes

» LO **11.1** Identify strategies for improving the quality of your decisions.

» LO **11.2** Implement plans to use for problem solving.

» LO **11.3** Recognize and correct problems that affect critical thinking.

Chapter Opening Example
page 289

Rich's situation at the opening of the chapter highlights that not all choices are "good" or "bad." Sometimes choices are merely different from one another. Have students really consider that as they approach the content of this chapter.

» LO **11.1** Identify strategies for improving the quality of your decisions
page 290

TEACHING TIP
page 290

Remember to refer to information discussed previously in the text to incorporate information about values and goals.

TEACHING TIP
page 291

The idea that there might be more than one right answer to a dilemma can be unsettling to first-year students. Convincing students to analyze their decision-making process systematically takes energy. What shared experience could you reference that would immediately focus the class on a decision-making moment?

TEACHING TIP
page 292

Point out that writing can serve to help students organize their ideas, which in turn can lead to better decision making.

DISCUSSION PROMPT
page 293

What connection exists between indecision and personal values?

TEACHING TIP
page 296

Refer back to information about learning styles. How do individual learning styles and preferences influence decision making?

DISCUSSION PROMPT
page 297

Ask your students to answer the questions on page xx relating to their test preparation habits. If the results don't match their intentions, encourage them to make a decision to change something.

STUDENT ALERT
page 297

First-year students come to your campus with a wide range of ideas about whether they will transfer to another institution. Be open to their questions and recognize that the time and connections on your campus will often be a deterrent to transferring.

» LO **11.2** Implement plans to use for problem solving
page 298

STUDENT ALERT
page 298

Many students are good at knowing they have problems, but can't always articulate the source of the issue or formulate a solid plan for solving the problem. It is important to reassure students that this situation is okay and incredibly normal.

TEACHING TIP   **page 298**

Take any newspaper article about a world event and ask your students to "identify the problem." Ask them to practice this skill daily.

DISCUSSION PROMPT   **page 299**

What kinds of concerns do your students believe fit into the category of "messy problems"?

TEACHING TIP   **page 299**

Many of your students may be tempted to share personal problems during this section of the course. By this point, they should have built a level of trust and camaraderie with their classmates, and the desire to share is natural. Be very careful about fostering a safe environment but also making sure conversations do not become uncomfortable for the class.

TEACHING TIP   **page 302**

As with wring papers or reading books, many first-year students will not embrace the "refinement" process. Once they have " said it, done it, or decided it," they are often reluctant to revisit it.

≫ LO **11.3** Recognize and correct problems that affect critical thinking   **page 304**

STUDENT ALERT   **page 304**

Critical thinking is a hard concept. While it is important for students to get a general sense of what it means to be a critical thinker, it is equally important to stress that it takes time to develop this skill. It is one they will use the rest of their lives, so it is understandable that it cannot be learned overnight.

STUDENT ALERT   **page 305**

Distinguishing an opinion from a fact can present difficulties. TRY IT 4 gives your students a chance to examine the power of language, as well as its developmental nature.

DISCUSSION PROMPT   **page 307**

Ask students to think alone for 2-3 minutes about a time when they jumped to a conclusion. Then ask them to share with a classmate why they did so, and what the outcome was. What would they do differently in the future?

STUDENT ALERT   **page 307**

False assumptions lead to many faulty conclusions. Ask your students why they have relied on similar faulty correlations.

IN-CLASS ACTIVITY

Group Problem Solving

Have the class brainstorm critical problems facing your campus—parking, growth, tuition increases, faculty hiring and firing policies, privacy issues concerning the use of e-mail, controversial speakers being invited to your campus, etc.—whatever issues your students will be drawn to. Have the students choose sides or research their positions and debate the issues in class. Instruct your students to focus on logical arguments and realistic solutions to the problems.

ADDITIONAL JOURNAL EXERCISE

Why College?

Have students complete journal entries about their decision to come to school. What motivated them to

Making Good Decisions

make this decision? Was it a difficult one? What are some of the problems associated with this decision? How did you solve those problems?

IN-CLASS ACTIVITY

Locus of Control*

It is a common tendency among first-year college students to see outside forces as controlling their destiny. This activity allows students to express their feelings about control in areas that influence their lives. It could be important to acknowledge that the level of "control" we feel might change, depending on our most immediate experiences. If a pattern of feeling "out of control" is felt with every prompt, the student should take that as a serious warning. As with the Values Continuum exercise, this activity works well using a scale of one to five

*Adapted from Katy Murphy's "Gaming: A Faculty Primer," presented at the First Year Experience Conference, Columbia, South Carolina, February 1995.

to reflect the level of control or else as a simple forced choice exercise, with two possible choices: "Complete Control" or "Out of Control."

PROCEDURE:

STEP 1: Place signs with one to five on the walls around the room or divide the room with one side designated "Complete Control" and the other "Out of Control."

STEP 2: State the prompt and let students move to the place in the room that best reflects their feelings. If appropriate, allow them to share their concerns.

Suggested prompts for locus of control issues: relationships with family, romantic relationships, money, time, class assignments, health, eating habits, sleep, selecting a major or study area, past choices, future decisions.

Diversity and Your Relationships with Others

12

Learning Outcomes

» LO 12.1 Discuss why the increasing racial, ethnic, and cultural diversity of society is important to you.

» LO 12.2 Utilize strategies to become more at ease with differences and diversity.

» LO 12.3 Build lasting relationships and deal with conflict.

Chapter Opening Example
page 313

Barack Obama is a great example of defining oneself based on accomplishments, while still celebrating your own background. Have students think of other culturally diverse celebrities or public figures.

» LO 12.1 Discuss why the increasing racial, ethnic, and cultural diversity of society is important to you page 314

DISCUSSION PROMPT page 314

What backgrounds do your students bring to the classroom? Ask them to describe their high school, families, and home communities.

DISCUSSION PROMPT page 315

Ask your students: What are the defining characteristics of your culture?

» LO 12.2 Utilize strategies to become more at ease with differences and diversity page 317

STUDENT ALERT page 320

Remind your class how important respectful language is when discussing sensitive Prompts. Most students *want* to be culturally sensitive but may not have had proper guidance up to this point on appropriate terminology.

DISCUSSION PROMPT page 322

Have students talk about instances in which assumptions made on the basis of first impressions or general appearance were proven incorrect. What did they learn from this experience?

TEACHING TIP page 323

Films, lectures, novels, and other outside readings are valuable activities that can help your students evaluate their cultural competence.

TEACHING TIP page 324

Journaling is one of the most effective ways to teach this chapter and receive an honest appraisal from your students.

» LO 12.3 Build lasting relationships and deal with conflict page 325

DISCUSSION PROMPT page 326

Few prompts inspire college students more than relationships. Be prepared for lots of discussion, but try to direct it toward positive comments, and insist on good listening practice from non-speakers.

STUDENT ALERT page 327

Listening has become a lost art for students. Their busy, electronic, multimedia world has not taught them the value of "supportive silence." Model this skill throughout the section and have students practice it in class.

TEACHING TIP page 329

Through the term, you're talking about building community and about having your students become a part

12 Diversity and Your Relationships with Others

of this academic community. This is a good checkpoint. If students in your class still feel disconnected, more serious intervention may be warranted.

DISCUSSION PROMPT   page 330

Ask your students how they deal with conflict. Before you teach new strategies for dealing with conflict, it's important to assess students' past experiences and attitudes toward conflict.

TEACHING TIP   page 332

This is an excellent time to make career connections. Much of workplace success is based on a person's ability to incorporate win-win attitudes and practices into everyday working situations.

TEACHING TIP   page 334

Making students aware of campus resources, such as a counseling center, is one of the most important functions of this class and this text. If your school does not offer this resource, be prepared with references for students who may need this assistance.

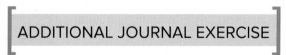

ADDITIONAL JOURNAL EXERCISE

The Relationship In Life*

Ask students to consider the relationships in their lives. What about those relationships is positive? Negative? How do the relationship patterns they are creating in

*Adapted from Katy Murphy's "Gaming: A Faculty Primer," presented at the First Year Experience Conference, Columbia, South Carolina, February 1995.

college reflect the connections they already know in their personal lives?

IN-CLASS ACTIVITY

What If?

This activity promotes awareness of gender differences and allows your class to discuss stereotypes and biases. This is a focused Think/Pair/Share activity.

PROCEDURE

STEP 1: Distribute 3 × 5 index cards to each student. Instruct them to close their eyes and image that they wake up tomorrow as the opposite sex.

STEP 2: Ask them to write eight to ten statements about how their life would be different (appearance, behavior, goals/dreams, eating habits, leisure activities, friends, etc.).

STEP 3: Then, by each statement they should put a "+" if it is a positive difference or a "−" if it is a negative difference.

STEP 4: Have students discuss their statements first in pairs (preferably a male and a female). Then discuss the findings as a class.

STEP 5: How might this exercise assist your students in developing an understanding for someone who is transgendered?

Money Matters

Learning Outcomes

» LO **13.1** Explain the purpose of a budget and outline how to prepare and stick to one.

» LO **13.2** Discuss the help available to pay for your college education.

» LO **13.3** Analyze the value of a college education.

Chapter Opening Example   page 339

Flores's situation is not uncommon. As important as their education is, many students have a myriad of other responsibilities and stressors, many of which are financial.

» LO **13.1** Explain the purpose of a budget and outline how to prepare and stick to one   page 340

DISCUSSION PROMPT   **page 340**

What history and experiences do your students bring to this subject? Have they ever lived on a budget? Held a job? Had a checking account? Had a credit card? Finding out the answers to these questions will help you determine your approach to this chapter.

TEACHING TIP   **page 341**

This "Journal Reflections" has practical information that each student should (but may not) know. Have your students answer these questions in class. List the figures on the board. How realistic are your students?

TEACHING TIP   **page 342**

Can your students recall a situation in which they had to sacrifice and save money for something really special? What was their financial goal? How did they make it happen?

TEACHING TIP   **page 343**

Suggest that your students keep track of their expenditures on a time management chart. This activity should reveal times during the day or week that your students are most likely to spend money.

STUDENT ALERT   **page 343**

Caution students about hidden costs, like telephone bills and parking tickets. These are two areas that constantly cause financial woes for students.

STUDENT ALERT   **page 347**

First-year students are often unaware of job opportunities on campus. The benefits are many—extra cash, a sense of belonging, a source of personal references, a broader sense of responsibility. Find out what resources are available on your campus, and share the information with the class, through guest speakers, student presentations, or a campus tour.

DISCUSSION PROMPT   **page 350**

Why does our culture support the notion of living on borrowed funds? Why are we not better savers?

STUDENT ALERT   **page 351**

How many students in your class carry credit cards? Are these issued in their name or their parents'? What experiences can your students share with one another?

13 Money Matters

TEACHING TIP   **page 351**

Consider bringing play money to class to demonstrate the point made in TRY IT 3. It will be more dramatic with dollars changing hands among class members.

» LO 13.2 Discuss the help available to pay for your college education   **page 354**

STUDENT ALERT   **page 355**

Every college campus has its own financial aid packaging formula, designed to conform to state and federal guidelines. Encourage students who are applying for aid to find out about your institution's policies.

STUDENT ALERT   **page 357**

Students should be encouraged to pursue sources of aid from their hometowns, counties, parishes, and commonwealths. These resources are often small, but they can make a difference, and they may not be listed on a Web site or in a university financial aid office.

STUDENT ALERT   **page 358**

Deadlines are critical, particularly with federal aid. Many sources are available on a first come, first served basis. Also, summer school is often considered separately from aid available for the academic year. Check out the policies on your campus.

DISCUSSION PROMPT   **page 359**

Direct the conversation to the discussion about the value of a college education in Chapter 1.

TEACHING TIP   **page 361**

TRY IT 5 is a useful exercise. Consider using it as a "Forced Choice" activity that will have your students on their feet and moving around the classroom.

» LO 13.3 Analyze the value of a college education   **page 362**

ADDITIONAL JOURNAL EXERCISE

Goals and Money

Encourage students to look at the personal and academic goals they wrote during the earlier chapters of this book. Ask them to put a dollar amount by each goal. Ask them to discuss how they arrived at these figures.

IN-CLASS ACTIVITY

Ways of Saving Money

This is a simple brainstorming activity that can enlighten not only your students but also give you new ways to save money!

PROCEDURE:

STEP 1: Ask students to work in small groups (three to five each) and come up with their top ten (realistic) ways of spending too much money in your particular town on a given weekend. Give them large sheets of paper or poster board and have them write their ideas down in descending order, from ten to one.

STEP 2: Ask each group to announce their results (David Letterman–style) to the rest of the class. Post the ideas around the room.

STEP 3: Return to group work and ask your students to brainstorm as many ways as they can rethink of to spend less money. Encourage them to think differently and creatively (such as "make less money and I will spend less money"). You might also want them to make a list of "free or nearly free" entertainment options available. Ask them to record all their suggestions.

STEP 4: Report the ideas. Ask two students to record the suggestions and make a huge list of "ways to save money," and hang it in the classroom so they can all be reminded on a regular basis how to save their dollars.

14 Stress, Health, and Wellness

Learning Outcomes

» LO **14.1** Explain what stress is and how to control it.

» LO **14.2** Discuss what is involved in keeping fit and healthy, and why this is important to do.

» LO **14.3** Identify the main threats to health and well-being.

» LO **14.4** Analyze the components of sexual health.

Chapter Opening Example   page 367

Louisa's day is likely to sound familiar to many students. It is vitally important to make sure students understand that they are not alone in with these challenges. This chapter can help underline the sense of belonging stressed throughout the course.

» LO **14.1** Explain what stress is and how to control it   page 368

TEACHING TIP   page 369

Stress is one of the leading reasons college students visit an infirmary or a counseling center on college campuses. Spend time talking about the "daily hassles" identified in Figure 14.1 in an effort to determine ways to develop a healthy lifestyle.

TEACHING TIP   page 372

Do not forget to give some attention to those students who do not feel stress in their lives. Sliding through life, always taking the easy way out, and never expecting the best of ourselves is certainly not a way to avoid stress.

DISCUSSION PROMPT   page 372

What makes us feel good? For a few minutes, have your class write down as many healthy ideas as they can think of, then share them with the class.

TEACHING TIP   page 373

Identifying the factors that cause stress is more difficult than it seems, and what is stressful to one person is not always stressful to someone else. Help your students (or let them help each other) find the real causes of stress.

TEACHING TIP   page 373

Do the mediation activity in class (Table 14.1) or invite a colleague from your counseling center to do it with your class. You may want to schedule this activity near the exam period at the end of the semester.

DISCUSSION PROMPT   page 375

What does keeping your promises, keeping your commitments, really mean? The current generation of college students sometimes is accused of not knowing what it means to be committed to keeping a promise. Ask them to respond to this idea.

» LO **14.2** Discuss what is involved in keeping fit and healthy, and why this is important to do   page 378

STUDENT ALERT   page 378

The idea of health can be challenging for students with hectic lives. This would be a great time to bring in a guest lecturer to talk about the benefits associated with good nutrition and regular exercise.

TEACHING TIP   page 378

Does your institution have a Wellness Center? If so, visit it with your class.

TEACHING TIP   page 379

Ask your students to keep a nutrition log and find someone on your campus who can evaluate it. They may be amazed at students' eating habits.

TEACHING TIP   page 380

Ask students to draw their favorite walking routes on campus or in town and exchange maps with one another.

STUDENT ALERT   page 381

Communal living in a residence hall usually changes students' sleeping habits. What coping mechanisms have your students discovered?

» LO 14.3 Identify the main threats to health and well-being   page 382

TEACHING TIP   page 382

Before you begin this section of the chapter, get specific facts about drugs and alcohol use on your campus. This information will give you more credibility when talking with your students.

TEACHING TIP   page 382

Ask your students who smoke to consider stopping that habit now. Invite them to write about their progress in their journals.

STUDENT ALERT   page 383

Who enforces the laws regarding illegal drug use on your campus—local or campus police? Have students research campus drug policies and bring this information to class.

TEACHING TIP   page 385

Denial of behavior remains a big part of the problem in dealing with drug and alcohol abuse. Encourage students to keep a journal. They may find it easier to face their thoughts in private than in public.

» LO 14.4 Analyze the components of sexual health   page 387

STUDENT ALERT   page 388

After students complete TRY IT 5, they will have a better understanding of campus resources involved in health and wellness issues. Do they understand the commitment to confidentiality that most professionals bring to discussions involving sexual behavior? If students do not trust the system, they will not use it.

TEACHING TIP   page 389

Invite a nurse or doctor who is comfortable talking to college students to address issues related to sexually transmitted diseases.

DISCUSSION PROMPT   page 391

The issue of violence in relationships of college-age students is a difficult but important one. Open the floor to your students and encourage them to share their views.

STUDENT ALERT   page 392

Many states have specific laws that apply to sex and alcohol/drug use. Do your students know the facts?

Stress, Health, and Wellness

ADDITIONAL JOURNAL EXERCISE

Long-Term Habits

What habits do you have that you would not want to pass on to your own children? Why? What habits do you hope to pass on to your children?

IN-CLASS ACTIVITY

Short Relaxation Technique: Quick Muscle Tensing

Tense every muscle group in your body. Hold your breath and hold the tension while you slowly count to five. Then relax and exhale. Take several slow, deep breaths, and then tense again. Allow yourself at least 30 seconds to enjoy the resulting feeling of relaxation.

Strategies for Success for Student Athletes

Learning Outcomes

» LO **A.1** Identify the special advantages of being a student athlete that help meet challenges in college life.

» LO **A.2** Explain how to deal most effectively with course instructors and time management issues.

» LO **A.3** Discuss the best ways to seek and use help.

» LO **A.4** Analyze strategies for dealing with pain, injury, and the potential of burnout.

Chapter Opening Example

page A-1

In many ways, student athletes are full-time students who also do the equivalent of a full-time job. The ability to manage this load can be overwhelming. Strategies for success are important for both personal achievement and loyalty to the team.

» LO **A.1** Identify the special advantages of being a student athlete that help meet challenges in college life
page A-2

TEACHING TIP   **page A-2**

Athletes are not a homogeneous group of students. Diversity is represented by different sports, different skills, different career choices, and different levels of academic preparedness. Perhaps the only thing they have in common is that they are all student athletes.

STUDENT ALERT   **page A-3**

Student athletes are often lumped together. It is imperative for you to approach them as individuals if you are to be a trusted academic mentor.

TEACHING TIP   **page A-3**

Do not miss an opportunity to explore time management skills in this chapter. There are many student athletes who are outstanding time managers and who may have a great deal to teach your class.

TEACHING TIP   **page A-3**

Academic support services differ greatly from campus to campus. The placement of these services says much about the campus philosophy regarding academic support. Ask your students to list the resources available to support their academic successes. Are there services available only to student athletes, or are they available to all students? What advantages or disadvantages result from the manner in which these services can be accessed?

DISCUSSION PROMPT   **page A-3**

Isolation and loneliness are often issues for student athletes because of team obligations and expectations. Balancing the demands of the sport and the rich world of co-curricular offerings on a college campus is extremely tough. Explore this topic with your students.

DISCUSSION PROMPT   **page A-4**

Ask student athletes to discuss their thoughts about the expectation to be role models.

TEACHING TIP   **page A-5**

Ask your student athletes to report regularly on their "points of pride" resulting from their participation in sports. Cut out articles in local student newspapers highlighting their successes and post them in the classroom or your office. Let them know that you know what is going on.

A Strategies for Success for Student Athletes

TEACHING TIP   page A-5

Student athletes are responsible not only to their campus plan for degree completion but also to the NCAA. Ask a university official familiar with NCAA academic eligibility standards to facilitate a discussion about academic planning.

»LO A.2 Explain how to deal most effectively with course instructors and time management issues page A-6

STUDENT ALERT   page A-6

Assist your student athletes by acknowledging that you know they are responding simultaneously to public scrutiny of their athletic accomplishments and faculty evaluations of their academic progress. It takes maturity and time to understand all the dynamics involved. Encourage them to find an upperclassman to be a mentor.

TEACHING TIP   page A-6

Travel can be a time management "black hole," or it can provide substantial blocks of time for studying. Ask your students to share tips for maximizing this time.

DISCUSSION PROMPT   page A-6

Ask students to generate a list of ways that technology can enhance their academic performance. How is technology used to enhance athletic performance?

»LO A.3 Discuss the best ways to seek and use help page A-7

STUDENT ALERT   page A-7

Student athletes are competitive and may find it difficult to ask for help. Reassure them that all students need help with different skills and that they are no different.

TEACHING TIP   page A-10

Trust and accessibility are essential elements for students seeking academic assistance. Teammates are a rich and ready resource to be considered.

TEACHING TIP   page A-13

Encourage student athletes to approach a tutoring session with the same level of preparation that they would approach a practice for their sport.

TEACHING TIP   page A-13

Right or wrong, fair or unfair, athletes are judged far more publicly than are others regarding academic integrity. Emphasize the importance of academic honesty beyond exams and tests.

TEACHING TIP   page A-13

Encourage first-year students to ask upper-class students to serve as tutors or academic mentors.

»LO A.4 Analyze strategies for dealing with pain, injury, and the potential of burnout page A-15

STUDENT ALERT   page A-15

Student athletes need to be their own best health advocates. They may hear conflicting information from the institution's infirmary and the athletic trainer. In the end, student athletes must live with the decisions relating to their bodies.

STUDENT ALERT   page A-16

Student athletes may be less willing than their classmates to use group therapy or individual counseling. They have learned to play with physical pain, and the psychological implications of this attitude may have lasting repercussions.

TEACHING TIP   page A-16

Bring an alternative health care provider to class who can provide additional options for your students to consider for health, such as a campus wellness coordinator, nutritionist, biofeedback specialist, etc.

Strategies for Success for Student Athletes

A

DISCUSSION PROMPT   page A-17

What is the difference between a team-building initiation ritual and hazing? Don't make an assumption that hazing doesn't occur on your campus just because you don't hear about it. You may be "out of the loop."

TEACHING TIP   page A-17

Does your campus have a sports psychologist? Consider inviting this person to class.

Taking Charge of Your Career

Learning Outcomes

» LO **C.1** Identify your ideal career and job.

» LO **C.2** Analyze strategies for finding and getting a job.

» LO **C.3** Discuss how to maximize your job interviewing skills.

Chapter Opening Example

page C-1

Darla's interview scenario in the opening reading of this chapter highlights an aspect of education that students can easily lose sight of: the ultimate goal of finding a job. Often students (and instructors) get caught up in the daily grind and can forget what they began school for in the first place. Helping students prepare for the transition to their professional careers is one very important element of a well-rounded education. It is not enough for students to know how to succeed at a job; they also need to know how to *get* that job.

» LO **C.1** Identify your ideal career and job

page C-2

TEACHING TIP
page C-2

Broaden the context of career planning from the beginning of this chapter. Students often connect careers with post-graduation decisions and we want them to begin that process of self-discovery now! There is no such thing as too soon for students to begin having serious consideration for their careers.

» LO **C.2** Analyze strategies for finding and getting a job

page C-3

TEACHING TIP
page C-6

In the personal interviews section, there is a great list of questions to ask someone in a field in which students may be interested. Remind students that these questions work equally well when they interview for jobs. Often students think they should merely be answering questions in an interview, but this is not the case. Tell them these are great question to use as a jumping off point when they are in interviews.

DISCUSSION PROMPT
page C-7

After reviewing Table C.1, take a survey of students' current plans for their future careers. It might be very

interesting for the class as a whole to discuss the similarities between top growing jobs. What characteristics do these jobs have in common? Are there benefits to know the top growing jobs, even if they are not of current interest to you?

TEACHING TIP
page C-8

Discuss the concept of an informational interview. Instead of asking for a job, you are becoming informed about the work–which may increase or decrease your desire to pursue this type of work.

STUDENT ALERT
page C-10

Students may want to consider keeping an electronic file of class projects and presentations (group or individual), as well as a paper copy.

TEACHING TIP
page C-12

Explore the idea of computer screening of résumés and job opportunities. What words are essential in this stage of the career search?

TEACHING TIP
page C-12

Ask students to go online and find sample résumés for positions they would like to explore.

C Taking Charge of Your Career

TEACHING TIP   **page C-15**

Discuss with students the importance of using verbs to describe their accomplishments. Ask them to review the words on the list and share the list.

TEACHING TIP   **page C-19**

So much emphasis is placed on résumés that the cover letter is sometimes forgotten. Don't underestimate the power of this first impression.

TEACHING TIP   **page C-22**

Many college career centers now offer online services to students; you can review job postings of employers who have relationships with your institution. Does your institution have this service?

TEACHING TIP   **page C-23**

Some Web sites are more complex than others. Consider your audience. If you are teaching first-year students, make sure the intricacies of the site are not discouraging. A class activity would include how to search different sites.

» LO C.3   Discuss how to maximize your job interviewing skills   **page C-24**

STUDENT ALERT   **page C-24**

Remind students to prepare questions for interviews. This is an excellent way to demonstrate that they did their homework and are engaged in knowing more about the potential employer.

TEACHING TIP   **page C-27**

Again, your institution may offer important resources in a career resource or development center. Does the center conduct mock interviews? Can it videotape the session?

Transferring Strategies: Making the Leap from Community College to a Four-Year School

Learning Outcomes

>> LO **T.1** Discuss the strategies for choosing a specific college or university to transfer to.

>> LO **T.2** Explain how to transfer credits.

>> LO **T.3** Identify ways to adjust to a new college.

Chapter Opening Example
page T-1

Transferring schools can be a reality for many college students for a variety of reasons. It is important to be supportive of the process and help students make the best choices possible.

>> LO **T.1** Discuss strategies for choosing a specific college or university to transfer to
page T-2

STUDENT ALERT
page T-2

Not all career choices require a four-year degree. It is important for students to assess their true educational needs in light of the career they hope to pursue.

TEACHING TIP
page T-2

Ask the class to generate of possible internship sites or opportunities in the area to assist them in making better choices about their future work environment.

STUDENT ALERT
page T-4

Making decisions can be stressful. Remind your students that decisions can always be revisited.

TEACHING TIP
page T-5

Consider inviting an academic advisor or transfer specialist from your campus or neighboring four-year institution to class to answer questions.

DISCUSSION PROMPT
page T-8

Transfer students will (theoretically) spend less time on a campus than those who entered as freshmen. Ask your students to discuss what is gained and lost by making the decision to move to another campus.

STUDENT ALERT
page T-8

Ask students to determine if their intended transfer institution has a special orientation session for transfers or other ways to bring transfer students together. If not, encourage them to begin such an effort.

TEACHING TIP
page T-10

Not only can some applications be downloaded, completed, and mailed in, but some institutions even provide students with the opportunity to submit applications online. Hold class in a computer lab and show students the different options.

TEACHING TIP
page T-11

The transfer process requires planning and is an excellent opportunity for reinforcing time management lessons.

STUDENT ALERT
page T-11

Remind students not to skip any required steps when applying to another institution. It will delay their acceptance.

TEACHING TIP
page T-12

There is a difference between campus-based and federal/FAFSA-based financial aid packages. Tell students not to assume that an aid package from one school will look like the aid package from another school. Also,

Transferring Strategies: Making the Leap from Community College to a Four-Year School

financial aid information is not shared by institutions; it is the student's responsibility to apply and send information to *each* campus.

» LO **T.2** Explain how to transfer credits   page T-14

STUDENT ALERT   page T-14

Remind students that the question, "Will my credits transfer?" is different from "How do my credits transfer?" Students may receive 30 transfer credits, but only 10 of these credits could be used toward the specific program of study or major they hope to pursue.

TEACHING TIP   page T-14

Remind students to explore credit for out-of-class experiences they might have under their belts—travel abroad, service learning opportunities, leadership roles, internships, etc.

TEACHING TIP   page T-15

Many public institutions have an online resource page that gives information about how specific two-year institution courses will be counted at four-year institutions.

TEACHING TIP   page T-18

Remind students to "be polite, be persistent, and provide documentation" when seeking specific recognition of credit.

TEACHING TIP   page T-18

When making an appeal for course credit, remind students to offer realistic substitutions and explanations.

It seldom helps to be angry or become overly emotional in an appeal process.

» LO **T.3** Identify ways to adjust to a new college   page T-19

STUDENT ALERT   page T-19

It is easy, particularly in the beginning, to criticize a new institution because it is different from what has already been experienced.

DISCUSSION PROMPT   page T-20

Invite students to make a list of their strengths and weaknesses as a brainstorming exercise in class. Many transfer students experience a drop in their grade point average the first semester of transfer work but improve in subsequent semesters. Remind them that their experience makes them more mature learners, which should lead them to seek additional support earlier.

STUDENT ALERT   page T-20

Residential campuses seldom have the same level of parking that commuter campuses have–remind students that they may need to adjust their expectations about transportation options.

STUDENT ALERT   page T-21

Even though transfer students have already attended at least one orientation, it is essential for them to attend the orientation program at their new institution. This is a great time to meet other students and solve problems before classes begin.